OXFORD DICTION

COMPUTING

FOR LEARNERS OF ENGLISH

Edited by Sandra Pyne
and Allene Tuck

Phonetics Editor
Michael Ashby

Oxford University Press

Oxford University Press, Walton Street, Oxford OX2 6DP

Oxford New York Athens Auckland Bangkok Bombay Calcutta
Cape Town Dar Es Salaam Delhi Florence Hong Kong Istanbul
Karachi Kuala Lumpur Madras Madrid Melbourne Mexico City
Nairobi Paris Singapore Taipei Tokyo Toronto

OXFORD and OXFORD ENGLISH are
trade marks of Oxford University Press

The British National Corpus is a collaborative project involving
Oxford University Press, Longman, Chambers, the Universities
of Oxford and Lancaster and the British Library.

ISBN 0 19 4314413

Typeset in Great Britain by Tradespools Limited, Frome, Somerset
Printed in Great Britain by Richard Clay Ltd, Bungay, Suffolk

Contents

Preface

This is the first dictionary of computing written especially for learners of English to be published by Oxford University Press. It is the second dictionary in a series, following the *Oxford Dictionary of Business English for Learners of English.*

In researching and writing this dictionary, it has been necessary to draw on the combined expertise of people in the world of computing and those involved in teaching English as a foreign language. The result is a dictionary that is comprehensive and up-to-date in its coverage of words and phrases used in computing. Clear explanations of the grammar and meaning of words, along with authentic examples showing how words are really used make this dictionary a useful tool for helping to read, write speak and understand the English used in computing today.

We would like to thank the following people for their careful and committed work in the making of this dictionary: John Jaworski, Bill Coumbe, John Acton and Kathryn Phillips-Miles. We would also like the acknowledge the work of the large team of people involved in the production of the dictionary once the text was complete.

User's Guide to the Dictionary

This dictionary is intended for learners of English of intermediate to advanced level who need to understand, speak, read and write the English used in computing. It will be a valuable reference work for people who use computers and people who study computing. Words and phrases are explained clearly and simply using a limited number of words which are easy to understand.

To ensure that the words and examples included in this dictionary are modern and authentic, this dictionary has been compiled with the help of the British National Corpus, a collection of 100 000 000 words of both written and spoken English. Many of the examples in the dictionary are corpus-based.

This dictionary has been specially designed so that it is easy to use. The headword is followed by a definition and examples. If more detailed information on grammar or pronunciation is needed, or if cross references, collocates, plurals, synonyms, parts of the verb or spelling and American variants are required, they have all been conveniently placed together in the separate language column.

Sandra Pyne
Allene Tuck

Oxford, 1995

A *abbr*

1 ► **ampere**
2 the letter which represents the decimal number 10 in hexadecimal notation

/eɪ/
2 ► **base 16**

---

abandon *verb* (operations)
to leave a file without saving the data it contains, or to leave a program before it has finished executing: *abandon the file and revert to the saved version*

/əˈbændən/
abandon, abandoning, abandoned
note transitive verb
► **abort, quit**

---

abbr *abbr*
► **abbreviation**

note used in written English only

☆**abbreviation** *noun*
a short form of a word or phrase: *'DTP' is an abbreviation for 'desktop publishing'.*

/ə,briːviˈeɪʃn/
pl abbreviations
abbr abbr, abbrev
◄ use an **abbreviation**
► **acronym, mnemonic**

---

abend *noun*
► **abnormal end**

/ˈæbend/

---

abnormal end *noun*
an unexpected end to a program caused by an error in the program or data: *This batch of processing included 8 successful runs and 3 abnormal ends.*

/æb,nɔːml ˈend/
pl abnormal ends
syn abend

☆**abort** *verb* (operations)
to stop a program while it is running: *The operators aborted the program at an early stage.* ○ *The program aborted because the data was in the wrong format.*

/əˈbɔːt/
abort, aborting, aborted
note transitive or intransitive verb
◄ **abort** an operation, a program
► **abandon, cancel, interrupt², terminate 1**

---

absolute address *noun* (hardware)
1 the fixed place where an item of data is always stored: *find any absolute address in the computer's memory* **2** the name, number or code of this place: *The machine-code instructions contain the absolute addresses for all the items of data required by the program.*

/,æbsəluːt əˈdres/
pl absolute addresses
syn direct address, machine address
► **address, relative address**

---

absolute addressing *noun*
a way of accessing data by using its ABSOLUTE ADDRESS: *The program uses absolute addressing.*

/,æbsəluːt əˈdresɪŋ/
note not used with *a* or *an*. No plural and used with a singular verb only.
syn direct addressing
► **indirect addressing**

---

absolute assembler *noun* (software)
a program that converts assembly language into machine code by using the same part of memory

/,æbsəluːt əˈsemblə(r)/
pl absolute assemblers
► **assembler**

---

absolute code *noun* (software)
a programming code that can be executed directly by the CPU: *a program written in absolute code*

/,æbsəluːt ˈkəʊd/
note no plural

---

abbr abbreviation   **pl** plural   **syn** synonym   ► see   ◄ collocate (*word often used with the headword*)

	⋈ use, write **absolute code**
	▶ **low-level language, machine code**
absolute loader *noun* (software) a program that always loads another program into the same absolute address	/ˌæbsəluːt ˈləʊdə(r)/ **pl** absolute loaders **▶** **loader**
absolute value *noun* (mathematics and logic) the size of a number that ignores if it is positive or negative: *The absolute value of -8.44 and 8.44 is 8.44.* ○ *a function that returns the absolute value of a number*	/ˌæbsəluːt ˈvæljuː/ **pl** absolute values
abstract data type *noun* (software) a data type that is defined by the data it contains and the operations that can be performed on it. Changes in abstract data types can be made without creating errors in the code that uses it: *change the definition of the abstract data type*	/ˌæbstrækt ˈdeɪtə taɪp/ **pl** abstract data types **abbr** ADT
AC *abbr* **▶** **alternating current**	/ˌeɪ ˈsiː/ **note** pronounced as individual letters
ACC *abbr* **▶** **accumulator**	/ˌeɪ siː ˈsiː/ **note** pronounced as individual letters
☆**accept** *verb* (system operation) to receive something as correct or suitable: *The computer won't accept the password.*	/əkˈsept/ **accept, accepting, accepted** **note** transitive verb **⋈** **accept** a disk, file
acceptance testing *noun* (hardware/software) an amount of time in the development of a computer system for checking that it works in the way required in the contract: *After the installation of the network there was a period for acceptance testing to identify any possible problems.* ○ *The time allowed for carrying out acceptance testing is three months.*	/əkˈseptəns ˌtestɪŋ/ **note** no plural **⋈** an **acceptance testing** period, routine, scheme **▶** **requirements specification, systems analysis**
☆**access**[1] *noun* (user operation) the process of looking at (reading) or recording or changing (writing) data: *Enter a password to gain access to the database.* ○ *Access to confidential files is restricted to senior staff members.*	/ˈækses/ **note** not used with *a* or *an*. No plural and used with a singular verb only. **⋈** allow, deny, gain, have, restrict **access**; read-only, write-only **access** **▶** **asynchronous access, carrier sense multiple access, cyclic access, disk access, parallel access, random access, sequential access, serial access**
☆**access**[2] *verb* to use a computer system or part of it in order to look at (read) or to record or change (write) data: *The system cannot be accessed by unauthorized users.* ○ *access the computer via a remote host* ○ *use the pull-down menus to access other files*	/ˈækses/ **access, accessing, accessed** **note** transitive verb

	⋈ **access** a computer, database, hard disk, program, system
	▶ **enter, log on**

access charge *noun*

the price paid to use a computer system: *pay an access charge to use a bulletin board* ○ *The access charge is made up of an amount per minute plus an amount for storage.*

/'ækses tʃɑːdʒ/
pl access charges
▶ **connect time**

access code *noun*

a group of letters and/or numbers that are needed to gain access to a computer system or part of it: *input an access code at the initial prompt screen* ○ *The access code includes a secret password.*

/'ækses kəʊd/
pl access codes
⋈ allocate, use an **access code**
▶ **password**

access control *noun*

1 the control of requests from users or programs to use parts of a computer system: *Permission to use certain data files is restricted by access control.* **2** (*software*) the software that controls access requests

/'ækses kən,trəʊl/
note usually singular
2 ⋈ an **access control** module, routine

accessible *adjective*

able to be reached, entered or used: *Most university computers are accessible via the Internet.*

/ək'sesəbl/
⋈ an **accessible** computer, file, system

access mechanism *noun*

a device that places the READ HEAD (= part of the disk drive that transfers information from the storage medium) in the correct place on a magnetic disk

/'ækses ,mekənɪzəm/
pl access mechanisms
⋈ adjust, maintain, repair the **access mechanism**
syn actuator

access method *noun*

the way data items are read from a file or data structure: *The company is developing a simple data access method for all databases.*

/'ækses ,meθəd/
pl access methods
⋈ a record at a time **access method**
syn access type
▶ **ISAM, random access, sequential access, serial access, SQL**

access path *noun*

the route to a particular file, starting from the ROOT DIRECTORY (= the place where the first details of a disk are stored): *The access path C:ØMAILØTEXT shows that the file TEXT is on drive C, in directory MAIL.*

/'ækses pɑːθ/
pl access paths
⋈ specify the **access path**
▶ **directory, pathname, subdirectory**

access request *noun*

a message to the operating system asking for the use of a data file: *The access request failed because the file was already in use.*

/'ækses rɪ,kwest/
pl access requests
⋈ act *on*, make an **access request**

access time *noun*

the time taken for a data item to be supplied after it has been requested: *an average access time of less than 100 milliseconds*

/'ækses taɪm/
pl access times
⋈ measure, record the **access time**
▶ **disk access time, latency**

---

abbr abbreviation   **pl** plural   **syn** synonym   ▶ see   ⋈ collocate (*word often used with the headword*)

access type *noun*
▶ **access method**

/'ækses taɪp/

---

accounting file *noun*
a file on a multi-user computing system that records the resources used for each job: *The system administrator checked the accounting file to see how often the database had been accessed.*

/ə'kaʊntɪŋ faɪl/
pl accounting files
◪ access, update the **accounting file**
▶ **audit**

☆**accumulator** *noun* (hardware)
a register that holds the results of operations done by the ARITHMETIC AND LOGIC UNIT (= the part of the CPU where mathematical operations are done): *store bytes/results in an accumulator*

/ə'kju:mjəleɪtə(r)/
pl accumulators
abbr ACC

☆**accuracy** *noun*
the correctness of a calculation or result: *calculate to an accuracy of four decimal places*

note 'Accuracy' is not the same as 'precision'. 'Accuracy' is how correct a result is. 'Precision' is how detailed a result is.

/'ækjərəsi/
note no plural
◪ test *for* **accuracy**
▶ **precision**

ACIA *abbr* (applications/communications)
an asynchronous communications interface adaptor. An integrated circuit that is used in a SERIAL COMMUNICATIONS pathway.

/ˌeɪ si: aɪ 'eɪ/
note pronounced as individual letters

ACK *abbr*
the ASCII character which shows POSITIVE ACKNOWLEDGEMENT (= a message reporting successful receipt of data): *The receiving unit sent back the ACK character.*

/æk/
note pronounced as a single word
▶ **control character**

---

acknowledge *verb*
to show or report that a message has been successfully received

/ək'nɒlɪdʒ/
acknowledge, acknowledging, acknowledged
note transitive verb
◪ **acknowledge** a fax, message, transmission

---

acknowledgement *noun*
a message that reports the result of a data transmission

/ək'nɒlɪdʒmənt/
pl acknowledgements
◪ receive, send, transmit an **acknowledgment**
▶ **negative acknowledgement, positive acknowledgement**

☆**acoustic coupler** *noun* (hardware)
a device attached to a telephone line that connects computers to the telephone system by converting computer signals to sound and sounds to computer signals: *use an acoustic coupler to convert digital signals to audio tones*

note Acoustic couplers are now usually replaced by modems.

/əˌku:stɪk 'kʌplə(r)/
pl acoustic couplers
◪ connect, use an **acoustic coupler**
▶ **modem**

ACR abbr
audio cassette recorder

/ˌeɪ siː ˈɑː/
note pronounced as individual
letters

ACR interface noun
an audio cassette recorder interface. A device that allows a
computer to store programs and data on an ordinary cassette
recorder: *Many early home computers used an ACR interface.*

/ˌeɪ siː ˈɑːr ˌɪntəfeɪs/
pl ACR interfaces
◄ install, use an **ACR interface**
► **interface**

☆**acronym** noun
a word formed from the first letters of a group of words: *The
acronym 'ROM' stands for 'Read Only Memory'.*

/ˈækrənɪm/
pl acronyms
◄ an **acronym** *for* something
► **abbreviation, mnemonic**

---

activate verb
to make something start to work: *The ON switch activates the
modem.* ○ *Infected programs activate the virus when started up.* ○
activate the circuit by passing an electric current through it

/ˈæktɪveɪt/
**activate, activating,
activated**
note transitive verb
◄ **activate** a printer, process,
program

☆**active** adjective
working or being used: *make the window active by clicking on it*

/ˈæktɪv/
◄ an **active** display, file, program,
window

---

activity ratio noun
the number of data items that are used by a process compared
to the total number of data items that are stored: *an increase in
the activity ratio*

/ækˈtɪvəti ˌreɪʃiəʊ/
pl activity ratios
◄ measure, record the **activity
ratio**

---

actual address noun
► **absolute address**

/ˌæktʃuəl əˈdres/

---

actual instruction noun
the machine code instruction that is executed after any
INDIRECT ADDRESSING or INDEXING

/ˌæktʃuəl ɪnˈstrʌkʃn/
pl actual instructions
◄ decode, execute the **actual
instruction**
► **addressing, index register**

---

actuator noun
► **access mechanism**

/ˈæktʃueɪtə(r)/

ACU abbr
► **automatic calling unit**

/ˌeɪ siː ˈjuː/
note pronounced as individual
letters

Ada noun
a high-level computer programming language designed for
military systems: *algorithms programmed in Ada*

note Ada is an imperative, procedural language which was
designed in the late 1970s and early 1980s.

/ˈeɪdə/
note not used with *a* or *an*. No
plural and used with a singular
verb only.
(also **ADA**)
◄ program *in* **Ada**; an **Ada**
compiler, program

---

abbr abbreviation   **pl** plural   **syn** synonym   ► see   ◄ collocate (*word often used with the headword*)

adapter noun
► adaptor

/ə'dæptə(r)/

---

adaptive channel control noun (applications)
a method of sharing pathways in a communications network according to the needs of the users

/ə,dæptɪv 'tʃænl kən,trəʊl/
note no plural
► **multiplexing**

---

adaptive control system noun (applications)
a method of control that uses FEEDBACK or other information to alter the way a system operates: *use an adaptive control system so that the communications network is self-regulating*

/ə,dæptɪv kən'trəʊl ,sɪstəm/
pl adaptive control systems
◄ implement, install, maintain, use an **adaptive control system**

---

adaptive routing noun
the ability of a network to choose the path that a message takes by responding to conditions at the time, and not by working in a fixed way following fixed procedures: *If there is a line failure, adaptive routing is used to make sure that messages are not delayed.*

/ə,dæptɪv 'ru:tɪŋ/
note no plural
◄ use **adaptive routing**; an **adaptive routing** algorithm, technique
► **alternate route**

☆**adaptor** noun (hardware)
a device such as an add-in board that allows a computer to be connected to another device: *use an adaptor to connect the machine to the network*

/ə'dæptə(r)/
pl adaptors
(also **adapter**)
◄ connect, install, use an **adaptor**
► **enhanced graphics adaptor**

---

adaptor board noun
a PRINTED CIRCUIT BOARD added to a computer to allow it to communicate with an external device: *install a video adaptor board*

/ə'dæptə bɔ:d/
pl adaptor boards
(also **adapter board**)
◄ install, maintain, test, use an **adaptor board**
syn adaptor card

---

adaptor card noun
► adaptor board

/ə'dæptə kɑ:d/

---

adaptor plug noun
a device that connects equipment with different plugs and SOCKETS (= a device which a plug fits into)

/ə'dæptə plʌg/
pl adaptor plugs
(also **adapter plug**)
► **gender changer**

☆**ADC** abbr
► analog-to-digital converter

/,eɪ di: 'si:/
note pronounced as individual letters

A/D converter abbr
► analog-to-digital converter

/,eɪ 'di: kən,vɜ:tə(r)/

---

add verb
1 to put something together with something else, so that capacity, size or value is increased: *add a hard disk drive to the PC to increase data storage capacity* **2** to put numbers or amounts together to get a total: *add 3 and 4 to get 7 ○ add 2 to 3 to make 5*

/æd/
add, adding, added
note transitive verb
◄ **add** something *to* something

addend noun (mathematics)
an addend is a number which is added to another number called an AUGEND

/'ædend/
pl addends
▶ **accumulator, operand**

☆**adder** noun (hardware)
the part of a computer that adds binary digits

/'ædə(r)/
pl adders
◄ a 4-bit **adder**
▶ **arithmetic and logic unit, full adder, half adder, parallel adder, serial adder**

---

add-in noun
▶ **add-on**

/'æd ɪn/

---

addition noun
the process of adding something, especially two or more numbers

/ə'dɪʃn/
pl additions
◄ perform an **addition**
▶ **addend, augend**

---

addition record noun
a data item in a CHANGE FILE (= a file in batch processing) that identifies a record to add to the MASTER FILE

/ə'dɪʃn ˌrekɔːd/
pl addition records
◄ access, read, write an **addition record**
▶ **audit trail**

---

add-on noun
a device that is added to a system to increase the work it can do: *A floating point processor is available as an add-on.* ○ *The games console comes with an add-on keyboard which can be used for word processing.* ○ *upgrade the PC with add-on memory*

/'æd ɒn/
pl add-ons
◄ buy, install an **add-on**; an **add-on** module, package, product, unit
syn add-in
▶ **built-in**

---

add-on board noun
▶ **expansion board**

/'æd ɒn bɔːd/

---

add-on module noun (hardware/software)
a separate piece of hardware or software that can be added to a computer system to increase its power or functions: *The system has additional MIDI capability via an add-on module.*

/ˌæd ɒn 'mɒdjuːl/
pl add-on modules
▶ **expansion board, upgrade**

☆**address¹** noun
1 (hardware) a place where a particular item of data is stored and which is identified by a name, number or code: *each memory location has a numeric address* ○ *The operating system is loaded into unused addresses between 640K and 1MB.* **2** this name, number or code **3** a unique name, number or code that belongs to a device on a network: *the machine's address is 193.63.59.166*

/ə'dres/
pl addresses
1,2 ◄ identify, locate an **address**
syn storage location, store address
▶ **absolute address, base address, byte address, memory, relative address, virtual address**
3 ▶ **IP address**

☆**address²** verb (system operation)
to refer to a device or an item of data by its address: *The system addresses the data through a code rather than a number.*

/ə'dres/
address, addressing, addressed

---

abbr abbreviation   **pl** plural   **syn** synonym   ▶ see   ◄ collocate (*word often used with the headword*)

	note transitive verb
	◄ **address** a location, memory, screen, store

addressability *noun* (graphics)
the number of ADDRESSABLE POINTS on a display screen: *When choosing a graphics program it is important to consider the addressability of the screen.*

/əˌdresə'bɪləti/

note not used with *a* or *an*. No plural and used with a singular verb only.

◄ high, low **addressability**

▶ **pixel**

---

addressable *adjective* (applications/graphics)
able to be addressed: *build applications with four gigabytes of addressable memory*

/ə'dresəbl/

▶ **all-points addressable**

---

addressable cursor *noun* (applications)
a cursor which is controlled by software that allows the user to move the cursor anywhere on the screen

/əˌdresəbl 'kɜːsə(r)/

pl addressable cursors

---

addressable point *noun*
a point or PIXEL on a display screen which can be addressed directly without affecting the surrounding points or pixels: *There are 640 by 1 024 addressable points on the screen.*

/əˌdresəbl 'pɔɪnt/

pl addressable points

◄ clear, set an **addressable point**

☆**address bus** *noun* (hardware)
a pathway used for sending addresses from one part of the computer to another. Computers usually have up to 64 address buses: *carry memory address information on an address bus*

/ə'dres bʌs/

pl address buses

◄ carry data *on/via* an **address bus**

syn bus address line

▶ **databus**

---

address decoder *noun* (hardware)
an electronic device that decodes an address signal to a memory location on one or more RAM chips

/ə'dres diːˌkəʊdə(r)/

pl address decoders

---

address field *noun* (software)
1 (*networks*) the part of a PACKET (= group of bits that forms part of a message) that contains an address **2** (*programming*) the part of an instruction that contains the address: *the address field of a machine code instruction*

/ə'dres fiːld/

pl address fields

syn operand field

---

address format *noun* (software)
the type of addressing used in an instruction: *A standard address format is used for identifying the track on a magnetic disk.*

/ə'dres ˌfɔːmæt/

pl address formats

syn instruction format

☆**addressing** *noun*
1 (*software*) the process of identifying the location in memory of an item of data **2** (*applications*) the process of identifying the place where a message has to go in a communications network

/ə'dresɪŋ/

note no plural

1 ◄ flat, hierarchical, logical **addressing**

▶ **absolute addressing, augmented addressing, symbolic addressing**

---

addressing capacity *noun*
the amount of memory that can be addressed: *an addressing capacity of 640 kilobytes ○ a process that exceeds the addressing capacity of the computer*

/ə'dresɪŋ kəˌpæsəti/

pl addressing capacities

▶ **address space**

addressing level *noun* (applications)
the level in a multilevel ADDRESSING MODE at which a terminal, cable connection, path, etc is addressed: *The addressing level for the network branch is below that for the network path.*

/əˈdresɪŋ ˌlevl/
pl addressing levels

---

addressing method *noun* (applications)
▶ **addressing mode**

/əˈdresɪŋ ˌmeθəd/

---

addressing mode *noun*
1 (*software*) the way of giving the computer the location of an item of data: *The addressing mode a programmer specifies depends on the system architecture.* **2** (*applications*) the way of giving the place where a message is to be sent in a communications network: *adopt the best addressing mode for the communications system*

/əˈdresɪŋ məʊd/
pl addressing modes
syn addressing method, addressing scheme
1 ▶ **absolute addressing, actual instruction, addressing, augmented addressing, immediate addressing, implied addressing, index addressing, relative addressing, symbolic addressing**

---

addressing scheme *noun*
▶ **addressing mode**

/əˈdresɪŋ skiːm/

---

address mapping *noun* (system operation)
the process of changing a VIRTUAL ADDRESS into an ABSOLUTE ADDRESS (= the fixed place where data is stored): *Virtual memory and cache memory use types of address mapping.*

/əˈdres ˌmæpɪŋ/
note no plural
▶ **address translation**

---

address mark *noun*
▶ **index mark**

/əˈdres mɑːk/

---

address modification *noun* (software)
the process of changing the ADDRESS FIELD (2) in an instruction so that each time the instruction is executed it can refer to a different address

/əˈdres mɒdɪfɪˌkeɪʃn/
note no plural
▶ **addressing**

---

address register *noun* (hardware)
a register in memory where an address is held and used to select the next address to be written to or read from: *During the execution of an instruction by the CPU, the address register holds the contents of the address field.*

/əˈdres ˌredʒɪstə(r)/
pl address registers

---

address space *noun* (hardware)
the range of locations in memory that can be addressed: *a 16-bit microprocessor that gives an address space of more than 1 megabyte ○ an 8-bit microcomputer with an address space of 64K*

/əˈdres speɪs/
pl address spaces
▶ **addressing capacity**

---

address translation *noun*
the process of changing the address of a data item or an instruction to an address in the main memory: *an address translation that is done in a single clock cycle*

/əˈdres trænsˌleɪʃn/
note no plural
◂ carry out, perform an **address translation**; an **address translation** algorithm, routine, scheme
syn address mapping

---

abbr abbreviation **pl** plural **syn** synonym ▶ see ◂ collocate (*word often used with the headword*)

add time *noun* (system operation)
the time it takes a computer to find the sum of two numbers: *Microcomputers are often rated by comparing their add times.*

/'æd taɪm/
pl add times
▶ **computer power**

---

adjacency *noun*
1 a direct connection in a network **2** in optical character recognition, a measure of the closeness of characters: *The adjacency of this lettering will result in many inaccuracies in the optical character reading process.*

/ə'dʒeɪsnsi/
note no plural
2 ▶ **kerning**

---

adjacent *adjective*
connected by a direct data link in a network: *adjacent terminals*

/ə'dʒeɪsnt/

ADP *abbr* (system operation)
automatic data processing

/ˌeɪ diː 'piː/
note pronounced as individual letters

ADT *abbr*
▶ **abstract data type**

/ˌeɪ diː 'tiː/
note pronounced as individual letters

AFIPS *abbr* (organizations)
American Federation of Information Processing Societies

/ˌeɪ ef ˌaɪ piːˈes/
note pronounced as individual letters

☆**AI** *abbr*
▶ **artificial intelligence**

/ˌeɪ 'aɪ/
note pronounced as individual letters

AIX *noun*
(*trade mark*) (*software*) an operating system developed by IBM for use on IBM workstations, minicomputers and mainframes: *AIX supports multitasking and is successful on network systems.*

/ˌeɪ aɪ 'eks/
note pronounced as individual letters
note no plural
◣ run, use **AIX**
▶ **DOS, UNIX**

---

alarm *noun* (system operation)
a message or sound that warns of an operation that might cause damage or could be impossible to execute: *The alarm sounded when the disk with a virus was inserted into the disk drive.*

/ə'lɑːm/
pl alarms

---

alert box *noun* (system operation)
a box with a message for the user that appears on the screen in a graphical user interface application: *acknowledge an alert box by clicking OK*

/ə'lɜːt bɒks/
pl alert boxes
◣ acknowledge, click *on* the **alert box**
syn message box
▶ **dialog box**

---

algebra *noun* (mathematics and logic)
a type of mathematics in which letters and symbols are used to represent numbers, sets of numbers, and the operations between them: *Most programming languages use a form of algebra for calculations.*

/'ældʒɪbrə/
note no plural

---

algebraic *adjective*
connected with ALGEBRA

/ˌældʒɪ'breɪɪk/
◣ an **algebraic** equation, expression, formula
▶ **algorithm, Boolean algebra**

algebraic language *noun* (software)
a programming language that is written in a form similar to
ALGEBRA: *ALGOL is an algebraic language.*

/ˈældʒɪˌbreɪk ˈlæŋgwɪdʒ/
pl algebraic languages
syn context-free language
▶ **programming language**

☆**ALGOL** *noun*
an ALGORITHMIC LANGUAGE which is mainly used for scientific
and mathematical work: *generate ALGOL source code*

note The word ALGOL is made of the words 'algorithmic
language'. It is a high-level imperative procedural language
which influenced the design of later languages such as Pascal
and Ada.

/ˈælgɒl/
note no plural
◄ program *in*, write **ALGOL**; an
ALGOL compiler, program

---

algorithm *noun*
a set of unambiguous rules to solve a problem in a finite
number of steps: *a sorting algorithm*

/ˈælgərɪðəm/
pl algorithms
◄ design, express, write down an
algorithm
▶ **flow chart, programming
language, pseudocode**

---

algorithmic *adjective*
connected with ALGORITHMS

/ˌælgəˈrɪðmɪk/

---

algorithmic language *noun*
a programming language that is written in a form similar to
an ALGORITHM

/ˈælgəˌrɪðmɪk ˈlæŋgwɪdʒ/
pl algorithmic languages

---

alias *noun* (software/hardware)
an alternative name for a file, device, command, etc: *In some
systems, an alias is represented as an icon on the desktop.* ○ *Use an
alias that is easy to remember instead of a long and complicated
command.*

/ˈeɪliəs/
pl aliases
◄ an **alias** list

---

aliasing *noun* (applications/graphics)
an effect which makes the lines in screen graphics look rough,
especially on LOW RESOLUTION screens

/ˈeɪliəsɪŋ/
note no plural
▶ **antialiasing, dithering,
graphical user interface,
resolution**

---

align *verb* (software/hardware)
1 to move something so that it is opposite or parallel to
something else: *The printer automatically aligns the paper before
printing any text.*
2 ▶ **justify 1**

/əˈlaɪn/
align, aligning, aligned
note transitive verb

---

alignment *noun*
1 (*hardware*) the adjustment of the disk drive so that the READ/
WRITE HEAD operates without error: *The hard disk crash was
attributed to a problem with the alignment.*
2 ▶ **justification**

/əˈlaɪnmənt/
note no plural
◄ out *of* **alignment**
2 ▶ **flush², justify, ragged text**

---

allocate *verb* (system operation)
to give resources such as memory or hardware to a program or
process: *allocate memory to the graphics program*

/ˈæləkeɪt/
**allocate, allocating,
allocated**
note transitive verb
◄ **allocate** disk space, memory
▶ **deallocate**

---

abbr abbreviation　　**pl** plural　　**syn** synonym　　▶ see　　◄ collocate (*word often used with the headword*)

allocation *noun* (user/system operation)
the process of giving resources such as time, hardware or memory to programs and processes: *The design of the new system optimises the allocation of memory.*

/ˌælə'keɪʃn/
note not used with *a* or *an*. No plural and used with a singular verb only.
◄ memory, storage **allocation**
► **resource allocation**

allocation routine *noun* (system operation)
a ROUTINE (= one part of a program) which controls the resources that are given to a process: *The allocation routine has been modified to improve the performance of the system.*

/ˌælə'keɪʃn ruː:,tiːn/
pl allocation routines

all-points addressable *adjective* (networks)
able to pass messages to all NODES (2)

/'ɔːl 'pɔɪnts ə'dresəbl/
◄ an **all-points addressable** network
► **addressability**

alphabetic *adjective*
relating to the letters of the alphabet: *There are twenty six alphabetic characters in English.* ○ *put the list in alphabetic order*

/ˌælfə'betɪk/
◄ an **alphabetic** character, code, string

alphageometric *adjective*
connected with the set of characters that is used to display graphics in VIDEOTEX systems: *Alphageometric codes sent to the videotex terminal produce simple graphical output.*

/'ælfə,dʒiːə'metrɪk/
◄ an **alphageometric** character, code
► **alphaphotographic**

☆**alphanumeric** *adjective*
containing both letters and numbers: *The user name can be up to twenty eight alphanumeric characters long.*

/ˌælfənju:'merɪk/
◄ an **alphanumeric** character, code, display, keyboard, sort, string: **alphanumeric** data
(*US* **alphameric**)
► **numeric**

alphaphotographic *adjective*
connected with the use of graphics characters to display pictures in VIDEOTEX systems: *alphaphotographic coding techniques*

/'ælfə,fəʊtə'græfɪk/
◄ an **alphaphotographic** character, code
► **alphageometric**

alpha testing *noun*
the first stage of testing a software package: *Alpha testing is usually done in-house and does not involve potential customers.*

/'ælfə ,testɪŋ/
note not used with *a* or *an*. No plural and used with a singular verb only.
◄ carry out, perform **alpha testing**
► **beta testing**

ALT *abbr*
► **alternate key**

/'ɔːlt/
note pronounced as a word

alternate key *noun*
a key on a computer or telex keyboard that is pressed at the same time as another key to access a range of characters and symbols: *The character obtained by holding down the alternate key and pressing 'A' is usually referred to as ALT-A.*

/ɔːl'tɜːnət kiː/
pl alternate keys
◄ hold down, press the **alternate key**
syn ALT
► **control key, shift**

alternate route *noun*
a second path between two NODES (= places in a communications network where two or more transmission channels meet) that can be used if equipment or a connection fails: *An adaptive routing algorithm selects an alternate route in the event of a line failure.*

/ɔːlˌtɜːnət ˈruːt/
pl alternate routes
◄ choose, follow, take an **alternate route**
► **adaptive routing**

alternating current *noun* (hardware)
an electric current that changes its direction and size many times each second. Electricity in this form has to be converted to a DIRECT CURRENT for use by a computer.

/ˌɔːltəneɪtɪŋ ˈkʌrənt/
pl alternating currents
abbr AC
◄ an **alternating current** connection, supply

☆**ALU** *abbr* (hardware)
► **arithmetic and logic unit**

/ˌeɪ el ˈjuː/
note pronounced as individual letters

AM *abbr*
► **amplitude modulation**

/ˌeɪ ˈem/
note pronounced as individual letters

ambiguity *noun*
the possibility of being understood in more than one way: *There were some ambiguities in the specification.*

/ˌæmbɪˈgjuːəti/
pl ambiguities
◄ resolve an **ambiguity**

ambiguous *adjective*
having more than one possible meaning: *Computer languages must not be ambiguous.*

/æmˈbɪgjuəs/
◄ an **ambiguous** specification, statement

ambiguous filename *noun*
a file name that identifies more than one file: *Ambiguous filenames may contain wildcard characters.*

/amˌbɪgjuəs ˈfaɪlneɪm/
pl ambiguous filenames

amp *abbr*
► **ampere**

/æmp/

ampere *noun* (hardware)
the international unit of electric current: *The current flowing through the coil is measured in amperes.* ○ *an electric current of 3 amps*

/ˈæmpeə(r)/
pl amperes
abbr A, amp
► **hertz, SI, volt**

ampersand *noun*
the character '&' used in writing as a short form of 'and'; often used as the logic symbol for AND: *The ampersand is found on most keyboards above the digit 7.*

/ˈæmpəsænd/
pl ampersands

amplifier *noun*
a device that makes something such as an electronic signal more powerful: *Signals on the transmission line are not very strong so amplifiers have been installed to boost them.*

/ˈæmplɪfaɪə(r)/
pl amplifiers
◄ adjust, maintain, use an **amplifier**

amplitude *noun*
the size or strength of a signal: *record an increase/a reduction in amplitude* ○ *measure amplitudes at certain critical frequencies*

/ˈæmplɪtjuːd/
pl amplitudes
◄ display, measure, modulate, record the **amplitude**

abbr abbreviation   **pl** plural   **syn** synonym   ► see   ◄ collocate (*word often used with the headword*)

amplitude modulation *noun*

a way of changing the AMPLITUDE of a CARRIER SIGNAL so that it can transmit information: *Radio programmes are broadcast using amplitude modulation.*

/ˈæmplɪtjuːd ˌmɒdjuˈleɪʃn/

note not used with *a* or *an*. No plural and used with a singular verb only.

abbr AM

⋈ transmit something *via*, use **amplitude modulation**

▶ **frequency modulation, modulation, phase modulation, pulse code modulation**

☆**analog** *adjective*

relating to constantly changing physical values, such as electrical signals, that are used for the storage and transmission of data: *Many voice telephone circuits which were analog are being replaced by digital equipment.*

/ˈænəlɒg/

(*UK* **analogue**)

⋈ an **analog** circuit; **analog** data

▶ **analog-to-digital converter, digital**

analog channel *noun*

a data transmission channel that carries analog signals

/ˈænəlɒg ˌtʃænl/

pl analog channels

⋈ send something *over*, transmit something *via* an **analog channel**; an **analog** circuit, recording

analog circuit *noun* (hardware)

an electronic circuit that works with analog signals and not binary digits

/ˈænəlɒg ˌsɜːkɪt/

pl analog circuits

▶ **digital circuit**

☆**analog computer** *noun* (hardware)

a computer that processes data represented by physical values, especially electrical signals: *The company is replacing its outdated analog computers with digital ones.*

/ˌænəlɒg kəmˈpjuːtə(r)/

pl analog computers

▶ **continuous, digital computer, discrete**

analog display *noun*

1 any form of output which is shown on a scale and not as a definite value in numbers: *a watch with an analog display* **2** a video display that can show all colours: *An analog display can show an infinite range of colours or shades of grey.*

/ˌænəlɒg dɪˈspleɪ/

pl analog displays

▶ **digital display**

analog input card *noun*

a printed circuit board that receives analog data and converts it to digital form for computer processing: *The temperature sensor communicates with the computer through an analog input card.*

/ˌænəlɒg ˈɪnpʊt kɑːd/

pl analog input cards

⋈ connect something *via*, install, maintain, use an **analog input card**

▶ **analog-to-digital converter**

analog output card *noun*

a printed circuit board that receives digital data from a computer system and changes it into an analog signal: *The sound system uses an analog output card to drive the loudspeaker.*

/ˌænəlɒg ˈaʊtpʊt kɑːd/

pl analog output cards

⋈ connect something *via*, install, maintain, use an **analog output card**

▶ **digital-to-analog converter**

analog representation *noun*

a value stored or transmitted as a continuously variable signal: *convert the digital data to an analog representation*

/ˈænəlɒg ˌreprɪzenˈteɪʃn/

pl analog representations

⋈ access, define, store, transmit an **analog representation**

analog signal   *noun*

a continuously varying physical signal that is used to carry data

note The physical value of an analog signal can be measured in voltage and current.

/ˈænəlɒg ˈsɪgnəl/
pl analog signals
◩ modulate, send, receive an **analog signal**
▶ **digital signal**

☆**analog-to-digital converter**   *noun*   (hardware)

a device that changes analog signals into digital signals: *The new computer has a built-in analog-to-digital converter to process incoming analog signals.*

/ˈænəlɒg tə ˈdɪdʒɪtl kənˈvɜːtə(r)/
pl analog-to-digital converters
abbr ADC, A/D converter
▶ **digital, digital-to-analog converter**

---

analogue   *adjective*
▶ **analog**

/ˈænəlɒg/

---

ancestor   *noun*

a NODE (1) (= a place where data is stored) in a tree diagram that is the parent, grandparent, etc of other nodes: *The path was defined by listing all the ancestors on the way up to the root.*

/ˈænsestə(r)/
pl ancestors
◩ an **ancestor** of a node
▶ **descendant, node, parent, tree**

---

ancestral file   *noun*

a copy of a file that is made and stored before the file is updated: *Look through the ancestral files to see when the change was made.*

/ænˈsestrəl ˈfaɪl/
pl ancestral files
◩ delete, make, save an **ancestral file**
▶ **backup, grandfather-father-son file system**

AND   *noun*   (logic)

a function with two or more inputs that gives an output of TRUE when all inputs are TRUE, and FALSE in all other cases: *The result of TRUE AND FALSE is FALSE.*

/ænd/
note not used with *a* or *an*. No plural and used with a singular verb only.
syn AND operation
▶ **Boolean operator, NAND**

AND circuit   *noun*
▶ **AND gate**

/ˈænd ˌsɜːkɪt/

AND gate   *noun*   (hardware)

an electronic circuit that performs an AND OPERATION on its inputs so that its output is logic 1 if and only if two or more inputs are all set to logic 1: *The chip provides four AND gates in a single 14 pin package.* ○ *A half-adder uses AND gates.*

/ˈænd geɪt/
pl AND gates
◩ connect something *to*, drive, replace something *by*, use an **AND gate**
syn AND circuit
▶ **gate**

AND operation   *noun*   (logic)

a logical operation combining two logical expressions. The combined expression P AND Q is true if and only if P and Q are both true: *The programming statement contains one AND operation.*

/ˈænd ɒpəˌreɪʃn/
pl AND operations
◩ do, implement, program an **AND operation**
syn conjunction
▶ **Boolean connective**

---

abbr abbreviation   **pl** plural   **syn** synonym   ▶ see   ◩ collocate (*word often used with the headword*)

animation *noun* (graphics)
images which move on a screen: *The animation is poor and jerky.*

/ˌænɪˈmeɪʃn/
note no plural
ᛐ computer, crude, realistic, realtime **animation**
▶ **graphics**

---

annotation *noun* (programming)
a note added to a program code to explain the instructions more clearly: *Add an annotation to make the code easier to understand.*

/ˌænəˈteɪʃn/
note no plural
ᛐ add, omit, read the **annotation**; an **annotation** symbol
▶ **comment, comment field**

ANSI *abbr*
American National Standards Institute

/ˈænsi/
note pronounced as a word

---

antialiasing *noun* (applications/graphics)
an automatic process which removes the rough edges of lines in screen graphics

/ˌæntiˈeɪliəsm̩/
note no plural
▶ **aliasing, graphical user interface, grey scale, resolution**

---

anti coincidence circuit *noun* (hardware)
a logic circuit whose output is TRUE if and only if one input is TRUE and the other input is FALSE

/ˌænti kəʊˈɪnsɪdəns ˌsɜːkɪt/
pl anti coincidence circuits
(also **anti-coincidence circuit**)
▶ **coincidence circuit, NEQ gate, XOR gate**

---

anti-glare shield *noun* (hardware)
a sheet of glass or plastic which is placed over a screen to reduce reflection: *All the VDUs in the office have an anti-glare shield to make the screen easier to read.*

/ˌænti ˈgleə ʃiːld/
pl anti glare shields
ᛐ use an **anti-glare shield**

---

anti-static device *noun* (hardware)
a device that protects a CHIP while it is being installed: *use an earthed plate as an anti-static device*

/ˌænti ˈstætɪk dɪˌvaɪs/
pl anti-static devices
ᛐ use, wear an **anti-static device**

---

anti-virus program *noun*
▶ **virus checking program**

/ˌænti ˈvaɪrəs ˌprəʊgræm/

APA *abbr*
▶ **all-points addressable**

/ˌeɪ piː ˈeɪ/
note pronounced as individual letters

API *abbr*
▶ **applications programming interface**

/ˌeɪ piː ˈaɪ/
note pronounced as individual letters

APL *noun*
a high-level computer programming language: *generate APL source code*

note APL is an acronym of 'A Programming Language'. It is a functional procedural language which was designed between 1957 and 1968.

/ˌeɪ piː ˈel/
note not used with *a* or *an*. No plural and used with a singular verb only.
ᛐ program in, write **APL**; an **APL** interpreter, program

append¹ *verb* (user)
to add data to the end of a file: *The file was appended to bring the information up to date.*

/ə'pend/
append, appending, appended
note transitive verb
ℍ **append** a document, file
▶ **insert**

☆**Apple** *noun*
(*trade mark*) (*organizations*) Apple Computer Incorporated, a major US manufacturer of personal computers

note Apple was the first company to bring a fully integrated system to the market place in 1983 with the launch of the Macintosh.

/'æpl/
note no plural
ℍ **Apple** Computer, Macintosh
▶ **IBM**

☆**application** *noun* (applications)
a computer program or set of programs designed for a particular type of real world job: *run an accounting application* ○ *design a database application*

/ˌæplɪ'keɪʃn/
pl applications
ℍ a business, an engineering, a graphics, a word processing **application**
▶ **system software, utility program**

---

application layer *noun*
one of the levels of structure of the International Standards Organization PROTOCOL for data communications. The application layer describes the standards for links between applications programs and transmission software.

/ˌæplɪ'keɪʃn leɪə(r)/
pl application layers
ℍ define, specify the **application layer**
▶ **data link layer, ISO OSI, network layer, physical layer, presentation layer, session layer, transport layer**

☆**applications program** *noun* (software)
a program that does a job such as word processing: *an invoicing applications program*

/ˌæplɪ'keɪʃnz ˌprəʊgræm/
pl applications programs
ℍ develop, run, use an **applications program**
▶ **application**

☆**applications programmer** *noun* (personnel)
a person who writes applications programs

/ˌæplɪ'keɪʃnz ˌprəʊgræmə(r)/
pl applications programmers
▶ **programmer, systems programmer**

---

applications programming interface *noun*
(*trade mark*) (*software/programming*) a way of putting HOOKS in the code of an application using standard names so programmers can use the code in their own applications: *This applications programming interface enables users to write custom software.*

/ˌæplɪ'keɪʃnz 'prəʊgræmɪŋ ˌɪntəfeɪs/
note no plural
abbr API

☆**applications software** *noun* (software)
programs that carry out specific tasks: *The personal computer has a word processing package, a spreadsheet program and other applications software.*

/ˌæplɪ'keɪʃnz ˌsɒftweə(r)/
note not used with *a* or *an*. No plural and used with a singular verb only.
▶ **software**

---

abbr abbreviation **pl** plural **syn** synonym ▶ see ℍ collocate (*word often used with the headword*)

APT *abbr*
automatically programmed tool

/ˌeɪ piː ˈtiː/
note pronounced as individual letters

Arabic number *noun*
▶ **Arabic numeral**

/ˌærəbɪk ˈnʌmbə(r)/

Arabic numeral *noun*
one of the figures 0, 1, 2, 3, 4, 5, 6, 7, 8 and 9 used in writing numbers: *In this word processing package, Arabic numerals or Roman numerals can be selected for page numbers.*

/ˌærəbɪk ˈnjuːmərəl/
pl Arabic numerals
M use, write *in* **Arabic numerals**
syn Arabic number
▶ **Roman numeral**

---

arbitration *noun* (operating systems)
the process of deciding which part of a system can use something which is shared, such as the system bus: *arbitration between competing processors* ○ *The arbitration is done by hardware switches.*

/ˌɑːbɪˈtreɪʃn/
note not used with *a* or *an*. No plural.
M bus, I/O, port **arbitration**

---

architecture *noun*
1 the basic ideas and principles that the design of a computer system is based on: *the architecture proposed by Von Neumann* ○ *fifth generation architectures* **2** the outline plan of a design for a computer which shows its major parts, for example the CPU and memory, and how they connect together: *the architecture of a personal computer* **3** the design plan of a logic chip at any level of detail: *The plan of the architecture of the new chip described its broad outline down to the physical layout of the logic gates.*

/ˈɑːkɪtektʃə(r)/
pl architectures
1 M layered, multiprocessor, network, parallel, sequential **architecture**
2 M describe, draw, improve the **architecture**
3 M functional, gate level, logical **architecture**
▶ **ASIC, uncommitted logic array**

☆**archive** *verb*
to move information that is not often needed to a tape or disk to keep it for the future: *archive the information to save storage space* ○ *It's not a good idea to archive documents that still need to be changed.*

/ˈɑːkaɪv/
archive, archiving, archived
M **archive** a document, a file, information
▶ **save**

☆**archived file** *noun* (software)
a file containing data or information that is not often needed and which is usually stored on disk or tape: *The archived files are on magnetic tape and they are stored in a fireproof cupboard.*

/ˌɑːkaɪvd ˈfaɪl/
pl archived files

---

area *noun* (programming)
in programming languages, a space for data objects: *registers stored in a save area*

/ˈeəriə/
pl areas

☆**argument** *noun* (software)
the words or numbers with a program instruction that make the computer execute the instruction in a particular way: *In the command 'select all', 'all' is the argument.* ○ *In the command 'ls-a', 'ls' means 'list files' and the argument '-a' means 'including hidden files'.*

/ˈɑːgjumənt/
pl arguments
▶ **statement**

---

arithmetic *noun* (mathematics)
the functions 'add', 'subtract', 'multiply' and 'divide' in mathematics: *The microprocessor provides facilities for performing arithmetic on bytes.* ○ *a business application that needs sophisticated arithmetic*

/əˈrɪθmətɪk/
note not used with *a* or *an*. No plural and used with a singular verb only.
M do, perform **arithmetic**

▶ **arithmetic operation, arithmetic operator, calculation, computation, fixed point arithmetic, floating point arithmetic**

☆**arithmetic and logic unit** *noun* (hardware)
the part of the CPU where mathematical operations are done: *The arithmetic and logic unit is able to add, subtract, multiply, divide, and compare.*

/ə,rɪθmətɪk ənd ˈlɒdʒɪk ˌjuːnɪt/
pl arithmetic and logic units
abbr ALU
(also **arithmetic unit**)
▶ **accumulator, register**

---

arithmetic mean *noun* (mathematics)
in statistics, a measure of the typical value of a set of quantities: *The arithmetic mean of 15 metres, 20 metres, and 16 metres is (15 + 20 + 16)/3 = 17 metres.*

/ˈærɪθˌmetɪk ˈmiːn/
pl arithmetic means
◄ calculate, compute, estimate, work *out* the **arithmetic mean**

---

arithmetic operation *noun* (mathematics)
an operation on numbers that uses the rules of ARITHMETIC: *perform an arithmetic operation on decimal digits* ○ *The computer has a special chip to speed up arithmetic operations.*

/ˈærɪθˌmetɪk ɒpəˌreɪʃn/
pl arithmetic operations
◄ carry *out*, execute, perform an **arithmetic operation**
▶ **logic operation**

---

arithmetic operator *noun* (mathematics)
a symbol which represents an arithmetic operation: '+', '-', '*' and '/' are arithmetic operators ○ *put the arithmetic operators in the formula in the correct order*

/ˈærɪθˌmetɪk ˌɒpəreɪtə(r)/
pl arithmetic operators
◄ change, correct, replace the **arithmetic operator**
▶ **logic operator**

---

arithmetic overflow *noun* (software)
a computer error which occurs if the result of a calculation is too big to be stored in the available memory: *A flag is set if an arithmetic overflow occurs.*

/ˈærɪθˌmetɪk ˌəʊvəfləʊ/
pl arithmetic overflows
◄ cause, indicate, prevent an **arithmetic overflow**
▶ **error condition, overflow bit, overflow check, overflow error**

---

arithmetic shift *noun*
a machine code instruction that moves the binary digits of a numeric data item so that information about whether the number is positive or negative is kept: *an arithmetic shift right by three places*

/ˈærɪθˌmetɪk ʃɪft/
pl arithmetic shifts
▶ **cyclic shift**

☆**arithmetic unit** *noun*
▶ **arithmetic and logic unit**

/ˈærɪθˌmetɪk ˌjuːnɪt/
pl arithmetic units

---

arm *verb* (system operation)
to switch on a device or system so that it is ready to react to a signal: *arm the alarm system* ○ *The control unit was not armed.*

/ɑːm/
arm, arming, armed
note transitive verb
◄ **arm** a device, transmitter

ARPA *abbr*
(*US*) Advanced Research Projects Agency, part of the US Department of Defense

/ˈɑːpə/
note pronounced as a word
▶ **DARPA**

---

abbr abbreviation   **pl** plural   **syn** synonym   ▶ see   ◄ collocate (*word often used with the headword*)

ARPANET *noun*
Advanced Research Projects Agency Network; the first major packet-switched network: *The virus jammed computers linked to the Pentagon-supported ARPANET network.* ○ *restore connections between ARPANET and other networks*

note ARPANET was established by the US Defense Advanced Research Projects Agency in the early 1970s, and was the prototype of many of today's networks.

/ˈɑːpənet/
note pronounced as a word (also **Arpanet**)
◄ use **ARPANET**

☆**array** *noun*
a DATA STRUCTURE containing data items of the same type in a certain order. All items share the same name and individual items are accessed by their position: *an array to hold integer values*

note A programmer can define an array as a list of items in order (a one-dimensional array) or as a table with rows and columns (a two-dimensional array). Many programming languages allow arrays with three or more dimensions.

/əˈreɪ/
pl arrays
◄ access, define, dimension an **array**; an **array** *of* items, *of* numbers
syn subscripted variable
▶ **dimension statement, matrix, one-dimensional array, two-dimensional array**

---

array bounds *noun*
the largest number allowed for one ARRAY DIMENSION

note In a two-dimensional array, the array bounds can be thought of as the number of rows and columns in the data structure.

/əˈreɪ baʊndz/
pl array bounds
note usually plural
◄ declare, define, exceed the **array bounds**

---

array dimension *noun*
the number of pieces of information that must be supplied by the programmer to access an element in an array: *The element NAME (7, 12) is part of the array NAME which has array dimension two.*

note The term 'array dimension' is sometimes used as a synonym of 'array bound'.

/əˈreɪ daɪˌmenʃn/
pl array dimensions
note usually plural
◄ declare, define the **array dimensions**
▶ **array, array bounds, dimension statement, one-dimensional array, two-dimensional array**

---

array element *noun*
an individual member of an array. Each array element has an index number, for example A [8] is the eighth element of the array A: *an algorithm that computes the location of a particular array element*

/əˈreɪ ˌelɪmənt/
pl array elements
◄ order, read, replace an **array element**
▶ **array, index**

☆**array processor** *noun* (hardware)
a computer system with several processors linked together to process large numbers of arrays: *The computer images are stored into hard disk memory by an array processor.* ○ *high-speed two-dimensional array processors*

/əˈreɪ ˌprəʊsesə(r)/
pl array processors

---

arrow key *noun*
▶ **cursor control key**

/ˈærəʊ kiː/

☆**artificial intelligence** *noun* (applications/science)
the theory and practice of how computers can be made to copy intelligent human behaviour: *Developments in artificial intelligence will create systems that use natural human languages.*

/ˌɑːtɪˌfɪʃl ɪnˈtelɪdʒəns/
abbr AI
note not used with *a* or *an*. No plural and used with a singular verb only.

○ *Some AI features of the system include reasoning and learning, game playing and visual perception.* ○ *use artificial intelligence in engineering*

syn machine intelligence
▶ **computer science, expert system, knowledge base, neural network**

---

ascender *noun*
the part of tall letters such as b, d and h that rises above short letters such as s, c and e when they are LOWER CASE

/ə'sendə(r)/
pl ascenders
◄ allow space *for* the **ascender**
▶ **descender**

---

ascending sort *noun*
the process of arranging a list of data items so that the lower values come before the higher values: *An ascending sort is the default in this sorting utility.* ○ *an alphabetical and numerical ascending sort*

/ə,sendɪŋ 'sɔ:t/
pl ascending sorts
◄ carry *out*, execute, perform an **ascending sort**
▶ **descending sort, sort**

☆**ASCII** *abbr*
American Standard Code for Information Interchange. A standard code that is used to represent letters and numbers, etc so that data can be transferred between computers using different programs: *save a file in ASCII* ○ *translate data into ASCII code*

note ASCII is an 8 bit binary code, although some systems do not use the eighth bit under normal operating modes.

/'æski/
note pronounced as a word
(also **ascii**)
◄ an **ASCII** character, character set, code, format
▶ **Baudot code, EBCDIC**

☆**ASCII file** *noun* (software)
a file that contains only the ASCII code for letters and numbers, etc: *load data into an ASCII file*

/'æski faɪl/
pl ASCII files
(also **ascii file**)
◄ convert data *from/to* an **ASCII file**

ASCII keyboard *noun*
any keyboard that generates the 7-bit ASCII value of the character represented by any of the keys: *When the key labelled A is pressed an ASCII keyboard will generate the 7-bit code 1000001.*

/'æski 'ki:bɔ:d/
pl ASCII keyboards
▶ **keyboard**

ASIC *abbr*
application specific integrated circuit

/'eɪsɪk/
note pronounced as a word

---

aspect ratio *noun*
1 a measure of how wide a display screen is, compared to how high it is: *The standard TV display has the aspect ratio of 4:3.* **2** a measure of how wide an image or a character displayed on screen is, compared to how high it is: *Simple dot-matrix printer characters have an aspect ratio of 6:9.*

/'æspekt ,reɪʃiəʊ/
pl aspect ratios

ASR *abbr*
automatic send receive. (Of a device or terminal) that can send or receive messages automatically.

/,eɪ es 'ɑ:/
note pronounced as individual letters
◄ an **ASR** device, teletypewriter, terminal

---

assemble *verb*
1 to make something out of smaller parts: *The final stage of producing the computer is to assemble the printed circuit boards on the chassis.* **2** to translate a computer program written in assembly language into machine code

/ə'sembl/
assemble, assembling, assembled
note transitive verb

---

abbr abbreviation   **pl** plural   **syn** synonym   ▶ see   ◄ collocate (*word often used with the headword*)

	1 ⋈ **assemble** a computer
	2 ⋈ **assemble** a program, routine, subroutine
	▶ compile, high-level language, interpret, low-level language, machine code, object code, source code

assemble-and-go *adjective*
(of an assembler program) that can start the execution of a translated program as soon as the translation is complete, without the user giving any further commands: *Assemble-and-go systems are very convenient for beginning programmers.*

/ə,sembl ənd ˈgəʊ/
⋈ **assemble-and-go** system
▶ compile-and-go

☆**assembler** *noun* (software)
a program that translates assembly language into machine code: *a program converted by an assembler*

/əˈsemblə(r)/
pl assemblers
⋈ convert something *by*, translate something *by* an **assembler**
▶ compiler, interpreter, machine code, object code, source code

---

assembler language *noun*
▶ **assembly language**

/əˈsemblə ˌlæŋgwɪdʒ/

☆**assembly** *noun* (software/operations)
the process of translating assembly language into machine code

/əˈsembli/
note usually singular
⋈ **assembly** time
▶ compiler, machine code, source code

☆**assembly language** *noun*
a low-level computer programming language that is translated by an assembler into machine code: *write routines in assembly language* ○ *a high-performance assembler that can compile 1 000 lines per second of assembly language code*

/əˈsembli ˌlæŋgwɪdʒ/
pl assembly languages
⋈ program *in*, write **assembly language**; an **assembly language** program, routine, subroutine
syn assembler language

☆**assembly program** *noun*
▶ **assembler**

/əˈsembli ˌprəʊgræm/

---

assembly routine *noun* (programming)
a ROUTINE that is written in assembly language

/əˈsembli ruːˌtiːn/
pl assembly routines
▶ **assembler**

---

assertion *noun*
1 a statement in LOGIC PROGRAMMING that gives a true fact which the program can use: *A false assertion indicates an error in the program.* **2** the act of putting the signal representing TRUE onto one of the inputs of a LOGIC CIRCUIT **3** a program statement that defines a particular condition at a certain stage of a program: *use assertions for verification*

/əˈsɜːʃn/
pl assertions
1 ⋈ delete, deduce something *from*, include an **assertion**
▶ knowledge base
2 ⋈ an **assertion** *of* an input
3 ▶ argument, statement

☆**assign** *verb*

1 to give some work to a person or a device: *She was assigned the task of reprogramming the computer.* ○ *Printing the invoices was assigned to the network printer.* **2** to give a variable a value: *assign the value '0' to the variable COUNT* ○ *assign a variable*

/əˈsaɪn/
assign, assigning, assigned
1 note transitive verb
⋈ **assign** a job, task
2 note transitive or intransitive verb
⋈ **assign** an initial value, a number, a string, a value

☆**assignment** *noun*

1 the act of giving some work to a person or a device: *The assignment of three programmers to the coding meant the job was finished sooner.* **2** a job or piece of work: *The assignment was finished in record time.* **3** the act of giving a value to a variable in a programming language: *The assignment of '0' to X caused the error.*

/əˈsaɪnmənt/
pl assignments
1 ⋈ alter, change, give an **assignment**
2 ⋈ undertake, work *on* an **assignment**
3 ⋈ make, program an **assignment**

---

assignment statement *noun*

a statement in a programming language that gives a value to a variable: *In BASIC, assignment statements can be prefixed by the word LET, as in LET X = 0.*

/əˈsaɪnmənt ˌsteɪtmənt/
pl assignment statements
⋈ insert, make, use, write an **assignment statement**
▶ **statement**

---

associative addressing *noun*

a method of addressing using the contents of a location instead of the address: *Associative addressing techniques are important in large databases.*

/əˌsəʊʃiətɪv əˈdresɪŋ/
note not used with *a* or *an*. No plural and used with a singular verb only.
⋈ **associative addressing** methods, routines, techniques
syn content addressing
▶ **associative memory, associative processor**

---

associative memory *noun* (hardware)

high-speed memory in which information is addressed by part of its contents rather than by its address: *The index is held in associative memory.*

/əˌsəʊʃiətɪv ˈmeməri/
note no plural
syn associative storage, content-addressable file, content-addressable file store, content-addressable memory, content-addressable storage

---

associative processor *noun*

a processor that uses the methods of ASSOCIATIVE ADDRESSING: *use a fast associative processor to manage the database*

/əˌsəʊʃiətɪv ˈprəʊsesə(r)/
pl associative processors
⋈ use an **associative processor**
▶ **associative memory**

---

associative search *noun*

a search ALGORITHM that directly accesses the content of the data items being searched instead of using their addresses

/əˌsəʊʃiətɪv ˈsɜːtʃ/
pl associative searches
⋈ carry out, perform an **associative search**; an **associative search** algorithm, method, technique
▶ **associative addressing, associative processor**

---

associative storage *noun*

▶ **associative memory**

/əˌsəʊʃiətɪv ˈstɔːrɪdʒ/

---

asterisk *noun*
the character '*' used in computing to show multiplication:
The asterisk is found on most keyboards above the digit '8'. ○ *An asterisk is often used as a wildcard.*

/'æstərɪsk/
pl asterisks
ℍ print, write an **asterisk**

asynchronous *adjective*
(of a device or method) that transmits or receives data and does not use a clock to time when the data is transmitted or received: *The transmissions of data to peripheral devices are asynchronous.* ○ *There is an asynchronous protocol incorporated into the system.*

/eɪs'ɪŋkrənəs/
ℍ an **asynchronous** circuit, interface; **asynchronous** access
▶ **synchronous, XON/XOFF**

asynchronous access *noun*
a way of organizing a lot of requests for access to a computer system without using timing signals. Access is not limited to specific times, but can happen as soon as a connection can be made: *a LAN node that allows asynchronous access for up to 16 remote PC users*

/eɪˌsɪŋkrənəs 'ækses/
note not used with *a* or *an*. No plural and used with a singular verb only.
ℍ an **asynchronous access** server

asynchronous communication *noun*
the sending and receiving of data when it is ready, rather than at fixed times: *The system allows asynchronous communication in a local area network.*

/eɪˈsɪŋkrənəs kəˌmjuːnɪˈkeɪʃn/
note not used with *a* or *an*. No plural and used with a singular verb only.
ℍ employ, use **asynchronous communication**
▶ **start bit, synchronous communication**

asynchronous communications interface adaptor *noun*
▶ **ACIA**

/eɪˈsɪŋkrənəs kəˌmjuːnɪˈkeɪʃnz 'ɪntəfeɪs əˌdæptə(r)/

asynchronous mode *noun*
a way of sending and receiving data without using timing signals: *Computer terminals usually operate in asynchronous mode.*

/eɪˈsɪŋkrənəs məʊd/
note not used with *a* or *an*. No plural and used with a singular verb only.
ℍ communicate *in*, operate *in*, use **asynchronous mode**
▶ **synchronous**

asynchronous transmission *noun*
1 the exchange of data when it is ready, rather than at fixed times: *Most printers receive data by asynchronous transmission.* **2** a piece of data that is sent as soon as it is ready to be sent, and not at a fixed time: *The log-in requests are made as asynchronous transmissions.*

/eɪˈsɪŋkrənəs trænsˈmɪʃn/
1 note not used with *a* or *an*. No plural and used with a singular verb only.
ℍ **asynchronous transmission** protocols, methods
▶ **synchronous transmission 1**
2 pl asynchronous transmissions
ℍ make, send an **asynchronous transmission**
▶ **synchronous transmission 2**

AT *abbr*
advanced technology

/ˌeɪ 'tiː/
note pronounced as individual letters
▶ **XT**

ATE *abbr*
▶ **automatic test equipment**

/ˌeɪ tiː 'iː/
note pronounced as individual letters

ATL *abbr*
automated tape library

/ˌeɪ tiː 'el/
note pronounced as individual letters

ATM *abbr*
automatic teller machine

/ˌeɪ tiː 'em/
note pronounced as individual letters

A to D *abbr*
analog-to-digital

/ˌeɪ tə 'diː/

---

atom *noun*
1 something that cannot be made simpler without losing its important properties **2** the basic unit of code or data in LISP and similar programming languages. Atoms cannot be divided into smaller units, but can be combined to form lists: *An atom in LISP is any string of characters, or the special atom NIL.*

/'ætəm/
pl atoms

1 ⋈ break down *into*, build up *from* **atoms**
2 ⋈ access, define, delete, read an **atom**

▶ **LISP, list processing**

---

attribute *noun*
1 an item of information that controls the way graphics or text are displayed by a computer: *Screen attributes are 16 colours and 40 lines by 80 characters.* **2** (*database*) in a DATA MODEL, a data item which can be accessed only after the key to the ENTITY is known: *The entity STAFF MEMBER has one key field which is the unique identifying number, and several attributes such as NAME, ADDRESS and SALARY.*

/'ætrɪbjuːt/
pl attributes

1 ⋈ have, possess an **attribute**
2 ⋈ access, edit, update an **attribute**

---

audio *adjective*
of hearing or sound: *The multimedia PC has audio output.*

/'ɔːdiəʊ/
⋈ **audio** input, output, tape
▶ **video**

---

audio board *noun*
an EXPANSION BOARD (= a printed circuit board added to a computer to increase its functions) that allows a computer to produce sound: *Speech synthesis requires an audio board.*

/'ɔːdiəʊ bɔːd/
pl audio boards
⋈ install, maintain, use an **audio board**
▶ **analog output card**

---

audit *noun*
a check on a system to make sure that it is secure and that the data is accurate: *A computer audit checks that there has been no unauthorized use of the computer facilities.*

/'ɔːdɪt/
pl audits
⋈ carry out, do an **audit**
▶ **accounting file**

---

audit trail *noun*
a record of how a system has been used: *The systems administrator used the audit trail to check which members of staff were logged on when the system crashed.* ○ *Security staff at the bank consulted the audit trail to find details of all the illegal transactions.*

/'ɔːdɪt treɪl/
pl audit trails
⋈ create, record, save an **audit trail**
▶ **addition record, journal file**

---

augend *noun* (mathematics and logic)
an augend is a number which is added to another number called an ADDEND

/'ɔːgend/
pl augends

---

abbr abbreviation **pl** plural **syn** synonym ▶ see ⋈ collocate (*word often used with the headword*)

▶ **accumulator, addition, operand**

---

augmented addressing *noun*

a way of accessing storage locations in a large amount of memory by joining the ADDRESS FIELDS of two or more shorter instructions

/ɔːgˌmentɪd əˈdresɪŋ/

note not used with *a* or *an*. No plural and used with a singular verb only.

Ɫ employ, use **augmented addressing**

▶ **addressing capacity**

---

authenticate *verb*

to prove that something is genuine: *Each electronic mail message is accompanied by a coded signature to authenticate it.*

/ɔːˈθentɪkeɪt/

authenticate, authenticating, authenticated

note transitive verb

Ɫ **authenticate** an identity, a message, a signature

▶ **verify**

---

author *noun* (personnel)

1 a person who writes programs: *The software house employs 3 multimedia authors.* **2** a person who uses an AUTHOR LANGUAGE to prepare exercises for students: *The teacher was the author of the computer-based learning materials.*

/ˈɔːθə(r)/

pl authors

▶ **programmer**

---

authoring tool *noun* (software)

software that is used for tasks such as the preparation of teaching materials, without the need to work in a programming language: *Authoring tools are achieving new importance in the production of CD-ROMs for educational purposes.*

/ˈɔːθərɪŋ tuːl/

pl authoring tools

▶ **author language**

Ɫ use, work *with* an **authoring tool**

---

authorization *noun*

the right to use a computer system: *the database cannot be accessed without authorization*

/ˌɔːθəraɪˈzeɪʃn/

note not used with *a* or *an*. No plural and used with a singular verb only.

(also **authorisation**)

Ɫ grant, have **authorization**

---

authorization code *noun*
▶ **password**

/ˌɔːθəraɪˈzeɪʃn kəʊd/

---

authorize *verb*

to give permission to use a computer system: *The systems administrator authorized access to the file server.*

/ˈɔːθəraɪz/

authorize, authorizing, authorized

note transitive verb

---

author language *noun*

a computer programming language that can be used to prepare teaching materials: *An author language can be used by any teacher or trainer because programming skills are not required.* ○ *PILOT is a well-known author language.*

/ˈɔːθə ˌlæŋgwɪdʒ/

pl author languages

(also **authoring language**)

Ɫ program *in*, use, write *in* an **author language**

auto *combining form*
automatic. Able to work without direct human control.
/ˈɔːtəʊ/

auto advance *noun*
the ability of a printer to move the paper up when the end of a line is reached without a signal from the computer
/ˌɔːtəʊ ədˈvɑːns/
note not used with *a* or *an*. No plural and used with a singular verb only.
⧓ disable, enable, switch *off*, switch *on* **auto advance**
▶ **line feed**

auto-answer *noun*
a feature of many modems that allows a computer to respond when data arrives and no operator is present: *Auto-answer is essential for unattended services such as bulletin boards.*
/ˌɔːtəʊ ˈɑːnsə(r)/
note not used with *a* or *an*. No plural and used with a singular verb only.

autobaud *noun*
a feature of a modem where the BAUD RATE (= speed of transmission) of a message is automatically measured as it arrives and the PROTOCOL (= the code that allows the message to be received) is changed to the same speed
/ˈɔːtəʊbɔːd/
note not used with *a* or *an*. No plural and used with a singular verb only.
▶ **modem**

auto-dial *noun*
a feature of modems which allows a telephone number to be dialled automatically, usually to communicate with another computer: *The software records any telephone number dialled so that in future the auto-dial feature can be used.*
/ˈɔːtəʊ daɪl/
note Not used with *a* or *an*. No plural and used with a singular verb only
syn automatic calling unit

auto log in *noun*
a feature of software which supplies passwords and user identification so the user does not have to enter them each time a system is accessed: *To connect to the bulletin board, use the auto log in feature.* ○ *access electronic mail via auto log in*
/ˌɔːtəʊ ˈlɒg ɪn/
note not used with *a* or *an*. No plural and used with a singular verb only.
(also **auto log on**)
⧓ set up, use **auto log in**; **auto log in** ability, data, parameters
▶ **auto-dial, log in**

auto log-on *noun*
▶ **auto log in**
/ˌɔːtəʊ ˈlɒg ɒn/

automate *verb*
to use machines to do the work of people: *The effect of new technology was to automate many of the clerical tasks.*
/ˈɔːtəmeɪt/
automate, automating, automated
⧓ an **automated** process, system
▶ **automation**

automated tape library *noun*
a device that stores magnetic data tapes and loads them onto a tape drive when a request is made by a user; no human action is needed to load the tape: *make a request to the automated tape library*
/ˌɔːtəmeɪtɪd ˈteɪp ˌlaɪbrəri/
pl automated tape libraries
abbr ATL
⧓ load a tape *from* the **automated tape library**

automatic *adjective*
(of a machine, etc) that can work by itself without direct human control: *a system with automatic processing capabilities*
/ˌɔːtəˈmætɪk/
⧓ **automatic** equipment, machinery

automatic calling unit *noun*
▶ **auto-dial**

/ˌɔːtəˌmætɪk ˈkɔːlɪŋ ˌjuːnɪt/
abbr ACU

automatic data logging *noun*
▶ **logging**

/ˌɔːtəˌmætɪk ˈdeɪtə ˌlɒgɪŋ/

automatic test equipment *noun* (hardware)
an electronic device that usually contains a microprocessor
and which is able to check a complex circuit for faults: *The
diagnosis on a printed circuit board was performed using automatic
test equipment.*

/ˌɔːtəˌmætɪk ˈtest ɪˌkwɪpmənt/
note not used with *a* or *an*. No
plural and used with a singular
verb only.
abbr ATE
◪ install, use **automatic test
equipment**
▶ **test equipment**

automation *noun*
the use of machines instead of people to do work: *The software
deals with everything from the automation of newspaper and
magazine orders to customer billing.*

/ˌɔːtəˈmeɪʃn/
note not used with *a* or *an*. No
plural and used with a singular
verb only.
◪ office **automation**
▶ **computerization**

automaton *noun*
1 a device which reads a string of symbols, checks the string is
in the correct form, and produces an output string

note In this sense, the 'device' is a mathematical idea, not a
mechanical or electronic machine. It is used to prove
theoretical results about computers.

2 any automatic device

note In this sense, the word automaton is used especially for a
device that behaves in a way that is very unlike the way a
person behaves.

/ɔːˈtɒmətən/
pl automata
pl automatons
1 ◪ implement, study an
automaton
▶ **Turing machine**
2 ◪ behave *like* an **automaton**

auto redial *noun*
a feature of a modem that allows a number to be dialled again
automatically if the telephone line is busy or engaged the first
time the number is dialled: *This modem's auto redial feature will
retry the transmission after a pause of two minutes.*

/ˌɔːtəʊ ˈriːdaɪl/
note not used with *a* or *an*. No
plural and used with a singular
verb only.
▶ **modem**

auto repeat *noun*
the ability of a computer keyboard to send the same character
to the computer again and again when the key is held down

/ˌɔːtəʊ rɪˈpiːt/
note not used with *a* or *an*. No
plural and used with a singular
verb only.
◪ disable, enable, switch *on*,
switch *off* **auto repeat**

auto restart *noun*
the ability of a computer system to reload its operating system
automatically, especially when power returns after a power
failure

/ˌɔːtəʊ ˈriːstɑːt/
note not used with *a* or *an*. No
plural and used with a singular
verb only.
◪ disable, enable, switch *off*,
switch *on* **auto restart**
syn auto start

auto start *noun*
▶ **auto restart**

/ˌɔːtəʊ ˈstɑːt/

auxiliary *adjective* (hardware/software)
(of a device, etc) that can give give extra help or support:
connect an auxiliary printer if the laser printer fails

/ɔːgˈzɪliəri/
◄ an **auxiliary** device; **auxiliary** support

---

auxiliary memory *noun* (hardware)
memory that is cheaper and usually slower than main
memory and is often a type of EXTERNAL MEMORY (= memory
that is outside the CPU): *access auxiliary memory through input
and output channels*

/ɔːgˌzɪliəri ˈmeməri/
note no plural
syn auxiliary store, auxiliary storage, external storage
► **random access storage device, primary memory**

---

auxiliary processor *noun*
an extra processor in a computer system that helps the main
processor by doing some of the calculations, or by managing
some part of the system: *The auxiliary processor handles the
updating of the screen display.*

/ɔːgˌzɪliəri ˈprəʊsesə(r)/
pl auxiliary processors
◄ install, use, work *with* an **auxiliary processor**
► **coprocessor, multi-processor system**

---

auxiliary storage *noun*
► **auxiliary memory**

/ɔːgˌzɪliəri ˈstɔːrɪdʒ/

---

auxiliary store *noun*
► **auxiliary memory**

/ɔːgˌzɪliəri ˈstɔː(r)/
pl auxilary stores

---

availability *noun*
1 a measure of how easy or difficult it is to use a computer
system when it is needed: *increase the availability of computers
with word processing facilities in the self-access centre* **2** a
measure of how easy or difficult it is to get something,
especially a piece of software: *The availability of sophisticated
word processing packages is good.*

/əˌveɪləˈbɪləti/
note not used with *a* or *an*. No plural and used with a singular verb only.
1 ◄ augment, check, increase **availability**
2 ◄ bad, excellent, good, poor, ready **availability**

---

available list *noun*
a list kept by the operating system which records computer
resources that are not being used

/əˌveɪləbl lɪst/
pl available lists
◄ access, update the **available list**
► **contention**

---

axis *noun*
1 an imaginary line through the middle of something which
turns: *The axis of rotation of the disk drive is vertical.* **2** one of the
reference lines on a graph that has a scale: *the x-axis ○ the
y-axis*

/ˈæksɪs/
pl axes
1 ◄ **axis** *of* rotation
2 ◄ calibrate, draw the **axis**
► **coordinate[1], X-axis, Y-axis, Z-axis**

---

azerty keyboard *noun* (hardware)
a keyboard where the top row of letter keys starts from the left
with AZERTY: *an azerty keyboard layout*

/əˌzɜːti ˈkiːbɔːd/
pl azerty keyboards
► **keyboard, qwerty keyboard**

---

abbr abbreviation   **pl** plural   **syn** synonym   ► see   ◄ collocate (*word often used with the headword*)

b *abbr* /biː/
▶ bit

B *noun* /biː/
1 a high-level computer programming language

1 ℍ program *in* B; a B compiler,
program; B source code
▶ CPL

note B is an imperative procedural language which was
developed from BCPL in the early 1970s. The programming
language C was developed from B.

2 ▶ byte

backbone network *noun* (networks) /ˈbækbəʊn ˌnetwɜːk/
the part of a wide area network that connects a number of
local area networks: *set up a backbone network to connect
industrial research networks throughout Europe* ○ *integrate remote
networks into an existing backbone network*

pl backbone networks
ℍ install, maintain, make use *of*,
use a **backbone network**
syn trunk network
▶ **bus network, site network**

backend *noun* /ˈbækend/
the part of a computer system which processes data: *archiving
operations happen in the backend*

pl backends
ℍ process *in* the **backend**

backend processor *noun* /ˌbækend ˈprəʊsesə(r)/
a processing unit added to a system to do the work of the
central processing unit for a special function, for example
arithmetic calculations or database management: *The system
uses a backend processor to speed up calculations.*

pl backend processors
ℍ fit, include, use a **backend
processor**
▶ coprocessor

background *noun* /ˈbækɡraʊnd/
the part of the display on screen which is behind the text and
graphics: *Text is displayed using black characters on a white
background.* ○ *change the default background from grey to blue*

pl backgrounds
ℍ change, choose, decide *on*,
select the **background**;
background colour
syn ground
▶ **display, foreground**

background job *noun* (system operation) /ˈbækɡraʊnd dʒɒb/
▶ **background task**

background printing *noun* (system operation) /ˌbækɡraʊnd ˈprɪntɪŋ/
the process of printing stored files when the FOREGROUND
PROGRAM is not using the printer: *Background printing is going on
while the next file is being read and sorted.*

note not used with *a* or *an*. No
plural and used with a singular
verb only.
ℍ allow, operate, use
background printing
▶ **print spooling**

background processing *noun* /ˌbækɡraʊnd ˈprəʊsesɪŋ/
the processing of tasks which happens when the system is not
working on a FOREGROUND PROGRAM in a multitasking
environment: *Background processing that the system can do
includes spooling and printing documents.*

note not used with *a* or *an*. No
plural and used with a singular
verb only.
ℍ carry out, control, organize the
background processing
▶ **foreground processing,
multitasking, precedence**

background program *noun*

a program that is executed when the system is not working on the FOREGROUND PROGRAM in a multitasking environment: *The background program is e-mail software which is scanning for new mail while the user is working on a spreadsheet program.*

/'bækgraʊnd ˌprəʊgræm/
pl background programs
ᴹ queue, run, store the **background programs**

---

background task *noun* (system operation)

a task which is suitable for BACKGROUND PROCESSING in a multitasking environment

/'bækgraʊnd tɑːsk/
pl background tasks
ᴹ run, treat something *as a* **background task**
syn background job

---

backing storage *noun* (hardware)
▶ **backing store**

/'bækɪŋ ˌstɔːrɪdʒ/

☆**backing store** *noun* (hardware)

a separate memory where a permanent record of the information in the main memory can be made. This information can be referred to, but must be accessed to work on: *bring programs on backing store into main memory*

/'bækɪŋ stɔː(r)/
syn backing storage
▶ **random access storage device, roll in**

---

backplane *noun* (hardware)

the part of a computer that holds the PRINTED CIRCUIT BOARDS: *The circuit board plugs into the backplane.* ○ *The backplane holds the motherboard.*

/'bækpleɪn/
pl backplanes
ᴹ assemble, build, connect something *to a* **backplane**

☆**backspace¹** *noun* (hardware)

the key usually marked with an arrow or the abbreviation 'BkSp' on a computer keyboard: *press the backspace key*

note Pressing the backspace key will move the cursor to the left and, in most programs, will delete any characters there.

/'bækspeɪs/
note not used with *a* or *an*. No plural and used with a singular verb only.
abbr BkSp
ᴹ a **backspace** facility, key
▶ **cursor control key, delete¹, insert¹, shift¹**

☆**backspace²** *verb* (user operation)

to move a cursor to the left by one or more spaces: *One way to delete characters is to backspace.*

/'bækspeɪs/
backspace, backspacing, backspaced
note intransitive verb
ᴹ **backspace** one character
▶ **delete², insert²**

---

backspace character *noun* (system)

the character BS in ASCII code which moves the cursor one space to the left

/'bækspeɪs ˌkærəktə(r)/
pl backspace characters
abbr BS
ᴹ decode, transmit a **backspace character**
▶ **ASCII, tab character**

☆**backspace key** *noun* (hardware)
▶ **backspace¹**

/'bækspeɪs kiː/

---

backtracking *noun*

a way of finding an answer to a problem by following a SEARCH PATH. If the first path followed does not give an answer to the problem, the system goes back to another path and searches

/'bæktrækɪŋ/
note not used with *a* or *an*. No plural and used with a singular verb only.

---

abbr abbreviation   **pl** plural   **syn** synonym   ▶ see   **ᴹ** collocate (*word often used with the headword*)

forward again: *Backtracking is an essential part of the Prolog language.*

▶ a **backtracking** algorithm, method, program

▸ **search, tree**

☆**backup¹** *noun*

1 a copy of a disk, file, program, etc for use in case the original is damaged: *a backup of important files* **2** the process of making such a copy: *The machine can't be used for anything else while it is doing the backup.*

/ˈbækʌp/
(also **back-up**)

1 pl backups

▶ do, keep, make a **backup**; a **backup** copy, file

2 note usually singular

☆**backup²** *verb*

to make a copy of a disk, file, program, etc for use in case the original is lost or damaged: *Always backup work at the end of the day.*

/ˈbækʌp/
backup, backing up, backed up

note transitive verb

▶ **back up** a disk, file, program; **back up** data *to* disk, etc

---

backup procedure *noun*

the way of making a backup copy: *The backup procedure is very simple.*

/ˈbækʌp prəˌsiːdʒə(r)/
pl backup procedures

▶ carry out, follow, omit the **backup procedure**

Backus-Naur form *noun*

a method of describing the GRAMMAR **(1)** (= word order or structure) of a computer programming language

note Backus-Naur Form is a well-known metalanguage, and was invented by John Backus and Peter Naur in the definition of ALGOL 60.

/ˌbækəs ˈnaʊə fɔːm/
note not used with *a* or *an*. No plural and used with a singular verb only.

abbr BNF

▶ define, write *in* **Backus-Naur form**

▸ **metalanguage**

---

backward error correction *noun*

a way of correcting errors in transmitted data. If the device that receives the message finds errors, a message is sent back to the device that transmitted the message asking it to transmit the correct data.

/ˌbækwəd ˈerə kəˈrekʃn/
note not used with *a* or *an*. No plural and used with a singular verb only.

▶ use **backward error detection**

syn backward error protection

▸ **forward error correction**

---

backward error protection *noun*

▸ **backward error correction**

/ˌbækwəd ˈerə prəˈtekʃn/

---

badge reader *noun*

a device for reading information from a small object often made of metal or plastic, called a badge, that usually carries information about a person's identity: *Insert an identification badge into the badge reader to gain access to the computer room.*

/ˈbædʒ ˌriːdə(r)/
pl badge readers

---

bag *noun* (mathematics)

a collection of things in which anything can occur more than once: *Two variables are needed to describe each thing in a bag - one for the name of the thing and for the number of times it occurs.*

/bæg/
pl bags

▶ implement, use a **bag**

▸ **set**

---

balanced binary tree *noun*
▶ **B-tree**

/ˈbælənst ˈbaɪnəri ˈtriː/

---

balanced tree *noun*
▶ **B-tree**

/ˌbælənst ˈtriː/

---

band *noun*
1 (*system operation*) a range of frequencies between two known limits: *The radio station broadcasts on the 90.2-92.4MHz band.* **2** (*hardware*) a group of tracks on a disk near or next to each other: *There are two sectors in the band.*

/bænd/
pl bands
1 ⋈ define, licence a **band**
▶ **bandpass filter, bandwidth, frequency**
2 ▶ **track**

---

band matrix *noun* (mathematics)
a type of MATRIX (= arrangement of items in rows and columns) in which most items are zero, and all the non-zero items are in a narrow band between the top left and the bottom right corners: *If the data is in the form of a band matrix then special programs can be used to save memory and computation time.*

/ˈbænd ˌmeɪtrɪks/
pl band matrices
pl band matrixes
⋈ recognize, write *as* a **band matrix**
▶ **sparse array**

---

band pass filter *noun*
an electronic circuit that cuts off all parts of a signal with frequencies outside a fixed range: *a band pass filter which cuts certain frequencies by 60%*

/ˌbænd pɑːs ˈfɪltə(r)/
pl band pass filters
⋈ use a **band pass filter**
▶ **bandwidth**

---

bandwidth *noun*
1 the range of frequencies that can be passed by a TRANSMISSION CHANNEL (= link between two devices that allows data to be sent): *Bandwidth is measured in hertz or kilohertz.*

note Bandwidth is measured as the difference between the highest and lowest frequencies in a range of frequencies.

2 a measure of the quantity of data that can be sent in a certain amount of time: *The project needs higher bandwidth communication equipment for data exchange between institutions.*

/ˈbændwɪdθ/
pl bandwidths
1,2 ⋈ a high, low, narrow, wide **bandwidth**
▶ **baud rate, bit rate**

---

bank switching *noun* (hardware)
a way of addressing a large amount of memory. The memory is divided into sections called banks. The processor first selects a bank, and then only this bank is addressed: *use bank switching to address 2 MB of memory*

/ˈbæŋk ˌswɪtʃɪŋ/
note not used with *a* or *an*. No plural and used with a singular verb only.
⋈ use **bank switching**
▶ **addressing, memory**

---

banner *noun*
the first page of a printed document which identifies the document

/ˈbænə(r)/
pl banners
⋈ print, read, separate *at* a **banner**
▶ **burst, listing**

---

bar chart *noun* (graphics)
a display of information which shows values as vertical or horizontal bars: *design a bar chart that shows the company's sales figures*

/ˈbɑː tʃɑːt/
pl bar charts
⋈ design, draw, show a **bar chart**
syn bar graph
▶ **graphics**

---

abbr abbreviation   **pl** plural   **syn** synonym   ▶ see   ⋈ collocate (*word often used with the headword*)

bar code *noun*
a series of lines printed on a product or its packaging that can be read by a computer system. It is used to record details of the sale, or to check the price or number of items left in stock: *scan the bar code with a light pen*

/ˈbɑː kəʊd/
pl bar codes
◪ read, scan a **bar code**
▶ **readable**

bar code reader *noun* (hardware)
a device that reads a BAR CODE: *a hand-held bar code reader*

/ˈbɑː kəʊd ˌriːdə(r)/
pl bar code readers
syn wand

bar graph *noun*
▶ **bar chart**

/ˈbɑː grɑːf/

☆**base** *noun* (mathematics and logic)
1 a number that is used to build up a system of numbers, for example 10 in the decimal system or 2 in the binary system: *The numbers in base 5 are 0, 1, 2, 3 and 4.* **2** the middle layer of a BIPOLAR TRANSISTOR

/beɪs/
pl bases
1 ▶ **binary notation, decimal notation, hexadecimal notation**

base address *noun* (software)
an address held in the BASE REGISTER for use in RELATIVE ADDRESSING: *The base address must be changed each time a new process is run.*

/ˈbeɪs əˌdres/
pl base addresses
◪ change, reset, write the **base address**
▶ **address, addressing**

base addressing *noun*
▶ **relative addressing**

/ˌbeɪs əˈdresɪŋ/

baseband modem *noun* (hardware)
a modem that sends and receives data directly, without using a CARRIER SIGNAL

/ˌbeɪs bænd ˈməʊdem/
pl baseband modems

baseband network *noun*
a network in which digital messages are sent using a single transmission channel, without using a CARRIER SIGNAL

/ˌbeɪs bænd ˈnetwɜːk/
pl base band networks
◪ use, transmit *over* a **baseband network**

base limit register *noun*
a register which stores the upper and lower limits of the range of memory addresses available to the program: *An error occurs if the process attempts to access addresses outside the limits set in the base limit register.*

/ˈbeɪs ˌlɪmɪt ˌredʒɪstə(r)/
pl base limit registers
◪ access, read, write *to* a **base limit register**
▶ **segmentation, segmented address**

base register *noun*
a register which holds the BASE ADDRESS to be used in BASE ADDRESSING: *a 32-bit base register* ○ *the updated contents of the base register*

/ˈbeɪs ˌredʒɪstə(r)/
pl base registers
◪ read, use, write *to* the **base register**
▶ **base addressing, register**

base 2 *noun* (mathematics)
a number system using the two digits 0 and 1 only. The base 2 system is used in BINARY NUMBERS: *The base 2 digits 0 and 1 correspond to the off/on states of electronic switches.*

/ˌbeɪs ˈtuː/
note no plural
◪ change *to*, convert *to*, express *in*, write in **base 2**; a **base 2** fraction, number, representation, system
syn binary system
▶ **binary fraction**

base 8 *noun* (mathematics)
a number system using the eight digits 0 to 7 only. The base 8 system is used in the OCTAL system: *The base 8 system was often used in the earliest computers.*

/ˌbeɪs ˈeɪt/
note no plural
◄ change *to*, convert *to*, express *in*, write *in* **base 8**; a **base 8** fraction, number, representation, system
► **octal**

base 10 *noun* (mathematics)
a number system using 0 to 9 only. The base 10 system is the basis of the decimal system: *convert all numbers to base 10*

/ˌbeɪs ˈten/
note no plural
◄ change *to*, convert *to*, written *in* **base 10**; a **base 10** fraction, number, representation, system
► **decimal**

base 12 *noun*
a way of writing numbers using the digits 0 to 9 with two extra symbols for 10 and 11: *The denary number 100 is written as 84 in base 12.*

/ˌbeɪs ˈtwelv/
note not used with *a* or *an*. No plural and used with a singular verb only.

base 16 *noun* (mathematics)
a number system using the sixteen hexadecimal numbers. These are represented by the numbers 0 to 9, followed by the letters A to F: *write addresses in hexadecimal, using base 16 digits*

/ˌbeɪs sɪkˈstiːn/
note No plural
◄ change *to*, convert *to*, write *in* **base 16**; a **base 16** address, number, representation, system
► **hexadecimal**

☆**BASIC** *noun*
Beginner's All-Purpose Symbolic Instruction Code. A high-level computer programming language which was designed to be an easy introduction to programming

note BASIC is an imperative procedural language which is usually translated by an interpreter.

/ˈbeɪsɪk/
note not used with *a* or *an*. No plural and used with a singular verb only.
(also **Basic**)
◄ program *in*, write *in* **BASIC**; **BASIC** source code

basic input output system *noun*
► **BIOS**

/ˈbeɪsɪk ˈɪnpʌt ˈaʊtpʌt ˌsɪstəm/

☆**batch** *noun* (operations)
a group of programs which are processed together:
Transactions are collected over a period of time and processed as a batch.

/bætʃ/
pl batches
◄ a **batch** application, file, job, number, program, queue, system; **batch** control

batch mode *noun*
► **batch processing**

/ˈbætʃ məʊd/

☆**batch processing** *noun* (system)
a way of running a group of programs (a batch) at the same time without instructions from the user: *Batch processing is used in database management systems.*

/ˈbætʃ ˌprəʊsesɪŋ/
note no plural
◄ sequential **batch processing**
syn batch mode
► **real-time processing**

battery *noun* (hardware)
a device which provides electric power without connection to a main electricity supply: *a calculator battery ○ a six-volt battery*

/ˈbætri/
pl batteries
◄ connect, replace a **battery**

abbr abbreviation   **pl** plural   **syn** synonym   ► see   ◄ collocate (*word often used with the headword*)

battery backed *adjective*
having a battery which will supply electricity if the main
power supply is lost or not available: *The real-time clock is
battery backed.*

/ˌbætri ˈbækt/
⋈ **battery backed** RAM

battery backup *noun*
the use of a battery to provide electric power for volatile
devices which lose data when the main power is turned off:
*Battery backup is used so that RAM can hold data when the
computer is switched off.*

/ˌbætri ˈbækʌp/
pl battery backups
⋈ install, use a **battery backup**
▶ **volatile memory**

baud *noun*
the unit for measuring the speed of data transmission, usually
of a modem

note In binary data transmission, one baud is approximately
equal to one bit per second; because of start and stop bits, this
is not the same as one bit of message data per second.

/bɔːd/
note not used with *a* or *an*. No
plural and used with a singular
verb only.

baudot code *noun*
the system for coding messages using five bits for each
character. It is used in telegraph communications.

/ˈbɔːdəʊ kəʊd/
note not used with *a* or *an*. No
plural and used with a singular
verb only.
(also **Baudot code**)
⋈ transmit *via*, use **baudot code**

baud rate *noun*
the speed of data transmission, measured in BAUD: *The baud rate
is fixed at 9 600 bits per second.*

/ˈbɔːd reɪt/
pl baud rates
⋈ a high, low **baud rate**
▶ **bandwidth, bit rate, split
baud rate**

BBS *abbr*
bulletin board system

/ˌbiː biː ˈes/
note pronounced as individual
letters
▶ **bulletin board**

BCD *abbr*
▶ **binary coded decimal**

/ˌbiː siː ˈdiː/
note pronounced as indvidual
letters

BCD adder *noun*
a device that adds two BINARY CODED DECIMAL digits: *There are
eight BCD adders on the chip.*

/ˌbiː siː diː ˈædə(r)/
pl BCD adders
⋈ design, use a **BCD adder**
▶ **adder, carry**

BCH *abbr*
block control header

/ˌbiː siː ˈeɪtʃ/
note pronounced individual
letters

BCH code *abbr*
▶ **Bose-Chaudhuri-Hocquengham code**

/ˌbiː siː ˈeɪtʃ kəʊd/

BCPL *noun*
a high-level computer programming language developed from
CPL

note BCPL is an imperative procedural language.

/ˌbiː siː piː ˈel/
note pronounced as indvidual
letters not used with *a* or *an*. No
plural and used with a singular
verb only.
⋈ program *in* **BCPL**; a **BCPL**
compiler, program

BCS *abbr*
basic control system

/ˌbiː siː 'es/
note pronounced as individual letters

BDC *abbr*
▶ **binary-to-decimal conversion**

/ˌbiː diː 'siː/
note pronounced as individual letters

---

beep *noun*
a short sound made by a device as a signal to the operator, especially if there is a problem: *Two beeps are sounded if the printer is not switched on.*

/biːp/
pl beeps
◄ give, sound a **beep**
syn bleep

Beginner's All-Purpose Symbolic Instruction Code
noun
▶ **BASIC**

/bɪˈɡɪnəz ˈɔːl ˌpːpəs sɪmbɒlɪk ɪnˈstrʌkʃn kəʊd/

---

beginning of file *noun* (software)
a character that is used to mark the start of a section of data: *The text characters follow immediately after the beginning of file is transmitted.*

/bɪˌɡɪnɪŋ əv 'faɪl/
note no plural
abbr BOF
◄ a **beginning of file** character, marker, symbol

---

beginning of information mark *noun*
a symbol or code that shows where a set of data begins

/bɪˈɡɪnɪŋ əv ˌɪnfəˈmeɪʃn maːk/
pl beginning of information marks
abbr BIM
◄ read, write a **beginning of information mark**

---

beginning of tape *noun* (software)
a character or code that is used to mark the start of a usable part of a tape: *Recording does not start until the beginning of tape has been read.*

/bɪˌɡɪnɪŋ əv 'teɪp/
note no plural
abbr BOT
◄ a **beginning of tape** character, code, signal

---

bell character *noun* (software)
an ASCII character that allows the computer to BEEP, usually when there is a problem

/'bel ˌkærəktə(r)/
pl bell characters
◄ read, write a **bell character**

---

bells and whistles *noun* (applications)
extra features added to a system to make it more attractive to users: *The application comes complete with all the usual bells and whistles.*

/ˌbelz ənd 'wɪslz/
note plural noun, used with a plural verb

---

benchmark *noun* (hardware/software)
a measurement of the features of software or hardware which is used to compare performance: *The company was the first to produce a system which scored a century on the benchmark.*

/'bentʃmaːk/
pl benchmarks
◄ adopt, choose, define a **benchmark**

---

benchmarking *noun* (applications)
the complete process of comparing the processing power of different systems: *The company applies benchmarking across all its computer systems.*

/'bentʃmaːkɪŋ/
note not used with *a* or *an*. No plural and used with a singular verb only.
◄ the **benchmarking** data, program, results

---

abbr abbreviation   **pl** plural   **syn** synonym   ▶ see   ◄ collocate (*word often used with the headword*)

benchmark problem *noun* (applications)
a task designed to compare the performance of different pieces of software or hardware. The results of a benchmark problem will give information on processing power: *Calculating pi to a thousand decimal places is a good benchmark problem for comparing maths packages.*

/ˈbentʃmɑːk ˌprɒbləm/
pl benchmark problems
ꓮ invent, propose, suggest a **benchmark problem**

---

benchmark testing *noun* (applications)
a way of comparing hardware or software by making them perform the same task: *The company will run the benchmark testing on the two packages to compare processing power next week.*

/ˌbentʃmɑːk ˈtestɪŋ/
note not used with *a* or *an*. No plural and used with a singular verb only.
ꓮ do, report *on*, run the **benchmark testing**

---

bespoke *adjective*
(of software) written or modified to meet the particular requirements of a customer

/bɪˈspəʊk/
▶ **custom-built**

---

best fit *noun* (sytem operation)
a way of choosing the area of PRIMARY MEMORY to be used by a process. The operating system searches for the smallest unused area that can hold the code and data of the process.

/ˌbest ˈfɪt/
note not used with *a* or *an*. No plural and used with a singular verb only.
ꓮ the **best fit** method, strategy
▶ **fragmentation, memory management**

---

beta testing *noun*
the process of testing new software before it is sold to the public: *The beta testing was carried out by a small group of experts.* ○ *The product is now in the last stages of beta testing.*

/ˈbiːtə ˌtestɪŋ/
note not used with *a* or *an*. No plural and used with a singular verb only.
▶ **acceptance testing, alpha testing**

---

bias *noun*
1 (*hardware*) a fixed DIRECT CURRENT which an electronic device uses to set a REFERENCE (2) (= a fixed value that is compared to other values): *Adjust the bias so that the current through the transistor is 2 mA.* ○ *Without the reference provided by bias, the logic gate would not know the difference between 0 and 1.* **2** (*mathematics*) an error that can make the results either all too high or all too low: *Apart from the random variations, there is also a bias towards the low side.*

/ˈbaɪəs/
note usually singular
1 ꓮ adjust, alter, calculate, fix the **bias**
2 ꓮ allow *for*, correct *for*, guard *against* a **bias**

---

biased *adjective*
1 (*hardware*) having a BIAS 1 applied: *The transistor is biased so that the collector current is 2mA.* **2** (*mathematics*) having a BIAS (2): *The results are too biased to be of any value.*

/ˈbaɪəst/
1 ꓮ the **biased** base, gate, input
2 ꓮ a **biased** calculation, method, result

---

bidirectional *adjective*
able to function or move in either direction: *The bidirectional ports can be programmed to serve as inputs or outputs.*

/ˌbaɪdəˈrekʃənl/
ꓮ a **bidirectional** line, port, signal, terminal

---

bidirectional bus *noun* (systems)
a bus that can carry data between two devices in either direction: *The memory and CPU are connected by a bidirectional bus.*

/ˈbaɪdəˌrekʃənl ˈbʌs/
pl bidirectional buses
ꓮ connected *to*, linked *by*, transmit *via* the **bidirectional bus**

bifurcation *noun*
1 the process of dividing a collection of things into two parts: *Repeated bifurcations are used to form the binary tree.* 2 a pair of contrasting values, for example true/false or off/on: *use the bifurcation black/white instead of the grey scale*

/ˌbaɪfəˈkeɪʃn/
pl bifurcations

1 ⋈ a binary, Boolean, logical **bifurcation**; a **bifurcation** algorithm, method

billion *noun*
1 (*US*) one thousand million: 100 000 000, or 10^9 2 (*UK*) one million million: 1 000 000 000 000, or 10^{12}

/ˈbɪljən/
pl billions

BIM *abbr*
▶ **beginning of information mark**

/ˌbiː aɪ ˈem/
note pronounced as individual letters

☆**binary** *adjective*
connected with a system of numbers based on the number 2

/ˈbaɪnəri/
⋈ a **binary** signal; **binary** arithmetic, logic, notation
▶ **base 2**

binary adder *noun*
a device that adds two binary numbers: *The output of the binary adder is placed in register A.*

/ˌbaɪnəri ˈædə(r)/
pl binary adders
⋈ build, design, use a **binary adder**
▶ **binary number, half adder**

binary coded decimal *noun*
the representation of the decimal digits 0 to 9 by binary numbers: *In binary coded decimal, 1001 represents decimal 9.*

/ˈbaɪnəri ˈkəʊdɪd ˈdesɪml/
note not used with *a* or *an*. No plural and used with a singular verb only.
abbr BCD
⋈ convert a number, etc *to*, express a number, etc *in* **binary coded decimal**
▶ **binary representation**

binary conversion *noun* (software)
the process of changing data to or from the binary number system: *Binary conversion is needed so that the output is displayed in decimals.*

/ˌbaɪnəri kənˈvɜːʃn/
pl binary conversions
⋈ a **binary conversion** algorithm, method, process

binary counter *noun* (hardware)
a device that counts in binary numbers so that the output increases by one each time an input signal is received: *A binary counter displays the number of pulses fed into it.*

/ˌbaɪnəri ˈkaʊntə(r)/
pl binary counters
⋈ a 16-bit, high-speed, rising-edge **binary counter**
▶ **counter**

☆**binary digit** *noun*
▶ **bit**

/ˌbaɪnəri ˈdɪdʒɪt/

binary dump *noun*
a display of the contents of registers or memory in binary notation: *a binary dump on screen/on paper*

/ˌbaɪnəri ˈdʌmp/
pl binary dumps
⋈ call, display, examine a **binary dump**
▶ **debug, hexadecimal dump**

---

abbr abbreviation **pl** plural **syn** synonym ▶ see ⋈ collocate (*word often used with the headword*)

binary encoding *noun*
the representation of a character by a string of binary digits:
The string 1000001 is the ASCII encoding of the character A. ○
*Set the printer switches to match the binary encoding used by the
computer.*

/ˌbaɪnəri ɪnˈkəʊdɪŋ/
pl binary encodings
◣ decode, define, interpret the
binary encoding
▶ **binary coded decimal,
binary format, binary
representation, protocol,
EBCDIC**

binary exponent *noun* (mathematics)
the CHARACTERISTIC of a binary representation of a number

/ˌbaɪnəri ɪksˈpəʊnənt/
pl binary exponents
◣ a negative, a positive, an
unsigned, an 8-bit **binary
exponent**

binary file *noun*
a file in which the bytes do not represent characters, for
example a file of binary numbers. They must be converted to
TEXT FILES before being displayed on screen: *save the data to a
binary file*

/ˌbaɪnəri ˈfaɪl/
pl binary files
◣ convert something *to*, load,
store something *as*, write
something *as* a **binary file**
▶ **ASCII file, file, file
conversion**

binary format *noun*
a fixed order of a string of binary digits which is used to
structure data: *Both numbers and text must be stored in a binary
format that is understood by the computer.*

/ˌbaɪnəri ˈfɔːmæt/
pl binary formats
◣ agree, choose a **binary format**
▶ **protocol**

binary fraction *noun* (mathematics)
a FRACTION written in binary notation so it can be processed by
a computer: *convert the decimal fraction to a binary fraction*

/ˌbaɪnəri ˈfrækʃn/
pl binary fractions
◣ represent, store, write *as* a
binary fraction
▶ **binary number, binary point**

binary logic *noun* (mathematics)
logic which uses variables that can only have the two values
TRUE and FALSE represented by 0 and 1: *Boolean algebra is one
kind of binary logic.*

/ˌbaɪnəri ˈlɒdʒɪk/
pl binary logic

☆**binary notation** *noun* (mathematics and logic)
the representation of numbers using only the 0 and 1 of the
binary system: *The number 13 in binary notation is 1101.*

/ˌbaɪnəri nəʊˈteɪʃn/
note usually singular
▶ **base 2**

☆**binary number** *noun*
a number written using the binary digits 0 and 1 only: *The
addresses are stored as 16-bit binary numbers.*

/ˌbaɪnəri ˈnʌmbə(r)/
pl binary numbers
◣ convert something *to*, work
with a **binary number**

binary operation *noun*
1 an operation using variables that can have only two values,
for example binary 0 and 1

2 ▶ **dyadic operation**

/ˌbaɪnəri ɒpəˈreɪʃn/
pl binary operations
1 ◣ carry out, execute a **binary
operation**
▶ **arithmetic operation, binary
number, Boolean algebra**

binary operator *noun*
an operator that uses two pieces of data in a calculation or
function

/ˌbaɪnəri ˈɒpəreɪtə(r)/
pl binary operators

	⋈ define, use a **binary operator**; a character, logical, numeric, relational **binary operator**

syn dyadic operator

▶ **operand, unary operator**

---

binary point *noun* (mathematics)

a dot character in a string of binary digits. The digits following the dot represent a BINARY FRACTION: *The system always assumes that the binary point is between bits 7 and 8.*

/ˌbaɪnəri ˈpɔɪnt/

pl binary points

⋈ assume, insert, omit, position the **binary point**

▶ **binary fraction, fixed point**

---

binary representation *noun*

any representation of numbers and their signs using the binary digits 0 and 1 only. The digits are arranged in a format that is understood by the computer: *the two's complement binary representation*

/ˈbaɪnəri ˌreprɪzenˈteɪʃn/

pl binary representations

⋈ convert something *to*, use a **binary representation**

▶ **binary coded decimal, binary number, biquinary code**

---

binary search *noun*

a way of finding an item in an ordered list of data. The middle of the list is compared with the item to establish which half of the list contains the item. The same process is repeated on that half until the item is found: *If the items are in alphabetical order then a binary search is simple and fast.*

/ˌbaɪnəri ˈsɜːtʃ/

pl binary searches

⋈ a **binary search** algorithm, method, procedure

▶ **search key, sequential search**

☆**binary system** *noun*

▶ **base 2**

/ˈbaɪnəri ˌsɪstəm/

---

binary thresholding *noun*

a way of displaying shades of grey as either black or white. All greys that are whiter than a certain value are shown as white, and all greys that are darker than a certain value are shown as black: *Binary thresholding ensures a good contrast when text is displayed.*

/ˌbaɪnəri ˈθreʃhəʊldɪŋ/

note not used with *a* or *an*. No plural and used with a singular verb only.

▶ **bifurcation 2**

---

binary-to-decimal conversion *noun*

the process of changing a number from binary form into decimal form

/ˈbaɪnəri tə ˈdesɪml kənˈvɜːn/

note usually singular

abbr BDC

⋈ a **binary-to-decimal conversion** algorithm, chip, procedure

▶ **decimal-to-binary conversion**

---

binary tree *noun*

a TREE where each data item has no more than two DESCENDANTS (= linked data items): *The binary tree encodes the mid-point information needed for searching.*

/ˌbaɪnəri ˈtriː/

pl binary trees

⋈ access, define, implement, traverse, update a **binary tree**

▶ **data structure**

---

bind *verb* (programming)

to associate each of the symbols used for variables and procedures in a program with addresses in memory: *The compiler binds the symbols used in the program.* ○ *The names of the functions must bind to their addresses at run time.*

/baɪnd/

bind, binding, bound

note transitive verb

⋈ **bind** the procedure, symbol, variable

---

abbr abbreviation   **pl** plural   **syn** synonym   ▶ see   ⋈ collocate (*word often used with the headword*)

binding time *noun* (programming)
the time it takes to BIND a symbol to an address

/'baɪndɪŋ taɪm/
pl binding times
ℍ avoid, reduce the **binding time**

BIOS *abbr* (software)
basic input output system. The part of the operating system
that controls input and output: *The BIOS can be configured to
shut the machine down if it has been inactive for a certain amount
of time.* ○ *store BIOS programs in ROM*

/'baɪɒs/
note pronounced as a word not
used with *a* or *an*. No plural and
used with a singular verb only
(also **Bios**)
ℍ access, install, use the **BIOS**
syn basic input output system

---

bipolar *adjective*
having two opposite states, such as positive or negative:
*Semiconductors are produced in one of two bipolar forms called
n-type and p-type.* ○ *the bipolar terminals of a battery*

/ˌbaɪˈpəʊlə(r)/
ℍ a **bipolar** chip, electrode,
junction, state
▶ **unipolar**

---

bipolar signal *noun* (systems)
a signal sent using both positive and negative VOLTAGE levels: *a
bipolar signal which represents a stream of bits*

/baɪˌpəʊlə ˈsɪgnəl/
pl bipolar signals
ℍ decode, receive, transmit
something *as* a **bipolar signal**
▶ **data transmission**

---

bipolar transistor *noun* (hardware/electronics)
a transistor with three layers: *The fastest integrated circuits use
bipolar transistors as the switching elements.*

note The three layers of a bipolar transitor are the 'emitter',
the 'collector', and the middle layer is the 'base'.

/baɪˌpəʊlə trænˈzɪstə(r)/
pl bipolar transistors
ℍ use, wire up a **bipolar
transistor**
▶ **field effect transistor**

---

biquinary code *noun* (software)
a 7-bit binary code used to represent the decimal digits 0 to 9

/baɪˌkwɪnəri ˈkəʊd/
pl biquinary codes
ℍ convert something *to*, decode,
use **biquinary code**
▶ **binary representation**

---

bistable¹ *noun* (hardware)
an electronic circuit that has the two stable output states 'on'
or 'off'. Each time an input signal is received the output is
switched to the other state: *each chip has two bistables* ○ *outputs
from the bistable are used to operate voltage switches*

note The two states of a bistable are usually represented by
binary 0 and 1.

/baɪˈsteɪbl/
pl bistables
(also **bistable device**)
ℍ build, design, set, use a
bistable
syn flip-flop

---

bistable² *adjective*
having two stable states

/'baɪsteɪbl/
ℍ a **bistable** circuit, device,
storage element

BISYNC *abbr*
binary synchronous communications protocol

/'baɪsɪŋk/
note pronounced as a word

☆**bit** *noun* (hardware)

a basic unit of data represented as either of the two values 0 or 1 in the binary system. Bits are used in computing because digital computers represent data in terms of the presence (1) or absence (0) of an electrical signal.

note 'Bit' is a short form of the words 'binary digit'. In computing, 'bit' is used more often than 'binary digit'. There are usually 8 bits in a byte.

/bɪt/
pl bits
◣ store, use **bits**
▶ **byte, check bit, parity bit**

---

bit addressing *noun* (software)

the process of addressing a single selected bit within a word. The instruction must indicate the position of the required bit as well as the address of the word: *Some processors have bit addressing which allows the value of individual bits to be read and changed without affecting any other bits.*

/'bɪt ə,dresɪŋ/
note not used with *a* or *an*. No plural and used with a singular verb only.
◣ alter *by*, make use *of* **bit addressing**
▶ **address, bit, word**

---

bit density *noun*

the number of bits that can be stored in a certain amount of storage space: *increase the bit density of disks to 1.28MB of storage* ○ *The bit density of magnetic tape is measured in bits per inch.*

/'bɪt ,densəti/
pl bit densities
◣ double, increase the **bit density**
▶ **bit, bits per inch**

---

bit error *noun*

an error in a single bit, especially an error in one bit in a block of transmitted data: *a bit error in a stream of data*

/'bɪt ,erə(r)/
pl bit errors
◣ allow *for*, cause, detect a **bit error**; **bit error** rate

---

bit map *noun*

1 a image such as a picture that is held in storage with a fixed number of bits for each PIXEL in the image: *A black-and-white image can be stored as a bit map using one bit for each pixel.* **2** a table recording which areas of a disk or other storage device are full. A single bit is set to 1 if an area is full or 0 if it is not full: *Use of a bit map is important for efficient disk access.*

/'bɪt mæp/
pl bit maps
1 ◣ store something *as* a **bit map**
syn bit-mapped graphics
2 ◣ access, maintain a **bit map**
syn disk map

---

bit-mapped font *noun*

a set of characters displayed on screen or printed on paper where each character is represented as a BIT MAP (1)

/,bɪt mæpt 'fɒnt/
pl bit-mapped fonts
◣ install, load, use a **bit-mapped font**

---

bit-mapped graphics *noun*
▶ **bit map 1**

/,bɪt mæpt 'græfɪks/

BITNET *noun*

a large public network used for sending electronic mail between universities in North America and Europe: *exchange messages using BITNET* ○ *subscribe to BITNET*

/'bɪtnet/
note not used with *a* or *an*. No plural and used with a singular verb only.
◣ send data *via*, subscribe to, use **BITNET**
▶ **JANET, Internet**

---

bit pattern *noun*

the order of the bits in a WORD: *The ASCII code uses a fixed bit pattern to represent each character.* ○ *This bit pattern is 10101101001100011000000.*

/'bɪt ,pætn/
pl bit patterns
◣ the agreed, standard, usual **bit pattern**

---

abbr abbreviation   **pl** plural   **syn** synonym   ▶ see   ◣ collocate (*word often used with the headword*)

bit rate *noun*
a measure of the speed of transmission of binary digits: *output can be generated at the bit rate the application requires*

/ˈbɪt reɪt/
pl bit rates
ᴍ a fast, a higher, an insufficient **bit rate**
▶ **baud rate, bits per second**

---

bit slice architecture *noun* (hardware/systems)
an architecture (= the basic ideas and principles the design of a computer is based on) that uses several small processors to make a larger processor: *Using bit slice architecture, a 32 bit CPU can be built from four low-cost 8-bit microprocessors.*

/ˈbɪt slaɪs ˌɑːkɪtektʃə(r)/
pl bit slice architectures
(also **bit slice microprocessor**)
ᴍ a cheap, practical **bit slice architecture**

---

bits per inch *noun*
the number of bits that fit into an inch of space on a disk or on tape: *The measurement of data storage capacity was bits per inch.*

/ˌbɪts pər ˈɪntʃ/
abbr bpi
note not used with *a* or *an*. No plural and used with a singular verb only.

---

bits per second *noun*
a measure of the speed of data transmission: *a 2400 bps modem*

/ˌbɪts pə ˈsekənd/
abbr bps
note not used with *a* or *an*. No plural and used with a singular verb only.

---

bit stream *noun*
a series of binary digits sent over a transmission channel: *Data is sent to the disk drive as a bit stream.* ○ *a bit stream that can be easily translated from one format to another*

note The term 'bit stream' is often used to show that the bits are not grouped into larger units such as character codes.

/ˈbɪt striːm/
pl bit streams
ᴍ receive, send, transmit *as a* **bit stream**

---

bit string *noun*
a number of bits, for example the ordered bits representing a single ASCII character, an address, a file, or a block of data: *The bit string must be decoded into text characters.*

/ˈbɪt strɪŋ/
pl bit strings
ᴍ package *as*, send, store *as a* **bit string**

---

bit stuffing *noun* (software)
the process of adding of extra bits to blocks of data to make each block a standard length. The extra bits are added to the data before transmission and removed by the receiver: *Bit stuffing is used to make synchronization easier.*

/ˈbɪt ˌstʌfɪŋ/
note not used with *a* or *an*. No plural and used with a singular verb only.

BIX *abbr*
Byte Information Exchange

/bɪks/
note pronounced as a word

☆**BkSp** *abbr*
▶ **backspace**[1]

note used in written English only

---

black box *noun* (hardware)
a device whose function is understood by the user, although the internal structure of the device and exactly how it works is not known: *A computer can be thought of as a black box because most people know what it does, but not how it does it.*

/ˌblæk ˈbɒks/
pl black boxes

black box testing *noun* (system operation)
the testing of a procedure whose code is not known to the tester. The tester only requires the procedure to give the right output from the input: *input data for the black box testing*

/ˌblæk ˈbɒks ˌtestɪŋ/
note not used with *a* or *an*. No plural and used with a singular verb only.

⋈ perform, specify, use **black box testing**

---

blank disk *noun* (hardware)
a computer disk that has no data stored on it because it is new or because all existing data has been deleted: *format a blank disk*

/ˌblæŋk ˈdɪsk/
pl blank disks

---

blank tape *noun* (hardware)
a magnetic tape that has no data recorded on it because it is new or because all existing data has been deleted

/ˌblæŋk ˈteɪp/
pl blank tapes

---

blast *verb*
▶ **burn**

/blɑːst/

---

bleep *noun*
▶ **beep**

/bliːp/

---

blink *verb*
to switch a character on screen on and off so the user notices it: *The cursor blinks once every second.*

/blɪŋk/
blink, blinking, blinked
note intransitive verb
⋈ the insertion point, warning message **blinks**

☆**block** *noun*
1 a collection of data items that are accessed, stored or transferred as a single unit **2** a group of statements in a certain order in a high-level computer programming language that function as a single unit: *nested blocks*

/blɒk/
pl blocks
1 ⋈ a fixed length, variable length **block**; a **block** header; **block** length, size, transfer
▶ **blocking factor, interblock gap**
2 ⋈ code, write a **block**; **block** structure
▶ **block-structured language**

---

block code *noun* (software)
a type of code used for ERROR DETECTION (= finding mistakes in data) and ERROR CORRECTION (= changing data to the correct form)

/ˈblɒk kəʊd/
pl block codes
⋈ encode *using*, decode *using* **block code**

---

block copy *noun*
1 the process of copying the data in one area of memory to another area of memory without erasing the original data: *perform a block copy to relocate the code* **2** (*word processing*) the process of copying a piece of text to another place in a document without erasing the original text: *use a block copy operation to repeat the first three paragraphs*

/ˌblɒk ˈkɒpi/
note no plural
⋈ perform, undo, use a **block copy**

---

block diagram *noun* (systems)
a diagram showing the main parts of a computer or system and its connections. The parts are shown as labelled boxes and the connections as lines joining them: *The block diagram of the computer's architecture shows how circuits and processors relate.* ○ *The block diagram shows how the terminals connect with the network.*

/ˌblɒk ˈdaɪəgræm/
pl block diagrams
⋈ draw, show, use a **block diagram**
▶ **flowchart**

---

abbr abbreviation **pl** plural **syn** synonym ▶ see ⋈ collocate (*word often used with the headword*)

blocked process *noun* (system operation)
a process which is unable to run because the resources it needs
are not available: *The blocked processes are held in a queue.*

/ˌblɒkt ˈprəʊses/
pl blocked processes
⋈ delete, free, store the **blocked
process**

---

blocking factor *noun* (software)
the size of a BLOCK (1): *The PC has a blocking factor of 512 bytes.*

/ˈblɒkɪŋ ˌfæktə(r)/
pl blocking factors
▶ **record**

---

block retrieval *noun*
the transfer of a block of data to a store which has a faster
access time, for example from disk to main memory, or from
main memory to CACHE

/ˌblɒk rɪˈtriːvl/
pl block retrievals
⋈ allow time *for*, execute, perform
a **block retrieval**

---

block-structured language *noun*
a high-level computer programming language that is
organized in separate units or BLOCKS (2): *Algol is a block-
structured language.*

/ˈblɒk ˌstrʌktʃəd ˈlæŋgwɪdʒ/
pl block-structured languages
⋈ program in a **block-
structured language**
▶ **Algol**

---

blow *verb*
▶ **burn**

/bləʊ/

---

blow up *verb*
1 to make something explode: *The power surge blew up the
computer and caused a small fire.* ○ *The printer blew up.* **2** to make
an image, etc larger: *blow up the picture so it fills the whole
screen*

/ˌbləʊ ˈʌp/
**blow up, blowing up, blew
up, blown up**
1 note transitive or intransitive
verb
2 note transitive verb
⋈ **blow up** graphics, pictures

BNF *abbr*
▶ **Backus-Naur form**

/ˌbiː en ˈef/
note pronounced as individual
letters

---

board *noun*
▶ **printed circuit board**

/bɔːd/

BOF *abbr*
▶ **beginning of file**

/ˌbiː əʊ ˈef/
note pronounced as individual
letters

---

boilerplate *noun* (word processing)
a piece of standard text that is added to documents: *a paragraph
that will be useful in a future boilerplate* ○ *boilerplates of all the
product specifications*

/ˈbɔɪləpleɪt/
pl boilerplates
⋈ include, make up, write a
boilerplate
▶ **template**

---

bold¹ *noun*
one of the features of a font which relates to the weight of text
on screen or on the printed page. Bold text is darker than other
text: *print the headings in bold so they stand out* ○ *make the
quotations in the text bold italic*

/bəʊld/
note no plural
▶ **italic¹**

bold² *adjective*
(of text, etc) which is created with the bold feature of a font

/bəʊld/
⋈ **bold** lettering, text, type
▶ **italic²**

---

bomb *noun* (software)
a piece of code which destroys data or a program: *A bomb has been inserted into the software to stop unlicensed copying.*

/bɒm/
pl bombs
⋈ put *in*, set *off*, trigger a **bomb**
▶ **logic bomb, virus**

☆**Boolean algebra** *noun* (mathematics and logic)
a system of logic that is very important to computer operations. In Boolean algebra, VARIABLES have either the value TRUE or the value FALSE. These values are shown by the binary digits 1 and 0. The relationship between the variables is expressed by using BOOLEAN CONNECTIVES including AND, OR and NOT.

note Boolean algebra is named after the mathematician George Boole (1815-1864)

/ˌbuːliən ˈældʒɪbrə/
note no plural
syn digital logic
▶ **truth value**

Boolean connective *noun* (mathematics and logic)
▶ **Boolean operator**

/ˌbuːliən kəˈnektɪv/

Boolean expression *noun* (mathematics and logic)
a logical statement that can have the value TRUE or FALSE: *A simple version of the instruction is given as a Boolean expression.*

/ˌbuːliən ɪkˈspreʃn/
pl Boolean expressions
⋈ evaluate, represent, simplify a **Boolean expression**

Boolean function *noun*
▶ **Boolean operation**

/ˌbuːliən ˈfʌŋkʃn/

Boolean operation *noun* (mathematics and logic)
an operation on a logical expression which is performed using the rules of BOOLEAN ALGEBRA: *Most languages support the Boolean operations AND, OR, and NOT.*

/ˌbuːliən ɒpəˈreɪʃn/
pl Boolean operations
⋈ do, perform, program, represent a **Boolean operation**
syn Boolean function

Boolean operator *noun*
a symbol or word such as AND, OR and NOR used in BOOLEAN ALGEBRA to join simple statements together and show the operations that are performed on the statements

note Boolean operators are often written in upper case letters to show the difference between them and the words as they are used in ordinary language.

/ˌbuːliən ˈɒpəreɪtə(r)/
pl Boolean operators
⋈ a formula *using*, a symbol *for* a **Boolean operator**
syn Boolean connective

Boolean value *noun* (mathematics)
either of the two values TRUE or FALSE. In computers these values may be represented by 1 and 0, and in electronics by high/low or on/off: *If the Boolean value is FALSE, the process is aborted.*

/ˌbuːliən ˈvæljuː/
pl Boolean values
⋈ work out the **Boolean value**
▶ **Boolean algebra**

Boolean variable *noun* (software)
1 a logical variable which has the value TRUE or FALSE **2** a data type that has only two values represented by a one-bit WORD **(1)**. The bit values 1 and 0 correspond to the BOOLEAN VALUES TRUE and FALSE

/ˌbuːliən ˈveəriəbl/
pl Boolean variables
1 ⋈ define, express *as*, represent *as* a **Boolean variable**
2 ⋈ declare, program *as* a **Boolean variable**

☆**boot¹** noun

the process of making a computer ready for use when it is first switched on: *The first boot failed.*

/buːt/
pl boots
syn start up
▶ **cold boot, reboot, warm boot**

☆**boot²** verb (operations/systems)

to make a computer ready for use when it is first switched on: *boot the computer* ○ *The system won't boot because of an error.*

/buːt/
boots, booting, booted
note transitive and intransitive verb
syn boot up, start up
▶ **bootstrap loader, crash²**

☆**bootstrap loader** noun

a program that runs automatically when a computer is booted. It checks the hardware then passes control to another program which usually loads the operating system.

/ˈbuːtstræp ˌləʊdə(r)/
pl bootstrap loaders

boot up verb
▶ **boot²**

/ˌbuːt ˈʌp/

border noun

the area that surrounds a window on screen

/ˈbɔːdə(r)/
pl borders
▶ **scroll bar**

Bose-Chaudhuri-Hocquenghem code noun (software)

a code that allows some errors in transmitted data to be found and corrected so the data does not have to be transmitted again

/ˈbəʊs ˈtʃaʊdəri ˈ(h)ɒkɒŋgem kəʊd/
pl Bose-Chaudhuri-Hocquengham codes
abbr BCH code
▶ **error correcting code**

BOT abbr
▶ **beginning of tape**

/ˌbiː əʊ ˈtiː/
note pronounced as individual letters

bottom of stack noun

the data item in a STACK which is the last item that can be accessed. When the bottom of stack is removed, the stack will be empty.

/ˌbɒtəm əv ˈstæk/
note not used with *a* or *an*. No plural and used with a singular verb only.
ⵉ access, pop, remove the **bottom of stack**
▶ **data structure, last in, first out, pop, push, top of stack**

bottom-up design noun

a method of creating software or computer systems by starting with the smallest units and joining them together to make larger units

/ˈbɒtəm ˌʌp dɪˈzaɪn/
note not used with *a* or *an*. No plural and used with a singular verb only.
ⵉ **bottom-up design** principles, techniques
syn bottom-up development

bottom-up development noun
▶ **bottom-up design**

/ˈbɒtəm ˌʌp dɪˈveləpmənt/

bottom-up programming *noun*
a way of developing computer programs by starting with simple statements and adding them to more than one ROUTINE (= part of a program). The routines are then joined together to make a complete program: *Interactive computing encourages bottom-up programming.*

/ˈbɒtəm ˌʌp ˈprəʊɡræmɪŋ/

note not used with *a* or *an*. No plural and used with a singular verb only.

◄ **bottom-up programming** methods, techniques

---

bounce *noun* (hardware)
a fault in the operation of CONTACTS[1] when they do not stay closed but keep opening and closing, often causing the character that is generated by pressing a key on a keyboard once to be repeated

/baʊns/

pl bounces

◄ avoid, overcome, prevent, remedy, solve, take account *of* **bounce**

► **contact bounce, debounce**

---

bound *noun*
a limit to the area of memory that can be used, often the highest or lowest memory address that a program can access when it is executed

/baʊnd/

pl bounds

◄ cross, define, exceed, set a **bound**

---

boundary protection *noun*
► **bound protection**

/ˈbaʊndri prəˌtekʃn/

---

bound protection *noun*
a way of controlling access to memory locations in which two registers, called bound registers, hold information about the highest and lowest addresses that may be accessed by the program that is being executed

/ˌbaʊnd prəˈtekʃn/

note no plural

◄ enforce, implement **bound protection**

syn boundary protection

---

bpi *abbr*
► **bits per inch**

/ˌbiː piː ˈai/

note pronounced as individual letters

Bps *abbr*
bytes per second

/ˌbiː piː ˈes/

► **baud rate**

---

bps *abbr*
► **bits per second**

/ˌbiː piː ˈes/

---

braces *noun*
another word for BRACKETS, especially the curly brackets { }: *ignore comments enclosed in braces* ○ *The formula inside braces denotes a variable.*

/ˈbreɪsɪz/

note usually plural

◄ enclosed something *in*, surround something *with* **braces**

---

brackets *noun*
a pair of symbols such as ( ), [ ] or { }: *Work out the equation in brackets.*

/ˈbrækɪts/

note usually plural

◄ enclose something *in*, surround something *with* **brackets**; a leading, trailing **bracket**

► **round brackets, square brackets**

---

branch *noun* (software)
1 a link in a tree that joins two items together **2** a point at which a program can take one of two paths: *The branch in this program leads to a result or to a loop.*

/brɑːntʃ/

pl branches

1 ► **leaf, node, root**

2 ◄ a program **branch**; a **branch** instruction

syn jump, jump instruction

► **directory**

---

abbr abbreviation   **pl** plural   **syn** synonym   ► see   ◄ collocate (*word often used with the headword*)

branchpoint *noun* (software)
a point in a program where a BRANCH **(2)** may occur: *There are two branchpoints inside the loop.*

/'brɑ:ntʃpɔɪnt/
pl branchpoints
◢ come *to*, reach, recognize something *as* a **branchpoint**

---

breadboard *noun* (hardware)
a board which was used for designing and testing electronic circuits where COMPONENTS could be added or taken away easily as the design changed or improved. A modern breadboard contains connected holes which hold electronic components: *build the experimental circuit with a breadboard*

/'bredbɔ:d/
pl breadboards
◢ demonstrate *with*, prototype *as*, put something together *on* a **breadboard**

---

breadth-first search *noun*
a way of searching trees in which all the NODES **(1)** at the same level are searched before going down to search the next level: *Items are located by a breadth-first search.*

/'bredθ ˌfɜ:st 'sɜ:tʃ/
pl breadth-first searches
◢ do, try, use a **breadth-first search**

---

break *noun*
an action that causes a program to stop running. It may be caused by an error, a program call or by the user pressing the BREAK KEY: *There is a break at this point.*

/breɪk/
pl breaks
◢ cause, come *to*, introduce a **break**

---

breaker *noun*
▶ **circuit breaker**

/'breɪkə(r)/

---

break in *verb*
to interrupt a process that has stopped responding to user input

/ˌbreɪk 'ɪn/
break in, breaking in, broke in, broken in
note intransitive verb
◢ **break in** *to* a loop, *to* a program
▶ **break key**

---

break key *noun* (hardware)
a key on standard keyboards which can be used to stop a computer executing a program: *Pressing the break key takes the user back to the start of the program.*

/'breɪk ki:/
pl break keys
◢ press, use the **break key**

☆**breakpoint** *noun*
a place in a program where it is forced to stop, usually while the program is being tested or DEBUGGED

/'breɪkpɔɪnt/
pl breakpoints
◢ insert, set a **breakpoint**; a **breakpoint** halt, instruction

---

☆**bridge** *noun* (hardware)
a device that connects two similar networks and allows them to exchange data without electronic problems or loss of power: *use a bridge to link two local area networks in different buildings*

/brɪdʒ/
pl bridges
◢ connect *via*, install, use a **bridge**
▶ **gateway**

---

bridgeware *noun*
software or hardware supplied by a computer manufacturer to allow buyers of new computers to continue to use their old software: *The bridgeware is designed to reformat files to make them IBM compatible.*

/'brɪdʒweə(r)/
note not used with *a* or *an*. No plural and used with a singular verb only.
◢ supply, use **bridgeware**
syn bridging product

bridging *noun*
the process of joining two networks with a BRIDGE

/ˈbrɪdʒɪŋ/
note not used with *a* or *an*. No plural and used with a singular verb only.
⧓ **bridging** protocols

bridging product *noun*
► **bridgeware**

/ˈbrɪdʒɪŋ ˌprɒdʌkt/

brightness *noun*
the part of a VIDEO SIGNAL that contains information about the level of lightness and darkness of images on screen: *The quality of surrounding light affects the brightness of the screen.*

/ˈbraɪtnəs/
note not used with *a* or *an*. No plural and used with a singular verb only.
⧓ adjust, set the **brightness**
► **contrast, hue, saturation**

British Standards Institution *noun* (organizations)
a organization that tests and sets safety standards for materials, products and manufacturing processes: *equipment approved by the British Standards Institution*

/ˌbrɪtɪʃ ˈstændədz ɪnstɪˌtjuːʃn/
note no plural
abbr BSI
⧓ meet the standards *of* the **British Standards Institution**; **British Standards Institution** regulations, specifications

British Telecom *noun* (organizations)
a provider of telephone and communication services

/ˌbrɪtɪʃ ˈtelikɒm/
note no plural
abbr BT
⧓ a **British Telecom** leased line, service, telephone
► **common carrier**

broadband *adjective*
having a wide BANDWIDTH (= range of frequencies): *transmit broadband signals* ○ *develop broadband services such as videophones*

/ˈbrɔːdbænd/
⧓ **broadband** communications, components, equipment, technology, transmissions

broadband network *noun*
a type of network where different types of transmissions travel through the same cable, allowing large amounts of data to be transmitted in a short time. The transmissions remain separate because they travel at different FREQUENCIES: *The company is using its global broadband network to link services.*

/ˌbrɔːdbænd ˈnetwɜːk/
pl broadband networks
⧓ send *via*, transmit *via*, use a **broadband network**
► **base band network, frequency division multiplexing**

broadcast¹ *noun*
a signal sent at the same time to a number of receivers: *a television/a radio broadcast*

/ˈbrɔːdkɑːst/
pl broadcasts
⧓ make, transmit a **broadcast**; a **broadcast** network

broadcast² *verb*
1 to send a signal to a number of receivers at the same time: *The BBC World Service broadcasts to most countries in the world.* ○ *The Olympics are broadcast live via satellite.* **2** to send a message to all computers on a network: *The data is decoded and broadcast over a wide area network.*

/ˈbrɔːdkɑːst/
broadcast, broadcasting, broadcast
note transitive or intransitive verb

1 ⋈ **broadcast** a radio/TV programme

2 ⋈ **broadcast** an e-mail message, a signal

---

browser *noun* (software)
software that reads and displays HYPERTEXT and HYPERMEDIA documents on the INTERNET: *Click on the 'home' icon on the browser to get back to the home page of the Internet site.*

/ˈbraʊzə(r)/
pl browsers
▶ **World Wide Web**

---

brush *noun* (hardware)
a mechanical connector that passes power to a moving part of a computer: *A fixed brush passes current to the rotating spindle of the disk drive.*

/brʌʃ/
pl brushes
⋈ align, install, maintain a **brush**

BS *abbr*
▶ **backspace character**

note used in written English only

BSI *abbr*
▶ **British Standards Institution**

/ˌbiː es ˈaɪ/
note pronounced as individual letters

BT *abbr*
▶ **British Telecom**

/ˌbiː ˈtiː/
note pronounced as individual letters

B-tree *noun*
a BINARY TREE where all the NODES (1) have exactly two branches

/ˈbiː triː/
pl B-trees
syn balanced binary tree, balanced tree
⋈ implement, structure something *as* a **B-tree**

---

bubble jet printer *noun* (hardware)
a type of printer that forces very small dots of ink out of its PRINT HEAD to form the shape of letters and characters, etc: *The notebook has a built-in bubble jet printer.*

/ˈbʌbl dʒet ˌprɪntə(r)/
pl bubble jet printers
▶ **printer**

☆**bubble memory** *noun* (hardware)
a form of memory in which bits are held in bubbles on magnetic material

/ˈbʌbl ˌmeməri/
note usually singular
syn magnetic bubble memory

---

bubble sort *noun*
a way of sorting a list of data items by looking at two items next to each other and changing them over until there are no items in the wrong place. The smallest item will go to the top of the list and the largest item will go to the bottom of the list.

/ˈbʌbl sɔːt/
note usually singular
⋈ execute, perform, program a **bubble sort**
syn exchange selection sort
▶ **sort**

---

bucket *noun*
an area in memory containing a number of records next to each other in a data file: *search a bucket sequentially ○ a bit bucket*

/ˈbʌkɪt/
pl buckets
⋈ access, fill, save, search a **bucket**
▶ **hashing, index**

☆**buffer** *noun* (hardware)
a part of the memory that is used to store data for a short time, usually while it is being moved from one place to another: *The results are output to the buffer and then transferred to the printer.*

/ˈbʌfə(r)/
pl buffers
ᴎ **buffer** size, storage
syn data buffer
▶ **communications buffer, memory, output buffer**

---

buffered device *noun* (hardware)
a PERIPHERAL that has a buffer that acts as a temporary store for the data being transferred between the peripheral and the computer

/ˌbʌfəd dɪˈvaɪs/
pl buffered devices

---

buffered I/O *noun*
part of the computer's memory that acts as a buffer for the input and output PORTS[1] of the computer. This allows slow PERIPHERALS to operate with the much faster central processing unit of the computer: *The keyboard of the new computer uses the buffered I/O to allow the user to input data faster than the computer can process it.*

/ˌbʌfəd ˌaɪ ˈəʊ/
note no plural

---

buffered memory *noun* (hardware)
backing storage in which the movement of data to or from main memory takes place in large blocks rather than individual bytes

/ˌbʌfəd ˈmeməri/
note no plural

---

buffering *noun*
the process of using a buffer to input and output data between devices: *Buffering improves the speed of access to slow peripherals.*

/ˈbʌfərɪŋ/
note no plural and used with a singular verb only
ᴎ implement, use **buffering**
▶ **double buffering**

---

buffer register *noun*
▶ **memory buffer register**

/ˈbʌfə ˌredʒɪstə(r)/

☆**bug** *noun*
a problem or error in a computer program or system: *test a program for bugs*

/bʌg/
pl bugs
ᴎ eliminate, find, introduce, sort out a **bug**
▶ **debug, error, glitch, virus**

---

built-in *adjective*
(of something) that is part of something else and does not need to be added separately: *The computer has a built-in fax modem.* ○ *The plotter contains a built-in microprocessor.* ○ *The language provides built-in syntax checking.*

/ˌbɪlt ˈɪn/
ᴎ a **built-in** disk drive, display, function, printer
▶ **add-on**

---

built-in function *noun* (software/programming)
a calculation or operation that is already part of a high-level computer programming language and does not need to be written by the programmer: *Mathematical operations such as sine and cosine are usually available as built-in functions.* ○ *Complex calculations are usually based upon built-in functions.*

/ˌbɪlt ɪn ˈfʌŋkʃn/
pl built-in functions
ᴎ invoke, make use *of*, use a **built-in function**

---

bulk memory *noun*
▶ **mass storage**

/ˈbʌlk ˌmeməri/

---

bulk storage *noun*
▶ **mass storage**

/ˌbʌlk ˈstɔːrɪdʒ/

---

abbr abbreviation   **pl** plural   **syn** synonym   ▶ see   ᴎ collocate (*word often used with the headword*)

bullet *noun*
a character such as diamond, square or circle which is used to mark important items in a document: *The paragraphs marked with bullets contain the most important information in the document.*

/'bʊlɪt/
(also **bullet point**)
pl bullets
ᴎ add a **bullet**

bulletin board *noun*
a network service that allows users with a shared interest to send and receive messages or to obtain software, etc: *access utilities and software via a bulletin board* ○ *download software from a bulletin board*

/'bʊlətɪn bɔːd/
pl bulletin boards
ᴎ download software *from*, post a message *to*, send a message *to*, subscribe *to*, use a **bulletin board**
▶ **teleconferencing**

bundle *verb*
to add hardware and/or software to a new computer at no extra cost: *Speakers and a CD-ROM were bundled with the multimedia PC.*

/'bʌndl/
bundle, bundling, bundled
note transitive verb

bundled software *noun* (software)
software that is supplied with a new computer at no extra cost: *The bundled software that comes with the new computer includes spreadsheet and word processing packages.*

/ˌbʌndld 'sɒftweə(r)/
note not used with *a* or *an*. No plural and used with a singular verb only.
ᴎ supply **bundled software**
▶ **applications software, unbundled software**

bureau *noun*
a company that sells the services of its own computing equipment to other companies: *The payroll is processed by a computer bureau.*

/'bjʊərəʊ/
pl bureaux
pl bureaus
ᴎ buy services *from*, contract, use a **bureau**

burn *verb*
to write data or code into ROM or ERASABLE PROM: *burn a ROM chip during manufacture*

/bɜːn/
burn, burning, burned
note transitive verb
▶ **programmable read only memory, ROM**
syn blast, blow, burn in

burn in *verb*
▶ **burn**

/ˌbɜːn 'ɪn/

burst *verb*
to separate sheets of continuous stationery: *The payslips are burst as they leave the line printer.*

/bɜːst/
burst, bursting, burst
note transitive verb
ᴎ **burst** a listing, printout
syn decollate
▶ **stationery**

burster *noun* (hardware)
a device that separates continuous stationery after printing: *The burster separates the customer copy of the invoice from the file copy.*

/'bɜːstə(r)/
pl bursters
ᴎ pass stationery *through* a **burster**
syn decollator
▶ **stationery**

burst mode *noun*
a way of sending data down a data channel as one unit and
not as separate pieces of data

note Burst mode allows high-speed data transmissions.

/'bɜːst məʊd/
note not used with *a* or *an*. No
plural and used with a singular
verb only.

ᴎ operate *in* **burst mode**
▶ **multiplex**

---

burst rate *noun*
1 (*data transmission*) the maximum speed at which data can be
transmitted over a data channel: *The burst rate can only be
achieved for short periods of continuous transmission.* **2** the
number of characters per second that a printer can print on a
single line

/'bɜːst reɪt/
pl burst rates
1,2 ᴎ decrease, increase,
measure the **burst rate**
syn burst speed
▶ **throughput**

---

burst speed *noun*
▶ **burst rate**

/'bɜːst spiːd/

☆**bus** *noun* (hardware)
a hardware pathway which connects one part of the computer
to another. Data travels along buses and the operation of buses
is usually controlled by the microprocessor: *a 32-bit bus* ○ *a bus
which carries data and addresses*

/bʌs/
pl buses
syn highway, trunk
▶ **address bus, data bus, input/
output bus, memory bus**

---

bus address line *noun*
▶ **address bus**

/ˌbʌs əˈdres laɪn/

---

bus architecture *noun*
▶ **bus topology**

/'bʌs ˌɑːkɪtektʃə(r)/

---

bus driver *noun*
a device which prepares a data signal so that it can be put on a
bus

/'bʌs ˌdraɪvə(r)/
pl bus drivers
ᴎ install, replace a **bus driver**

---

bus master *noun*
the device that puts data onto a bus

/'bʌs ˌmɑːstə(r)/
pl bus masters
ᴎ install a **bus master**
▶ **bus slave**

---

bus network *noun* (hardware)
a network where each NODE **(2)** is linked to a bus which is the
central line of communication, sometimes called the BACKBONE
NETWORK: *Ethernet systems are bus networks.* ○ *monitor activity
on the line in a bus network*

/'bʌs ˌnetwɜːk/
pl bus networks
ᴎ configure a network *as*, use *a*
bus network
▶ **backbone network,
network topology, ring
network, star network, tree
network**

---

bus slave *noun*
a device that receives data from a bus: *The bus master sends data
along the bus to the bus slaves.*

/'bʌs sleɪv/
pl bus slaves
ᴎ install a **bus slave**
▶ **bus master**

---

bus structure *noun* (hardware)
any type of bus network such as a tree network or a linear
network

/'bʌs ˌstrʌktʃə(r)/
pl bus structures

---

abbr abbreviation   **pl** plural   **syn** synonym   ▶ see   ᴎ collocate (*word often used with the headword*)

> ⋈ implement a **bus structure**; parallel, serial **bus structure**
>
> ▶ **bidirectional bus**

---

bus terminator *noun* (hardware)
a device connected to the end of a bus which creates an electrical circuit to ensure the bus transmits data correctly: *add a bus terminator to the last device in a SCSI bus*

/'bʌs ˌtɜːmɪneɪtə(r)/
pl bus terminators

⋈ connect, install a **bus terminator**

▶ **terminator 2**

---

bus topology *noun*
a way of arranging a local area network with all nodes attached to a single bus

/'bʌs təˌpɒlədʒi/
pl bus topologies

⋈ structure a network *as a* **bus topology**

syn bus architecture

▶ **network topology**

---

busy *adjective*
in use; engaged: *The line was busy.* ○ *A priority interrupt claims the CPU even when it is busy.*

/'bɪzi/

⋈ a **busy** signal, state

---

busy signal *noun*
a message sent by a device to show that it is working and is not ready to receive more data or commands: *A busy signal from the printer means that it is still processing the last data sent.*

/'bɪzi ˌsɪɡnəl/
pl busy signals

⋈ receive, send, transmit a **busy signal**

☆**byte** *noun* (hardware)
a unit of data, usually a group of 8 bits: *The basic unit of storage is the 8-bit byte.* ○ *one byte of memory*

/baɪt/
pl bytes

abbr B

▶ **character, gulp, kilobyte, megabyte, nibble, terabyte, word**

---

byte address *noun*
the location of a byte in the computer's memory: *a byte address of 1FCC*

/'baɪt əˌdres/
pl byte addresses

---

byte machine *noun* (hardware)
a computer which has a byte as a basic unit of storage and processing

/'baɪt məˌʃiːn/
pl byte machines

⋈ design, program a **byte machine**

▶ **word machine**

Cc

☆**C** *noun*
1 a high-level computer programming language

note C is an imperative procedural language which was designed in the early 1970s.

2 the letter which represents the decimal number 12 in hexadecimal notation

/siː/
1,2 note no plural

1 ⋈ program *in* C; a C compiler, library, program, shell; C software development products, source code

▶ **B, CPL, BCPL, UNIX**

---

cable *noun* (hardware)
a collection of wires surrounded by plastic. A cable connects devices to each other so that data can pass between them, or it

/'keɪbl/
pl cables

⋈ a power supply, printer **cable**

connects a device to a power supply: *This cable connects the keyboard to the computer.*

▶ **connector, fibre optic cable, wire**

---

cable television *noun* (hardware)
a system that transmits television programmes into homes using cables

/ˌkeɪbl ˈtelɪvɪʒn/
note no plural

ꓧ receive, subscribe *to*, watch **cable television**; a **cable television** line, network, operator, station

---

cabling diagram *noun*
a plan of the cables that connect PERIPHERALS to a computer, or the COMPONENTS inside a computer to each other: *The cabling diagram shows clearly how the disk drive is connected to the disk controller.*

/ˈkeɪblɪŋ ˌdaɪəgræm/
pl cabling diagrams

ꓧ draw, label a **cabling diagram**

☆**cache** *noun* (hardware)
a part of memory that stores copies of data that is often needed while a program is running. This data can be accessed very quickly.: *The 8k of internal cache memory is used as a very fast storage space.* ○ *The program sets up a cache.* ○ *64Kb of on-chip cache*

/kæʃ/
pl caches

ꓧ a **cache** buffer, memory

▶ **disk cache, memory, secondary store**

☆**CAD** *abbr*
▶ **computer aided design**

/kæd/
note pronounced as a word

☆**CADCAM** *abbr* (applications)
computer aided (or assisted) design/computer aided (or assisted) manufacturing. A process where computers are used to design and produce products by transmitting the design data to the machines that make the product: *set up a CADCAM system in a factory*

/ˈkædkæm/
note pronounced as a word

▶ **CIM**

CAFS *abbr*
▶ **content-addressable file store**

/ˌsiː eɪ ef ˈes/
note pronounced as individual letters

☆**CAI** *abbr* (applications)
computer aided instruction. The use of computers and programs for preparing lessons and other material for students: *The college makes use of CAI in its education programmes.*

/ˌsiː eɪ ˈaɪ/
note pronounced as individual letters

☆**CAL** *abbr* (applications)
computer assisted (or aided or augmented) learning. The use of computers and programs for testing, practice and other ways of learning: *A microcomputer is used for CAL in the classroom.*

/kæl/
note pronounced as a word

ꓧ a **CAL** package; **CAL** facilities, software

▶ **courseware**

---

calculate *verb*
to use mathematical operations on numbers in order to produce a result: *use the computer to calculate the ratio* ○ *calculate the costs accurately* ○ *calculate in base 10*

/ˈkælkjuleɪt/
calculate, calculating, calculated

note transitive or intransitive verb

ꓧ **calculate** an amount, an answer, a figure, a percentage, a result

---

abbr abbreviation   **pl** plural   **syn** synonym   ▶ see   ꓧ collocate (*word often used with the headword*)

calculation *noun*
a mathematical operation on numbers that produces a result: *The computer was designed to do scientific calculations.*

/ˌkælkjuˈleɪʃn/
pl calculations
⋈ carry out, perform a **calculation**

calculator *noun*
a small electronic instrument or software application for doing mathematical calculations: *a hand-held calculator* ○ *The computer's desk accessories include a calculator.* ○ *an on-screen calculator*

/ˈkælkjuleɪtə(r)/
pl calculators
⋈ a desk, pocket **calculator**

☆**CALL** *abbr* (applications)
computer assisted (or aided) language learning. The use of computers in teaching and learning a foreign language: *use CALL in the teaching of English as a foreign language* ○ *Computer assisted language learning can be useful in providing simple drill-and-practice exercises for students.*

/kɔːl/
note pronounced as a word

call¹ *noun*
a statement in a program that executes a SUBROUTINE or function

/kɔːl/
pl calls
⋈ a **call** *to* a function, *to* a subroutine

call² *verb*
1 to send a message to a computing device: *The auto dial modem called the main computer.* **2** to bring a SUBROUTINE or function into operation: *call any of the C subroutines*

/kɔːl/
call, calling, called
note transitive verb
1 **⋈** **call** a computer, telephone number
2 **⋈** **call** a function, library routine, subroutine

call by address *noun*
▶ **call by reference**

/ˌkɔːl baɪ əˈdres/

call by name *noun* (software/programming)
a method of PARAMETER PASSING (= a way of giving a value to a subroutine) where the information given to the SUBROUTINE is accessed each time that it is needed. The value of the subroutine may change each time it is used.

/ˌkɔːl baɪ ˈneɪm/
note no plural
⋈ implement, pass parameters *by*, use **call by name**; a **call by name** algorithm, code, protocol
syn pass by name

call by reference *noun* (software/programming)
a method of PARAMETER PASSING (= a way of giving a value to a subroutine) where the value given to the subroutine is the address of the parameter in memory. There will only be one copy of the parameter and changes to the parameter made in the subroutine will remain after the subroutine has ended: *a language that supports call by reference*

/ˌkɔːl baɪ ˈrefərəns/
note not used with *a* or *an*. No plural and used with a singular verb only.
⋈ implement, pass parameters *by*, use **call by reference**; a **call by reference** algorithm, code, program, protocol
syn call by address, pass by address, pass by reference

call by value *noun* (software/programming)
a method of PARAMETER PASSING (= a way of giving a value to a subroutine) where the information given to the SUBROUTINE is

/ˌkɔːl baɪ ˈvæljuː/
note no plural

the value of the PARAMETER at that time. Calculations in the subroutine cannot change the original parameter.

> ⋈ implement, pass parameters *by*, use **call by value**; a **call by value** algorithm, code, program, protocol
>
> **syn** pass by value

---

call duration *noun*
the length of time that a call lasts: *The call duration was 25 seconds.*

> /ˌkɔːl djuˈreɪʃn/
> **pl** call durations
> ⋈ measure, time the **call duration**

---

called party *noun*
the person or device receiving a call

> /ˌkɔːld ˈpɑːti/
> **pl** called parties
> ⋈ advise, invoice the **called party**

---

caller *noun*
the person or device making a call: *The caller disconnected before the call was completed.*

> /ˈkɔːlə(r)/
> **pl** callers

---

calling sequence *noun* (software/programming)
the machine code statements that allow a function or SUBROUTINE (= one part of a program) to be executed. The calling sequence must record where the FUNCTION CALL or SUBROUTINE CALL was made, so that when the function or subroutine is complete, operations can continue from the correct place in the program.

> /ˈkɔːlɪŋ ˌsiːkwəns/
> **pl** calling sequences
> ⋈ define a **calling sequence**
> ▶ call¹, return¹ 2, return address

---

calling up *noun*
the process of accessing data in a computer: *The calling up of this file could take some time as it is so long.*

> /ˌkɔːlɪŋ ˈʌp/
> **note** no plural
> ⋈ a **calling up** procedure, process, system
> ▶ access¹

☆CAM *abbr* (applications)
computer assisted (or aided) manufacturing. The use of computers in all or part of the manufacturing process: *set up a CAM system*

> /kæm/
> **note** pronounced as a word
> **note** not used with *a* or *an*. No plural and used with a singular verb only.
> ▶ CADCAM

---

camera-ready copy *noun*
a document that needs no changes and is ready to be printed: *The printer produces camera-ready copy.* ○ *camera-ready copy on film*

> /ˌkæmərə redi ˈkɒpi/
> **note** not used with *a* or *an*. No plural and used with a singular verb only.
> **abbr** CRC

CAN *abbr*
▶ **cancel character**

> /kæn/
> **note** pronounced as a word

☆cancel *verb*
to stop something before it happens or before it is complete: *cancel the instruction to print*

> /ˈkænsl/
> **cancel, cancelling, cancelled**
> (*US* **cancel, canceling, canceled**)
> **note** transitive verb
> ⋈ **cancel** an instruction, an operation, a request

---

abbr abbreviation   **pl** plural   **syn** synonym   ▶ see   ⋈ collocate (*word often used with the headword*)

cancel character noun
an ASCII character used in a message to show that the previous character is wrong and should be ignored: *correct errors in the data by sending a cancel character*

note The backspace key on a terminal usually sends the cancel character.

/ˈkænsl ˌkærəktə(r)/
pl cancel characters
abbr CAN
◄ input, send, type a **cancel character**
► **delete character**

cancellation noun
the act of stopping something before it happens or before it is complete

/ˌkænsəˈleɪʃn/
pl cancellations

☆**capacity** noun (hardware)
the amount of data a computer or PERIPHERAL can store or process: *The capacity of this tape is 2.4 gigabytes.*

/kəˈpæsəti/
pl capacities
► **memory capacity**

capital noun
a letter in large format such as A, B and C: *'BIG' in this sentence is written with a capital B, I and G.* ○ *use a capital to begin the sentence* ○ *The heading should be written in block capitals.*

/ˈkæpɪtl/
pl capitals
abbr caps
syn upper case
► **lower case**

caps abbr
► **capital**

/kæps/

Caps Lock key noun (hardware)
the key on a keyboard allowing text to be written continuously in capital letters: *Press the Caps Lock key to write the heading in capital letters.*

/ˌkæps ˈlɒk kiː/
note usually singular

caption noun
a small piece of text of usually one or two lines that is printed by a photograph, picture or a larger piece of text: *What does the caption say?* ○ *The caption is printed in the margin next to the paragraph.*

/ˈkæpʃn/
pl captions

☆**capture**[1] noun
the process of recording data in electronic form: *a data capture system* ○ *automatic data capture techniques*

/ˈkæptʃə(r)/
note not used with *a* or *an*. No plural and used with a singular verb only.
◄ data, text **capture**
► **enter, input**

☆**capture**[2] verb
to record data in electronic form: *capture the text by keying it to disk*

/ˈkæptʃə(r)/
capture, capturing, captured
note transitive verb
◄ **capture** an image; **capture** data, text
► **enter**

CAR abbr
► **current address register**

/ˌsiː eɪ ˈɑː/
note pronounced as individual letters

---

card *noun* (hardware)
an electronic circuit board that is added to a computer to increases its functions or capabilities: *fit the card into the computer's expansion slot*

/kɑːd/
pl cards
◄ a fax, memory, sound, video **card**
► **expansion board**

---

card cage *noun* (hardware)
a container that holds printed circuit boards inside a computer

/'kɑːd keɪdʒ/
pl card cages

---

card code *noun* (hardware)
the combination of holes on a PUNCHED CARD

/'kɑːd kəʊd/
pl card codes

---

card image *noun*
a copy of information on a card that exists in part of the computer's memory

/'kɑːd ˌɪmɪdʒ/
pl card images

---

card punch *noun* (hardware)
a machine used for making holes in a PUNCHED CARD (= a piece of card with small holes that represent data)

note Card punches are old fashioned and are not often used.

/'kɑːd pʌntʃ/
pl card punches

---

card reader *noun* (hardware)
an input device for reading punched cards which translates the holes in the card into data a computer can process: *The computer operator took the pile of punched cards from the box and placed them into the card reader.*

/'kɑːd ˌriːdə(r)/
pl card readers

---

caret *noun*
the 'ʌ' symbol usually found on the key marked '6' on computer keyboards: *press shift and 6 to get the caret*

/'kærət/
pl carets

---

carriage *noun* (hardware)
the part of a printer or typewriter that holds and moves the piece of paper that is being printed

/'kærɪdʒ/
pl carriages

---

carriage control *noun*
a set of instructions or codes to the computer that control the movement of the CARRIAGE

/'kærɪdʒ kənˌtrəʊl/
note not used with *a* or *an*. No plural and used with a singular verb only.

---

carriage return *noun*
a CONTROL CHARACTER that tells the computer or printer to move to the beginning of the current line

/ˌkærɪdʒ rɪ'tɜːn/
pl carriage returns
abbr CR
► **line feed, newline character**

---

carrier *noun*
► **carrier signal**

/'kæriə(r)/

---

carrier detect *noun*
► **data carrier detect character**

/ˌkæriə dɪ'tekt/

---

carrier sense multiple access *noun*
► **CSMA**

/'kæriə 'sens 'mʌltɪpl 'ækses/

---

carrier sense multiple access with collision detection *noun*
► **CSMA-CD**

/'kæriə 'sens 'mʌltɪpl 'ækses wɪð kə'lɪʒn dɪˌtekʃn/

---

abbr abbreviation   **pl** plural   **syn** synonym   ► see   ◄ collocate (*word often used with the headword*)

carrier signal *noun*
a steady signal sent along a data transmission channel which carries information only when it is altered in some way; this alteration is called MODULATION: *The modem automatically disconnected because it could no longer sense a carrier signal.*

/'kæriə ˌsɪɡnəl/
pl carrier signals
ℍ detect, sense a **carrier signal**
syn carrier, carrier wave, data carrier

carrier wave *noun*
▶ **carrier signal**

/'kæriə weɪv/

carry *noun* (mathematics and logic)
a digit that is created when the result of an addition is larger than the number base being used

note In binary notation the addition of 1 and 1 will give a result 0 and a carry of 1 to take to the next position, making 10 (2 in decimal notation).

/'kæri/
pl carries
▶ **flag**

carry bit *noun*
the number remaining when two 8-bit binary numbers are added together

/'kæri bɪt/
pl carry bits
▶ **full adder, half adder**

☆**cartridge** *noun* (hardware)
a container that holds and protects material such as magnetic tape

/'kɑːtrɪdʒ/
pl cartridges

cartridge drive *noun* (hardware)
a PERIPHERAL which uses either a disk or tape in a cartridge. The cartridge can be removed for security or for transferring information to other computers: *transfer data from a hard disk to a cartridge drive for the backup*

/'kɑːtrɪdʒ draɪv/
pl cartridge drives

cartridge font *noun* (hardware)
a font for a printer which is supplied in a cartridge that fits into the printer: *plug the cartridge font into the printer*

/'kɑːtrɪdʒ fɒnt/
pl cartridge fonts

cartridge tape *noun* (hardware)
magnetic tape which is contained in a cartridge and is used to make backups of the data on a hard disk, or to transfer data from one computer to another: *use a cartridge tape to make a backup copy of the day's work*

/'kɑːtrɪdʒ teɪp/
pl cartridge tapes

cascade¹ *noun*
a group of devices connected together so that the output of one device is the input to the next device, and so on

/kæˈskeɪd/
pl cascades

cascade² *verb*
to have several windows containing different applications or data open on screen at the same time. Some windows may be hidden behind other windows: *cascade the windows to avoid opening the application each time it is needed*

/kæˈskeɪd/
cascade, cascading, cascaded
note transitive verb
ℍ **cascade** applications, windows
▶ **tile**

cascade carry *noun*
a carry signal output by an ADDER (= the part of the computer that adds binary digits) that is the result of a carry signal that is input from the previous stage of processing

/kæˌskeɪd 'kæri/
pl cascade carries
syn ripple through carry

CASE *abbr*
computer assisted software engineering

/keɪs/
note pronounced as a word

---

case change *noun* (hardware)
the key on a keyboard that is used to change from LOWER CASE
to UPPER CASE and from upper case to lower case

/'keɪs tʃeɪndʒ/
note usually singular

---

case folding *noun*
the process of changing the characters in a section of text so
that they are all UPPER CASE or all LOWER CASE: *One stage of
cleaning up the raw data is to carry out case folding on the text
items.*

/'keɪs ˌfəʊldɪŋ/
note not used with *a* or *an*. No
plural and used with a singular
verb only.
ⵖ carry out, perform **case
folding**

---

case sensitive *adjective*
(of a process or program) that recognizes and is affected by text
keyed in UPPER CASE or LOWER CASE: *The password software is case
sensitive and passwords will only be accepted if they are entered in
lower case.*

/ˌkeɪs 'sensətɪv/
ⵖ a **case sensitive** file name,
identifier, variable name; **case
sensitive** input

---

case statement *noun* (software/programming)
a statement in some programming languages such as Pascal
which allows different groups of statements to be executed
when a named variable takes different values: *The user input
should be 'Y' or 'N' and a case statement executes different
instructions depending on whether the input is either of these.*

/'keɪs ˌsteɪtmənt/
pl case statements
ⵖ execute, program, use a **case
statement**

CASE tools *noun* (software/programming)
computer assisted software engineering tools. A computer
program used to help programmers plan and design software:
*A new CASE standard allows developers to integrate and deploy
their CASE tools across different CASE environments.*

/'keɪs tuːlz/
note usually plural

---

cassette *noun* (hardware)
a hard plastic container which holds magnetic tape: *make a
backup on a cassette* ○ *buy a music cassette*

/kə'set/
pl cassettes
ⵖ read data *from*, transfer data *to*
a **cassette**

---

cassette drive *noun* (hardware)
the PERIPHERAL device which reads data from and writes data to
a cassette tape: *Insert a cassette into the cassette drive to make a
security backup.*

/kə'set draɪv/
pl cassette drives

---

cassette tape *noun* (hardware)
the narrow magnetic tape that stores data and is contained in
a cassette: *backup onto cassette tape*

/kə'set teɪp/
pl cassette tapes

CAT *abbr*
computer aided testing

/cæt/
note pronounced as a word

---

catastrophic error *noun*
a problem that makes a program crash or erases files: *A virus
caused the catastrophic error.*

/'kætəˌstrɒfɪk 'erə(r)/
pl catastrophic errors
▶ **crash**[1]

---

catastrophic failure *noun*
the complete failure of a computer system: *A cold boot was the
only way to restore the system after a catastrophic failure.*

/'kætəˌstrɒfɪk 'feɪljə(r)/
pl catastrophic failures
▶ **crash**[1]

---

abbr abbreviation   **pl** plural   **syn** synonym   ▶ see   ⵖ collocate (*word often used with the headword*)

cathode ray tube *noun* (hardware)
a device that produces images on a screen: *The monitor contains a cathode ray tube.*

/ˌkæθəʊd ˈreɪ tjuːb/
pl cathode ray tubes
abbr CRT
▶ **display¹, liquid crystal display, monitor, VDU**

CBL
computer based learning

/ˌsiː biː ˈel/
note pronounced as individual letters

CBT *abbr*
computer based training

/ˌsiː biː ˈtiː/
note pronounced as individual letters

CCD *abbr*
▶ **charge coupled device**

/ˌsiː siː ˈdiː/
note pronounced as individual letters

CCP *abbr*
▶ **command console processor**

/ˌsiː siː ˈpiː/
note pronounced as individual letters

☆**CD** *abbr* (hardware)
a compact disc. A small disk which contains digital data that is read by a laser. This data can be music, or in multimedia CDs it can be images, text and sound. CDs can also contain various types software such as virus-checking programs: *The computer can run music CDs and multimedia CDs.* ○ *The software to compress files came as freeware on a CD.*

note In 'compact disc' and phrases containing it, 'disc' is spelt with a 'c'. In all other cases it is spelt with a 'k', as in 'floppy disk' and 'hard disk', etc.

/ˌsiː ˈdiː/
pl CDs
◄ an audio, an interactive, a multimedia **CD**; a **CD** drive, player
syn optical disc
▶ **disk**

☆**CD-I** *abbr* (hardware)
compact disc interactive. A type of CD-ROM that displays sound, images and text through a television: *CD-I outputs directly to a TV screen.* ○ *CD-I can deliver video.*

/ˌsiː diː ˈaɪ/
note pronounced as individual letters
note usually singular
◄ **CD-I** mode, software

☆**CD-ROM** *abbr* (hardware)
compact disc read-only memory. A compact disc which is a popular format for multimedia products and stores sound, images and text, etc: *a CD-ROM version of the software* ○ *multimedia CD-ROM publishing* ○ *The application is available on a CD-ROM.*

/ˌsiː diː ˈrɒm/
pl CD-ROMs
◄ a **CD-ROM** product, system, title

CD-ROM drive *noun* (hardware)
part of the computer that holds the CD-ROM and passes the information it contains to the computer: *The CD-ROM drive was bundled with the multimedia computer.* ○ *The PC has an inbuilt CD-ROM drive.*

/ˌsiː diː ˈrɒm draɪv/
pl CD-ROM drives
▶ **disk drive, floppy disk drive, hard disk drive**

---

cell *noun*
1 an individual unit in a computer's memory that can store a single piece of data **2** (*applications*) an area in a spreadsheet which contains data: *enter the counting formula into the cell*

/sel/
pl cells
1 syn store location

centralized processing *noun*
the processing of data in one place which all the users on a
network have access to

/ˌsentrəlaɪzd 'prəʊsesɪŋ/
note not used with *a* or *an*. No
plural and used with a singular
verb only

---

central memory *noun*
▶ **primary memory**

/ˌsentrəl 'meməri/

☆**central processing unit** *noun*
▶ **CPU**

/ˌsentrəl 'prəʊsesɪŋ ˌjuːnɪt/

---

central processor *noun*
▶ **CPU**

/ˌsentrəl 'prəʊsesə(r)/

Centronics interface *noun*
(*trade mark*) a PARALLEL INTERFACE normally used for a printer

/sen,trɒnɪks 'ɪntəfeɪs/
pl Centronics interfaces

CGA *abbr*
▶ **colour graphics adaptor**

/ˌsiː dʒiː 'eɪ/
note pronounced as individual
letters

---

chad *noun*
the paper that is removed when holes are made in cards or
tape: *throw away the chad*

/tʃæd/
note not used with *a* or *an*. No
plural and used with a singular
verb only.
▶ **paper tape, punched card**

---

chain *noun*
a series of items such as files, data or instructions that are
linked in some way

/tʃeɪn/
pl chains

---

chained file *noun*
a file in which an entry contains information and an address
referring to the next entry that has the same information. This
means that identical data can be accessed very quickly.

/ˌtʃeɪnd 'faɪl/
pl chained files

---

chained list *noun*
▶ **linked list**

/ˌtʃeɪnd 'lɪst/

---

chain printer *noun* (hardware)
a type of LINE PRINTER with characters on a metal chain. The
characters are printed when paper and ink are pushed against
the moving metal chain: *The earliest chain printer had a speed of
150 lines per minute.*

/'tʃeɪn ˌprɪntə(r)/
pl chain printers

---

change file *noun*
a file in batch processing that contains a collection of records.
It is used to update a MASTER FILE.

/'tʃeɪndʒ faɪl/
pl change files
▶ **transaction file**

---

change record *noun*
a record that contains new information which is used to
update a MASTER FILE

/'tʃeɪndʒ ˌrekɔːd/
pl change records

---

abbr abbreviation   **pl** plural   **syn** synonym   ▶ see   ◣ collocate (*word often used with the headword*)

channel¹ *noun* (hardware)
a physical path along which data is transmitted and received. If the channel is inside the computer, it is usually a type of bus. If the channel is outside the computer, it can be a cable or a certain FREQUENCY that carries a signal: *The channel carries analog data.*

/'tʃænl/
pl channels
⋈ send data *over*, transmit data *via* a **channel**; a communications, data, transmissions **channel**
▶ **data channel**

channel² *verb*
to carry data and signals, etc along a communications link: *Information is channelled from the computer to the printer.*

/'tʃænl/
channel, channelling, channelled
(*US* **channel, channeling, channeled**)
note transitive verb
⋈ **channel** data, information

channel adaptor *noun* (hardware)
a device that allows hardware using different communications channels to be connected together so that data can be transferred between them: *The channel adaptor is based on modern chip technology.*

/'tʃænl ə,dæptə(r)/
pl channel adaptors
(also channel apapter)

channel controller *noun*
hardware that manages the access by one device to the physical connection with another device: *A channel controller is installed on the motherboard.*

/'tʃænl kən,trəʊlə(r)/
pl channel controllers
⋈ install, replace a **channel controller**

channel switching *noun*
the process of changing from one communications channel to another

/'tʃænl ,swɪtʃɪŋ/
note not used with *a* or *an*. No plural and used with a singular verb only.

☆**character** *noun*
1 a letter, number or symbol displayed on screen or printed on paper: *The filename must not contain more than eight characters.*
2 ▶ **control character**

/'kærəktə(r)/
pl characters
1 display, print, type a **character**; a **character** code, set, string
▶ **alphanumeric**

character code *noun* (software)
the number that is used by a computer to represent a character: *In ASCII, the character code for 'A' is 65.*

/'kærəktə kəʊd/
pl character codes
⋈ define, use a **character code**
▶ **character set**

character device *noun* (hardware)
a device such as a keyboard or printer that processes data one complete character at a time. The range of characters produced by the device is limited by the character set of the device.

/'kærəktə dɪ,vaɪs/
pl character devices

character display *noun*
a part of device that can only show complete characters from its character set. It cannot display graphics: *The hand-held machine has an 80-line character display.*

/'kærəktə dɪ,spleɪ/
pl character displays

character generator *noun*
the part of ROM that transfers dots representing a character to the display unit

/'kærəktə ,dʒenəreɪtə(r)/
pl character generators

characteristic *noun*

the part of a FLOATING POINT NUMBER that stores the power to which the number must be raised: *In the decimal floating point number 3.14159X10^{12} the characteristic is 12.*

/ˌkærəktəˈrɪstɪk/

pl characteristics

⋈ access, store, increment the **characteristic**

syn exponent

▶ **mantissa**

---

character printer *noun* (hardware)

a printer that can only print complete characters from its character set. It cannot print graphics: *The address labels for the mail-shot were produced on a character printer.*

/ˈkærəktə ˌprɪntə(r)/

pl character printers

▶ **printer**

---

character recognition *noun*

the ability of a system to recognize characters and transfer them to a computer for processing

/ˈkærəktə rekəgˌnɪʃn/

note not used with *a* or *an*. No plural and used with a singular verb only.

▶ **magnetic ink character recognition, optical character recognition**

---

character set *noun* (software)

the characters that can be printed or displayed by a computer system: *Six data bits encode a character set consisting of the digits 0 to 9.*

note A character set is both the printed characters and the codes that represent the characters.

/ˈkærəktə set/

pl character sets

⋈ define a **character set**

▶ **ASCII, extended character set**

---

characters per inch *noun*

a measurement of the number of characters that will fit into a line that is one inch long: *print at 10 characters per inch*

/ˌkærəktəz pər ˈɪntʃ/

note no plural

abbr cpi

▶ **monospace font, pitch, proportional font**

---

characters per second *noun*

a measurement of the printing speed of a character-based output device: *a dot matrix printer with a speed of 240 characters per second*

/ˌkærəktəz pə ˈsekənd/

note no plural

abbr cps

▶ **throughput**

---

character string *noun*

▶ **string**

/ˈkærəktə strɪŋ/

---

charge coupled device *noun* (hardware)

an electronic device that may be given a charge by shining light onto it. It is used in document scanners and video cameras, and also as a storage device.

/ˈtʃɑːdʒ ˈkʌpld dɪˈvaɪs/

pl charge coupled devices

abbr CCD

⋈ charge, read data *from*, use a **charge coupled device**: **charge coupled device** memory

---

chart *noun*

a map, plan or other diagram of an object or a process: *The spreadsheet data was displayed as a chart.*

/tʃɑːt/

pl charts

⋈ display something *as*, draw, read a **chart**

▶ **flow chart**

---

chassis *noun* (hardware)

a frame that supports the individual components of a computer: *The chassis holds the motherboard and the expansion slots.*

/ˈʃæsi/

pl chassis

⋈ attach *to*, connect *to*, earth, ground the **chassis**

---

abbr abbreviation   **pl** plural   **syn** synonym   ▶ see   ⋈ collocate (*word often used with the headword*)

check¹ *noun*
a test to make sure that something is correct or in a certain condition: *Checks are carried out weekly on all equipment to make sure it is working correctly.*

/tʃek/
pl checks
◄ carry out, make, perform a **check**

check² *verb*
to make sure that something is correct or in a certain condition: *check the value of the variables* ○ *check that the network is operating* ○ *check the backup procedures and make any necessary adjustments*

/tʃek/
check, checking, checked
note transitive verb
◄ **check** a result, value

check bit *noun*
a binary digit added to any item of binary data to make sure that it is entered or transmitted correctly. The bit depends on the rest of the data item and if the data is changed the bit will no longer be correct: *add a check bit to a block of transmitted data*

/ˈtʃek bɪt/
pl check bits
◄ add, check, read, use a **check bit**
► **error detection, parity check**

check character *noun*
a character added to an item of data to make sure that it is entered or transmitted correctly. The character depends on the rest of the item and if the data is changed the character will no longer be correct.

/ˈtʃek ˌkærəktə(r)/
pl check characters
◄ add, read, use a **check character**
► **check digit, error detection**

check digit *noun*
a digit added to an item of data to make sure that it is entered or transmitted correctly. The digit depends on the rest of the data item and if the data is changed the digit will no longer be correct: *The International Standard Book Number includes one of the digits 0 to 9 or X as a check digit.*

/ˈtʃek ˌdɪdʒɪt/
pl check digits
◄ add, check, read, use a **check digit**
► **error detection**

checkpoint *noun* (software/programming)
an instruction in a machine language program that makes execution stop so that the programmer can inspect the values of the variables: *Checkpoints were inserted into the program when it was debugged but were removed when the final version was produced.*

/ˈtʃekpɔɪnt/
pl checkpoints
◄ insert, remove a **checkpoint**
syn breakpoint

checkpoint dump *noun*
a listing or display of all or part of memory when a program is stopped at a CHECKPOINT: *The checkpoint dump shows whether the program is updating the variables.*

/ˌtʃekpɔɪnt ˈdʌmp/
pl checkpoint dumps
◄ print a **checkpoint dump**

check sum *noun*
a way of finding errors in a DATA TRANSMISSION by treating the data as numbers and calculating their total. The total is calculated before and after data is transmitted or stored. When the results of both calculations are different, an error has occurred: *The checksum was re-computed and did not agree with the transmitted one which indicated a transmission error.*

/ˈtʃek sʌm/
pl check sums
(also **checksum**)
◄ calculate, compute a **check sum**
syn check total
► **hash total**

check total *noun*
► **check sum**

/ˈtʃek təʊtl/

chief programmer team *noun* (personnel)
a group of people producing software under the direction of a
leader: *A chief programmer team is strongly recommended for
major projects.*

/ˌtʃiːf ˈprəʊgræmə tiːm/
pl chief programmer teams
◢ belong *to*, lead, work *as* a **chief
programmer team**

---

child *noun*
a NODE[1] in a data structure which is linked to a node at a
higher level: *Any node with a child is a parent.*

/tʃaɪld/
pl children
◢ create, delete, link something *to*
a **child**
▶ **parent**

☆**chip** *noun* (hardware)
a small piece of SILICON with a complex electrical circuit, called
an integrated circuit, which is used in computers. It can do the
work of a very large number of electrical COMPONENTS in a small
space: *Revolutionary advances in the manufacture of chips have
improved the speed, size and reliability of computers.*

/tʃɪp/
pl chips
◢ a kilobit, megabit **chip**
syn integrated circuit, microchip,
silicon chip
▶ **large scale integration,
medium scale integration,
memory chip,
microprocessor, small scale
integration, super large
scale integration, ultra large
scale integration, very large
scale integration**

---

chip architecture *noun*
the design and layout of an integrated circuit (chip): *8-bit chip
architecture*

/ˈtʃɪp ˌɑːkɪtektʃə(r)/
pl chip architectures
◢ design, specify the **chip
architecture**

---

chip set *noun* (hardware)
a number of integrated circuits (chips) connected together to
form a single component of a computer system: *Upgrading a
computer may involve changing the chip set.*

/ˈtʃɪp set/
pl chip sets
◢ install, remove a **chip set**

---

chip socket *noun* (hardware)
a component mounted on a PRINTED CIRCUIT BOARD into which
an integrated circuit (chip) can be placed: *Some of the memory
chip sockets are empty.*

/ˈtʃɪp ˌsɒkɪt/
pl chip sockets
◢ connect, replace a **chip socket**

---

chop *verb*
to reduce the number of decimal places in a number by
ignoring all digits beyond a given point: *chop 3.14159 to 3.14*

/tʃɒp/
chop, chopping, chopped
note transitive verb
◢ **chop** an answer, a number, a
result
▶ **round**

---

chop round to zero *verb*
▶ **truncate**

/ˈtʃɒp ˈraʊnd tə ˈzɪərəʊ/

---

chroma *noun*
the part of a television signal which carries information about
colour: *adjust the chroma level*

/ˈkrəʊmə/
note not used with *a* or *an*. No
plural and used with a singular
verb only.

---

abbr abbreviation   **pl** plural   **syn** synonym   ▶ see   ◢ collocate (*word often used with the headword*)

CIM *abbr*
1 computer integrated manufacturing. The use of computers to control the manufacturing process: *The CIM system controls resource management.* 2 computer input MICROFILM. This microfilm contains data which is SCANNED and converted into codes for computer processing.

/ˌsiː aɪ ˈem/
note pronounced as individual letters

---

cipher *noun*
1 a system for putting data into a form so it cannot be read without a key: *A cipher was used for important information in the document.*

note A cipher is often incorrectly referred to as a 'code'. A code replaces one word with another, and is not intended to ensure secrecy, while a cipher operates on individual letters and is intended to make the message secret. Many people use both words to mean the same thing.

2 a message that has been put into another form so that is impossible to read without a key: *a secure cipher*

/ˈsaɪfə(r)/
pl ciphers
(also **cypher**)
1 ◪ use a **cipher**
▶ **code, data encryption standard, encryption, encypher**
2 ◪ transmit, turn a message *into* a **cipher**
syn ciphertext
▶ **plain text**

---

cipher key *noun*
▶ **key 2**

/ˈsaɪfə kiː/

---

ciphertext *noun*
▶ **cipher 2**

/ˈsaɪfətekst/

CIR *abbr*
▶ **current instruction register**

/ˌsiː aɪ ˈɑː/
note pronounced as individual letters

☆**circuit** *noun* (hardware)
a path, such as a wire, that an electric current can move through: *measure the current flowing in the circuit* ○ *a 30-amp power circuit*

/ˈsɜːkɪt/
pl circuits
◪ connect, flow *along* a **circuit**: a bipolar, a closed, an electric, an electronic, a short, a unipolar **circuit**

---

circuit analyser *noun* (hardware)
equipment that measures electrical circuits, usually to test if they are working correctly: *measure voltage, current and resistance with a circuit analyser*

/ˈsɜːkɪt ˌænəlaɪzə(r)/
pl circuit analysers
(*US* **circuit analyzer**)
◪ test *with*, use a **circuit analyser**

---

circuit board *noun* (hardware)
a flat card used as a base on which electronic COMPONENTS are placed and then connected together by wires: *a circuit board which plugs into the standard disk drive* ○ *the circuit board is mounted on the base panel* ○ *the layout of components on a circuit board*

/ˈsɜːkɪt bɔːd/
pl circuit boards
◪ design, install, manufacture a **circuit board**
syn circuit card
▶ **chip, expansion board, printed circuit board**

---

circuit breaker *noun* (hardware)
a switch that controls the flow of an electric current. If an electric current becomes too high, a circuit breaker stops it from flowing to protect against damage: *test the operation of the circuit breakers*

/ˈsɜːkɪt ˌbreɪkə(r)/
pl circuit breakers
◪ close, open, reset, trip a **circuit breaker**
syn breaker

circuit card *noun*
▶ **circuit board**

/ˈsɜːkɪt kɑːd/

---

circuit diagram *noun*
a plan that shows how the COMPONENTS of an electrical system are connected

/ˈsɜːkɪt daɪəgræm/
pl circuit diagrams

◄ draw, draw *up*, follow, read a **circuit diagram**

---

circuitry *noun* (hardware)
a system of electric or electronic CIRCUITS: *There is a lot of complex circuitry in modern computers.*

/ˈsɜːkɪtri/
note not used with *a* or *an*. No plural and used with a singular verb only.

◄ design, examine the **circuitry**

---

circuit switching *noun*
a way of sending messages over telephone lines or a network. A fixed path between the sender and receiver is used for the whole message: *Most voice telephone communications use circuit switching*

/ˈsɜːkɪt ˌswɪtʃɪŋ/
note not used with *a* or *an*. No plural and used with a singular verb only.

▶ **packet switching, switching**

---

circular buffer *noun*
an area of storage used to hold data for a short time during transfer between parts of a system which operate at different speeds. New data is added until the area becomes full; if the earlier data has been used, it is then OVERWRITTEN (2) with more data.

/ˌsɜːkjələ ˈbʌfə(r)/
pl circular buffers

◄ access, fill, use a **circular buffer**

▶ **buffer**

---

circular list *noun*
a list DATA STRUCTURE where the last data item is linked back to the first data item

/ˌsɜːkjələ ˈlɪst/
pl circular lists

◄ access, implement, update a **circular list**

---

circular shift *noun*
▶ **rotate operation**

/ˌsɜːkjələ ˈʃɪft/

---

circulating register *noun*
a storage location where any movement (shift) of binary digits left or right makes those bits that are moved out reappear at the other end of the register

/ˈsɜːkjəleɪtɪŋ ˌredʒɪstə(r)/
pl circulating registers

◄ access, store bits *in a* **circulating register**

☆**CISC** *abbr* (hardware)
a complex instruction set computer. A computer designed to use a microprocessor with a large INSTRUCTION SET which allows software to be simpler and shorter but involves longer processing times: *Most PCs use CISC processors.*

/sɪsk/
note pronounced as a word
pl CISCs
(also **cisc**)

◄ a CISC chip, processor, system; CISC architecture

▶ **instruction code, RISC**

---

clean copy *noun* (hardware)
1 a copy of a printed document without notes or changes that may have been added by hand: *print a clean copy of the program listing* **2** a printed version of data, especially text for input to a computer, which has been VERIFIED so that it is reliable: *It is important to use clean copy for input of substantial volumes of text.*

/ˌkliːn ˈkɒpi/
1 pl clean copies
2 note usually singular

---

clean room *noun*
a room which contains nothing that can affect delicate equipment: *The electronic components are kept in a clean room*

/ˈkliːn ruːm/
pl clean rooms

---

abbr abbreviation   **pl** plural   **syn** synonym   ▶ see   ◄ collocate (*word often used with the headword*)

where they cannot be damaged by dust or dirt. ○ *wear protective clothing in the clean room*

⋈ enter, leave, work *in* a **clean room**

☆**clear¹** *verb*

1 to remove data from the computer's memory: *If memory is not cleared, values left from a previous program may affect the execution.*

note In computer programming, 'clear' often means 'set equal to zero'.

2 to remove information that is displayed on the screen: *The program clears the screen before displaying the menu.* **3** to give up control of a transmission line after a message has been sent: *After transmission, the line is cleared.*

/klɪə(r)/
clear, clearing, cleared
note transitive verb
1 ⋈ **clear** an array, the memory, the screen, a variable
▶ **unset**
2 ⋈ **clear** a data channel, line

---

clear² *adjective*

1 not in use at a certain time and available to be used: *The line was clear.* **2** easy to understand: *The instructions on screen were clear and helpful.* **3** (of a signal) free from noise

/klɪə(r)/
1 ⋈ a **clear** data channel, line
2 ⋈ **clear** instructions, orders
3 ⋈ a **clear** picture, signal, transmission

---

clear to send character *noun*

a signal used in the RS-232C, PROTOCOL (= a set of signals and rules that control data transmission) to show that a device is ready to receive a message: *When the printer has output all the data in its buffer it returns a clear to send character.*

/ˌklɪə tə ˈsend ˌkærəktə(r)/
pl clear to send characters
abbr CTS
⋈ receive, send, transmit a **clear to send character**

☆**click** *verb* (operations)

to press a button on a mouse: *Place the cursor in the box and click once to open the file.*

/klɪk/
click, clicking, clicked
note intransitive verb
⋈ **click** *on* an icon, *on* the mouse; **click** *inside* a box or window, etc
▶ **double-click, drag, highlight**

---

client *noun*

1 a person or company who pays for goods and services: *Most of the company's clients are small businesses.* **2** a REMOTE TERMINAL that is linked to a server

/ˈklaɪənt/
pl clients
1 ⋈ deal with, service a **client**
2 ⋈ a remote **client**

---

client-server *noun*

a system of CLIENTS (2) that are linked to servers. The client sends a request to the server which the server processes and then returns the result to the client: *In the client-server system, the server receives requests from clients anywhere on the network.* ○ *Client-servers communicate using a common protocol.*

note One example of a client-server system is an Internet browser where a request is sent from the client (the user's computer) to the server (which could be anywhere in the world). The server processes the client's request and sends back the result which is displayed on the client's screen. The advantage of client-server systems are that they allow access to a wide variety of resources such as data and processing.

/ˌklaɪənt ˈsɜːvə(r)/
pl client-servers
⋈ a distributed **client-server**

---

clip *verb*

to reduce the size of an image on screen to make it fit into a space of a fixed size: *The graphic was clipped so it could be fitted into a page of text.*

/klɪp/
clip, clipping, clipped
note transitive verb

clock *noun*   /klɒk/
▶ **real-time clock, system clock**

---

clocking *noun*   /'klɒkɪŋ/
the action of driving a COMPONENT by timing signals from a
clock: *Clocking of the expansion boards needs to be at an
appropriate clock rate.*

note not used with *a* or *an*. No
plural and used with a singular
verb only.

H **clocking** rate, speed

▶ **synchronization,
synchronous**

---

clock track *noun*   (hardware)   /'klɒk træk/
a series of marks along the edge of a document designed for an
OPTICAL MARK READER to adjust the speed at which the document
is scanned

pl clock tracks

H print, read a **clock track**

---

clone *noun*   (hardware)   /kləʊn/
a computer made by one company that is exactly the same as
one originally made by a different company: *The software runs
on an IBM clone.*

pl clones

H a Macintosh, PC **clone**

▶ **original equipment
manufacturer**

---

close *verb*   /kləʊz/
to stop working on a file or application, etc: *close the spreadsheet
○ The system closes automatically when the user logs off.*

close, closing, closed

note transitive or intransitive
verb

H **close** an application, a data
channel, a document, a file

▶ **quit**

---

closed *adjective*   /kləʊzd/
not able to be accessed: *a closed bulletin board*

---

closed subroutine *noun*   (software/programming)   /ˌkləʊzd 'sʌbruːtiːn/
a SUBROUTINE that is stored away from the main program.
Whenever this subroutine is needed, the current position in
the main program is saved and execution continues with the
subroutine. Only one copy of a closed subroutine is needed by
a program.

pl closed subroutines

H program, use a **closed
subroutine**

▶ **calling sequence, open
subroutine**

---

closed user group *noun*   /ˌkləʊzd 'juːzə gruːp/
a group of computer users sharing a database or BULLETIN BOARD
(= a network service that allows users with a shared interest to
communicate) who have access to information that is not
available to others: *Only members of the closed user group know
the password.*

pl closed user groups

abbr CUG

H belong *to* a **closed user group**

▶ **user group**

---

cluster *noun*   /'klʌstə(r)/
1 a set of PERIPHERALS controlled by a single processor or a
group of processors that are linked together **2** a set of disk
storage locations next to one another: *Clusters are a convenient
measure of the amount of disk space occupied by a file.*

pl clusters

1 H arrange *in*, control, manage
a **cluster**

2 H access, read, write a **cluster**

---

abbr abbreviation   **pl** plural   **syn** synonym   ▶ see   H collocate (*word often used with the headword*)

CLUT *abbr*
▶ **colour look-up table**

note used in written English only

CMI *abbr*
computer managed instruction

/ˌsiː em ˈaɪ/
note pronounced as individual letters

CMOS *abbr*
complementary metal-oxide semiconductor

/ˈsiːmɒs/
note pronounced as a word

---

coaxial cable *noun* (hardware)
a pair of electrical wires where one wire is completely enclosed within the other wire so that the outer wire can prevent interference to the signal on the central wire: *The television is connected to the aerial by a coaxial cable.*

/kəʊ ˈæksɪəl ˌkeɪbl/
pl coaxial cables
abbr coax

☆**COBOL** *noun* (software/programming)
a high-level computer programming language designed for business and commercial use

note COBOL is an imperative procedural language which was designed in the 1960s by the Committee on Data Systems Languages (CODASYL). The word 'COBOL' comes from the the words 'Common Business Oriented Language'.

/ˈkəʊbɒl/
note not used with *a* or *an*. No plural and used with a singular verb only.
◄ program in, write **COBOL**; a **COBOL** compiler, program; **COBOL** source code

---

CODASYL *abbr*
Committee (or sometimes Conference) on Data Systems Languages. This body defined the COBOL programming language.

/ˈkəʊdəsɪl/
note pronounced as a word

☆**code¹** *noun*
1 a system of figures, words and symbols, etc that is used to represent other figures, words and symbols, etc: *A very common code for computing purposes is ASCII which uses numbers to represent characters.* **2** a general term for computer programming instructions: *test the code of the new software*

/kəʊd/
1 pl codes
◄ ASCII, binary, computer **code**
2 note not used with *a* or *an*. No plural and used with a singular verb only.
◄ compile, produce, write **code**
▶ **lines of code, machine code, source code**

☆**code²** *verb* (software)
to put one system of figures, words and symbols, etc into another system of figures, words and symbols, etc especially to write computer programming instructions: *The test required us to code the mathematical equation into a computer program.*

/kəʊd/
codes, coding, coded
note transitive verb
◄ **code** a function, program, subroutine
syn encode
▶ **decode, encrypt**

---

code area *noun*
the part of memory used to store programs: *A code area is allocated to user programs by the operating system.*

/ˈkəʊd ˌeərɪə/
pl code areas
◄ a protected **code area**

CODEC *abbr*
coder-decoder

/ˈkəʊdek/
note pronounced as a word

code conversion *noun*
the process of changing the codes used for characters from one set to another: *code conversion between ASCII and EBCDIC*

/ˈkəʊd kənˌvɜːʃn/
pl code conversions
⧓ carry out, perform a **code conversion**
▶ **character code**

code length *noun*
the number of symbols or bits that correspond to a coded character: *ASCII has a fixed code length of eight bits*

/ˈkəʊd leŋθ/
pl code lengths
⧓ fixed, variable **code length**
▶ **ASCII**

code set *noun*
the complete set of all available instructions in a machine code

/ˈkəʊd set/
pl code sets
⧓ define, list the **code set**

coding *noun* (software/programming)
the process of turning something into code, especially changing an ALGORITHM into part of a computer program

/ˈkəʊdɪŋ/
note not used with *a* or *an*. No plural and used with a singular verb only.
⧓ complex, efficient, inefficient **coding**
syn encoding

coding form *noun*
▶ **coding sheet**

/ˈkəʊdɪŋ fɔːm/

coding sheet *noun*
a printed form used by computer programmers for writing program statements. The layout of the sheet helps to produce clear, understandable programs: *a FORTRAN coding sheet*

/ˈkəʊdɪŋ ʃiːt/
pl coding sheets
⧓ plan out a program *on*, use, write *on* a **coding sheet**
syn coding form

coding standards *noun*
▶ **programming standards**

/ˈkəʊdɪŋ ˌstændədz/

coincidence circuit *noun* (hardware)
a logic circuit whose output is TRUE if and only if all inputs are TRUE and none of the inputs is FALSE

/kəʊˈɪnsɪdəns ˌsɜːkɪt/
pl coincidence circuits
▶ **anti coincidence circuit, AND gate**

☆**cold boot** *verb* (hardware)
to start or restart a computer system and clear the memory: *If the computer crashes, cold boot it by switching it off and on again.* ○ *The computer was cold booted after the interruption when all the data was lost.*

/ˌkəʊld ˈbuːt/
cold boot, cold booting, cold booted
note transitive verb
syn cold start
▶ **boot, reboot**

cold fault *noun* (hardware)
an error in a computer system that is found as soon as the system is switched on: *The cold fault was caused by the power surge.*

/ˌkəʊld ˈfɔːlt/
pl cold faults
⧓ detect a **cold fault**

cold standby *noun* (hardware)
the state of a computer system when it is switched on but not ready to run: *The backup computer is in cold standby and will need to be properly configured before it can be used.*

/ˌkəʊld ˈstændbaɪ/
note no plural

cold start *noun*
▶ **cold boot**

/ˌkəʊld ˈstɑːt/

---

collate *verb*
to place a set of things in order, especially pages of a printout or records in a data file: *Many photocopiers collate multiple copies of documents.*

/kəˈleɪt/
collate, collating, collated
note transitive verb
Ⅺ **collate** a data set
▶ **sort**

---

collating sequence *noun*
the order in which things are placed when being COLLATED: *The collating sequence of this word processor treats upper and lower case characters differently.*

/kəˈleɪtɪŋ ˌsiːkwəns/
pl collating sequences
Ⅺ define, follow, use a **collating sequence**

---

collator *noun*
a mechanical device that puts printouts or punch cards into a certain order

note Mechanical collators are old fashioned and are not often used.

/kəˈleɪtə(r)/
pl collators

---

collect *verb*
to bring things together in one place

/kəˈlekt/
collect, collecting, collected
note transitive verb
Ⅺ **collect** data
▶ **data collection**

---

collision *noun*
1 a situation where two or more messages are sent on a network at the same time and interfere with each other: *To avoid collisions, the sender first checks that no message is currently being sent.* **2** a situation where an attempt is made to store a data item in a place that is already occupied: *If a collision occurs, a hashing algorithm finds an alternative location.*

/kəˈlɪʒn/
pl collisions
1 ▶ **contention, CSMA**
1,2 Ⅺ avoid, cause, detect a **collision**

---

collision detection *noun*
the process of recognizing that a COLLISION has happened or is about to happen: *Collision detection is essential to make sure that messages are not lost or corrupted on a network.*

/kəˈlɪʒn dɪˌtekʃn/
note no plural
Ⅺ **collision detection** algorithms, techniques
▶ **CSMA-CD**

---

colour display *noun*
an output device such as a screen, etc that can display more than two colours: *A high resolution colour display means computer graphics can enhance illustrations.*

/ˈkʌlə dɪˌspleɪ/
pl colour displays
Ⅺ an LCD **colour display**
▶ **monochrome**

---

colour graphics adaptor *noun*
the first video interface for a PC that displayed both colours and graphics: *The software requires a colour graphics adaptor display and will not work properly with a monochrome display.*

note The colour graphics adaptor can display four colours at the same time with a screen resolution of 320 by 200 pixels, or just two colours with a screen resolution of 640 by 200 pixels.

/ˌkʌlə ˈɡræfiks əˌdæptə(r)/
pl colour graphics adaptors
(also colour graphics adapter)
abbr CGA
Ⅺ a **colour graphics adaptor** display
▶ **EGA, VGA**

colour look-up table *noun*
a table of values used by the computer or printer to produce graphics or an image in a particular colour or set of colours: *alter the colour look-up table to emphasize details on a satellite picture*

/ˌkʌlə 'lʊk ʌp ˌteɪbl/
pl colour look-up tables
abbr CLUT

colour monitor *noun* (hardware)
a display screen that is able to show information in colour: *The pie-chart was displayed on the colour monitor with each section of the pie-chart in a different colour.*

/ˈkʌlə ˌmɒnɪtə(r)/
pl colour monitors

colour printer *noun* (hardware)
a printer that can produce text and graphics in colour. The printed colours may not exactly match the colours of the computer display.

/ˈkʌlə ˌprɪntə(r)/
pl colour printers
▶ **printer**

colour saturation *noun*
the depth of a colour which is one of three features that control how a displayed colour appears; the others features are HUE and BRIGHTNESS

/ˌkʌlə sætʃə'reɪʃn/
pl colour saturations
◄ adjust, increase, measure the **colour saturation**

column *noun*
1 a vertical line of character positions on a display screen: *an 80-column display* **2** a vertical line of CELLS in a spreadsheet: *This column contains the tax figures.*

/ˈkɒləm/
pl columns
1,2 ◄ access, copy, delete, fill, highlight, select, print a **column**

COM *abbr*
computer output microfilm

/kɒm/
note pronounced as a word

COMAL *noun*
Common Algorithmic Language. A high-level computer programming language designed for educational use: *program in COMAL*

note COMAL is an imperative procedural language and is usually translated by an interpreter.

/ˈkəʊmæl/
note no plural
◄ program *in* **COMAL**; a **COMAL** interpreter, program; **COMAL** source code

combinational *adjective*
related to adding two or more things together, especially electronic signals: *Combinational techniques were used to implement the logic circuits.*

/ˌkɒmbɪ'neɪʃənl/
◄ a **combinational** algorithm, circuit, method; **combinational** logic
▶ **gate**

combinatorics *noun* (mathematics)
the branch of mathematics related to counting possible combinations of a number of things: *Combinatorics helps in studying the behaviour of algorithms as the number of data items that are processed increases.*

/ˌkɒmbɪnə'tɒrɪks/
note not used *a* or *an*. No plural and used with a singular verb only.
◄ study, use **combinatorics**; a theorem in **combinatorics**

☆**command** *noun* (software)
a direct instruction to the computer from the user which is made through the operating system: *enter the command 'ls' to see the contents of the current directory*

/kə'mɑːnd/
pl commands
◄ abort, cancel, enter, modify, select, type in a **command**; a **command** key, name

command console processor *noun* (software)
the software that receives commands from a user's terminal and passes it to the operating system: *The command console processor performs a check on the command syntax.*

/kə'mɑːnd ˌkɒnsəʊl ˌprəʊsesə(r)/
pl command console processors

---

abbr abbreviation   **pl** plural   **syn** synonym   ▶ see   ◄ collocate (*word often used with the headword*)

	abbr CCP
	◄ execute, invoke the **command console processor**
command control language *noun* ▶ **control language**	/kə,mɑːnd kən'trəʊl ˌlæŋgwɪdʒ/
command control program *noun* ▶ **control program**	/kə,mɑːnd kən'trəʊl ˌprəʊgræm/
command driven *adjective* able to be controlled by a series of commands, not by choices from a menu: *command driven applications* ○ *a command driven interface*	/kə'mɑːnd drɪvn/
command file *noun* a data file made of the text of one or more operating system commands; these commands can be executed automatically one after the other: *execute the command file by specifying the command file name.*	/kə'mɑːnd faɪl/ **pl** command files
command file processor *noun* (software) the part of the operating system which reads the commands in a COMMAND FILE and executes them	/kə'mɑːnd faɪl ˌprəʊsesə(r)/ **pl** command file processors ◄ execute, prepare a **command file processor**; call, invoke the **command file processor** ▶ **batch file**
command interface *noun* a way of controlling a computer in which the user types commands which are then executed; after this, the computer waits for another command: *interact with the computer through a command interface*	/kə'mɑːnd ˌɪntəfeɪs/ **pl** command interfaces ▶ **menu-driven**
command interpreter *noun* the software that reads a user's command, checks that it is correct, and then passes control to the software that will execute the command: *The command interpreter is not case-sensitive.*	/kə'mɑːnd ɪn,tɜːprɪtə(r)/ **pl** command interpreters ◄ call, invoke the **command interpreter** ▶ **command processor**
command language *noun* ▶ **job control language**	/kə'mɑːnd ˌlæŋgwɪdʒ/
command line *noun* **1** the place on a display screen where the user's commands will appear when typed: *place the cursor on the command line* **2** the line of text typed by the user as a command	/kə'mɑːnd laɪn/ **pl** command lines **1** ◄ type *at/on* the **command line** **2** ◄ interpret, process a **command line**
command mode *noun* the state software is in when it is ready to receive commands from the user: *After a processing phase, the package returns to command mode.*	/kə'mɑːnd məʊd/ **note** usually singular ◄ change *to*, enter, get out *of*, move *to* **command mode** ▶ **edit mode**

command processor *noun*
the software that executes a command entered by the user

/kəˈmɑːnd ˌprəʊsesə(r)/
pl command processors
ᴎ call, invoke a **command processor**
▶ **command interpreter**

---

command prompt *noun*
the characters that appear on the display screen to tell the user that a command is expected: *In DOS, the command prompt is the '>' character, usually prefaced by the current disk name: 'C:>'*

/kəˈmɑːnd prɒmpt/
pl command prompts
ᴎ display, type *at* a **command prompt**

---

command window *noun*
an area of screen where commands will appear when entered by the user: *The command window displays the previous commands as well as the current one being executed.* ○ *make the command window active*

/kəˈmɑːnd ˌwɪndəʊ/
pl command windows
ᴎ select, type *in* a **command window**

☆**comment** *noun* (software/programming)
a computer programming language statement or part of a statement that the computer does not use. This allows the programmer to add an explanation of the program to the statements that will be executed: *In BASIC, comments are preceded by the word 'REM'.*

/ˈkɒment/
pl comments
ᴎ an in-line, a tail-end **comment**; a **comment** statement

---

comment field *noun*
a part of an assembly language instruction that the computer does not use, and so it can be used by the programmer to add notes and comments on the program

/ˈkɒment fiːld/
pl comment fields
ᴎ add, complete, fill a **comment field**

---

comment out *verb* (software/programming)
to make parts of a high-level computer programming language into comment statements: *comment out all the diagnostic statements*

note Commenting out is often done during program testing so that long printouts are not produced on every trial run of the program.

/ˌkɒment ˈaʊt/
comment out, commenting out, commented out
note transitive verb

---

common *adjective*
able to be shared by two or more users, systems or parts of a system: *Results are left in a common storage area.* ○ *Staff in the office share a common printer.*

/ˈkɒmən/
ᴎ a **common** area of memory

---

common carrier *noun*
an organization such as a telephone company that provides communications services but is not responsible for the contents of the messages it carries: *Most common carriers are regulated by their governments.*

/ˌkɒmən ˈkæriə(r)/
pl common carriers
ᴎ use a **common carrier**
syn public carrier

---

common language *noun*
a programming language that can be translated on several different types of computer: *Most personal computers have BASIC as a common language.*

/ˌkɒmən ˈlæŋgwɪdʒ/
pl common languages
ᴎ share a **common language**

---

common LISP *noun*
a high-level computer programming language

note Common LISP is an informal standard version of LISP.

/ˌkɒmən ˈlɪsp/
note not used with *a* or *an*. No plural and used with a singular verb only.

---

abbr abbreviation   **pl** plural   **syn** synonym   ▶ see   ᴎ collocate (*word often used with the headword*)

▶ program *in*, write **Common LISP**; a **Common LISP** interpreter, program; **Common LISP** source code

▶ **LISP**

---

communication *noun*

1 sending or exchanging information or data: *Communication between network users is helped by an efficient e-mail system.* **2** a message: *an e-mail communication*

/kə,mju:nɪˈkeɪʃn/

1 note not used *a* or *an*. No plural and used with a singular verb only.

▶ data **communication**

2 pl communications

▶ an electronic, a telephone, a written **communication**

☆**communications** *noun*

the methods that are used for sending or exchanging information or data: *Digital exchanges have improved telephone communications.*

/kə,mju:nɪˈkeɪʃnz/

note plural noun, used with a plural verb

▶ a **communications** system; satellite **communications**

---

communications buffer *noun* (hardware)

an area of memory that can store data that is waiting to be sent, or data that has been received and is waiting to be processed: *a modem with a built-in communications buffer*

/kə,mju:nɪˈkeɪʃnz ,bʌfə(r)/

pl communications buffers

▶ hold *in*, read *from*, write *to* a **communications buffer**

---

communications card *noun* (hardware)

a printed circuit board that can be added to a computer to allow it to send data to other computers: *The communications card allows the computer to access the network.*

/kə,mju:nɪˈkeɪʃnz ,kɑ:d/

pl communications cards

▶ install a **communications card**

syn communications board

---

communications channel *noun*

a link which is used for sending data between computers: *The communications channel uses radio links to send data.*

/kə,mju:nɪˈkeɪʃnz ,tʃænl/

pl communications channels

(also **communication channel**)

▶ receive data *over*, send data *over* a **communications channel**

---

communications control unit *noun*

a device that controls the transmission of data in a network by choosing the correct PROTOCOL and routes through the network, etc

/kəˈmju:nɪ,keɪʃnz kənˈtrəʊl ,ju:nɪt/

pl communications control units

(also **communication control unit**)

syn communications link control

---

communications link control *noun*

▶ **communications control unit**

/kə,mju:nɪˈkeɪʃnz lɪŋk kənˌtrəʊl/

---

communications network *noun*

▶ **network**

/kə,mju:nɪˈkeɪʃnz ,netwɜ:k/

---

communications network processor *noun*

▶ **communications processor**

/kə,mju:nɪˈkeɪʃnz ,netwɜ:k ,prəʊsesə(r)/

communications port *noun* (hardware)
a place in a computer that can be linked to a COMMUNICATIONS
CHANNEL to allow the transfer of data: *attach a modem to a
communications port*

note A communications port often includes the buffers and
the software which control the port, as well as the hardware.

/kə,mjuːnɪˈkeɪʃnz ˌpɔːt/
pl communications ports
(also **communication port**)
ᴎ configure, install a
communications port
▶ **port¹**

communications processor *noun*
a device which receives data from a computer and prepares it
for transmission before sending it to the COMMUNICATIONS
CONTROL UNIT: *A communications processor may format the data
and insert control characters before sending the data on.*

/kə,mjuːnɪˈkeɪʃnz
ˌprəʊsesə(r)/
pl communications processors
ᴎ send to, use a
communications processor
syn communications network
processor

communications system *noun*
a number of computers that can send messages and data to
each other: *install a communications system that allows users to
exchange e-mail messages*

/kə,mjuːnɪˈkeɪʃnz ˌsɪstəm/
pl communications systems
ᴎ install, maintain, use a
communications system

☆**compact disc** *noun*
▶ **CD**

/ˌkɒmpækt ˈdɪsk/

compacting algorithm *noun* (software)
a program, method or formula that is used to reorganize data
stored on disk or in main memory so that any free storage
locations are put together

/kəmˈpæktɪŋ ˌælgərɪðəm/
pl compacting algorithms
ᴎ execute a **compacting
algorithm**
▶ **defragmentation**

compaction *noun*
▶ **defragmentation**

/kəmˈpækʃn/

comparator *noun*
a device that is used for comparing two items or quantities to
determine whether they are the same: *a comparator that
measures electrical pulses* ○ *The character recognition system has a
comparator that decides if two words are the same.*

/kəmˈpærətə(r)/
pl comparators
ᴎ an analog, a digital
comparator

comparison *noun*
the act or process of looking at the similarities and differences
between two or more things: *These new disks are much better in
comparison with the old ones.* ○ *There is no comparison between the
two systems.* ○ *If a comparison is drawn between the two
processors, the newer one performs much better.*

/kəmˈpærɪsn/
pl comparisons

compatibility *noun*
the ability of computers and devices or computers and
programs to work together

/kəm,pætəˈbɪləti/
note no plural
▶ **clone**

☆**compatible** *adjective*
1 (of software and hardware) that are able to work together,
especially software that can be used with different hardware:
*The data can be transmitted over telephone lines that are linked to
any compatible receiver.* **2** (of software and hardware) that meet
certain standards: *The specification of this PC makes it IBM
compatible.*

/kəmˈpætəbl/
1 **ᴎ** PC **compatible**
2 ▶ **clone, standards**

abbr abbreviation   **pl** plural   **syn** synonym   ▶ see   **ᴎ** collocate (*word often used with the headword*)

compilation *noun*
the process of translating the SOURCE CODE of a high-level
language into machine code

/ˌkɒmpɪˈleɪʃn/
pl compilations
note not used with *a* or *an*. No
plural and used with a singular
verb only.
◪ **compilation** time

---

compilation error *noun*
a mistake or problem which occurs when a high-level
language is translated into machine code

/ˌkɒmpɪˈleɪʃn ˌerə(r)/
pl compilation errors

---

compilation time *noun*
the amount of time taken to translate a high-level language
into MACHINE CODE

/ˌkɒmpɪˈleɪʃn taɪm/
note usually singular

---

compile *verb*
1 to translate a high-level computer language into MACHINE
CODE so that it can be understood by the computer. This is
usually done by decoding all statements at the same time. **2** to
collect information and organize it in a certain way: *It took
weeks to compile the new customer database.*

/kəmˈpaɪl/
**compile, compiling,
compiled**
note transitive verb
1 ▶ **interpret**
2 ◪ **compile** a database, list,
report; **compile** information,
statistics

---

compile-and-go *adjective*
(of a program) that executes a program as soon as it has been
translated, without an instruction from the user: *Compile-
and-go systems are very convenient for beginning programmers.*

/kəmˌpaɪl ənd ˈgəʊ/
◪ a **compile-and-go** system
▶ **assemble-and-go**

---

compiled language *noun* (software/programming)
a computer programming language where all statements are
translated by a COMPILER before any part of it is executed:
FORTRAN is usually a compiled language.

/kəmˌpaɪld ˈlæŋgwɪdʒ/
pl compiled languages
◪ translate, use, write *in a*
compiled language
▶ **interpreted language**

---

compile phase *noun*
the period of time during a program run in which the
instructions are translated from a high-level language to
MACHINE CODE

/kəmˈpaɪl feɪz/
pl compile phases

---

compiler *noun* (software)
a piece of software that translates a program written in a high-
level computer programming language into a MACHINE CODE
program

/kəmˈpaɪlə(r)/
pl compilers
▶ **optimizing compiler, object
code, source code,
interpreter**

---

compiler diagnostics *noun*
a section in a COMPILER that helps the computer programmer to
find any faults

/kəmˈpaɪlə ˌdaɪəgˈnɒstɪks/
note plural noun, used with a
plural verb

---

complex *adjective*
1 very difficult to understand or explain: *Computers can deal
with problems that are too complex for the human brain.* **2** made
of many different parts: *A computer is a complex machine.*

/ˈkɒmpleks/
1 ◪ a **complex** instruction,
program, operation, job
2 ◪ a **complex** circuit, network,
system

☆**complex instruction set computer** *noun*
▶ **CISC**

/ˈkɒmpleks ɪnˌstrʌkʃn set
kəmˈpjuːtə(r)/

complexity measure *noun*
the amount of resources used by a program

note Complexity measures combine the memory used with the time taken to process data in a mathematical formula to quantify the demands that a calculation makes on a system.

/kəm'pleksəti ˌmeʒə(r)/
pl complexity measures
◄ calculate a **complexity measure**

---

component *noun* (hardware)
a small device or individual part that a machine is made of:
build a computer from separate components

/kəm'pəʊnənt/
pl components
◄ a computer, electrical, electronic, machine **component**

---

component density *noun*
a measure of the number of electronic COMPONENTS on a printed circuit board in relation to its area: *This circuit board is very simple, so component density is low.*

/kəmˌpəʊnənt 'densəti/
note not used with *a* or *an*. No plural and used with a singular verb only.
◄ average, high, low **component density**

---

compress *verb*
to make something smaller so that it uses less space or resources: *compress the files to create more room on the hard disk* ○ *techniques that compress digital TV signals* ○ *some files compress better than others*

/kəm'pres/
note transitive or intransitive verb
◄ **compress** a file, signal

---

compression *noun* (software)
the act of making data occupy less space: *Compression can save up to 80% of the space needed to store graphics files.* ○ *data compression that doubles hard disk space*

/kəm'preʃn/
compress, compressing, compression
note not used with *a* or *an*. No plural and used with a singular verb only.
◄ image, video **compression**; **compression** algorithms, software, techniques
syn data compression

---

computable *adjective*
able to be calculated; having a ALGORITHM which will give a result when processed by a computer

/kəm'pjuːtəbl/
◄ a **computable** number, problem

---

computation *noun*
1 the operations on numbers and data usually done by a computer: *The amount of computation the data requires exceeds the capacity of the system.* **2** an operation on numbers and data that produces a result: *The computation gave an unexpected result.*

/ˌkɒmpju'teɪʃn/
1 note not used with *a* or *an*. No plural and used with a singular verb only.
2 pl computations

---

computational error *noun*
a mistake made when data is processed: *A bug in the program caused the computational errors.*

/'kɒmpjuˌteɪʃənl 'erə(r)/
pl computational errors

---

compute *verb*
to calculate, usually by using a computer: *compute the coordinates of the position of objects*

/kəm'pjuːt/
compute, computing, computed
note transitive verb

---

compute bound *adjective*
(of a program) that is unable to execute very quickly because the CPU is not powerful enough: *A compute bound process will run faster if the CPU is upgraded.* ○ *The compute bound microprocessor was overloaded with computations.*

/kəm'pjuːt baʊnd/
syn CPU bound, processor bound
▶ **input/output bound**

---

abbr abbreviation   **pl** plural   **syn** synonym   ▶ see   ◄ collocate (*word often used with the headword*)

☆**computer** *noun* (hardware)
an electronic machine that can store, process and display data
and control other machines and processes: *All the information
is stored on computer.*

/kəm'pju:tə(r)/
pl computers
M controlled *by*, stored *on*
computer
▶ analog computer, central
processing unit, digital
computer, generation,
mainframe, microcomputer,
minicomputer, personal
computer, supercomputer

☆**computer aided design** *noun* (applications)
the use of computers and programs to produce drawings and
to design products: *Computer aided design allows the production
of goods which are more creative and cost-effective.*

/kəm'pju:tə(r) 'eɪdɪd dɪ'zaɪn/
note not used with *a* or *an*. No
plural and used with a singular
verb only.

☆**computer aided instruction** *noun*
▶ CAI

/kəm'pju:tə(r) 'eɪdɪd
ɪn'strʌkʃn/

☆**computer aided manufacturing** *noun*
▶ CAM

/kəm'pju:tə(r) 'eɪdəd
ˌmænju'fæktʃərɪŋ/

computer animation *noun*
displaying one computer image on a screen very quickly after
another one to create a moving image: *Computer animation was
used in the feature film to make robots look more realistic.*

/kəm'pju:tə(r) ˌænɪ'meɪʃn/
note not used with *a* or *an*. No
plural and used with a singular
verb only.

computer architecture *noun*
▶ architecture 1,2

/kəmˌpju:tə(r) 'ɑ:kɪtektʃə(r)/

☆**computer assisted design** *noun*
▶ computer aided design

/kəm'pju:tə(r) ə'sɪstɪd dɪ'zaɪn/

computer assisted language learning *noun*
▶ CALL

/kem'pju:tə(r) ə'sɪstɪd
'læŋgwɪdʒ ˌlɜ:nɪŋ/

computer assisted learning *noun*
▶ CAL

/kəm'pju:tə(r) ə'sɪstɪd 'lɜ:nɪŋ/

☆**computer assisted manufacturing** *noun*
▶ CAM

/kəm'pju:tə(r) ə'sɪstɪd
mænju'fæktʃərɪŋ/

computer conference *noun*
▶ conference

/kəmˌpju:tə 'kɒnfərəns/

computer crime *noun*
1 using a computer to do things which are against the law:
several companies have fallen victim to computer crime **2** an act of
using a computer to do something which is against the law:
*The criminal's computer crimes included accessing and changing
restricted data.*

/kəm'pju:tə kraɪm/
1 note not used with *a* or *an*. No
plural and used with a singular
verb only.
M commit, detect, investigate,
prevent, punish **computer
crime**; an increase *in*
computer crime
2 pl computer crimes

---

computer engineer *noun*
a person who designs or maintains computer hardware

/kəmˈpjuːtər endʒɪˌnɪə(r)/
pl computer engineers
ᴴ contract, employ a **computer engineer**

---

computer family *noun* (hardware)
a group of computers that are similar in design: *The company will introduce the next generation of its supercomputer family next year.*

/kəmˈpjuːtə ˌfæməli/
pl computer families
ᴴ a business, personal **computer family**

---

computer file *noun*
▶ **file**

/kəmˈpjuːtə faɪl/

---

computer fraud *noun*
1 using a computer to do things which are against the law, often to get money: *Millions of pounds are lost every year through computer fraud.* **2** an act of using a computer to do things which are against the law, often to get money: *The police are investigating several computer frauds in the same company.*

/kəmˈpjuːtə frɔːd/
1 note not used with *a* or *an*. No plural and used with a singular verb only.
ᴴ commit, detect, investigate, prevent, punish **computer fraud**
2 pl computer frauds

---

computer-generated *adjective* (software)
produced by a computer

/kəmˌpjuːtə ˈdʒenəreɪtd/
ᴴ a **computer-generated** film, model, random number; **computer-generated** graphics, punctuation, text

---

☆**computerization** *noun* (operations)
the use of computers to do work previously done by people, or to control other machines and processes: *The computerization of the company's distribution system has made it more efficient.*

/kəmˌpjuːtəraɪˈzeɪʃn/
note not used with *a* or *an*. No plural and used with a singular verb only.
(also **computerisation**)
▶ **automation**

☆**computerize** *verb* (operations)
to use computers to do work formerly done by people or to control other machines: *Funds are needed to computerize the library service.*

/kəmˈpjuːtəraɪz/
computerize, computerizing, computerized
(also **computerise**)
note transitive verb
ᴴ **computerize** a factory, an office
▶ **automate**

---

computer literacy *noun*
the ability to use a computer and understand how it works: *Some degree of computer literacy is required for the job.* ○ *computer literacy which extends to the ability to program*

/kəmˌpjuːtə ˈlɪtərəsi/
note not used with *a* or *an*. No plural and used with a singular verb only.
ᴴ full, minimal **computer literacy**

---

computer literate *adjective*
able to use a computer and understand how it works: *Candidates for the job should be computer literate.* ○ *People who were not very computer literate found the system difficult to use.*

/kəmˌpjuːtə ˈlɪtərət/
ᴴ a **computer literate** employee, secretary, person

---

abbr abbreviation   **pl** plural   **syn** synonym   ▶ see   ᴴ collocate (*word often used with the headword*)

computer network *noun*
▶ **network**

/kəmˈpjuːtə ˌnetwɜːk/

---

computer power *noun*
the speed and capacity of a computer. This can be measured in different ways including the number of instructions a computer can execute in a certain time, the number of bits that can be processed at once and how much RAM the computer has: *The more computer power is available, the faster business can be transacted.*

/kəmˈpjuːtə ˌpaʊə(r)/

note not used with *a* or *an*. No plural and used with a singular verb only.

Ӿ measure **computer power**; immense, inadequate **computer power**

▶ **megaflops, MIPS**

☆**computer program** *noun*
▶ **program**[1]

/kəmˈpjuːtə ˌprəʊɡræm/

☆**computer programmer** *noun*
▶ **programmer**

/kəmˈpjuːtə ˌprəʊɡræmə(r)/

---

computer science *noun*
the theories and principles of how computers are designed and how they work: *consult an expert in the field of computer science*

/kəmˌpjuːtə ˈsaɪəns/

note not used with *a* or *an*. No plural and used with a singular verb only.

Ӿ specialize *in*, study, teach **computer science**

▶ **artificial intelligence**

---

computer services *noun*
support for computer systems that is provided by a department in an organization, or by one company for other companies: *The computer equipment is administered by computer services.*

/kəmˈpjuːtə ˌsɜːvɪsɪz/

note plural noun

Ӿ a **computer services** agency, bureau, business, company, department

---

computer simulation *noun*
1 the use of program which can represent a physical object or the conditions of a situation so that realistic reactions to different types of input can be seen: *Computer simulation is frequently used to help train pilots.* **2** a representation of a physical object or a situation by a computer program: *test the theory using a computer simulation*

/kəmˈpjuːtə ˌsɪmjuˈleɪʃn/

1 note not used with *a* or *an*. No plural and used with a singular verb only.

2 pl computer simulations

---

computer system *noun*
a central processor and the PERIPHERALS such as disk drives, keyboards and monitors that work together

/kəmˈpjuːtə ˌsɪstəm/

pl computer systems

Ӿ buy, install, set up a **computer system**

▶ **configuration**

---

concatenate *verb*
to join two or more sets of data together by adding one to the end of the other: *concatenate data structures*

/kənˈkætəneɪt/

concatenate, concatenating, concatenated

note transitive verb

Ӿ **concatenate** data, sets, strings

▶ **string concatenation**

concatenation *noun*
1 the act of joining two or more sets of data together, usually by adding one to the end of the other: *Concatenation of the strings 'down' and 'load' gives 'download'* **2** the result of joining two things together: *'Download' is the concatenation of 'down' and 'load'.*

/kənˌkætə'neɪʃn/
pl concatenations
1 ◄ carry out, perform **concatenation**
2 ◄ print out, store the **concatenation**
► **string concatenation**

concentrator *noun* (hardware/communications)
a device that combines several signals from different places into one signal and then transmits it: *access a network concentrator*

/'kɒnsntreɪtə(r)/
pl concentrators
◄ send signals *via* a **concentrator**
► **bridge, gateway, multiplexer**

conceptual schema *noun*
► **logical schema**

/kənˌseptʃuəl 'skiːmə/

concordance *noun*
1 a list produced by a computer that contains every word in a particular text in alphabetical order: *Look at the concordance to see how many times the word 'computer' appears in the text.* **2** a list produced by a computer that shows all the examples of an individual word in a text. This word is usually in the centre of the page or screen in a line of text: *run a concordance on the word 'server'* ○ *sort the concordance left/right*

/kən'kɔːdəns/
pl concordances
1,2 ◄ examine, look *at*, print out, produce a **concordance**; a **concordance** line, program

concurrent *adjective*
happening or working at the same time: *There are 100 concurrent users on the network.*

/kən'kʌrənt/
◄ **concurrent** execution, operation, processing, programming

conditional *adjective*
depending on the existence of a certain situation: *Using this software is conditional on having a computer powerful enough to support it.*

/kən'dɪʃənl/

conditional branch *noun* (software/programming)
an instruction in a programming language that changes the order in which instructions are executed: *If the loop is to be executed again, a conditional branch transfers control to the start.*

/kənˌdɪʃənl 'brɑːntʃ/
pl conditional branches
◄ follow, insert, obey, remove a **conditional branch**
syn conditional jump, conditional transfer
► **branch, unconditional branch**

conditional breakpoint *noun* (software/programming)
the point where execution stops when certain conditions are found, usually when a program is DEBUGGED

/kənˌdɪʃənl 'breɪkpɔɪnt/
pl conditional breakpoints

conditional compilation *noun* (software/programming)
a translation of a high-level language program that will only take place if certain conditions exist, for example if another program has been successfully executed

/kən'dɪʃənl ˌkɒmpɪ'leɪʃn/
pl conditional compilations
◄ request a **conditional compilation**; a **conditional compilation** command, instruction
► **compilation**

---

abbr abbreviation   **pl** plural   **syn** synonym   ► see   ◄ collocate (*word often used with the headword*)

conditional jump *noun*
▶ **conditional branch**

/kən,dɪʃəln ˈdʒʌmp/

---

conditional statement *noun* (software/programming)
a statement in a program that tells a computer to do
something if certain conditions exist: *An 'If... Then' statement
in BASIC is a conditional statement.*

/kən,dɪʃənl ˈsteɪtmənt/
pl conditional statements

---

conditional transfer *noun*
▶ **conditional branch**

/kən,dɪʃənl ˈtrænsfɜː(r)/

---

condition code register *noun*
a register that contains the state of the central processing unit
after the last instruction has been executed

/kənˈdɪʃn kəʊd ˌredʒɪstə(r)/
pl condition control registers

---

conference *noun*
a group of computer users with the same interests who use a
network or a BULLETIN BOARD to send messages: *The computer
conference takes place on BITNET.* ○ *The conference members are
expected to contribute regularly.*

/ˈkɒnfərəns/
pl conferences
ℳ belong *to*, contribute *to*, join a
conference

---

conferencing *noun*
the use of a network or BULLETIN BOARD to exchange messages
with other members of a group with the same interests:
Conferencing has improved the flow of ideas among students.

/ˈkɒnfərənsɪŋ/
note not used with *a* or *an*. No
plural and used with a singular
verb only.
ℳ make use of, take part in
conferencing; conferencing
facilities
▶ **teleconferencing**

---

confidence interval *noun*
▶ **confidence level**

/ˈkɒnfɪdəns ,ɪntəvl/

---

confidence level *noun*
a measure of the ACCURACY of the result of a calculation on
data: *This statistical sample is large enough to obtain a 95 per cent
confidence level.*

/ˈkɒnfɪdəns ,levl/
pl confidence levels
syn confidence interval

☆**configuration** *noun* (hardware/software)
the hardware units and/or the software programs that make
up a computer system

/kən,fɪgəˈreɪʃn/
pl configurations
ℳ system **configuration**
▶ **computer system**

---

configure *verb*
1 (*hardware*) to arrange a computer, computer system or the
different parts making up a computer system in a particular
way **2** (*software*) to make software work in the way the user
prefers: *configure the word processing software so a prompt to save
appears on screen every 10 minutes*

/kənˈfɪgə(r)/
configure, configuring,
configured
note transitive verb
1 ℳ **configure** a circuit board,
computer system, printer
2 ℳ **configure** a package,
program

---

congestion *noun*
the situation that exists when a computer system is not
powerful enough to process all the work it is required to do

/kənˈdʒestʃən/
note not used with *a* or *an*. No
plural and used with a singular
verb only.
▶ **compute bound**

conjunction *noun*
▶ **AND operation**

/kənˈdʒʌŋkʃn/

☆**connect** *verb*
1 to join or link two devices: *The cable connects the mouse to the keyboard.* **2** to open a communications link between two systems or devices: *log in and then connect to the Internet*

/kəˈnekt/
connect, connecting, connected
1 note transitive verb
ᴎ **connect** something *to/with* something
2 note intransitive verb
ᴎ **connect** *to* a network, etc
▶ **disconnect**

---

connect charge *noun*
the price paid by a user for the time spent using a remote computer system: *The total charge is made up of a connect charge and a charge for disk storage.*

/kəˈnekt tʃɑːdʒ/
pl connect charges
ᴎ make, pay a **connect charge**

☆**connection** *noun*
1 a link between two things: *The network connection is usually very reliable.* **2** the act of linking two things together, usually so that they can communicate: *The connection happened without problems.*

/kəˈnekʃn/
pl connections
1 ᴎ an electrical, a physical **connection**
2 ᴎ break, make, restore a **connection**

---

connectivity *noun*
the ability of different systems or pieces of equipment to be linked together

/kəˈnektɪvəti/
note no plural
ᴎ database, mainframe, network, PC-to-Unix **connectivity**; a **connectivity** package; **connectivity** products, software

---

connector *noun* (hardware)
a device like a plug that connects one piece of equipment to another and is usually found at the end of a cable

/kəˈnektə(r)/
pl connectors

---

connect time *noun*
the amount of time a user spends using a remote computer system: *a connect time of eight minutes* ○ *A month's free connect time is given to new subscribers.*

/kəˈnekt taɪm/
pl connect times
ᴎ measure, record, use up **connect time**
▶ **access charge**

---

consecutive *adjective*
following one after another in an ordered way and without interruptions: *6, 7, and 8 are consecutive numbers* ○ *run three consecutive programs*

/kənˈsekjətɪv/
ᴎ a **consecutive** file, number, program

---

console *noun*
pieces of equipment including a keyboard and visual display unit that the operator uses to communicate with the computer: *input data at the console*

/ˈkɒnsəʊl/
pl consoles
ᴎ a video game **console**

---

constant¹ *noun*
a data item that always has the same value: *The data item is a constant and does not change its value when the program is executed.*

/ˈkɒnstənt/
pl constants
ᴎ an absolute **constant**

---

abbr abbreviation   **pl** plural   **syn** synonym   ▶ see   ᴎ collocate (*word often used with the headword*)

constant² *adjective*
1 that does not change: *The printer produces text at a constant rate.* **2** continuous: *The database requires constant updating.*

/'kɒnstənt/
1 ⋈ **constant** rate, speed, velocity
▶ **variable**
2 ⋈ **constant** maintenance

---

construct *verb*
to build a machine or device by putting different parts together: *construct a computer from separate components*

/kən'strʌkt/
construct, constructing, constructed
note transitive verb
⋈ **construct** a circuit board, computer, device, system

---

consultant *noun* (personnel)
a person who has a lot of knowledge and experience in a particular area and gives professional advice

/kən'sʌltənt/
pl consultants
⋈ call in, contract, hire, work *as* a **consultant**; a computer, an engineering, a programming, a systems **consultant**

---

consumables *noun* (hardware)
small items used in computing such as cables and floppy disks: *buy consumables by mail order*

/kən'sju:məblz/
note plural noun
⋈ buy, purchase, sell, store, use **consumables**

---

contact¹ *noun*
the part of a switch or CONNECTOR which, when it touches a similar part of another switch or connector, allows an electrical current or signal to pass

/'kɒntækt/
pl contacts

---

contact² *verb*
to communicate with a person or device: *contact the users on the network*

/'kɒntækt/
note transitive verb
⋈ **contact** a device, an operator, a user

---

contact bounce *noun*
an error that occurs when a key on a keyboard is pressed only once but more than one character is generated: *A faulty switch caused contact bounce.* ○ *The extra pulses of electricity are due to contact bounce.*

/'kɒntækt baʊns/
note not used with *a* or *an*. No plural and used with a singular verb only.
⋈ avoid, overcome, prevent, remedy, solve, take account *of* **contact bounce**
▶ **bounce**

---

content-addressable file *noun*
▶ **associative memory**

/'kɒntent ə'dresəsbl 'faɪl/

---

content-addressable file store *noun*
▶ **associative memory**

/'kɒntent ə'dresəbl 'faɪl stɔ:(r)/

---

content-addressable memory *noun*
▶ **associative memory**

/'kɒntent ə'dresəbl 'meməri/

---

content-addressable storage *noun*
▶ **associative memory**

/'kɒntent ə'dresəbl 'stɔ:rɪdʒ/

---

content addressing *noun*
▶ **associative addressing**

/'kɒntent ə,dresɳ/

contention *noun*

a situation which occurs when there is competition for the use of a communications channel or network RESOURCES. This can be one way of controlling the use of resources, or it may cause problems such as COLLISIONS (1) when there are not enough communications channels.

/kən'tenʃn/

note not used with *a* or *an*. No plural and used with a singular verb only.

◄ be delayed *by*, resolve **contention**

---

contention delay *noun*

an amount of time when a system or part of it cannot be used because of CONTENTION

/kən'tenʃn dɪˌleɪ/

pl contention delays

---

context-dependent *adjective*

(of a code or grammar, etc) that has a particular meaning which can only be understood in a certain environment

/ˌkɒntekst dɪ'pəndənt/

◄ a **context-dependent** expression, language, operation, symbol

---

context-dependent language *noun*
(software/programming)

a programming language where the meaning of a combination of letters or symbols depends on the letters and symbols that come before and/or after that combination

/'kɒntekst dɪ'pendənt 'læŋgwɪdʒ/

pl context-dependent languages

◄ define, design, write a **context-dependent language**

► **context-free language**

---

context-free *adjective*

(of a code or grammar, etc) that has a meaning that can be understood without being affected by what comes before or after it

/ˌkɒntekst 'friː/

◄ a **context-free** code, grammar, operation, symbol

► **context-dependent**

---

context-free language *noun* (software/programming)

a programming language where the meaning of a combination of letters or symbols does not depend on the symbols that come before or after it

/ˌkɒntekst friː 'læŋgwɪdʒ/

pl context-free languages

◄ define, design, write a **context-free language**: **context-free language** interpretation, syntax

---

context-sensitive help *noun*

help or information the user needs to solve the exact problem they have at the time they access help, not just a general help index which makes the user search for the type of help they need: *get context-sensitive help with a hot key*

/'kɒntekst 'sensətɪv 'help/

note not used with *a* or *an*. No plural and used with a singular verb only.

◄ access, call up, request, switch *off/on* **context-sensitive help**

► **on-line help**

---

context switching *noun*

1 changing from one environment to another when one computer process starts another automatically: *preserve the values of variables when context switching takes place* **2** changing from one set of screen layout and menu choices to another, when a user moves from one software package to a different software package: *Context switching is made easier if software follows a standard design.*

/'kɒntekst ˌswɪtʃɪŋ/

1,2 note not used with *a* or *an*. No plural and used with a singular verb only.

1,2 ◄ experience, initiate, undergo **context switching**; **context switching** difficulties

---

contiguous *adjective*

sharing a boundary: *contiguous areas of disk storage* ○ *bytes of contiguous memory*

/kən'tɪgjuəs/

◄ **contiguous** graphics; **contiguous** *to/with* something

---

contiguous data *noun*

data that is stored in a group of disk SECTORS that are next to one another

/kənˌtɪgjuəs 'deɪtə/

note not used with *a* or *an*. No plural and used with a singular verb only.

---

abbr abbreviation   **pl** plural   **syn** synonym   ► see   ◄ collocate (*word often used with the headword*)

contiguous file *noun*
a file that is stored in a group of disk SECTORS that are next to
one another

/kən,tɪgjuəs 'faɪl/
pl contiguous files

---

contingency *noun*
an event that might happen in the future: *Staff in the
information technology department are prepared for every
contingency.*

/kən'tɪndʒənsi/
pl contingencies
⋈ deal *with*, plan *for* a
contingency; an unexpected,
unforeseen **contingency**;
contingency arrangements,
measures

---

contingency plan *noun*
decisions that have been made on how to react to a situation
that might occur in the future: *The systems analyst drew up
several contingency plans to cope with possible problems when the
new system was introduced.*

/kən'tɪndʒənsi plæn/
pl contingency plans
⋈ agree, discuss, draft, draw *up*,
prepare, work *out* a
contingency plan

☆**continuous** *adjective*
without breaks or interruptions: *Put a continuous roll of paper in
the fax machine.*

/kən'tɪnjuəs/
⋈ a **continuous** process, signal;
continuous stationery

---

continuous data stream *noun*
a method of ASYNCHRONOUS data transmission where the data
items follow one another without being divided up: *Continuous
data streams usually have a high transmission speed.*

/kən,tɪnjuəs 'deɪtə striːm/
pl continuous data streams
⋈ send *as*, transmit *as* a
continuous data stream

---

continuous feed *noun* (hardware)
the process of moving continuous stationery through a printer
without breaks or interruptions

/kən,tɪnjuəs 'fiːd/
note no plural
▶ cut sheet feeder, feed,
stationery

---

continuous speech recognition *noun*
a system used by a computer to recognize and understand
continuous human speech, not just individual words: *build a
continuous speech recognition system* ○ *The continuous speech
recognition software only recognizes a limited set of words.*

/kən,tɪnjuəs 'spiːtʃ
rekəg,nɪʃn/
note not used with *a* or *an*. No
plural and used with a singular
verb only.
abbr CSR
▶ speech recognition

---

continuous speech understanding *noun*
the ability of a computer to receive speech as input, to separate
the speech into individual words, and to recognize those words

/kən,tɪnjuəs 'spiːtʃ
ʌndə,stændɪŋ/
note not used with *a* or *an*. No
plural and used with a singular
verb only.
abbr CSU
⋈ implement, progress *in*
**continuous speech
understanding**; **continuous
speech understanding**
algorithms, software,
techniques, technology

contrast noun

the difference between pure white and deep black on a television or display screen: *Increasing the contrast makes it easier to distinguish the outlines of objects on screen.*

/ˈkɒntrɑːst/

note not used with *a* or *an*. No plural and used with a singular verb only.

◄ **contrast** adjustment, control

▶ **brightness**

---

control block noun

▶ **file control block**

/kənˈtrəʊl blɒk/

---

control bus noun (hardware)

a bus that carries CONTROL SIGNALS between the CPU, memory and input/output devices: *send a reset signal on the control bus to all devices on the network*

/kənˈtrəʊl bʌs/

pl control buses

◄ place a signal *on*, transmit a signal *via* a **control bus**

▶ **bus**

---

control character noun

1 any character sent with a message which is not part of that message, but which tells the device that receives the message to do something: *The form feed (FF) control character makes the printer space to the top of the next sheet of paper.* **2** one of the ASCII characters with codes between 0 and 31: *The control character EOT (ASCII 4) marks the end of a transmission.*

/kənˈtrəʊl ˌkærəktə(r)/

pl control characters

1 ◄ receive, send, transmit a **control character**; a graphics, printer **control character**

syn device control character

2 ▶ **control key**

---

control cycle noun

the actions that happen again and again when an instruction is copied from memory to the CPU, translated and executed: *A faster microprocessor chip means that the control cycle is speeded up.*

/kənˈtrəʊl ˌsaɪkl/

pl control cycles

◄ implement, obey the **control cycle**

▶ **CPU cycle**

---

control data noun

data that contains instructions on how to control a device or send a signal: *control data that routes and synchronizes other data*

/kənˈtrəʊl ˌdeɪtə/

note used with a plural or a singular verb

◄ access, store, update the **control data**

---

control driven adjective (hardware)

(of a device) that can follow a set of instructions when it receives a single control signal

/kənˌtrəʊl ˈdrɪvn/

◄ **control driven** hardware

---

control field noun

the area of memory where CONTROL DATA is stored

/kənˈtrəʊl fiːld/

pl control fields

◄ access, update the **control field**

---

control key noun (hardware)

a key on a computer keyboard that is pressed at the same time as another key to access functions: *To kill the window, press the control key and C.*

/kənˈtrəʊl kiː/

pl control keys

abbr CTRL

◄ hit, hold *down*, press the **control key**

---

control language noun (software/programming)

a high-level computer programming language used in programs that control mechanical or electrical equipment

/kənˈtrəʊl ˌlæŋgwɪdʒ/

pl control languages

◄ program *in*, write *in* a **control language**; a **control language** program, translator

syn command control language

---

abbr abbreviation   **pl** plural   **syn** synonym   ▶ see   ◄ collocate (*word often used with the headword*)

controller *noun* (hardware)
a device which controls the access of other devices to parts of a
computer system: *The controller manages the printing process.*

/kən'trəʊlə(r)/
pl controllers
⋈ a data, disk, display, printer
controller

---

control line *noun* (hardware)
one of the wires in a data bus that is used to carry control
signals: *Timing signals are sent on the control line.*

/kən'trəʊl laɪn/
pl control lines
⋈ send a signal *over*, test a
control line
▶ **control bus**

---

control memory *noun* (hardware)
a very expensive, high-speed form of memory that is used to
hold MICROCODE

/kən'trəʊl ˌmeməri/
pl control memories

---

control panel *noun* (software)
a program that the user can access in order to make changes
to certain parts of the system such as screen colour and the
time and date: *select the control panel from the menu ○ go to the
control panel to change the desktop pattern*

/kən'trəʊl ˌpænl/
pl control panels
▶ **configure**

---

control program *noun* (software)
a computer program that controls mechanical or electronic
devices

note 'Control program' was the first name for what is now
called an operating system.

/kən'trəʊl ˌprəʊɡræm/
pl control programs
⋈ code, execute, write a **control
program**
syn command control program
▶ **control language**

---

control sequence *noun* (software)
a number of characters used by a device or program to control
how the device works or how the program processes data:
*Sending the appropriate control sequences sets the printer into italic
mode.*

note The first character in a control sequence is a control
character.

/kən'trəʊl ˌsiːkwəns/
pl control sequences
⋈ act *on*, receive, send, transmit a
control sequence
▶ **control character**

---

control signal *noun* (software)
a signal sent to a device that controls its operation: *Some wires
on the bus are reserved for control signals.*

/kən'trəʊl ˌsɪɡnəl/
pl control signals
⋈ act *on*, receive, send, transmit a
control signal
▶ **control bus**

---

control store *noun*
▶ **control memory**

/kən'trəʊl stɔː(r)/

---

control structure *noun* (software/programming)
one or more statements in a programming language that
control how the program is executed: *Most languages have a
simple 'JUMP' or 'GOTO' control structure. ○ 'IF...THEN'
statements, 'FOR...NEXT' loops and 'WHILE...DO' loops are the
commonest control structures in high-level languages.*

/kən'trəʊl ˌstrʌkʃə(r)/
pl control structures
⋈ define, describe, execute a
control structure

---

control total *noun*
a number calculated from data to be processed by adding
together the NUMERIC VALUES in one of the fields of each data
item. This number is checked during the processing to make
sure that no data has been changed or missed.

/kən'trəʊl ˌtəʊtl/
pl control totals
⋈ calculate, check, read the
control total
▶ **data validation**

☆**control unit** *noun* (hardware)
the part of the CPU that decodes program instructions and
controls the way they are executed

/kən'trəʊl ˌjuːnɪt/
pl control units

---

control word *noun*
a WORD (= part of memory treated as a single unit by the CPU)
that holds information about the use of part of a computer
system, such as areas of memory: *Control words are used by the
operating system to avoid two different programs trying to use the
same resource.*

/kən'trəʊl wɜːd/
pl control words
M access, update a **control word**

---

convention *noun*
the way something is usually done: *The convention in e-mail
addresses is to put the name or number of the receiver first.*

/kən'venʃn/
pl conventions
M break, breach, follow, obey,
understand a **convention**
▶ **standards**

---

conversational mode *noun*
▶ **interactive**

/ˌkɒnvə'seɪʃənl məʊd/

---

conversion *noun*
a change, especially from one system to another, or from one
form to another: *code conversion between ASCII and EBCDIC*

/kən'vɜːʃn/
pl conversions
M carry out, implement a
conversion
▶ **code conversion, data
conversion, file conversion,
media conversion, software
conversion**

---

conversion equipment *noun* (hardware)
hardware that changes data from one form to another: *The
conversion equipment allows data on PC disks to be read by a
Macintosh.*

/kən'vɜːʃn ɪˌkwɪpmənt/
note not used with *a* or *an*. No
plural and used with a singular
verb only.
M install, use **conversion
equipment**

---

conversion program *noun* (software)
software that changes data or a program from one form to
another: *The conversion program allows software to run on
different platforms.*

/kən'vɜːʃn ˌprəʊɡræm/
pl conversion programs
M execute, invoke, write a
conversion program

---

conversion table *noun* (software)
a DATA STRUCTURE used by a CONVERSION PROGRAM that lists data
items as they should be before and after CONVERSION

/kən'vɜːʃn ˌteɪbl/
pl conversion tables
M access, compile, update the
conversion table
syn translation table

☆**convert** *verb*
to change from one system to another or from one form to
another: *convert from EBCDIC to ASCII* ○ *The disks convert easily
from one format to another with the new conversion equipment.*

/kən'vɜːt/
**convert, converting,
converted**
note transitive or intransitive
verb
M **convert** A *into* B, A *to* B,
between A *and* B, *from* A *to* B

---

converter *noun* (hardware)
hardware that changes signals or data from one standard or
format to another: *an analog-to-digital converter*

/kən'vɜːtə(r)/
pl converters

---

abbr abbreviation   **pl** plural   **syn** synonym   ▶ see   M collocate (*word often used with the headword*)

	⋈ pass data *through*, use a **converter**

coordinate¹ *noun*

one of a set of numbers or letters, etc used to show a position on a graph or chart: *The x-coordinate shows time.* ○ *The y-coordinate represents processing speed.*

/kəʊˈɔːdɪnət/

pl coordinates

⋈ measure, plot, read *off* a **coordinate**

▶ **axis, X-coordinate, Y-coordinate, Z-coordinate**

coordinate² *verb*

to organize people, devices and processes, etc so that they work together efficiently: *coordinate the implementation of the new system*

/kəʊˈɔːdɪneɪt/

coordinate, coordinating, coordinated

note transitive verb

⋈ **coordinate** a project, task

coprocessor *noun* (hardware)

an extra processor that works with the CPU to provide more functions: *use a floating point coprocessor to do faster calculations*

/ˌkəʊˈprəʊsesə(r)/

pl coprocessors

⋈ install a **coprocessor**; **coprocessor** architecture, chips

syn maths coprocessor

▶ **auxiliary processor, dual processor**

☆**copy¹** *noun*

1 a device, data or software, etc that is exactly the same as other devices, data or software, etc: *make a backup copy of the files* ○ *sell illegal copies of software* ○ *The PC is an exact copy of PCs made by IBM.* **2** the text of a document: *read through the copy to check for errors*

/ˈkɒpi/

1 pl copies

⋈ make, save a **copy**

▶ **clone**

2 note not used with *a* or *an*. No plural and used with a singular verb only.

▶ **hard copy**

☆**copy²** *verb*

to reproduce data so that it exists in more than one place: *copy the text to the clipboard* ○ *copy stored data back to main memory* ○ *The large file was copied across five floppy disks.*

/ˈkɒpi/

copy, copying, copied

note transitive or intransitive verb

⋈ **copy** data *to* disk

copy protection *noun*

ways of making software impossible to copy

/ˈkɒpi prəˌtekʃn/

note not used *a* or *an*. No plural and used with a singular verb only.

⋈ add, implement **copy protection**

▶ **dongle, write protect**

copyright *noun*

the legal right of one person or organization to produce, sell and copy, etc a piece of original work or part of it, such as a computer program: *Who holds the copyright of the software?*

/ˈkɒpiraɪt/

note singular noun, used with a singular verb

⋈ be *in/out of*, establish, hold, own the **copyright**; a breach *of*, an infringement *of* **copyright**; **copyright** permission

▶ **patent**

CORAL *noun*
a high-level computer programming language designed for controlling REAL-TIME SYSTEMS

note CORAL was based on an early version of ALGOL and is an imperative procedural language.

/ˈkɒrəl/
note not used with *a* or *an*. No plural and used with a singular verb only.
ℍ program *in*, write **CORAL**; a **CORAL** compiler, program; **CORAL** source code

---

core memory *noun* (hardware)
a form of memory found in SECOND GENERATION computers where data was stored in magnetic rings called cores

note The term 'core memory' was also used to refer to main memory in later computers which used more advanced technology for storage.

/ˌkɔː ˈmeməri/
note not used with *a* or *an*. No plural and used with a singular verb only.
syn core store
▶ **memory**

---

coresident *adjective*
(of a program) that is in main memory at the same time as another program

/ˌkəʊˈrezɪdənt/

---

core store *noun*
▶ **core memory**

/ˌkɔː ˈstɔː(r)/

---

coroutine *noun*
a SUBROUTINE which may be CALLED² (2) (= brought into operation) several times and which begins to execute from the point that was reached when it was called before

/ˈkəʊruːtiːn/
pl coroutines
ℍ call, invoke a **coroutine**

---

correct¹ *verb*
to make an error or mistake right: *The validation process showed that several errors had to be corrected in the data.*

/kəˈrekt/
correct, correcting, corrected
note transitive verb
ℍ **correct** an error, a mistake

---

correct² *adjective*
right or true: *get the correct output from reliable input data*

/kəˈrekt/
ℍ a **correct** answer, result

---

correctness proof *noun*
information that shows a computer program executes without errors: *The correctness proof shows the complex piece of software works properly under all circumstances.*

/kəˈrektnəs pruːf/
pl correctness proofs
ℍ carry out, design, perform a **correctness proof**

---

correlation *noun*
1 the connection or relation between the behaviour of two things: *There is an obvious correlation between the number of users on the network and the number of times the computers crash.* **2** a statistical measurement of the relation between two variable quantities: *There is a positive correlation between prices and interest rates.*

/ˌkɒrəˈleɪʃn/
pl correlations
1 ℍ a clear, direct, general, significant, strong **correlation**
2 ℍ an inverse, a negative, a positive, a statistical, a zero **correlation**

---

corrupt¹ *verb*
to damage data or a device holding data, usually accidentally: *The disk will corrupt if it is overloaded.* ○ *A system crash has corrupted all the data in the database.*

/kəˈrʌpt/
corrupt, corrupting, corrupted
note transitive or intransitive verb
ℍ **corrupt** a disk, file, program; **corrupt** data, memory, software

---

abbr abbreviation   **pl** plural   **syn** synonym   ▶ see   ℍ collocate (*word often used with the headword*)

corrupt² *adjective*

(of data or a device holding data) that has been damaged: *It was impossible to access the files on the corrupt hard disk.* ○ *The corrupt program instructions don't execute properly.*

/kəˈrʌpt/

◣ a **corrupt** disk, file, program

---

corruption *noun*

the process of damaging data or a device holding data: *The corruption of the master file made it necessary to restore the backup copy.*

/kəˈrʌpʃn/

note not used with *a* or *an*. No plural and used with a singular verb only.

◣ detect, recover *from* **corruption**

syn data corruption

---

counter *noun*

1 an electronic device that stores a number which is increased by one each time the counter receives an electronic signal **2** a variable that holds a number which is increased or decreased as a LOOP¹ (2) is executed: *The loop terminates when the counter reaches zero.*

/ˈkaʊntə(r)/

pl counters

1 ◣ access, increment, read a **counter**

2 ◣ a loop **counter**

---

couple *verb*

to join together or link two or more devices, etc so that they are able to work together: *The systems were coupled.*

/ˈkʌpl/

couple, coupling, coupled

note transitive verb

◣ **couple** devices, systems

▶ **decouple**

---

coupled *adjective*

(of devices, etc) that are joined together so that they are able to work together: *coupled systems*

/ˈkʌpld/

---

coupler *noun*

a device that joins two devices, etc together: *The coupler provides electrical connections between the two systems.*

/ˈkʌplə(r)/

pl couplers

◣ connect, install a **coupler**

---

courseware *noun*

the teaching material used in CAL (= computer assisted learning): *The courseware is available as a series of self-instruction modules.* ○ *Courseware that teaches languages is available in the resources room of the college.*

/ˈkɔːsweə(r)/

note not used with *a* or *an*. No plural and used with a singular verb only.

◣ a **courseware** author, designer; CAL, multimedia **courseware**

CP *abbr*

▶ **control program**

/ˌsiː ˈpiː/

note pronounced as individual letters

CPA *abbr*

▶ **critical path analysis**

/ˌsiː piː ˈeɪ/

note pronounced as individual letters

---

cpi *abbr*

▶ **characters per inch**

/ˌsiː piː ˈaɪ/

note pronounced as individual letters

CPL *noun*
a high-level computer programming language designed for applications software and systems software

note CPL is an imperative procedural language and was designed at the Universities of Cambridge and London in 1963. Improvements in CPL led eventually to the C language.

/ˌsiː piː ˈel/
note not used with *a* or *an*. No plural and used with a singular verb only.
◄ program in **CPL**; a **CPL** compiler, program
► B, BCPL, C

CPS *abbr*
► characters per second

/ˌsiː piː ˈes/
note pronounced as individual letters

cps *abbr*
► cycles per second

/ˌsiː piː ˈes/
note pronounced as individual letters

☆**CPU** *abbr* (hardware)
the central processing unit. The part of a computer that controls all the other parts of the system. It consists of a control unit, an arithmetic and logic unit and storage devices: *a 40-MHz CPU* ○ *an engineering calculation that requires a lot of CPU time* ○ *input and output devices connected to the central processing unit*

/ˌsiː piː ˈjuː/
note pronounced as individual letters
pl central processing units
syn central processor, processor
► mainframe

CPU bound *adjective*
► compute bound

/ˌsiː piː ˈjuː baʊnd/

CPU cycle *noun*
the smallest unit of time that is recognized by the CPU, usually the time taken to execute the simplest instruction: *measure the CPU cycle in milliseconds*

/ˌsiː piː ˈjuː saɪkl/
pl CPU cycles
◄ improve, time the **CPU cycle**
► control cycle

CPU time *noun*
the amount of time that a process controls the CPU, not including the time spent waiting for data to be retrieved from memory: *CPU time was high because a lot of calculation was being done.* ○ *The process requires 0.4 seconds of CPU time.*

/ˌsiː piː ˈjuː taɪm/
note not used with *a* or *an*. No plural and used with a singular verb only.
◄ charge *for*, measure **CPU time**

CR *abbr*
► carriage return

/ˌsiː ˈɑː/
note pronounced as individual letters

☆**crash¹** *noun* (software)
a sudden end to a program: *All the data was lost in the crash.*

/kræʃ/
pl crashes
◄ **crash** protected
► disk crash, failure, hang up, system crash

☆**crash²** *verb* (system operation)
to fail suddenly: *The computer crashed and had to be rebooted.*

/kræʃ/
crash, crashing, crashed
note intransitive verb
► system crash

CRC *abbr*
► camera-ready copy

/ˌsiː ɑː ˈsiː/
note pronounced as individual letters

abbr abbreviation **pl** plural **syn** synonym ► see ◄ collocate (*word often used with the headword*)

CRC *abbr*
▶ cyclic redundancy check

/ˌsiː ɑː ˈsiː/
note pronounced as individual letters

CRC *noun*
▶ camera-ready copy

/ˌsiː ɑː ˈsiː/
note pronounced as individual letters

---

create *verb*
to make and open a new data file or record which may then have data written to it: *create a temporary file*

/kriˈeɪt/
create, creating, created
note transitive verb
ᴎ **create** a document, file, record

---

critical path analysis *noun*
a method of planning and managing large projects by breaking the project into a number of smaller tasks. The time taken by each task is calculated and the possible timing problems are identified: *Graphical methods are frequently used in critical path analysis.*

note The 'critical path' is the sequence of tasks that will make the overall project take longer if any of these tasks is delayed; not all tasks will be on the critical path.

/ˌkrɪtɪkl ˈpɑːθ əˌnæləsɪs/
note not used with *a* or *an*. No plural and used with a singular verb only.
ᴎ **critical path analysis** methods, techniques
syn critical path method

---

critical path method *noun*
▶ critical path analysis

/ˌkrɪtɪkl ˈpɑːθ ˌmeθəd/

CR/LF *abbr*
carriage return line feed

note used in written English only
▶ **carriage return, line feed**

---

cross assembler *noun* (software)
an assembler program that runs on one computer but produces machine code for another

/ˌkrɒs əˈsemblə(r)/
pl cross assemblers
▶ **cross compiler**

---

cross check¹ *noun*
a result that is obtained by checking something a second time: *The cross check showed errors in the original result.*

/ˌkrɒs ˈtʃek/
pl cross checks
ᴎ perform, run a **cross check**

---

cross check² *verb*
to check something a second time using a different method: *cross check the addition of the figures by adding them again in the reverse direction* ○ *The results were cross checked against previous results.*

/ˌkrɒs ˈtʃek/
cross check, cross checking, cross checked
note transitive verb
ᴎ **cross check** a calculation, result

---

cross compiler *noun* (software)
a COMPILER program that runs on one computer but produces machine code for another computer called the OBJECT COMPUTER

/ˌkrɒs kəmˈpaɪlə(r)/
pl cross compilers
ᴎ translate by, use a **cross compiler**
▶ **cross assembler**

---

cross coupling *noun*
a connection between two logic devices that allows the output of each device to become the input of the other device

note A cross coupling between two gates allows them to operate as a bistable.

/ˌkrɒs ˈkʌplɪŋ/
pl cross couplings
▶ **bistable¹**

cross hatching *noun*
a way of showing a grey area on screen or on paper by drawing horizontal and vertical lines close together: *fill in the blank space with cross hatching*

/ˈkrɒʃ ˌhætʃɪŋ/
note not used with *a* or *an*. No plural and used with a singular verb only.

◄ draw, produce, shade *as* **cross hatching**

---

cross reference generator *noun* (software)
software used in programming that makes a list of all NAMES (1) used in the program with the addresses that they are stored at: *The cross reference generator will help to test the program.*

note Cross reference generators are often part of assemblers or compilers.

/ˌkrɒʃ ˈrefərəns ˌdʒenəreɪtə(r)/
pl cross reference generators
◄ call, execute, invoke, use a **cross reference generator**

---

cross talk *noun*
signals from one transmission channel that move to another and cause errors: *cross talk on a telephone line* ○ *cross talk corrupted the transmission*

/ˈkrɒʃ tɔːk/
note not used with *a* or *an*. No plural and used with a singular verb only.

CR-ROM drive *noun*
a mechanical device, similar to an audio CD player, which allows a computer to read a CD-ROM: *Internal CD-ROM drives generally transfer data faster than external ones.* ○ *a double-speed CD-ROM drive* ○ *a quad-speed CD-ROM drive*

/ˌsiː diː ˈrɒm draɪv/
pl CD-ROM drives
◄ install, load, use a **CD-ROM drive**
► **disk drive**

CRT *abbr*
► **cathode ray tube**

/ˌsiː ɑː ˈtiː/
note pronounced as individual letters

---

crunch *verb*
(*informal*) to do calculations, especially on a large amount of data: *crunch the data*

/krʌntʃ/
crunch, crunching, crunched
note transitive verb
► **number crunching**

---

cryogenic memory *noun* (hardware)
a form of memory in which very high processing speeds are achieved by operating at extremely low temperatures

/ˈkraɪəˌdʒenɪk ˌmeməri/
note no plural

---

cryptanalysis *noun*
ways of reading coded messages

/ˌkrɪptəˈnæləsɪs/
note not used with *a* or *an*. No plural and used with a singular verb only.
◄ **cryptanalysis** methods, techniques
► **cipher, code²**

---

cryptography *noun*
ways of turning text into coded messages

note Cryptography is ways of writing secret messages, but it is often used to mean ways of reading them.

/krɪpˈtɒɡrəfi/
note not used with *a* or *an*. No plural and used with a singular verb only.
◄ **cryptography** system, techniques
► **cipher, encoding, encryption**

---

abbr abbreviation   **pl** plural   **syn** synonym   ► see   ◄ collocate (*word often used with the headword*)

cryptography algorithm *noun*
an ALGORITHM that is used to turn a PLAINTEXT message into a
secret message: *The DES (Data Encryption Standard) is an
American cryptography algorithm.*

/krɪpˈtɒɡrəfi ˌælɡərɪðəm/
pl cryptography algorithms
ᴍ define, employ, use a
cryptography algorithm

cryptography key *noun*
the information that must be known before a coded message
can be read: *use a cryptography key to decrypt coded data*

/krɪpˈtɒɡrəfi kiː/
pl cryptography keys
ᴍ apply, discover, find, use, work
out the **cryptography key**
syn key
▶ **code², decryption**

CSMA *abbr*
carrier sense multiple access. A way of exchanging
information on a network. Messages are sent to all computers
which know that a message is being sent because they detect a
CARRIER SIGNAL.

/ˌsiː es em ˈeɪ/
note pronounced as individual
letters
note not used with *a* or *an*. No
plural and used with a singular
verb only.
▶ **protocol**

CSMA-CD *abbr*
carrier sense multiple access with collision detection. A way of
ensuring that messages are not sent from two or more
computers on a network at the same time. If a collision occurs,
each computer has to wait before sending the message again.

/ˈsiː es em ˌeɪ siː ˈdiː/
note pronounced as individual
letters

CSR *abbr*
▶ **continuous speech recognition**

/ˌsiː es ˈɑː(r)/
note pronounced as individual
letters

CSU *abbr*
▶ **continuous speech understanding**

/ˌsiː es ˈjuː/
note pronounced as individual
letters

CTRL *abbr*
▶ **control key**

note used in written English only

CTS *abbr*
▶ **clear to send character**

/ˌsiː tiː ˈes/
note pronounced as individual
letters

CU *abbr*
▶ **control unit**

/ˌsiː ˈjuː/
note pronounced as individual
letters

CUG *abbr*
▶ **closed user group**

/ˌsiː juː ˈdʒiː/
note pronounced as individual
letters

current address register *noun* (hardware)
a register in the CPU that holds the address of the machine
code instruction that is to be executed next

/ˌkʌrənt əˈdres ˌredʒɪstə(r)/
pl current address registers
abbr CAR
ᴍ access, increment, read, update
the **current address register**
syn sequence control register,
instruction counter, instruction
register, next instruction
register², program counter

current directory *noun*
the list of files (called a directory) that will be accessed in any
file operation unless the user names another directory: *The
Unix command 'pwd' returns the name of the current directory.* ○
display a list of files in the current directory

note Only one directory can be current at any time.

/ˌkʌrənt dəˈrektəri/
pl current directories

(also **current working
directory**)

Ⅎ access, look *at/in* the **current
directory**

syn default directory

▶ **directory, root directory**

---

current instruction register *noun*
a register in the CPU that is used to hold a copy of instructions
that are decoded and executed: *an instruction fetched from
memory to the current instruction register*

/ˌkʌrənt ɪnˈstrʌkʃn
ˌredʒɪstə(r)/
pl current instruction registers

abbr CIR

Ⅎ access, update the **current
instruction register**

☆**cursor** *noun* (software)
a marker on a screen that can be moved and shows where the
next item to be typed will appear: *Insert the cursor at the
beginning of the line.* ○ *Move the cursor to the top of the screen.*

note Cursors are common in character-based interfaces.

/ˈkɜːsə(r)/
pl cursors

Ⅎ insert, move, place, position the
cursor

▶ **insertion point, mouse,
trackball**

☆**cursor control key** *noun* (hardware)
any of the four keys with arrows on a computer keyboard
which can be used to control the cursor: *Use the cursor control
keys to move the cursor left, right, up, or down.*

/ˌkɜːsə kənˈtrəʊl kiː/
pl cursor control keys

Ⅎ hit, press, use the **cursor
control key**

syn arrow key

▶ **down arrow, left arrow,
right arrow, up arrow**

---

custom-built *adjective* (hardware)
made for one customer to do a particular job: *A custom-built
computer system was necessary to do such a specialized job.*

/ˌkʌstəm ˈbɪlt/
Ⅎ **custom-built** apparatus,
equipment

▶ **bespoke**

---

custom design *noun*
hardware or software designed for one customer usually
because there is no standard equipment, etc available to do the
work required: *The terminals were manufactured to a custom
design.*

/ˌkʌstəm dɪˈzaɪn/
pl custom designs

Ⅎ prepare, produce a **custom
design**

---

customize *verb*
to change a system so that it works in the way the user wants:
customize the PC by adding a video card

/ˈkʌstəmaɪz/
**customize, customizing,
customized**

note transitive verb

Ⅎ **customize** a display, machine,
printout, system; **customize**
software

▶ **configure, user-definable**

---

custom PROM *noun*
▶ **custom ROM**

/ˌkʌstəm ˈprɒm/

---

abbr abbreviation   **pl** plural   **syn** synonym   ▶ see   Ⅎ collocate (*word often used with the headword*)

custom ROM noun
ROM chips designed and made for one customer: *produce custom ROMs*

/ˌkʌstəm 'rɒm/
pl custom ROMS
ᴍ blow, burn, manufacture a **custom ROM**
► **PROM**

☆**cut** verb
to remove a piece of selected text or graphics from a document: *highlight the text and cut it* ○ *cut the last sentence on screen*

/kʌt/
cut, cutting, cut
note transitive verb
ᴍ **cut** a box, an image, a paragraph, a word
► **paste, word processing**

☆**cut and paste** verb
to remove a piece of selected text or graphics from a document and move it to another place: *cut and paste from one document to another*

/ˌkʌt ənd 'peɪst/
cut and paste, cutting and pasting, cut and pasted
note transitive verb

cut sheet feeder noun (hardware)
a device attached to a printer which passes single sheets of paper into a printer

/ˌkʌt 'ʃiːt ˌfiːdə/
pl cut sheet feeders
► **continuous feed**

cybernetics noun
a comparison of systems in technology with natural living systems

note Studies in cybernetics compare control and communication systems in humans and animals with the control and communications systems used by mechanical and electronic devices.

/ˌsaɪbə'netɪks/
note singular noun used with a singular verb
ᴍ research *into*, study **cybernetics**
► **artificial intelligence, neural network**

cycle noun
one of the basic steps in a process that repeats over and over again: *Mains current in the UK oscillates at 50 cycles per second (50Hz).*

/'saɪkl/
pl cycles
► **hertz**

cycle count noun
the number of completed cycles: *The loop stops executing when the cycle count reaches 100.*

/'saɪkl kaʊnt/
pl cycle counts
ᴍ record, update the **cycle count**

cycle shift noun
► **rotate operation**

/'saɪkl ʃɪft/

cycles per second noun
a measure of how fast something repeats in a second: *Alternating current in Europe oscillates at 50 cycles per second and 60 cycles per second in the US.*

note Cycles per second is measured in hertz. One cycle per second equals one hertz, so 50 cycles per second is written as 50Hz, etc

/ˌsaɪklz pə 'sekənd/
note not used with *a* or *an*. No plural and used with a singular verb only.
ᴍ a rate *of* n, change *at* n **cycles per second**

cycle stealing noun
a fast way to access data without using the CPU; the CPU is stopped for one or more of its ɪɴsᴛʀᴜᴄᴛɪᴏɴ ᴄʏᴄʟᴇs while data is transferred directly to or from memory: *Cycle stealing is a very efficient method of transferring data blocks.*

/'saɪkl ˌstiːlɪŋ/
note not used with *a* or *an*. No plural and used with a singular verb only.
ᴍ implement, use **cycle stealing**
► **DMA**

cycle time noun
the time taken to finish one complete cycle in a repeating
operation: *a 50MHz cycle time*

/ˈsaɪkl taɪm/
pl cycle times
◣ improve, reduce the **cycle time**
▶ **address time**

cyclic access noun
access to data that can only happen at fixed points in a cycle of
events

/ˌsaɪklɪk ˈækses/
note usually singular
◣ a **cyclic access** device; **cyclic
access** storage

cyclic binary code noun
▶ **Gray code**

/ˈsaɪklɪk ˈbaɪnəri ˈkəʊd/

cyclic check noun
a method of ERROR DETECTION that examines single bits of
transmitted data at regular times: *A cyclic check examines every
eighth bit of the data.*

/ˌsaɪklɪk ˈtʃek/
pl cyclic checks
◣ implement, perform, use a
cyclic check
▶ **cyclic redundancy check**

cyclic code noun
▶ **Gray code**

/ˌsaɪklɪk ˈkəʊd/

cyclic redundancy check noun
the most common ERROR DETECTION method for data being
transmitted. Each block of data is treated as if it was a number,
and a value based on this number is calculated and added to
the data before it is transmitted. When the data is received,
this value is recalculated; if it is not the same as the original
calculation then an error has occurred and a request to
transmit the data again is made.

/ˌsaɪklɪk rɪˈdʌndənsi tʃek/
pl cyclic redundancy checks
abbr CRC
◣ carry out, perform a **cyclic
redundancy check**
▶ **parity check**

cyclic shift noun
▶ **rotate operation**

/ˌsaɪklɪk ˈʃɪft/

cylinder noun
the tracks of data that lie one above another on a disk with
many surfaces: *All data in one cylinder can be read without
moving the read/write heads.*

/ˈsɪlɪndə(r)/
pl cylinders
◣ move the head *to*, read data
from a **cylinder**

cypher noun
▶ **cipher**

/ˈsaɪfə(r)/

Dd

D abbr
the letter which represents the decimal number 13 in
hexadecimal notation

/ˈdiː/

DAC abbr
▶ **digital-to-analog converter**

/dæk/
note pronounced as a word

D/A converter noun
▶ **digital-to-analog converter**

/ˌdiː ˈeɪ kənˌvɜːtə(r)/

abbr abbreviation   **pl** plural   **syn** synonym   ▶ see   ◣ collocate (*word often used with the headword*)

daisy chain *noun*
a group of devices which are linked by a single line of
communication so signals pass from the first device to the
second device and from the second device to the third device,
etc

/ˈdeɪzi tʃeɪn/
pl daisy chains
◄ connect devices *in* a **daisy
chain**

daisy chain bus *noun* (hardware)
a bus that links devices in a DAISY CHAIN: *The mouse and keyboard
are linked to a daisy chain bus.*

/ˈdeɪzi tʃeɪn bʌs/
pl daisy chain buses
◄ modify, receive, transmit data
on a **daisy chain bus**

daisy chain interrupt *noun*
an INTERRUPT[1] to a CPU in a DAISY CHAIN: *determine which device
caused the daisy chain interrupt*

/ˌdeɪzi tʃeɪn ˈɪntəˈrʌpt/
pl daisy chain interrupts
◄ receive a signal *on* a **daisy
chain interrupt**; **daisy chain
interrupt** line

daisywheel printer *noun* (hardware)
a printer that produces text by hitting individual letters
against paper in a similar way to a typewriter: *The business
letters were printed on a daisywheel printer.*

/ˈdeɪziwiːl ˌprɪntə(r)/
pl daisywheel printers
► dot matrix printer, laser
printer

DARPA *abbr*
(*US*) Defense Advanced Research Projects Agency

/ˈdɑːpə/
note pronounced as a word
► ARPANET

DASD *abbr*
► direct access storage device

/ˌdiː eɪ es ˈdiː/
note pronounced as individual
letters

DAT *abbr*
digital audio tape

/dæt/
note pronounced as a word

☆**data** *noun*
numbers and text, etc that can be organized in a certain way
to allow storage and processing by a computer: *feed data into
the computer*

note There is a difference between data and information. Data
is what the computer processes without understanding the
content. Information is the result of the processing and it has
meaning for people who use it. In informal situations,
'information' and 'data' are used to mean the same thing.

/ˈdeɪtə/
note plural noun but usually
used with a singular verb. The
singular *datum* is rarely used.
◄ access, analyse, process,
retrieve, store **data**
► datum

data access *noun*
the right to use data stored in a computer

/ˈdeɪtə ˌækses/
note not used with *a* or *an*.No
plural and used with a singular
verb only.
◄ gain, have **data access**; **data
access** permission, privileges,
rights

data acquisition *noun*
► data capture

/ˈdeɪtə ækwɪˌzɪʃn/

data administrator *noun* (personnel)
the person responsible for managing data processing in a
company

/ˈdeɪtə ədˌmɪnɪstreɪtə(r)/
pl data administrators

☆**databank** *noun*
a large amount of data, usually on one subject, which is stored on computer: *Police records are kept in a central databank.*

/'deɪtəbæŋk/
pl databanks

◄ retrieve information *from*, store information *in* a **databank**

☆**database** *noun*
a store of facts and information held in a computer: *The database is used by the project manager to control the work done by different people.* ○ *extract information from the database* ○ *sort the statistics in the database*

/'deɪtəbeɪs/
pl databases

◄ access, build *up*, manage, retrieve information *from*, search, set up, update, use a **database**

► **hierarchical database, network database, relational database, databank**

---

database administrator *noun* (personnel)
a person who manages a database system and is responsible for the security of the database and access to it, etc

/'deɪtəbeɪs əd,mɪnɪstreɪtə(r)/
pl database administrators
abbr DBA

► **systems analyst**

---

database language *noun* (software/programming)
one of the languages used to describe the structure of a database or to access the data contained in the database: *Structured Query Language is a database language*

/'deɪtəbeɪs ,læŋgwɪdʒ/
pl database languages

◄ define, program *in*, write *in*, use a **database language**

► **data manipulation language**

---

database machine *noun*
a computer with software that is specially designed to store and process large collections of data

note Rapid processing, the ability to transfer large amounts of data and fast flexible storage are important characteristics of database machines.

/'deɪtəbeɪs mə,ʃiːn/
pl database machines

◄ build, use a **database machine**

► **database, database management system**

---

database management system *noun*
software that allows the user to store, update and retrieve information held in a database: *The database management system supports different file organization methods.*

/,deɪtəbeɪs 'mænɪdʒmənt ,sɪstəm/
pl database management systems
abbr DBMS

◄ install a **database management system**

---

data buffer *noun*
► **buffer**

/'deɪtə ,bʌfə(r)/

---

data bus *noun*
a bus that is used to carry data

/'deɪtə bʌs/
pl data buses
► **bus**

---

data capture *noun* (user operation)
the process of putting information into a computer: *Data capture is done by keying text to disk.*

/'deɪtə ,kæptʃə(r)/
note not used with *a* or *an*. No plural and used with a singular verb only.

◄ a **data capture** device, system
syn data acquisition

---

abbr abbreviation   **pl** plural   **syn** synonym   ► see   ◄ collocate (*word often used with the headword*)

data carrier *noun*
▶ **carrier signal**

/'deɪtə ˌkæriə(r)/

---

data carrier detect character *noun*
a standard RS-232C signal that is used to show the existence of a CARRIER SIGNAL on a communications channel: *When the receiving device senses a carrier signal on the transmission line it returns a data carrier detect character.*

/'deɪtə ˌkæriə dɪ'tekt ˌkærəktə(r)/
pl data carrier detect characters
abbr DCD
ᴍ receive, send, transmit a **data carrier detect character**
▶ **carrier signal**

---

data chaining *noun*
a method of storing data as a LINKED LIST in which each data item has a POINTER to the next data item in order

note Data chaining allows a data set to be sorted without moving the data around in memory.

/'deɪtə ˌtʃeɪnɪŋ/
note not used with *a* or *an*. No plural and used with a singular verb only.
ᴍ **data chaining** algorithms, methods, techniques

☆**data channel** *noun*
a communications link that can be used to transmit data

/'deɪtə ˌtʃænl/
pl data channels
ᴍ send, receive over a **data channel**; a high-speed, limited-capacity, two-way **data channel**
▶ **channel, duplex, simplex**

---

data collection *noun*
the act or process of transferring data to a computer in order to form a database: *scan the data into the computer as part of the data collection*

/'deɪtə kəˌlekʃn/
note not used with *a* or *an*. No plural and used with a singular verb only.

---

data compaction *noun*
▶ **defragmentation**

/'deɪtə kəmˌpækʃn/

---

data compression *noun*
▶ **compression**

/'deɪtə kəmˌpreʃn/

---

data conversion *noun*
the process of changing the way data is represented: *Data conversion between analog and digital is done by an analog-to-digital converter.*

/'deɪtə kənˌvɜːʃn/
note not used with *a* or *an*. No plural and used with a singular verb only.
▶ **conversion**

---

data corruption *noun*
▶ **corruption**

/'deɪtə kəˌrʌpʃn/

---

data description language *noun*
a high-level programming language that is used in a database system to describe the structure of the data and the links between data items: *write data definitions in a data description language* ○ *use a data description language to set up the users' views of data structures*

note Database systems usually have two database languages: a data description language and a data manipulation language.

/ˌdeɪtə dɪ'skrɪpʃn ˌlæŋgwɪdʒ/
pl data description languages
abbr DDL
ᴍ define data *in* a **data description language**; a global, non-procedural **data description language**
▶ **database language, data manipulation language, database**

data dictionary *noun*
a file that is used in a DATABASE MANAGEMENT SYSTEM to hold
information about all the databases in a database system,
including information about database structure and the
relationships between the types of data items

/ˈdeɪtə ˌdɪkʃənri/
pl data dictionaries
⋈ access, add *to*, create, modify,
record *in*, update a **data
dictionary**

data driven design *noun* (software/programming)
a method of designing large computer applications by
arranging the software in a way that is similar to the structure
of the data that will be processed

/ˈdeɪtə ˌdrɪvn dɪˈzaɪn/
note not used with *a* or *an*. No
plural and used with a singular
verb only.
⋈ **data driven design** methods,
techniques
▶ **functional design**

data element *noun*
▶ **data item**

/ˈdeɪtə ˌelɪmənt/

data encryption standard *noun*
an ALGORITHM that was developed in the US for encoding and
decoding data: *The data encryption standard is built into chips.*

/ˌdeɪtə ɪnˈkrɪpʃn ˌstændəd/
note no plural and used with a
singular verb only
abbr DES
⋈ conform *to*, employ the **data
encryption standard**
▶ **cryptography, coding,
encryption**

data entry *noun*
the process of putting data into a computer. This can be done
in different ways including keying to disk and optical character
recognition, etc.

/ˈdeɪtə ˌentri/
note not used with *a* or *an*. No
plural and used with a singular
verb only.
⋈ **data entry** clerk, department,
process, stage, supervisor
syn data preparation
▶ **data vetting, optical
character recognition**

data file *noun*
▶ **file**

/ˈdeɪtə faɪl/

data flow *noun*
the route followed by data as it passes through a data
processing system

/ˈdeɪtə fləʊ/
note usually singular
⋈ **data flow** path

data flowchart *noun*
a diagram showing the route taken by data through a data
processing system: *A data flowchart enables a systems analyst to
find places where problems could occur.*

/ˌdeɪtə ˈfləʊtʃɑːt/
pl data flowcharts
⋈ annotate, draw a **data
flowchart**
syn data flow diagram, systems
chart, systems flowchart
▶ **flowchart**

data flow diagram *noun*
▶ **data flowchart**

/ˈdeɪtə fləʊ ˌdaɪəgræm/

data format *noun*
the way data is organized when it is stored or transmitted

/ˈdeɪtə ˌfɔːmæt/
pl data formats

abbr abbreviation   **pl** plural   **syn** synonym   ▶ see   ⋈ collocate (*word often used with the headword*)

> ◄ conform *to*, define, follow a **data format**
> ► **characteristic, floating point, mantissa**

data integrity *noun*

the degree to which data is reliable and not CORRUPT[2]: *Data integrity is an important part of security procedures.*

/ˌdeɪtə ɪnˈtegrəti/

note not used with *a* or *an*. No plural and used with a singular verb only.

◄ ensure, maintain **data integrity**

syn integrity

► **data security**

data item *noun*

a single piece of data or information such as a name or number

/ˈdeɪtə ˌaɪtəm/

pl data items

syn data element

data link *noun*

a connection between two devices to allow data to pass between them: *a data link between the computer and the printer*

/ˈdeɪtə lɪŋk/

pl data links

◄ install, maintain, use a **data link**

data link layer *noun*

one of the sections of the International Standards Organization PROTOCOL for data communications. The data link layer describes standards for hardware and software used for communication.

/ˈdeɪtə lɪŋk ˌleɪə(r)/

note not used with *a* or *an*. No plural and used with a singular verb only.

◄ define, specify the **data link layer**

► **physical layer, network layer, transport layer, session layer, presentation layer, application layer**

data logging *noun*
► **logging**

/ˈdeɪtə ˌlɒgɪŋ/

data management *noun*

the control of data by hardware and software at all stages in a data processing system

/ˌdeɪtə ˈmænɪdʒmənt/

note not used with *a* or *an*. No plural and used with a singular verb only.

◄ effective, poor **data management**

► **database administrator**

data manipulation language *noun*
(software/programming)

a high-level programming language used in a database system to access and process the data items

note Database systems usually have two database languages: a data description language and a data manipulation language.

/ˈdeɪtə məˌnɪpjuˈleɪʃn ˌlæŋgwɪdʒ/

pl data manipulation languages

abbr DML

◄ define *in*, write *in* a **data manipulation language**

► **database language, data description language, database**

data model *noun*
a plan of the types of data items held in a database and the links between those items

/'deɪtə ˌmɒdl/
pl data models
◄ amend, construct a **data model**
► **data description language, schema**

data node *noun*
► **node 1**

/'deɪtə nəʊd/

data packet *noun*
► **packet**

/'deɪtə ˌpækɪt/

data path *noun*
the connections in a computer or system that are used for the transmission of data from one place to another

/'deɪtə pɑːθ/
pl data paths
◄ follow, mark, route the **data path**

data preparation *noun*
► **data entry**

/'deɪtə prepəˌreɪʃn/

data processing *noun*
► **processing**

/'deɪtə ˌprəʊsesɪŋ/

data protection *noun*
ways of keeping data private and secure: *comply with laws for data protection*

/ˌdeɪtə prə'tekʃn/
note not used with *a* or *an*. No plurals and used with a singular verb only.
◄ **data protection** guidelines, legislation
► **data security, data integrity**

data rate *noun*
the maximum speed at which data can be transmitted over a transmission channel: *The link has a 9 600 baud data rate.*

/'deɪtə reɪt/
pl data rates
◄ set, specify the **data rate**

data record *noun*
► **record¹**

/'deɪtə ˌrekɔːd/

data reduction *noun*
changes made to original data so that it uses less memory and can be processed more easily: *Data reduction caused the word 'street' to be abbreviated to 'St.' in the address database.*

/'deɪtə rɪˌdʌkʃn/
note not used with *a* or *an*. No plural and used with a singular verb only.
◄ a **data reduction** algorithm, method, module, phase
► **data validation, data vetting**

data retrieval *noun*
the use of SORTING and SELECTING methods to get information from a data file: *The telecommunications directory enquiries service uses fast data retrieval techniques.*

/'deɪtə rɪˌtriːvl/
note not used with *a* or *an*. No plural and used with a singular verb only.
◄ **data retrieval** algorithms, methods, techniques, software

abbr abbreviation   **pl** plural   **syn** synonym   ► see   ◄ collocate (*word often used with the headword*)

data security *noun*

ways of protecting data against damage and unauthorized access: *The growth of network access to computer systems has increased the need for effective data security.*

/ˌdeɪtə sɪˈkjʊərəti/

note not used with *a* or *an*. No plural and used with a singular verb only.

⋈ efficient, poor **data security**

syn security

▶ **data protection**

---

data set ready *noun*

a signal from a device that shows it is ready to receive data: *send the data set ready signal from the modem to the computer*

/ˌdeɪtə set ˈredi/

note not used with *a* or *an*. No plural and used with a singular verb only.

abbr DSR

▶ **data terminal ready**

---

data storage *noun*

▶ **storage**

/ˈdeɪtə ˌstɔːrɪdʒ/

---

data stream *noun*

data transmitted serially, one binary digit at a time: *The data stream can be corrupted by noise on the line.* ○ *a high-speed data stream*

note A data stream is treated as a sequence of bits. The divisions of the bits into characters or words is usually ignored during transmission.

/ˈdeɪtə striːm/

pl data streams

⋈ receive, send, transmit a **data stream**

syn stream

---

data structure *noun*

a collection of data items that behaves as one single item. Usually the whole data structure is given one name and has links or POINTERS (= information about the location of a data item) that show how the data items are related to each other: *search for a string in the data structure*

note Common data structures are lists, trees, queues, arrays and stacks.

/ˈdeɪtə ˌstrʌktʃə(r)/

pl data structures

⋈ access, choose, define, implement, traverse, update a **data structure**; a global, hierarchical **data structure**

▶ array, dequeue, dynamic data structure, information structure, list, queue[1], stack, static data structure, tree

---

data terminal ready *noun*

a signal from a device that shows that it is ready to send data

/ˈdeɪtə ˌtɜːmɪnl ˈredi/

note not used with *a* or *an*. No plural and used with a singular verb only.

abbr DTR

▶ **data set ready**

---

data transfer *noun*

the process of moving data from one place to another: *data transfer via satellite*

/ˈdeɪtə ˌtrænsfɜː(r)/

note not used with *a* or *an*. No plural and used with a singular verb only.

⋈ implement, perform **data transfer**; **data transfer** methods, operations, software

---

data transfer rate *noun*

the speed at which data is moved from one place to another: *The system supports a data transfer rate of up to 600Kb per second.*

note Data transfer rate is usually measured in bits per second.

/ˌdeɪtə ˈtrænsfɜː ˈreɪt/

pl data transfer rates

⋈ define, measure, specify the **data transfer rate**

data transmission *noun*
1 the process of sending data from one place to another using a data link: *Reliable methods of data transmission are essential for network operations.* 2 the data which is sent over a data link: *The data transmission included the latest financial accounts.*

/'deɪtə trænsˌmɪʃn/
1 note not used with *a* or *an*. No plural and used with a singular verb only.
◄ **data transmission** methods, operation, software
2 pl data transmissions
◄ receive, send a **data transmission**

---

data type *noun*
the sort of data that can be stored in a variable

/'deɪtə taɪp/
pl data types
◄ copy, define, inherit a **data type**; a string, logical, numeric **data type**
► **abstract data type, strongly typed, type declaration, weakly typed**

---

data validation *noun*
the process of checking that data in a computer system is correct: *run the sales data through a data validation program*

note Data validation checks that the data is consistent and accurate within certain parameters; it does not check that data has been input correctly (this is data vetting). A common data validation technique is the range check which ensures that data items fall in a possible range of values.

/'deɪtə vælɪˌdeɪʃn/
note not used with *a* or *an*. No plural and used with a singular verb only.
◄ **data validation** algorithms, methods, techniques
► **data reduction**

---

data vetting *noun*
the process of checking data that has been input to a computer system to make sure that no mistakes have been made while entering it

note Data vetting only checks that the data that has been input is an exact copy of what should have been input; it does not interpret the data to see if it makes sense (this is data validation).

/'deɪtə ˌvetɪŋ/
note not used with *a* or *an*. No plural and used with a singular verb only.
◄ **data vetting** algorithms, methods, techniques
► **data reduction**

---

datum *noun*
a single character or number, etc which is coded so that it can be processed by a computer: *a numeric datum*

note The single noun 'datum' is only found in formal situations; it is now common to use 'data' as a singular and plural noun.

/'deɪtəm/
pl data
◄ define, measure, print, record a **datum**
► **data**

---

daughter board *noun*
a printed circuit board that is connected to the MOTHERBOARD (= the main printed circuit board) of a computer: *install the graphics adaptor as a daughter board in an unused expansion slot on the motherboard*

/'dɔːtə bɔːd/
pl daughter boards
◄ connect, install, plug *in* a **daughter board**
► **expansion board, expansion slot, motherboard**

DBA *abbr*
► **database administrator**

/ˌdiː biː 'eɪ/
note pronounced as individual letters

DBMS *abbr*
► **database management system**

/ˌdiː biː em 'es/
note pronounced as individual letters

---

abbr abbreviation   **pl** plural   **syn** synonym   ► see   ◄ collocate (*word often used with the headword*)

DC *abbr*
▶ **direct current**

/ˌdiː ˈsiː/
note pronounced as individual letters

DCD *abbr*
▶ **data carrier detect character**

/ˌdiː siː ˈdiː/
note pronounced as individual letters

DCE *abbr*
data circuit terminating equipment

/ˌdiː siː ˈiː/
note pronounced as individual letters

DDE *abbr*
▶ **direct data entry**

/ˌdiː diː ˈiː/
note pronounced as individual letters

DDL *abbr*
▶ **data description language**

/ˌdiː diː ˈel/
note pronounced as individual letters

---

dead halt *noun* (operations)
a step in a computer program that makes execution stop. The only way of continuing is to reboot the computer.

/ˌded ˈhɔːlt/
pl dead halts
ʜ come *to* a **dead halt**
▶ **abend, catastrophic error, catastrophic failure, crash**

---

deadlock *noun*
▶ **deadly embrace**

/ˈdedlɒk/

---

deadly embrace *noun*
the situation in MULTIPROGRAMMING where two tasks are prevented from executing further because each needs resources allocated to the other: *use a modern operating system that avoids the problems of a deadly embrace*

/ˌdedli ɪmˈbreɪs/
pl deadly embraces
ʜ encounter, get *into* a **deadly embrace**
syn deadlock

---

deallocate *verb*
to take away resources such as memory or hardware from a program or process: *deallocate memory from the application*

/ˌdiːˈæləkeɪt/
deallocate, deallocating, deallocated
note transitive verb
ʜ **deallocate** a device, memory page, printer
▶ **allocate**

---

deblock *verb*
to remove an individual data record from a BLOCK (= a set of data items that are stored as a single unit): *deblock the compressed data so that it can be processed*

/ˌdiːˈblɒk/
deblock, deblocking, deblocked
note transitive verb
ʜ **deblock** a compressed file
▶ **data compression**

---

debounce *verb*
to process input from a keyboard to make sure that a key pressed once does not generate more than one character: *debounce circuits in the keyboard hardware*

/ˌdiːˈbaʊns/
debounce, debouncing, debounced
note transitive verb
ʜ **debounce** a keyboard
▶ **bounce**

debug *verb* (software)
to correct errors in a program or system: *debug the software during beta testing*

/ˌdiːˈbʌg/
debug, debugging, debugged

note transitive verb

◣ **debug** a program, system

▶ **bug**

---

decimal *adjective*
connected with a system of numbers based on the number 10: *a decimal arithmetic operation*

/ˈdesɪml/
◣ a**decimal** point; **decimal** notation

▶ **base 10, binary coded decimal, binary to decimal conversion, hexadecimal**

---

decimal-to-binary conversion *noun*
the process of changing a number written or stored in decimal notation to one of the same value in binary notation

/ˈdesɪml tə ˈbaɪnəri kənˈvɜːʃn/
note usually singular

◣ use **decimal-to-binary conversion**

---

decision box *noun*
a symbol in a FLOW CHART that shows where a choice has to be made in a process and what the result will be: *Decision boxes are usually diamond-shaped.*

/dɪˈsɪʒn bɒks/
pl decision boxes

◣ draw a **decision box**

---

decision support system *noun* (applications/business)
a system designed to combine information from an organization's database with a manager's database to help in making future decisions: *manage projects with the help of a decision support system*

/dɪˌsɪʒn səˈpɔːt ˌsɪstəm/
pl decision support systems

abbr DSS

◣ blame, consult, develop a **decision support system**

▶ **expert system, management information system**

---

decision table *noun*
a table which shows how the values of variables cause different routes to be taken through the program or process

/dɪˈsɪʒn teɪbl/
pl decision tables

◣ compile, draw *up* a **decision table**

▶ **decision tree**

---

decision tree *noun*
a diagram which shows the information in a DECISION TABLE as a picture

/dɪˈsɪʒn triː/
pl decision trees

◣ draw, represent *as* a **decision tree**

---

deck *noun*
1 a pile of punched cards: *load the deck into the card reader*

2 ▶ **tape deck**

/dek/
pl decks

1 ◣ arrange *as*, load a **deck**

---

declaration *noun* (software/programming)
a statement in a computer programming language that tells the software translator how much storage the data will need, the DATA STRUCTURES used, or the type of data held in named variables

note Declarations are often processed when the program is translated rather than when it is executed.

/ˌdekləˈreɪʃn/
pl declarations

◣ include, insert, make a **declaration**

syn declarative statement

▶ **translator**

---

abbr abbreviation   **pl** plural   **syn** synonym   ▶ see   ◣ collocate (*word often used with the headword*)

declare *verb*

1 to make a statement that shows that a variable or a DATA STRUCTURE exists: *In this program, the first statement declares the variable A and assigns it the value 1.* 2 to make a statement in a computer program asking for resources to be made available to the program: *In this program, the use of the network printer was declared.*

/dɪˈkleə(r)/
declare, declaring, declared
note transitive verb

---

decode *verb*

to change something in code to its original form so that it can be understood: *decode encoded text into plaintext* ○ *decode the message*

/ˌdiːˈkəʊd/
decode, decoding, decoded
note transitive verb
▶ **code**

☆**decoder** *noun* (hardware)

1 a device that is used to choose one of several possible signals for transmission 2 a device or program that changes coded data into its uncoded form: *The decoder unscrambles the signal for input into the VDU.*

/ˌdiːˈkəʊdə(r)/
pl decoders
▶ **scramble**

---

decoding *noun*

the process of changing data that has been ENCODED back into its original form: *decoding the data took a lot of computer time*

/ˌdiːˈkəʊdɪŋ/
note not used with *a* or *an*. No plural and used with a singular verb only.
◄ a **decoding** algorithm, module, routine
▶ **conversion, encryption**

---

decollate *verb*
▶ **burst**

/ˌdiːkəˈleɪt/

---

decollator *noun*
▶ **burster**

/ˌdiːkəˈleɪtə(r)/

---

decompiler *noun* (software)

a program that tries to generate source code from assembly language code or machine code: *A decompiler may be useful in debugging a program.*

/ˌdiːkəmˈpaɪlə(r)/
pl decompilers
◄ execute, use a **decompiler**

---

decouple *verb*

to separate two devices, etc which are joined: *decouple the systems so that they run independently*

/ˌdiːˈkʌpl/
decouple, decoupling, decoupled
note transitive verb
◄ **decouple** devices, systems
▶ **couple**

---

decoupled *adjective*

of two devices, etc that have been separated

/ˌdiːˈkʌpld/
◄ **decoupled** devices, systems
▶ **coupled**

---

decrement *verb*

to take a number away from a numeric variable that is being used as a COUNTER (2): *decrement by 2* ○ *decrement the counter until it reaches zero*

/ˈdekrɪmənt/
decrement, decrementing, decremented
note transitive or intransitive verb
◄ **decrement** *by* 1, 2, 3 etc., a counter, loop variable, variable
▶ **increment**

decryption *noun*
the process of changing information that has a special code
back into its original form so that it can be easily understood:
use decryption techniques to understand secret messages

/ˌdiːˈkrɪpʃn/
note not used with *a* or *an*. No
plural and used with a singular
verb only.

◄ a **decryption** algorithm,
technique

dedicated *adjective*
(of software and hardware) that is only used for one particular
task or purpose: *The dedicated file server only makes files available
to network users.*

/ˈdedɪkeɪtɪd/
◄ a **dedicated** machine, server;
dedicated software

dedicated channel *noun*
a DATA TRANSMISSION link that is used by a small number of
users, or for a special purpose only: *The bank uses dedicated
channels for communication between head office and other
branches.*

/ˌdedɪkeɪtɪd ˈtʃænl/
pl dedicated channels
◄ transmit *over*, use a **dedicated
channel**

dedicated word processor *noun* (hardware/software)
a computer system that is only able to process text and so can
only run word processing programs: *The computer is configured
to be a dedicated word processor.*

/ˌdedɪkeɪtɪd ˈwɜːd ˌprəʊsesə(r)/
pl dedicated word processors
◄ buy, use a **dedicated word
processor**

default¹ *noun* (software/operations/system)
the choices made automatically by the software, such as
screen colour and font size, etc unless the user changes them:
change the default font ○ *configure the software if the default option
isn't suitable* ○ *Page numbers are printed in the margins by default.*

/dɪˈfɔːlt/
pl defaults
◄ a **default** drive, font, option,
setting, value

default² *verb* (software)
to make an automatic choice without instructions from the
user: *The computer's start-up program defaults to the hard disk.* ○
The word processing program defaults to double spacing.

/dɪˈfɔːlt/
**default, defaulting,
defaulted**
note intransitive verb

default directory *noun*
► **current directory**

/dɪˌfɔːlt dəˈrektəri/

deferred addressing *noun*
► **indirect addressing**

/dɪˌfɜːd əˈdresɪŋ/

definition *noun*
1 the amount of detail that can be shown on a screen: *flat
screen technology gives excellent definition* **2** a description of
something that explains exactly what it is: *a data definition*

/ˌdefɪˈnɪʃn/
1 note not used with *a* or *an*. No
plural and used with a singular
verb only.
◄ high, low **definition**
► **resolution**
2 pl definitions
► **macro definition**

defragmentation *noun*
the process of reorganizing data stored on disk or in main
memory so that any free storage locations are put together:
defragmentation can speed up disk access

/ˈdiːˌfrægmenˈteɪʃn/
note not used with *a* or *an*. No
plural and used with a singular
verb only.
◄ carry out, perform
defragmentation; a

---

abbr abbreviation **pl** plural **syn** synonym ► see ◄ collocate (*word often used with the headword*)

defragmentation algorithm, routine, utility

syn compaction, data compaction

---

degradation *noun*

a loss of quality: *a degradation in picture quality* ○ *Degradation of software happens when it is copied again and again.*

/ˌdegrəˈdeɪʃn/

note no plural

⋈ **degradation** *in* data, an image, a signal

---

del *abbr*

▶ **delete**[1]

note used in written English only

---

delay[1] *noun*

an amount of time when an action or process stops, usually because the system is very busy, or because there is a problem: *expect a delay when connecting to the Internet when it is heavily used in the afternoon* ○ *e-mail may be subject to delays when the server is down*

/dɪˈleɪ/

pl delays

⋈ be subject *to*, encounter, suffer a **delay**

---

delay[2] *verb*

to stop an action or process for an amount of time, usually because the system is very busy, or because there is a problem: *Printing is delayed because there is a long print queue.*

/dɪˈleɪ/

delay, delaying, delayed

note transitive verb

⋈ a long, a short, an unnecessary **delay**

---

delay-line storage *noun* (hardware)

a slow form of storage found in FIRST GENERATION computers

note Delay-line storage involves a group of bits represented by electrical pulses moving in a conducting medium such as nickel wire or a column of mercury.

/dɪˈleɪ laɪn ˈstɔːrɪdʒ/

note no plural

☆**delete**[1] *noun*

the key that is used used to remove words, etc from a text or files from a hard disk: *press the delete key*

/dɪˈliːt/

note not used with *a* or *an*. No plural and used with a singular verb only.

abbr del

syn delete key

▶ **backspace**[1]

☆**delete**[2] *verb* (user operation)

1 to remove a letter, word or line, etc from a piece of text: *delete a mistake in the memo* **2** to remove files from a magnetic disk, etc: *delete unwanted files to make space on the hard disk*

/dɪˈliːt/

delete, deleting, deleted

note transitive verb

▶ **erase**

---

delete character *noun* (software)

one of the characters that can be typed from the keyboard to tell the program to ignore the character that was typed last

/dɪˈliːt ˌkærəktə(r)/

pl delete characters

⋈ input, repeat, type a **delete character**

▶ **cancel character**

☆**delete key** *noun*

▶ **delete**[1]

/dɪˈliːt kiː/

☆**delimiter** *noun* (software)

a character such as a comma that marks the beginning or end of individual items in a program or set of data: *put a delimiter between the program instructions*

/dɪˈlɪmɪtə(r)/

pl delimiters

⋈ a field, record **delimiter**

demand paging *noun* (software)

a systems software operation where blocks of data are transferred from disk into memory only when they are requested: *implement memory management for demand paging*

note Demand paging allows the computer to run large programs by keeping part of the program on backing store until it is needed. When a new part is loaded, it replaces an unwanted part already in memory.

/dɪˌmɑːnd ˈpeɪdʒɪŋ/

note not used with *a* or *an*. No plural and used with a singular verb only.

⋈ implement, use **demand paging**; **demand paging** algorithms, techniques

▶ **virtual memory**

---

demodulate *verb*

to return a MODULATED signal to its original form

/ˌdiːˈmɒdjuleɪt/

demodulate, demodulating, demodulated

note transitive verb

⋈ **demodulate** a carrier wave, signal

▶ **amplitude modulation, carrier signal, frequency modulation, modem, phase modulation, pulse code modulation, modulate**

---

demodulation *noun*

the process of returning a MODULATED signal to its original form

/ˈdiːˌmɒdjuˈleɪʃn/

note not used with *a* or *an*. No plural and used with a singular verb only.

⋈ **demodulation** *of* a carrier signal, *of* a wave

▶ **amplitude modulation, carrier signal, frequency modulation, modulation, phase modulation, pulse code modulation**

---

demodulator *noun* (hardware)

a device which returns a MODULATED signal to its original form

/ˌdiːˈmɒdjuleɪtə(r)/

pl demodulators

⋈ receive a signal *via*, use a **demodulator**

▶ **modulator**

---

demountable disk *noun* (hardware)

a disk that can be taken out of the computer:

/diːˌmaʊntəbl ˈdɪsk/

pl demountable disks

---

denary notation *noun*

the system of writing numbers using BASE 10

/ˌdiːnəri nəʊˈteɪʃn/

note not used with *a* or *an*. No plural and used with a singular verb only.

⋈ count *in*, express a number *in* **denary notation**

▶ **decimal**

---

density *noun*

the amount of space available on a disk for recording data: *a hard disk with a high recording density*

/ˈdensəti/

note not used with *a* or *an*. No plural and used with a singular verb only.

⋈ bit, packing, recording **density**

▶ **double-density disk, high-density disk**

---

dependent *adjective*
able to change when something else changes

/dɪˈpendənt/
ᴹ a **dependent** variable

---

dequeue *noun*
a DATA STRUCTURE arranged as a list of data items in a certain order where items may only be added or accessed at one end of the list or the other, but not elsewhere: *a dequeue of data items to be processed*

note The word 'dequeue' comes from the words 'double ended queue'.

/ˈdiːkjuː/
pl dequeues
ᴹ define, empty, implement, update, use a **dequeue**
syn double ended queue
▶ **dynamic data structure, queue**

DES *abbr*
▶ **data encryption standard**

/ˌdiː iː ˈes/
note pronounced as individual letters

---

descendant *noun*
a data item in a tree that is linked by a POINTER from another data item. The descendant is at a lower level than the item that it is linked with: *Each data item in a binary tree has two descendants.*

/dɪˈsendənt/
pl descendants
ᴹ access, update a **descendant**
▶ **binary tree, data structure**

---

descender *noun*
the bottom or tail parts of letters such as p, q and g that fall below short letters such as s, c and e when they are LOWER CASE

/dɪˈsendə(r)/
pl descenders
ᴹ allow space *for* the **descender**
▶ **ascender**

---

descending sort *noun*
the process of arranging a list of data items so that the higher values come before the lower values: *a descending sort on dates* ○ *a descending sort on the key field*

/dɪˌsendɪŋ ˈsɔːt/
pl descending sorts
ᴹ carry out, execute, perform a **descending sort**
▶ **ascending sort, sort**

---

description *noun*
a statement that explains what something looks like, or how it behaves: *a description of the program logic*

/dɪˈskrɪpʃn/
pl descriptions
ᴹ make, write down a **description**
▶ **definition 2**

---

descriptor *noun* (software/programming)
an item of data that describes the type of data in a file or a field of a record: *a two character tag that acts as a descriptor of the data type*

/dɪˈskrɪptə(r)/
pl descriptors
ᴹ access, insert, update a **descriptor**; a **descriptor** record, word
▶ **data type**

---

design¹ *noun*
1 a plan of something before it is produced: *a design proposal for a new system* ○ *interactive software at the design stage* **2** the structure of hardware or software: *The system design works well.*

/dɪˈzam/
1 pl designs
ᴹ define, describe, draw *up*, propose a **design**; a **design** cycle, method, technique
▶ **computer aided design**
2 note not used with *a* or *an*. No plural and used with a singular verb only.
ᴹ chip, database **design**

☆**design²** verb

to plan something before it is produced: *A team of experts will design the new system.*

/dɪˈzaɪn/
design, designing, designed
note transitive verb
M **design** an algorithm, a circuit board, a component

desk check noun

the process of testing a computer program by studying a printed copy of it, and not executing the program on a computer: *A desk check revealed several branches of code that would never be executed, showing that the program could be improved.*

/ˈdesk tʃek/
pl desk checks
M carry out, perform, run a **desk check**
▶ **trace table, dry run**

desktop¹ noun

the background screen picture in modern personal computer systems: *icons sit on the desktop*

note The desktop is designed to look like an office desk with documents, files and folders.

/ˈdesktɒp/
pl desktops
M look at, update the **desktop**
▶ **graphical user interface**

desktop² adjective

small enough to fit onto an office desk

/ˈdesktɒp/
M a **desktop** computer, printer

☆**desktop publishing** noun

the use of a personal computer, printer and software to design, plan and print text that will be published in forms such as books and leaflets etc: *produce literature using a desktop publishing package*

/ˌdesktɒp ˈpʌblɪʃɪŋ/
note no plural
abbr DTP
M a **desktop publishing** package, system

despool verb

to print files which have been SPOOLED: *Despooling files is an off-line operation which does not slow the system down.*

/ˌdiːˈspuːl/
despool, despooling, despooled
note transitive verb
▶ **spool**

destination address noun (software/programming)

the address of the instruction in a computer program that will be obeyed after a jump or BRANCH (2) instruction is executed: *the destination address of the GOTO instruction*

/ˌdestɪˈneɪʃn əˌdres/
pl destination addresses
M access, branch *to*, jump *to* the **destination address**
▶ **address**

destructive adjective

(of a process) that destroys or OVERWRITES (2) data, etc used in a computer operation: *a destructive memory access operation*

/dɪˈstrʌktɪv/

destructive addition noun (software)

an addition operation that puts the answer into the same location as one of the two numbers being added, OVERWRITING (2) that number: *It can be convenient for an increment instruction to be implemented as a destructive addition.*

/dɪˌstrʌktɪv əˈdɪʃn/
pl destructive additions
M perform a **destructive addition**

destructive cursor noun

a cursor that removes text from a screen: *The destructive cursor passes over characters that have to be removed.*

/dɪˌstrʌktɪv ˈkɜːsə(r)/
pl destructive cursors
M implement, use a **destructive cursor**

---

abbr abbreviation   **pl** plural   **syn** synonym   ▶ see   M collocate (*word often used with the headword*)

destructive read *noun* an operation that accesses a memory location and removes the data that is read	/dɪˌstrʌktɪv 'riːd/ **pl** destructive reads **abbr** DRO ◪ perform a **destructive read** **syn** destructive readout
destructive readout *noun* ▶ **destructive read**	/dɪˌstrʌktɪv 'riːdaʊt/
detection *noun* the process of finding or identifying something: *Error detection is an important part of transmission protocols.*	/dɪ'tekʃn/ **note** not used with *a* or *an*. No plural and used with a singular verb only. ◪ **detection** algorithms, methods, techniques ▶ **error detection**
develop *verb* to design or improve something: *A big investment is needed to develop a new computer system.* ○ *After release, the software was developed further.*	/dɪ'veləp/ **develop, developing, developed** **note** transitive verb ◪ **develop** a product; **develop** hardware, software
developer *noun* a person or organization that designs or improves hardware or software: *The software developers are beta-testing the latest version of the program.*	/dɪ'veləpə(r)/ **pl** developers
development *noun* **1** the process of designing or improving something: *the development of fifth generation computers* **2** a new product: *The company's latest development is a new chip.*	/dɪ'veləpmənt/ **1 note** not used with *a* or *an*. No plural and used with a singular verb only. ◪ carry out **development**; a **development** period, phase, trial **2 pl** developments
development software *noun* (software) a set of programs that are used to write new programs	/dɪ'veləpmənt ˌsɒftweə(r)/ **note** not used with *a* or *an*. No plural and used with a singular verb only.
☆**device** *noun* (hardware) a small machine or piece of equipment, such as a keyboard, a disk drive, a server or a chip, etc: *a device for measuring data flow rates*	/dɪ'vaɪs/ **pl** devices ◪ an electronic, an input/output, a peripheral **device**; a **device** driver
device address *noun* (hardware) a location in a computer's memory that the CPU accesses to perform operations involving a particular device: *write data to the device address of the sound card to produce audio output*	/dɪˌvaɪs ə'dres/ **pl** device addresses ◪ access, read *from*, write *to* a **device address**
device code *noun* a pattern of bits in a MACHINE CODE instruction that identifies a PERIPHERAL: *Device codes are in the range 0 to 31.*	/dɪ'vaɪs kəʊd/ **pl** device codes ◪ allocate, refer *to* a **device code**

device control character *noun*
▶ **control character**

/dɪ,vaɪs kən'trəʊl ,kærəktə(r)/

---

device dependent *adjective* (software)
(of software) that will only execute correctly when used with certain devices, such as printers or display screens: *This software is device dependent and will only operate with a PostScript printer.*

/dɪ,vaɪs dɪ'pendənt/
◄ a **device dependent** interface, routine

---

device driver *noun* (software)
software that receives data before it is sent to a PERIPHERAL so that it can be converted into the correct format for that peripheral: *The printer needs an appropriate device driver.*

/dɪ'vaɪs ,draɪvə(r)/
pl device drivers
◄ install, remove a **device driver**

---

device independent *adjective*
(of software) that runs on different systems without needing any changes: *Device independent colour capabilities will be a part of the new operating system.*

/dɪ'vaɪs ,ɪndɪ'pendənt/
◄ a **device independent** bitmap, routine; **device independent** code, software
▶ **device dependent**

DFD *abbr*
▶ **data flow diagram**

/,di: ef 'di:/
note pronounced as individual letters

---

diagnosis *noun*
the result of identifying something, especially an error in a computer program or system: *The diagnosis from the disk checking program identified damaged directories.*

/,daɪəg'nəʊsɪs/
pl diagnoses
◄ **diagnosis** *of* an error, *of* a fault

---

diagnostic *noun*
a message displayed by a system that gives information about an error that has occurred: *Error messages and other diagnostics help to identify problems.*

/,daɪəg'nɒstɪk/
pl diagnostics
◄ display, print a **diagnostic**; a **diagnostic** error message, message

---

diagnostic program *noun*
a program that is executed when an error occurs in a computer system, and which tries to identify what caused the error: *examine the results of the diagnostic program*

/,daɪəg'nɒstɪk ,prəʊgræm/
pl diagnostic programs
◄ execute, load, run a **diagnostic program**

---

diagram *noun*
a drawing or plan that uses lines to explain ideas etc, or to show how something works: *a diagram of a circuit* ○ *a diagram that explains bus systems in the CPU*

/'daɪəgræm/
pl diagrams
◄ draw, explain, print a **diagram**; a colour, simple **diagram**
▶ **bar chart**

---

dial *verb* (operations)
to use a number to communicate with another telephone or device over a telephone line: *Remote users can dial in over a modem to access the network.* ○ *dial a bulletin board service*

/daɪl/
dial, dialling, dialled
(*US* **dial, dialing, dialed**)
note transitive or intransitive verb
◄ **dial** a computer, number

---

dialect *noun*
small changes in programming language that make it different from the original language: *Turbo Pascal is a dialect of Pascal.* ○ *program in a dialect of BASIC*

/'daɪəlekt/
pl dialects

---

abbr abbreviation   **pl** plural   **syn** synonym   ▶ see   ◄ collocate (*word often used with the headword*)

dial-in modem *noun* (hardware)
a modem connected to a central computer which remote users can access: *access a bulletin board via a dial-in modem*

/ˌdaɪl ɪn ˈməʊdem/
pl dial-in modems
◄ dial, use a **dial-in modem**

☆**dialog box** *noun* (applications)
a box that appears on the screen in a graphical user interface with different options for the user to choose: *select an option from the dialog box* ○ *cancel the dialog box*

/ˈdaɪəlɒg bɒks/
pl dialog boxes
  (also **dialogue box**)
◄ click *in* the **dialog box**
► **alert box, menu, WIMP**

---

dibit *noun*
a pair of binary digits: *the dibit 00*

/ˈdaɪ bɪt/
pl dibits
◄ send, transmit a **dibit**

---

dictionary *noun*
1 (*software/word processing*) the words in a SPELLCHECK program: *add words to the dictionary*
2 ► **data dictionary**

/ˈdɪkʃənri/
pl dictionaries
1 ► **thesaurus**

---

difference *noun*
1 the amount by which two values are not the same: *The difference in processing time between the computers is minimal.* **2** (*mathematics*) the number that remains when one number is taken from another: *The difference between 7 and 5 is 2.*

/ˈdɪfrəns/
pl differences
1 ◄ identify, list the **differences**
2 ◄ a negative, positive, zero **difference**

---

digit *noun* (mathematics and logic)
the numbers from 0 to 9: *The binary system uses only the digits 0 and 1.*

note In number representations like hexadecimal which uses letters of the alphabet, 'digit' can mean both letters and numbers.

/ˈdɪdʒɪt/
pl digits
◄ a binary, a hexadecimal, an octal **digit**
► **bit, number**

---

digital *adjective*
relating to the storage and transmission of data using DIGITS: *A digital computer processes binary data.*

/ˈdɪdʒɪtl/
◄ a **digital** print-out, reading, scale, watch
► **analog, digital-to-analog converter**

---

digital circuit *noun* (hardware)
an electronic circuit that works with binary digits and not analog signals

/ˌdɪdʒɪtl ˈsɜːkɪt/
pl digital circuits
► **analog circuit**

---

digital clock *noun*
a clock that shows the time as a series of numbers rather than as hands pointing to numbers: *The time according to the digital clock is 10:32.*

/ˌdɪdʒɪtl ˈklɒk/
pl digital clocks

---

digital communications *noun*
the process of transmitting and receiving digital data: *Digital communications have speeded up the transfer of data.*

/ˈdɪdʒɪtl kəˌmjuːnɪˈkeɪʃnz/
note used with a singular or plural verb

ᴍ a **digital communications** interface, link, network, processor

▶ **communication**

☆**digital computer** *noun* (hardware)
a computer that uses DISCRETE (= separate) units to represent data. These units are the binary digits (bits) 0 and 1

/ˌdɪdʒɪtl kəmˈpjuːtə(r)/
pl digital computers

▶ **analog computer, continuous**

---

digital display *noun*
a display device that shows digits: *This alarm clock has a digital display.*

/ˌdɪdʒɪtl dɪˈspleɪ/
pl digital displays

ᴍ output *to* a **digital display**

---

digital logic *noun*
▶ **Boolean algebra**

/ˌdɪdʒɪtl ˈlɒdʒɪk/

---

digital plotter *noun*
a PLOTTER that receives signals in digital form

/ˌdɪdʒɪtl ˈplɒtə(r)/
pl digital plotters

---

digital recording *noun*
1 the process of storing data such as text, graphics and sound as a set of binary digits (bits): *The studio has all the latest equipment for digital recording.* **2** data such as text, graphics and sound that is held as a set of binary digits (bits): *The digital recording on the compact disc lasts for 74 minutes.*

/ˌdɪdʒɪtl rɪˈkɔːdɪŋ/
1 note not used with *a* or *an*. No plural and used with a singular verb only.

ᴍ use **digital recording**; **digital recording** methods, techniques, technology

2 pl digital recordings

ᴍ make a **digital recording**

---

digital signal *noun*
a signal that carries data using only a fixed number of possible values: *Binary digital signals use only two values, often represented as 1 or 0.*

note All electronic signals are corrupted in transmission. A digital signal can be easily corrected because its exact value is one of a number of known possible values. This allows data to be transmitted very accurately.

/ˌdɪdʒɪtl ˈsɪgnəl/
pl digital signals

ᴍ code *as*, send *as* a **digital signal**; a **digital signal** processor

---

digital signal processing *noun*
the analysis and interpretation of signals that have been transmitted digitally: *The satellite data undergoes digital signal processing.*

/ˌdɪdʒɪtl ˈsɪgnəl ˌprəʊsesɪŋ/
note not used with *a* or *an*. No plural and used with a singular verb only.

ᴍ perform **digital signal processing**

☆**digital-to-analog-converter** *noun* (hardware)
a device for converting DISCRETE digital signals to continuous analog signals

/ˈdɪdʒɪtl tu ˈænəlɒg kənˈvɜːtə(r)/
pl digital-to-analog converters
abbr DAC, D/A converter

▶ **analog, analog-to-digital converter**

☆**digitize** *verb* (system operation)
to convert data into digital form usually by using an ANALOG-TO-DIGITAL CONVERTER: *use the scanner to digitize this photograph*

/ˈdɪdʒɪtaɪz/
digitize, digitizing, digitized
note transitive verb

---

abbr abbreviation   **pl** plural   **syn** synonym   ▶ see   ᴍ collocate (*word often used with the headword*)

digitized *adjective*
(of data) that has been converted into digital form

/ˈdɪdʒɪtaɪzd/

ᴎ a **digitized** image, photograph, signal

---

digitizer *noun* (hardware)
a device that converts data into digital form: *a scanning digitizer*

/ˈdɪdʒɪtaɪzə(r)/

pl digitizers

▶ **video digitizer**

---

digitizing *noun*
the process of converting data into digital form

/ˈdɪdʒɪtaɪzɪŋ/

note not used with *a* or *an*. No plural and used with a singular verb only.

DIL *abbr*
▶ **dual in-line package**

/dɪl/

note pronounced as a word

---

dimension statement *noun* (software/programming)
the programming language statement that is used to DECLARE 1 the ARRAY DIMENSION and ARRAY BOUNDS of an array

/daɪˈmenʃn ˌsteɪtmənt/

pl dimension statements

ᴎ insert, program, use a **dimension statement**

---

dingbat *noun*
a symbol such as a box, star or arrow, etc that is used to decorate a page: *insert dingbats between paragraphs*

/ˈdɪŋbæt/

pl dingbats

ᴎ a **dingbat** character, font

▶ **graphics**

DIP *abbr*
▶ **dual in-line package**

/dɪp/

note pronounced as a word

DIP switch *noun*
dual in-line package switch. A switch that is connected to a CIRCUIT BOARD and is used to select different options, such as setting a printer to parallel or serial operation.

/ˈdɪp swɪtʃ/

pl DIP switches

ᴎ set the **DIP switch** *to* open/closed

☆**direct access** *noun*
▶ **random access**

/dəˌrekt ˈækses/

---

direct access storage device *noun*
▶ **random access storage device**

/dəˈrekt ˈækses ˈstɔːrɪdʒ dɪˌvaɪs/

---

direct address *noun*
▶ **absolute address**

/dəˌrekt əˈdres/

---

direct addressing *noun*
▶ **absolute addressing**

/dəˌrekt əˈdresɪŋ/

---

direct current *noun* (hardware)
electric current that flows in one direction only: *a radio powered by direct current from a battery*

/dəˌrekt ˈkʌrənt/

note not used with *a* or *an*. No plural and used with a singular verb only.

abbr DC

ᴎ a **direct current** connection, supply

▶ **alternating current**

direct data entry *noun*
the act or process of transferring information directly to a disk by using the keyboard

/dəˌrekt ˈdeɪtə ˌentri/
note not used with *a* or *an*. No plural and used with a singular verb only.
abbr DDE

---

directive *noun* (software/programming)
a command in a computer program that controls the translation process and which is not translated into an executable instruction

note Directives may select compiler options such as the production of a diagnostic listing, a memory map or a printed name table, etc.

/dəˈrektɪv/
pl directives
ᴴ add, insert a **directive**

---

direct memory access *noun*
► **DMA**

/dəˌrekt ˈmeməri ˌækses/

☆**directory** *noun* (software)
a place where files are kept in a computer: *look through the list of filenames in the directory*

/dəˈrektəri/
pl directories
ᴴ a disk **directory**
syn file directory
► **file, subdirectory**

---

disable *verb*
to deliberately stop a system or part of it from working: *disable the computer to prevent access to files*

/dɪsˈeɪbl/
disable, disabling, disabled
note transitive verb
ᴴ **disable** a computer, a fax, an interrupt, a keyboard, a machine, a modem, a printer
► **enable**

---

disable interrupt *noun* (software)
an instruction that causes the CPU to ignore any INTERRUPTS: *Some routines issue a disable interrupt before they begin execution.*

/dɪsˌeɪbl ˈɪntərʌpt/
pl disable interrupts
ᴴ insert, program a **disable interrupt**
syn inhibit interrupt
► **interrupt**

---

disassemble *verb*
to convert a program written in machine code into assembly language

/ˌdɪsəˈsembl/
disassemble, disassembling, disassembled
note transitive verb
► **assemble**

☆**disassembler** *noun* (software)
a program which converts machine code back into assembly language

/ˌdɪsəˈsemblə(r)/
pl disassemblers
ᴴ **disassembler** language
► **assembler, compiler, low-level language, source code**

☆**disc** *noun*
► **CD**

/dɪsk/

---

abbr abbreviation   **pl** plural   **syn** synonym   ► see   ᴴ collocate (*word often used with the headword*)

disconnect *verb*
1 to separate two devices: *disconnect the printer by unplugging it from the computer* 2 to close a communications link between two systems or devices: *log out then disconnect from the Internet*

/ˌdɪskə'nekt/
disconnect, disconnecting, disconnected

1 note transitive verb
ℍ **disconnect** a computer, printer

2 note intransitive verb
ℍ **disconnect** *from* a network, etc
▶ **connect**

---

discrete *adjective*
existing in separate identifiable units: *Bits are discrete units of data processed by computers.*

/dɪ'skriːt/
ℍ a **discrete** bit, value, variable

---

discrete data *noun* (mathematics)
readings or measurements that have only a limited number of possible values

/dɪˌskriːt 'deɪtə/
note plural noun usually used with a singular verb

---

disinfect *verb*
to find and remove any virus that may be in a part of a computer system: *disinfect a disk* ○ *disinfect the system software*

/ˌdɪsɪn'fekt/
disinfect, disinfecting, disinfected

note transitive verb
▶ **virus checking**

☆**disk** *noun* (hardware)
a storage device with a magnetic surface that records information received electronically: *insert a disk into the disk drive* ○ *The data is stored on disk.*

/dɪsk/
pl disks
(also **disc**)
ℍ copy data *to*, read data *from*, save data *to*, store data *on*, write data *to* **disk**
▶ **CD, floppy disk, hard disk, magnetic disk**

☆**disk access** *noun*
the transfer of data to or from a magnetic disk: *a network requiring a large number of disk accesses*

/'dɪsk ˌækses/
pl disk accesses
ℍ make a **disk access**
▶ **access[1], random access**

---

disk access time *noun*
the time taken to supply a data item from a magnetic disk: *The disk controller has 2Mb of memory which boosts disk access times.*

/ˌdɪsk 'ækses taɪm/
pl disk access times
▶ **access time**

---

disk cache *noun*
a part of RAM that holds information read from a disk: *The most frequently used information on disk is held in the disk cache.*

note A disk cache allows information held on disk to be accessed more quickly than from a disk in a disk drive. A disk cache does not hold whole files.

/'dɪsk kæʃ/
pl disk caches
▶ **cache, RAM disk**

---

disk capacity *noun*
the amount of space on a disk for storing data: *The floppy disk has a disk capacity of 1.4 Mb.* ○ *The disk capacity of the CD is 650 Mb.*

/'dɪsk kəˌpæsəti/
note usually singular
▶ **double-density disk, high-density disk**

disk cartridge *noun*
a removable container with a disk inside

/'dɪsk ˌkɑːtrɪdʒ/
pl disk cartridges

---

disk controller *noun*
an electronic circuit that controls reading writing operations
to a disk in the disk drive

/'dɪsk kənˌtrəʊlə(r)/
pl disk controllers
⋈ a caching, a fast, an intelligent
disk controller

---

disk crash *noun*
a crash caused when the READ/WRITE HEAD (= part of the disk
drive that transfers information to the computer) touches the
surface of the disk, damaging the disk and the data on it

/'dɪsk kræʃ/
pl disk crashes
syn head crash
▶ **crash**

☆**disk drive** *noun* (hardware)
a device that passes data to or from a disk and a computer. A
microcomputer usually has two types of disk drive, a HARD DISK
DRIVE and a FLOPPY DISK DRIVE: *insert the floppy into the A or B disk
drive* ○ *a malfunction in the hard disk drive*

/'dɪsk draɪv/
pl disk drives
⋈ a magnetic **disk drive**
syn disk unit, drive, physical disk
drive
▶ **CD-ROM drive**

---

disk error *noun*
a fault in a disk: *The file couldn't be copied onto the disk because of
the disk error.* ○ *The disk error was the result of the faulty magnetic
coating on the disk.*

/'dɪsk erə(r)/
pl disk errors
⋈ cause, identify a **disk error**

---

diskette *noun*
▶ **floppy disk**

/dɪ'sket/

---

disk formatting *noun* (operations)
the process of recording information onto a disk so that it is
possible to read data to or write data from it. Disk formatting is
done by the operating system or a utility program

/'dɪsk ˌfɔːmætɪŋ/
note no plural
⋈ a **disk formatting** program,
routine, utility

---

disk map *noun*
▶ **bit map 2**

/'dɪsk mæp/

☆**disk operating system** *noun*
▶ **DOS**

/ˌdɪsk 'ɒpəreɪtɪŋ ˌsɪstəm/

---

disk pack *noun* (hardware)
a set of disks in a protective container that is mainly used with
mainframes and minicomputers

/'dɪsk pæk/
pl disk packs
⋈ remove the **disk pack**
syn pack

---

disk partition *noun*
a part of a hard disk that has been divided into two or more
sections that function as separate devices: *The security program
takes a copy of disk partition information during installation.*

/'dɪsk pɑːˌtɪʃn/
pl disk partitions
⋈ create a **disk partition**

☆**disk sector** *noun*
the smallest area of storage on a disk: *a disk sector that can hold
512 bytes of data*

/'dɪsk ˌsektə(r)/
pl disk sectors
⋈ access, delete, update a **disk
sector**
syn sector

---

abbr abbreviation   **pl** plural   **syn** synonym   ▶ see   ⋈ collocate (*word often used with the headword*)

disk track *noun*
one of the many small rings on the surface of a disk: *Once a disk is formatted the data can be recorded in circular disk tracks.*

/'dɪsk træk/
pl disk tracks
ℍ address a **disk track**; a circular, parallel, spiral **disk track**
syn track
▶ **sector**

disk unit *noun*
▶ **disk drive**

/'dɪsk ˌjuːnɪt/

dispatcher *noun* (software)
the ROUTINES that control how the CPU is used in some multitasking operating systems

/dɪ'spætʃə(r)/
pl dispatchers

☆**display¹** *noun* (hardware)
1 a screen or device for showing data or images: *a monitor with a colour display* **2** data or graphics shown on a screen: *a display in the form of a bar chart*

/dɪ'spleɪ/
pl displays
1 ▶ **cathode ray tube, liquid crystal display, monitor, VDU**

☆**display²** *verb*
to show data or graphics etc on a screen or other device: *display the results on screen* ○ *The sales figures were displayed using an overhead projector.*

/dɪ'spleɪ/
display, displaying, displayed
note transitive verb
ℍ **display** a character, an image; **display** data, graphics, information

display adaptor *noun*
▶ **video adaptor**

/dɪ'spleɪ əˌdæptə(r)/

display attribute *noun*
a feature that affects the way a character looks on screen: *select the bold italic display attribute for text*

/dɪ'spleɪ ˌætrɪbjuːt/
pl display attributes

display terminal *noun*
the part of a computer containing the visual display unit: *a colour display terminal*

/dɪ'spleɪ ˌtɜːmɪnl/
pl display terminals
▶ **cathode ray tube, liquid crystal display, monitor, VDU**

dithering *noun*
a way of creating different shades of grey on a MONOCHROME display or printer or adding more colours on a colour display or printer

/'dɪðərɪŋ/
note not used with *a* or *an*. No plural and used with a singular verb only.
▶ **aliasing, grey scale**

DMA *abbr*
direct memory access. A way of transferring data to or from memory without using the CPU: *use direct memory access for fast file copying*

/ˌdiː em 'eɪ/
note pronounced as individual letters
note not used with *a* or *an*. No plural and used with a singular verb only.
ℍ **DMA** methods, techniques
▶ **cycle stealing**

DML *abbr*
▶ **data manipulation language**

/ˌdiː em 'el/
note pronounced as individual letters

☆**document** *noun*
1 a computer file that contains text and graphics, etc and has a unique filename that identifies it: *create a new document and name it* ○ *save the document to disk* 2 a letter, etc that is written on a computer using a word processing application: *file all the documents that are memos or contracts* ○ *edit the document on-screen*

/ˈdɒkjumənt/
pl documents
1 create, load, save a **document**

☆**documentation** *noun*
the information that explains how to use software or hardware: *The set-up instructions are in the documentation.* ○ *The documentation is contained in a four-page README.DOC.*

/ˌdɒkjumenˈteɪʃn/
note not used with *a* or *an*. No plural and used with a singular verb only.
◪ hardware, on-disk, software, technical **documentation**
syn program documentation
▶ **manual, on-line help**

document processing *noun*
the editing and formatting of text and graphics in a file: *Document processing software was used to prepare the publicity material.*

note Document processing usually allows charts, spreadsheets and graphics to be included in text. Document processing packages are usually more powerful than word processing packages but less powerful than desktop publishing applications.

/ˈdɒkjumənt ˌprəʊsesɪŋ/
note no plural
◪ a **document processing** application, package, system

document reader *noun* (hardware)
a device which reads documents and converts the information into computer data: *pass the letter through the document reader*

/ˈdɒkjumənt ˌriːdə(r)/
pl document readers
▶ **optical character recognition, magnetic character recognition**

do loop *noun* (software/programming)
a block of statements in a programming language that is executed a fixed number of times

note The name comes from the DO statement in FORTRAN. In BASIC, the equivalent statement is the FOR ... NEXT loop.

/ˈduː luːp/
pl do loops
◪ execute, perform, repeat a **do loop**
syn for next loop
▶ **loop¹ 2**

domain *noun*
1 a part of a network which is under the control of one central processor: *Certain users are denied access privileges to the secure files domain.* 2 (database) the set of values that an ATTRIBUTE (2) can have: *The domain of EMPLOYEE NUMBER only contains seven-digit numbers.*

/dəˈmeɪn/
pl domains
1 ◪ a hardware, public, software **domain**
▶ **public domain software**
2 ◪ an alphabetic, an alphanumeric, a numeric **domain**

dongle *noun* (hardware)
a chip or circuit in a device that is connected to the main computer and contains a code that is checked by copyright software before it will run: *The dongle plugs into the printer port.*

/ˈdɒŋl/
pl dongles
◪ buy, fit, install a **dongle**

abbr abbreviation   **pl** plural   **syn** synonym   ▶ see   ◪ collocate (*word often used with the headword*)

do nothing instruction *noun* (software/programming)
a programming language statement, usually in a low-level language, which has no effect. It may be used to show the place in a program where an instruction can be put, or it can use up extra processing time.

/ˌduː 'nʌθɪŋ ɪnˌstrʌkʃn/
pl do nothing instructions
M add, delete, insert a **do nothing instruction**
syn no operation instruction, null instruction, null operation

---

☆**DOS** *abbr*
1 disk operating system. The part of an operating system that controls and manages files and programs on disk.
2 ▶ MS-DOS

/dɒs/
note pronounced as a word

---

dot addressable *adjective* (hardware)
(of a printer or screen) that allows any single PIXEL to be controlled without affecting surrounding pixels: *A dot addressable printer is necessary for graphics.*

/ˈdɒt əˌdresəbl/

☆**dot matrix printer** *noun* (hardware)
a printer that produces text by printing very small dots very close together to form characters: *print out drafts of the document on the dot matrix printer*

/ˌdɒt 'meɪtrɪks ˌprɪntə(r)/
pl dot matrix printers
M a 9-pin, 24-pin **dot matrix printer**
syn matrix printer
▶ daisy-wheel printer, laser printer

☆**dots per inch** *noun*
▶ dpi

/ˌdɒts pər 'ɪntʃ/

---

double buffering *noun*
the process of using two buffers to improve access times to slow PERIPHERALS that are used very often. For example, while the computer is filling one buffer, the printer will be emptying the other.

/ˌdʌbl 'bʌfərɪŋ/
note no plural and used with a singular verb only
M employ, use **double buffering**
▶ buffer

---

double-click *verb* (operations)
to press a button on a mouse twice very quickly: *Double-click on the mouse to open a new file.* ○ *start the application by double-clicking on the icon*

/ˌdʌbl 'klɪk/
double-click, double-clicking, double-clicked
note intransitive verb
M **double-click** *on* an icon, *on* the mouse; **double-click** *inside* a box, window
▶ click, drag, highlight

☆**double density disk** *noun* (hardware)
a disk with the capacity for storing double the normal amount of data: *insert a double density disk into the disk drive*

note A double density disk can store half as much data as a high density disk.

/ˈdʌbl 'densəti 'dɪsk/
pl double density disks
M a 5¼ inch, a 3½ inch, a formatted, an unformatted **double density disk**
▶ disk, DSDD, DSHD, hard disk, high density disk

---

double ended queue *noun*
▶ dequeue

/ˈdʌbl ˌendɪd 'kjuː/

---

double length word *noun*
two WORDS **(1)** that store a single unit of data

/ˌdʌbl 'leŋθ 'wɜːd/
pl double length words
syn double word

double precision *noun*

a way of storing numerical data using DOUBLE LENGTH WORDS to allow more decimal places to be stored

/,dʌbl prɪ'sɪʒn/

note not used with *a* or *an*. No plural and used with a singular verb only.

◄ **double-precision** arithmetic, data, storage

► **extended precision, precision, single precision**

---

double-sided disk *noun* (hardware)

a disk that can store and record information on both sides

/'dʌbl ,saɪdɪd 'dɪsk/

pl double sided disks

► **disk, single-sided disk**

---

double word *noun*

► **double length word**

/,dʌbl 'wɜːd/

---

doubly-linked list *noun*

a list where each data item contains two POINTERS (1), one to the next item and one to the previous item in the list

/'dʌbli lɪŋkt 'lɪst/

pl doubly-linked lists

◄ access, delete something *from*, insert something *into*, traverse a **doubly-linked list**

► **linked list**

☆**down arrow** *noun* (hardware)

the CURSOR CONTROL KEY with an arrow pointing down

/'daʊn ,ærəʊ/

pl down arrows

◄ hold, press the **down arrow**

► **left arrow, Pg Up, Pg Dn, right arrow, up arrow**

☆**download** *verb* (system operation)

to send a program or some data from a central computer to a terminal or smaller computer: *download the program to another computer* ○ *download programs from a Bulletin Board System via a modem*

/,daʊn'ləʊd/

download, downloading, downloaded

note transitive verb

► **upload**

---

downloadable *adjective*

able to be sent from a central computer to a smaller computer or terminal

/,daʊn'ləʊdəbl/

◄ **downloadable** fonts, programs, software

☆**down time** *noun* (system operation)

the time during which a computer or computer system is not working: *The e-mail directory update will increase server down time by an hour.*

/'daʊn taɪm/

note not used with *a* or *an*. No plural and used with a singular verb only.

---

downwards compatible *adjective*

(of software or hardware) that can work correctly with earlier versions of software or hardware: *The latest version of the word processing package is fully downwards compatible with earlier versions.*

/,daʊnwəds kəm'pætəbl/

(US **downward compatible**)

◄ **downwards compatible** equipment, hardware, software

► **upwards compatible**

☆**DP** *abbr*

► **data processing**

/,diː 'piː/

note pronounced as individual letters

---

abbr abbreviation **pl** plural **syn** synonym ► see ◄ collocate (*word often used with the headword*)

☆**dpi** *abbr*

dots per inch. The number of dots per inch that a screen can display or a printer can print. This is used as a measure of screen or printer RESOLUTION: *The laser printer offers near-typeset quality of 600 dpi.* ○ *The colour dot matrix printer is capable of 180 dpi.*

/ˌdiː piː ˈaɪ/
note pronounced as individual letters

DPM *abbr*

data processing manager

/ˌdiː piː ˈem/
note pronounced as individual letters

---

draft quality *adjective*

(of printed text) that does not have the clearest characters possible: *The draft quality text was only the first rough version of the document.*

note Dot matrix printers usually have a draft mode to print draft quality text.

/ˈdrɑːft ˌkwɒləti/
▶ **letter quality**

---

drag *verb* (operations)

to move an icon, text or graphics, etc from one part of the screen to another, or to move the cursor over text, etc to select it. This is done by holding down the mouse button and moving the mouse at the same time: *To eject the floppy disk, drag the floppy disk icon to the waste basket.* ○ *drag the cursor down the page to highlight the text*

/dræg/
drag, dragging, dragged
note transitive verb
◄ **drag** an icon, a window

☆**DRAM** *abbr* (hardware)

dynamic random access memory. A form of RAM that has to be REFRESHED (1) at regular intervals: *The notebook comes with 16MB DRAM.* ○ *The computer has four spare DRAM slots for memory upgrades.*

/ˈdiː ræm/
▶ **static memory, RAM, memory**

---

drive *noun*
▶ **disk drive**

/draɪv/

---

driver *noun* (software)

software that controls the transfer of data between a computer and a PERIPHERAL

/ˈdraɪvə(r)/
pl drivers
◄ install, remove a **driver**; a printer, screen **driver**
syn handler

DRO *abbr*
▶ **destructive read**

note used in written English only

---

drop dead halt *noun* (software/programming)

1 an instruction from the user that makes the program stop executing without being able to start again: *issue a drop dead halt instruction* **2** an error that makes a program stop executing without being able to start again: *reboot after the drop dead halt*

/ˈdrɒp ded ˈhɔːlt/
pl drop dead halts
▶ **abend, catastrophic error, catastrophic failure, crash**

---

drop out *noun* (hardware)

the situation that occurs when a small piece of disk or tape is not correctly magnetized so that information cannot be stored accurately

/ˈdrɒp aʊt/
note usually singular
▶ **disk error**

---

drum plotter *noun* (hardware)

a type of PLOTTER (= a device that converts data into graphs) where paper is wrapped around the drum with pens moving up and down to record data

/ˈdrʌm ˌplɒtə(r)/
pl drum plotters
▶ **bar chart, flatbed plotter, graph, graph plotter**

dry run *noun*
the process of testing a computer program without using real data: *a dry run of the payroll program*

/ˌdraɪ ˈrʌn/
pl dry runs
⋈ execute, perform, schedule a **dry run**
syn dummy run

DS DD *abbr* (hardware)
double-sided double-density. A measure of the storage capacity of a floppy disk.

/ˌdiː es diː ˈdiː/
note pronounced as individual letters
⋈ a **DS DD** disk
▶ double-density disk, DS HD, high-density disk, single-sided disk

DS HD *abbr* (hardware)
double-sided high-density. A measure of the storage capacity of a floppy disk.

/ˌdiː es eɪtʃ ˈdiː/
note pronounced as individual letters
⋈ a **DS HD** disk
▶ double density disk, DS DD, high density disk, single-sided disk

DSP *abbr*
digital signal processor

/ˌdiː es ˈpiː/
note pronounced as individual letters

DSR *abbr*
▶ data set ready

/ˌdiː es ˈɑː(r)/
note pronounced as individual letters

☆**DSS** *abbr*
▶ decision support system

/ˌdiː es ˈes/
note pronounced as individual letters

DTE *abbr*
data terminal equipment

/ˌdiː tiː ˈiː/
note pronounced as individual letters

☆**DTP** *abbr*
▶ desktop publishing

/ˌdiː tiː ˈpiː/
note pronounced as individual letters

DTR *abbr*
data terminal ready

/ˌdiː tiː ˈɑː(r)/
note pronounced as individual letters

dual in-line package *noun* (hardware)
the standard way of fitting an INTEGRATED CIRCUIT into a device that can be connected to an integrated circuit board

/ˈdjuːəl ɪn ˈlaɪn ˌpækɪdʒ/
pl dual in-line packages
abbr DIL, DIP
⋈ insert, remove a **dual in-line package**

dual processor *noun* (hardware)
a computer system that has two processors so that it can work more quickly

/ˌdjuːəl ˈprəʊsesə(r)/
pl dual processors

---

abbr abbreviation   **pl** plural   **syn** synonym   **▶** see   **⋈** collocate (*word often used with the headword*)

▶ **auxiliary processor,
coprocessor**

☆**dumb terminal** *noun*
▶ **terminal**

/ˌdʌm 'tɜːmɪnl/

dummy argument *noun*
▶ **formal parameter**

/ˌdʌmi 'ɑːgjumənt/

dummy run *noun*
▶ **dry run**

/ˌdʌmi 'rʌn/

dummy variable *noun*
▶ **formal parameter**

/ˌdʌmi 'veəriəbl/

dump¹ *noun*
1 data that is moved from one device or area of storage to
another: *a dump of the end-of-year accounts* **2** a printout of the
contents of some or all of a computer's memory: *a memory
dump*

/dʌmp/
pl dumps
2 ꟷ a file, hex, memory, storage
dump; dump an action, a
check
▶ **screen dump**

☆**dump²** *verb* (system operation/user)
to move data from one device or area of storage to another:
dump the contents of the file to the printer

/dʌmp/
dump, dumping, dumped
note transitive verb
ꟷ **dump** data *to* a disk, printer

duodecimal *adjective*
a system of numbers based on the number 12

/ˌdjuːəʊ'desɪml/
ꟷ a **duodecimal** number, system
▶ **base 12, decimal**

☆**duplex** *adjective* (data transmission)
(of data) that is able to be sent over a data channel in both
directions at the same time

/'djuːpleks/
note no plural
ꟷ **duplex** mode, operation,
transmissions
syn full duplex
▶ **half duplex channel, simplex**

duplex channel *noun*
a data channel that allows DUPLEX transmission

/ˌdjuːpleks 'tʃænl/
pl duplex channels
ꟷ send data *over*, transmit data
via, use a **duplex channel**
syn full duplex channel
▶ **half duplex channel, simplex
channel**

dyadic operation *noun* (software/programming)
an operation that needs two OPERANDS (= pieces of data): *a
dyadic operation that adds two numbers*

/daɪˌædɪk ɒpə'reɪʃn/
pl dyadic operations
ꟷ encode, execute, perform a
dyadic operation
syn binary operation
▶ **monadic operation, operand
field, opcode**

dyadic operator *noun* ▶ **binary operator**	/daɪˌædɪk ˈɒpəreɪtə(r)/
dynamic allocation *noun* a situation where the resources of a computer or system are used when they are needed while a program is running	/daɪˌnæmɪk æləˈkeɪʃn/ **note** not used with *a* or *an*. No plural and used with a singular verb only. ⋈ implement, use **dynamic allocation** ▶ **static allocation**
dynamic buffer *noun* a buffer whose size can change to become bigger or smaller depending on how much it is needed	/daɪˌnæmɪk ˈbʌfə(r)/ **pl** dynamic buffers ▶ **buffer**
dynamic data structure *noun* a DATA STRUCTURE (= a collection of data items considered as one single item) that is not fixed in size and can grow larger or smaller during the execution of a program **note** Lists, queues, trees and stacks are usually dynamic data structures, but arrays are not.	/daɪˌnæmɪk ˈdeɪtə ˌstrʌkʃə(r)/ **pl** dynamic data structures ⋈ access, choose, define, implement, traverse, update a **dynamic data structure** ▶ **static data structure**
dynamic dump *noun* a DUMP¹ (2) (= a printout of the contents of memory) produced at certain times while a program is running	/daɪˌnæmɪk ˈdʌmp/ **pl** dynamic dumps
☆**dynamic RAM** *noun* ▶ **DRAM**	/daɪˌnæmɪk ˈræm/
dynamic storage allocation *noun* a way of giving extra main memory to a program while it is running	/daɪˌnæmɪk ˈstɔːrɪdʒ æləˌkeɪʃn/ **note** not used with *a* or *an*. No plural and used with a singular verb only. ▶ **static allocation**

Ee

E *abbr* the letter which represents the decimal number 14 in hexadecimal notation	/ˈiː/
EAROM *abbr* electrically alterable read only memory	/ˌiː ˈeɪ rɒm/
earth¹ *noun* the electrical state of having no VOLTAGE: *Electrical components may be connected to earth to complete a circuit.*	/ɜːθ/ **note** not used with *a* or *an*. no plural and used with a singular verb only. (US **ground**) ⋈ connect *to*, make a connection *to* **earth**; *an* earth connection, wire

abbr abbreviation   **pl** plural   **syn** synonym   ▶ see   ⋈ collocate (*word often used with the headword*)

earth² *verb*

to connect a wire to a place that has no voltage: *Domestic electrical appliances must usually be earthed for safety.*

/ɜːθ/

earth, earthing, earthed

note transitive verb

(*US* **ground**)

◄ **earth** a circuit, wire

EBCDIC *abbr*

Extended Binary-Coded Decimal Interchange Code

/'ebsiːdɪk/

note pronounced as a word

---

echo¹ *noun*

1 a signal sent back to the sender on the same transmission channel that carried the original signal: *The echo was sent back to the main computer on the network to test that network connections were working correctly.* **2** a type of fault on a telephone line that causes speech or data to be repeated, making the message difficult or impossible to understand: *The echo caused the message to be distorted.* ○ *There is a very bad echo on the line.*

/'ekəʊ/

pl echoes

1 ◄ send back, transmit *via* an **echo**

---

echo² *verb*

1 to send a signal back to the sender over the same transmission channel, usually to confirm that it has been correctly received **2** to repeat speech or data on a telephone line which makes it difficult or impossible to understand: *The line echoes badly.*

/'ekəʊ/

echo, echoing, echoed

1 note transitive verb

◄ **echo** a character, transmission; **echo** data

2 note intransitive verb

---

echo check *noun*

a way of checking that data has been transmitted without errors. This is done by sending transmitted data back to the sender: if there are any differences between the data that was originally sent and the data sent back, an error has occurred: *The communications software is responsible for the echo checks.*

/'ekəʊ tʃek/

pl echo checks

◄ carry out, make use of an **echo check**

---

echo suppression *noun*

the use of electronic circuits to remove an ECHO¹ (2) from a telephone line or transmission channel: *The modem has built in echo suppression.*

/'ekəʊ sə,preʃn/

note no plural

◄ **echo suppression** circuit, modem

ECL *abbr*

electronic cabling link

/,iː siː 'el/

note pronounced as individual letters

---

edge connector *noun* (hardware)

the CONTACTS¹ at the edge of a printed circuit board which fit into an EXPANSION SLOT on a computer

/'edʒ kə,nektə(r)/

pl edge connectors

☆**edit** *verb* (user operation)

to change or modify text or data in a file or an instruction in a program: *edit the file to bring the figures up to date* ○ *edit the document and save the changes*

/'edɪt/

edit, editing, edited

note transitive verb

► line editor, text editor

---

edit key *noun* (hardware)

a key that can be pressed to allow some editing function to be performed on text, such as deleting a character. An edit key may also be used to switch to EDIT MODE.

/'edɪt kiː/

pl edit keys

◄ press, use the **edit key**

edit mode *noun*
the state word processing software is in when a user can make changes such as deleting blocks of text

/'edɪt məʊd/
note usually singular
◄ change *to*, enter, get out *of*, move *to* **edit mode**
▶ **command mode**

editor *noun* (software)
a software program that allows a user to make changes to a file

/'edɪtə(r)/
pl editors
◄ an HTML, an SGML **editor**
▶ **line editor, text editor**

EDP *abbr*
▶ **electronic data processing**

/ˌiː diː ˈpiː/
note pronounced as individual letters

EEPROM *abbr*
electrically erasable PROM

/ˈiːprɒm/
note pronounced as a word
▶ **EPROM**

EEROM *abbr*
electrically erasable ROM

/ˈiːrɒm/
note pronounced as a word

EFT *abbr*
▶ **electronic funds transfer**

/ˌiː ef ˈtiː/
note pronounced as individual letters

EGA *abbr*
▶ **enhanced graphics adaptor**

/ˌiː dʒiː ˈeɪ/
note pronounced as individual letters

80 column printer *noun* (hardware)
a printer which can print no more than 80 characters per line

/ˌeɪti kɒləm ˈprɪntə(r)/
pl 80 column printers

elastic banding *noun* (applications/graphics)
a way of changing the shape of an object on screen by holding it and pulling it to another part of the screen

/ɪˌlæstɪk ˈbændɪŋ/
note not used with *a* or *an*. No plural and used with a singular verb only.
syn rubber banding

electronic data processing *noun* (applications)
the use of computers to input, store and process data: *Use of the computer system for electronic data processing takes the form of cataloguing books in the library.*

/ɪˌlektrɒnɪk ˈdeɪtə ˌprəʊsesɪŋ/
note not used with *a* or *an*. No plural and used with a singular verb only.
abbr EDP
◄ **electronic data processing** algorithms, methods, systems

electronic funds transfer *noun* (applications)
the use of computer systems to transfer money from one person or organization to another person or organization: *The use of electronic funds transfers has made banking one of the largest users of computing.*

/ɪˌlektrɒnɪk ˈfʌndz ˌtrænsfɜː(r)/
pl electronic funds transfers
abbr EFT
◄ carry out an **electronic funds transfer**

☆**electronic mail** *noun*
▶ **e-mail**

/ɪˌlektrɒnɪk ˈmeɪl/

electronic point of sale *noun*
▶ **EPOS**

/ɪˈlektrɒnɪk ˈpɔɪnt əv ˈseɪl/

abbr abbreviation   **pl** plural   **syn** synonym   ▶ see   ◄ collocate (*word often used with the headword*)

electronic publishing *noun*
the production of books, etc in a form that can be read by a computer: *The company's electronic publishing activities include making academic journals available in electronic form on the Internet.* ○ *The electronic publishing done by division includes several multimedia titles on CD-ROM.*

/ɪ,lektrɒnɪk ˈpʌblɪʃɪŋ/
note no plural

electrostatic printer *noun* (hardware)
a printer that charges the paper with a certain type of electricity and uses ink with an opposite charge to make the ink stick to the paper: *send the map to the electrostatic printer*

/ɪ,lektrəʊˈstætɪk ˈprɪntə(r)/
pl electrostatic printers
▶ **printer**

☆**e-mail¹** *noun*
1 electronic mail. Data and messages sent to users on a computer network: *send e-mail over the Internet* **2** a way of sending messages and data to users on a network: *communicate by e-mail* ○ *send a fax by e-mail* **3** a message or data sent to a user on a network: *E-mails requesting help with computers are sent to the systems analyst all the time.*

/ˈiː meɪl/
(also **Email, E-mail, email**)
1,2 note no plural
◄ delete, forward, send, receive **e-mail**
3 pl e-mails

☆**e-mail²** *verb*
to send electronic mail messages to users on a computer network: *The group administrator e-mailed details of a meeting to all members of the department.*

/ˈiː meɪl/
e-mail, e-mailing, e-mailed
note transitive verb

☆**embed** *verb* (hardware)
to put a device in another device or system: *embed the compact disc drive between the monitor and the hard disk drive*

/ɪmˈbed/
embed, embedding, embedded
note transitive verb

embedded computer *noun*
▶ **embedded system**

/ɪm,bedɪd kəmˈpjuːtə(r)/

embedded program *noun*
a computer program that executes on an EMBEDDED SYSTEM

/ɪm,bedɪd ˈprəʊgræm/
pl embedded programs
◄ design, load, write an **embedded program**

embedded system *noun*
a computer system built into a piece of non-computing equipment to control it: *The machine tool is monitored by an embedded system.*

/ɪm,bedɪd ˈsɪstəm/
pl embedded systems
◄ design, implement, install an **embedded system**
syn embedded computer

empty list *noun*
a list that does not contain any data items

note An empty list is usually written as 'nil' or as ().

/,empti ˈlɪst/
pl empty lists
◄ access, construct, delete an **empty list**
syn null list

empty string *noun*
a string that does not contain any characters: *an array with empty strings*

/,empti ˈstrɪŋ/
pl empty strings
◄ enter, print, test *for* an **empty string**
syn null string

emulate *verb*

to make one system act in the same way as another: *The new computer system was emulated on another computer during the design phase.*

/ˈemjuleɪt/

emulate, emulating, emulated

note transitive verb

◣ **emulate** a computer, system; **emulate** hardware, software

---

☆**emulator** *noun* (hardware/software)

hardware and software that allow a computer to operate as if it were a different type of computer: *Emulators are often used in computer development.*

/ˈemjuleɪtə(r)/

pl emulators

▶ **simulator, terminal emulation, virtual**

---

enable *verb*

to make a device or part of a system able to work: *enable the mouse by switching on the mouse key on the control panel*

/ɪˈneɪbl/

enable, enabling, enabled

note transitive verb

◣ **enable** a computer, a fax, an interrupt, a keyboard, a machine, a modem, a printer

▶ **disable**

---

encipher *verb*

to change data or a message into a CIPHER (2)

/ɪnˈsaɪfə(r)/

encipher, enciphering, enciphered

note transitive verb

☆**encode** *verb*

▶ **code²**

/ɪnˈkəʊd/

---

encoder *noun* (hardware/software)

a program or a computer system that converts data into a form accepted by a computer: *an integrated video encoder*

/ɪnˈkəʊdə(r)/

pl encoders

---

encoding *noun*

▶ **coding**

/ɪnˈkəʊdɪŋ/

---

encrypt *verb*

to change data into code, especially to prevent unauthorized access to the data: *encrypt the file directories* ○ *encrypt the data on the hard disk to ensure that it is secure* ○ *The system encrypts the password the first time the data transfer program is run.*

/ɪnˈkrɪpt/

encrypt, encrypting, encrypted

note transitive verb

---

encryption *noun*

the process of changing data into code, especially to prevent unauthorized access to the data: *Data encryption allows data to be saved to disk in encoded form.* ○ *Network security is offered through data encryption and user passwords.*

/ɪnˈkrɪpʃn/

note no plural

syn file encryption

▶ **data encryption standard**

☆**end** *noun* (hardware)

a key used move the cursor to the end of a document or page: *press 'end' to get to the bottom of the text*

/end/

note Not used with *a* or *an*. No plural and used with a singular verb only.

syn end key

▶ **cursor control key, home**

---

end around carry *noun*

the part of a ROTATE OPERATION which moves a bit (binary digit) out of one end of a word and puts it into the other end of the word

/ˈend əˌraʊnd ˈkæri/

pl end around carries

◣ execute, perform an **end around carry**

---

abbr abbreviation **pl** plural **syn** synonym ▶ see ◣ collocate (*word often used with the headword*)

☆**end key** *noun* ▶ **end**	/'end kiː/
endless loop *noun* ▶ **infinite loop**	/,endləs 'luːp/
end of field marker *noun* ▶ **field separator**	/,end əv 'fiːld ,mɑːkə(r)/
end of file *noun* (software) a character or set of characters that is used to show where the data in a file ends	/,end əv 'faɪl/ **note** no plural **abbr** EOF ◀ an **end of file** marker ▶ **file, header**
end of text character *noun* the CONTROL CHARACTER with ASCII code number 3 which is used to mark the end of a piece of text	/,end əv 'tekst ,kærəktə(r)/ **pl** end of text characters **abbr** ETX ◀ receive, send, transmit, type an **end of text character**
end of transmission character *noun* the CONTROL CHARACTER with ASCII code number 4 which is used to mark the end of a transmission	/,end əv trænsˈmɪʃn ,kærəktə(r)/ **note** not used with *a* or *an*. No plural and used with a singular verb only. **abbr** EOT ◀ insert, send, transmit the **end of transmission character**
end user *noun* ▶ **user**	/'end ,juːzə(r)/
enhanced graphics adaptor *noun* (hardware) a GRAPHICS ADAPTOR which allows a screen to display 16 colours and text: *The enhanced graphics adaptor is built into the PC to give sharper characters and improved colours.*	/ɪn,hɑːnst 'græfiks ə,dæptə(r)/ **pl** enhanced graphics adaptors (also enhanced graphics adapter) **abbr** EGA ▶ **VGA**
enorder traversal *noun* ▶ **symmetric traversal**	/en,ɔːdə trəˈvɜːsl/
ENQ *abbr* the ASCII symbol number 5 for enquiry	**note** used in written English only
☆**enter¹** *noun* (hardware) the key that is pressed to tell the operating system to execute a command or to mark the end of a paragraph in a word processing program	/'entə(r)/ **note** not used with *a* or *an*. No plural and used with a singular verb only. ▶ **return¹**
☆**enter²** *verb* (user operation) to put information into a computer using a keyboard or other device: *enter figures into a spreadsheet* ○ *enter data in the database*	/'entə(r)/ **enter, entering, entered** **note** transitive verb ◀ **enter** data, figures, information, words ▶ **insert, install, load, retrieve**

enter key *noun*
▶ **enter**[1]

/'entə kiː/

---

entity *noun* (database)
an item that has data stored with it: *In the staff database, STAFF MEMBER is one of the entities with data including the name, address and salary of each person in the company.*

/'entəti/
pl entities
◄ define an **entity**; an **entity** diagram
▶ **attribute 2**

---

entry level system *noun*
the hardware and software that is offered for sale to individuals or companies who are starting to use computers or want to use a computer in a new area: *The retailer recommends a certain combination of hardware and software as an entry level system for computer aided design.*

/'entri levl ˌsɪstəm/
pl entry level systems
◄ buy, sell, use an **entry level system**

---

entry point *noun* (software/programming)
the instruction in a SUBROUTINE or FUNCTION that is executed first when the subroutine is called: *The subroutine offers a choice of entry points.*

/'entri pɔɪnt/
pl entry points
◄ branch *to*, jump *to* an **entry point**

---

envelope *noun*
the way sound changes when it is heard on a computer system: *Careful adjustment of the sound envelope makes a computer generated noise sound like a musical instrument.*

/'envələʊp/
pl envelopes
◄ amplitude, pitch **envelope**; adjust, define, reproduce an **envelope**

☆**environment** *noun*
the resources, physical layout and organization of hardware in a computer system: *work in a Macintosh environment*

/ɪn'vaɪrənmənt/
pl environments
◄ an applications, a mainframe, a network, an object-oriented, a Unix, a windows-based **environment**

EOF *abbr*
▶ **end of file**

/ˌiː əʊ 'ef/
note pronounced as individual letters

EOT *abbr*
▶ **end of transmission character**

/ˌiː əʊ 'tiː/
note pronounced as individual letters

EPOS *abbr* (hardware/software)
electronic point of sale. A system that uses computer hardware and software for stock control and pricing, etc: *install an electronic point of sale system*

/'iː pɒs/
note pronounced as a word

EPROM *noun* (hardware)
erasable programmable read-only memory. PROGRAMMABLE READ-ONLY MEMORY which can be cleared by the user so that a new program can be written in the same part of memory: *EPROMS can be rewritten a limited number of times.*

/'iː prɒm/
pl EPROMs
◄ blow, burn, erase, install, read *from*, write *to* an **EPROM**
syn erasable PROM

---

abbr abbreviation   **pl** plural   **syn** synonym   ▶ see   **◄** collocate (*word often used with the headword*)

EPS *abbr*
encapsulated postscript

/ˌiː piː ˈes/

note pronounced as individual letters

EQ circuit *abbr*
▶ **EQ gate**

/ˌiː ˈkjuː ˌsɜːkɪt/

EQ gate *abbr*
equivalence gate. An electronic circuit whose output is logic 1 if and only if all its inputs have the same value: all logic 1 or all logic 0: *a four input EQ gate chip*

/ˌiː ˈkjuː geɪt/

pl EQ gates

ᴎ a fast, single-chip **EQ gate**

syn equivalence gate

▶ **equivalence**

---

equivalence *noun*
a logical operation combining two logical expressions: *The figure shows the truth table for the equivalence operator.*

note The usual symbols for equivalence are '<=>' or three parallel bars. A<=>B is TRUE if and only if A and B always have the same truth values, so if A is TRUE then B is TRUE, and if A is FALSE then B is FALSE.

/ɪˈkwɪvələns/

note usually singular

ᴎ an **equivalence** function, operator, symbol

---

equivalence gate *noun*
▶ **EQ gate**

/ɪˈkwɪvələns geɪt/

---

erasable *adjective*
1 (of data) that is able to be removed from a disk or file, etc
2 (of a storage device) that can have data removed from it

/ɪˈreɪzəbl/

2 ᴎ erasable circuitry, computer memory; an **erasable** chip, compact disc, optical disk drive

---

erasable PROM *noun*
▶ **EPROM**

/ɪˌreɪzəbl ˈprɒm/

---

erasable storage *noun* (hardware)
any type of memory that can be reused by removing the data stored in it, and replacing that data with new data

/ɪˌreɪzəbl ˈstɔːrɪdʒ/

note no plural

☆**erase** *verb* (system operation)
to remove data permanently from a file or disk

/ɪˈreɪz/

erase, erasing, erased

note transitive verb

▶ **delete²**

☆**error** *noun*
a mistake, especially one that stops a program from executing or brings a computer system to a HALT¹: *an error in the command line*

/ˈerə(r)/

pl errors

ᴎ check *for*, read *for* an **error**; an **error** message

▶ **bug**

---

error checking *noun*
the process of identifying mistakes in data: *The error checking identified several parity errors.*

/ˈerə ˌtʃekɪŋ/

note no plural

ᴎ an **error checking** algorithm, routine; **error checking** hardware, software

▶ **validate, verify, vet**

error condition *noun*

the state that a program or device is in when an error has occurred: *One small error condition such as a user out of disk quota can cause several system errors.* ○ *When an operand is unsuitable for processing, the hardware automatically signals an error condition for treatment by software.*

/'erə kən,dıʃn/
pl error conditions
⋈ cause, deal *with*, enter, recover *from*, resolve, signal an **error condition**

---

error correcting code *noun* (software)

a method of coding data which allows errors to be corrected during storage or transmission

/'erə kə,rektıŋ 'kəʊd/
pl error correcting codes
(also **error correction code**)
⋈ design, use an **error correcting code**
▶ **parity check**

---

error correction *noun*

the process of finding mistakes in data and changing the data to the correct form

/'erə kə,rekʃn/
note no plural
⋈ an **error correction** algorithm, code, protocol, routine; **error correction** hardware, software

---

error detection *noun*

the process of finding mistakes in data

/'erə dı,tekʃn/
note no plural
⋈ an **error detection** algorithm, code, protocol, routine; **error detection** hardware, software

---

error handling *noun*

the use of special ROUTINES to correct errors in hardware or software so that a program can continue to execute: *Error handling allows the program to recover from run-time errors.*

/'erə ,hændlıŋ/
note no plural
⋈ an **error handling** module, routine
syn error recovery

---

error rate *noun*

the number of errors in a data transmission compared to the total amount of data that was sent: *a six per cent error rate*

/'erə reıt/
pl error rates
⋈ a high, low, satisfactory, unsatisfactory **error rate**

---

error recovery *noun*
▶ **error handling**

/'erə rı,kʌvəri/

---

esc *abbr*
▶ **escape¹**

note used in written English only

☆**escape¹** *noun* (hardware)

a key on a keyboard which is used to cancel an operation or to exit a program, etc: *press 'escape' to return to the main menu* ○ *hit 'escape' to exit the program*

/ı'skeıp/
note not used with *a* or *an*. No plural and used with a singular verb only.
abbr esc
▶ **return**

☆**escape²** *verb* (user operation)

to leave an operation, command or program, etc

/ı'skeıp/
escape, escaping, escaped
note intransitive verb
⋈ **escape** *from* a program, etc
▶ **exit, quit**

---

abbr abbreviation   **pl** plural   **syn** synonym   ▶ see   ⋈ collocate (*word often used with the headword*)

escape code *noun*
► **escape sequence**

/ɪˈskeɪp kəʊd/

☆**escape key** *noun*
► **escape**[1]

/ɪˈskeɪp kiː/

---

escape sequence *noun* (software)
a number of CONTROL CHARACTERS in a certain order which are
sent as part of a data transmission to show that the characters
that follow these control characters must be processed
differently: *After sending an escape sequence, the following
characters may be interpreted as graphics characters.*

/ɪˈskeɪp ˌsiːkwəns/
pl escape sequences
◪ receive, send, transmit an
escape sequence
syn escape code

Ethernet *noun*
(*trade mark*) (*network*) a type of local area network: *PC users are
connected by Ethernet to the server.*

/ˈiːθənet/
note no plural
(also **ethernet**)
◪ be connected *to*, install, send
data *over* **Ethernet**; an
Ethernet adaptor, backbone,
cable, card, connection,
controller, interface, port,
system
► **local area network,
protocol, thick Ethernet,
thin Ethernet**

ETX *abbr*
► **end of text character**

/ˌiː tiː ˈeks/
note pronounced as individual
letters

---

even parity *noun*
► **parity 1**

/ˌiːvn ˈpærəti/

---

event *noun*
something that happens in a computer system. This may be
detected by software and cause some other action to happen:
*The event of a key being pressed causes the software to identify
which key it is.*

/ɪˈvent/
pl events
◪ cause, respond *to*, service an
event; **event** driven

---

exchangeable disk *noun* (hardware)
a hard disk that can be removed from the disk drive

note A floppy disk is also an exchangeable disk but the term is
always used to talk about hard disks.

/ɪksˌtʃeɪndʒəbl ˈdɪsk/
pl exchangeable disks
◪ back up *onto*, insert, remove,
replace an **exchangeable disk**

---

exchange selection sort *noun*
► **bubble sort**

/ɪksˌtʃeɪndʒ sɪˈlekʃn sɔːt/

---

exclusive OR *noun*
► **EXOR operation**

/ɪkˌskluːsɪv ˈɔː(r)/

---

executable program *noun* (software)
a program that can be run: *an executable program written in a
high-level language*

/ˌeksɪkjuːtəbl ˈprəʊɡræm/
pl executable programs
► **compile, translate**

☆**execute** *verb* (system operation)
to run a program or an instruction: *The computer executes the
program.* ○ *A bug stops the program from executing.*

/ˈeksɪkjuːt/
**execute, executing,
executed**

	note transitive or intransitive verb
	◪ **execute** a phase, step
	▶ **fetch-execute cycle**

---

execution error *noun* (system operation)
mistake that happens while a program is running: *check for execution errors*

/ˌeksɪˈkjuːʃn ˌerə(r)/
pl execution errors
◪ detect an **execution error**
▶ **bug, compilation error**

---

execution time *noun*
the amount of time it takes a program, etc to execute: *extra memory usually improves execution time* ○ *measure the execution time required by each algorithm to process the documents*

/ˌeksɪˈkjuːʃn taɪm/
pl execution times
◪ improve, measure, shorten the **execution time**

---

executive program *noun*
▶ **operating system**

/ɪgˈzekjətɪv ˌprəʊgræm/

☆**exit** *verb* (software)
(*user operation*) to leave a program and return to a directory or operating system, etc: *exit a word processing program* ○ *hit escape to exit*

/ˈeksɪt/
exit, exiting, exited
note transitive or intransitive verb
◪ **exit** a program
▶ **escape², quit**

EXOR *noun*
▶ **EXOR operation**

/ˈeksɔː(r)/

EXOR circuit *noun*
▶ **EXOR gate**

/ˈeksɔː ˌsɜːkɪt/

EXOR gate *noun* (hardware)
an electronic circuit whose output is logic 0 if and only if its inputs (two or more) are all set to logic 0 or are all set to logic 1. Otherwise its output is 1. This action corresponds to an EXOR OPERATION: *The chip provides four EXOR gates in a single 14-pin package.*

/ˈeksɔː geɪt/
pl EXOR gates
syn XOR gate
◪ connect *to*, drive, use an **EXOR gate**
syn EXOR circuit, XOR gate
▶ **OR gate**

EXOR operation *noun* (mathematics)
exclusive OR operation. A logical operation combining two logical expressions. The combined expression P EXOR Q is FALSE if and only if expression P and expression Q are both FALSE or both TRUE. Otherwise it is TRUE: *The statement contains three EXOR operations.*

/ˈeksɔː(r) ˌɒpəˌreɪʃn/
pl EXOR operations
◪ do, implement, program an **EXOR operation**
syn exclusive OR, EXOR, XOR
▶ **Boolean Connective, OR operation**

☆**expanded memory** *noun* (hardware)
additional memory that is accessed through an adaptor: *make use of expanded memory*

/ɪkˌspændɪd ˈmeməri/
note no plural
▶ **memory**

---

abbr abbreviation   **pl** plural   **syn** synonym   ▶ see   ◪ collocate (*word often used with the headword*)

expanded memory manager *noun*
software in the operating system which controls access to
extra memory that is added to overcome the limitations of the
basic PC memory

/ɪk,spændɪd 'meməri
,mænɪdʒə(r)/
pl expanded memory managers
◣ install an **expanded memory manager**
▶ **expanded memory**

---

expansion board *noun* (hardware)
a printed circuit board that is added to a computer to increase
its performance or to allow it to be connected to another
device: *an expansion board for high-resolution graphical display* ○
an expansion board with extra RAM

/ɪk'spænʃn bɔːd/
pl expansion boards
◣ communicate *via*, install, use
an **expansion board**
syn add-on board, expansion card
▶ **expansion slot,
motherboard, daughter
board**

---

expansion card *noun*
▶ **expansion board**

/ɪk'spænʃn kɑːd/

---

expansion slot *noun*
a place inside a computer where an EXPANSION BOARD is
connected: *plug the high-resolution graphics board into an unused
expansion slot*

/ɪk'spænʃn slɒt/
pl expansion slots
◣ connect an expansion board *to*,
plug an expansion board *into* an
expansion slot
▶ **daughter board, edge
connector, motherboard**

☆**expert system** *noun* (software/applications)
a computer program or set of computer programs that are
designed to include the knowledge and reasoning of experts
and are used to help solve problems in certain areas, such as
medicine and banking, etc: *an expert system that deals with
project management tasks*

/,ekspɜːt 'sɪstəm/
pl expert systems
◣ build, feed data *into*, use, write
an **expert system**; a diagnostic
expert system
syn intelligent knowledge-based
system
▶ **artificial intelligence,
decision support system,
knowledge-based system**

---

exponent *noun*
▶ **characteristic**

/ɪk'spəʊnənt/

☆**export** *verb* (user operation)
to move information from one program or system to another:
export the file in ASCII

/ɪk'spɔːt/
export, exporting, exported
note transitive verb
▶ **import**

---

extended character set *noun* (software)
a set of CHARACTER CODES allowing the user to store and display
characters such as foreign letters and mathematical symbols
which are not normally found on the computer keyboard

/ɪk,stendɪd 'kærəktə set/
pl extended character sets
◣ define, use an **extended
character set**
▶ **character set**

☆**extended memory** *noun*
▶ **expanded memory**

/ɪk,stendɪd 'meməri/

extended precision *noun*
the use of more than one memory location for storing a
number to allow the number to be represented more
accurately

note Extended precision is common in scientific programming
languages.

/ɪkˌstendɪd prɪˈsɪʒn/
note no plural
◄ **extended precision**
  algorithms, data,
  representations
► **double precision, precision**

☆**extension** *noun* (software)
the set of three characters placed after a dot at end of a
filename. An extension can be added by the user or
automatically. It usually shows what a program can do with a
file: *identify the file by making the extension the first three letters of
your name* ○ *The extension .EXE on the file NETSCAPE.EXE
shows that the program is executable and can be loaded and run.*

note Extensions are most often used in the DOS operating
system.

/ɪkˈstenʃn/
pl extensions
◄ a .BAS, .DOC, .EPS, .TXT
  extension
syn filename extension

extent *noun*
the amount of memory occupied by a data file or program

/ɪkˈstent/
note usually singular
◄ exceed, measure, record the
  extent
syn file extent

external interrupt *noun*
an INTERRUPT[1] (= a signal to the CPU asking for attention) that
comes from outside the computer system: *The network generated
an external interrupt.*

/ɪkˌstɜːnl ˈɪntərʌpt/
pl external interrupts
◄ cause, handle, issue, respond *to*
  an **external interrupt**;
  an **external interrupt** request,
  service routine, signal, system
► **internal interrupt**

external memory *noun*
memory that is outside the CPU, such as disk or tape: *The
computer has five external memory devices including the network
file server.*

/ɪkˌstɜːnl ˈmeməri/
note usually singular
◄ access, back up *onto*, store *in/on*
  external memory

external schema *noun*
► **logical schema**

/ɪkˌstɜːnl ˈskiːmə/

external storage *noun*
► **auxiliary memory**

/ɪkˌstɜːnl ˈstɔːrɪdʒ/

Ff

F *abbr*
the letter which represents the decimal number 15 in
hexadecimal notation

/ef/

f *abbr*
► **femto**

/ef/

face *noun*
► **typeface**

/feɪs/

abbr abbreviation　　**pl** plural　　**syn** synonym　　► see　　◄ collocate (*word often used with the headword*)

facsimile *noun*
▶ **fax**[1]

/fæk'sɪməli/

☆**facsimile transmission** *noun*
▶ **fax**[1]

/fæk'sɪməli træns,mɪʃn/

---

fail-safe system *noun*
a computer system that is designed to save important data if part of the system breaks down or if power is lost: *A fail-safe system is important in safety-critical applications.*

/'feɪl seɪf ,sɪstəm/
pl fail-safe systems
Ⅺ design, operate a **fail-safe system**

---

fail-soft system *noun*
▶ **fault tolerant system**

/'feɪl sɒft ,sɪstəm/

☆**failure** *noun*
a situation where a computer system or device stops working, usually because of loss of power

/'feɪljə(r)/
pl failures
Ⅺ a mechanical, system **failure**; **failure** rate
▶ **crash, fault**

FALSE *noun* (logic)
one of the two values that a logical expression can have in formal logic

note Logical FALSE is written in capital letters to show that it is different from the word 'false' used in ordinary language.

/fɔːls/
note not used with *a* or *an*. No plural and used with a singular verb only.
Ⅺ assign the value, evaluate *to*, take the value **FALSE**
▶ **TRUE**

---

family *noun*
a set of computers from one manufacturer: *The IBM 360 family.* ○ *Early computers in the family had small memories and slow processing speeds.* ○ *The software is compatible with every computer in the family.*

/'fæməli/
pl families

---

fan-in *noun* (hardware)
1 the number of inputs to a circuit

note The simplest binary addition circuit has a fan-in of two.

2 the number of places in a computer program from which a subroutine or module may be CALLED: *This module has a high fan-in.*

/'fæn ɪn/
note usually singular
1,2 Ⅺ a high, low **fan-in**

---

fan-out *noun* (hardware)
1 the number of outputs from a circuit

note The simplest binary addition circuit has a fan-out of two: a 'sum' output and a 'carry' output. Logic circuits with a fan-out of one are called 'gates'.

2 the number of SUBROUTINES or modules CALLED from a particular part of a computer program: *This module has a low fan-out.*

/'fæn aʊt/
note usually singular
1,2 Ⅺ a high, low **fan-out**

fatal error *noun*

a failure in a computer program which makes the program
stop executing, or a failure in a physical device which causes
the computer system to fail. A fatal error cannot be corrected
by the program or system; it must be done by the user or
programmer: *The fatal error caused the program to abort.* ○ *A fatal
error has occurred.*

/ˌfeɪtl ˈerə(r)/
pl fatal errors

---

father file *noun*

an older version of a SON FILE

/ˈfɑːθə faɪl/
pl father files
▶ **grandfather-father-son file**

☆**fault** *noun*

a problem with a device or in a program: *The crash was caused
by a fault in the disk drive.* ○ *The fault in the program was solved by
rewriting a line of code.*

/fɔːlt/
pl faults
ⴴ detect, find a **fault**
▶ **bug, failure**

---

fault tolerant system *noun*

a computer system which continues to work after one or more
COMPONENTS has failed

note If a fault tolerant system continues to work at a reduced
level, the system is said to be in a state of graceful degradation.

/ˈfɔːlt ˌtɒlərənt ˈsɪstəm/
pl fault tolerant systems
ⴴ provide a **fault tolerant
system**
syn graceful degradation, fail-soft
system
▶ **fail-safe system**

☆**fax¹** *noun*

a document which is transmitted over telephone lines in
digital form to a fax machine. Faxes can be sent from one fax
machine to another, or from a computer with the necessary
hardware and software: *confirm receipt of the fax*

/fæks/
pl faxes
ⴴ receive, send, transmit a **fax**

☆**fax²** *verb*

to send a fax: *fax the information from the computer terminal*

/fæks/
fax, faxing, faxed
note transitive verb
ⴴ **fax** a document

---

faxboard *noun* (hardware)

a device attached to a computer that enables it to send faxes

/ˈfæksbɔːd/
pl faxboards
ⴴ add, install, use a **faxboard**

---

fax machine *noun* (hardware)

a device that can send documents over phone lines in digital
form and also receive and print them: *The fax machine has run
out of paper.*

/ˈfæks məˌʃiːn/
pl fax machines
ⴴ install, use a **fax machine**

FCB *abbr*
▶ **file control block**

/ˌef siː ˈbiː/
note pronounced as individual
letters

FDC *abbr*
▶ **floppy disk controller**

/ˌef diː ˈsiː/
note pronounced as individual
letters

FDM *abbr*
▶ **frequency division multiplexing**

/ˌef diː ˈem/
note pronounced as individual
letters

---

abbr abbreviation   **pl** plural   **syn** synonym   ▶ see   ⴴ collocate (*word often used with the headword*)

feasibility study *noun*

a study of the costs and performance of a computer system to assess whether it will be useful in a certain situation: *The feasibility study proved that the system was too expensive for the new company and that the old system was more cost-efficient.* ○ *Investors require a detailed feasibility study before they will decide to invest in the project.* ○ *The results of research formed the first part of the feasibility study.*

/ˌfiːzəˈbɪləti ˌstʌdi/
pl feasibility studies

◄ carry out, conduct, commission, disregard, draw up, undertake a **feasibility study**

---

feed *verb*

to put something into something else, especially paper into a printer or data into a computer: *the printer automatically feeds in stationery* ○ *feed the raw data into the statistics program*

/fiːd/
feed, feeding, fed
note transitive verb

---

feedback *noun*

1 information about the way something works. This information can be used to make changes: *feedback from customers about the latest release of the software* **2** data passed from a device which is measuring something back to a computer program that controls the behaviour or operation of that thing: *Temperature sensors provide continuous feedback for the heating device.*

/ˈfiːdbæk/
note no plural

1,2 ◄ act on, get, obtain **feedback**

2 ◄ continuous, intermittent, negative, positive **feedback**

---

feedback loop *noun*

the route taken by data that is fed back to a controlling device that causes a change: *The feedback loop is from the heater, which warms the air, via sensors which report the current temperature and back to the heater to decide if it can be turned off for a time.*

/ˈfiːdbæk ˌluːp/
pl feedback loops

◄ follow a **feedback loop**

---

feeder *noun* (hardware)

a device that feeds something into something else, especially paper into a printer: *An envelope feeder is an optional extra with this printer.*

/ˈfiːdə(r)/
pl feeders

◄ install a **feeder**; a sheet, envelope **feeder**

► **continuous feed, cut sheet feeder**

---

female connector *noun* (hardware)

a device which is used when electrical connections are made between cables and computers, etc and which a MALE CONNECTOR fits into: *use a female connector on the live side of a high-voltage electrical connection*

/ˌfiːmeɪl kəˈnektə(r)/
pl female connectors

◄ connect *to*, plug *into*, use a **female connector**

syn female socket

---

female socket *noun*
► **female connector**

/ˌfiːmeɪl ˈsɒkɪt/

---

femto *prefix*

1 (*UK*) one thousand million millionth or one thousand billionth

note Expressed as a number, femto is 10^{-15}, said as 'ten to the minus fifteen'.

2 (*US*) one million billionth or one thousand trillionth

/ˈfemtəʊ/
abbr f

◄ a **femto** second

► **pico, nano**

FEP *abbr*
► **front-end processor**

/ˌef iː ˈpiː/
note pronounced as individual letters

FET *abbr*
▶ **field effect transistor**

/ˌef iː ˈtiː/

note pronounced as individual letters

---

fetch¹ *noun*
the process of bringing data or an instruction from a memory location to the CPU

/fetʃ/

pl fetches

◄ perform a **fetch**

syn fetch instruction

---

fetch² *verb* (programming)
to bring data or an instruction from a memory location to the CPU: *fetch the next instruction from store*

/fetʃ/

fetch, fetching, fetched

note transitive verb

◄ **fetch** an instruction; **fetch** data

---

fetch execute cycle *noun*
▶ **instruction cycle**

/ˌfetʃ ˈeksɪkjuːt ˌsaɪkl/

---

fetch instruction *noun*
▶ **fetch¹**

/ˈfetʃ ɪnˌstrʌkʃn/

FF *abbr*
▶ **form feed**

note used in written English only

---

fibre optic cable *noun* (hardware)
a cable made of long thin pieces of glass or clear plastic which carry signals of light that are MODULATED so that they transmit data: *use fibre optic cables to increase the volume and speed of data transmission*

/ˌfaɪbə(r) ˈɒptɪk ˌkeɪbl/

pl fibre optic cables

◄ install, transmit data *on/over* a **fibre optic cable**

(*US* **fiber optic cable**)

---

fibre optics *noun* (hardware)
the technology that allows MODULATED signals of light to move along a FIBRE OPTIC CABLE to transmit data

/ˌfaɪbə(r) ˈɒptɪks/

note not used with *a* or *an*. No plural and used with a singular verb only.

(*US* **fiber optics**)

---

fiche *noun*
▶ **microfiche**

/fiːʃ/

☆**field** *noun* (software)
1 a part of a record that represents an item of data: *In the database, STAFF MEMBER is a key field that has a unique number.* **2** the area in which a magnetic or electrical force is present: *the particle's magnetic field*

/fiːld/

pl fields

1 ▶ **file**

---

field effect transistor *noun* (hardware)
a type of TRANSISTOR used in switches and amplifiers: *A field effect transistor is very effective in amplifying small signals.*

/ˈfiːld ɪˌfekt trænˈzɪstə(r)/

pl field effect transistors

abbr FET

◄ an array *of*, a chip *containing* **field effect transistors**

---

field engineer *noun* (personnel)
a person who maintains and repairs computers at the place where they are used: *A field engineer helps to minimize down time in the event of computer failures.*

/ˈfiːld endʒɪˌnɪə(r)/

pl field engineers

◄ contract, employ a **field engineer**

---

abbr abbreviation   **pl** plural   **syn** synonym   ▶ see   ◄ collocate (*word often used with the headword*)

field marker *noun*
▶ field separator

/ˈfiːld ˌmɑːkə(r)/

---

field separator *noun*
a character that marks the end of a field in a data record

/ˈfiːld ˌsepəreɪtə(r)/
pl field separators

M insert, read, write a **field separator**

syn field marker, end of field marker

---

field tested *adjective*
(of hardware and software) that has been used and tested in a real situation, not just in a laboratory or factory: *A major strength of the new software is that it is extensively field tested.*

/ˈfiːld ˌtestɪd/

FIFO *abbr*
▶ first in, first out

/ˈfaɪfəʊ/
note pronounced as a word

☆**fifth generation** *noun* (hardware)
a stage of computer design of machines and systems that include fast processing, large memory and user interaction by sound and touch: *Expert systems will be a key element of computers of the fifth generation.*

note Fifth generation computers are expected to be used in the twenty-first century.

/ˈfɪfθ ˌdʒenəˈreɪʃn/
pl no plural

▶ first generation, fourth generation, second generation, third generation

---

☆**file** *noun* (software)
a collection of data in electronically recorded form which is the basic unit of storage in a computer system. A file can be a program, a document created by a user or data used by a program, etc: *The document is in a file on the hard disk of computer 14.* ○ *The screensavers are in a file in the system folder on the hard disk.*

/faɪl/
pl files

M an ASCII, a binary **file**: access, amend, back up, change, create, delete, open, save, update a **file**

syn data file, computer file, program file

▶ directory, end of file, subdirectory

---

file control block *noun*
a part of memory that contains information about files, such as the name of the file and its location on disk

/ˌfaɪl kənˈtrəʊl blɒk/
pl file control blocks
abbr FCB

M access, read, write the **file control block**

syn control block

---

file conversion *noun*
the process of changing the layout or format of a data file so that it may be accessed by a different program from the one that created it

/ˈfaɪl kənˌvɜːʃn/
note not used with *a* or *an*. No plural and used with a singular verb only.

M carry out **file conversion**

---

file directory *noun*
▶ directory

/ˈfaɪl dəˌrektəri/

---

file encryption *noun*
▶ encryption

/ˈfaɪl ɪnˌkrɪpʃn/

file extent *noun* ▶ **extent**	/ˈfaɪl ɪkˌstent/
file gap *noun* an area of empty storage space between files held on backing storage	/ˈfaɪl gæp/ **pl** file gaps ⋈ insert, skip a **file gap** **syn** inter file gap
file handling routine *noun* (software) software that carries out operations on data files such as opening, updating, closing, deleting and creating them	/ˈfaɪl ˌhændlɪŋ ruːˌtiːn/ **pl** file handling routines ⋈ program, use, execute a **file handling routine**
file maintenance *noun* the process of updating a data file	/ˈfaɪl ˌmeɪntənəns/ **note** not used with *a* or *an*. No plural and used with a singular verb only. ⋈ perform **file maintenance**; a **file maintenance** routine; **file maintenance** software
file management system *noun* (software) the part of the operating system that keeps a record of where a data file is held on backing storage	/ˈfaɪl ˌmænɪdʒmənt ˌsɪstəm/ **pl** file management (systems) ⋈ invoke, use a **file management system**
☆**filename** *noun* (software) the name given to a program or data file: *a Macintosh filename that can be up to 254 characters long* ○ *the DOS filename is WIN.EXE*	/ˈfaɪlneɪm/ **pl** filenames ⋈ change, choose a **filename** ▶ **directory, extension**
filename extension *noun* ▶ **extension**	/ˈfaɪlneɪm ɪkˌstenʃn/
file protection *noun* ways of preventing unauthorized changes to a data file including PASSWORD PROTECTION for computer systems and WRITE PROTECTING files on disk	/ˈfaɪl prəˌtekʃn/ **note** not used with *a* or *an*. No plural and used with a singular verb only. ⋈ implement, install **file protection**; a **file protection** routine; **file protection** hardware, software
file recovery *noun* the process of accessing data files which have been damaged or deleted	/ˈfaɪl rɪˌkʌvəri/ **note** not used with *a* or *an*. No plural and used with a singular verb only. ⋈ carry out, perform **file recovery**
file recovery routine *noun* (software) software that allows access to a file that has been damaged or deleted: *The file recovery routine is part of the operating system.*	/ˌfaɪl rɪˈkʌvəri ruːˌtiːn/ **pl** file recovery routines ⋈ execute a **file recovery routine** **syn** file recovery utility

abbr abbreviation **pl** plural **syn** synonym ▶ see ⋈ collocate (*word often used with the headword*)

file recovery utility *noun*
▶ file recovery routine

/ˈfaɪl rɪˌkʌvəri juːˌtɪləti/

☆**file server** *noun*
▶ server

/ˈfaɪl ˌsɜːvə(r)/

---

file structure *noun*
the way that data items are arranged in a file

/ˈfaɪl ˌstrʌkʃə(r)/
pl file structures
M choose, implement a **file structure**

---

file transfer *noun*
the movement of a file from one area of memory to another: *Before the hard disk can be replaced, there must be a file transfer of all data on the old disk to the network.*

/ˈfaɪl ˌtrænsfɜː(r)/
pl file transfers
M perform a **file transfer**

---

file transfer protocol *noun*
▶ FTP

/ˈfaɪl ˌtrænsfɜː ˌprəʊtəkɒl/

---

file update *noun*
changes made to the data in a file: *File updates happen every day to keep data current.*

/ˈfaɪl ˌʌpdeɪt/
pl file updates
M perform a **file update**; a regular, scheduled **file update**

---

fill *verb*
1 to use all the space on a disk or tape, etc: *fill the tape with data that can be archived* **2** to make an area of a graphics display all the same colour or pattern

/fɪl/
fill, filling, filled
note transitive verb
2 M **fill** with a colour
syn flood fill, region fill

☆**filter** *noun*
1 (*hardware*) an electronic circuit which removes certain parts of a signal: *The filter removes frequencies above 10KHz.* **2** (*software*) a part of a program that selects data that is needed from a larger file or database: *use a filter to locate files on new employees*

/ˈfɪltə(r)/
pl filters
1,2 M employ, pass through, use a **filter**

---

find *verb*
to locate the position of something: *find the file name in the directory* ○ *find the data item in the look up table*

/faɪnd/
find, finding, found
note transitive verb

☆**firmware** *noun* (*hardware*)
permanent software that is held in ROM: *The new operating system is supplied as firmware.*

/ˈfɜːmweə(r)/
pl no plural
M program, upgrade the **firmware**
▶ hardware, software

☆**first generation** *noun* (*hardware*)
a stage in computer design of early machines which used electronic valves and had small memories

note First generation computers were built in the early 1950s.

/ˌfɜːst dʒenəˈreɪʃn/
note no plural
▶ fifth generation, fourth generation, second generation, third generation

---

first in, first out *adjective*
of a DATA STRUCTURE (= a collection of data items considered as one single item) where only the first item added can be accessed first: *a first in, first out queue* ○ *a first in, first out list*

/ˌfɜːst ˈɪn ˌfɜːst ˈaʊt/
abbr FIFO
▶ last in, first out, pop, push, queue 2, stack

fixed disk *noun*
► **hard disk**

/ˌfɪkst 'dɪsk/

---

fixed format *adjective*
(of input to a computer) that must obey certain layout rules such as the order of items and the number of characters in an item: *A fixed format address field.* ○ *A fixed format header gives general information about the file.*

/ˌfɪkst 'fɔːmæt/
◄ a **fixed format** record

---

fixed-format record *noun*
one record in a data file which has the same number of fields of the same size as other records in the file

note It is easy to locate any fixed format record in a file because its position can be calculated directly.

/'fɪkst 'fɔːmæt 'rekɔːd/
pl fixed format records
◄ access, delete, update a **fixed-format record**

---

fixed-head disk *noun*
a magnetic disk where the READ/WRITE HEAD does not move across the disk. The head can only move towards or away from one DISK TRACK, so a different read/write head is needed for each track.

/ˌfɪkst hed 'dɪsk/
pl fixed head disks
◄ a **fixed-head disk** drive
► **moving head disk**

---

fixed-head drive *noun* (hardware)
a disk drive in which a separate READ/WRITE HEAD for every DISK TRACK ; this makes access time very short

/ˌfɪkst hed 'draɪv/
pl fixed head disks
► **moving-head drive**

---

fixed-length record *noun*
a record that occupies a fixed amount of storage space which is not affected by the amount of data the record contains

/ˌfɪkst leŋθ 'rekɔːd/
pl fixed length records
◄ access, delete, update a **fixed-length record**
► **fixed format record**

---

fixed-length word *noun*
one of the areas of computer storage that takes up the same space as all others, and which is accessed as a single unit

note A fixed-length word is always a predetermined number of bits for any given computer system.

/ˌfɪkst leŋθ 'wɜːd/
pl fixed length words
◄ access, read, write a **fixed-length word**

---

fixed point *noun*
a method of representing numbers with FRACTIONS where the position of the decimal or binary point is stored with the digits

/ˌfɪkst 'pɔɪnt/
note not used with *a* or *an*. No plural and used with a singular verb only.
◄ a **fixed-point** calculation, number, representation
► **floating point**

☆**fixed-point arithmetic** *noun* (mathematics)
a form of arithmetic in which numbers are represented in FIXED POINT

/ˌfɪkst pɔɪnt ə'rɪθmətɪk/
note no plural
► **floating-point arithmetic**

---

fixed-point number *noun*
a number represented in fixed point form: *Fixed-point numbers can be calculated very quickly.*

note Although it is used often, this term is only informal: it is not the number that is fixed point, but the method of representing it.

/ˌfɪkst pɔɪnt 'nʌmbə(r)/
pl fixed point numbers
◄ store as a **fixed point number**
► **floating-point number**

---

abbr abbreviation   **pl** plural   **syn** synonym   ► see   ◄ collocate (*word often used with the headword*)

fixed-point operation *noun*
a machine code instruction that carries out an arithmetic operation on fixed point numbers: *ADD is the fixed point operation of addition*

/ˌfɪkst pɔɪnt ɒpəˈreɪʃn/
pl fixed point operations
⋈ execute, perform a **fixed-point operation**
▶ **floating-point operation**

fixed word length *noun*
the number of bits used for a FIXED LENGTH WORD

/ˌfɪkst ˈwɜːd leŋθ/
pl fixed word lengths
⋈ define the **fixed word length**

☆**Fkey** *abbr*
▶ **function key**

/ˈef kiː/

flag *noun*
a bit stored in hardware or software that is used to show the state of some part of the system: *The operating system checks the flag before it allows access to a shared resource.*

/flæg/
⋈ clear, read, set, unset a **flag**; an error, an overflow, a zero **flag**
syn semaphore
▶ **flag bit**

flag bit *noun*
a single bit which is used as a FLAG: *The status word is made up of flag bits.*

/ˈflæg bɪt/
pl flag bits
⋈ clear, read, set, unset a **flag bit**

flatbed plotter *noun*
a type of PLOTTER (= a device that converts data into graphs) with paper on a flat surface with pens moving over the paper to record data

/ˌflætbed ˈplɒtə(r)/
pl flatbed plotters
▶ **bar chart, drum plotter, graph plotter**

flat file *noun*
a data file where the data items are simple items and do not have any internal structure of their own: *A flat file can be thought as a two-dimensional array.*

/ˌflæt ˈfaɪl/
pl flat files
⋈ access, structure *as* a **flat file**; a **flat file** system

flat pack *noun* (hardware)
a type of chip that can be put directly onto a PRINTED CIRCUIT BOARD

/ˈflæt pæk/
pl flat packs
⋈ install a **flat pack**

flavour *noun*
a particular type of something, usually software: *Which flavour of Lisp is installed on the system?* ○ *Pascal comes in a variety of flavours.*

/ˈfleɪvə(r)/
pl flavours
(*US* **flavor**)

flicker¹ *noun*
a small movement of light that is repeated frequently, usually on a screen: *reduce the flicker on the screen to an acceptable level* ○ *The flicker on the VDU is tiring on the eyes.*

/ˈflɪkə(r)/
pl flickers

flicker² *verb*
to change in brightness by a small amount: *The light bulb was flickering.* ○ *The screen is old and flickers a lot.*

/ˈflɪkə(r)/
flicker, flickering, flickered
note intransitive verb
⋈ **flicker** badly, excessively

flicker free *adjective*
(of a display screen) that is REFRESHED (2) so quickly the user does not see the image move: *The new screen is flicker free.*

/ˈflɪkə friː/
⋈ a **flicker free** display, monitor, screen

flip-flop *noun*
▶ **bistable**[1]

/ˈflɪp flɒp/

---

float *verb*
to change a stored number from FIXED POINT to FLOATING POINT

note Many computer programming languages have a function FLOAT to perform this operation.

/fləʊt/
float, floating, floated
ꟶ **float** a number
▶ **floating point**

---

floating point *noun*
a method of representing numbers with FRACTIONAL parts. A fixed number of decimal places, called the MANTISSA is stored with a power, called a CHARACTERISTIC, which scales the number.

note For example, to store the number 3.14159 in floating point, the significant figures 314159 would be held with a characteristic that showed that the decimal point should be inserted to make the number 3.14159 rather than 31.4159 or 314.159 etc.

/ˌfləʊtɪŋ ˈpɔɪnt/
note not used with *a* or *an*. No plural and used with a singular verb only.
ꟶ a **floating-point** number, representation, calculation
▶ **fixed point**

☆**floating-point arithmetic** *noun* (mathematics)
a form of arithmetic in which numbers are represented in FLOATING POINT: *The compiler runs on a processor using floating-point arithmetic.*

/ˌfləʊtɪŋ pɔɪnt əˈrɪθmətɪk/
note no plural

---

floating-point number *noun*
a number represented in FLOATING POINT form

note Although it is used often, this term is only informal: it is not the number that is floating-point, but the method of representing it.

/ˌfləʊtɪŋ pɔɪnt ˈnʌmbə(r)/
pl floating point numbers
ꟶ store as a **floating-point number**
▶ **fixed-point number**

---

floating-point operation *noun*
a machine code instruction that executes an arithmetic operation on floating point numbers: *FADD is the floating-point operation of addition.*

/ˌfləʊtɪŋ pɔɪnt ɒpəˈreɪʃn/
pl floating point operations

---

floating-point processor *noun* (hardware)
special hardware that is part of the CPU or a separate device that is designed to perform floating point operations quickly: *an add-on floating point processor*

/ˌfləʊtɪŋ pɔɪnt ˈprəʊsesə(r)/
pl floating point processors
ꟶ buy, install a **floating-point processor**

---

floating-point underflow *noun*
the error that occurs when the result of a calculation using FLOATING-POINT ARITHMETIC is too small to be stored

note Floating-point underflow can usually be detected and trapped as a recoverable error; often the action taken is to store the small number as a zero.

/ˌfləʊtɪŋ pɔɪnt ˈʌndəfləʊ/
note not used with *a* or *an*. No plural and used with a singular verb only
ꟶ cause, trap **floating-point underflow**

---

flood fill *verb*
▶ **fill 2**

/ˈflʌd fɪl/

---

floppy *noun*
▶ **floppy disk**

/ˈflɒpi/

---

abbr abbreviation   **pl** plural   **syn** synonym   ▶ see   ꟶ collocate (*word often used with the headword*)

☆**floppy disk** *noun* (hardware)
a removable magnetic disk inside a flat plastic case which is used to store data: *A copy of the report is stored on floppy disk.*

/ˌflɒpi ˈdɪsk/
pl floppy disks
◪ copy *onto*, insert, read *from*, save *to*, store *on*, use, write *to* a **floppy disk**
syn floppy, diskette
▶ **disk, double-density disk, hard disk, high-density disk, magnetic disk**

floppy disk controller *noun*
the hardware that controls access to a floppy disk: *The floppy disk controller is accessed by the filing system portion of the operating system.*

/ˌflɒpi ˈdɪsk kənˌtrəʊlə(r)/
pl floppy disk controllers
abbr FDC
◪ access, test a **floppy disk controller**

floppy disk drive *noun*
the part of a computer where a floppy disk is inserted so data can be written to or read from it: *install a new floppy disk drive* ○ *insert the disk in the floppy disk drive*

/ˌflɒpi ˈdɪsk draɪv/
pl floppy disk drives
▶ **CD-ROM drive, disk drive, hard disk drive**

FLOPS *abbr*
floating point operations per second

/flɒps/
note pronounced as a word

flow¹ *noun*
a continuous movement of something, especially data or electricity: *The modem can cope with a flow of data of up to 9 600 baud.* ○ *a steady flow of electricity*

/fləʊ/
pl flows
◪ **flow** rate

flow² *verb*
to move continuously, usually at the same speed: *The electric current flows through the circuit.*

/fləʊ/
flow, flowing, flowed
note intransitive verb

☆**flowchart** *noun* (software)
a diagram of the order of operations in a program or system, etc: *The configuration of the system is shown in the flowchart representing the hardware.* ○ *show the variables and feedback in a systems flowchart*

/ˈfləʊtʃɑːt/
pl flowcharts
◪ annotate, draw, print a **flowchart**; a data, program **flowchart**
syn flow diagram
▶ **block diagram**

flow control *noun*
the organization of data flow to data buffers so that data transfer happens in the most efficient way: *Flow control is necessary to prevent loss of data.*

/ˈfləʊ kənˌtrəʊl/
note not used with *a* or *an*. No plural and used with a singular verb only.
◪ perform **flow control**

flow diagram *noun*
▶ **flowchart**

/ˈfləʊ ˌdaɪəgræm/

flush¹ *verb* (software)
to clear the data stored in a part of the system's memory, especially data stored in a buffer: *flush data into the main memory*

/flʌʃ/
flush, flushing, flushed
note transitive verb
◪ **flush** a buffer, the memory; **flush** data

flush² *adjective* (applications/word processing)
(of word processed text) that is arranged on a page so that either the left side or the right side is parallel to the edge of the page

/flʌʃ/
▶ **align, justify, ragged left, ragged right**

FM *abbr*
▶ **frequency modulation**

/ˌef ˈem/
note pronounced as individual letters

---

folder *noun* (software/system operation)
the place where files and programs are kept: *give the folder a name to identify the contents* ○ *connect to the public folder of machine 5* ○ *The screensavers are in the system folder on the hard disk.*

note 'Folder' is used mainly with reference to Macintosh systems. PC users would call a folder a 'directory'.

/ˈfəʊldə(r)/
pl folders
◄ access, create, delete a **folder**
▶ **directory**

☆**font** *noun*
all the features of text on screen or on a page: *the default font is 12 point Helvetica*

note A font has four features: 'style', such as italic; 'typeface', such as Geneva; 'size', such as 12 point and 'weight', such as bold.

/fɒnt/
pl fonts
(also **fount**)
◄ a computerized, digitized, screen **font**
▶ **bit-mapped font, italic, typeface**

---

font cartridge *noun* (hardware)
a device that can be added to a printer which contains one or more fonts: *The printer has a Postscript font cartridge.*

/ˈfɒnt ˌkɑːtrɪdʒ/
pl font cartridges
◄ add, insert, plug *in*, remove a **font cartridge**
▶ **Postscript**

---

footer *noun* (applications/word processing)
text automatically added to the bottom of every page of printed text: *include the title of the document and the page number in the footer*

/ˈfʊtə(r)/
pl footers
◄ insert, use a **footer**
▶ **header**

---

footprint *noun*
the area on a desk that a computer occupies: *The laptop has a small footprint.*

/ˈfʊtprɪnt/
pl footprints

---

foreground *noun*
the main features of a displayed image, such as text or graphics, that are not part of the BACKGROUND: *The application offers a choice of 256 colours for the foreground.*

/ˈfɔːɡraʊnd/
note usually singular
◄ change, choose, decide *on*, select the **foreground**; **foreground** colour
▶ **display**

---

foreground processing *noun* (operations)
the processing of the current tasks by a system in a multitasking environment: *The foreground processing is data input.*

/ˈfɔːɡraʊnd ˌprəʊsesɪŋ/
note not used with *a* or *an*. No plural and used with a singular verb only.
◄ do, schedule the **foreground processing**
▶ **background processing, multitasking**

---

foreground program *noun*
the current program that is running a multitasking environment: *The foreground program the user is working on is a word processing application while the printer is spooling documents in the background.*

/ˈfɔːɡraʊnd ˌprəʊɡræm/
pl foreground programs
◄ execute, store a **foreground program**
▶ **background program, multitasking**

---

abbr abbreviation   **pl** plural   **syn** synonym   ▶ see   ◄ collocate (*word often used with the headword*)

form noun
a document that contains spaces where the user is expected to put information: *The form requests product feedback from users of the new application.*

/fɔ:m/
pl forms
◣ complete, fill *in/out*, submit a **form**; an electronic, a printed **form**

---

formal argument noun
▶ **formal parameter**

/ˌfɔ:ml 'ɑ:gjumənt/

---

formal parameter noun
a variable which is used when a SUBROUTINE, function or procedure is written, but will be replaced by another variable when the subroutine is executed: *The formal parameters are listed in brackets after the function name.*

/ˌfɔ:ml pə'ræmɪtə(r)/
pl formal parameters
◣ define, insert a **formal parameter**

syn dummy argument, dummy variable, formal argument
▶ **parameter**

☆**format¹** noun
1 a structure for storing or processing data: *the format of the video is VHS* ○ *The company only produces electronic products in a CD-ROM format.* **2** the way in which text and graphics, etc appears on screen or on a printed page: *a format consisting of three columns*

/'fɔ:mæt/
pl formats
◣ a file, instruction **format**
1 ▶ **unformatted 1**
2 ▶ **layout, unformatted 2**

☆**format²** verb (user operation)
1 to prepare a disk, etc to receive data. This is usually done by the operating system or a utility program: *format a 1.4Mb floppy disk* **2** to give text a certain layout: *format the text so it is centred*

/'fɔ:mæt/
format, formatting, formatted
note transitive verb
◣ **format** a disk, tape
▶ **disk formatting**

---

form feed noun
an instruction to a printer to move to the next page: *send a form feed instruction to the printer* ○ *press the form feed button on the printer*

/'fɔ:m fi:d/
pl form feeds
abbr FF
◣ do, execute a **form feed**

---

form letter noun (applications)
a document which is designed to be sent to many people: *The invoices are sent out monthly with a covering form letter.*

/'fɔ:m ˌletə(r)/
pl form letters
◣ print, send a **form letter**
▶ **mail merge**

---

formula noun
a rule showing how to solve a problem, especially a rule expressed in mathematical symbols which allows a value to be calculated: *The density of air at height h is found using the formula: density = 1.225 (1 - 0.001h).* ○ *the spreadsheet formula A1 + B2*

/'fɔ:mjələ/
pl formulas
pl formulae
◣ define, delete, insert rearrange, use a **formula**; a complicated, difficult, mathematical, simple **formula**

---

for next loop noun
▶ **do loop**

/ˌfɔ: 'nekst ˌlu:p/

FORTH *noun* (software/programming)
a programming language that uses POSTFIX NOTATION and
requires the programmer to work directly with the program
STACK

note FORTH is an interpreted structured language that was
developed in the late 1960s.

/ˈfɔːθ/
note not used with *a* or *an*. No
plural and used with a singular
verb only.
(also **Forth**)
ꓱ program *in* **FORTH**

☆**FORTRAN** *noun* (software/programming)
a high-level programming language used in science and
engineering

note The word FORTRAN comes from the words 'formula
translation'. It is an imperative procedural language and was
designed in the late 1950s. It was one of the first third-
generation languages.

/ˈfɔːtræn/
note not used with *a* or *an*. No
plural and used with a singular
verb only.
ꓱ program *in* **FORTRAN**; a
FORTRAN program;
FORTRAN source code

forward error correction *noun*
a way of finding and correcting errors in transmitted data that
uses information sent with the data

/ˌfɔːwəd ˈerə kəˌrekʃn/
note not used with *a* or *an*. No
plural and used with a singular
verb only.
ꓱ use **forward error correction**
syn forward error protection
▶ **backward error correction,
error correction**

forward error protection *noun*
▶ **forward error correction**

/ˌfɔːwəd ˈerə prəˌtekʃn/

forward reference *noun*
the use of an IDENTIFIER in a low-level language that refers to a
location later in the program

/ˌfɔːwəd ˈrefərəns/
pl forward references
ꓱ make a **forward reference**

fount *noun*
▶ **font**

/faʊnt/

4GL *abbr*
▶ **fourth generation language**

/ˌfɔː dʒiː ˈel/

☆**fourth generation** *noun* (hardware)
a stage in computer design where computers have integrated
circuits, large memories and connections to networks

note Fourth generation computers began appearing in the
mid-1970s.

/ˌfɔːθ dʒenəˈreɪʃn/
note no plural
▶ **fifth generation, first
generation, second
generation, third generation**

fourth generation language *noun*
a high-level computer programming language that makes it
easy for a user who is not an expert to write programs: *The
company intends to release a new version of its fourth generation
language.* ○ *fourth generation language development tools*

note Fourth generation languages should not be confused
with fourth generation computers. Languages are usually
classified as machine code (first generation), assembly
language (second generation), high-level language (third
generation) and fourth generation languages which are above
standard high-level languages such as C and Pascal, etc.

/ˈfɔːθ dʒenəˈreɪʃn ˈlæŋgwɪdʒ/
pl fourth generation languages
abbr 4GL
ꓱ design, program *in*, write *in*, use
a **fourth generation
language**; **fourth generation
language** software

abbr abbreviation   **pl** plural   **syn** synonym   ▶ see   ꓱ collocate (*word often used with the headword*)

fraction *noun* (mathematics)
a number that is not a whole number: *the fraction .75 in the decimal number 1.75*

/'frækʃn/
pl fractions

---

fragmentation *noun*
the creation of areas of unused addresses in memory as data of different sizes is taken in and out of memory. Since these areas are often too small to hold any new data, memory is made less efficient: *The operating system tries to keep fragmentation to a minimum.* ○ *Slow access to the file was caused by fragmentation.*

/ˌfrægmen'teɪʃn/
note not used with *a* or *an*. No plural and used with a singular verb only.
◄ avoid, deal with **fragmentation**
▶ **defragmentation**

---

frame *noun*
1 one complete television picture: *In the UK, television is transmitted at 25 frames per second; in the US it is 30.* **2** a block of data that is transmitted together with information about the address and error correction methods: *send a number of frames sequentially over the network* **3** the area on a magnetic tape occupied by a single character: *A frame extends across the width of the tape.*

/freɪm/
pl frames
1,2 ◄ receive, transmit a **frame**
3 ◄ read, write a **frame**

---

frame buffer *noun*
a storage area capable of holding one FRAME **1** of video information

/'freɪm ˌbʌfə(r)/
pl frame buffers
◄ hold data *in*, read data *from* a **frame buffer**

---

frame grabber *noun*
▶ **video digitizer**

/'freɪm ˌgræbə(r)/

---

free format *adjective*
(of input to a computer) that is able to be typed as the user wishes, not following any rules: *The address field is free format.* ○ *Data keyed in free format mode requires spaces or commas between each item.* ○ *The database search query can be presented in English in free format (such as phrases and sentences) as no special syntax forms are imposed on the searcher.*

/ˌfriː 'fɔːmæt/

---

freeware *noun* (software)
computer software that is offered free of charge or for a small charge to cover the cost of disks, etc. Users of freeware may not be allowed to copy or distribute it: *A variety of freeware is downloadable from the Internet.*

/'friːweə(r)/
note not used with *a* or *an*. No plural and used with a singular verb only.
◄ download, use **freeware**
▶ **proprietary software, public domain software, shareware**

---

frequency *noun*
a measure of how often something repeats in a fixed amount of time. Frequency is usually measured in HERTZ: *The system clock has a frequency of 90MHz.* ○ *the frequency of light in a laser beam*

/'friːkwənsi/
pl frequencies
◄ calculate, increase, measure the **frequency**; high, low **frequency**

frequency division multiplexing *noun*
a way of combining several data transmissions into a single
signal by sending messages on separate CARRIER SIGNALS at
different frequencies at the same time

note Frequency division multiplexing is used in analog
transmissions such as communication over telephone lines.

/ˈfriːkwənsi dɪˈvɪʒn
ˈmʌltɪpleksm̩/
note not used with *a* or *an*. No
plural and used with a singular
verb only

abbr FDM

◄ **frequency division
multiplexing** protocols,
techniques

▶ **time division multiplexing,
multiplexer**

---

frequency modulation *noun*
a way of changing the frequency of a CARRIER SIGNAL so that it
can transmit information

/ˈfriːkwənsi ˌmɒdjuˈleɪʃn/
note not used with *a* or *an*. No
plural and used with a singular
verb only.

abbr FM

◄ transmit *via*, use **frequency
modulation**

▶ **amplitude modulation,
modulation, phase
modulation, pulse code
modulation**

---

friction *noun*
the energy that is produced when two things rub together

/ˈfrɪkʃn/
note not used with *a* or *an*. No
plural and used with a singular
verb only.

☆**front-end processor** *noun* (hardware)
a small processor that receives data from several input devices
and puts it in order so it is ready to be processed by a larger
computer

/ˌfrʌnt end ˈprəʊsesə(r)/
pl front-end processors
abbr FEP

▶ **backend processor**

FTP *abbr*
file transfer protocol. An agreed set of standards for
transferring files from one computer to another over a
network: *post material to an FTP site on the Internet* ○ *get a piece
of shareware by anonymous FTP*

/ˈef tiː ˈpiː/
note pronounced as individual
letters
(also **ftp**)

◄ connect *via*, follow, obey, use
FTP; anonymous **FTP**

---

full adder *noun*
a logic circuit used in a computer to add binary digits (bits)

note A full adder has three bits as input and produces two
outputs: a sum and carry bit.

/ˌfʊl ˈædə(r)/
pl full adders

▶ **carry bit, half adder**

---

full duplex *adjective*
▶ **duplex**

/ˌfʊl ˈdjuːpleks/

---

full duplex channel *noun*
▶ **duplex channel**

/ˌfʊl ˈdjuːpleks ˌtʃænl/

---

full motion video *noun*
a video signal which can be processed in real time and can be
displayed fast enough to give the impression of smooth
movements

/ˈfʊl ˈməʊʃn ˈvɪdiəʊ/
note not used with *a* or *an*. No
plural and used with a singular
verb only.

◄ display, manipulate **full
motion video**; digital, full
frame **full motion video**

---

abbr abbreviation   **pl** plural   **syn** synonym   ▶ see   ◄ collocate (*word often used with the headword*)

☆**function¹** *noun*

1 a mathematical formula that takes one or more values as an input and produces a single result as an output 2 a group of computer programming language statements that performs a particular computation

note A function is very similar to a subroutine except that the result of a function is usually obtained by using the name of the function as if it were a variable.

/ˈfʌŋkʃn/
pl functions

1 ⋈ define, evaluate a **function**; a logarithm, sine **function**

2 ⋈ an add-on, a built-in, a user-defined **function**; call, define, invoke a **function**

▶ nested function, parameter

---

function² *verb*

to operate correctly: *The system functions well.*

/ˈfʌŋkʃn/
function, functioning, functioned

note intransitive verb

⋈ **function** intermittently, reliably

---

functional *adjective*

1 (of computers and systems) that work correctly: *When tested, the equipment was all functional.* 2 (of a programming language) that is organized as separate functions: *Logo is a high-level functional language.*

/ˈfʌŋkʃənl/

1 ⋈ a **functional** computer, network, printer

2 ⋈ a **functional** language; **functional** programming

▶ logic programming, query language, object-oriented, imperative

---

functional design *noun*

a description of a computer system that explains how parts of the system work together: *a functional design that meets the specifications*

/ˌfʌŋkʃnl dɪˈzaɪn/
pl functional designs

⋈ draw up, offer, prepare, propose a **functional design**

▶ data driven design

---

functional specification *noun*

an explanation of how a computer system should work when a new system is being designed: *Drawing up a functional specifcation is part of the design phase of the project.*

/ˈfʌŋkʃənl ˌspesɪfɪˈkeɪʃn/
pl functional specifications

⋈ follow, prepare, write a **functional specification**

▶ functional testing

---

functional testing *noun*

the process of checking that a computer system or part of the system works in the way described in the FUNCTIONAL SPECIFICATION: *The functional testing showed that there were minor problems to be resolved in the system.*

/ˌfʌŋkʃənl ˈtestɪŋ/

note not used with *a* or *an*. No plural and used with a singular verb only.

⋈ carry out, perform **functional testing**

---

function call *noun*

the statement in a computer programming language that causes a function to be executed

note A function call will usually give the parameters to be used by the function.

/ˈfʌŋkʃn kɔːl/
pl function calls

⋈ make a **function call**

▶ calling sequence, parameter, return², subroutine call

☆**function key** *noun* (hardware)

one of several keys on a keyboard, each marked with 'F' and a number, that can be used to do something, such as access help in a program or save a file: *press the function key F1 to return to the main menu*

/ˈfʌŋkʃn kiː/
pl function keys
abbr Fkey

	⋈ hold *down*, press, use a **function key**
	syn programmable function key
	▶ **cursor control key, menu**

fuse¹ *noun*
a part of an electric circuit that breaks or burns if there is an increase in power. This stops the power reaching and damaging computers and other equipment: *put a 13-amp fuse in the plug*

/fjuːz/
pl fuses
⋈ blow, replace a **fuse**
▶ **surge**

fuse² *verb*
1 to join two or more things together, usually by heating them: *The chip was fused onto the circuit board.* **2** to stop devices from working because a FUSE¹ has broken: *The faulty cable connection fused the whole office. The circuit has fused.*

/fjuːz/
fuse, fusing, fused
1,2 note transitive or intransitive verb
1 ⋈ **fuse** two connections
2 ⋈ **fuse** lights, equipment

fusible link *noun* (hardware)
a small connection in an UNCOMMITTED LOGIC ARRAY or other programmable device which can be FUSED² 1 to permanently program the device

/ˌfjuːzəbl ˈlɪŋk/
pl fusible links
⋈ blow, fuse a **fusible link**

fuzzy logic *noun*
a type of logic that is used to try to make computers behave like the human brain: instead of using only the two truth values TRUE and FALSE, fuzzy logic tries to represent a value between TRUE and FALSE, such as 'possibly true' or 'probably false', etc: *The anti-virus tool employs fuzzy logic to combat computer viruses.* ○ *The software uses neural network learning to generate fuzzy logic rules.*

/ˌfʌzi ˈlɒdʒɪk/
note not used with *a* or *an*. No plural and used with a singular verb verb only.
⋈ implement, incorporate, use **fuzzy logic**; a **fuzzy logic** algorithm, chip
syn fuzzy theory, multiple valued logic
▶ **artificial intelligence, expert system, logic**

fuzzy theory *noun*
▶ **fuzzy logic**

/ˌfʌzi ˈθɪəri/

Gg

☆**G** *abbr*
▶ **giga**

/dʒiː/

games paddle *noun*
▶ **paddle**

/ˈɡeɪmz ˌpædl/

gap *noun*
▶ **interblock gap**

/ɡæp/

garbage *noun* (operations)
(*informal*) data or information that is not useful or is CORRUPT²: *The output is garbage.*

/ˈɡɑːbɪdʒ/
note not used with *a* or *an*. No

abbr abbreviation   **pl** plural   **syn** synonym   ▶ see   ⋈ collocate (*word often used with the headword*)

	plural and used with a singular verb only.

gas discharge display *noun* ▶ **plasma display**	/ˈgæs dɪsˌtʃɑːdʒ dɪˌspleɪ/

gas panel display *noun* ▶ **plasma display**	/ˈgæs ˌpænl dɪˌspleɪ/

gas plasma display *noun* ▶ **plasma display**	/ˈgæs ˈplæzmə dɪˌspleɪ/

☆**gate** *noun* an electronic device which will output a signal that is related to the input signal. Gates allow computer chips to do arithmetic and logic operations: *design a gate to perform different types of logic functions* ○ *gates that implement logic operations including AND, NOT and OR*	/geɪt/ **pl** gates **⋈** a **gate** input, output **syn** logic gate, logic element ▶ **AND gate, EQ gate, fan-out 1, OR gate, NAND gate, NEQ gate, NOR gate, NOT gate, XOR gate, XNOR gate**

gate array *noun* a number of GATES on a single integrated circuit **note** Shift registers, arithmetic units and other complex logic devices are fabricated as gate arrays.	/ˈgeɪt əˌreɪ/ **pl** gate arrays **⋈** design, fabricate, make, use a **gate array** **syn** logic array

gate delay *noun* the time taken for the output of a gate to show the correct signal after the input signals have been received	/ˈgeɪt dɪˌleɪ/ **pl** gate delays **⋈** shorten, wait *for* the **gate delay** **syn** propagation delay, propagation time

☆**gateway** *noun* (hardware) a device that links two (usually wide area) networks, changing the data to make it compatible with the PROTOCOL (= agreed signals and rules that control data transmission) of the other network, if necessary: *an e-mail gateway*	/ˈgeɪtweɪ/ **pl** gateways **⋈** send data *via*, use a **gateway**

gather *verb* to collect things together, especially to receive data from different places: *The analysis program uses data gathered from three different sources.*	/ˈgæðə(r)/ **gather, gathering, gathered** **note** transitive verb **⋈** **gather** data, facts, information

GB *abbr* ▶ **gigabyte**	**note** used in written English only

gender changer *noun* (hardware) a device that allows two female connectors or two male connectors to be joined together: *use a gender changer with sockets at both ends to connect two male connectors together*	/ˈdʒendə ˌtʃeɪmdʒə/ **pl** gender changers ▶ **adaptor plug**

general-purpose interface bus *noun* a bus that is a standard interface for communication between items of laboratory equipment: *The data logger was connected to the PC by a general-purpose interface bus.*	/ˈdʒenrəl ˈpɜːpəs ˈɪntəfeɪs bʌs/ **pl** general-purpose interface buses **abbr** GPIB **⋈** connect devices *via*, use a **general-purpose interface bus**

general-purpose register *noun* (hardware)
a register that can be used for any purpose, or one that is not used by the operating system for any specific purpose: *The programmer used machine code to access the general-purpose register.*

/'dʒenrəl 'pɜːpəs 'redʒɪstə(r)/
pl general purpose registers
ϻ address, load, use a **general-purpose register**
syn general register

---

general register *noun*
▶ **general-purpose register**

/ˌdʒenrəl 'redʒɪstə(r)/

☆**generate** *verb* (system operation)
to produce something: *select the correct menu option to generate a table on screen*

/'dʒenəreɪt/
generate, generating, generated
note transitive verb

☆**generation** *noun* (hardware)
a stage in computer development: *Experts are already talking of the sixth generation of computers of the next century.*

/ˌdʒenə'reɪʃn/
pl generations
▶ **fifth generation, first generation, fourth generation, second generation, third generation**

☆**generator** *noun* (software)
a program which automatically creates another program with a command from the user: *This game package has a generator to provide variations of the game.*

/'dʒenəreɪtə(r)/
pl generators
ϻ a game, sort **generator**

---

generic *adjective*
1 (of hardware and software) that is compatible with a wide range of hardware or software: *Third-generation computers were processors that used generic software and hardware.* **2** (of hardware and software) that is not produced by a well-known company: *Customers know there is a difference between name brand personal computers and generic machines.*

/dʒə'nerɪk/
ϻ **generic** hardware, products, software

---

geostationary orbit satellite *noun*
▶ **synchronous orbit satellite**

/dʒiːəʊ'steɪʃnri 'ɔːbɪt 'sætəlaɪt/

☆**giga** *prefix*
a thousand million, 10^9

/ 'ɡɪɡə/
▶ **kilo, mega, tera**

---

gigabit *noun* (hardware)
one thousand million bits

note In computing, because of the use of the binary system, a gigabit is 2^{30}, or 1 073 741 824 bits. There are eight gigabits in a gigabyte.

/'ɡɪɡəbɪt/
pl gigabits

---

gigabyte *noun* (hardware)
one thousand million bytes

note In computing, because of the use of the binary system, a gigabyte is 2^{30}, or 1 073 741 824 bytes.

/'ɡɪɡəbaɪt/
pl gigabytes

---

gigaflops *noun*
one thousand million basic FLOATING-POINT OPERATIONS per second: *The supercomputer has over 16 000 small processors working at once and can achieve speeds of over eight gigaflops.*

/'ɡɪɡəflɒps/
note plural noun used with a plural verb

---

abbr abbreviation   **pl** plural   **syn** synonym   ▶ see   **ϻ** collocate (*word often used with the headword*)

GIS *abbr*
geographical information system

/ˌdʒiː aɪ 'es/
note pronounced as individual letters

GKS *abbr*
graphics kernel system

/ˌdʒiː keɪ 'es/
note pronounced as individual letters

☆**glitch** *noun*
a small problem in general, or sometimes a problem caused by a SURGE: *The debugging process failed to remove a glitch in the software.*

/glɪtʃ/
pl glitches
◄ an electronic, a technical **glitch**
► **bug**

☆**global** *adjective*
connected with a whole document, file, program or system, etc: *run a global check on the system*

/'gləʊbl/
◄ a **global** backup, format, parameter
► **local 2**

global edit *noun*
► **global search and replace**

/ˌgləʊbl 'edɪt/

global scope *noun* (software/programming)
the range of a variable over a whole program so that any subroutine or function can use the contents of the variable: *Declaring a variable GLOBAL in the programming language C gives it global scope.*

/ˌgləʊbl 'skəʊp/
note not used with *a* or *an*. No plural and used with a singular verb only.
◄ declare a variable *with* **global scope**
► **local scope, scope**

global search and replace *noun* (applications)
a process where the computer searches for a word or string of characters in a document or file and replaces it with another word or string that the user has chosen: *do a global search and replace to replace the word 'secretary' with 'administrator'* ○ *The global search and replace is case insensitive.*

/'gləʊbl 'sɜːtʃ ənd rɪ'pleɪs/
note no plural
◄ a **global search and replace** function, operation
syn global edit
► **search, word processing**

global variable *noun*
a variable whose value can be accessed and changed by all parts of a program

/ˌgləʊbl 'veəriəbl/
pl global variables
◄ access, declare, define, use a **global variable**
► **local variable, scope**

golfball *noun* (hardware)
a metal ball in a printer or typewriter with characters on its surface. When the printer or typewriter is used, the golfball hits a piece of material with ink on it, called a ribbon, onto the paper to produce printed text: *type the document with an electric golfball machine*

/'gɒlfbɔːl/
pl golfballs
◄ a **golfball** printer, typewriter

GOTO *noun*
► **GOTO instuction**

/'gəʊtuː/

GOTO instruction *noun*
a high-level programming language instruction which causes a jump to another place in the program

/'gəʊtuː ɪnˌstrʌkʃn/
pl GOTO instructions
(also **GOTO statement**)

⋈ delete, insert, program, replace, use a **GOTO instruction**

syn GOTO

GPIB *abbr*
▶ **general-purpose interface bus**

/ˌdʒiː piː aɪ ˈbiː/
note pronounced as individual letters

GPR *abbr*
▶ **general-purpose register**

/ˌdʒiː piː ˈɑː/
note pronounced as individual letters

---

graceful degradation *noun*
▶ **fault tolerant system**

/ˈɡreɪsfl ˌdegrəˈdeɪʃn/

---

grammar *noun*
1 the word order or structure of the statements of a programming language. Grammar is only concerned with structure and not meaning. **2** the rules for writing a computer programming language. A grammar is usually written in a METALANGUAGE or expressed as production rules.

/ˈɡræmə(r)/
1 note no plural
2 pl grammars
syn ·syntax
▶ **semantics**

---

grammar check *noun*
the process of making sure that a computer program follows the grammar rules of the programming language: *A grammar check detects syntax errors.*

/ˈɡræmə ˌtʃek/
pl grammar checks
⋈ carry out, perform a **grammar check**
syn syntax check

---

grandfather-father-son file system *noun*
a set of files that is used to keep important data safe. The newest version of the data is written to a file called the son file. The previous son file is kept but becomes the father file. The previous father file is also kept but becomes the grandfather file. The previous grandfather file, which holds data that has been updated three times, is then deleted: *The payroll data is archived using a grandfather-father-son file system.*

/ˈɡrænfɑːðə ˈfɑːðə ˈsʌn faɪl sɪstəm/
pl grandfather-father-son file systems
⋈ implement, rotate *under*, use a **grandfather-father-son file system**

---

granularity *noun* (hardware)
a measure of the amount of memory used as a single unit by a particular process: *fine granularity of disk storage uses space efficiently*

/ˌɡrænjuˈlærəti/
note no plural
⋈ coarse, fine **granularity**

☆**graphical user interface** *noun* (applications)
a type of user interface that allows the user to select commands, etc by clicking on icons and menus. The use of a graphical user interface means commands do not have to be entered from the keyboard, although some icon and menu functions can be accessed from the keyboard, sometimes by using MACROS.

/ˌɡræfɪkl ˈjuːzə(r) ˌɪntəfeɪs/
pl graphical user interfaces
⋈ **graphical user interface** technology
▶ **disk operating system, human-computer interface, user interface, WIMP**

---

graphic language *noun*
a high-level computer programming language which includes commands for drawing graphics: *a graphic language with commands to draw lines, circles, ellipses and squares*

/ˈɡræfɪk ˌlæŋɡwɪdʒ/
pl graphic languages
(also **graphics language**)
⋈ program *in*, use a **graphic language**

---

abbr abbreviation   **pl** plural   **syn** synonym   ▶ see   ⋈ collocate (*word often used with the headword*)

graphic processor *noun*
▶ **graphics processor**

/'græfɪk ˌprəʊsesə(r)/

☆**graphics** *noun*
images that can be displayed on a computer screen: *graphics made up of simple lines and bright colours* ○ *the graphics are stored as a bit map*

/'græfɪks/

note plural noun used with a plural verb

◂ 3D, colour, computer **graphics**; a **graphics** department, display

syn graphics display, image

---

graphics adaptor *noun* (hardware)
a circuit board fitted to a computer to produce the signals to display graphics on a screen: *The software is compatible with all graphics adaptors.*

/'græfɪks ə'dæptə(r)/

pl graphics adaptors

(also **graphics adapter**)

◂ connect, install, use a **graphics adaptor**

syn graphics board, graphics card

▶ **adaptor, enhanced graphics adaptor, video graphics adaptor**

---

graphics board *noun*
▶ **graphics adaptor**

/'græfɪks bɔːd/

---

graphics card *noun*
▶ **graphics adaptor**

/'græfɪks kɑːd/

---

graphics character *noun*
a text character with an internal CHARACTER CODE that can be displayed in text-only systems, but which can be used to make simple images on screen

/'græfɪks ˌkærəktə(r)/

pl graphics characters

◂ delete, display, insert a **graphics character**

---

graphics coprocessor *noun*
▶ **graphics processor**

/'græfɪks kəʊˌprəʊsesə(r)/

---

graphics display *noun*
▶ **graphics**

/'græfɪks dɪˌspleɪ/

---

graphics pad *noun*
▶ **graphics tablet**

/'græfɪks pæd/

---

graphics processor *noun* (hardware)
a separate processor that controls the display of graphics without using the computing power that is being used for other processes: *improve the system by adding a graphics processor to speed up the display*

/'græfɪks ˌprəʊsesə(r)/

pl graphics processors

◂ add, build *in*, install a **graphics processor**

syn graphic processor, graphics coprocessor

---

graphics tablet *noun* (hardware)
an electronic device with a pen that acts like an electronic piece of paper. The user, often a designer, uses the pen to draw on the graphics tablet and the images are transferred from the tablet to the computer screen: *copy the map using the graphics tablet and store it in the computer* ○ *use a graphics tablet for large scale graphics*

/'græfɪks ˌtæblət/

pl graphics tablets

◂ draw *on*, use a **graphics tablet**

syn graphics pad, tablet

▶ **puck**

☆**graph plotter** *noun* (hardware)
an electronic device connected to a computer that records
information as lines on paper: *output statistical data to a graph
plotter*

/ˈɡrɑːf ˌplɒtə(r)/
pl graph plotters
▶ **bar chart, drum plotter,
flatbed plotter**

Gray code *noun*
a method of coding numbers using binary digits where only a
single bit changes between decimal numbers that follow each
other

note To change from 7 (0111) to 8 (1000) in ordinary binary
means changing all four bits from 1 to 0 or from 0 to 1. In
Gray code, 7 is 0100 and 8 is 1100, so only one of the bits is
different.

/ˈɡreɪ kəʊd/
note no plural
Ḥ code *in*, transmit *by*, use **Gray
code**
syn cyclic binary code, cyclic code

---

grey scale *noun* (hardware)
the number of shades of grey between black and white on a
monitor or in pictures, etc. If the grey scale is larger, the
quality is better: *a scanner with improved grey scale capability*

/ˈɡreɪ skeɪl/
(*US* **gray scale**)
note usually singular
Ḥ a large, small **grey scale**; a
grey scale display, monitor
▶ **dithering**

---

ground¹ *noun*
1 ▶ **earth¹**
2 ▶ **background**

/ɡraʊnd/

---

ground² *verb*
▶ **earth²**

/ɡraʊnd/

---

groupware *noun* (software)
software which enables a group of people connected to a
network to work on the same task, wherever they are in the
world: *share information on a daily basis by using groupware*

/ˈɡruːpweə(r)/
note no plural
Ḥ a **groupware** package

---

guard bit *noun*
a single bit in a data item that shows whether the user can
update the item or not

/ˈɡɑːd bɪt/
pl guard bits
Ḥ clear, reset, set a **guard bit**

☆**GUI** *abbr*
▶ **graphical user interface**

/ɡuːi/
note pronounced as a word

---

guide *noun*
1 a component that keeps a moving object on the correct path:
*The paper passes between two guides to align it before it enters the
printer.* 2 a helpful book or manual: *a guide to word processing*

/ɡaɪd/
pl guides
1 Ḥ travel *between* a **guide**
2 Ḥ read, study a **guide**

☆**gulp** *noun* (hardware)
(*informal*) several bytes, usually two bytes: *The data takes up
gulps of memory.*

/ɡʌlp/
pl gulps
▶ **byte, nibble, word**

---

abbr abbreviation   **pl** plural   **syn** synonym   ▶ see   Ḥ collocate (*word often used with the headword*)

Hh

☆**hack** *verb*
to access to data in a computer system without AUTHORIZATION: *hack into a computer system*

/hæk/
hack, hacking, hacked
note intransitive verb

☆**hacker** *noun* (personnel)
(*informal*) **1** a person who uses computers to access data without AUTHORIZATION: *The hacker manipulated the code to access the database illegally.*

note 'Hacker' was not originally used to describe people who accessed systems without authorization, although it is now mainly used in that negative way. Some computer experts think that the correct word for someone who accesses a computer system without authorization is 'cracker'.

2 a person skilled in programming: *find a hacker to unravel the machine code*

/'hækə(r)/
pl hackers
◪ a computer, professional **hacker**

---

half adder *noun* (hardware)
a logic circuit used in a computer to add binary digits (bits)

note A half adder has two bits as input and produces two outputs: a sum and a carry bit.

/,hɑːf'ædə(r)/
pl half adders
▶ **carry bit, full adder**

---

half duplex channel *noun* (data transmission)
a data channel that allows data to be transmitted in both directions but not at the same time

/,hɑːf'djuːpleks ,tʃænl/
pl half duplex channels
◪ send data *over*, transmit data *via*, use a **half duplex channel**
▶ **duplex channel, simplex channel**

---

half word *noun*
part of a WORD (**1**) which can be accessed as a single unit

note A half word is not always exactly half of a word but is some part of a word.

/,hɑːf'wɜːd/
pl half words
◪ access, process, store data *in a* **half word**

---

halt¹ *noun*
an interruption or stop in a system or program, usually because of an error: *The halt was caused by stack overflow.*

/hɔːlt/
pl halts
◪ bring something *to a* **halt**

---

halt² *verb*
to stop or interrupt, usually because of an error: *the system halted* ○ *halt the execution of the program*

/hɔːlt/
halt, halting, halted
note transitive or intransitive verb
◪ **halt** an operation, a program
▶ **halt instruction**

---

halt instruction *noun* (software/programming)
an instruction in a computer program that causes execution to stop: *insert a halt instruction in the program*

/'hɔːlt ɪnˌstrʌkʃn/
pl halt instructions
◪ code, delete, insert, program a **halt instruction**

Hamming code *noun*
a code used in data transmission that can detect and correct any single error in transmission. Hamming code is mainly used in TELETEXT systems.

/'hæmɪŋ kəʊd/
note no plural
◪ use **Hamming code**
▶ **error correcting code**

hand-held computer *noun* (hardware)
a computer which is small enough to be held in the user's hand

/ˌhænd held kəmˈpjuːtə(r)/
pl hand-held computers

---

handler *noun*
▶ **driver**

/ˈhændlə(r)/

---

handshake *noun*
a signal that is sent from one device to another device to show that data can be transmitted: *A ready to send (RTS) signal is part of the handshake involved in starting a data transmission.*

/ˈhændʃeɪk/
pl handshakes
◄ a hardware, software **handshake**
▶ **protocol**

---

handshaking *noun*
the exchange of control signals between two devices that shows data can be transmitted: *Handshaking ensures that both devices are operating to the same protocol.*

/ˈhændʃeɪkɪŋ/
note not used with *a* or *an*. No plural and used with a singular verb only.
◄ practise **handshaking**; a **handshaking** protocol, signal
▶ **protocol**

---

hang up¹ *noun*
the failure of software or a computer system to respond to the user: *In case of a hang up, it is necessary to reboot the computer.*

/ˈhæŋ ʌp/
pl hang ups
◄ cause, experience, suffer a **hang up**

---

hang up² *verb*
1 to finish using a telephone line so that it is free for other users: *Many modems hang up automatically after the transmission has finished.* ○ *hang up the phone when the call is finished*
2 (hardware) to stop working, usually because of an error: *The computer often hangs up.*

/ˌhæŋ ˈʌp/
hang up, hanging up, hung up
1 note transitive or intransitive verb
2 note intransitive verb
▶ **crash**

☆**hard copy** *noun* (hardware)
permanent material such as paper, film or disk that contains data or information: *correct the errors on the hard copy* ○ *keep a hard copy in case the disk is lost or damaged*

/ˌhɑːd ˈkɒpi/
pl hard copies
◄ print **hard copy**; **hard copy** output
▶ **copy¹ 2, printout, soft copy**

☆**hard disk** *noun* (hardware)
a magnetic disk inside a computer that stores data and programs. A hard disk stores more information and retrieves it more quickly than a floppy disk: *save the data on hard disk* ○ *All the files are held on the hard disk.*

/ˌhɑːd ˈdɪsk/
pl hard disks
◄ save *to*, use, work *on* the **hard disk**
syn fixed disk, physical hard disk
▶ **disk, floppy disk**

---

hard disk drive *noun* (hardware)
a disk drive that passes data to or from the hard disk and the computer

/ˌhɑːd ˈdɪsk draɪv/
pl hard disk drives
◄ install, maintain a **hard disk drive**
▶ **CD-ROM drive, disk drive, floppy disk drive**

---

hard error *noun*
an error that is caused because a piece of hardware stops working or because hardware that is not compatible with a system is used

/ˌhɑːd ˈerə(r)/
pl hard errors

---

abbr abbreviation   **pl** plural   **syn** synonym   ▶ see   ◄ collocate (*word often used with the headword*)

	⋈ diagnose, suffer *from* a **hard error**
	▶ **hard failure**

hard failure *noun*
▶ **hardware failure**

/ˌhɑːd ˈfeɪljə(r)/

---

hard return *noun* (applications/word processing)
a CARRIAGE RETURN character that the user types to start a new line of text. If the text is changed, the position of the hard return does not change.

/ˌhɑːd rɪˈtɜːn/
pl hard returns
⋈ delete, insert **hard return**
▶ **return**[1] **1, soft return, word wrap**

---

hard space *noun* (applications/word processing)
the character that is typed by a user to create a space between words. If the text is changed, the location of the space does not change: *hit the space bar to type a hard space*

/ˌhɑːd ˈspeɪs/
pl hard spaces
⋈ delete, insert a **hard space**
▶ **soft space, nonbreaking space, kerning**

☆**hardware** *noun* (hardware)
the electrical and mechanical parts of a computer system, including the screen, the keyboard and the hard disk

/ˈhɑːdweə(r)/
note not used with *a* or *an*. No plural and used with a singular verb only.
⋈ a piece of **hardware**; computer **hardware**
▶ **peripheral, software**

---

hardware compatible *adjective*
(of one computer) that can work with the programs of another computer without any changes to either computer: *all the computers in the office must be hardware compatible*

/ˌhɑːdweə kəmˈpætəbl/
⋈ a **hardware compatible** computer

---

hardware configuration *noun* (hardware)
the way in which the hardware in a computer system is arranged: *The software can operate in any hardware configuration the user wants.* ○ *The main hardware configuration includes a 16MB 486 processor with a 1 200 dpi laser printer.*

/ˈhɑːdweə kənˌfɪɡəˌreɪʃn/
pl hardware configurations
⋈ alter, improve, upgrade the **hardware configuration**

---

hardware dependent *adjective*
(of programs and devices) that only work with a certain type of hardware

/ˌhɑːdweə dɪˈpendənt/
⋈ a **hardware dependent** assembly language, computer component, device, program

---

hardware failure *noun* (hardware)
a failure of a computer system caused by a HARD ERROR

/ˈhɑːdweə ˌfeɪljə(r)/
pl hardware failures
⋈ diagnose, suffer *from* a **hardware failure**
syn hard failure
▶ **crash**[1]

---

hardware interrupt *noun*
a signal sent by a hardware device asking the CPU for attention: *The computer's memory failure generated a high-priority hardware interrupt.*

/ˌhɑːdweə(r) ˈɪntərʌpt/
pl hardware interrupts
⋈ generate, respond *to* a **hardware interrupt**; an external, internal **hardware interrupt**

	► **interrupt**[1], **software interrupt**

hardwired *adjective*
(of functions) that are built into a system and are not provided by software: *Machine code instructions correspond to the basic operations hardwired in the computer.*

/ˈhɑːdwaɪd/
M **hardwired** circuitry, logic, instructions

---

hardwired logic *noun* (hardware)
logic circuits that are a permanent part of the computer hardware and are not programmed by software: *Most basic gate circuits are hardwired logic.*

/ˌhɑːdwaɪəd ˈlɒdʒɪk/
note not used with *a* or *an*. No plural and used with a singular verb only.
M build, use **hardwired logic**
► **logic**

---

hashing *noun*
a way of using a data item in a calculation to give its expected position in a list or table: *Hashing can improve access times to large tables.*

/ˈhæʃɪŋ/
note not used with *a* or *an*. No plural and used with a singular verb only.
M implement, use **hashing**; a **hashing** algorithm, calculation, code, method
► **collision**

---

hash total *noun*
a value that is calculated from a set of data before and after it is processed. If the value that is calculated before processing is not the same as the total that is calculated when processing has finished, an error has occurred.

/ˈhæʃ ˌtəʊtl/
pl hash totals

HCI *abbr*
► **human-computer interface**

/ˌeɪtʃ siː ˈaɪ/
note pronounced as individual letters

---

head *noun*
1 the first item in a list: *The atom A is the head of the list (A, B, (C, D))*

2 ► **read/write head**

/hed/
pl heads
1 M access, delete, print the **head**
► **tail**

---

head alignment *noun*
the process of placing the READ/WRITE HEAD in the correct position in the disk drive so that data can be transferred from a disk to the computer or from the computer to a disk

/ˈhed əˌlaɪmmənt/
note not used with *a* or *an*. No plural and used with a singular verb only.

---

head crash *noun*
► **disk crash**

/ˈhed kræʃ/

☆**header** *noun*
1 (*software*) a piece of code that marks the beginning of a file: *The file has a fixed format header giving general information about the file and its format.* **2** (*applications*) text that is automatically added to the top of every page of a printout and can be the title of the document or page number, etc: *The header contains the name of the author and the date the document was printed.*

/ˈhedə(r)/
pl headers
1 ► **end of file**
2 **syn** running head
► **footer, message header, start of header character**

---

abbr abbreviation   **pl** plural   **syn** synonym   ► see   M collocate (*word often used with the headword*)

header label *noun*
▶ **label**

/'hedə ,leɪbl/

---

header record *noun*
▶ **label**

/'hedə ,rekɔːd/

---

heap *noun*
an area of memory reserved for DYNAMIC DATA STRUCTURES

note A heap is not structured. When memory is needed for a new element, any available memory can be taken from anywhere in the heap.

/hiːp/
pl heaps
ʍ draw something *from*, replace something *on* the **heap**

☆**help** *noun*
a way of answering users' questions about a program either with ON-LINE HELP or a MANUAL: *The package comes with a comprehensive help and a tutorial.*

/'help/
note Not used with *a* or *an*. No plural and used with a singular verb only.
▶ **context-sensitive help**

---

help file *noun*
▶ **on-line help**

/'help faɪl/

---

hertz *noun*
the SI unit of frequency where one hertz is equal to one cycle per second

/'hɜːts/
note not used with *a* or *an*. No plural and used with a singular verb only.
abbr Hz
ʍ measure *in* **hertz**
▶ **cycles per second, MIPS**

---

heuristic *noun*
a program which is designed to learn and improve its way of working as it is executed again and again: *Heuristics are central to artificial intelligence and expert systems development.*

/hjuːˈrɪstɪk/
pl heuristics
ʍ execute, program as a **heuristic**
syn heuristic program

---

heuristic program *noun*
▶ **heuristic**

/hjuːˌrɪstɪk 'prəʊgræm/

☆**HEX** *abbr*
▶ **hexadecimal**

/heks/
note pronounced as a word

☆**hexadecimal** *noun*
a system of numbers based on the number 16: *data coded in hexadecimal*

/ˌheksə'desɪml/
note not used with *a* or *an*. No plural and used with a singular verb only.
abbr HEX, hex
ʍ **hexadecimal** characters, notation, numbers
▶ **base 16**

---

hexadecimal conversion *noun*
to change a number to or from HEXADECIMAL notation: *Hexadecimal conversion of the byte FF into denary gives 255.*

/'heksəˌdesɪml kən'vɜːʃn/
note not used with *a* or *an*. No plural and used with a singular verb only.
ʍ carry out, perform **hexadecimal conversion**

hexadecimal dump *noun*
a display of the contents of registers or memory in hexadecimal notation: *Hexadecimal dumps are used in debugging to see if memory is being altered as expected.* ○ *a hexadecimal dump on screen/on paper*

/ˈheksəˌdesɪml ˈdʌmp/
pl hexadecimal dumps
ᴍ perform, print, request a **hexadecimal dump**
▶ **binary dump, debug**

hidden file *noun* (software)
a file which is an important part of the operating system and is marked so that it does not appear on any list of files. This protects it from being deleted or changed.

/ˌhɪdn ˈfaɪl/
pl hidden files
syn invisible file

hidden line removal *noun* (applications/graphics)
the process of removing edges and surfaces of a THREE-DIMENSIONAL object which should not be visible from certain positions in order to make the image look more realistic.

/ˌhɪdn ˈlaɪn rɪˌmuːvl/
note not used with *a* or *an*. No plural and used with a singular verb only.
ᴍ carry out, perform **hidden line removal**

hierarchical *adjective*
connected with things arranged in a HIERARCHY: *This software package has options arranged as a set of hierarchical menus.*

/ˌhaɪəˈrɑːkɪkl/
ᴍ **hierarchical** classification, structure

☆**hierarchical database** *noun* (data representation)
a database in which the data is structured in a HIERARCHY. The importance of the data is the main feature in a hierarchical database rather than its alphabetical or numerical order.

/ˈhaɪəˌrɑːkɪkl ˈdeɪtəbeɪs/
pl hierarchical databases
ᴍ arrange, order a **hierarchical database**
▶ **databank, network database, relational database**

hierarchical file system *noun*
a way of storing data by putting files into directories or folders

note A hierarchical file system allows a user to structure their data files in a way which reflects their use, and to give them names so they can be easily identified.

/ˈhaɪəˌrɑːkɪkl ˈfaɪl ˌsɪstəm/
pl hierarchical file systems
ᴍ store in, structure as a **hierarchical file system**
▶ **directory, folder, path, subdirectory**

hierarchical menu *noun*
a menu which has choices leading to further menus

/ˈhaɪəˌrɑːkɪkl ˈmenjuː/
pl hierarchical menus
ᴍ choose *from* a **hierarchical menu**; **hierarchical menu** choices, options

☆**hierarchy** *noun* (data representation)
a system in which data items are stored in a certain order: *The top of the hierarchy consists of the most important items.*

/ˈhaɪərɑːki/
pl hierarchies
ᴍ a complex, simple **hierarchy**

high density disk *noun* (hardware)
a floppy disk that can store one megabyte or more of data

note A high density disk can store nearly twice as much as a double density disk.

/ˈhaɪ ˈdensətɪ ˈdɪsk/
pl high density disks
ᴍ a 5¼ inch, a 3½ inch, a formatted, an unformatted **high density disk**
▶ **floppy disk, double density disk, DS DD, DS HD**

---

abbr abbreviation   **pl** plural   **syn** synonym   ▶ see   ᴍ collocate (*word often used with the headword*)

☆**high-level language** *noun* (programming)
a programming language, such as Basic, Pascal and C, that consists of statements that are very close to human language, and so not very close to machine code: *translate high-level languages into machine code with a compiler*

/ˌhaɪ levl ˈlæŋgwɪdʒ/
pl high-level languages
ℍ understand, write a **high-level language**
syn problem-oriented language
▶ **assembly language, compile, interpreter, low-level language, machine code, source code**

☆**highlight** *verb* (user operation)
to change the colour or brightness of a piece of text or a menu item, etc: *highlight the word to be deleted* ○ *select the menu option by highlighting it*

/ˈhaɪlaɪt/
note transitive verb
ℍ **highlight** a letter, word
▶ **drag, select**

high-resolution *adjective* (hardware)
(of a screen or a printer) that can produce very good quality images or text: *The high-resolution screen displays graphics very clearly.* ○ *print graphics on a high resolution laser printer*

/ˌhaɪ rezəˈluːʃn/
abbr high-res
ℍ a **high-resolution** printer, screen
▶ **high-resolution**

☆**high-tech** *adjective*
(*informal*) (of technology or equipment, etc) that is very modern: *a sophisticated high-tech office with all the latest computers, photocopiers and fax machines* ○ *a high-tech production process controlled almost completely by computers*

/ˌhaɪ ˈtek/
ℍ a **high-tech** industry, machine, system
▶ **state-of-the-art, technology**

highway *noun*
▶ **bus**

/ˈhaɪweɪ/

hi-res *abbr*
▶ **high-resolution**

/ˌhaɪ ˈrez/

hit *noun*
a successful search in a database: *The search produced four hits.*

/hɪt/
pl hits
ℍ achieve, score a **hit**

hit rate *noun*
the proportion of HITS compared to failures in a database search: *a 20 per cent hit rate*

/ˈhɪt reɪt/
pl hit rates
ℍ a high, low **hit rate**

Hollerith code *noun*
a coding system for representing numbers and characters as holes punched onto cards

note Hollerith code was first used before computers in mechanical tabulators and sorting machines used for the US census.

/ˈhɒlərɪθ ˌkəʊd/
note not used with *a* or *an*. No plural and used with a singular verb only.
ℍ use, punch in **Hollerith code**

☆**home** *noun* (hardware)
a key which is used to move the cursor to the beginning of a document or page: *press home to place the cursor at the beginning of the memo*

/həʊm/
note not used with *a* or *an*. No plural and used with a singular verb only.
syn home key
▶ **end, page down, page up**

☆**home computer** *noun* (hardware)
a computer that can be used at home: *work from home using a home computer* ○ *multimedia CD-ROMs for the home computer*

/ˌhəʊm kəmˈpjuːtə(r)/
pl home computers
▶ **PC, teleworking**

☆**home key** *noun*
▶ **home**

/'həʊm kiː/

---

home page *noun*
the first page of information on an organization, university or individual, etc on the WORLD WIDE WEB. A home page usually contains an introduction to the other pages and links to related information: *The university's home page has hyperlinks to other related sites on the Internet.*

/ˌhəʊm 'peɪdʒ/
pl home pages
▶ **browser, HTML, World Wide Web**

---

hook *noun*
a place in a program where a programmer can put ROUTINES

/hʊk/
pl hooks
◄ insert a function/module/routine *into* a, provide a **hook**

---

horizontal axis *noun*
▶ **X-axis**

/'hɒrɪˌzɒntl 'æksɪs/

---

horizontal redundancy check *noun*
a CYCLIC REDUNDANCY CHECK that is used on the whole of a single data item, rather than on the same part of each data item: *On a magnetic tape system a horizontal redundancy check is applied across each character.*

/'hɒrɪˌzɒntl rɪ'dʌndənsi tʃek/
pl horizontal redundancy checks
abbr HRC
◄ apply a **horizontal redundancy check**
syn longitudinal redundancy check
▶ **vertical redundancy check**

---

horizontal scrolling *noun*
the process of moving text on screen or in a window from one side of the screen or window to the other. This usually happens when a document is too wide for both sides to be seen at the same time: *Horizontal scrolling allows the left part of the large spreadsheet to be seen on the screen.*

/'hɒrɪˌzɒntl 'skrəʊlɪŋ/
note not used with *a* or *an*. No plural and used with a singular verb only.
▶ **vertical scrolling**

---

horizontal tabulation *noun*
the process of FORMATTING² (2) data into columns on screen or on paper: *Horizontal tabulation makes the figures easier to read.*

/'hɒrɪˌzɒntl ˌtæbju'leɪʃn/
note no plural
abbr HT

☆**host computer** *noun* (hardware)
a computer in a network that makes programs and data available to other computers in the network: *Packets of data are transferred from the host computer to each terminal.* ○ *The host computer is being scanned for new e-mail.*

/'həʊst kəmˌpjuːtə(r)/
pl host computers
◄ download data *from*, receive data *from*, send data *to*, upload data *to* a **host computer**

---

hot key *noun*
a key or combination of keys that can be pressed to take the user to a different program: *use the hot key 'Alt P' as a short cut to switch from the word processing program to the spreadsheet*

/'hɒt kiː/
pl hot keys
◄ define, press, use a **hot key**; a **hot key** combination, command
▶ **macro**

☆**housekeeping** *noun* (system operation)
the programs that keep a system working well: *a housekeeping routine that deallocates memory that is no longer needed* ○ *Housekeeping functions include updating the system clock from time to time.*

/'haʊskiːpɪŋ/
note no plural
◄ **housekeeping** actions, routines
▶ **operating system**

---

abbr abbreviation   **pl** plural   **syn** synonym   ▶ see   ◄ collocate (*word often used with the headword*)

HRC *abbr*
▶ **horizontal redundancy check**

/ˌeɪtʃ ɑː ˈsiː/
note pronounced as individual letters

HT *abbr*
the ASCII symbol number 9 for HORIZONTAL TABULATION

note used in written English only

HTML *abbr*
hypertext mark-up language

/ˌeɪtʃ tiː em ˈel/
note pronounced as individual letters

---

hue *noun*
the characteristic of a colour that makes it different from other colours

/hjuː/
pl hues
Ⱳ adjust, match, specify the **hue**
▶ **colour saturation**

---

human-computer interface *noun* (applications)
the communication between a user and a computer system:
design human-computer interface facilities

/ˌhjuːmən kəmˈpjuːtə(r) ˌɪntəfeɪs/
pl human-computer interfaces
abbr HCI
(also **human-machine interface**)
▶ **graphical user interface, interactive, user-interface**

---

hybrid computer *noun* (hardware)
a computer that contains both analog and digital circuits, such as a PC

/ˈhaɪbrɪd kəmˌpjuːtə(r)/
pl hybrid computers
Ⱳ build, design, use a **hybrid computer**

☆**hypermedia** *noun* (applications)
the combination of sound, graphics and video (= multimedia) to present information that is linked, enabling the user to move from one piece of information to another: *The hypermedia page on programming is linked to related topics on specific programming languages.*

note 'Hypermedia' is a combination of the words 'hypertext' and 'multimedia'.

/ˌhaɪpəˈmiːdiə/
note no plural
Ⱳ a **hypermedia** application; **hypermedia** software, technology

---

☆**hypertext** *noun*
text stored in a computer system that contains links that allow the user to move from one piece of text to another: *put a hypertext document on the Internet ○ construct hypertext links ○ click on a link in a hypertext document*

/ˈhaɪpətekst/
note no plural
Ⱳ **hypertext** software
▶ **browser, multimedia, text**

---

hyphen *noun*
the character '-' found on keyboards which is used in printing certain compound words such as 'in-house' or in marking the end of the first part of a whole word that starts on one line and continues on the line below

/ˈhaɪfən/
pl hyphens
Ⱳ delete, insert a **hyphen**
▶ **soft hyphen, underscore**

Hz *abbr*
▶ **hertz**

/hɜːts/

IAS *abbr*
▶ **immediate access store**

/ˌaɪ eɪ 'es/
note pronounced as individual letters

IBG *abbr*
▶ **interblock gap**

/ˌaɪ biː 'dʒiː/
note pronounced as individual letters

IBM *abbr*
(*trade mark*) (*organizations*) International Business Machines. A company that produces personal computers.

/ˌaɪ biː 'em/
note pronounced as individual letters

IC *abbr*
▶ **integrated circuit**

/ˌaɪ 'siː/
note pronounced as individual letters

☆**icon** *noun* (applications)
a small picture on a screen that represents a program, an option or a file: *drag the disk icon to the wastebasket icon to eject the disk* ○ *click on the printer icon*

/'aɪkɒn/
pl icons
◄ click *on*, drag, select an **icon**
▶ **graphical user interface, WIMP**

ID *abbr*
▶ **identification**

/ˌaɪ 'diː/
note pronounced as individual letters

☆**identification** *noun* (system operation)
1 the process of checking that a computer user has the right to use a system: *Strict rules of identification have to be followed to gain access to classified data.* **2** the process of one computer checking that it is able to communicate with another computer: *obtain transmission protocol information during identification*

/aɪˌdentɪfɪ'keɪʃn/
note not used with *a* or *an*. No plural and used with a singular verb only.
abbr ID
1 ▶ **password, personal identification device, personal identification number**

☆**identifier** *noun* (software)
a name used to identify a set of data or a PERIPHERAL: *The identifier of the list is 'freespace'.* ○ *The identifier of the server is 'drongo'.*

/aɪ'dentɪfaɪə(r)/
pl identifiers
◄ a program, statement **identifier**
▶ **variable name**

---

idle *adjective*
(of a device) that is switched on but is not in use

/'aɪdl/
◄ an **idle** device, moment, state

---

idle time *noun*
a amount of time when a device is switched on but is not used

/'aɪdl taɪm/
note usually singular
◄ record **idle time**
▶ **down time, up time**

IH *abbr*
▶ **interrupt handler**

/ˌaɪ 'eɪtʃ/
note pronounced as individual letters

IKBS *abbr*
▶ **intelligent knowledge-based system**

/ˌaɪ keɪ biː 'es/
note pronounced as individual letters

---

illegal character *noun*
a character which is not recognized by an application, or cannot be used as part of the grammar of a language: *Error 46 means there is an illegal character in a command line.*

/ɪˌliːgl 'kærəktə(r)/
pl illegal characters
◄ input, recognize, type an **illegal character**

---

abbr abbreviation   **pl** plural   **syn** synonym   ▶ see   ◄ collocate (*word often used with the headword*)

☆**illegal operation** *noun* (system operation)
an action that the operating system or program will not allow
the computer to do: *writing data to a protected disk is an illegal
operation* ○ *The illegal operation caused the system to halt.*

/ɪ,liːgl ɒpəˈreɪʃn/
pl illegal operations
◪ perform an **illegal operation**

☆**image** *noun* (applications)
1 a copy of something, especially part of memory: *The RAM
disk holds an image of the files from the floppy disk in main
memory.*

2 ▶ **graphics**

/ˈɪmɪdʒ/
pl images

image enhancement *noun*
the process of analysing a video signal to remove NOISE and to
improve the contrast of the picture to make it clearer: *Image
enhancement was needed to improve the pictures on the security
camera to identify the criminals.*

/ˈɪmɪdʒ ɪn,hɑːnsmənt/
note not used with *a* or *an*. No
plural and used with a singular
verb only.
◪ carry out, perform **image
enhancement**
▶ **image processing, contrast**[2]

image processing *noun*
the analysis of the data contained in a picture or video signal:
Image processing requires fast computers with a lot of storage.

/ˈɪmɪdʒ ,prəʊsesɪŋ/
note not used with *a* or *an*. No
plural and used with a singular
verb only.
◪ perform, carry out **image
processing**; an **image
processing** algorithm, method,
technique; **image processing**
software

image scanner *noun*
▶ **scanner**

/ˈɪmɪdʒ ,skænə(r)/

imaging *noun*
the process of capturing, storing and displaying an image on
screen: *build up a display of a human brain using imaging
techniques*

/ˈɪmɪdʒɪŋ/
note not used with *a* or *an*. No
plural and used with a singular
verb only.
◪ carry out, perform **imaging**; an
imaging technique, method;
imaging software; digital,
magnetic resonance,
diagnostic, document, thermal
imaging

immediate access store *noun* (hardware)
memory from which the CPU can access data almost
immediately: *The immediate access store has an access time of 50
nanoseconds.*

/ɪ,miːdiət ˈækses stɔː(r)/
note not used with *a* or *an*. No
plural and used with a singular
verb only.
abbr IAS
◪ place data *in*, read data *from*,
store data *in*, write data *to*
immediate access store

immediate address *noun*
the address field of a machine code instruction which is used as
data, and not as the address at which the data is found

/ɪ,miːdiət əˈdres/
pl immediate addresses
▶ **implied addressing, indirect
addressing**

immediate addressing *noun*

a method of addressing in machine code where the address field of the instruction is used as data, and not as the address at which the data is found: *Simple increment instructions usually use immediate addressing.*

/ɪˌmiːdiət əˈdresɪŋ/

note not used with *a* or *an*. No plural and used with a singular verb only.

◣ implement, program using, use **immediate addressing**

immediate operand *noun*

the address part of an instruction used in IMMEDIATE ADDRESSING: *Simple increment instructions usually use immediate operands.*

/ɪˌmiːdiət ˈɒpərænd/

pl immediate operands

◣ access, use an **immediate operand**

impact printer *noun* (hardware)

a printer that produces text by hitting characters against a piece of material with ink on it, called a ribbon, onto paper

/ˈɪmpækt ˌprɪntə(r)/

pl impact printers

▶ **nonimpact printer, printer**

imperative *adjective*

(of a programming language) that has a set of instructions on how to execute ALGORITHMS: *Fortran is an imperative high-level language.*

/ɪmˈperətɪv/

◣ an **imperative** language, operation, statement

▶ **logic programming, query language, object-oriented**

implement *verb*

to start using a plan or a computer system, etc: *The development plan was implemented as soon as it was agreed.* ○ *implement a new system that can read bar codes*

/ˈɪmplɪment/

implement, implementing, implemented

note transitive verb

implementation *noun*

the act of starting to use a plan or computer system, etc: *Implementation of the system was scheduled for January 1998.*

/ˌɪmplɪmenˈteɪʃn/

note not used with *a* or *an*. No plural and used with a singular verb only.

◣ plan *for*, schedule **implementation**

implied addressing *noun*

a type of addressing that makes the execution time of certain machine code instructions faster because the data for the instruction is always found in the same place

note The location in an instruction using implied addressing is usually one of the CPU registers.

/ɪmˌplaɪd əˈdresɪŋ/

note not used with *a* or *an*. No plural and used with a singular verb only.

◣ use **implied addressing**

▶ **immediate addressing, indirect addressing**

☆**import** *verb*

to move data from one system or program to another system or program. This will only be successful if the system or program receiving the data can support the format of this data

/ɪmˈpɔːt/

import, importing, imported

note transitive verb

◣ **import** a bitmap, file

▶ **export**

inches per second *noun*

a measure of the speed of something: *Professional audio recording tape travels at 15 inches per second.*

/ˌɪntʃɪz pə ˈsekənd/

note not used with *a* or *an*. No plural and used with a singular verb only.

abbr ips

◣ measure *in* **inches per second**

abbr abbreviation   **pl** plural   **syn** synonym   ▶ see   ◣ collocate (*word often used with the headword*)

inclusive OR *noun*
a GATE whose single ouput is set to TRUE if any one or more of its inputs is TRUE

/ɪnˌkluːsɪv 'ɔː(r)/
pl inclusive ORs
◀ an **inclusive OR** circuit, gate
▶ **exclusive OR**

---

incoming traffic *noun* (software/communications)
messages and data received by a device from a network or communication channel: *There is a lot of incoming traffic at the start of the day.*

/ˌɪnkʌmɪŋ 'træfɪk/
note not used with *a* or *an*. No plural and used with a singular verb only.
◀ heavy, light **incoming traffic**
▶ **traffic density**

☆**incompatible** *adjective*
(of hardware or software) that are not able to work together: *The program was written for a Mac and is therefore incompatible with a PC.*

/ˌɪnkəm'pætəbl/
◀ **incompatible** with a computer, etc
▶ **compatible**

---

increment¹ *noun*
1 an amount added to a register or counter: *In a FOR NEXT loop, the increment is specified in the STEP variable.* **2** a regular increase in a scale or axis: *The X-axis is marked in increments of 10.*

/'ɪŋkrəmənt/
pl increments
2 ◀ mark an **increment**
▶ **decrement**

---

increment² *verb*
to add a number (usually 1) to a numeric register: *increment the loop counter by one after each iteration*

/'ɪŋkrəment/
increment, incrementing, incremented
note transitive verb
◀ **increment** a counter, register
▶ **decrement**

---

indent¹ *noun*
the amount of white space before the first character on a printed line: *Quotations have an indent of 2cm.*

/'ɪndent/
pl indents
◀ adjust, insert, set an **indent**

---

indent² *verb*
to put a piece of text further from the left of the page than the rest of the text on the page: *Quotations in the text are indented by 2 cm from the margin.* ○ *If the paragraph is indented, it will be seen more clearly.*

/ɪn'dent/
indent, indenting, indented
note transitive verb
◀ **indent** a paragraph; **indent** text

---

independent *adjective*
(of a device or system, etc) that is not controlled by another device or system

/ˌɪndɪ'pendənt/
◀ an **independent** device, system; **independent** behaviour

---

☆**index** *noun* (software)
an ordered list that contains information about the physical location of an item of data in memory or on disk: *When searching or sorting the database, the program uses the index rather than the full database.*

/'ɪndeks/
pl indexes
pl indices
◀ access, build, construct, make, update an **index**
▶ **primary index, secondary index**

indexed *adjective*
(of data) that is able to be accessed by using an INDEX or an INDEX REGISTER

/'ɪndekst/
⋈ an **indexed** instruction, sequential file

---

indexed addressing *noun*
a way of changing an address calculated by the CPU before it is used to access a storage location. The contents of an index register are added to the address to give a new address which is then used for accessing a storage location.

/ˌɪndekst ə'dresɪŋ/
note not used with *a* or *an*. No plural and used with a singular verb only.
⋈ use **indexed addressing**
▶ **address modification, indirect addressing**

---

indexed sequential access method *noun*
▶ **ISAM**

/'ɪndekst sɪ'kwenʃl 'ækses ˌmeθəd/

---

index generation *noun*
the process of calculating a numeric value that shows where in a list or table a data item should be accessed or stored

/'ɪndeks dʒenə,reɪʃn/
note not used with *a* or *an*. No plural and used with a singular verb only.
1 ⋈ an **index generation** algorithm; **index generation** software

---

index hole *noun*
a small round hole near the large hole in the centre of a floppy disk. The index hole marks the beginning of the first data SECTOR on the disk. It also allows the SYNCHRONIZATION of read and write operations with the movement of the disk.

/'ɪndeks həʊl/
pl index holes
⋈ read the **index hole**

---

indexing *noun*
the use of INDEXES and INDEX REGISTERS in accessing data items: *Indexing allows faster access to structured data items such as arrays.*

/'ɪndeksɪŋ/
note not used with *a* or *an*. No plural and used with a singular verb only.
⋈ use **indexing**; an **indexing** method, routine

---

index mark *noun*
a code on the track of a magnetic disk that is placed just before the address of a section of data: *The index mark is placed on the disk during formatting.*

/'ɪndeks mɑːk/
pl index marks
syn address mark

---

index register *noun*
a special register in the CPU which is used to calculate addresses. The contents of the index register may be added to the address already available to give a new address. The new address is then used for accessing a storage location.

/'ɪndeks ˌredʒɪstə(r)/
pl index registers
⋈ load, use an **index register**
▶ **address modification, indirect addressing, actual instruction**

---

index sequential file *noun*
a file that may be accessed by ISAM: *The bigger collections of data are in index sequential files.*

/'ɪndeks sɪ'kwenʃl 'faɪl/
pl index sequential files
⋈ access, store data in, update an **index sequential file**

---

abbr abbreviation   **pl** plural   **syn** synonym   ▶ see   ⋈ collocate (*word often used with the headword*)

indirect addressing *noun*

a method of changing an address calculated by the CPU before it is used to access a storage location. Instead of using the address field of an instruction as the location of the data, the field contains the address of a location which contains a further address. It is this last address which is used as the location of the data.

note Indirect addressing can be used to allow access to a wider range of addresses than can be stored in the space reserved in an instruction word.

/ˈɪndəˌrekt əˈdresɪŋ/

note not used with *a* or *an*. No plural and used with a singular verb only.

⋈ use **indirect addressing**

▶ **actual instruction**

---

infect *verb*

to put a virus into a computer

/ɪnˈfekt/

infect, infecting, infected

note transitive verb

⋈ **infect** a disk, program

---

inference engine *noun* (software)

the part of an EXPERT SYSTEM which uses the rules and facts stored in the system to make decisions

/ˈɪnfərəns ˌendʒɪn/

pl inference engines

⋈ employ, invoke, use an **inference engine**

▶ **knowledge base**

---

infinite loop *noun* (software/programming)

a block of statements in a computer programming language that is executed again and again until the program HALTS[2]: *The program could not break out of the infinite loop.*

/ˌɪnfɪnət ˈluːp/

pl repeat until loops

⋈ execute, perform, repeat an **infinite loop**

syn endless loop

▶ **loop[1] 2, while loop, do loop, repeat until loop, nested loop, loop body, loop variable**

---

infix notation *noun*

the usual way of writing operations on numbers, with the operator between the two OPERANDS: *addition in infix notation is written as 2+3*

/ˈɪnfɪks nəʊˌteɪʃn/

note not used with *a* or *an*. No plural and used with a singular verb only.

⋈ read, translate *from/into*, write *in* **infix notation**

▶ **postfix notation, prefix notation**

---

informatics *noun*

the subjects that relate to information technology, such as computing, technology and mathematics

/ˌɪnfəˈmætɪks/

note plural noun used with a singular verb

---

information *noun*

data that has meaning for people: *The computer can turn statistical data into information on a graph that is easy for people to understand.*

note There is a difference between data and information. Data is what the computer processes without understanding the content. Information is the result of the processing and it has meaning for people who use it. In informal situations, 'information' and 'data' are used to mean the same thing.

/ˌɪnfəˈmeɪʃn/

note not used with *a* or *an*. No plural and used with a singular verb only.

⋈ process, receive **information**; an **information** explosion; **information** processing, theory

▶ **data**

information management system *noun* (software)
software for storing, updating and accessing information

/ˈɪnfəˌmeɪʃn ˈmænɪdʒmənt ˌsɪstəm/
pl information management systems
◣ build, run, use an **information management system**
▶ **database**

---

information processing *noun*
the processing of data, especially by computers, in order to obtain information from it

/ˌɪnfəˈmeɪʃn ˌprəʊsesɪŋ/
note not used with *a* or *an*. No plural and used with a singular verb only.
◣ carry out, perform **information processing**
▶ **data processing**

☆**information retrieval** *noun* (applications)
the process of finding and usually displaying information stored in a computer system:

/ˌɪnfəˈmeɪʃn rɪˌtriːvl/
note no plural
◣ on-line **information retrieval**
▶ **search**

---

information structure *noun*
a way of organizing information as data in a computer

/ˌɪnfəˈmeɪʃn ˌstrʌktʃə(r)/
pl information structures
◣ represent data *as*, update an **information structure**

☆**information technology** *noun*
▶ **IT**

/ˌɪnfəˈmeɪʃn tekˌnɒlədʒi/

---

inhibit interrupt *noun*
▶ **disable interrupt**

/ɪnˌhɪbɪt ˈɪntərʌpt/

---

in-house *adjective*
connected with one company only and not involving anything from outside that company: *In-house text processing facilities are cheaper and more efficient than out-of-house ones.*

/ˈɪn haʊs/
◣ **in-house** services, operations, facilities

---

initialize *verb*
1 to give a value to a variable at the start of a program: *initialize the counter to zero* **2** to make a device ready for use: *The first stage of connecting to the Internet is initializing the modem.*

/ɪˈnɪʃəlaɪz/
initialize, initializing, initialized
(also **initialise**)
note transitive verb
1 ◣ **initialize** an array, a variable
2 ◣ **initialize** a disk, printer
▶ **disk formatting**

---

initial program loader *noun*
a short MACHINE CODE program that loads the operating system from backing store

/ɪˌnɪʃl ˈprəʊgræm ˌləʊdə(r)/
pl initial program loaders
abbr IPL
◣ execute, invoke, load an **initial program loader**

---

abbr abbreviation   **pl** plural   **syn** synonym   ▶ see   ◣ collocate (*word often used with the headword*)

initial value *noun*
the value that is given to a variable at the start of a program:
Each element in the array is given an initial value of zero.

/ɪˌnɪʃl 'væljuː/
pl initial values
⋈ assign, give, set an **initial value**

---

ink-jet printer *noun*
a printer that forces ink through a narrow opening to print
text, etc: *a document produced by an ink-jet printer* ○ *an ink-jet printer squirts ink onto the paper*

/'ɪŋk dʒet ˌprɪntə(r)/
pl ink-jet printers
▶ **nonimpact printer, printer**

---

inline code *noun* (software/programming)
statements in a computer program that are in the main part of
the program and are not contained in a SUBROUTINE or
procedure

/ˌɪnlaɪn 'kəʊd/
note not used with *a* or *an*. No
plural and used with a singular
verb only.
⋈ code *as*, execute, write **inline code**

---

in-line processing *noun*
processing data as it becomes available, rather than processing
it at a fixed time

/ˌɪnlaɪn 'prəʊsesɪŋ/
note not used with *a* or *an*. No
plural and used with a singular
verb only.
⋈ perform **in-line processing**
▶ **asynchronous**

---

inner loop *noun* (software/programming)
a LOOP[1] (2) that is contained inside another loop: *The program
executes an inner loop.*

/ˌɪnə 'luːp/
pl inner loops
⋈ execute, perform, program an **inner loop**
▶ **nested loop, outer loop**

---

inorder traversal *noun*
▶ **symmetric traversal**

/ɪnˌɔːdə trə'vɜːsl/

☆**input[1]** *noun* (software)
1 the data that is put into a computer for processing: *enter
input via a keyboard* **2** the act of putting data into a computer:
prepare information for input

/'ɪnpʊt/
1 note usually singular
abbr I/P
⋈ data, electrical **input**
2 note not used with *a* or *an*. No
plural and used with a singular
verb only.
▶ **output[1]**

☆**input[2]** *verb*
to put data into a computer for processing: *input figures into the
spreadsheet*

/'ɪnpʊt/
input, inputting, input *or*
inputted
note transitive verb
⋈ **input** data
▶ **output[2]**

---

input area *noun* (hardware)
a part of memory reserved for data to be received

/'ɪnpʊt ˌeəriə/
pl input areas
⋈ access, load *into*, read *from* the **input area**
▶ **buffer**

input bound *adjective* (system operation)
(of a program) whose execution speed is limited by the time taken to input data

note Most keyboard operations, for example, are input bound because human typing speed will always be much slower than computer processing speed.

/'ɪmpʊt baʊnd/
◄ an **input bound** process, program; **input bound** software
▶ **input/output bound**

☆**input device** *noun* (hardware)
a piece of equipment, such as a mouse or keyboard, that is used for inputting data into a computer

/'ɪmpʊt dɪˌvaɪs/
pl input devices
▶ **output device, peripheral**

☆**input/output** *adjective*
connected with the part of a computer system that is used to pass data to and from the central processing unit

/ˌɪmpʊt 'aʊtpʊt/
abbr I/O
◄ an **input/output** channel, device, file, port, system

---

input/output bound *adjective* (system operation)
(of a program) whose execution speed is limited by the time taken to input and/or output data: *upgrade the system to avoid the processing becoming input/output bound* ○ *The microprocessor is input/output bound because the disk drive is too slow.*

/ˌɪmpʊt 'aʊtpʊt baʊnd/
abbr I/O bound
◄ an **input/output bound** process, program
▶ **compute bound**

---

input/output buffer *noun*
an area of storage which is used for data that is sent to or received from a PERIPHERAL

/ˌɪmpʊt 'aʊtpʊt ˌbʌfə(r)/
pl input/output buffers
◄ access, load *into* an **input/output buffer**
syn I/O buffer
▶ **buffer, output buffer**

---

input/output bus *noun*
the links between a computer and its peripheral devices; both data and CONTROL SIGNALS travel over the input/output bus

/ˌɪmpʊt 'aʊtpʊt bʌs/
pl input/output buses
syn I/O bus
◄ send *on*, transmit *over* an **input/output bus**

---

input/output controller *noun*
hardware that directs the transmission of data between the computer and PERIPHERALS: *A new faster input/output controller has improved transfer times.*

/ˌɪmpʊt 'aʊtpʊt kənˌtrəʊlə(r)/
pl input/output controllers
syn I/O controller
◄ install, use an **input/output controller**

---

input/output coprocessor *noun*
▶ **input/output processor**

/'ɪmpʊt 'aʊtpʊt kəʊ'prəʊsesə(r)/

---

input/output processor *noun* (hardware)
a processor that only controls input and output operations: *Use of an input/output processor allows the central processor to concentrate on computation.*

/ˌɪmpʊt 'aʊtpʊt ˌprəʊsesə(r)/
pl input/output processors
abbr IOP
syn I/O coprocessor, I/O processor, input/output coprocessor

---

abbr abbreviation   **pl** plural   **syn** synonym   ▶ see   ◄ collocate (*word often used with the headword*)

input port *noun*
a PORT[1] that allows a computer to receive data from an
external device: *connect the keyboard to an input port*

/'ɪnpʊt pɔːt/
pl input ports
ᴍ address, connect *to*, receive
from an **input port**
▶ **output port, port[1]**

---

input tagging *noun*
the process of adding a TAG[1] 2 to an item of data as it is entered
into a computer system to describe that item of data

/'ɪnpʊt ˌtægɪŋ/
note not used with *a* or *an*. No
plural and used with a singular
verb only.

---

ins *abbr*
▶ **insert[1]**

note used in written English only

☆**insert[1]** *noun* (hardware/word processing)
the key that is used to add words, etc to a text: *press insert to
avoid typing over existing text*

/'ɪnsɜːt/
note not used with *a* or *an*. No
plural and used with a singular
verb only.
abbr ins
ᴍ the **insert** key
▶ **backspace[1], cursor control
keys, delete[1], shift**

☆**insert[2]** *verb* (user operation)
1 to place or fit something into something else: *insert the disk
into drive A* **2** to add a letter, word or line to a piece of text:
insert a word in the middle of a line

/ɪn'sɜːt/
insert, inserting
pl inserted
note transitive verb
1,2 ᴍ **insert** something
between, in, into something
▶ **enter[2], delete[2]**

---

insertion point *noun*
the place in text, usually marked by a CURSOR, where new text
will be added, especially in a graphical interface: *The insertion
point can be moved by the arrow keys or by the mouse.*

/ɪn'sɜːʃn pɔɪnt/
pl insertion points
ᴍ change, move the **insertion
point**
▶ **cursor**

---

insertion sort *noun*
a method of sorting data where each data item from the
unsorted list is taken and placed in its correct position in a
growing list of items that have already been sorted

/ɪn'sɜːʃn sɔːt/
pl insertion sorts
ᴍ carry out, perform, use an
insertion sort
▶ **sort**

☆**insert key** *noun*
▶ **insert[1]**

/ɪn'sɜːt kiː/

---

insert mode *noun*
the state of a word processing program in which new
characters are added to the text without deleting those that
follow

note In insert mode, Z typed between the letters SP will give
SZP. In overtype mode, the result would be SZ.

/ɪn'sɜːt məʊd/
note not used with *a* or *an*. No
plural and used with a singular
verb only.
ᴍ be in, enter, select **insert mode**
▶ **overtype mode**

☆**install** *verb*
1 to put a piece of software in a computer system, usually on the hard disk: *The new program came with instructions on how to install it.* **2** to place a computer system or piece of equipment in a position so that is ready to be used: *more powerful processors will be installed next year* ·

/ɪnˈstɔːl/
install, installing, installed
note transitive verb
1 ꓧ **install** an operating system, a program
▶ **load**

---

installation *noun*
1 the process of putting a piece of software in a computer: *The installation of the program took about ten minutes.* **2** the process of placing a computer system or piece of equipment in a position so that is ready to be used: *The installation of the new server took engineers the whole weekend to complete.* **3** a particular computer system: *Scientists visited the computer installation before visiting other parts of the factory.*

/ˌɪnstəˈleɪʃn/
1,2 note not used with *a* or *an*. No plural and used with a singular verb only.
3 pl installations
ꓧ manage, run an **installation**

☆**instruction** *noun* (software/programming)
a program statement that has been changed into machine code so that the CPU can understand the statement and execute it

/ɪnˈstrʌkʃn/
pl instructions
ꓧ carry out, interpret, perform, process an **instruction**
syn machine instruction
▶ **statement, command**

---

instruction code *noun* (software/programming)
a group of binary digits that can be understood by the computer and which makes it execute instructions: *translate the GOTO command into instruction code*

/ɪnˈstrʌkʃn kəʊd/
pl instruction codes
ꓧ add, insert, program an **instruction code**

---

instruction counter *noun*
▶ **current address register**

/ɪnˈstrʌkʃn ˌkaʊntə(r)/

---

instruction cycle *noun*
the events that are repeated in a certain order as machine code instructions are FETCHED from store, decoded and executed

/ɪnˈstrʌkʃn ˌsaɪkl/
pl instruction cycles
ꓧ implement, obey the **instruction cycle**
syn fetch execute cycle

---

instruction field *noun*
the part of a machine code instruction that holds the INSTRUCTION CODE: *a 6-bit instruction field*

/ɪnˈstrʌkʃn fiːld/
pl instruction fields
ꓧ define, fill the **instruction field**

---

instruction format *noun*
the way an instruction in machine code is represented, with fixed amounts of space for instruction codes and address fields, etc: *a choice of instruction formats* ○ *the instruction format for the 6502 processor*

/ɪnˈstrʌkʃn ˌfɔːmæt/
pl instruction formats
ꓧ define, describe, obey the **instruction format**

---

instruction register *noun*
▶ **current address register**

/ɪnˈstrʌkʃn ˌredʒɪstə(r)/

---

instruction repertoire *noun*
▶ **instruction set**

/ɪnˈstrʌkʃn ˌrepətwɑː(r)/

☆**instruction set** *noun* (software)
the set of instructions that a microprocessor can execute. Each microprocessor has its own instruction set: *an instruction set designed for a compatible range of computers* ○ *an instruction set that performs arithmetic operations in decimal*

/ɪnˈstrʌkʃn set/
note usually singular
ꓧ execute, implement an **instruction set**
syn instruction repertoire
▶ **RISC, CISC**

---

abbr abbreviation   **pl** plural   **syn** synonym   ▶ see   ꓧ collocate (*word often used with the headword*)

instruction time *noun*
the time taken for the CPU to fetch, decode and execute a
machine code instruction

/ɪnˈstrʌkʃn taɪm/
pl instruction times
◄ improve, shorten the
instruction time

---

in tandem *adverb*
operating or happening together: *The two processors operate in
tandem.* ○ *Development of software proceeded in tandem with the
design of the hardware.*

/ˌɪn ˈtændəm/
◄ develop, operate, perform **in
tandem**
► **tandem processors**

---

integer *noun*
1 (*mathematics*) a whole number that is positive, negative or
zero without a decimal or FRACTIONAL part: *the integers 0, 1, 2,
-7* **2** a DATA TYPE in some programming languages such as
FORTRAN that is used for whole numbers

/ˈɪntɪdʒə(r)/
pl integers
1 ◄ add, subtract an **integer**
2 ◄ store *as* an **integer**

---

integer arithmetic *noun* (mathematics)
mathematical calculations carried out using INTEGERS (1):
*Financial calculations in the spreadsheet are done in integer
arithmetic.*

/ˌɪntɪdʒə(r) əˈrɪθmətɪk/
note not used with *a* or *an*. No
plural and used with a singular
verb only.
◄ carry out, perform **integer
arithmetic**
► **floating point**

---

integer division *noun* (mathematics)
a mathematical operation on two whole numbers where one is
divided by the other but any FRACTIONS in the result are
ignored: *Integer division of 3 by 2 gives 1.*

/ˌɪntɪdʒə dɪˈvɪʒn/
pl integer divisions
◄ perform, carry out **integer
division**

☆**integrated circuit** *noun*
► **chip**

/ˌɪntɪɡreɪtɪd ˈsɜːkɪt/

---

integrated office *noun*
a business environment in which all communications and
accounting operations are done using a central computer
system, and where all parts of the business are linked by a
network

/ˌɪntɪɡreɪtɪd ˈɒfɪs/
pl integrated offices
◄ run, work *in* an **integrated
office**

---

integrated package *noun*
► **integrated software**

/ˌɪntɪɡreɪtɪd ˈpækɪdʒ/

---

integrated software *noun* (software)
separate software applications which have been designed to
work together by storing data in a way that allows it to be
shared and by using a common command structure: *The
integrated software offers word processing, spreadsheets and
databases that work together.*

/ˌɪntɪɡreɪtɪd ˈsɒftweə(r)/
note not used with *a* or *an*. No
plural and used with a singular
verb only.
◄ install, use **integrated
software**

---

integration *noun*
the process of designing pieces of hardware or software so that
they will work together

/ˌɪntɪˈɡreɪʃn/
note not used with *a* or *an*. No
plural and used with a singular
verb only.
◄ hardware, software
integration; an **integration**
method

integration testing *noun*
the part of the process of testing software that checks that
different parts of the software will work together

/ˌɪntɪˌɡreɪʃn ˈtestɪŋ/
note not used with *a* or *an*. No
plural and used with a singular
verb only.
Ⓜ carry out, perform **integration
testing**

---

integrity *noun*
▶ **data integrity**

/ɪnˈteɡrəti/

---

intelligent knowledge-based system *noun*
▶ **expert system**

/ɪnˈtelɪdʒənt ˈnɒlɪdʒ beɪst
ˈsɪstəm/

☆**intelligent terminal** *noun* (hardware)
a terminal that is capable of doing small processing operations,
such as error checking, before data is passed to the main
computer: *use communications software to make the PC an
intelligent terminal*

/ɪnˌtelɪdʒənt ˈtɜːmɪnl/
pl intelligent terminals
syn smart terminal
▶ **terminal**

☆**interactive** *adjective* (user operation/system operation)
connected with a two-way flow of data and information
between a system and a user, with the system responding to
the user's requests: *an interactive coursebook on CD-ROM* ○ *an
on-line interactive dictionary* ○ *interactive cable and satellite
television*

/ˌɪntərˈæktɪv/
Ⓜ **interactive** computing,
graphics, mode, multimedia,
processing, software, systems,
video
syn conversational mode
▶ **CD-I**

---

interactive system *noun*
a computer system which allows the user to communicate
with a program being executed by providing input or
interrupting the program, etc

/ˈɪntərˌæktɪv ˈsɪstəm/
pl interactive systems
Ⓜ use, work *on* an **interactive
system**

---

interblock gap *noun*
the empty space between blocks of data recorded onto a
storage device such as magnetic tape

/ˌɪntəblɒk ˈɡæp/
pl interblock gaps
abbr IBG
syn gap, interrecord gap

☆**interface¹** *noun*
1 the equipment including hardware and software that allows
two devices to be connected so that they can operate together
2 a common boundary between systems, devices and
programs: *The interface between the operating system and the
hardware.*

3 ▶ **graphical user interface**

/ˈɪntəfeɪs/
pl interfaces
1,2 Ⓜ an **interface** cable,
standard
▶ **ISO OSI, user interface**

☆**interface²** *verb* (system operation)
to connect one device with another: *The monitor comes equipped
to interface with various types of printer.* ○ *interface the plotter to
the computer*

/ˈɪntəfeɪs/
**interface, interfacing,
interfaced**
note transitive or intransitive
verb
Ⓜ **interface** *with* something
▶ **ACR interface**

---

interface board *noun*
▶ interface card

/'ɪntəfeɪs bɔːd/

---

interface card *noun* (hardware)
a printed circuit board that allows a computer to communicate with a PERIPHERAL such as a printer or a display screen: *a printer interface card* ○ *a video interface card*

/'ɪntəfeɪs kɑːd/
pl interface cards
ℍ install, maintain an **interface card**
syn interface board

---

interface routine *noun* (software)
software that helps a program written for one operating system to execute on another system

/'ɪntəfeɪs ruːˌtiːn/
pl interface routines
ℍ install, provide, use an **interface routine**

---

inter file gap *noun*
▶ file gap

/ˌɪntə faɪl 'gæp/

---

interlaced video *noun*
a method of displaying a video signal on a monitor or television by REFRESHING² all the even-numbered lines after all the odd-numbered ones: *Interlaced video reduces the impression of a flickering picture.*

/ˌɪntəleɪst 'vɪdiəʊ/
note not used with *a* or *an*. No plural and used with a singular verb only.
ℍ display, show **interlaced video**

---

interleaving *noun*
the process of dividing data into small sections which are stored separately so that the process of retrieving one data item does not slow down access to the next data item

/ˌɪntə'liːvɪŋ/
note not used with *a* or *an*. No plural and used with a singular verb only.
ℍ carry out, implement, use **interleaving**

---

interlock¹ *noun*
a software or hardware device that stops something from happening unless particular conditions exist: *There is an interlock which prevents the printer operating if the cover has been opened.*

/'ɪntəlɒk/
pl interlocks
ℍ a safety, security **interlock**; an **interlock** sensor, switch

---

interlock² *verb*
to prevent something happening unless particular conditions exist: *The printer transport is interlocked with the paper sensor so that the printer cannot function unless paper is loaded.*

/ˌɪntə'lɒk/
interlock, interlocking, interlocked
note transitive verb
ℍ **interlock** devices, processes

---

intermittent error *noun*
▶ transient error

/'ɪntəˌmɪtənt 'erə(r)/

---

internal *adjective*
(of a device or piece of code, etc) that is inside something else that is similar to it: *The internal modem is mounted inside the computer.*

/ɪn'tɜːnl/
ℍ an **internal** code, device, memory

---

internal character code *noun*
the number that is used to represent a character within the computer

/ɪnˌtɜːnl 'kærəktə kəʊd/
pl internal character codes
ℍ store something *as*, use the **internal character code**
▶ character code, ASCII

internal clock *noun* ▶ **real-time clock**	/ɪn,tɜ:nl ˈklɒk/
internal interrupt *noun* an INTERRUPT¹ (= a signal to the CPU asking for attention) that comes from inside the computer, not from an external device: *The time-of-day clock can generate an internal interrupt to allow tasks to be initiated at a set time.*	/ɪn,tɜ:nl ˈɪntərʌpt/ **pl** internal interrupts ◄ cause, handle, respond *to*, service an **internal interrupt**; an **internal interrupt** request, service routine, signal, system ▶ **external interrupt**
internal memory *noun* (hardware) memory that is a fixed and permanent part of the computer system	/ɪn,tɜ:nl ˈmeməri/ **note** no plural **syn** internal storage
internal modem *noun* (hardware) a modem used for data communications which is inside a computer: *An internal modem is included in PCs with Internet access.*	/ɪn,tɜ:nl ˈməʊdəm/ **pl** internal modems ◄ fit, install an **internal modem**
internal schema *noun* ▶ **physical schema**	/ɪn,tɜ:nl ˈski:mə/
internal storage *noun* ▶ **internal memory**	/ɪn,tɜ:nl ˈstɔ:rɪdʒ/
International Standards Organization *noun* ▶ **ISO OSI**	/ˈɪntə,næʃnəl ˈstændədz ,ɔ:gənaɪ,zeɪʃn/
Internet *noun* many small networks which are connected together to make a larger network that covers the world: *send international electronic mail via the Internet* ○ *buy a PC that is Internet-enabled for full access to Internet services* **note** Always referred to as 'the Internet'.	/ˈɪntənet/ **note** no plural ◄ access, surf the **Internet**; an **Internet** protocol, service, site ▶ **World Wide Web**
interpret *verb* to decode and execute a statement or instruction. This is usually done by decoding and executing a statement and then decoding and executing the next statement, etc: *The interpreter interpreted the high-level language into machine code.*	/ɪnˈtɜ:prɪt/ **interpret, interpreting, interpreted** **note** transitive verb ◄ **interpret** an instruction, a language, program ▶ **compile 1**
interpreted language *noun* (software/programming) a computer programming language where each statement is translated by an INTERPRETER and then executed one statement after another: *Postscript is an interpreted language.*	/ɪn,tɜ:prɪtɪd ˈlæŋgwɪdʒ/ **pl** interpreted languages ◄ translate, use, write *in* an **interpreted language** ▶ **compiled language**
interpreter *noun* (software) a piece of software that executes a program written in a high-level computer programming language. This is usually done one statement at a time, and the program is never translated as a whole. Because of this, the interpreter must remain in the computer with the user's program: *translate a program with an interpreter*	/ɪnˈtɜ:prɪtə(r)/ **pl** interpreters ◄ translate using, use an **interpreter** ▶ **compiler, object code, source code**

abbr abbreviation **pl** plural **syn** synonym ▶ see ◄ collocate (*word often used with the headword*)

interprocess communication *noun*
the ability of one task or process to share data with another
task or process. This is possible on a MULTITASKING computer:
*Interprocess communications are the key to modern integrated
software suites.*

/ˈɪntəˌprəʊses
kəˌmjuːnɪˈkeɪʃn/

note not used with *a* or *an*. No
plural and used with a singular
verb only.

◨ an **interprocess
communication** protocol,
method

---

interrecord gap *noun*
▶ **interblock gap**

/ˈɪntəˌrekɔːd ˈgæp/

☆**interrupt**[1] *noun* (hardware)
a signal from a program or a device that is sent to the CPU
asking for attention: *The printer sends an interrupt when its
buffer is empty.*

/ˈɪntərʌpt/

pl interrupts

◨ cause, handle, generate, issue,
respond *to* an **interrupt**; an
interrupt request, service
routine, signal, system

▶ **external interrupt,
hardware interrupt,
internal interrupt, software
interrupt**

☆**interrupt**[2] *verb*
1 (*user operation*) to stop a program, usually by pressing a
combination of keyboard keys: *press CTRL-C to interrupt the run*
2 (*system operation*) to stop a program because an instruction
generated within the computer has to control processing: *The
warning message showed processing had been automatically
interrupted.*

/ˌɪntəˈrʌpt/

**interrupt, interrupting,
interrupted**

note transitive verb

◨ **interrupt** a program, run

---

interrupt disable *noun*
a command that tells the CPU to ignore INTERRUPT[1] signals

/ˌɪntərʌpt dɪsˈeɪbl/

note usually singular

▶ **maskable interrupt,
nonmaskable interrupt**

---

interrupt enable *noun*
a command that tells the CPU to respond to INTERRUPT[1] signals

/ˌɪntərʌpt ɪˈneɪbl/

note usually singular

▶ **maskable interrupt,
nonmaskable interrupt**

---

interrupt flag *noun*
a single bit which is set to 1 to show that an INTERRUPT[1] has
happened

/ˈɪntərʌpt flæg/

pl interrupt flags

◨ read, reset, set the **interrupt
flag**

---

interrupt handler *noun* (software)
a short ROUTINE which processes INTERRUPT[1] requests and
identifies what has caused the interrupt, so that the correct
INTERRUPT SERVICE ROUTINE can be CALLED[2] (2)

/ˈɪntərʌpt ˌhændlə(r)/

pl interrupt handlers

abbr IH

◨ branch *to*, call, invoke the
interrupt handler

---

interrupt mask *noun*
a register holding information about INTERRUPT[1] signals that
have been ENABLED or DISABLED: *The interrupt mask can only affect
maskable interrupts.*

/ˈɪntərʌpt mɑːsk/

pl interrupt masks

◨ maintain, set an **interrupt
mask**

▶ **interrupt enable, maskable
interrupt**

interrupt priority *noun*

the importance of a particular INTERRUPT[1]: the most important interrupt will be processed first

/ˌɪntərʌpt praɪˈɒrəti/

pl interrupt priorities

⋈ assign, decide *on* an **interrupt priority**

▶ **interrupt handler**

---

interrupt service routine *noun* (software)

the code which is executed to perform a task that is required by an INTERRUPT[1]

/ˌɪntərʌpt ˈsɜːvɪs ruːˌtiːn/

pl interrupt service routines

⋈ call, invoke an **interrupt service routine**

▶ **interrupt handler**

---

interrupt vector *noun*

a location in memory that holds the address of the state of an INTERRUPT SERVICE ROUTINE: the INTERRUPT HANDLER will pass control to this address

/ˈɪntərʌpt ˌvektə(r)/

pl interrupt vectors

⋈ change, update the **interrupt vector**

---

in the field *adjective*

in a real situation, not in a laboratory or factory: *The hardware was extensively tested in the field by various clients and experts.*

/ˌɪn ðə ˈfiːld/

⋈ develop, test **in the field**

▶ **field tested**

---

inverse video *noun*

a situation where the normal background colour of the screen and the colour of the text, etc displayed on screen is changed: if the background colour of the screen is blue, and the displayed characters are yellow, inverse video would be a yellow screen with blue characters: *pull-down menus in inverse video* ○ *use inverse video to highlight parts of the text*

/ɪnˌvɜːs ˈvɪdiəʊ/

note not used with *a* or *an*. No plural and used with a singular verb only.

⋈ display text*in*, put characters *into*, show **in inverse video**

syn reverse video

---

invert *verb*

to change all the bits in a binary data item so that the 1s become 0s and the 0s become 1s

note Inverting a binary word is equivalent to the logical operation NOT.

/ɪnˈvɜːt/

invert, inverting, inverted

note transitive verb

⋈ **invert** a bit, bit pattern, word

▶ **NOT operation**

---

inverted commas *noun*

either of the pairs of symbols " " or ' ' used to surround speech or quotations in text, and often used to mark STRING data types in programming languages: " " *are double inverted commas* ○ ' ' *are single inverted commas*

/ɪnˌvɜːtɪd ˈkɒməz/

note plural noun, used with a plural verb

⋈ insert, place something *between/inside* **inverted commas**; double, matched, single **inverted commas**

---

inverted file *noun*

a file that uses an INDEX[1] (1) or several indexes, so that any field in any data item may be accessed directly

/ɪnˌvɜːtɪd ˈfaɪl/

pl inverted files

⋈ access, delete, update an **inverted file**

---

inverter *noun*

a hardware device that INVERTS its output

note An inverter may not always be a separate component: it can be an alternative output signal from a more complex component.

/ɪnˈvɜːtə(r)/

pl inverters

⋈ pass *through*, read the output *of*, use an **inverter**

---

abbr abbreviation **pl** plural **syn** synonym ▶ see ⋈ collocate (*word often used with the headword*)

inverter *noun*   /ɪn'vɜːtə(r)/
▶ **NOT gate**

invisible file *noun*   /ɪnˌvɪzəbl 'faɪl/
▶ **hidden file**

invoke *verb*   /ɪn'vəʊk/
to begin the execution of a program, a FUNCTION[1] or a
SUBROUTINE: *Pressing the hot key F1 at any time invokes the HELP
system.*

invoke, invoking, invoked
note transitive verb
ᴎ **invoke** a function, module,
program, subroutine

☆**I/O** *abbr*   /ˌaɪ 'əʊ/
▶ **input/output**

note pronounced as individual
letters

I/O bound *adjective*   /ˌaɪ 'əʊ baʊnd/
▶ **input/output bound**

I/O buffer *noun*   /ˌaɪ 'əʊ ˌbʌfə(r)/
▶ **input/output buffer**

I/O bus *noun*   /ˌaɪ 'əʊ bʌs/
▶ **input/output bus**

I/O controller *noun*   /ˌaɪ 'əʊ kənˌtrəʊlə(r)/
▶ **input/output controller**

I/O coprocessor *noun*   /'aɪ ˌəʊ kəʊ'prəʊsesə(r)/
▶ **input/output processor**

IOP *abbr*   /ˌaɪ əʊ 'piː/
▶ **input/output processor**

note pronounced as individual
letters

I/O processor *noun*   /ˌaɪ 'əʊ ˌprəʊsesə(r)/
▶ **input/output processor**

I/P *abbr*   /ˌaɪ 'piː/
▶ **input**

note pronounced as individual
letters

IP address *noun*   /ˌaɪ 'piː əˌdres/
Internet Protocol address. The number that identifies a
computer linked to the INTERNET: *The workstation has the IP
address 158.152.18.65.*

pl IP addresses
ᴎ decode, route *to* an **IP address**

IPL *abbr*   /ˌaɪ piː 'el/
▶ **initial program loader**

note pronounced as individual
letters

ips *abbr*   /ˌaɪ piː 'es/
▶ **inches per second**

note pronounced as individual
letters

ISAM *abbr*

indexed sequential access method. A way of accessing large data files in which the positions of each block of data are kept in an index. Random access is used to find the correct starting position, then serial access is used to find the data item wanted.

/'ɪsæm/

note pronounced as individual letters

ᴍ an **ISAM** application, data structure, file system

▶ **random access, serial access**

ISO OSI *abbr*

International Standards Organization Open Systems Interconnection. An organization which describes the ways in which different computer networks can be connected to each other using certain standards. The standards apply to seven layers of systems interconnection, starting from the bottom physical layer and moving up through other layers to the top application layer: *work towards a global communications network with the ISO OSI model*

note The ISO OSI model forms the basis of all the interconnections for most of the modern packet switching networks.

/ˌaɪ es 'əʊ ˌəʊ es 'aɪ/

note pronounced as individual letters

▶ **application layer, data link layer, network layer, physical layer, presentation layer, session layer, transport layer**

☆**IT** *abbr*

information technology. The study or use of electronic equipment, especially computers and also television, video and communication systems to process, transmit and receive information, etc: *use information technology to design and build systems and programs to meet the needs of users* ○ *The company has an information technology division.*

/ˌaɪ 'tiː/

note pronounced as individual letters

ᴍ apply, introduce, use **information technology**

▶ **informatics, information processing, technology, telecommunications**

---

italic¹ *noun*

one of the styles of a font

/ɪ'tælɪk/

note singular noun, used with a singular verb

▶ **bold¹, font**

---

italic² *adjective*

(of text, etc) which is created with the italic feature of a font: *The italic paragraph in the documentation contains all the technical details of the system.*

/ɪ'tælɪk/

ᴍ **italic** lettering, text, type, words

▶ **bold², font**

---

italics *noun*

text which is created by using the italic feature of a font: *the information in italics* ○ *put the footnotes in italics* ○ *Italics are used to highlight important details in the document.*

/ɪ'tælɪks/

note Plural noun used with a plural verb.

▶ **font**

---

item *noun*

one particular thing in a set of many things

/'aɪtəm/

pl items

ᴍ a data **item**; an **item** *in/on* a list, *in* a set

---

iteration *noun* (system operation)

the process of a computer executing a command or statement again and again until a result is obtained: *The analysis of the program operations showed nine iterations were performed.*

/ˌɪtə'reɪʃn/

pl iterations

▶ **loop**

---

abbr abbreviation   **pl** plural   **syn** synonym   ▶ see   ᴍ collocate (*word often used with the headword*)

iterative *adjective*

(of a statement or instruction, etc) that executes again and again: *an iterative instruction in a loop* ○ *the iterative run of the program*

/'ɪtərətɪv/

---

iterative process *noun*

a process that is repeated many times until a result is obtained

/ˌɪtərətɪv 'prəʊses/

pl iterative processes

ᴍ carry out, define, perform an **iterative process**

Jj

☆**jack** *noun* (hardware)

a special type of plug that connects one device to another: *The mouse jack fitted into the socket on the keyboard.* ○ *use a jack to make audio and video connections* ○ *a mini jack*

/'dʒæk/

pl jacks

ᴍ connect *via*, insert a **jack**

syn patch plug, jack plug

---

jack field *noun*

a collection of JACK SOCKETS: *use a jack field to make temporary connections*

/'dʒæk fiːld/

pl jack fields

ᴍ insert something *into*, use a **jack field**

syn jack panel

pl patch panel

▶ **jack**

---

jack panel *noun*

▶ **jack field**

/'dʒæk pænl/

---

jack plug *noun*

▶ **jack**

/'dʒæk plʌg/

---

jack socket *noun*

a circular SOCKET (= device with a set of holes into which something fits) for a JACK: *a mini jack socket*

/'dʒæk ˌsɒkɪt/

pl jack sockets

ᴍ insert something *into* a **jack socket**

JANET *abbr*

Joint Academic Network. The network connecting universities in the UK.

/'dʒænɪt/

note pronounced as a word

ᴍ access, connect *to*, disconnect *from*, link up *with*, use **JANET**

▶ **BITNET, e-mail, gateway, Internet**

JCL *abbr*

▶ **job control language**

/ˌdʒeɪ siː 'el/

note pronounced as individual letters

☆**job** (software)

an item of work which is processed as a single unit by a computer: *The computer processed the job overnight.*

/dʒɒb/

pl jobs

ᴍ a print **job**; a **job** stream

▶ **batch**

job control *noun*
the process of managing an ordered group of tasks that a
computer has to process: *Allocation of resources is one part of job
control.*

/ˈdʒɒb kənˌtrəʊl/
note not used with *a* or *an*. No
plural and used with a singular
verb only.

ꓱ **job control** language,
commands, algorithms

▶ **job**

---

job control language *noun*
a computer programming language which is used to control
the execution of computer programs, usually in
MULTIPROGRAMMING SYSTEMS

note A job control language usually requests particular
peripheral devices such as printers or disk drives and specifies
how errors will be handled.

/ˈdʒɒb kənˌtrəʊl ˌlæŋgwɪdʒ/
pl job control languages
abbr JCL

ꓱ program *in*, write **job control
language**; **job control
language** commands,
statements

syn command language

---

job priority *noun*
the importance of a task being executed in a computer system:
*A high job priority may cause a job to be processed before a lower
priority one submitted earlier.*

/ˈdʒɒb praɪˌɒrəti/
pl job priorities

ꓱ assign, schedule *according to* **job
priority**

▶ **job**

---

job queue *noun*
▶ **job stream**

/ˈdʒɒb kjuː/

---

job scheduling *noun*
the decisions that are made by the system about which tasks
should be executed first

/ˈdʒɒb ˌʃedjuːlɪŋ/
note not used with *a* or *an*. No
plural and used with a singular
verb only.

ꓱ **job scheduling** algorithms,
methods

▶ **job priority**

---

job stream *noun*
the list of tasks waiting to be processed by a computer or
system: *The job stream may be reordered depending on priorities
and availability of system resources.*

/ˈdʒɒb striːm/
pl job streams

ꓱ add *to*, delete *from*, update the
job stream

syn job queue

---

join *noun*
1 the place at which two things are connected: *There was a
weak join between the circuit board and the integrated circuit* **2** an
operation in a RELATIONAL DATABASE that combines elements
from two tables

/dʒɔɪn/
pl joins

1 ꓱ make, reinforce a **join**
syn junction
2 ꓱ carry out, perform a **join**

Joint Academic Network *noun*
▶ **JANET**

/ˈdʒɔɪnt ˈækədemɪk ˈnetwɜːk/

---

journal file *noun*
a record of all changes in data made in a computer system.
This may be used to help recover from errors: *Journal files
permit the recovery of almost all data in the event of disk failure.*

/ˈdʒɜːnlə faɪl/
pl journal files

ꓱ consult, keep, maintain, update
a **journal file**

▶ **audit trail**

---

abbr abbreviation   **pl** plural   **syn** synonym   ▶ see   ꓱ collocate (*word often used with the headword*)

☆**joystick** *noun* (hardware)
a device connected to a computer that the user holds and
moves to control actions on screen, especially in video games:
*The game had a joystick for guiding the plane through a simulated
landing.*

/ˈdʒɔɪstɪk/
pl joysticks
▶ **mouse, paddle**

jump *noun*
▶ **branch 2**

/dʒʌmp/

jumper *noun*
▶ **link¹ 2**

/ˈdʒʌmpə(r)/

jump instruction *noun*
▶ **branch 2**

/ˈdʒʌmp ɪn،strʌkʃn/

junction *noun*
▶ **join 1**

/ˈdʒʌŋkʃn/

justification *noun* (applications/word processing)
the process of arranging text, etc on screen or on paper so that
either the left side or the right side of the text is parallel with
the edge of the paper or screen: *In a spreadsheet, default
justification is right-justification for numbers and left-justification
for text.*

/،dʒʌstɪfɪˈkeɪʃn/
note not used with *a* or *an*. No
plural and used with a singular
verb only.
Ⱶ left, right **justification**
▶ **right justify, left justify**

☆**justify** *verb*
1 (*applications/word processing*) to arrange text on a page so
that either the left side or the right side of the text is parallel to
the edge of the page, or the text is centred on the page: *justify
the text so the left and right margins are straight* **2** (*hardware*) to
move the bit pattern stored in a register so that it is at the
correct end of the register: *justify the bits that make up the
password*

/ˈdʒʌstɪfaɪ/
justify, justifying, justified
note transitive verb
1 ▶ **left justify**

Kk

☆**K** *abbr*
▶ **kilo**

/keɪ/

Kb *abbr*
▶ **kilobyte**

note used in written English only

kbaud *abbr*
▶ **kilobaud**

note used in written English only

kernel *noun* (hardware)
the central part of the operating system that controls
important tasks such as managing memory and system
resources, etc

/ˈkɜːnl/
pl kernels

kerning *noun*
the reduction of space between some letters in a text so that
they look more evenly spaced and are easier to read

/ˈkɜːnɪŋ/
note not used with *a* or *an*. No
plural and used with a singular
verb only.
Ⱶ employ **kerning**

	▶ **monospace font, proportional font**

☆**key¹** *noun*

1 (*hardware*) any of the buttons on a word processor or computer keyboard that are pressed to type in information or a command: *hold down the shift key to type a capital letter* ○ *press this key to delete a word* ○ *hit the escape key to exit the program*
2 information that is used to code and decode a message: *discovering the key made it possible to crack the code*
3 (*software/database*) ▶ **key field**

/kiː/
pl keys
1 ⋈ hit, hold down, press, release a **key**
3 syn cipher key

☆**key²** *verb* (user operation)

to put information into a computer by typing on a keyboard: *The keyboarder keyed the data into the computer.* ○ *key the data to disk*

/kiː/
key, keying, keyed
note transitive verb
⋈ **key** *in* data/information
▶ **enter²**

☆**keyboard¹** *noun* (hardware)

a set of keys that represent the letters of the alphabet, numbers and symbols, etc which are arranged on a flat board and are connected to a computer: *data can be entered manually using a keyboard*

/ˈkiːbɔːd/
pl keyboards
⋈ use a **keyboard**
▶ ASCII keyboard, azerty keyboard, qwerty keyboard

☆**keyboard²** *verb* (user operation)

to put data into a computer or word processor using a keyboard: *get data keyboarded into the system*

/ˈkiːbɔːd/
keyboard, keyboarding, keyboarded
note transitive verb
▶ **enter²**

☆**keyboarder** *noun* (personnel)

a person who types information into a computer or word processor using a keyboard: *employ a new keyboarder* ○ *a fast and efficient keyboarder*

/ˈkiːbɔːdə(r)/
pl keyboarders
(also **keyboard operator**)

keyboard layout *noun*

the way in which the keys on a keyboard are arranged

/ˈkiːbɔːd ˌleɪaʊt/
pl keyboard layouts
⋈ a complicated, simple, standard **keyboard layout**

keyboard overlay *noun*

a piece of paper which shows the function of each key and can be put over the keys on a keyboard: *place the keyboard overlay over the function keys*

/ˈkiːbɔːd ˌəʊvəleɪ/
pl keyboard overlays

key field *noun* (software/database)

the field in a data record that shows it is the only one of its type: *The key field in each record in the database means that no record is duplicated.*

/ˈkiː fiːld/
pl key fields
syn key

☆**keypad** *noun* (hardware)

a type of keyboard that is small and sometimes hand-held with a small number of keys: *enter the PIN number using the keypad* ○ *The keyboard has a separate numeric keypad on the right hand side.*

/ˈkiːpæd/
pl keypads
(also **key pad**)
⋈ a numeric **keypad**

---

abbr abbreviation   **pl** plural   **syn** synonym   ▶ see   ⋈ collocate (*word often used with the headword*)

key to disk system *noun* (hardware)
a system that transfers data directly from the keyboard onto a disk without any processing taking place

/ˌkiː tə ˈdɪsk/
pl key to disk systems

---

keyword *noun* (software/programming)
a set of characters in a fixed order that have a special meaning in a programming language and often identify a statement: *In BASIC, assignment statements have the optional keyword LET.*

/ˈkiːwɜːd/
pl keywords
M define, type a **keyword**

---

keyword in context *noun* (applications)
a way of displaying a word that has been searched for; some of the text around the word will also be displayed: *use the text database to search for a keyword in context* ○ *A concordance shows a keyword in context.*

/ˌkiːwɜːd ɪn ˈkɒntekst/
pl keywords in context
abbr KWIC

☆**KHz** *abbr*
▶ **kilohertz**

note used in written English only

---

kill *verb*
1 to delete a file, etc **2** to stop a program while it is running

/kɪl/
kill, killing, killed
note transitive verb
1 **M** **kill** a file, directory, document
2 **M** **kill** a program

☆**kilo** *prefix* (hardware)
one thousand, 1 000

note In computing because of the use of the binary system, kilo represents 2^{10}, or 1 024.

/ˈkɪlə/
pl kilos
abbr K
▶ **giga, mega, tera**

---

kilobaud *noun*
1 000 baud; a measure of the speed of data transmission: *transfer rates close to 200 kilobaud*

/ˈkɪləbɔːd/
note singular noun used with a singular verb
abbr kbaud
▶ **baud**

---

kilobit *noun* (hardware)
one thousand bits

note In computing because of the use of the binary system, a kilobit is 2^{10}, or 1 024 bits. There are 8 kilobits in a kilobyte.

/ˈkɪləbɪt/
pl kilobits
abbr Kb

☆**kilobyte** *noun* (hardware)
one thousand bytes: *the chip has a 64-kilobyte memory*

note In computing because of the use of the binary system, a kilobyte is 2^{10}, or 1 024 bytes.

/ˈkɪləbaɪt/
pl kilobytes
abbr K, k
▶ **byte**

☆**kilohertz** *noun*
1 000 hertz

/ˈkɪləhɜːts/
note no plural
abbr KHz
▶ **Hz, megahertz**

---

kit *noun* (hardware)
(*informal*) computer hardware: *The information technology department will install the new kit next week.*

/kɪt/
note not used with *a* or *an*. No plural and used with a singular verb only.

☆**knowledge base** *noun* (software)
part of a software program used in EXPERT SYSTEMS. It contains
information or knowledge provided by experts in a particular
subject which is used to help solve problems: *build an adequate
knowledge base*

/ˈnɒlɪdʒ beɪs/
pl knowledge bases
► **artificial intelligence,
inference engine**

knowledge-based system *noun*
a computer system that uses a KNOWLEDGE BASE

/ˌnɒlɪdʒ beɪst ˈsɪstəm/
pl knowledge-based systems
► **expert system**

knowledge engineer *noun*
a professional person working in the area of EXPERT SYSTEMS

/ˈnɒlɪdʒ endʒɪˌnɪə(r)/
pl knowledge engineers
◄ contract, employ a **knowledge
engineer**

KWIC *abbr*
► **keyword in context**

/kwɪk/
note pronounced as a word

Ll

label *noun* (software/programming)
a character, word or symbol used in computer programming
to identify a variable or part of a program: *Line numbers are
used as labels in BASIC.*

/ˈleɪbl/
pl labels
◄ program **label**
syn header label, header record

lag *noun*
the amount of time that it takes for an image to disappear from
a computer screen: *a lag of less than a second*

/læg/
pl lags

☆**LAN** *abbr*
► **local area network**

/læn/
note pronounced as a word

landscape *adjective*
(of pages of a document) that are printed so that the top of the
page is one of the longer sides: *select the landscape option for
printing the spreadsheet*

/ˈlændskeɪp/
◄ **landscape** display, mode
► **portrait**

landscape monitor *noun* (hardware)
a screen in which the width is greater than the length: *The TV
has a landscape monitor.*

/ˈlændskeɪp ˌmɒnɪtə(r)/
pl landscape monitors
► **portrait monitor**

language translation *noun*
the act or process of translating text from one natural
language into another using a computer: *language translation is
possible with a specially-written program*

/ˈlæŋgwɪdʒ trænsˌleɪʃn/
note not used with a *a* or *an*. No
plural and used with a singular
verb only.
◄ a **language translation**
application, parser, program,
system
► **machine translation**

☆**laptop** *noun* (hardware)
a portable microcomputer that can use batteries: *integrate the
laptop into the network*

note A laptop is sometimes called a 'notebook'.

/ˈlæptɒp/
pl laptops
◄ carry, use a **laptop**; a **laptop**
computer, user, workstation
► **portable 1**

abbr abbreviation   **pl** plural   **syn** synonym   ► see   ◄ collocate (*word often used with the headword*)

large scale integration *noun* (hardware)
the process of putting between 500 and 10 000 COMPONENTS on an integrated circuit

/ˌlɑːdʒ skeɪl ɪntɪˈɡreɪʃn/
note no plural
abbr LSI
H **large scale integration** techniques, methods
► **circuit board, medium scale integration, printed circuit board, small scale integration, super large scale integration, ultra large scale integration, very large scale integration, wafer scale integration**

---

laser *noun*
a device that produces light at a certain FREQUENCY: *a laser beam* ○ *There have been rapid developments in lasers for fibre optic communications.*

/ˈleɪzə(r)/
H a high-power, low-power **laser**; **laser** energy, technology

---

☆**laser disk** *noun* (hardware)
a computer disk that stores data which can be read by a laser: *computer output to laser disk*

/ˈleɪzə dɪsk/
pl laser disks
abbr LD
► **CD, disk**

☆**laser printer** *noun* (hardware)
a printer that uses a laser to fix the ink to the paper: *use the laser printer to produce good quality publicity material*

/ˈleɪzə ˌprɪntə(r)/
pl laser printers
► **daisywheel printer, dot matrix printer**

---

last in, first out *adjective*
of a DATA STRUCTURE (= a collection of data items considered as one single item) where only the last item to be added can be accessed first

note The most common last in, first out structure is the stack.

/ˈlɑːst ˈɪn ˈfɜːst ˈaʊt/
abbr LIFO
H a **last in, first out** data structure, list
► **first in, first out, stack, pop, push**

---

latency *noun*
the amount of time a computer takes to execute an instruction from the moment that instruction is given

/ˈleɪtənsi/
pl latencies
H a decrease *in*, an increase *in* **latency**; a **latency** period
► **access time**

---

layer *noun*
a stage that data has to go through when it is being sent from one computer to another on a network. These different stages have been defined by the ISO OSI.

/ˈleɪə(r)/
pl layers
► **application layer, data link layer, network layer, physical layer, presentation layer, session layer, transport layer**

☆**layout** *noun*
the way in which text and pictures are arranged on a page or screen: *add space to make the layout clearer* ○ *change from a single column to a two-column layout*

/ˈleɪaʊt/
pl layouts

	◄ a grid, magazine, newspaper, page **layout**
	syn screen layout
	► **format²** 2
☆**LCD** *abbr* ► **liquid crystal display**	/ˌel si: ˈdi:/ **note** pronounced as individual letters
LD *abbr* ► **laser disk**	/ˌe ˈdɪː/ **note** pronounced as individual letters
leader *noun* **1** the beginning of a piece of magnetic tape: *The leader on the magnetic tape holds no data.* **2** a row of marks such as dots that connect information on one side of the screen or page to information on the other side of the screen or page: *The leaders on the contents page connect chapter numbers to chapter titles in the book.*	/ˈliːdə(r)/ **pl** leaders
leaf *noun* a data item in a tree that has no DESCENDANTS. A leaf is always furthest from the ROOT: *A four-leaf binary tree has at most eight leaves.*	/liːf/ **pl** leaves ◄ access, update a **leaf**
leased line *noun* a data transmission channel that is rented from a COMMON CARRIER organization: *The company's branches are linked on a telephone system using leased lines.* ○ *The leased line has a wider bandwidth so data can be transmitted more efficiently.*	/ˌliːst ˈlaɪn/ **pl** leased lines ◄ **leased line** services
least significant bit *noun* the binary digit with the smallest place value in a storage location or register: *test the least significant bit of the integer to see if it is odd or even*	/ˈliːst sɪgˈnɪfɪkənt ˈbɪt/ **pl** least significant bits **abbr** lsb ◄ access, read, set, update the **least significant bit**
least significant digit *noun* the digit with the smallest place value in a storage location or register	/ˈliːst sɪgˌnɪfɪkənt ˈdɪdʒɪt/ **pl** least significant digits **abbr** lsd ◄ access, read, set, update the **least significant digit**
☆**LED** *abbr* ► **light emitting diode**	/ˌel iː ˈdiː/ **note** pronounced as individual letters
left arrow *noun* (hardware) the CURSOR CONTROL KEY with an arrow pointing to the left: *Press the left arrow to move the cursor to the left.*	/ˌleft ˈærəʊ/ **pl** left arrows ◄ hold down, press the **left arrow** ► **down arrow, right arrow, up arrow**
left justify *verb* to arrange text, etc on screen or on paper so that the left side of the text is parallel with the edge of the paper or the screen	/ˌleft ˈdʒʌstɪfaɪ/ **left justify, left justifying,**

abbr abbreviation   **pl** plural   **syn** synonym   ► see   ◄ collocate (*word often used with the headword*)

left justified

note transitive verb

◄ **left justify** a document; **left justify** text

► **justify, right justify**

LET statement *noun*
a name for the ASSIGNMENT STATEMENT (= a statement that gives a value to a variable) in the BASIC programming language

/'let ˌsteɪtmənt/

pl LET statements

◄ insert, make, use, write a **LET statement**

► **assignment 3**

---

letter quality *adjective*
(of printed text) that has clear characters: *Final versions of the document for customers should be printed in letter quality text.*

/'letə ˌkwɒləti/

◄ **letter quality** mode, output

► **draft quality, near letter quality, print qulaity**

---

lexical analysis *noun*
the first part of the translation of a computer program in which the characters in the SOURCE CODE are grouped into items such as variable names, labels and operators, etc

/ˌleksɪkl əˈnæləsɪs/

pl lexical analyses

◄ carry out, perform **lexical analysis**; a **lexical analysis** phase, stage

► **compile, syntax analysis**

LF *abbr*
► **line feed**

note used in written English only

---

library *noun* (programming)
a set of ROUTINES stored in a file. A programmer can store routines in a library to avoid writing the same routines again and again: *The library contains standard and customized routines.*

/'laɪbri/

◄ identify, refer *to* a **library**; a software **library**

syn program library

► **tape library**

---

library program *noun* (software)
a computer program that is available to all users of a multiaccess computer system: *common utilities can be supplied as library programs*

/'laɪbrəri ˌprəʊgræm/

pl library programs

◄ execute, load, use a **library program**

---

library routine *noun* (software)
a function or SUBROUTINE that performs a common task and which is made available to all users of a multiaccess system: *Sorting programs are often provided as library routines.*

/'laɪbrəri ruːˌtiːn/

pl library routines

◄ execute, load, use a **library routine**

---

licence *noun*
1 an official document that shows a person or company, etc can use something such as a piece of software **2** an official document that gives permission for a company to produce hardware or software

/'laɪsns/

pl licences

1 ◄ apply *for*, buy, obtain a **licence**; a single-user **licence**

► **site licence, software licence**

2 ◄ produce something *under* **licence**; a **licence** agreement

---

LIFO *abbr*
► **last in, first out**

/'laɪfəʊ/

note pronounced as a word

LIFO stack *noun* /ˈlaɪfəʊ stæk/
▶ **stack**

☆light emitting diode *noun* (hardware)
a device that changes electrical energy into light: *clusters of super-bright light emitting diodes* ○ *There is an LED on the disk drive.*

/ˈlaɪt iˌmɪtɪŋ ˈdaɪəʊd/
pl light emitting diodes
abbr LED
▶ **liquid crystal display**

light pen *noun* (hardware)
a device like a pen that is sensitive to light and is used to touch a certain place on a screen to transfer information to the computer: *use the light pen to select the menu* ○ *point with a light pen*

/ˈlaɪt pen/
pl light pens
▶ **bar code reader, touch screen**

line *noun*
1 (hardware) a channel used to transmit power or data: *analog data sent over telephone lines* ○ *The electricity power lines came down in a storm causing a blackout which made all the computers crash.* **2** (software/programming) a program statement or instruction that is written on one line: *a line of code*

/laɪn/
pl lines
▶ **lines of code**

linear *adjective*
1 like a line **2** (mathematics) (of an algebraic expression) that does not have terms such as x^2 and y^3, but only has terms such as x and y: $3x^2 + y = 0$ *is not linear because it has an* x^2 *term*

3 ▶ **one-dimensional**

/ˈlɪniə(r)/
1 ⋈ a **linear** data structure, function, model, scale
2 ⋈ a **linear** equation, formula

linear list *noun*
a simple list where all of the items follow each other in a certain order: *the linear list (A, B, C, D, E, F)*

/ˌlɪniə ˈlɪst/
pl linear lists
⋈ order, print out a **linear list**
▶ **empty list, linked list**

linear programming *noun* (software/programming)
a mathematical way of finding solutions to problems where numerical values must be kept within limits, and the best solution within these limits is found: *Linear programming on large problems requires large powerful computers.*

/ˌlɪniə ˈprəʊɡræmɪŋ/
note not used with *a* or *an*. No plural and used with a singular verb only.
abbr LP
⋈ a **linear programming** algorithm, method; **linear programming** software

linear search *noun*
▶ **sequential search**

/ˌlɪniə ˈsɜːtʃ/

line driver *noun* (hardware)
an electronic device that converts data from a computer so it can be transmitted over a communications channel

/ˈlaɪn ˌdraɪvə(r)/
pl line drivers
⋈ maintain, use a **line driver**

line editor *noun* (software)
software that allows text to be edited one line at a time: *The line editor packaged with the operating system allows users to prepare command files.*

/ˈlaɪn ˌedɪtə(r)/
pl line editors
⋈ edit with, use a **line editor**
▶ **editor, text editor**

line feed *noun* (software)
a CONTROL CHARACTER that tells the computer or printer to move to the following line

/ˈlaɪn fiːd/
note not used with *a* or *an*. No

abbr abbreviation   **pl** plural   **syn** synonym   ▶ see   ⋈ collocate (*word often used with the headword*)

	plural and used with a singular verb only.
	abbr LF
	▶ **carriage return, newline character**

line level *noun* the strength of a signal on a transmission line: *The line level was too low to allow satisfactory transmission.*	/'laɪn levl/ **pl** line levels ◄ a low, high, satisfactory **line level**

line number *noun* a number used as a LABEL in some computer programming languages. The program statements are executed in the order of their line numbers: *line numbers cannot exceed 3 2767*	/'laɪn ˌnʌmbə(r)/ **pl** line numbers ◄ delete, insert, jump *to* a **line number**

☆**line printer** *noun* (hardware) a printer that prints a line of text at a time and not a letter at a time: *a line printer with an output of 2 000 lines per minute* ○ *a line printer capable of printing 1 32 characters per line*	/'laɪn ˌprɪntə(r)/ **pl** line printers ◄ use a **line printer** ▶ **dot matrix printer, laser printer, page printer**

lines of code *noun* the size of the source code of a computer program. This is measured by counting the number of lines in a printed list of the program: *The software comprises well over 20 000 lines of code.*	/'laɪnz əv 'kəʊd/ **note** not used with *a or an*. No plural and used with a singular verb only. ◄ count, estimate the number of **lines of code** ▶ **code¹ 2, line 2**

line spacing *noun* (applications/word processing) the space between two lines of text	/'laɪn ˌspeɪsɪŋ/ **note** not used with *a or an*. No plural and used with a singular verb only. ▶ **kerning**

line width *noun* the length of a line of text across a page or screen: *The application has a tool for choosing line width.*	/'laɪn wɪdθ/ **pl** line widths ◄ a **line width** measurement

link¹ *noun* **1** a path or channel that joins two devices: *the link to the printer from the PC* **2** a short piece of metal on a printed circuit board that can be placed in different positions to change the way the circuit works: *The link can be set in one of two positions depending on how much memory is available.* **3 ▶ pointer 2**	/lɪŋk/ **pl** links **1** ◄ make, use a **link** **2** ◄ break, make a **link** **syn** jumper

link² *verb* **1** to join two things together, especially two devices so that data can be sent from one to the other: *link the cable to the serial port on the printer* **2** to combine two separate programs, etc to make a single executable program: *programs developed by separate teams are linked together* ○ *link the routines to produce a program*	/lɪŋk/ **link, linking, linked** **note** transitive verb **1** ◄ **link** *to* the mainframe, *to* a printer ▶ **data link** **2** ◄ **link** automatically ▶ **link loader**

linked list   *noun*

a list where each data item contains a POINTER (2) to the next item in the list: *add new data items to a linked list by adjusting the pointers*

/ˌlɪŋkt ˈlɪst/
pl linked lists
ᴓ delete something *from*, insert something *into* a **linked list**
▶ **doubly-linked list**
syn chained list

link loader   *noun*

a LOADER program that combines machine code from different places: *The link loader combined code from the subroutine library with code from another program.*

/ˈlɪŋk ˌləʊdə(r)/
pl link loaders
ᴓ execute, run, use a **link loader**

☆liquid crystal display   *noun*   (hardware)

an electronic device that is used to display information in many calculators and portable computers, etc: *a backlit liquid crystal display* ○ *an LCD that reproduces colour*

/ˈlɪkwɪd ˈkrɪstl dɪˈspleɪ/
pl liquid crystal displays
abbr LCD
ᴓ a **liquid crystal display** screen
▶ **light emitting diode**

LISP   *noun*   (software/programming)

a high-level computer programming language designed for artificial intelligence research: *LISP source code*

note LISP is a functional procedural language which was designed in 1959. It has many versions, and is usually translated by an interpreter. The word LISP comes from the words 'list processing'.

/lɪsp/
note not used with *a* or *an*. No plural and used with a singular verb only.
ᴓ program in, write **LISP**; a **LISP** application, interpreter, program

list   *noun*

a DATA STRUCTURE with data items arranged in a certain order: *insert data into a list* ○ *a list operand*

/lɪst/
pl lists
ᴓ read something *from*, remove something *from* a **list**
▶ **empty list, linear list, linked list, sublist**

listing   *noun*   (hardware)

a printed copy of a program's SOURCE CODE

/ˈlɪstɪŋ/
pl listings
syn program listing

list processing   *noun*

computer programming methods that use a list as their basic data structure: *use list processing in artificial intelligence applications*

/ˈlɪst ˌprəʊsesɪŋ/
note not used with *a* or *an*. No plural and used with a singular verb only.
ᴓ **list processing** algorithms, methods, techniques
▶ **LISP**

literal   *noun*

an item in a programming language which is used exactly as it appears in the SOURCE CODE and is not changed by translation: *The most frequent literals in programs are quoted strings.*

/ˈlɪtərəl/
pl literals
ᴓ define a **literal**
▶ **compilation**

☆load   *verb*

to transfer a program from a floppy disk or a hard disk to the RAM of a computer: *load a program into the computer*

/ləʊd/
load, loading, loaded
note transitive verb
ᴓ **load** software
▶ **enter², install**

abbr abbreviation   **pl** plural   **syn** synonym   ▶ see   ᴓ collocate (*word often used with the headword*)

load-and-go *adjective*
(of a ROUTINE) that executes automatically when it is loaded

/ˌləʊd ənd ˈɡəʊ/

---

loader *noun* (software)
a program that is usually part of the operating system and
loads another program into memory so it can be executed:
install the software package using a loader program

/ˈləʊdə(r)/
pl loaders
◄ execute, run, use a **loader**

---

local *adjective*
1 connected with devices that are close: *files are stored on a local
computer* **2** connected with a single part of document, file,
program or system, etc

/ˈləʊkl/
1 ◄ **local** mode, terminal
► **global, remote**

☆**local area network** *noun* (hardware/networks)
a network that covers a small area, such as a single building:
send e-mail over a local area network ○ *The LAN links personal
computers to a shared printer, database and file server.*

/ˈləʊkl ˈeəriə ˈnetwɜːk/
pl local area networks
abbr LAN
(also **short haul network**)
◄ be linked *to*, share, use a **local
area network**
► **Ethernet, gateway, network,
node, wide area network**

---

local intelligence *noun*
the ability of a terminal connected to a network to do some
processing without accessing another computer: *a dumb
terminal with no local intelligence*

/ˌləʊkl ɪnˈtelɪdʒəns/
note not used with *a* or *an*. No
plural and used with a singular
verb only.
◄ have, use **local intelligence**

---

local scope *noun* (software/programming)
the range of a variable over part of a program only, not the
whole program

/ˌləʊkl ˈskəʊp/
note not used with *a* or *an*. No
plural and used with a singular
verb only.
◄ declare a variable *with* **local
scope**
► **global scope**

---

local variable *noun* (software/programming)
a variable whose value can only be accessed from the
SUBROUTINE or function where it is first created: *define local
variables in subroutines, functions and procedures* ○ *There are
different local variables with the same name in different
subroutines.*

/ˌləʊkl ˈveəriəbl/
pl local variables
◄ declare, define, use a **local
variable**
► **global variable, scope**

---

location *noun*
the address of an item of data in memory

/ləʊˈkeɪʃn/
pl locations
◄ address, define, identify, specify
a **location**

---

lock *verb*
to make it impossible to access, change or delete something
such as a data file: *lock the data file*

/lɒk/
lock, locking, locked
note transitive verb
◄ **lock** a data item

☆**log¹** *verb* (user operation)
1 to enter information in an official record: *The fault was logged
in the system diary.* **2** to spend a certain amount of time
working on a computer: *The keyboarder logged 50 hours on the
computer that week.*

/lɒɡ/
log, logging, logged
note transitive verb
► **access, log off, log on,
password**

log² *abbr*
▶ **logarithm**

/lɒg/

☆**logarithm** *noun* (mathematics)
any of a series of numbers that can represent another number
in order to make it easier to do a difficult multiplication or
division sum: *The programming language includes a function for
calculating natural logarithms.* ○ *log tables*

/ˈlɒgərɪðəm/
pl logarithms
abbr log
ᴎ a common, natural **logarithm**

---

logging *noun*
the process of recording data automatically at regular
intervals: *A logging utility records and prints reports of data
changes.* ○ *Telephone call logging is available so that all records can
be more easily processed for billing.* ○ *Temperature readings were
recorded every 15 minutes on logging equipment.*

/ˈlɒgɪŋ/
note not used with *a* or *an*. No
plural and used with a singular
verb only.
ᴎ **logging** devices, equipment
syn automatic data logging, data
logging

☆**logic** *noun* (mathematics and logic)
a system or set of principles that define the operations of a
computer: *high-speed programmable logic devices* ○ *Errors of logic
happen when BASIC understands what you said, but what you said
is not what you meant.*

/ˈlɒdʒɪk/
note no plural
ᴎ data, deductive, formal,
inductive, internal,
mathematical, symbolic **logic**
▶ **Boolean operation, FALSE,
fuzzy logic, TRUE**

---

logical *adjective*
1 connected with logic **2** (of a device or part of memory) that is
SIMULATED by software or is accessed by the user in a way that
hides physical problems: *The computer is linked to several logical
devices.*

/ˈlɒdʒɪkl/
1 **ᴎ** **logical** behaviour,
computation, consequences
2 **ᴎ** a **logical** disk drive
▶ **physical**

---

logical decision *noun* (software/mathematics and logic)
a choice between two paths through a program: *A logical
decision in a high-level programming language is usually expressed
as an IF statement.*

/ˌlɒdʒɪkl dɪˈsɪʒn/
pl logical decisions
ᴎ make a **logical decision**

---

logical expression *noun*
a statement with LOGICAL VARIABLES connected with AND, OR,
NOT and other LOGIC OPERATORS: *The logical expressions NOT (A
OR B) and (NOT A) AND (NOT B) are equivalent.*

/ˌlɒdʒɪkl ɪkˈspreʃn/
pl logical expressions
ᴎ expand, form, process a **logical
expression**

---

logical file *noun*
a file as it appears to the user; this may not be the same way
that it is held in memory: *Two separate files appeared as a single
logical file to the user.*

note A logical file represents the user's view of the data; a
physical file is the computer's view of the data.

/ˌlɒdʒɪkl ˈfaɪl/
pl logical files
ᴎ access, delete, read, update a
logical file

---

logical left shift *noun*
a LOGICAL SHIFT of bits that are held in a register to the left

note A logical left shift loses the most significant bit and
introduces a zero at the right hand end of the register.

/ˌlɒdʒɪkl ˈleft ʃɪft/
pl logical left shifts
ᴎ carry out, perform a **logical
left shift**
▶ **most significant bit, shift
instruction**

---

abbr abbreviation   **pl** plural   **syn** synonym   ▶ see   **ᴎ** collocate (*word often used with the headword*)

logical record *noun*
a data record in a file as the user sees it; this may not be the same way that it is held in memory: *The user does not see the links and pointers that are in a logical record.*

/ˌlɒdʒɪkl ˈrekɔːd/
pl logical records
◄ access, delete, read, update a **logical record**
► **physical record**

---

logical right shift *noun*
a LOGICAL SHIFT of bits that are held in a register to the right

note A logical right shift loses the least significant bit and introduces a zero at the left hand end of the register.

/ˌlɒdʒɪkl ˈraɪt ʃɪft/
pl logical right shifts
◄ carry out, perform a **logical right shift**
► **least significant bit, shift instruction**

---

logical schema *noun*
the layout of types of data in a database and the links between the data as the user sees them; this may be different from the way they are held in memory: *convert the data model into a logical schema*

/ˌlɒdʒɪkl ˈskiːmə/
pl logical schemas
pl logical schemata
◄ compile, draw up a **logical schema**
syn conceptual schema, external schema
► **database management system, schema, subschema, physical schema**

---

logical shift *noun*
an operation on a set of bits held in a register where bits are moved (shifted) left or right. The bits that move outside the register are lost and the new spaces that are created are filled with zeros.

/ˌlɒdʒɪkl ˈʃɪft/
pl logical shifts
◄ carry out, perform a **logical shift**
► **arithmetic shift, cyclic shift, logical left shift, logical right shift, shift instruction**

---

logical variable *noun* (software/programming)
a variable which can hold one of the two values TRUE or FALSE

note Logical variables are represented in memory by the numerical values 0 and 1.

/ˌlɒdʒɪkl ˈveəriəbl/
pl logical variables
◄ assign *to*, read the value *of* a **logical variable**
► **local variable, numeric variable, string variable, variable**

---

logic array *noun*
► **gate array**

/ˈlɒdʒɪk əˌrei/

---

logic bomb *noun*
a type of virus which stays in the computer's memory doing nothing until a certain operation makes it execute, causing it to damage data: *insert a logic bomb into the system*

/ˈlɒdʒɪk bɒm/
pl logic bombs
◄ leave, plant a **logic bomb**
► **hacker, Trojan horse**

---

logic circuit *noun*
an electronic circuit made of a number of GATES

/ˈlɒdʒɪk ˌsɜːkɪt/
pl logic circuits
◄ an input *to*, output *from* a **logic circuit**
► **uncommitted logic array**

logic diagram *noun*
a chart that shows how individual logic GATES are connected to form a more complicated logic circuit

/ˈlɒdʒɪk ˌdaɪəgræm/
pl logic diagrams
ᴍ draw, study a **logic diagram**
▶ **flow chart, gate, logic symbol**
syn logic flowchart

logic element *noun*
▶ **gate**

/ˈlɒdʒɪk ˌelɪmənt/

logic error *noun*
a mistake in the execution of a program caused by a poorly-designed logical decision: *The program crashed because of a logic error.*

/ˈlɒdʒɪk ˌerə(r)/
pl logic errors
ᴍ make, suffer from a **logic error**
▶ **logical decision**

logic flowchart *noun*
▶ **logic diagram**

/ˈlɒdʒɪk ˌfləʊtʃɑːt/

logic gate *noun*
▶ **gate**

/ˈlɒdʒɪk geɪt/

logic operand *noun*
a data item that represents a TRUTH VALUE (= one of the values TRUE or FALSE), and which is combined with other data items by a LOGIC OPERATOR: *In NOT X, the logic operand X is negated.*

/ˈlɒdʒɪk ˌɒpərænd/
pl logic operands
(also **logical operand**)
ᴍ combine *with*, use a **logic operand**
▶ **operand**

logic operation *noun*
an operation in a computer program which processes TRUTH VALUES to produce a further truth value: *AND, OR and NOT are common logic operations.*

/ˈlɒdʒɪk ɒpəˌreɪʃn/
pl logic operations
(also **logical operation**)
ᴍ perform a **logic operation**
▶ **arithmetic operation, gate, operation**

logic operator *noun*
a symbol or word used in mathematics or in a computer program to represent a LOGIC OPERATION: *The logic operator NOT negates X in the formula NOT X.*

/ˈlɒdʒɪk ˌɒpəreɪtə(r)/
pl logic operators
(also **logical operator**)
ᴍ insert, use a **logic operator**
▶ **logic operand, logical variable**

logic programming *noun*
the process of programming a computer using the rules of logic: *Prolog is a logic programming language.*

/ˈlɒdʒɪk ˌprəʊgræmɪŋ/
note not used with *a* or *an*. No plural and used with a singular verb only.
ᴍ a **logic programming** language, method, system
▶ **imperative, object-oriented, query language**

logic symbol *noun*
1 one of several standard symbols used in diagrams for a basic GATE circuit **2** one of several standard symbols used in logic expressions for a basic operations such as AND, OR and NOT, etc

/ˈlɒdʒɪk ˌsɪmbl/
pl logic symbols
1 ᴍ draw a **logic symbol**
2 ᴍ write a **logic symbol**

---

abbr abbreviation   **pl** plural   **syn** synonym   ▶ see   ᴍ collocate (*word often used with the headword*)

☆**log in** verb /ˌlɒg ˈɪn/
▶ **log on**

☆**LOGO** noun (software/programming) /ˈləʊgəʊ/

a high-level computer programming language which was designed to be used in education, especially to teach programming to children: *The child typed the simple LOGO command FORWARD 50.*

note LOGO is a functional procedural language which was designed in 1968. It is usually translated by an interpreter.

note not used with *a* or *an*. No plural and used with a singular verb only.

(also **Logo**)

ℍ program *in*, write **LOGO**; a **LOGO** graphic, interpreter, program

▶ **turtle**

☆**log off** verb (user operation) /ˌlɒg ˈɒf/

to stop using a computer on a network by entering certain instructions: *Log off to terminate the current session, but don't shut the computer down because it has to back up.*

log off, logging off, logged off

note intransitive verb

syn log out, sign off

☆**log on** verb (user operation) /ˌlɒg ˈɒn/

to start using a computer on a network by entering certain instructions: *log on by entering the password at the prompt*

log on, logging on, logged on

note intransitive verb

syn log in, sign on

log out verb /ˌlɒg ˈaʊt/
▶ **log off**

long haul network noun /ˌlɒŋ ˈhɔːl ˌnetwɜːk/
▶ **wide area network**

longitudinal redundancy check noun /ˈlɒndʒɪˌtjuːdɪml rɪˈdʌndənsi tʃek/
▶ **horizontal redundancy check**

look up verb /ˈlʊk ʌp/

to access a table using one data item so that value associated with that item can be read: *The compiler looks up the variable name in a table.*

look up, looking up, looked up

note transitive verb

ℍ **look up** a value, a data item

look-up table noun /ˈlʊk ʌp ˌteɪbl/

a DATA STRUCTURE that is designed so that accessing one data item gives the value of a related data item

pl look up tables

abbr LUT

ℍ access, build, construct, use a **look-up table**

▶ **name table**

loop¹ noun /luːp/

1 (hardware) an arrangement of computers in a network that are linked to each other in the form of a circle: *The network loop connects 12 terminals.* ○ *a loop configuration* **2** (software) a set of statements in a program that is executed again and again by the computer until the required result is obtained

pl loops

1 ℍ a network **loop**

▶ **node, ring network**

2 ℍ execute, perform a **loop**; a program **loop**

▶ **do loop, infinite loop, loop body, loop variable, nested loop, repeat until loop, while loop**

---

loop² *verb*
to execute a set of statements in a computer programming
language again and again until the required result is obtained:
loop 100 times ○ *loop until the file is empty* ○ *loop while a condition
holds*

/luːp/
loop, looping, looped
note intransitive verb

---

loop body *noun* (software)
the block of statements that is repeated in a LOOP¹ (2)

note The loop body does not include the statements
controlling the loop, such as FOR...NEXT.

/ˌluːp ˈbɒdi/
pl loop bodies
◄ execute, perform a **loop body**

---

looping program *noun* (software)
a program with instructions that are repeated over and over
again, usually with different data

/ˌluːpɪŋ ˈprəʊɡræm/
pl looping programs
◄ execute, print *out*, program a **looping program**
▶ infinite loop, loop, main loop

---

loop variable *noun* (software)
a variable that holds the value that is used to test whether a
LOOP¹ 2 should be repeated: *In the BASIC statement, FOR I= 1
TO 10, I is the loop variable.*

/ˈluːp ˌveəriəbl/
pl loop variables
◄ increment, test, update a **loop variable**
▶ loop body, repeat counter

---

lower case *noun*
letters that are small and not CAPITALS: *a, b and c are lower case*

/ˌləʊə ˈkeɪs/
note no plural
▶ case sensitive

☆**low-level language** *noun* (software/programming)
a computer programming language which is very close to the
computer's own basic instructions, and so not very close to
human language: *translate low-level languages into machine code
with an assembler*

/ˌləʊ levl ˈlæŋɡwɪdʒ/
pl low level languages
syn machine-oriented language
▶ assembly language, compile, high-level language, interpreter, machine code, source code

---

low-res *abbr* (hardware)
▶ **low resolution**

/ˌləʊ ˈrez/

---

low resolution *adjective* (hardware)
connected with hardware such as a screen or printer that
cannot produce clear, high-quality output: *The graphics were
not bold and sharp on the low resolution screen.* ○ *The image from
the low resolution printer was blurred with jagged edges.*

/ˈləʊ ˌrezəˈluːʃn/
abbr low res
◄ a **low resolution** printer, screen; **low resolution** graphics
▶ aliasing, high-resolution

LP *abbr*
▶ **linear programming**

/ˌel ˈpiː/
note pronounced as individual letters

---

lsb *abbr*
▶ **least significant bit**

/ˌel es ˈbiː/
note pronounced as individual letters

---

abbr abbreviation   **pl** plural   **syn** synonym   ▶ see   ◄ collocate (*word often used with the headword*)

| **lsd** *abbr* | /ˌel es ˈdiː/ |
| ▶ **least significant digit** | **note** pronounced as individual letters |

| **LSI** *abbr* | /ˌel es ˈaɪ/ |
| ▶ **large scale integration** | **note** pronounced as individual letters |

| **LU** *abbr* | /ˌel ˈjuː/ |
| logical unit | **note** pronounced as individual letters |

| **LUT** *abbr* | |
| ▶ **look-up table** | **note** used in written English only |

Mm

| ☆**M** *abbr* | /em/ |
| ▶ **mega** | |

MAC *abbr*	/mæk/
1 medium/media access control	**note** pronounced as a word
2 multiple access computer	
3 ▶ **message authentication code**	

☆**machine** *noun* (hardware)	/məˈʃiːn/
a piece of equipment, such as a computer, that does a certain kind of work and usually uses electricity as power	**pl** machines
	◄ operate, use a **machine**; an answering, a desktop, an electronic, a parallel **machine**
	▶ **device, virtual machine**

| **machine address** *noun* | /məˈʃiːn əˌdres/ |
| ▶ **absolute address** | |

☆**machine code** *noun* (software/programming)	/məˈʃiːn kəʊd/
the 0s and 1s (binary-coded commands) that are loaded and executed by a computer. Machine code is the only language the computer understands, and it is obtained by COMPILING assembly language or any high-level language.	**note** not used with *a* or *an*. No plural and used with a singular verb only.
	◄ program in, write **machine code**: **machine code** instructions, programs, routines, subroutines
	syn machine language
	▶ **assembly language, high-level language, object code, portability, source code**

| **machine instruction** *noun* | /məˌʃiːn ɪnˈstrʌkʃn/ |
| ▶ **instruction** | |

| **machine intelligence** *noun* | /məˌʃiːn ɪnˈtelɪdʒəns/ |
| ▶ **artificial intelligence** | |

☆**machine language** *noun* /məˈʃiːn ˌlæŋgwɪdʒ/
▶ **machine code**

---

machine-oriented language *noun* /məˈʃiːn ˈɔːrientɪd ˈlæŋgwɪdʒ/
▶ **low-level language**

☆**machine-readable** *adjective* /məˌʃiːn ˈriːdəbl/
▶ **readable**

---

machine translation *noun* /məˌʃiːn trænsˈleɪʃn/
the use of computers to convert text from one human language to another: *The development of reliable machine translation is invaluable to the European Union.*

note not used with *a* or *an*. No plural and used with a singular verb only.

◄ carry out, perform **machine translation**; **machine translation** logarithms, techniques

▶ **language translation**

☆**macro** *noun* (software) /ˈmækrəʊ/
1 a group of program instructions that can be stored as a unit. Macros are used for tasks that require many keystrokes or several options from menus: *set up a macro to save keying in a long pathname* ○ *make a macro for complicated instructions*

2 ▶ **open subroutine**

pl macros

1 ◄ define, expand, inset a **macro**; a **macro** command

syn macro instruction

▶ **hot key**

---

macro assembler *noun* (software) /ˈmækrəʊ əˌsemblə(r)/
software that produces program instructions by processing MACROS (1)

pl macro assembler

◄ execute a **macro assembler**

---

macro definition *noun* (software) /ˈmækrəʊ ˌdefɪˈnɪʃn/
a set of instructions that are grouped together under a single name; when this name is used in a program it will be replaced by this set of instructions

pl macro definitions

◄ make, program, write a **macro definition**

▶ **parameter**

---

macro expansion *noun* /ˌmækrəʊ ɪkˈspænʃn/
the set of instructions that replaces the name of a MACRO (1) when it is used in a program

pl macro expansions

note The ability to use variable parameters means that different macro expansions can result from separate uses of a macro.

---

macro instruction *noun* /ˈmækrəʊ ɪnˌstrʌkʃn/
▶ **macro 1**

---

macro language *noun* (software/proramming) /ˈmækrəʊ ˌlæŋgwɪdʒ/
a computer programming language that allows the programmer to make new instructions by combining instructions that already exist

pl macro languages

◄ program *in*, translate, write *in* a **macro language**

---

macro library *noun* (software) /ˈmækrəʊ ˌlaɪbrəri/
a LIBRARY of macros that can be used by a programmer so the programmer does not have to write the macro each time it needs to be used

pl macro libraries

◄ access, use a **macro library**

---

abbr abbreviation   **pl** plural   **syn** synonym   ▶ see   ◄ collocate (*word often used with the headword*)

☆**magnetic bubble memory** *noun*
► **bubble memory**

/mæg'nətɪk 'bʌbl 'meməri/

☆**magnetic disk** *noun* (hardware)
a flat circular device covered with magnetic material that is used to store data: *The computer program is resident on a magnetic disk.* ○ *The medium the text is held on is a magnetic disk.*

/mæg,netɪk 'dɪsk/
pl magnetic disks
◄ copy data *to*, read data *from*, save data *to*, store data *on*, write data *to* a **magnetic disk**
► **floppy disk, hard disk**

---

magnetic drum *noun* (hardware)
a device that is used for storing information. It is shaped like a tube and its outside surface is covered in magnetic material: *The form of backing store the system used was a magnetic drum.*

note Magnetic drums are not common today and have been replaced by disks.

/mæg,netɪk 'drʌm/
pl magnetic drums

---

magnetic ink character recognition *noun*
the process of reading text or characters printed in magnetic ink: *Magnetic ink character recognition is used to read the numbers at the bottom of bank cheques.*

/mæg'netɪk 'ɪŋk 'kærektə rekəg,nɪʃn/
note not used with *a* or *an*. No plural and used with a singular verb only.
abbr MICR

---

magnetic media *noun* (hardware)
devices that are used for storing data, such as magnetic disks or magnetic tape: *The bank uses magnetic media to archive the data.* ○ *Transactions are stored digitally on magnetic media.* ○ *improperly stored magnetic media degrades*

/mæg,netɪk 'mi:dɪə/
note plural noun, used with a plural verb

---

magnetic strip *noun* (hardware)
a line of magnetic material on a plastic card, such as a bank card, that contains information: *activate the lock with a magnetic strip identity card* ○ *The information is carried on a magnetic strip on the back of the credit card.*

/mæg,netɪk 'strɪp/
pl magnetic strips
◄ a damaged, machine-readable **magnetic strip**
syn magnetic stripe

---

magnetic stripe *noun*
► **magnetic strip**

/mæg,netɪk 'straɪp/

☆**magnetic tape** *noun* (hardware)
a storage medium made of a thin piece of plastic covered with magnetic material: *download data onto magnetic tape for long-term storage* ○ *a reel of magnetic tape*

/mæg,netɪk 'teɪp/
pl magnetic tapes
◄ load, rewind, spool, store data *on*, transfer data *to*, wind a **magnetic tape**

---

magnetic tape unit *noun* (hardware)
a device that reads data from or writes data to magnetic tape

/mæg,netɪk 'teɪp ,ju:nɪt/
pl magnetic tape units
syn tape device, tape unit

---

mail[1] *noun*
messages sent or received, especially electronic mail: *At start-up, the system shows if there is any mail in the in-basket.* ○ *The software scans the host computer for new mail.*

/meɪl/
note no plural
◄ receive, save, send **mail**
► **e-mail**[1]

mail² *verb*
to send a message, especially electronically: *mail a message over a network*

/meɪl/
mail, mailing, mailed
note transitive verb
▶ **e-mail²**

---

mailbox *noun*
the area of computer memory where electronic mail messages are held until the person they are sent to is ready to read them: *messages are saved in the mailbox*

/ˈmeɪlbɒks/
pl mailboxes
И delete mail *from*, save mail *in* a **mailbox**
▶ **e-mail**

☆**mail merge** *noun*
1 a program which produces copies of a document with individual differences such as names and addresses: *The monthly statements are produced by mail merge.* **2** the process of producing documents by using a MAIL MERGE (1) program: *do a publicity mail merge*

/ˈmeɪl mɜːdʒ/
pl mail merges
1 И a **mail merge** package, program

---

main body *noun* (software/programming)
the part of a computer program where execution begins and which CALLS² (2), SUBROUTINES, functions and other procedures

/ˌmeɪn ˈbɒdi/
pl main bodies
И list, program the **main body**

☆**mainframe** *noun* (hardware)
a powerful computer that can process very complex data. Mainframes are often the centre of a network which many smaller computers are connected to: *Workstation users can access and create files on the mainframe.*

/ˈmeɪnfreɪm/
pl mainframes
И a **mainframe** computer, environment, processor, system
▶ **PC**

---

main loop *noun* (software)
the part of a LOOPING PROGRAM that contains the important program instructions which are repeated again and again

/ˌmeɪn ˈluːp/
pl main loops
И execute, program, trace the **main loop**
▶ **nested loop, subroutine**

---

main memory *noun* (hardware)
very high speed VOLATILE MEMORY which is directly accessible from the CPU: *Data and instructions are held in main memory while a program is running.*

note Main memory is usually RAM which is semiconductor-based memory and can be written to and read from. Main memory is often just called 'RAM'.

/ˌmeɪn ˈmeməri/
note no plural
syn main store, primary memory, primary storage

---

main store *noun*
▶ **main memory**

/ˌmeɪn ˈstɔː(r)/

---

maintain *verb*
to keep a computer or system working well by checking it regularly and repairing anything that does not work properly

/meɪnˈteɪn/
maintain, maintaining, maintained
note transitive verb
И **maintain** a computer, machine, printer

---

maintenance *noun*
regular checks and repairs to a computer or system

/ˈmeɪntənəns/
note not used with *a* or *an*. No plural and used with a singular verb only.

	◄ **maintenance** costs, engineers, repairs; preventative **maintenance**
maintenance contract *noun* an agreement between a company using computers and another company who will regularly check and repair equipment so that it works correctly	/ˈmeɪntənəns ˌkɒntrækt/ **pl** maintenance contracts ◄ enter, negotiate, sign, take out a **maintenance contract**
make-up *noun* ► **page make-up**	/ˈmeɪk ʌp/
male connector *noun* (hardware) a device which is used when electrical connections are made between cables and computers, etc and which fits into a FEMALE CONNECTOR: *use a male connector on the side of the connection not carrying current*	/ˌmeɪl kəˈnektə(r)/ **pl** male connectors ◄ connect *to*, plug *into*, use a **male connector** **syn** male plug
male plug *noun* ► **male connector**	/ˌmeɪl ˈplʌg/
☆**management information system** *noun* (applications) a computer system that allows useful information to be recorded, stored and used by managers without the help of a computer specialist: *develop a management information system for effective monitoring and control of the business* ○ *The management information system helps to isolate and solve problems.*	/ˈmænɪdʒmənt ˌɪnfəˈmeɪʃn ˌsɪstəm/ **pl** management information systems **abbr** MIS ◄ blame, consult, develop, use a **management information system** ► **decision support system, expert system, knowledge based system**
mantissa *noun* the digits in a FLOATING POINT NUMBER. The size of the number is held in the CHARACTERISTIC: *In the decimal floating point number 3.14159×10^{12} the mantissa is 3.14159 and the characteristic is 12.*	/mænˈtɪsə/ **pl** mantissas **pl** mantissae ◄ define, store a **mantissa**
☆**manual** *noun* a book of instructions that explains how to use a computer or a computer program: *look up how to configure the software in the manual* ○ *The manual explains how to set up the system.*	/ˈmænjuəl/ **pl** manuals ◄ a hardware, software, user **manual** **syn** reference manual, user documentation, user manual ► **documentation, help, tutorial**
☆**MAR** *abbr* ► **memory address register**	/ˌem eɪ ˈɑː/ **note** pronounced as individual letters
margin *noun* the spaces at the side of a printed page that do not contain text: *add notes in the margin*	/ˈmɑːdʒɪn/ **pl** margins ◄ a narrow, wide **margin** ► **footer, header 2**

mark sensing *noun*

the process of recognizing marks made on paper, etc: *The mark sensing system reads pencil marks at certain positions on a sheet of paper.*

/'mɑːk ˌsensɪŋ/

note not used with *a* or *an*. No plural and used with a singular verb only.

⋈ a **mark sensing** device

▶ **magnetic ink character recognition, optical mark reader**

---

mask¹ *noun*

1 a pattern of binary digits which is used to select the bits in a location that should be read or ignored

note A 1 bit in a mask shows that a bit should be read, a 0 bit shows that it should be ignored.

2 a design for an integrated circuit

/mɑːsk/

pl masks

---

mask² *verb*

to use a pattern of binary digits to select bits in a location that should be read or ignored: *mask the instruction word to isolate the operation code*

note A 1 bit masks a bit that should be read, a 0 bit masks a bit that should be ignored.

/mɑːsk/

mask, masking, masked

note transitive verb

⋈ **mask** a location, register, word

---

maskable interrupt *noun* (hardware)

an INTERRUPT¹ that can be ignored: *The programmer set the system to ignore maskable interrupts.*

/ˌmɑːskəbl 'ɪntərʌpt/

pl maskable interrupts

⋈ cause, receive, respond *to* a **maskable interrupt**

▶ **nonmaskable interrupt**

---

mass memory *noun*

▶ **mass storage**

/ˌmæs 'meməri/

---

mass storage *noun*

a device or system that can hold or process large amounts of data: *use disk and tape for mass storage*

/ˌmæs 'stɔːrɪdʒ/

note no plural

⋈ a **mass storage** subsystem, unit

syn bulk memory, bulk storage, mass memory

---

master control program *noun*

▶ **operating system**

/ˌmɑːstə kən'trəʊl ˌprəʊɡræm/

---

master file *noun* (software)

a file in a database that contains important information about the database: *The database summary data is in the master file.*

/'mɑːstə faɪl/

pl master files

⋈ access, change, update the **master file**

---

master processor *noun* (hardware)

a computer or device that controls another computer or device: *The master processor controls the slave processor.*

/ˌmɑːstə 'prəʊsesə(r)/

pl master processors

---

master/slave system *noun* (hardware)

a system where one main computer controls other computers or devices that are connected to it: *view files on each computer in a master/slave system*

/ˌmɑːstə 'sleɪv sɪstəm/

pl master/slave systems

---

abbr abbreviation   **pl** plural   **syn** synonym   ▶ see   ⋈ collocate (*word often used with the headword*)

mathematical model *noun*
a set of FORMULAS that describe how a program works

/ˈmæθəˌmætɪkl ˈmɒdl/
pl mathematical models
⋈ build, construct a
mathematical model

maths coprocessor *noun*
▶ **coprocessor**

/ˌmæθs kəʊˈprəʊsesə(r)/

matrix *noun*
an arrangement of items such as numbers and other data in
rows and columns: *The display treats data as a matrix, with profit
in rows and dates in columns.*

/ˈmeɪtrɪks/
pl matrices
pl matrixes
▶ **two-dimensional array**

matrix printer *noun*
▶ **dot matrix printer**

/ˈmeɪtrɪks ˌprɪntə(r)/

☆**MB** *abbr*
▶ **megabyte**

note used in written English only

Mbps *abbr*
one million bits per second

note used in written English only
▶ **bits per second**

☆**MBR** *abbr*
▶ **memory buffer register**

/ˌem biː ˈɑː(r)/
note pronounced as individual
letters

☆**Mbyte** *abbr*
▶ **megabyte**

note used in written English only

MCP *abbr*
message control program

/ˌem siː ˈpiː/
note pronounced as individual
letters

MDR *abbr*
miscellaneous data record

/ˌem diː ˈɑː(r)/
note pronounced as individual
letters

mean *noun*
an average: *6+4+8 gives a mean of 6*

/miːn/
pl means
⋈ calculate, compute a **mean**

mean time between failures *noun*
a calculation of how often a device or system fails to operate:
calculate mean time between failures in thousands of hours

/ˌmiːn ˈtaɪm bɪˌtwiːn ˈfeɪljəz/
pl mean times between failures
⋈ improve, predict, record the
mean time between failures
abbr MTBF
▶ **mean time to repair**

mean time to repair *noun*
a calculation of how often a device or system will need to be
repaired

/ˌmiːn ˈtaɪm tə rɪˈpeə(r)/
pl mean times to repair
⋈ calculate, improve the **mean
time to repair**

media conversion *noun*
the process of copying data from one storage medium to another: *The media conversion involved copying data from disk to tape.* ○ *The older data undergoes media conversion before being archived.*

/'miːdɪə kən,vɜːʃn/
note no plural

---

medium scale integration *noun* (hardware)
the process of putting between 10 and 100 COMPONENTS on an integrated circuit

/,miːdɪəm skeɪl ɪntɪ'greɪʃn/
note no plural
abbr MSI
⋈ **medium scale integration** techniques, methods
▶ **circuit board, large scale integration, printed circuit board, small scale integration, super large scale integration, ultra large scale integration, very large scale integration, wafer scale integration**

---

meg *abbr*
(*informal*)
▶ **megabyte**

/meg/

☆**mega** *prefix*
one million, 10^6

/'megə/
abbr M
▶ **giga, kilo, tera**

---

megabit *noun* (hardware)
one million bits

note In computing, because of the use of the binary system, a megabit is 2^{20}, or 1 048 576 bits. There are 8 megabits in a megabyte.

/'megəbɪt/
pl megabits

☆**megabyte** *noun* (hardware)
one million bytes

note In computing, because of the use of the binary system, a megabyte is 2^{20}, or 1 048 576 bytes.

/'megəbaɪt/
pl megabytes
abbr MB, Mbyte

---

megaflops *noun*
millions of FLOATING POINT OPERATIONS per second; a measurement of computing speed

/'megəflɒps/
note plural noun used with a plural verb
▶ MIPS

☆**megahertz** *noun* (hardware)
one million hertz, equivalent to one million CYCLES PER SECOND: *a stand-alone computer that operates with a 66 megahertz processor* ○ *measure the speed of clocks in computers in megahertz*

/'megəhɜːts/
note no plural
abbr MHz

☆**memory** *noun* (hardware)
the part of a computer where data and instructions are stored: *There isn't enough memory to open the application.* ○ *The computer has 512K of memory.* ○ *upgrade the machine by adding more memory*

/'meməri/
note usually singular
⋈ **memory** capacity
▶ RAM, ROM

---

memory address *noun* (hardware)
a number that identifies a particular memory location: *locate a memory address*

/'meməri ə,dres/
pl memory addresses

---

abbr abbreviation   **pl** plural   **syn** synonym   ▶ see   ⋈ collocate (*word often used with the headword*)

☆**memory address register** *noun* (hardware)
the register in the CPU that holds the memory address of a
data item when an instruction is executed

/ˌmeməri əˈdres ˌredʒɪstə(r)/
pl memory address registers
abbr MAR
⋈ access, load, update the
memory address register

---

memory bank *noun* (hardware)
a collection of separate memory devices that are combined to
make a larger memory

/ˈmeməri ˌbæŋk/
pl memory banks

---

memory board *noun* (hardware)
a printed circuit board containing the memory chips and the
logic circuits which are used for writing and reading data
during the memory cycle: *a memory board that gives 2MB of
RAM* ○ *The upgrade kit includes a memory board.*

/ˈmeməri ˌbɔːd/
pl memory boards

☆**memory buffer register** *noun* (hardware)
a place in the CPU that holds an item of data while it is being
written to or read from memory: *a one-word memory buffer
register* ○ *a double length memory buffer register*

/ˈmeməri ˌbʌfə ˌredʒɪstə(r)/
pl memory buffer registers
abbr MBR
⋈ access, read data *from*, write
data *to* the **memory buffer
register**
syn buffer register

---

memory bus *noun* (hardware)
a bus that transfers data between registers on the memory
board: *a 128-bit memory bus* ○ *a high-performance memory bus*

/ˈmeməri bʌs/
pl memory buses
▶ **bus**

---

memory capacity *noun* (hardware)
the maximum amount of data, measured in bits and bytes, etc
that can be stored in memory: *The memory capacity of the
computer is 8 megabytes.* ○ *a system with 192MB memory
capacity*

/ˈmeməri kəˌpæsəti/
note usually singular

---

memory chip *noun* (hardware)
a chip that contains thousands of circuits that can be used to
store data

/ˈmeməri tʃɪp/
pl memory chips
syn RAM chip
▶ **microprocessor**

---

memory cycle *noun* (hardware)
a cycle in which a memory address is located so that
information can be read from or written to it

/ˈmeməri ˌsaɪkl/
pl memory cycles
▶ **cycle, hertz**

---

memory data register *noun* (hardware)
a register in the logic circuits that control memory, and where
an item of data is held until the next point in the MEMORY CYCLE
when the data can be either written into memory, or retrieved
from memory and used by a program

/ˈmeməri ˌdeɪtə ˌredʒɪstə(r)/
pl memory data registers

---

memory hierarchy *noun*
a way of organizing memory by reserving separate areas for
the operating system and applications programs, etc

/ˈmeməri ˌhaɪərɑːki/
note no plural
⋈ construct, define, structure a
memory hierarchy

memory management *noun* (hardware)
the ability of some CPUs to support DYNAMIC STORAGE ALLOCATION
and VIRTUAL MEMORY: *This processor has built-in memory
management facilities.*

/'meməri ˌmænɪdʒmənt/
note no plural
ℍ **memory management**
facilities, functions, tools,
utilities

☆**memory map** *noun* (hardware)
a part of memory that records the memory locations which
have been given to programs and other functions: *allocate an
address within the memory map*

/'meməri mæp/
pl memory maps

memory-mapped *adjective* (hardware)
(of programs, etc) that have been given a permanent location
in memory: *The screen display on this machine is memory-
mapped.*

/'meməri mæpt/
▶ **memory mapped I/O, video
memory**

memory-mapped I/O *noun* (hardware)
a way of controlling input to and output from a computer
which has PERIPHERALS that have been given particular
locations in memory. To send information to a particular
peripheral, a program writes information to the memory
location of that peripheral.

/'meməri mæpt ˌaɪ 'əʊ/
note no plural

memory-resident *adjective* (software)
(of a program) that is loaded into memory when the computer
is booted, and remains permanently in memory because it is
used very often: *memory-resident anti-virus software* ○ *switch
between motherboards by using a memory-resident facility*

/'meməri ˌrezɪdənt/
ℍ a **memory-resident** program,
utility

☆**menu** *noun* (applications)
a list of program commands. The user can select a command
by clicking on it, or by using keys on the keyboard: *select
options from the main menu* ○ *an interactive menu*

/'menjuː/
pl menus
ℍ choose, select a command, etc
from the **menu**; the main
menu
▶ **dialog box, function key,
graphical user interface,
pop-up menu, pull-down
menu, WIMP**

menu bar *noun* (applications)
a thin box at the top of the window of an application that
allows the user to access a menu: *select the HELP menu from the
menu bar*

/'menjuː bɑː/
pl menu bars

menu-driven *adjective* (applications)
(of a program) that allows the user to select a command from a
menu, not by typing in command lines: *The search software
with menu-driven commands is very user-friendly.*

/'menjuː ˌdrɪvn/
ℍ a **menu-driven** interface,
operation
▶ **command interface**

☆**merge** *verb* (system operation)
to combine two or more things, such as files, items of data or
systems, etc into one file, item of data or system, etc: *The
company wants to merge wide area networks with local area
networks to create a single network.* ○ *merge the two files to get an
up-to-date list of addresses* ○ *reorganize the file before merging
additions and removing deleted records*

/mɜːdʒ/
merge, merging, merged
note transitive verb
▶ **mail merge**

merge sort *noun*
a process that takes two or more sorted lists as input, combines
them, and produces a single sorted list as output

/'mɜːdʒ sɔːt/
pl merge sorts

---

abbr abbreviation   **pl** plural   **syn** synonym   ▶ see   ℍ collocate (*word often used with the headword*)

☆**message** *noun*

a unit of information which is transmitted electronically from one device to another, or from one person to another: *route the message through a physical link* ○ *an e-mail message*

/ˈmesɪdʒ/

pl messages

◣ forward, receive, reply *to*, send a **message**

▶ **packet switching**

---

message authentication code *noun*

a part of a transmitted message that proves its contents and the place it was sent from, etc are genuine

/ˈmesɪdʒ ɔːˌθentɪˈkeɪʃn kəʊd/

pl message authentication codes

◣ receive, send, transmit a **message authentication code**

---

message header *noun*

a unit of information at the beginning of an electronic message which identifies the code it is written in, its length and routing information, etc: *information in the message header included the time stamp*

/ˈmesɪdʒ ˌhedə(r)/

pl message headers

◣ examine, include, print a **message header**

▶ **header**

---

message switching *noun*

a method of sending messages over a network in which the message is held until it is complete and then sent by the best route, perhaps in several stages. There is no direct link between the sender and the receiver: *Message switching allows data to be held back until telephone charges are cheaper.*

/ˈmesɪdʒ ˌswɪtʃɪŋ/

note not used with *a* or *an*. No plural and used with a singular verb only.

◣ send a message *by*, use **message switching**

syn store and forward switching

▶ **packet switching, circuit switching**

---

metalanguage *noun*

a language that is used for describing the structure of other languages, especially computer programming languages: *Backus-Naur Form is a well-known metalanguage.*

/ˈmetəlæŋgwɪdʒ/

pl metalanguages

◣ write *in* a **metalanguage**; **metalanguage** syntax rules

▶ **grammar**

MFLOPS *abbr*

▶ **megaflops**

/ˈem ˌflɒps/

MHz *abbr*

▶ **megahertz**

note used in written English only

MICR *abbr*

▶ **magnetic ink character recognition**

/ˈmaɪkə(r)/

note pronounced as a word

---

micro- *combining form*

one millionth

/ˈmaɪkrəʊ/

☆**micro** *noun*

▶ **microcomputer**

/ˈmaɪkrəʊ/

☆**microchip** *noun*

▶ **chip**

/ˈmaɪkrəʊtʃɪp/

---

microcode *noun* (hardware)

the set of very basic instructions that is HARDWIRED into the CPU; machine code instructions are programmed as a number of microcode instructions

/ˈmaɪkrəʊkəʊd/

note no plural

◣ code *in*, program *in* **microcode**

syn microinstruction

☆**microcomputer** *noun* (hardware)
a small digital computer that contains one or more microprocessors: *use a microcomputer at home or at school* ○ *link the school microcomputer to external sources of information*

/ˈmaɪkrəʊkəmpjuːtə(r)/
pl microcomputers
abbr micro
Ⓜ a **microcomputer** network, system
▶ **mainframe, palmtop, PC**

---

microelectronics *noun* (hardware)
the technology that allows circuits to be made in very small sizes: *chip-based microelectronics*

/ˈmaɪkrəʊ ɪˌlekˈtrɒnɪks/
note singular noun, used with a singular verb

---

microfiche *noun*
a piece of MICROFILM that is framed by card, etc and can be read with a special machine: *a hardcopy version of the text on microfiche* ○ *view the collection of photographs on microfiche*

/ˈmaɪkrəʊfiːʃ/
note not used with *a* or *an*. No plural and used with a singular verb only.
syn fiche

---

microfilm *noun* (hardware)
a piece of HIGH-RESOLUTION film that is used to record text and images: *archived copies of documents are held on microfilm* ○ *a roll of microfilm*

/ˈmaɪkrəʊfɪlm/
note not used with *a* or *an*. No plural and used with a singular verb only.
Ⓜ capture *on*, copy *onto*, record *on* **microfilm**; a frame of, piece of, roll of **microfilm**

---

microfloppy *noun* (hardware)
a 3.5 inch floppy disk: *a microfloppy that holds 1.44 MB of data*

/ˈmaɪkrəʊflɒpi/
pl microfloppies
Ⓜ a double-sided, high-density, single-sided **microfloppy**
▶ **floppy disk**

☆**microinstruction** *noun*
▶ **microcode**

/ˈmaɪkrəʊɪnˌstrʌkʃn/

☆**microprocessor** *noun* (hardware)
a chip that contains all the functions of a computer's central processing unit: *a RISC microprocessor* ○ *microprocessor controlled systems*

/ˈmaɪkrəʊprəʊsesə(r)/
pl microprocessors
Ⓜ **microprocessor** chip
▶ **memory chip, RISC**

---

microprogram *noun* (hardware)
one of the basic programs stored in the CPU that executes machine code instructions. Microprograms are written in MICROCODE and are invisible to the user.

/ˈmaɪkrəʊprəʊgræm/
pl microprograms
Ⓜ execute, write a **microprogram**

☆**microsecond** *noun*
one millionth of a second: *Data can be retrieved from the hard disk in less than a tenth of a microsecond.*

/ˈmaɪkrəʊsekənd/
pl microseconds

Microsoft Corporation *noun*
(*trade mark*) (*organization*) a US software company specializing in programs and packages for personal computers

/ˈmaɪkrəʊsɒft kɔːpəˌreɪʃn/
abbr MS
▶ **MS-DOS**

---

abbr abbreviation   **pl** plural   **syn** synonym   ▶ see   Ⓜ collocate (*word often used with the headword*)

milli- *combining form*
one thousandth

/ˈmɪli/

---

millisecond *noun*
one thousandth of a second: *a system that operates on a millisecond timescale*

/ˈmɪlisekənd/
pl milliseconds

☆**minicomputer** *noun* (hardware)
a computer that is smaller and slower than a mainframe but larger and faster than a microcomputer. Minicomputers are often used as interfaces between mainframes and wide area networks: *a PC connected to a minicomputer host*

/ˈmɪnikəmpjuːtə(r)/
pl minicomputers
ℍ a front end, a network, an office **minicomputer**

---

minus sign *noun*
the symbol that is used to show that a number is negative or that a subtraction operation should happen: *The minus sign in front of the number '-0.743' shows that the result of the calculation was a negative number.*

/ˈmaɪnəs saɪn/
pl minus signs
ℍ insert, print a **minus sign**

MIPS *abbr*
millions of instructions per second; a measure of processor speed: *The workstation performs at 133 MIPS.* ○ *The 50 MHz computer is capable of 100 MIPS.* ○ *Overall system performance runs to 68 000 MIPS.*

/mɪps/
note pronounced as a word
▶ hertz, megaflops

☆**MIS** *abbr*
▶ management information system

/ˌem aɪ ˈes/
note pronounced as individual letters

MMI *abbr*
man machine interface

/ˌem em ˈaɪ/
note pronounced as individual letters

---

mnemonic *noun*
a short form of a programming language instruction or command that helps the programmer to remember it easily: *INCX is a mnemonic for 'increment the X register'.*

/nɪˈmɒnɪk/
pl mnemonics
ℍ substitute something *for*, use, write a **mnemonic**: **mnemonic** code
▶ abbreviation, acronym

☆**mode** *noun* (system operation)
a way of using a computer system or part of it: *run jobs in batch mode* ○ *operate in WYSIWYG mode* ○ *switch into standalone mode to run the spreadsheet*

/məʊd/
pl modes
ℍ expert, interactive, sequential **mode**

---

model¹ *noun*
a SIMULATION that describes how a system behaves so that a computer program can control the system or can explore the effects of changes to the system

/ˈmɒdl/
pl models
ℍ alter, change, construct, design a **model**

---

model² *verb*
to design a SIMULATION which describes how a system behaves so that a computer program can control the system or can explore the effects of changes to the system: *model the possible effects of changes to the system*

/ˈmɒdl/
model, modelling, modelled
(US **model, modeling, modeled**)
note transitive verb

M **model** an operation, a process, a system

☆**modem** *noun* (hardware)

A device that converts analog signals received via a telephone line into digital data that a computer can process. When the computer transmits digital data, a modem converts this into an analog signal that can travel on telephone lines: *download programs via a modem* ○ *The system boots remotely via an internal modem.* ○ *a modem link* ○ *The laptop has an integral fax modem.*

note The word 'modem' is formed from the words 'modulator/demodulator'.

/'məʊdem/

pl modems

M receive data, etc *by*, send data, etc *via*, transmit data, etc *by* (a) **modem**

---

modifier bit *noun* (software)

a part of a machine code instruction that shows if another part of the instruction, such as the address field, has to be changed before the instruction is executed

/'mɒdɪfaɪə bɪt/

pl modifier bits

M access, clear, set, unset the **modifier bit**

---

modify *verb*

to change something, especially to change the address given in a machine code instruction by INDEXING or INDIRECT ADDRESSING: *modify the address before the instruction is executed*

/'mɒdɪfaɪ/

modify, modifying, modified

note transitive verb

---

modular *adjective*

(of a program or system) that is divided into parts. Each part (module) is a working unit on its own and users may build a system to work in a certain way by combining separate modules: *Users can create systems to their own specification with a wide range of modular components.* ○ *The modular architecture will integrate 10 million transistors.*

/'mɒdjələ(r)/

M **modular** hardware, programs, systems

---

modular arithmetic *noun* (mathematics)

a form of counting in which the numbers restart from zero whenever a fixed limit is reached

/ˌmɒdjulə əˈrɪθmətɪk/

note not used with *a* or *an*. No plural and used with a singular verb only.

M carry out, perform **modular arithmetic**

---

modular programming *noun*

a type of STRUCTURED PROGRAMMING where the program is divided into small sections, called modules, which are coded and tested separately and then CALLED[2] (2) from the MAIN BODY of the program: *modular programming allows different programmers to work on separate modules*

/ˌmɒdjələ ˈprəʊɡræmɪŋ/

note not used with *a* or *an*. No plural and used with a singular verb only.

M practise **modular programming**

---

modulate *verb*

to change a CARRIER SIGNAL so it transmits data: *The modem modulates the signal before it is transmitted.*

/'mɒdjuleɪt/

modulate, modulating, modulated

note transitive verb

M **modulate** a carrier wave, signal

▶ **amplitude modulation, demodulate, frequency modulation, phase modulation, pulse code modulation**

---

abbr abbreviation   **pl** plural   **syn** synonym   ▶ see   M collocate (*word often used with the headword*)

modulation *noun*
the process of changing a CARRIER SIGNAL by adding another signal to it; the changes in the carrier signal represent data: *a modulation rate of 80 baud*

/ˌmɒdjuˈleɪʃn/

note not used with *a* or *an*. No plural and used with a singular verb only.

◄ **modulation** *of* a carrier signal, *of* a wave

► **amplitude modulation, frequency modulation, phase modulation, pulse code modulation, carrier signal, demodulation**

☆**modulator** *noun* (hardware)
a device which MODULATES a signal

/ˈmɒdjuleɪtə(r)/

pl modulators

◄ send a signal, etc *via*, transmit a signal, etc *via*, use a **modulator**

► **demodulator**

☆**module** *noun*
1 (*hardware*) a hardware COMPONENT of a computer system: *The system includes an integrated power supply module.* ○ *test each module separately before connecting it to the system* **2** (*software/programming*) a group of ROUTINES that perform different parts of the same task: *load the spell checking module in the word processing application* ○ *debug each module before adding it to the system*

/ˈmɒdjuːl/

pl modules

---

monadic operator *noun*
► **unary operator**

/mɒˌnædɪk ˈɒpəreɪtə(r)/

☆**monitor** *noun* (hardware)
a piece of eqipment with a screen that displays images, etc: *connect the camcorder to the monitor via a special connector* ○ *plug the monitor into an external VGA video port to view in colour*

/ˈmɒnɪtə(r)/

pl monitors

◄ a black and white, colour, monochrome, television, video **monitor**

► **screen, VDU**

---

monitor program *noun* (software)
an operating system

note This term is not often used; 'operating system' is more common.

/ˈmɒnɪtə ˌprəʊɡræm/

pl monitor programs

► **operating system**

---

monochrome *adjective*
(of a screen, etc) that only uses the colours black, white and grey: *a high-resolution monochrome screen* ○ *The company produces a wide range of colour and monochrome display monitors for computers.*

/ˈmɒnəkrəʊm/

◄ a **monochrome** display, image, picture, screen, terminal

► **colour display**

---

monospace font *noun*
a font which has characters that all occupy the same amount of horizontal space: *The letters 'i' and 'w' occupy the same amount of space in a monospace font.*

/ˌmɒnəʊspeɪs ˈfɒnt/

pl monospace fonts

(also **fixed-width font**)

► **font, kerning, proportional font**

MOS *abbr*
metal oxide semiconductor

/ˌem əʊ ˈes/

note pronounced as individual letters

most significant bit *noun*
the bit at the left end of a binary WORD **1** that has the largest place value when a number is stored

/'məʊst sɪg'nɪfɪkənt 'bɪt/
pl most significant bits
abbr msb
⋈ clear, set the **most significant bit**
▶ **least significant bit**

most significant character *noun*
the character at the left end of a group of characters stored in a memory location or data structure

/'məʊst sɪg'nɪfɪkənt 'kærəktə(r)/
pl most significant characters
⋈ access, delete, read, write the **most significant character**

motherboard *noun* (hardware)
the main printed circuit board of a computer where its important parts are found, such as the CPU and main memory *memory expansion is built into the motherboard* ○ *upgrade the machine by replacing the motherboard*

/'mʌðəbɔːd/
pl motherboards
⋈ attach something *to*, build something *into*, install, integrate something *onto*, replace the **motherboard**
▶ **daughter board**

☆**mouse** *noun* (hardware)
a small electronic device attached to a computer that is moved by hand to control the position of the cursor on screen. The buttons on the mouse are used to enter commands: *click on the mouse to open a file* ○ *the left/right(-hand) mouse button* ○ *configure the mouse for high sensitivity*

/maʊs/
pl mice
⋈ click *on*, double click *on*, move, use the **mouse**
▶ **joystick**

moving head disk *noun* (hardware)
a magnetic disk where the READ/WRITE HEAD moves across the disk and can access more than one TRACK

/'muːvɪŋ hed 'dɪsk/
pl moving head disks
▶ **fixed head disk**

moving head drive *noun* (hardware)
a device such as a disk drive where the READ/WRITE HEAD moves across the surface of the disk rather than being fixed in position

/'muːvɪŋ hed 'draɪv/
pl moving head drives
▶ **fixed head drive**

MPC *abbr*
multipath channel

/ˌem piː 'siː/
note pronounced as individual letters

MS *abbr*
▶ **Microsoft Corporation**

/ˌem 'es/
note pronounced as individual letters

ms *abbr*
▶ **millisecond**

note used in written English only

msb *abbr*
▶ **most significant bit**

/ˌem es 'biː/
note pronounced as individual letters

MS-DOS *abbr* (software)
(*trade mark*) Microsoft Disk Operating System, an operating system for IBM and IBM-compatible computers.

note MS-DOS is often called 'DOS'. It has a character-based interface which means commands must be typed in at the keyboard. Most users now avoid this type of interface by using a graphical user interface such as Windows.

/ˌem es 'dɒs/
note no plural
⋈ run, use **MS-DOS**; an **MS-DOS** command
▶ **operating system, Unix, Windows**

---

abbr abbreviation   **pl** plural   **syn** synonym   ▶ see   ⋈ collocate (*word often used with the headword*)

MSI *abbr*
► **medium scale integration**

/ˌem es ˈaɪ/
note pronounced as individual letters

MT *abbr*
► **magnetic tape**

/ˌem ˈtiː/
note pronounced as individual letters

MTBF *abbr*
► **mean time between failures**

/ˌem tiː biː ˈef/
note pronounced as individual letters

---

multi- *combining form*
more than one, or many: *a multi-access computer system* ○ *a multi-user environment*

/ˈmʌlti/

---

multi-address instruction *noun*
an instruction that has more than one address

/ˈmʌlti əˌdres ɪnˈstrʌkʃn/
pl multi-address instructions

(also **multiaddress instruction, multiple address instruction**)

---

multi-dimensional *adjective* (software/graphics)
(of an image, etc) that has width, depth and height and so does not look flat: *display complex data as multi-dimensional graphics and tables*

/ˌmʌlti daɪˈmenʃənəl/

---

multi-dimensional array *noun*
an ARRAY with more than one dimension (= the number of values that must be given to access a data item)

/ˈmʌlti daɪˌmenʃənəl əˈreɪ/
pl multi-dimensional arrays

► **one-dimensional array, two-dimensional array, three-dimensional array**

---

multi-drop circuit *noun* (hardware/networks)
a network in which a number of terminals can communicate with the central computer, but the terminals cannot communicate with each other directly

/ˈmʌlti ˈdrɒp ˈsɜːkɪt/
pl multi-drop circuits

► **network, local area network**

☆**multimedia** *noun* (applications)
the combination of sound, graphics and video to present information on a computer: *The multimedia system has an internal sound card.* ○ *create an interactive multimedia presentation for computer-based training* ○ *a multimedia CD-ROM* ○ *use multimedia in the classroom*

/ˌmʌltiˈmiːdiə/
note no plural

◄ a **multimedia** application, CD, PC, system, workstation; **multimedia** software, technology

► **hypermedia**

---

multipart *adjective*
having more than one part: *a multipart computer game*

/ˈmʌltipɑːt/

---

multipart form *noun*
forms used with IMPACT PRINTERS that consist of two or more sheets of paper, one on top of the other. The information printed on the top sheet is copied onto the sheets below: *multipart forms need bursting after they have passed through the printer* ○ *send the top copy of the multipart form to the customer*

/ˌmʌltipɑːt ˈfɔːm/
pl multipart forms

◄ load, print *onto* a **multipart form**

multipart stationery *noun*

stationery used with IMPACT PRINTERS that consists of two or more sheets of paper, one on top of the other. The information printed on the top sheet is copied onto the sheets below: *three-part multipart stationery*

/ˌmʌltipɑːt ˈsteɪʃənri/

note not used with *a* or *an*. No plural and used with a singular verb only.

▶ **stationery**

multiple¹ *noun* (mathematics)

a larger number that can be divided by a smaller number an exact number of times: *10 is a common multiple of 2 and 5* ○ *12, 18 and 24 are multiples of 6*

/ˈmʌltɪpl/

pl multiples

multiple² *adjective*

more than one, or many: *The software enables multiple users to access the network from any point.* ○ *multiple platforms and networks* ○ *issue multiple requests to the system*

/ˈmʌltɪpl/

M **multiple** licences, processors

▶ **multi-user**

multiple valued logic *noun*

▶ **fuzzy logic**

/ˈmʌltɪpl ˌvæljuːd ˈlɒdʒɪk/

multiplex *verb* (communications)

to combine one or more signals into a single transmission channel: *The signals are multiplexed before being transmitted over a satellite link.*

/ˈmʌltɪpleks/

multiplex, multiplexing, multiplexed

note transitive verb

M **multiplex** data, messages, signals

☆**multiplexer** *noun* (hardware/communications)

a device which allows different signals to be transmitted over the same channel at the same time. So that the signals are not mixed, they are separated by time, space or frequency.

/ˈmʌltɪpleksə(r)/

pl multiplexers

(also **multiplexor**)

abbr MUX

M install, use a **multiplexer**

▶ **concentrator, time division multiplexing, frequency division multiplexing**

multiplexing *noun* (communications)

a way of transmitting different signals over the same channel at the same time. So that the signals are not mixed, they are separated by time, space or frequency.

/ˈmʌltɪpleksɪŋ/

note not used with *a* or *an*. No plural and used with a singular verb only.

M **multiplexing** circuits, protocols, techniques

▶ **time division multiplexing, frequency division multiplexing**

multiplicand *noun* (mathematics)

a number that is multiplied by another number, called a MULTIPLIER: *In the sum 2×5=10, the number 2 is the multiplicand.*

/ˌmʌltɪplɪˈkænd/

pl multiplicands

multiplier *noun* (mathematics)

a number by which another number, called a MULTIPLICAND, is multiplied: *In the sum 2×5=10, the number 5 is the multiplier.*

/ˈmʌltɪplaɪə(r)/

pl multipliers

---

abbr abbreviation   **pl** plural   **syn** synonym   ▶ see   **M** collocate (*word often used with the headword*)

multiply *verb*
1 to make a number bigger by a certain number of times: *3 multiplied by 4 equals 12* ○ *multiply 4 by 8 to get 32* **2** to increase in size or capacity: *The virus in the computer will multiply.* ○ *multiply processing capacity by upgrading the computers*

/ˈmʌltɪplaɪ/
multiply, multiplying, multiplied
1 note transitive verb
M **multiply** A *and* B (together), A *by* B
2 note transitive or intransitive verb

---

multipoint configuration *noun* (hardware/networks)
an arrangement of terminals on a network where the terminals share the same physical connection to the main computer

/ˈmʌltɪpɔɪnt kənfɪgəˌreɪʃn/
pl multipoint configurations
M install, structure a network *as a* **multipoint configuration**
► **network topology, parallel processing**

---

multiprocessing *noun*
the situation when two or more PROCESSING UNITS work together: *multiprocessing on desktops and servers* ○ *use multiprocessing to increase speed*

/ˌmʌltɪˈprəʊsesɪŋ/
note not used with *a* or *an*. No plural and used with a singular verb only.
M symmetric **multiprocessing**

---

multiprocessor system *noun*
a computer system in which two or more PROCESSING UNITS work together

/ˌmʌltɪˈprəʊsesə ˌsɪstəm/
pl multiprocessor systems

---

multiprogramming *noun* (system software)
a way of executing two or more programs together. Each program is executed for a short amount of time (= a time slice) to allow more than one program to share processor time: *users' programs compete for resources in multiprogramming*

/ˌmʌltɪˈprəʊgræmɪŋ/
note not used with a *a* or *an*. No plural and used with a singular verb only.
M a **multiprogramming** computer, environment
► **time slice**

---

multiprogramming system *noun* (software)
an OPERATING SYSTEM that controls the way in which two or more programs are processed together

/ˌmʌltɪˈprəʊgræmɪŋ ˌsɪstəm/
pl multiprogramming systems

☆**multitasking** *noun* (system operation)
the ability of a computer to work on more than one task at the same time: *Multitasking allows the computer to retrieve e-mail while the user is working in another application.*

/ˈmʌltiˌtɑːskɪŋ/
note no plural
M **multitasking** in real time
syn tasking
► **background processing, context switching 1, foreground processing, simultaneous processing**

---

multithreading *noun* (software/programming)
a way of writing a program so that it uses more than one processor. This allows different parts (threads) of the program to be executed at the same time: *Multithreading improves the execution time of large complex programs.*

/ˌmʌltɪˈθredɪŋ/
note no plural
syn threading
► **thread**

☆**multi-user** *adjective* (hardware/software)
(of a computer or system) that can be used by more than one person at the same time

/ˌmʌltɪˈjuːzə(r)/
(also **multiuser**)
M a **multi-user** environment, network, site, system, terminal

multi-user operating system *noun*
(software/system software)
an operating system that allows more than one person to use
the system at the same time: *The multi-user operating system
supports 64 terminals.*

/ˌmʌltɪ juːzə(r) ˈɒpəreɪtɪŋ
ˌsɪstəm/
pl multi-user operating systems
Ⱨ execute, install, load a **multi-user operating system**

☆**multi-user system** *noun* (hardware)
a computer system that can be used by more than one person
at the same time: *install a multi-user system with several
terminals*

/ˈmʌltɪ ˈjuːzə ˈsɪstəm/
pl multi-user systems
(also **multiuser system**)
▶ **stand-alone**

MUX *abbr*
▶ **multiplexer**

/mʌks/
note pronounced as a word

Nn

n *abbr*

1 ▶ **nano**

2 ▶ **node**
3 number

/en/

NAK *abbr*
the ASCII character which shows NEGATIVE ACKNOWLEDGEMENT
(= a message reporting that data has not been successfully
received): *The receiving unit sent back the NAK character.*

note used in written English only
▶ **control character**

name table *noun*
a LOOK-UP TABLE which is used by a compiler to find the address
in memory of the data that is linked to a particular variable
name

/ˈneɪm ˌteɪbl/
pl name tables
Ⱨ access, fill, update a **name table**
syn symbol table

NAND *abbr*
▶ **NAND operation**

/nænd/
note pronounced as a word

NAND circuit *noun*
▶ **NAND gate**

/ˈnænd ˌsɜːkɪt/

NAND gate *noun* (hardware/logic)
a circuit or chip which performs a NAND OPERATION on its inputs.
If all the inputs to a NAND gate are 1, its output is 0. In all
other cases its output is 1: *The logic circuit is built entirely from
NAND gates.*

/ˈnænd geɪt/
pl NAND gates
Ⱨ drive, connect *to*, use a **NAND gate**
syn NAND circuit
▶ **gate, NOR gate**

NAND operation *noun* (logic)
a logical operation which is the same as an AND OPERATION
followed by a NOT OPERATION: *The statement contains three NAND
operations.*

note P NAND Q is equivalent to NOT (P AND Q). The
combined expression P NAND Q is FALSE if and only if the
expression P and the expression Q are both TRUE.

/ˈnænd ɒpəˌreɪʃn/
pl NAND operations
Ⱨ carry out, do, implement,
perform, program something *as*
a **NAND operation**
syn NAND
▶ **Boolean connective**

---

abbr abbreviation   **pl** plural   **syn** synonym   ▶ see   Ⱨ collocate (*word often used with the headword*)

nano *prefix*
1 (*UK*) one thousand millionth **2** (*US*) one billionth

note Expressed as a number, nano is 10^{-9}, said as 'ten to the minus nine'.

/ˈnænəʊ/
abbr n
ᴎ a nano **second**
▶ **femto, pico**

---

natural language *noun*
a language, such as French or English, that is used between people

/ˌnætʃrəl ˈlæŋgwɪdʒ/
pl natural languages
ᴎ speak, understand, use a **natural language**
▶ **language translation**

NDR *abbr*
▶ **nondestructive readout**

/ˌen diː ˈɑː(r)/
note pronounced as individual letters

---

near letter quality *noun*
text printed by a dot matrix printer that is nearly as good as text produced with a typewriter or DAISYWHEEL PRINTER: *The expensive printer offers draft and near letter quality.* ○ *a printer that gives near letter quality*

/ˌnɪə ˈletə ˌkwɒləti/
note not used with *a* or *an*. No plural and used with a singular verb only.
abbr NLQ
▶ **draft quality, letter quality, print quality**

---

negation *noun*
the process of making a positive number less than zero, or NEGATIVE

/nɪˈgeɪʃn/
note not used with *a* or *an*. No plural and used with a singular verb only
▶ **NOT gate**

---

negative *adjective*
(of a number or amount) that is less than zero: *The company recorded negative profits last year.*

/ˈnegətɪv/
ᴎ a **negative** figure, sign, sum
▶ **positive**

---

negative acknowledgement *noun*
a message that reports a failed transmission of a signal or data and shows that the signal or data must be sent again

/ˌnegətɪv əkˈnɒlɪdʒmənt/
pl negative acknowledgements
abbr NAK
ᴎ receive, send, transmit a **negative acknowledgment**
▶ **acknowledgement, positive acknowledgement**

---

negative number *noun*
a number that is less than zero: *-4 is a negative number*

/ˌnegətɪv ˈnʌmbə(r)/
pl negative numbers

NEQ *abbr*
▶ **NEQ gate**

/ˌen iː ˈkjuː/
note pronounced as individual letters

NEQ circuit *abbr*
▶ **NEQ gate**

/ˌen iː ˈkjuː ˌsɜːkɪt/

NEQ gate *abbr*

a nonequivalence gate. A logic circuit with two or more inputs and a single output. There is a signal on the output only when the signals on the inputs are not all the same.

note A nonequivalence gate is the same as an equivalence gate followed by a NOT gate.

/ˌen iː ˈkjuː geɪt/
⋈ assert the input *to*, read output *from* an **NEQ gate**
syn NEQ, NEQ circuit

---

nested *adjective*

(of something) that is contained within something else of the same type

/ˈnestɪd/

---

nested function *noun* (software/programming)

a function that is executed when it is CALLED² (2) from a statement in another function or subroutine: *Many languages only allow a small number of nested function calls.*

/ˌnestɪd ˈfʌŋkʃn/
pl nested functions
⋈ call, invoke a **nested function**
▶ **calling sequence, function**

---

nested loop *noun* (software/programming)

a LOOP¹ (2) which is part of the block of statements forming another loop

/ˌnestɪd ˈluːp/
pl nested loops
⋈ execute, perform a **nested loop**
▶ **inner loop, outer loop**

---

nested procedure *noun* (software/programming)

a PROCEDURE (= a separate part of a computer program that performs a task) which is CALLED² (2) from a statement in another procedure

/ˌnestɪd prəˈsiːdʒə(r)/
pl nested procedures
⋈ execute, perform a **nested procedure**; a **nested procedure** call

---

nested subroutine *noun* (software/programming)

a subroutine that is executed when it is CALLED² (2) from a statement in another subroutine or function: *Many languages only allow a small number of nested subroutines.*

/ˌnestɪd ˈsʌbruːtiːn/
pl nested subroutines
⋈ call, invoke a **nested subroutine**
▶ **calling sequence**

☆**network¹** *noun*

a number of computers, PERIPHERALS and other devices that are connected by cables, telephone lines and other communications links: *The office network allows users to share files and software, and to use a central printer.* ○ *Electronic mail messages can be sent over a global network.*

/ˈnetwɜːk/
pl networks
⋈ install, maintain, send data/ messages *over*, use a **network**; a commercial, a data, a digital, an international, a national, a software **network**; **network** analysis, architecture, communications, support, systems
▶ **Internet, local area network, wide area network**

☆**network²** *verb*

to connect devices in a network: *The whole building will be networked next weekend.*

/ˈnetwɜːk/
network, networking, networked
note transitive verb
⋈ **network** a company, an office

---

network address *noun*

the identification that must be attached to data transmitted over a network to make sure that it goes to the right place: *send the message to the network address 'jsmith@oxford.ac.uk'* ○ *the machine's network address is 158.685.097.4*

/ˈnetwɜːk əˌdres/
pl network addresses
⋈ add, attach, quote a **network address**

---

abbr abbreviation   **pl** plural   **syn** synonym   ▶ see   ⋈ collocate (*word often used with the headword*)

☆**network database** *noun*
a database where data items can be linked together in more
than one way

/ˌnetwɜːk ˈdeɪtəbeɪs/
pl network databases
◄ an extended, a non-relational
network database; **network
database** architecture,
structure

network layer *noun*
one of the levels of structure of the International Standards
Organization PROTOCOL for data communications. The network
layer describes how a network can be connected to another
larger network: *The network layer will have to deal with problems
such as routing data and making sure that packet sizes match.*

/ˈnetwɜːk ˌleɪə(r)/
note not used with *a* or *an*. No
plural and used with a singular
verb only.
◄ define, specify the **network
layer**
► **application layer, data link
layer, ISO OSI, physical
layer, presentation layer,
session layer, transport
layer**

network node *noun*
► **node 2**

/ˈnetwɜːk nəʊd/

network protocol *noun*
the set of rules for message formats and control signals that
computers must use to be able to communicate over a
network: *The network protocol decides what type of adaptor is
needed to connect the PC to the network.* ○ *Most organizations have
multiple networks that communicate using different network
protocols.*

/ˌnetwɜːk ˈprəʊtəkɒl/
pl network protocols
◄ define, follow, obey the
network protocol
► **control character, message
format, protocol**

network software *noun* (software)
software that is used to connect a user to a network

/ˌnetwɜːk ˈsɒftweə(r)/
note not used with *a* or *an*. No
plural and used with a singular
verb only.
◄ install, run, upgrade **network
software** ; error-correcting,
local area, wide area **network
software**; a **network
software** layer, suite
► **network, protocol**

network topology *noun*
the arrangement of NODES (2) in a local area network: *Each node
(PC, terminal or workstation) on the network can be replaced
because the network topology is flexible.*

/ˌnetwɜːk təˈpɒlədʒi/
pl network topologies
► **bus network, ring network,
star network, tree network**

neural net *abbr*
► **neural network**

/ˌnjʊərəl ˈnet/

neural network *noun*
a method of computing that tries to copy the way the human
brain works. A group of processing elements all receive data at
the same time, and links are made between elements as
repeated patterns are recognized: *a learning mechanism in a
neural network* ○ *Parallel processing is heavily used in neural
networks.*

/ˌnjʊərəl ˈnetwɜːk/
pl neural networks
abbr neural net
◄ design a **neural network**; a
neural network algorithm,
application; **neural network**
learning, technology
► **fuzzy logic, parallel
processing, pattern
recognition**

---

newline character *noun* (software)
a CONTROL CHARACTER that tells the computer or printer to move to the beginning of the next line

note The newline character is equivalent to the combination of carriage return and line feed.

/'nju:laɪn ˌkærəktə(r)/
note usually singular
abbr NL
▶ **carriage return, hard return, line feed, soft return, wrap**

---

next instruction register *noun*
▶ **current address register**

/ˌnekst ɪn'strʌkʃn ˌredʒɪstə(r)/
abbr NIR

☆**nibble** *noun* (hardware)
(*informal*) one half of a byte, or four bits: *The numbers are broken down for processing into nibbles.*

/'nɪbl/
pl nibbles
▶ **byte, gulp, word**

---

nil *noun*
a standard way of writing an EMPTY LIST (= a list with no data items) in languages such as Lisp

/nɪl/
note not used with *a* or *an*. No plural and used with a singular verb only.

---

nine's complement *noun*
a system for recording positive and negative numbers using the base ten numerals

note In nine's complement notation, negative numbers are represented by changing each digit of a positive number into the difference between that digit and 9. For example, using eight digits, -123 would be represented as 99999876 and -1 would be represented as 99999998, etc.

/ˌnaɪnz 'kɒmplɪmənt/
note no plural
(also **9's complement**)
◄ employ, use **nine's complement**; **nine's complement** arithmetic, notation, representation
▶ **one's complement, ten's complement, two's complement**

NIR *abbr*
▶ **next instruction register**

/ˌen aɪ 'ɑː/
note pronounced as individual letters

NL *abbr*
▶ **newline character**

note used in written English only

NLQ *abbr*
▶ **near letter quality**

/ˌen el 'kjuː/
note pronounced as individual letters

NMI *abbr*
▶ **non-maskable interrupt**

/ˌen em 'aɪ/
note pronounced as individual letters

☆**node** *noun*
1 a place in a data structure such as a tree or list where data is stored. Nodes are linked by POINTERS: *A tree that has 26 pointers leading from each node.* **2** a place in a communications network where two or more transmission channels meet. In a computer network, each computer will be at a node: *The laptop operates as a node on the network.*

/nəʊd/
pl nodes
1 ◄ access, store data *in* a **node**
syn data node
▶ **data structure**
2 ◄ configure, install, link a **node**
syn network node

---

abbr abbreviation **pl** plural **syn** synonym ▶ see ◄ collocate (*word often used with the headword*)

noise *noun*
the extra signals in a COMMUNICATIONS CHANNEL that are not part of any transmitted signals. Noise can damage the signals that are transmitted: *The information on the signal was distorted by noise.*

/nɔɪz/
note no plural
◄ be distorted *by*, be obscured *by* **noise**
► **signal**[1]

nonbreaking space *noun*
(applications/word processing)
a space that is put between two words that must appear on the same line in a piece of text: *A nonbreaking space must be inserted between 'Great' and 'Britain'.*

/ˈnɒnˌbreɪkɪŋ ˈspeɪs/
pl nonbreaking spaces
◄ delete, insert a **nonbreaking space**
► **hard space, soft space**

noncompatibility *noun*
a situation when pieces of hardware and software cannot work together

/ˈnɒnkəmˌpætəˈbɪləti/
note not used with *a* or *an*. No plural and used with a singular verb only.
► **compatibility**

nondestructive readout *noun* (hardware)
a read operation which copies the data being read instead of moving it

note Programming languages suggest that access to a variable is a nondestructive readout. This is not true, as the hardware must write the variable back to the same location as part of the access.

/ˈnɒndɪˌstrʌktɪv ˈriːdaʊt/
pl nondestructive readouts
abbr NDR

nonequivalence gate *noun*
► **NEQ gate**

/ˌnɒnɪˈkwɪvələns ˌɡeɪt/

nonimpact printer *noun* (hardware)
a printer such as a laser printer that produces text in a way that does not involve hitting characters against paper

/ˌnɒnˈɪmpækt ˈprɪntə(r)/
pl nonimpact printers
► **impact printer, printer**

nonmaskable interrupt *noun* (hardware)
an INTERRUPT[1] that cannot be ignored: *The nonmaskable interrupt had priority and could not be blocked by software.*

/ˈnɒnˌmɑːskəbl ˈɪntərʌpt/
pl nonmaskable interrupts
abbr NMI
► **maskable interrupt**

non-procedural language *noun*
(software/programming)
a programming language which is not arranged in procedures or blocks: *PROLOG is a non-procedural language.*

/ˈnɒnprəˌsiːdʒərəl ˈlæŋɡwɪdʒ/
pl non-procedural languages
◄ program *in*, write *in* a **non-procedural language**
► **procedural language, programming language**

non return to zero *noun*
a way of sending binary data (bits) as positive or negative VOLTAGES without the signal returning to zero VOLTS between bits

/ˈnɒn rɪˈtɜːn tə ˈzɪərəʊ/
note singular noun, used with a singular verb
abbr NRZ
◄ a **non return to zero** protocol, system
► **return to zero**

nonvolatile *adjective*
able to hold data when switched off: *a microprocessor with nonvolatile memory*

/ˌnɒnˈvɒlətaɪl/
◄ a **nonvolatile** disk, store
► **volatile**

nonvolatile storage *noun* (hardware)
memory that does not lose data when the computer system is
switched off

/ˈnɒnˌvɒlətaɪl ˌstɔːrɪdʒ/
note no plural

---

no operation instruction *noun*
▶ **do nothing instruction**

/ˈnəʊ ɒpəˈreɪʃn ɪnˌstrʌkʃn/

NOR *noun*
▶ **NOR operation**

/nɔː(r)/
note pronounced as a word

NOR circuit *noun*
▶ **NOR gate**

/ˈnɔː ˌsɜːkɪt/

NOR gate *noun* (hardware)
a circuit or chip whose output is 1 if all its inputs are 0,
otherwise its output is 0: *The logic circuit is built from NOR
gates.*

/ˈnɔː geɪt/
pl NOR gates
syn NOR circuit
▶ **NAND gate**

---

normal form *noun* (applications/databases)
1 the rules controlling the way information is stored in a
database

2 (*programming*) ▶ **Backus-Naur form**

/ˈnɔːml fɔːm/
1 note Not used with *a* or *an*. No
plural and used with a singular
verb only.
◄ fifth, first, fourth, second, third
normal form

---

normalization *noun*
the process of representing something in a standard form,
especially a FLOATING POINT NUMBER before it is stored:
Normalization is the last step in all floating point algorithms.

/ˌnɔːməlaɪˈzeɪʃn/
note no plural
◄ carry out, perform
normalization; a
normalization algorithm,
procedure, routine, subroutine

---

normalize *verb*
to represent something in standard form, especially to write a
FLOATING POINT NUMBER in the form 0.12345×10^6: *To enable
floating point numbers to be easily compared, they are normalized
before they are stored.*

/ˈnɔːməlaɪz/
**normalize, normalizing,
normalized**
note transitive verb
◄ **normalize** a binary number,
result
▶ **floating point notation**

NOR operation *noun* (mathematics)
a logical operation that is equivalent to NOT (P OR Q). The
expression P NOR Q is TRUE if and only if the expression P and
the expression Q are both FALSE: *The statement contains 3 NOR
operations.*

note P NOR Q is the same as an OR operation followed by a
NOT operation.

/ˈnɔː(r) ɒpəˌreɪʃn/
pl NOR operations
◄ carry out, do, implement,
perform, program *as a* **NOR
operation**
syn NOR
▶ **Boolean connective, AND,
NAND, OR, NOT, XNOR,
XOR**

NOT *noun*
▶ **NOT operation**

/nɒt/

☆**notation** *noun* (mathematics and logic)
a system of signs or symbols that is used to represent the
elements of a programming language

/nəʊˈteɪʃn/
note no plural

---

abbr abbreviation   **pl** plural   **syn** synonym   ▶ see   ◄ collocate (*word often used with the headword*)

◄ adopt, use the **notation**; algebraic, binary, decimal, hexadecimal, logical, programming **notation**

▶ **infix notation, postfix notation, prefix notation, reverse Polish notation**

NOT circuit *noun*
▶ **NOT gate**

/'nɒt ˌsɜːkɪt/

---

notebook *noun* (hardware)
a small portable computer that can use batteries: *work on the notebook while travelling*

note A notebook is sometimes called a 'laptop'.

/'nəʊtbʊk/
pl notebooks

◄ carry, use a **notebook**; a **notebook** computer, user, workstation

---

NOT gate *noun* (hardware)
a circuit or chip whose output is 0 if the input is 1, and whose output is 1 if its input is 0

/'nɒt geɪt/
pl NOT gates
syn inverter, NOT circuit
▶ **NAND gate, NOR gate**

NOT operation *noun* (mathematics/and logic)
a logical operation which changes the TRUTH VALUE of a logical expression to its opposite. The expression NOT P is FALSE if the expression P is TRUE, and NOT P is TRUE if P is FALSE: *The two NOT operations in succession leave the truth value unchanged.*

/'nɒt ˌɒpəˌreɪʃn/
pl NOT operations

◄ carry out, do, implement, perform, program a **NOT operation**

syn NOT
▶ **Boolean connective**

NRZ *abbr*
▶ **non return to zero**

/ˌen ɑː ˈzed/
note pronounced as individual letters

---

ns *abbr*
▶ **nanosecond**

note used in written English only

NTSC *abbr*
National Television Standards Committee. An organization that decided on the standard method of transmitting colour television pictures in North America and Japan: *conform to NTSC standards* ○ *The video is NTSC compatible.*

/ˌen tiː es ˈsiː/
note pronounced as individual letters
▶ **PAL**

NUL *abbr*
the ASCII symbol 0 which represents the NULL CHARACTER

/nʌl/
note pronounced as a word

---

null *adjective*
relating to zero: *null output*

/nʌl/
◄ a **null** matrix, result, sequence, set, string

---

null character *noun*
a character that represents nothing or zero: *The null character separates blocks of information held in memory.* ○ *The string ends with a null character.*

/'nʌl ˌkærəktə(r)/
pl null characters

---

null instruction *noun*
▶ **do nothing instruction**

/'nʌl ɪnˌstrʌkʃn/

null list *noun*
▶ empty list

/ˌnʌl ˈlɪst/

---

null modem *noun*
▶ null modem cable

/ˌnʌl ˈməʊdem/

---

null modem cable *noun* (hardware)
a cable that links two computers and allows them to
communicate without a modem: *use a null modem cable to link
the portable computer to the desktop machine in the office*

/ˌnʌl ˈməʊdem ˌkeɪbl/
pl null modem cables

◪ connect, link something
with/to, send data over a **null
modem cable**

syn null modem

---

null operation *noun*
▶ do nothing instruction

/ˌnʌl ɒpəˈreɪʃn/

---

null string *noun*
▶ empty string

/ˌnʌl ˈstrɪŋ/

☆**number**[1] *noun* (mathematics and logic)
1 a symbol or word that represents a quantity and is often
used in calculations: *let the variable equal the number 4* ○ *add the
numbers together* **2** a symbol or word that which identifies
something: *machine number 14* ○ *The Internet address of the
company is the number 100066.1603.*

/ˈnʌmbə(r)/
pl numbers

1 ◪ an even, odd **number**

▶ base, batch number, binary
number, digit, fixed point
number, floating point
number

☆**number**[2] *verb*
to give a number or numbers to something: *The pages are
numbered automatically.*

/ˈnʌmbə(r)/
**number, numbering,
numbered**

note transitive verb

◪ **number** items, pages,
paragraphs

---

number base *noun*
the number on which a particular number system or NOTATION
is based: *The binary system has a number base of two.* ○ *The
decimal system has a number base of ten.*

/ˈnʌmbə beɪs/
pl number bases

☆**number crunching** *noun*
(*informal*) the process of doing a lot of mathematical
calculations in a short space of time: *use a powerful computer
that can cope with a lot of number crunching*

/ˈnʌmbə ˌkrʌntʃɪŋ/
note singular noun, used with a
singular verb

◪ a **number crunching**
application, process, system,
task

▶ crunch

---

numeric *adjective*
relating to numbers: *arrange in numeric order*

/njuːˈmerɪk/
(also **numerical**)

◪ a **numeric** keypad, operand,
value; **numeric** ability, code,
format, order, output

---

numeric control *noun*
a method of controlling machine tools by computer. The
particular operation to be done by the machine tool is stored in
numeric form on magnetic disk or punched cards.

/njuːˌmerɪk kənˈtrəʊl/
note not used with a or an. No
plural and used with a singular
verb only.

◪ computer **numeric control**

---

abbr abbreviation   **pl** plural   **syn** synonym   ▶ see   ◪ collocate (*word often used with the headword*)

numeric keypad *noun* (hardware)
the keys that are usually on the right hand side of the keyboard and are used for entering numbers

/njuː,merɪk 'kiːpæd/
pl numeric keypads

numeric value *noun*
the number that is represented by a letter or symbol: *Let Y have the numeric value of 36.*

/njuː,merɪk 'væljuː/
pl numeric values

numeric variable *noun* (programming)
a set of locations in the computer's memory which can hold a number. Data is stored in a numeric variable by using an ASSIGNMENT STATEMENT.

/njuː,merɪk 'veərɪəbl/
pl numeric variables
Ħ assign something *to*, increment, read the value *of* a **numeric variable**
▶ **logical variable, string variable, variable**

☆**Num Lock key** *noun* (hardware)
the Numeric Lock key. A key on a computer keyboard that turns the NUMERIC KEYPAD on or off.

/'nʌm lɒk kiː/
note no plural
Ħ press, toggle the **Num Lock key**
▶ **Caps Lock key**

Oo

object *noun* (software/programming)
a region of storage with associated SEMANTICS: *The declaration 'int i' shows that 'i' is an object of type 'int'.*

note In C++ object-oriented programming, an object can be an instance of something in a class, so a class may define the behaviour of many objects (or instances).

/'ɒbdʒɪkt/
pl objects

object code *noun* (software)
a computer program that has been translated into machine code and can be executed by the computer

/'ɒbdʒɪkt kəʊd/
note not used with *a* or *an*. No plural and used with a singular verb only.
Ħ execute, translate something *into* **object code**
syn object program
▶ **assemble, compile, machine code, source code**

object computer *noun* (hardware)
the computer which uses the machine code produced for it by a COMPILER or CROSS COMPILER on another computer

/,ɒbdʒɪkt kəm'pjuːtə(r)/
pl object computers
Ħ **object computer** language
▶ **object language, object program**
syn target computer

object file *noun* (software)
a file that contains OBJECT CODE

/'ɒbdʒɪkt faɪl/
pl object files
Ħ create, delete an **object file**
syn object module

object language *noun* (software/programming)
the language into which a program is translated before it is executed. Object language is usually low-level language such as machine code.

/ˈɒbdʒɪkt ˌlæŋgwɪdʒ/
pl object languages
◄ compile a program, etc *into*, translate a program, etc *into* the **object language**
syn target language
► **source language**

---

object module *noun*
► **object file**

/ˈɒbdʒɪkt ˌmɒdjuːl/

---

object-oriented *adjective*
(of software) that is able to use OBJECTS: *The new system will have object-oriented functions.* ○ *The company supplies and supports object-oriented software.*

/ˌɒbdʒɪkt ˈɔːrientɪd/
abbr OO
◄ **object-oriented** programming, software; an **object-oriented** application, database, operating system
► **functional 2, imperative, logic programming, query language**

---

object program *noun* (software/programming)
the machine code program that is produced when a high-level or assembly language program is translated: *An object program is usually smaller than the original source code.*

/ˈɒbdʒɪkt ˌprəʊgræm/
pl object programs
◄ compile a program, etc *into*, translate a program, etc *into* an **object program**
syn object code, target program
► **source code**

☆**OCR** *abbr*
► **optical character recognition**

/ˌəʊ siː ˈɑː(r)/
note pronounced as individual letters

OCR font *noun*
a font with specially designed characters that can be easily read by OPTICAL CHARACTER RECOGNITION systems

/ˌəʊ siː ˈɑː fɒnt/
pl OCR fonts

---

octal *adjective*
connected with a system of numbers based on the number 8

/ˈɒktl/
◄ an **octal** number, scale, system
► **base 8, decimal**

---

odd *adjective* (mathematics)
(of a number) that cannot be divided exactly by two: *5, 7 and 11 are all odd*

/ɒd/

---

odd parity *noun*
► **parity 1**

/ˌɒd ˈpærəti/

OEM *abbr*
► **original equipment manufacturer**

/ˌəʊ iː ˈem/
note pronounced as individual letters

---

office automation *noun*
the use of machines or computers in an office, sometimes taking the place of people: *Increasing office automation means that less people will be needed.*

/ˈɒfɪs ˌɔːtəˈmeɪʃn/
note not used with *a* or *an*. No plural and used with a singular verb only.

---

abbr abbreviation **pl** plural **syn** synonym ► see ◄ collocate (*word often used with the headword*)

☆**off-line** *adjective* (hardware)

connected with devices or computers that are not controlled by or cannot communicate with other devices or computers: *The workstation is off-line because it has been temporarily disconnected from the network.*

/'ɒf laɪn/

◪ an **off-line** terminal, workstation; **off-line** printing, processing, storage

▶ **on-line**

---

off-line processing *noun*

computer operations that are not directly controlled by the CPU

/ˌɒf laɪn 'prəʊsesɪŋ/

note not used with *a* or *an*. No plural and used with a singular verb only.

▶ **on-line processing**

---

offset *noun*

a number that is used in RELATIVE ADDRESSING to show how far a data item is from a fixed location usually called the BASE ADDRESS

/'ɒfset/

note not used with *a* or *an*. No plural and used with a singular verb only.

◪ a bit, byte **offset**

OK button *noun*

a place in a DIALOG BOX that the user clicks on to select an option or function, etc

/ˌəʊ 'keɪ ˌbʌtn/

pl OK buttons

▶ **icon**

OMR *abbr*

▶ **optical mark recognition**

/ˌəʊ em 'ɑː(r)/

note pronounced as individual letters

---

on-board computer *noun*

a computer that is part of a vehicle or other machine

/ˌɒn bɔːd kəm'pjuːtə(r)/

pl on-board computers

---

one-dimensional *adjective*

able to be identified by just one index or PARAMETER (2)

/ˌwʌn daɪ'menʃənəl/

◪ a **one-dimensional** data structure

syn linear

▶ **array, data structure, two-dimensional array**

---

one-dimensional array *noun* (software)

a DATA STRUCTURE containing data items of the same type. All items share the same name and individual items are accessed by giving one number to locate their position in the array: *The element NAME(7) is part of a one-dimensional array called NAME.*

note A programmer may think of a one-dimensional array as a list of items in order.

/'wʌn daɪ'menʃənəl ə'reɪ/

pl one-dimensional arrays

◪ access, define, use a **one-dimensional array**

syn vector

▶ **array, array bounds, array dimension, two-dimensional array**

---

one-pass compiler *noun* (software)

a program that translates language written by the programmer into a language that the computer can understand in a single process, not in different stages

/ˌwʌn pɑːs kəm'paɪlə(r)/

pl one-pass compilers

▶ **compile**

---

one's complement *noun*

a system for recording positive and negative binary numbers

note In one's complement notation, negative numbers are represented by changing each bit of a positive number from 1 to 0 or from 0 to 1. For example, the one's complement of 001110 is 110001.

/ˌwʌnz 'kɒmplɪmənt/

note no plural

(also **1's complement**)

◪ employ, use **one's complement; one's complement** arithmetic, notation

▶ **nine's complement, ten's complement, two's complement**

☆**on-line** *adjective* (hardware)

connected with devices or computers that are controlled by or can communicate with other devices and computers: *The new network provides on-line access to information on the Internet.*

/ˌɒn ˈlaɪn/

◪ an **on-line** database, help file, information service, system, terminal; **on-line** access, retrieval, storage, transaction processing, updating

▶ **off-line**

---

on-line help *noun*

advice or instructions on how to use a program that can be accessed while that program is being used: *Problems with the software force the user to refer to on-line help.*

/ˌɒn laɪn ˈhelp/

note not used with *a* or *an*. No plural and used with a singular verb only.

◪ access, read, request **on-line help**

syn help file

▶ **context-sensitive help**

---

on-line processing *noun*

data processing using computers or machines that are directly controlled by a central computer: *The on-line processing of payments to the bank is done via a dedicated modem link.*

/ˌɒn laɪn ˈprəʊsesɪŋ/

note not used with *a* or *an*. No plural and used with a singular verb only.

---

on-line storage *noun* (hardware)

a BACKING STORE that is permanently connected to the computer: *Modules that no longer need to be maintained in on-line storage can be archived.*

/ˌɒn laɪn ˈstɔːrɪdʒ/

note not used with *a* or *an*. No plural and used with a singular verb only.

◪ direct **on-line storage**

---

on-line system *noun* (hardware)

a computer system that allows users to send and receive data and information on a network: *On-line systems are used for financial transactions across the world.*

/ˌɒn laɪn ˈsɪstəm/

pl on-line systems

◪ crash, install, maintain, support an **on-line system**

OO *abbr*

▶ **object-oriented**

/ˌəʊ ˈəʊ/

note pronounced as individual letters

O/P *abbr*

▶ **output**

/ˌəʊ ˈpiː/

note pronounced as individual letters

---

op code *abbr*

▶ **operation code**

/ˈɒp kəʊd/

---

open file *noun*

a file that has been created and is ready to use

/ˌəʊpən ˈfaɪl/

pl open files

◪ access, read data *from*, write data *to* an **open file**

---

open subroutine *noun* (software)

a SUBROUTINE that is copied into different parts of the main program if it is used more than once

note Although once quite important, open subroutines are rarely found today.

/ˌəʊpən ˈsʌbruːtiːn/

pl open subroutines

◪ call, insert, use, write an **open subroutine**

syn macro

▶ **closed subroutine, function**

---

abbr abbreviation   **pl** plural   **syn** synonym   ▶ see   ◪ collocate (*word often used with the headword*)

open system *noun*
a computer system that is designed to allow different operating systems on different computers to work together: *The open system runs different applications and offers links to mainframe systems.*

/ˌəʊpən ˈsɪstəm/
pl open systems

Open Systems Interconnection *noun*
the name given to the work of the International Standards Organization in designing PROTOCOLS to allow different computers to communicate over networks: *conform to Open Systems Interconnection protocols*

/ˈəʊpən ˈsɪstəmz ˌɪntəkəˈnekʃn/
note not used with *a* or *an*. No plural and used with a singular verb only.
abbr OSI
◄ implement **Open Systems Interconnection**; **Open Systems Interconnection** methods, protocols

operand *noun*
a piece of data that is processed in an operation: *In the sum 1+2, the operands are 1 and 2 and the operation is addition.*

/ˈɒpərænd/
pl operands
◄ an illegal, out-of-range **operand**
▶ dyadic operation, logic operand

operand field *noun* (software)
the part of a machine code instruction which defines the data item the instruction refers to: *a six-bit operand field* ○ *the address in the operand field*

/ˈɒpərænd fiːld/
pl operand fields
◄ access, decode the **operand field**
▶ absolute addressing, immediate addressing, indirect addressing, operand

☆**operating system** *noun* (software)
software that controls the use of hardware RESOURCES by applications or other system software

/ˈɒpəreɪtɪŋ ˌsɪstəm/
pl operating systems
abbr OS
◄ a network **operating system**
syn executive program, master control program, supervisor
▶ disk operating system, MS-DOS, network, system software, Unix

☆**operation** *noun*
1 the calculation executed by a single machine code instruction: *perform the SHIFT operation* ○ *execute the ADD operation* **2** the mathematical or logical way of producing a result from one or more OPERANDS: *carry out a multiplication operation*

/ˌɒpəˈreɪʃn/
pl operations
1 ◄ carry out, execute, implement an **operation**
2 ◄ an arithmetic, a mathematical **operation**
▶ logic operation

☆**operational** *adjective* (system operation)
(of a device or computer) that is working or ready to work: *an operational system* ○ *The printer is operational.*

/ˌɒpəˈreɪʃənl/
◄ **operational** mode

operation code *noun* (software)

the pattern of binary digits in a machine code instruction that shows the operation that is to be performed: *The program error was caused by trying to execute an invalid operation code.* ○ *The format of the operation code occupies the first 2 bytes.*

/ˌɒpəˈreɪʃn kəʊd/
pl operation codes
abbr op code
◄ access, decode, identify the **operation code**; a 6-bit, 2-byte **operation code**
syn order code

☆**operator** *noun*

1 (*personnel*) a person who uses a machine, device or computer, etc: *a computer operator* **2** (*mathematics and logic*) a symbol or character that shows an operation on two or more numbers or data items, etc: *In the sum 5-4, the operator is the minus sign.*

/ˈɒpəreɪtə(r)/
pl operators
▶ **operand**

---

operator precedence *noun*

the ORDER OF PRECEDENCE for mathematical or logical operations: *Multiplication has higher operator precedence than addition.*

/ˌɒpəreɪtə ˈpresɪdəns/
note usually singular
◄ equal, higher, lower **operator precedence**

☆**optical character recognition** *noun* (hardware)

a process where a machine SCANS printed material and encodes it into electronic form: *Optical character recognition makes input processing rates faster.* ○ *produce optical character recognition software*

/ˌɒptɪkl ˈkærəktə rekəɡˌnɪʃn/
note no plural
abbr OCR
▶ **magnetic ink character recognition**

☆**optical disc** *noun*
▶ **CD**

/ˌɒptɪkl ˈdɪsk/

---

optical mark reader *noun* (hardware)

a device that is used to recognize marks made in particular places on special forms: *The forms are fed into an optical mark reader.*

/ˌɒptɪkl ˈmɑːk ˌriːdə(r)/
pl optical mark readers
▶ **mark sensing**

---

optical mark recognition *noun*

the process of identifying and encoding marks made on special forms for computer processing

/ˌɒptɪkl ˈmɑːk rekəɡˌnɪʃn/
note not used with *a* or *an*. No plural and used with a singular verb only.
abbr OMR

---

optical scanner *noun* (hardware)

a device that reads characters and encodes them so they can be processed by a computer

/ˌɒptɪkl ˈskænə(r)/
pl optical scanners
▶ **scanner**

---

optimization *noun*

the process of making something as efficient and effective as possible

/ˌɒptɪmaɪˈzeɪʃn/
note not used with *a* or *an*. No plural and used with a singular verb only.

---

optimize *verb*

to make something as efficient and effective as possible: *The company bought new computers in an effort to optimize production.*

/ˈɒptɪmaɪz/
optimize, optimizing, optimized
note transitive verb

---

optimizing compiler *noun* (software)

a COMPILER that produces machine code that is as fast and efficient as possible: *translate the program using an optimizing compiler*

/ˌɒptɪmaɪzɪŋ kəmˈpaɪlə(r)/
pl optimizing compilers

---

abbr abbreviation   **pl** plural   **syn** synonym   ▶ see   ◄ collocate (*word often used with the headword*)

☆**option** noun (software)

a choice made by a user to control a program: *The main options are displayed on a menu bar at the top of the screen.* ○ *select the 'copy' option*

/ˈɒpʃn/
pl options
◄ a menu **option**

---

option key noun (hardware)

a key on a computer keyboard that is pressed at the same time as another key to access a range of characters and symbols

note The option key works in a similar way to the shift and alternate keys.

/ˈɒpʃn kiː/
pl option keys
◄ hit, hold down, press, release the **option key**

OR noun
► **OR operation**

/ɔː(r)/

OR circuit noun
► **OR gate**

/ˈɔː ˌsɜːkɪt/

---

order code noun
► **operation code**

/ˈɔːdə kəʊd/

---

order of precedence noun

a list of operations that shows which are more important, and should be performed before others: *The order of precedence for interrupt requests will usually give power-fail interrupts the highest priority.*

/ˌɔːdər əv ˈpresɪdəns/
pl orders of precedence
◄ define, implement, refer *to* an **order of precedence**
► **interrupt, operator precedence**

OR gate noun (hardware)

an electronic circuit whose output is logic 0 if and only if two or more of its inputs are set to logic 0. Otherwise its output is 1. This action corresponds to an OR OPERATION: *The chip provides four OR gates in a single 14-pin package.*

/ˈɔː geɪt/
pl OR gates
◄ connect *to*, drive, replace something *by*, use an **OR gate**
syn OR circuit
► **AND gate, NOR gate**

---

original equipment manufacturer noun

a company that makes parts of computers or systems which are usually bought by another company to make complete computers or systems: *The original equipment manufacturer develops customized network software for its clients.*

/əˈrɪdʒənl ɪˈkwɪpmənt mænjuˌfæktʃərə(r)/
pl original equipment manufacturers
abbr OEM
► **third party**

OR operation noun (mathematics)

a logical operation combining two logical expressions. The combined expression P OR Q is FALSE if and only if expression P and expression Q are both FALSE. Otherwise it is TRUE: *The statement contains three OR operations.*

/ˈɔː(r) ˌɒpəˌreɪʃn/
pl OR operations
◄ do, implement, program an **OR operation**
syn OR
► **Boolean connective**

---

orphan noun

the first line of a piece of text which is printed at the bottom of a page and is separated from the rest of the text which is on the next page: *The layout of the text is designed to avoid orphans.*

/ˈɔːfn/
pl orphans
◄ allow, suppress **orphans**
► **widow**

OS abbr
► **operating system**

/ˌəʊ ˈes/
note pronounced as individual letters

oscillator *noun* (hardware)
an electronic device that produces a regular signal that can be used to SYNCHRONIZE other devices: *The oscillator frequency determines how fast the system operates.*

/ˈɒsɪleɪtə(r)/
pl oscillators
⋈ install an **oscillator**

OSI *abbr*
▶ **Open Systems Interconnection**

/ˌəʊ es ˈaɪ/
note pronounced as individual letters

outer loop *noun* (software/programming)
a LOOP¹ (2) that contains another loop: *Each execution of the outer loop involves ten repetitions of the inner loop.*

/ˌaʊtə ˈluːp/
pl outer loops
⋈ execute, perform, program an **outer loop**
▶ **inner loop, nested loop**

outgoing traffic *noun*
messages and data sent from a computer over a network or communication channel: *There is a lot of outgoing traffic at the start of the day.*

/ˌaʊtgəʊɪŋ ˈtræfɪk/
note not used with *a* or *an*. No plural and used with a singular verb only.
⋈ heavy, light **outgoing traffic**
▶ **traffic density**

☆**output¹** *noun*
1 (*software*) the results of a processing operation performed by a computer. The output is usually displayed on screen or printed on paper. **2** (*hardware*) an electrical signal that is passed out of a computer system: *The output is between 8 and 25 volts.*

/ˈaʊtpʊt/
note usually singular
abbr O/P
▶ **input**

☆**output²** *verb* (system operation)
to send the results of a processing operation to a screen or a printer: *key the changes in the text and output it to the laser printer*

/ˈaʊtpʊt/
output, outputting, output
note transitive verb
▶ **input, write**

output bound *adjective* (system operation)
(of a program) whose execution speed is limited by the time taken to output data

/ˈaʊtpʊt baʊnd/
⋈ an **output bound** process, program; **output bound** software
▶ **input-output bound**

output buffer *noun* (hardware)
a temporary storage area in which data is held before being displayed, printed or transmitted to another device: *The output buffer is 95 bytes long.*

/ˈaʊtpʊt ˌbʌfə(r)/
pl output buffers
▶ **buffer**

☆**output device** *noun* (hardware)
a piece of equipment, such as a printer or screen, that displays or prints the results of a computer operation: *The printer is the main output device in most computer systems.*

/ˌaʊtpʊt dɪˈvaɪs/
pl output devices
▶ **input device**

output port *noun*
a PORT¹ (= a place in a computer that a device can be connected to) that allows a computer to send data to an external device: *connect the printer to the output port*

/ˈaʊtpʊt pɔːt/
pl output ports
⋈ address, connect a device, etc *to*, send data *to* an **output port**
▶ **input port, port**

---

abbr abbreviation   **pl** plural   **syn** synonym   ▶ see   **⋈** collocate (*word often used with the headword*)

overflow *noun*
an error that occurs because the result of a mathematical calculation is too big for the computer to represent it with PRECISION: *incrementing the register caused an overflow* ○ *The overflow generated an interrupt which activated the overflow recovery routine.*

/ˈəʊvəfləʊ/
pl overflows
▶ **carry, underflow**

---

overflow bit *noun*
a single bit that is set to 1 if an OVERFLOW happens. This bit may be tested by the programmer so that overflow errors can be corrected: *Failure to clear the overflow bit caused the program to crash.*

/ˈəʊvəfləʊ bɪt/
pl overflow bits
Ⓜ access, clear, reset, set, test the **overflow bit**
syn overflow flag

---

overflow check *noun*
the examination of an OVERFLOW BIT to look for signs of an OVERFLOW

/ˈəʊvəfləʊ tʃek/
pl overflow checks

---

overflow error *noun*
an error that occurs because of an OVERFLOW

/ˈəʊvəfləʊ ˌerə(r)/
pl overflow errors

---

overflow flag *noun*
▶ **overflow bit**

/ˈəʊvəfləʊ flæg/

---

overlay *noun*
▶ **segment**[1]

/ˈəʊvəleɪ/

---

overprint[1] *noun*
a situation where characters, text or colour are printed on top of other characters, text or colour that have already been printed

/ˈəʊvəprɪnt/
pl overprints

---

overprint[2] *verb*
to print more characters, text or colour on top of characters, text or colour that have already been printed: *overprint the heading in red to make it stand out more*

/ˌəʊvəˈprɪnt/
overprint, overprinting, overprinted
note transitive verb

---

overrun *noun*
an error that occurs when data is transmitted too quickly and the receiving device cannot accept the data

/ˈəʊvərʌn/
pl overruns

---

overstrike *verb*
to type or print one character on top of another character to create a new character that is a combination of the two individual characters: *overstrike an 'S' with a vertical line to get a dollar sign*

/ˈəʊvəstraɪk/
overstrike, overstriking, overstruck
note transitive verb
Ⓜ **overstrike** a character, symbol

---

overtype mode *noun*
the state of a word processing program in which new characters are added to the text by replacing those that follow

note In insert mode, Z typed between the letters SP will give SZP. In overtype mode, the result would be SZ.

/ˈəʊvətaɪp məʊd/
note not used with *a* or *an*. No plural and used with a singular verb only.
Ⓜ be *in*, enter, select **overtype mode**
▶ **insert mode**

☆**overwrite** *verb*

1 to replace a character on the screen with another character by using the keyboard: *Text to the right of the cursor can be overwritten.* **2** (*system operation*) to replace an item of data in memory or on disk by putting another item of data in its place: *The original data in the file was lost when it was overwritten.*

/ˌəʊvəˈraɪt/
overwrite, overwriting, overwrote, overwritten
note transitive verb
1 **overwrite** a character, letter, number, symbol
2 **overwrite** a file, record

Pp

p *abbr*
▶ **pico**

/piː/

pack¹ *noun*
1 a number of punched cards
2 ▶ **disk pack**

/pæk/
pl packs

pack² *verb*
to reduce the amount of storage space taken up by data or information: *pack individual bits into a single byte*

/pæk/
pack, packing, packed
note transitive verb
◄ **pack** something *into* a data item, etc
▶ **unpack**

package *noun*
▶ **software package**

/ˈpækɪdʒ/

packed decimal *noun*
a way of encoding decimal numbers in binary form to save storage space. One byte represents two decimal digits: *four numeric bits are packed two to a byte to produce a packed decimal byte string*

/ˌpækt ˈdesɪml/
pl packed decimals
◄ a **packed decimal** instruction, operand, string

packet *noun*
a group of binary digits forming part of a message. The group is transmitted together, but not always by the same route as other packets which form part the same message: *The data transmission is split into packets of equal size.*

note Packets of data are sometimes called 'datagrams'.

/ˈpækɪt/
pl packets
◄ send, split data *into* **packets**

packet assembler/disassembler *noun*
▶ **PAD**

/ˈpækɪt əˈsemblə ˌdɪsəˈsemblə(r)/

packet switching *noun*
a method of sending messages over telephone lines or a network by dividing the messages into units of digital data of fixed length, called packets. The packets are sent separately over the network, by any route that is available, and put together to form the complete message when they arrive: *Packet switching is used on most wide area networks.*

/ˈpækɪt ˌswɪtʃɪŋ/
note no plural
◄ a **packet switching** link, network, system
▶ **circuit switching**

abbr abbreviation   **pl** plural   **syn** synonym   ▶ see   ◄ collocate (*word often used with the headword*)

packing density *noun*

a measure of how much data can be held on a magnetic medium such as disk or tape: *adding records will increase the packing density* ○ *measure packing density in bits per inch*

/ˈpækɪŋ ˌdensəti/

note not used with *a* or *an*. No plural and used with a singular verb only.

▶ **single density**

PAD *abbr*

packet assembler/disassembler. A device that splits messages into packets so they can be transmitted over a PACKET SWITCHING network, and joins the packets together again when they are received: *The packet assembler/disassembler receives data in serial form from asynchronous terminals.*

/pæd/

⧓ send data *to*, use a **PAD**

---

pad *noun*

a group of keys arranged together on a keyboard: *The cursor pad can be used instead of a mouse.*

/pæd/

pl pads

⧓ cursor, number **pad**

▶ **keypad, numeric keypad**

---

pad character *noun*

a character that is added to a block of data as often as necessary to make the data a standard size: *The last block of the message will not necessarily be of the correct length and will be filled out with pad characters.*

/ˈpæd ˌkærəktə(r)/

pl pad characters

⧓ add, fill out something *with* a **pad character**

---

paddle *noun* (hardware)

a device that can be moved or turned in order to control a cursor or arrow on the screen

/ˈpædl/

pl paddles

⧓ move, operate, turn a **paddle**

syn games paddle

▶ **joystick, mouse**

---

page *noun* (hardware)

a block of memory with a fixed size

/peɪdʒ/

pl pages

⧓ address a **page**

---

page break *noun* (software)

a command to a printer to stop printing text on one page at a certain point and continue on a new page. Page breaks can be automatic or inserted by the user: *insert a page break to avoid splitting a paragraph*

/ˈpeɪdʒ breɪk/

pl page breaks

⧓ delete, insert a **page break**

---

page description language *noun*

a language that is used to describe the layout of a printed page, including the position and size of the text and graphics, etc: *The page makeup software supports a page description language.*

/ˌpeɪdʒ dɪˈskrɪpʃn ˌlæŋgwɪdʒ/

pl page description languages

abbr PDL

⧓ be compatible *with*, translate something *into* a **page description language**

☆**page down** *noun* (hardware)

the key marked 'Pg Dn' on a computer keyboard which is used to move the cursor to the bottom of the page or screen: *Press the page down key to get to the end of the page.*

/ˌpeɪdʒ ˈdaʊn/

note not used with *a* or *an*. No plural and used with a singular verb only.

abbr Pg Dn

▶ **cursor control key, page up**

---

page fault *noun*

an INTERRUPT[1] signal that is generated when a PAGE of data is requested but it is not in main memory

/ˈpeɪdʒ fɔːlt/

pl page faults

⧓ cause, respond *to* a **page fault**

page make-up *noun* (software)
the process of combining text and graphics on screen to make a page of a document, usually before it is printed: *paste in pictures and lay out text using the page make-up facility* ○ *The DTP package handles page make-up.*

/'peɪdʒ ˌmeɪkʌp/
note not used with *a* or *an*. No plural and used with a singular verb only.
ᴎ a **page make-up** package, system
syn make-up

page printer *noun*
a printer that forms and prints a whole page of text or graphics at one time: *The artwork was printed out on a page printer.* ○ *connect the PCs to the page printer*

/'peɪdʒ ˌprɪntə(r)/
pl page printers
▶ **printer**

page table *noun*
a list of PAGES and their location in main memory

/'peɪdʒ ˌteɪbl/
pl page tables

☆**page up** *noun* (hardware)
the key marked 'Pg Up' on a computer keyboard which is used to move the cursor to the top of the page or screen: *Press the page up key to get to the beginning of the page.*

/ˌpeɪdʒ 'ʌp /
note not used with *a* or *an*. No plural and used with a singular verb only.
abbr Pg Up
▶ **cursor control key, page down**

pagination *noun*
the process of dividing a document or letter, etc into separate pages and sometimes adding numbers to each page

/ˌpædʒɪ'neɪʃn/
note not used with *a* or *an*. No plural and used with a singular verb only.
ᴎ automated **pagination**

paging *noun* (software)
a way of dividing data into blocks of a fixed size called PAGES. Some pages are held in main memory and some are held on disk. System software makes sure that the pages required by the user are in main memory when they are needed.

note Paging is one way of creating virtual memory.

/'peɪdʒɪŋ/
note not used with *a* or *an*. No plural and used with a singular verb only.
▶ **virtual memory**

paging algorithm *noun*
an ALGORITHM that is used by the MEMORY MANAGEMENT system when making a section of memory into a PAGE

/ˌpeɪdʒɪŋ 'ælgərɪðəm/
pl paging algorithms

paint¹ *noun*
the different colours that can be used in a graphics program

/peɪnt/
note not used with *a* or *an*. No plural and used with a singular verb only.

paint² *verb*
to apply colour to an image on a computer screen: *click on the palette to paint the drawing*

/peɪnt/
paint, painting, painted
note transitive verb
ᴎ **paint** an image

PAL *abbr*
phase alternating line. The standard method of transmitting colour television pictures in the UK and most of Europe and Asia: *conform to PAL standards*

/pæl/
note pronounced as a word
ᴎ encode signals, etc in **PAL**
▶ **NTSC**

---

abbr abbreviation   **pl** plural   **syn** synonym   ▶ see   ᴎ collocate (*word often used with the headword*)

palette *noun*
a selection of colours that are available to be displayed on a computer screen: *a 256 colour palette*

/ˈpælət/
pl palettes

---

palmtop *noun* (hardware)
a smaller version of a NOTEBOOK computer which can be held in one hand

/ˈpɑːmtɒp/
pl palmtops
▶ **laptop, notebook**

---

paper feed *noun*
the part of a printer where paper is placed ready to be printed: *The printer will not work if there are too many sheets of paper in the paper feed.*

/ˈpeɪpə fiːd/
pl paper feeds

---

paper jam *noun* (hardware)
a problem caused by paper not being able to move through a printer or other device: *The printer stopped working because there was a paper jam.*

/ˈpeɪpə dʒæm/
pl paper jams
Ⓜ fix the **paper jam**

---

paperless office *noun*
an office where not much paper is used because most of the work is done by computers or other electronic devices

/ˌpeɪpələs ˈɒfɪs/
pl paperless offices

---

paper tape *noun* (hardware)
a continuous strip of paper holding data coded as punched holes

note The use of paper tape is an old-fashioned way of transferring information to a computer.

/ˌpeɪpə ˈteɪp/
note not used with *a* or *an*. No plural and used with a singular verb only.
Ⓜ feed, insert, punch, read **paper tape**

---

parallel access *noun*
1 a data transmission where several bits are sent at the same time: *Many printers use parallel access, receiving 8 bits of data at a time.*

2 ▶ **random access**

/ˌpærəlel ˈækses/
2 note not used with *a* or *an*. No plural and used with a singular verb only.
Ⓜ a **parallel access** cable, connection, port
▶ **serial access**

---

parallel adder *noun* (hardware)
an adder that adds all digits of two binary numbers at the same time, not one after the other

/ˌpærəlel ˈædə(r)/
pl parallel adders
▶ **adder, serial adder**

---

parallel computer *noun* (hardware)
a computer that is able to execute several program instructions at the same time because it has more than one processor: *a parallel computer with 400 processors which can perform 400 million arithmetical calculations in a second*

/ˌpærəlel kəmˈpjuːtə(r)/
pl parallel computers
Ⓜ a massively **parallel computer**

---

parallel data transmission *noun*
▶ **parallel transmission**

/ˌpærəlel ˈdeɪtə trænsˌmɪʃn/

---

parallel interface *noun*
a device that transfers bits at the same time (in parallel) and not one after the other

/ˌpærəlel ˈɪntəfeɪs/
pl parallel interfaces
Ⓜ attach a connector *to*, fit, insert, set the parameters *of* the **serial interface**
syn parallel port
▶ **serial interface**

parallel port *noun*
▶ **parallel interface**

/ˈpærəlel pɔːt/

---

parallel printer *noun* (hardware)
a printer that is connected to a computer by a PARALLEL
INTERFACE

/ˌpærəlel ˈprɪntə(r)/
pl parallel printers
▶ **printer, serial printer**

☆**parallel processing** *noun* (system operation)
the execution of several program instructions at the same time
by the computer's CPU: *Parallel processing is a method of
increasing processing speed.*

/ˌpærəlel ˈprəʊsesɪŋ/
note no plural
ᴹ massively, scalable **parallel
processing**; a **parallel
processing** application;
parallel processing power,
software
▶ **serial processing**

---

parallel running *noun*
the process of running an old and a new computer system at
the same time so that the new system can be checked before it
becomes the only system used

/ˌpærəlel ˈrʌnɪŋ/
note not used with *a* or *an*. No
plural and used with a singular
verb only.

---

parallel transmission *noun*
the process of transmitting a group of bits over different
transmission channels at the same time: *Most printers receive
data by parallel transmission.*

/ˌpærəlel trænsˈmɪʃn/
pl parallel transmissions
ᴹ **parallel transmission**
methods, protocols
syn parallel data transmission
▶ **serial transmission**

---

parameter *noun*
1 a piece of information that is given to a SUBROUTINE, function
or procedure when it is CALLED[2] (2). The parameters are used in
the subroutine for calculations, or to control the action of the
subroutine: *a numeric parameter* ○ *a string parameter* **2** a
variable in a formula or mathematical expression which
controls the value of that expression

/pəˈræmɪtə(r)/
pl parameters
1 ᴹ define, specify a **parameter**
▶ **formal parameter,
parameter passing**
syn argument
2 ᴹ specify a **parameter**
▶ **constant**

---

parameter driven *adjective*
(of software) that is controlled by the value of one or more
pieces of information set by the user: *a parameter driven
communications program*

/pəˈræmɪtə ˌdrɪvn/
ᴹ a **parameter driven** program
▶ **configure**

---

parameter passing *noun*
the method of giving a value to a SUBROUTINE, function or
procedure: *most assemblers allow parameter passing*

/pəˈræmɪtə ˌpɑːsɪŋ/
note no plural
ᴹ a **parameter passing**
mechanism, method;
parameter passing code,
software
▶ **call by name, call by value,
call by reference, formal
parameter**

---

parametrize *verb*
to organize a computation so that the output is controlled by
the value of one or more input PARAMETERS: *parametrize by
Cartesian coordinates*

/pəˈræmɪtəraɪz/
**parametrize, parametrizing,
parametrized**
note transitive verb

---

abbr abbreviation   **pl** plural   **syn** synonym   ▶ see   ᴹ collocate (*word often used with the headword*)

	◄ **parametrize** a function, problem
parent *noun* something immediately above or more important than something else: *a parent node in a data structure*	/ˈpeərənt/ **pl** parents ◄ inherit features *from* a **parent**
parent directory *noun* (software) the directory in a filing system which contains the current directory	/ˈpeərənt də,rektəri/ **pl** parent directories ◄ access, delete, enter, store files *in* the **parent directory**
parent node *noun* the NODE (1) in a TREE data structure immediately above the current node: *The root node has no parent node.*	/ˈpeərənt nəʊd/ **pl** parent nodes ◄ access, update the **parent node**
parity *noun* **1** the state of being odd or even: *5 has odd parity* **2** an error checking procedure used by devices that receive and transmit data: *parity is one parameter of data transmission*	/ˈpærəti/ **note** no plural **2 syn** even parity, odd parity
parity bit *noun* an extra bit added to a group of bits sent between computers. The parity bit helps the computer that receives the data to check for errors in the data: *The protocol specifies seven-bit characters with even parity.* ○ *set the parity bit to 1*	/ˈpærəti bɪt/ **pl** parity bits ◄ add, check a **parity bit**
parity check *noun* the process of testing transmitted data to check that it has the correct PARITY. If the parity is not correct, the data contains errors: *The parity check on the data failed so all the data had to be retransmitted.*	/ˈpærəti tʃek/ **pl** parity checks ◄ carry out, perform a **parity check**
parity error *noun* an error in the transmission of data that is detected when one or more characters does not have the correct PARITY: *Noise on the transmission line caused a number of parity errors.*	/ˈpærəti ,erə(r)/ **pl** parity errors ◄ cause, detect a **parity error**
parse *verb* to separate a high-level programming language statement into parts that will be processed as individual units when it is converted into machine code: *parse expressions and statements*	/pɑːz/ **parse, parsing, parsed** **note** transitive verb ◄ **parse** code, input ► compiler, interpreter, machine code, grammar, translator
parsing *noun* the process of separating a high-level programming language statement into parts that will be processed individually when it is translated into machine code: *Parsing is the first stage of translation.*	/ˈpɑːzɪŋ/ **note** not used with *a* or *an*. No plural and used with a singular verb only. ◄ a **parsing** algorithm ► compiler, interpreter, grammar, translator
partition *noun* (hardware) a part of memory that has different functions from other parts of memory: *divide a hard disk into partitions*	/pɑːˈtɪʃn/ **pl** partitions

☆**Pascal** *noun* (software)

a high-level computer programming language that was used in the development of microcomputers: *translate Pascal into machine code*

note Pascal is an imperative procedural language designed for structured programming. It was developed between 1968 and 1971.

/pæˈskæl/

note no plural

ℍ program *in*, write **Pascal**; a **Pascal** compiler, interface, program

---

pass¹ *noun*

1 a single analysis of the source code of a program during COMPILATION: *a one-pass compiler* ○ *a second pass* **2** a single execution of the instructions in a LOOP¹ **(2)**: *one pass of the loop* **3** any single run through a set of items: *the first pass through the data*

/pɑːs/

pl passes

1,2,3 ℍ make a **pass**

---

pass² *verb*

to copy or transfer values from a main program to a SUBROUTINE, function or procedure: *pass a parameter*

/pɑːs/

pass, passing, passed

note transitive verb

▶ **call, parameter passing**

---

pass by address *verb*
▶ **call by reference**

/ˌpɑːs baɪ əˈdres/

---

pass by name *verb*
▶ **call by name**

/ˌpɑːs baɪ ˈneɪm/

---

pass by reference *verb*
▶ **call by reference**

/ˌpɑːs baɪ ˈrefərəns/

---

pass by value *verb*
▶ **call by value**

/ˌpɑːs baɪ ˈvæljuː/

☆**password** *noun* (user operation)

a string of characters that is entered into a computer or computer system in order to access it: *enter a user name and password to get into the system* ○ *each user has a secret personal password*

/ˈpɑːswɜːd/

pl passwords

ℍ change, choose, use a **password**

syn authorization code

▶ **access code, identification**

---

password protection *noun*

a way of controlling access to information held in a computer system by making each user enter a password to gain access to the system: *set up password protection to prevent unauthorized access to files* ○ *a screensaver with password protection*

/ˌpɑːswɜːd prəˈtekʃn/

note not used with *a* or *an*. No plural and used with a singular verb only.

☆**paste** *verb* (system operation)

to copy or transfer a piece of selected text or graphics from a buffer or memory into a document, often when the text or graphics have been cut from another document: *paste text into the e-mail window* ○ *cut and paste between different programs*

/peɪst/

paste, pasting, pasted

note transitive verb

▶ **cut, cut and paste**

---

patch panel *noun*
▶ **jack field**

/ˈpætʃ ˌpænl/

---

abbr abbreviation **pl** plural **syn** synonym ▶ see ℍ collocate (*word often used with the headword*)

patent *noun*
an official document that gives a person or a company the
right to make or sell a certain product such as a computer, and
prevents others from making or selling the same product: *The
product is protected by patent.* ○ *The patent on the software expires
in 10 years and will have to be renewed.*

/ˈpeɪtnt/
pl patents
ℍ apply *for*, grant, hold, infringe,
issue, obtain, take *out* a **patent**
▶ **copyright**

☆**path** *noun*
1 the route between two nodes in a DATA STRUCTURE or a
network: *In a star network the path between two nodes passes
through the central node.* **2** (*software/programming*) the sequence
of steps followed when a program is executed: *Test all possible
paths through a program.*

/pɑːθ/
pl paths
1, 2 ℍ follow, trace, traverse a
path

☆**pathname** *noun*
the full description of the location of a file, showing the disk
drive and the directories which must be accessed to reach the
file: *Files with pathname C:ØPERSONALØLETTERS are found in
the directory called LETTERS within the directory PERSONAL
held on drive C.*

/ˈpɑːθneɪm/
pl pathnames
ℍ give, quote, specify a **path
name**

pause¹ *noun*
a temporary stop in a process: *The pause facility allows the user
to interrupt the program.*

/pɔːz/
pl pauses
ℍ create, request a **pause**

pause² *verb*
to stop something for a short time usually so that it can be
restarted from the place it was stopped: *the program is set to
pause automatically* ○ *pause the tape*

/pɔːz/
pause, pausing, paused
note transitive or intransitive
verb
ℍ **pause** the execution

☆**PC** *abbr* (hardware)
1 a personal computer. The general name for a
microcomputer designed for home or business use: *The PC has
a hard disk, two floppy disk drives and a CD-ROM drive.*

note The abbreviation PC is generally understood to refer to a
specific range of personal computers originally manufactured
by IBM.

2 ▶ **program counter**

/ˌpiː ˈsiː/
note pronounced as individual
letters
pl PCs
1 ℍ buy, own, use a **personal
computer**
▶ **desktop, laptop, mainframe,
microcomputer,
minicomputer, palmtop**

☆**PCB** *abbr*
▶ **printed circuit board**

/ˌpiː siː ˈbiː/
note pronounced as individual
letters

PCL *abbr*
(*trademark*) Printer Control Language

/ˌpiː siː ˈel/
note pronounced as individual
letters

PDL *abbr*
▶ **page description language**

/ˌpiː diː ˈel/
note pronounced as individual
letters

peek *verb*
to read a binary pattern directly from a particular memory
location, usually in a high-level language that does not
normally allow access to memory except by using VARIABLES

/piːk/
peek, peeking, peeked
note transitive verb
ℍ **peek** *at* a location, *at* a binary
pattern
▶ **poke**

pel *noun*
▶ **pixel**

/pel/

---

pen plotter *noun* (hardware)
a device that moves a pen across a piece of paper and is
controlled by a computer: *The map is output from the computer
to a pen plotter.*

/'pen ˌplɒtə(r)/
pl pen plotters
▶ **graph plotter, plotter**

☆**peripheral** *noun* (hardware)
a piece of equipment, such as a printer or keyboard, that is
attached to a computer and is used to transfer information into
or out of the computer: *output the map to any suitable peripheral
such as the plotter*

/pə'rɪfərəl/
pl peripherals
◄ an on-line, input, output
peripheral; a **peripheral**
application, device
▶ **input device**

---

peripheral bound *adjective*
(of a program) that is not able to execute very quickly because
the processor is limited by the speed of peripheral devices it is
accessing: *A faster disk drive would prevent the program being
peripheral bound.*

/pə'rɪfərəl baʊnd/
◄ a **peripheral bound** process,
program
▶ **input bound, output bound,**
compute bound

---

peripheral transfer *noun*
the movement of data between a computer and a PERIPHERAL

/pəˌrɪfərəl 'trænsfɜː(r)/
note not used with *a* or *an*. No
plural and used with a singular
verb only.

---

permanent file *noun*
data that is held on a BACKING STORE, such as a hard disk, and
which will not be deleted after the execution of a program that
accesses it

/ˌpɜːmənənt 'faɪl/
pl permanent files
◄ access, create, update a
permanent file
▶ **temporary file**

---

permanent storage *noun* (hardware)
a form of storage, such as a floppy disk, in which information
can be stored for a long time

/ˌpɜːmənənt 'stɔːrɪdʒ/
note no plural
▶ **nonvolatile storage, volatile**
memory

☆**personal computer** *noun*
▶ **PC**

/ˌpɜːsənl kəm'pjuːtə(r)/

---

personal identification device *noun* (hardware)
a piece of equipment, such as a card, that can be recognized by
a computer and authorizes a person to use the computer: *Each
operator has a small card which is their own personal identification
device.*

/'pɜːsənl aɪˌdentɪfɪ'keɪʃn
dɪˌvaɪs/
pl personal identification devices
abbr PID
▶ **password**

☆**personal identification number** *noun*
a secret number that is entered into a computer system to
allow someone to use it: *Bank customers can obtain money from
a machine by inserting a plastic card and entering their personal
identification number.*

/'pɜːsənl aɪˌdentɪfɪ'keɪʃn
ˌnʌmbə(r)/
pl personal identification numbers
abbr PIN, PIN number
◄ enter, key in a **personal**
identification number
▶ **password**

---

abbr abbreviation   **pl** plural   **syn** synonym   ▶ see   ◄ collocate (*word often used with the headword*)

☆**Pg Dn** *abbr*
► **page down**

note used in written English only

☆**Pg Up** *abbr*
► **page up**

note used in written English only

phase alternating line *noun*
► **PAL**

/'feɪz ˌɔːltəneɪtɪŋ 'laɪn/

phase modulation *noun*
a way of changing a CARRIER SIGNAL so that it can be used to
transmit data. This is done by moving the position of the wave
in relation to time and a fixed value.

/'feɪz mɒdjuˌleɪʃn/
note usually singular
► **amplitude modulation,
frequency modulation,
modulation, pulse code
modulation**

phosphorus *noun* (hardware)
a material found in a CATHODE RAY TUBE that produces light
when it comes into contact with electricity: *a phosphorous-
coated screen*

/'fɒsfərəs/
note no plural

physical *adjective*
(of a device or component) that forms part of the hardware of a
computer or system and is not SIMULATED by software

/'fɪzɪkl/
► **logical 2**

physical disk drive *noun*
► **disk drive**

/ˌfɪzɪkl 'dɪsk draɪv/

physical hard disk *noun*
► **hard disk**

/ˌfɪzɪkl hɑːd 'dɪsk/

physical layer *noun*
one of the levels of structure in the International Standards
Organization PROTOCOL for data communications. The physical
layer gives information about standards of the interface
between the data and hardware connections: *Adaptor boards
for other physical layer and computer system interfaces will be
added to the system.*

/ˌfɪzɪkl 'leɪə(r)/
note not used with *a* or *an*. No
plural and used with a singular
verb only.
⋈ define, specify the **physical
layer**
► **application layer, data link
layer, ISO OSI, network
layer, presentation layer,
session layer, transport
layer**

physical record *noun*
a record in a data file as it is stored in the computer; it contains
information about data formats which are not shown to the
user: *The physical record is part of the computer database.*

/ˌfɪzɪkl 'rekɔːd/
pl physical records
⋈ access, maintain, update a
physical record
► **logical record**

physical schema *noun*
the layout of types of data in a database and the links between
them as they are held in memory; this may be different from
the way the user sees them: *the physical schema of file
organization*

/ˌfɪzɪkl 'skiːmə/
pl physical schemas
pl physical schemata
⋈ compile, draw up a **physical
schema**
syn internal schema
► **database management
system, logical schema,
schema, subschema**

pico *prefix*
1 (*UK*) one million millionth or one billionth **2** (*US*) one trillionth

note Expressed as a number, pico is 10^{-12}, said as 'ten to the minus twelve'.

/'piːkəʊ/
abbr p
⋈ a pico **second**
▶ **femto, nano**

---

picture *noun*
a method that is used in some high-level programming languages of describing the format of a data item by giving an example of it: *In COBOL, the declaration PIC 99 gives a picture of a numeric data item with two decimal digits.*

/'pɪktʃə(r)/
pl pictures
⋈ define a **picture**

---

picture element *noun*
▶ **pixel**

/'pɪktʃər ˌelɪmənt/

PID *abbr*
▶ **personal identification device**

/ˌpiː aɪ 'diː/
note pronounced as individual letters

---

piggy-back *verb*
1 to place one COMPONENT or device on top of another to save space: *The printed circuit boards are piggy-backed on the motherboard.* **2** to allow one operation to carry the results of another operation: *Acknowledgements of previous transmissions are piggy-backed onto new transmissions.*

/'pɪgi bæk/
piggy-back, piggy-backing, piggy-backed
note transitive verb
1 ⋈ **piggy-back** integrated circuits

---

piggyback board *noun* (hardware)
a small printed circuit board that is designed to save space by carrying one integrated circuit above another

/'pɪgibæk bɔːd/
pl piggyback boards
⋈ mount a circuit, etc *on* a **piggyback board**

PILOT *noun* (software)
a high-level computer programming language designed to be used for preparing teaching materials

note PILOT is an acronym of 'Programmed Inquiry, Learning or Teaching'. It is an imperative procedural language and was designed in the 1960s at the University of California.

/'paɪlət/
note no plural
⋈ program *in* PILOT; a PILOT interpreter, program
▶ **author language, CAL**

---

pin *noun* (hardware)
1 one of the CONNECTORS on an integrated circuit: *a 24-pin chip*
2 a short metal part of a MALE CONNECTOR that fits into a FEMALE CONNECTOR or SOCKET: *a 3-pin plug*

/pɪn/
pl pins

☆**PIN** *abbr*
▶ **personal identification number**

/pɪn/
note pronounced as a word

---

pinfeed *noun*
▶ **sprocket feed**

/'pɪnfiːd/

PIN number *abbr*
▶ **personal identification number**

/'pɪn ˌnʌmbə(r)/

---

pipelining *noun*
the execution of instructions in stages, with parts of several instructions processed at the same time: *Pipelining offers a significant increase in overall execution speed.*

/'paɪplaɪnɪŋ/
note not used with *a* or *an*. No plural and used with a singular verb only.

---

abbr abbreviation   **pl** plural   **syn** synonym   ▶ see   ⋈ collocate (*word often used with the headword*)

piracy *noun*
the copying and/or selling of software without permission
from the owner of the COPYRIGHT or PATENT: *Attempts to prevent
software piracy include increased prosecutions under software
piracy laws.*

/ˈpaɪrəsi/
note no plural

pirate *verb*
to copy and/or sell software without permission from the
owner of the COPYRIGHT or PATENT: *pirate software and CDs on the
black market*

/ˈpaɪrət/
pirate, pirating, pirated
note transitive verb
⋈ **pirate** programs, software

pitch *noun*
the number of characters in a font, often a MONOSPACE FONT,
that fit into an inch: *a 10-pitch font has 10 characters per inch*

/pɪtʃ/
note usually singular
► **characters per inch**

pixel *noun*
the smallest single point on a visual display screen. A pixel can
be given colour and brightness, etc independently of all other
points on the screen: *graphics made of a pattern of pixels on a grid*
○ *a 640 by 480 pixel 16-colour screen*

/ˈpɪksl/
pl pixels
⋈ display, set, unset a **pixel**
syn pel, picture element, point
► **addressable point**

PL/1 *noun* (software)
a high-level computer programming language that is designed
for use in science and business

note PL/1 is an abbreviation of 'Programming Language
number 1'. PL/1 is an imperative procedural language that
was designed in the 1960s.

/ˌpiː el ˈwʌn/
note no plural
⋈ program *in* PL/1; a **PL/1**
compiler, program
► **COBOL**

plaintext *noun*
a message in a form that can be read by a person, before it is
turned into a CIPHER (2): *The cipher was successfully broken, and
the secret messages could be turned back into plaintext.*

/ˈpleɪntekst/
note not used with *a* or *an*. No
plural and used with a singular
verb only.
⋈ decipher *into*, read **plaintext**

plasma display *noun* (hardware)
a flat display screen made of two pieces of glass or plastic with
a layer of gas between the glass or plastic. Electricity passes
through the gas to form characters on the screen: *The plasma
display is strong enough to be used in a portable computer.*

note Plasma displays can only show characters, usually in red
or orange.

/ˈplæzmə dɪˌspleɪ/
pl plasma displays
⋈ show *on* a **plasma display**
syn gas plasma display, gas
discharge display, gas panel
display

platform *noun* (hardware)
a type of computer or program used as a standard for a
particular computer system: *an application developed on different
platforms* ○ *an IBM PC platform* ○ *a Mac platform*

/ˈplætfɔːm/
pl platforms
⋈ a computer, desktop, hardware,
mainframe, software **platform**

platter *noun* (hardware)
a metal disk that forms part of a hard disk: *The distance between
the read/write head and the platter is about 20 microns.* ○ *a high
capacity drive with several platters in the disk-head assembly*

/ˈplætə(r)/
pl platters

plot *verb*
to put points on a graph to create a diagram or graphics on
screen

/plɒt/
plot, plotting, plotted
note transitive verb

	⋈ **plot** a bar chart, data point, histogram

☆**plotter** *noun* (hardware)
a device that turns data from a computer into a graph, usually on paper: *The plotter is shared between several computers.* .

/ˈplɒtə(r)/
pl plotters
⋈ a graph **plotter**
▶ **digital plotter, drum plotter, flatbed plotter**

plug compatible *adjective*
(of software or hardware) that is specially made so it can be used with different computers or systems without needing to be changed: *Plug compatible machines made by different manufacturers can all use the same software.* ○ *a plug compatible printer*

/ˌplʌg kəmˈpætəbl/
⋈ a **plug compatible** board, keyboard

point¹ *noun*
1 a location or place: *a point on the x-axis* **2** a dot symbol used to separate a whole number from the decimal or binary part of a number in a FRACTION

3 ▶ **pixel**

/pɔɪnt/
pl points
1 ⋈ coordinates *of* a **point**
2 ⋈ insert a **point**

point² *verb*
to indicate the position of something, especially using a POINTING DEVICE: *move the arrow on screen to point to the menu*

/pɔɪnt/
point, pointing, pointed
note intransitive verb

pointer *noun*
1 a symbol on screen, such as an arrow, that is controlled by a POINTING DEVICE **2** a variable that contains information about the location of another data item in a DATA STRUCTURE: *In a binary tree, each data item has no more than two pointers.*

/ˈpɔɪntə(r)/
pl pointers
2 ⋈ follow, maintain, update a **pointer**
syn link

pointing device *noun* (hardware)
a device such as a mouse that is used with a graphical user interface to control a POINTER (1) on screen

/ˈpɔɪntɪŋ dɪˌvaɪs/
pl pointing devices
⋈ click *with*, point *with*, use a **pointing device**

poke *verb*
to put a byte of data directly into a memory location. Programming languages do not usually allow this because it is normally the program and not the user that decides where data is stored: *Poking a zero byte into a special location allows the game to be played without time limits.*

/pəʊk/
poke, poking, poked
note transitive verb
⋈ **poke** a binary pattern, code
▶ **peek**

Polish notation *noun*
a PREFIX NOTATION for mathematical and logical operations in which the operator is written before the OPERANDS: *In Polish notation, the operation of adding 2 to 3 is written '+ 2 3'.*

/ˌpəʊlɪʃ nəʊˈteɪʃn/
note not used with *a* or *an*. No plural and used with a singular verb only.
⋈ use, write *in* **Polish notation**
▶ **reverse Polish notation**

polling *noun* (software)
a process in MULTIPROGRAMMING where the operating system looks at each task in turn to see if it needs attention: *If polling determines that a task needs to execute, it is allocated a time slice.*

/ˈpəʊlɪŋ/
note not used with *a* or *an*. No plural and used with a singular verb only.
⋈ a **polling** algorithm, sequence

---

abbr abbreviation   **pl** plural   **syn** synonym   ▶ see   ⋈ collocate (*word often used with the headword*)

polling interval *noun*
the period of time between two POLLING operations on one task

/ˈpəʊlɪŋ ˌɪntəvl/
pl polling intervals
⋈ optimize, shorten the **polling interval**

---

pop *verb*
to access and remove the data item which is the TOP OF STACK:
pop a data item off the stack

/pɒp/
pop, popping, popped
note transitive verb
⋈ **pop** a data item, value
▶ **push**

---

pop-up menu *noun* (applications)
a menu that can appear in certain places on the screen,
usually when the user clicks on these places, although some
pop-up menus appear automatically: *In this program, a pop-up
menu appears automatically whenever the user is required to make
a choice.* ○ *position the cursor in the text and click the right-hand
mouse button to get the pop-up menu*

/ˌpɒp ʌp ˈmenjuː/
pl pop-up menus
▶ **menu, pull-down menu**

---

port¹ *noun*
a place in a computer that a PERIPHERAL can be connected to,
allowing data to be transferred between the computer and the
peripheral: *The unit plugs into the parallel printer port of the PC.*

/pɔːt/
pl ports
⋈ a communications, an input, a printer **port**
▶ **input port, output port, serial port, parallel port**

---

port² *verb*
to transfer software successfully from one computer to another
computer of a different type: *When the software package had been
tested, a month was scheduled to confirm that it could be ported to
other models.*

/pɔːt/
port, porting, ported
note transitive verb
⋈ **port** programs, software

---

portability *noun*
the ability to use hardware in different places, or software on
different types of computer: *The portability of the laptop allows
the user to work on it while travelling.* ○ *Portability is a major
design problem for applications software.*

/ˌpɔːtəˈbɪləti/
note not used with *a* or *an*. No plural and used with a singular verb only.
⋈ have, possess **portability**

---

portable *adjective*
(of a device) that is small enough to be carried from place to
place: *Portable computers have rechargeable batteries so that they
can be used where there is no mains current.*

/ˈpɔːtəbl/
1 ⋈ a **portable** calculator, printer, telephone

☆**portable computer** *noun* (hardware)
a computer designed to be carried from one place to another:
The portable computer has a battery life of five hours.

/ˌpɔːtəbl kəmˈpjuːtə(r)/
pl portable computers
syn transportable computer
▶ **laptop**

---

portable program *noun*
▶ **portable software**

/ˌpɔːtəbl ˈprəʊgræm/

---

portable software *noun* (software)
software that needs some or perhaps no changes to run on
different types of computer: *The highly portable software needed
no changes to run on different platforms.*

/ˌpɔːtəbl ˈsɒftweə(r)/
note not used with *a* or *an*. No plural and used with a singular verb only.

	⋈ transfer **portable software**: highly, moderately, non **portable software**
	syn portable program

porting *noun*

the process of transferring software from one computer to another computer of a different type: *The porting of the operating system to a different platform was difficult.*

/ˈpɔːtɪŋ/

note not used with *a* or *an*. No plural and used with a singular verb only.

⋈ perform the **porting**

▶ **portable, platform**

---

portrait *adjective*

(of a document page) that is printed so that the top of the page is one of the shorter sides: *Alter the page set-up from landscape to portrait.*

/ˈpɔːtreɪt/

note not used with *a* or *an*. No plural and used with a singular verb only.

⋈ **portrait** display, mode

▶ **landscape**

---

portrait monitor *noun* (hardware)

a screen in which the length is greater than the width: *use a portrait monitor with a desktop publishing application*

/ˈpɔːtreɪt ˌmɒnɪtə(r)/

pl portrait monitors

▶ **landscape monitor**

POS *abbr*

point of sale

note used in written English only

---

positive *adjective* (mathematics)

(of a number or amount) that is more than zero

/ˈpɒzətɪv/

⋈ a **positive** figure, sign, sum

▶ **negative**

---

positive acknowledgement *noun* (communications)

a message that reports a successful transmission of data and shows that the next item can be sent: *If no errors are found in the message, a positive acknowledgement is sent back.*

/ˌpɒzətɪv əkˈnɒlɪdʒmənt/

pl positive acknowledgements

abbr ACK

⋈ receive, send, transmit a **positive acknowledgement**

▶ **acknowledgement, negative acknowledgement**

---

postfix notation *noun*

a way of writing operations on numbers, with the operator following the two OPERANDS: *addition in postfix notation is written as '2 3 +'*

/ˈpəʊstfɪks nəʊˌteɪʃn/

note not used with *a* or *an*. No plural and used with a singular verb only.

⋈ read, translate *from/into*, write *in* **postfix notation**

▶ **infix notation, prefix notation, reverse Polish notation**

---

post-order traversal *noun*

a path through a BINARY TREE that accesses each data item in turn. A particular item is accessed only after the items reached through its two DESCENDANTS are accessed.

/ˌpəʊst ɔːdə trəˈvɜːsl/

pl post-order traversals

⋈ perform a **post-order traversal**

▶ **pre-order traversal, symmetric traversal**

---

abbr abbreviation   **pl** plural   **syn** synonym   ▶ see   ⋈ collocate (*word often used with the headword*)

postprocessor *noun*

a device or piece of software that processes data that has already been processed by another device or piece of software: *The final stage of processing - preparing the data for output to the printer - is done by the postprocessor.*

/ˌpəʊst ˈprəʊsesə(r)/
pl post processors
  (also **post-processor**)
⛹ pass data *through/to* a **postprocessor**
▶ **preprocessor**

---

power spike *noun*
▶ **surge**

/ˈpaʊə spaɪk/

☆**power supply** *noun* (hardware)

a source of energy, usually electricity, that is used to run devices and machines, etc: *Turn the computer off and then disconnect it from the power supply.*

/ˈpaʊə səˌplaɪ/
pl power supplies
⛹ cut off the **power supply**; an emergency, an internal, a main, a supplementary, an uninterrupted **power supply**

---

power surge *noun*
▶ **surge**

/ˈpaʊə sɜːdʒ/

---

power surge protector *noun* (hardware)

a device that stops a POWER SURGE damaging a computer

/ˈpaʊə sɜːdʒ prəˌtektə(r)/
pl power surge protectors
⛹ install a **power surge protector**
▶ **fuse**[1], **uninterruptable power supply**

---

power transient *noun*
▶ **transient**[1]

/ˈpaʊə ˌtrænziənt/

---

power up *verb*

to switch on a piece of electrical equipment: *remove all floppy disks from the drives before powering up the computer*

/ˌpaʊər ˈʌp/
power up, powering up, powered up
note transitive verb
⛹ **power up** a computer, device, printer
▶ **cold start**

---

precedence *noun*

the order in which two operations happen

/ˈpresɪdəns/
note usually singular
⛹ equal, higher, lower, programming **precedence**
▶ **order of precedence, operator precedence**
syn priority

---

precision *noun*

the exactness of a measurement or calculation, etc: *Although the result was one of great precision, it was wrong because it had been calculated from incorrect data.* ○ *The speed and precision of the system's calculations is impressive.*

note 'Precision' is not the same as 'accuracy'. 'Precision' is how detailed a result is. 'Accuracy' is how correct a result is.

/prɪˈsɪʒn/
pl no plural
▶ **accuracy**

---

precompiled *adjective*

(of a computer program) that has already been translated from a high-level language into MACHINE CODE, so that it may execute without further translation: *The software is supplied on disk as precompiled code.*

/ˌpriːkəmˈpaɪld/
⛹ a **precompiled** module; **precompiled** code, software
▶ **preprocessor, source code**

prefix *noun*
a code at the beginning of a message or record: *The data file DT/CORRESPONDENCE has the prefix DT.*

/'priːfɪks/
pl prefixes
▶ **suffix**

---

prefix notation *noun*
a way of writing operations on numbers, with the operator before the two OPERANDS: *Addition in prefix notation is written as '+ 2 3'.*

/'priːfɪks nəʊˌteɪʃn/
note not used with *a* or *an*. No plural and used with a singular verb only.
◄ read, translate something *from/ into*, write **prefix notation**
▶ **infix notation, Polish notation, postfix notation**

---

preformatted *adjective* (hardware)
(of a disk or tape, etc) that has been formatted before the first time it is used

/ˌpriːˈfɔːmætɪd/
▶ **format²**

---

preformatted disk *noun* (hardware)
a disk that contains all the information necessary to make it ready for immediate use

/ˈpriːˌfɔːmætɪd ˈdɪsk/
pl preformatted disks

---

pre-order traversal *noun*
a path through a BINARY TREE that accesses each data item in turn. Any particular item is accessed before the items reached through its two DESCENDANTS are accessed.

/ˌpriːɔːdə trəˈvɜːsl/
pl pre-order traversals
◄ perform a **pre-order traversal**
▶ **post-order traversal, symmetric traversal**

---

preprinted stationery *noun* (hardware)
stationery such as forms that has standard text printed on it: *The order for preprinted stationery included invoices with the company's tax number and address printed on them.*

/ˌpriːprɪntɪd ˈsteɪʃənri/
note not used with *a* or *an*. No plural and used with a singular verb only.
◄ order, purchase **preprinted stationery**

---

preprocessor *noun*
a device or piece of software that performs a first stage of processing data before passing the data to another device or piece of software: *The preprocessor expands the macros in the program.*

/ˌpriːˈprəʊsesə(r)/
pl preprocessors
(also **pre-processor**)
◄ pass data *through/to* a **preprocessor**
▶ **postprocessor**

---

presentation graphics package *noun* (software)
software that helps a user to design and print charts and displays to use at meetings: *The sales manager used a presentation graphics package to prepare and present the annual report to the shareholders.*

/ˈpreznˌteɪʃn ˈgræfɪks ˌpækɪdʒ/
pl presentation graphics packages
◄ use a **presentation graphics package**

---

presentation layer *noun*
one of the levels of structure of the International Standards Organization PROTOCOL for data communications. The presentation layer describes standards on how data is presented: *The presentation layer provides details of the agreed transfer syntax that all communications systems understand.*

/ˌpreznˈteɪʃn ˌleɪə(r)/
note not used with *a* or *an*. No plural and used with a singular verb only.
◄ define, specify the **presentation layer**
▶ **application layer, data link layer, ISO OSI, network**

---

abbr abbreviation   **pl** plural   **syn** synonym   ▶ see   ◄ collocate (*word often used with the headword*)

layer, physical layer, session layer, transport layer

---

preventative maintenance *noun*

regular checking of equipment in order to find and repair faults before they become serious

/prɪˌventətɪv ˈmeɪntənəns/

note not used with *a* or *an*. No plural and used with a singular verb only.

◄ carry out **preventative maintenance**

---

primary index *noun* (software/data structure)

a table that is used to access data items held in a SEQUENTIAL FILE. The data items are stored in the file in the same order as the entries in the table: *The primary index is a table of employees' insurance numbers and secondary indexes contain names and job titles.* ○ *access data files by using a primary index*

/ˌpraɪməri ˈɪndeks/

pl primary indexes

pl primary indices

◄ access, build, construct, make, update the **primary index**

► **secondary index**

---

primary key *noun*

a field in a data record which has a different value for each record stored; knowing the value of the primary key allows access to just one record: *Data items are often stored in primary key order.*

/ˌpraɪməri ˈkiː/

pl primary keys

◄ access, use the value *of* the **primary key**

syn unique identifier

► **primary index, secondary key**

☆**primary memory** *noun*

► **main memory**

/ˌpraɪməri ˈmeməri/

---

primary storage *noun*

► **main memory**

/ˌpraɪməri ˈstɔːrɪdʒ/

---

primitive *noun* (programming)

one of the basic statements that can be used in some high-level programming languages to make longer statements

/ˈprɪmətɪv/

pl primitives

◄ employ, use a **primitive**

---

print¹ *noun*

1 letters and numbers, etc that have been printed, usually on paper: *The print is clear and easy to read.* **2** a command in a word processing application that sends a document to be printed: *select the print command from the menu*

/prɪnt/

note not used with *a* or *an*. No plural and used with a singular verb only.

1 ◄ fine, large, small **print**

---

print² *verb*

to produce letters and numbers, etc using a printer: *print all the files so they exist as hard copy*

/prɪnt/

print, printing, printed

◄ **print** a copy, a document, an invoice, a letter, a page

---

print buffer *noun* (hardware)

a part of the computer's memory that stores text that is ready to be sent to a printer

/ˈprɪnt ˌbʌfə(r)/

pl print buffers

☆**printed circuit board** *noun*

a flat piece of material such as plastic which holds chips and other small electronic components

note A printed circuit board is made of insulated material so it does not conduct electricity. Metal tracks which carry electricity are printed onto the circuit board to connect chips and components together. Printed circuit boards are one of the most basic parts of modern computers and they remove the need for wires.

/ˌprɪntɪd ˈsɜːkɪt bɔːd/

pl printed circuit boards

abbr PCB

◄ design, install, manufacture a **printed circuit board**; a multi-layer, a single-layer **printed circuit board**

syn board

► **expansion board**

☆**printer** *noun* (hardware)
a machine that is linked to a computer that produces words, pictures and symbols, etc on paper

/'prɪntə(r)/
pl printers

⋈ connect *to*, disconnect *from*, set the **printer**; a bit-mapped, desktop, high-speed, logic-seeking, 1 200 dpi **printer**

▶ **daisywheel printer, dot matrix printer, electrostatic printer, impact printer, ink-jet printer, laser printer, nonimpact printer, page printer, thermal printer**

---

printer plotter *noun* (hardware)
a printer that can be used as a PLOTTER

/ˌprɪntə 'plɒtə(r)/
pl printer plotters

---

print hammer *noun* (hardware)
a part of an IMPACT PRINTER that hits the characters against a piece of material with ink on it, called a ribbon, onto paper

/'prɪnt ˌhæmə(r)/
pl print hammers

---

print head *noun* (hardware)
the mechanical part of a printer that controls the printing of characters on paper: *Eight rows of horizontal dots are printed in a single movement of the print head across the paper.*

/'prɪnt hed/
pl print heads

⋈ a 24-dot, 128-nozzle, refillable **print head**

▶ **printer**

☆**printout** *noun* (hardware)
paper that contains printed information from a computer: *a monthly printout of sales figures* ○ *a printout of text downloaded from the Internet*

/'prɪntaʊt/
pl printouts
(also **print-out**)

⋈ computer **printout**

▶ **hard copy, soft copy**

---

print quality *noun*
the quality of characters produced by a printer, usually measured from clear and easy to read LETTER QUALITY to poorer DRAFT QUALITY: *300 dpi print quality* ○ *A matrix printer is sufficient for reasonable print quality.* ○ *The print quality from the laser printer is excellent.*

/'prɪnt ˌkwɒləti/
note not used with *a* or *an*. No plural and used with a singular verb only.

⋈ good, high, inferior, low, poor, superior **print quality**

---

print server *noun* (hardware)
a computer that is part of a network and is only used for managing requests from other computers in the network to use the printer: *printing is controlled by the print server* ○ *a dedicated print server*

/'prɪnt ˌsɜːvə(r)/
pl print servers

⋈ **print server** software

▶ **server**

---

print spooling *noun*
the process of moving data to be printed to a temporary storage place on a disk. The data is then sent from the disk to the printer under the control of the operating system: *bypass print spooling and connect directly to the printer*

/'prɪnt ˌspuːlɪŋ/
note not used with *a* or *an*. No plural and used with a singular verb only.

---

priority *noun*
▶ **precedence**

/praɪ'ɒrəti/

---

abbr abbreviation　　**pl** plural　　**syn** synonym　　▶ see　　⋈ collocate (*word often used with the headword*)

priority interrupt *noun*
a signal that is sent to the CPU by a device to request action or to report completion of a task, and which is processed before other INTERRUPTS[1]

/praɪˌɒrəti ˈɪntərʌpt/
pl priority interrupts
ᴍ cause, respond to, service a **priority interrupt**
▶ nonmaskable interrupt

---

privileged instruction *noun* (software)
a machine code instruction which is allowed to access areas of data that cannot be accessed from user programs: *The operating system makes extensive use of privileged instructions.* ○ *Privileged instructions include all instructions concerned with clocks and interval timers.*

/ˌprɪvəlɪdʒd ɪnˈstrʌkʃnz/
pl privileged instructions
ᴍ disable, enable, execute, use a **privileged instruction**

---

problem-oriented language *noun*
▶ high-level language

/ˈprɒbləm ˌɔːriəntɪd ˈlæŋgwɪdʒ/

---

procedural language *noun* (software)
a programming language that gives the instructions to compute a result rather than the result that is needed: *Ada is a high-level procedural language.*

/prəˌsiːdʒərəl ˈlæŋgwɪdʒ/
pl procedural languages
▶ non-procedural language, programming language

---

procedure *noun* (software/programming)
1 a way of performing a task that usually does not change each time the task is performed: *The procedure for logging on to the network always involves entering a user name and password.*

2 ▶ routine

/prəˈsiːdʒə(r)/
pl procedures
1 ᴍ define, follow, obey a **procedure**

---

procedure call *noun* (software/programming)
a statement in a main program which stops it from executing in order to execute a PROCEDURE. When the procedure has been executed, execution continues again from the same place in the main program: *a recursive procedure call*

/prəˈsiːdʒə kɔːl/
pl procedure calls
ᴍ execute a **procedure call**
syn routine call
▶ call

---

procedure declaration *noun* (software)
the programming language statements that show where the instructions making up a procedure begin and end. It may also define the data type of any results computed by the procedure.

/prəˈsiːdʒə dekləˌreɪʃn/
pl procedure declarations
ᴍ make, include, insert a **procedure declaration**
▶ declaration

☆**process[1]** *noun*
the work a computer program does on data: *the process of extracting figures from a spreadsheet*

/ˈprəʊses/
pl processes
ᴍ a computing, mathematical, sorting **process**
▶ operation

☆**process[2]** *verb* (software/system operation)
to make a computer program work on data in order to produce a result

/ˈprəʊses/
process, processing, processed
note transitive verb
ᴍ **process** data, information

---

process control *noun*
the use of a computer to control a physical process such as the operation of machinery: *The manufacturing of materials in the factory is under process control.*

/ˈprəʊses kənˌtrəʊl/
note not used with *a* or *an*. No plural and used with a singular verb only.
ᴍ **process control** hardware, methods, software; a **process control** computer, system

☆**processing** *noun* (system operation) the work that a program does on data in order to produce an output	/ˈprəʊsesɪŋ/ **note** no plural **M** image, text **processing** **syn** data processing ▶ **CPU, data processing, parallel processing, serial processing, word processing**
processing unit *noun* a part of a computer which processes data	/ˌprəʊsesɪŋ ˈjuːnɪt/ **pl** processing units **M** install, use a **processing unit** **syn** processor ▶ **coprocessor**
☆**processor** *noun* ▶ **processing unit**	/ˈprəʊsesə(r)/
processor bound *adjective* ▶ **compute bound**	/ˈprəʊsesə baʊnd/
☆**program**[1] *noun* (software) a set of instructions that can be understood by a computer and perform a certain task or function: *write a special program to analyse the data* ○ *load the program into the computer*	/ˈprəʊɡræm/ **pl** programs (*UK* **programme**) **M** design, download, execute, write a **program** **syn** computer program, stored program ▶ **application, lines of code, software**
☆**program**[2] *verb* (user operation) to write a list of instructions in a programming language that enables a computer to perform certain tasks or functions: *program the computer to sort data alphabetically*	/ˈprəʊɡræm/ **program, programming, programmed** (*US* **program, programing, programed**) **note** transitive verb **M** **program** a computer, system
program counter *noun* ▶ **current address register**	/ˈprəʊɡræm ˌkaʊntə(r)/
program documentation *noun* ▶ **documentation**	/ˈprəʊɡræm ˌdɒkjumənˈteɪʃn/
program file *noun* ▶ **file**	/ˈprəʊɡræm faɪl/
program flowchart *noun* ▶ **flowchart**	/ˌprəʊɡræm ˈfləʊtʃɑːt/
program generator *noun* software that creates the source code of a computer program	/ˈprəʊɡræm ˌdʒenəreɪtə(r)/ **pl** program generators **M** execute, use a **program generator**

abbr abbreviation   **pl** plural   **syn** synonym   ▶ see   **M** collocate (*word often used with the headword*)

program library *noun*
► library

/'prəʊgræm ˌlaɪbrəri/

---

program listing *noun*
► listing

/'prəʊgræm ˌlɪstɪŋ/

---

programmable *adjective*
(of a computer or device) that is capable of accepting
instructions to control how it works: *the programmable CD-
player allows the user to change the order tracks are played in*

/'prəʊgræməbl/

⋈ a **programmable** fax machine,
keyboard, logic device,
microprocessor, mouse, remote
control device

---

programmable function key *noun*
► function key

/ˌprəʊgræməbl 'fʌŋkʃn kiː/

---

programmable logic array *noun*
► uncommitted logic array

/ˌprəʊgræməbl 'lɒdʒɪk əˌreɪ/

---

programmable read-only memory *noun* (hardware)
a form of ROM which can be written to by the user with a
special device called a PROM programmer. Once data has been
written to PROM in this way, it may be read but not changed.

/'prəʊgræməbl 'riːd əʊnli
'meməri/

note no plural

abbr PROM

⋈ blow, burn, erase, install, read
data *from*, write data *to*
**programmable read-only
memory**

► EPROM, ROM

☆**programmer** *noun* (personnel)
a person who writes or designs programs for a computer

/'prəʊgræmə(r)/

pl programmers

► **applications programmer,
systems programmer**

☆**programming** *noun* (user operation)
the process of writing and testing programs for computers:
machines designed for end-user programming

/'prəʊgræmɪŋ/

note not used with *a* or *an*. No
plural and used with a singular
verb only.

⋈ automatic, operator, structured
programming

► **software**

☆**programming language** *noun* (software)
a language that can be used for writing instructions that a
computer can process and execute

/'prəʊgræmɪŋ ˌlæŋgwɪdʒ/

pl programming languages

⋈ learn, use, write *in* a
programming language; a
programming language
compiler, interpreter,
translator; **programming
language** grammar, software,
semantics, syntax

► **grammar, high-level
language, low-level
language, natural language,
semantics**

programming standards *noun*
rules followed by computer programmers who are working in
a team so that their work can be understood by other
programmers

note Programming standards usually cover the choice of
variable names, labels and comments.

/ˈprəʊɡræmɪŋ ˌstændədz/
note plural noun used with a
plural verb
◄ adopt, follow, propose a set of
programming standards
syn coding standards
▶ **comment, label, variable**

---

program run *noun*
▶ **run**[1]

/ˈprəʊɡræm rʌn/

---

program statement *noun*
▶ **statement**

/ˈprəʊɡræm ˌsteɪtmənt/

☆**PROLOG** *noun* (software)
a high-level computer programming language designed for
artificial intelligence and database use

note PROLOG is an acronym of 'Programming Logic'. It is a
non-procedural logical programming language that is usually
translated by an interpreter. It was designed in 1972.

/ˈprəʊlɒɡ/
note not used with *a* or *an*. No
plural and used with a singular
verb only.
◄ program *in*, write **PROLOG**; a
PROLOG interpreter, machine,
program

PROM *abbr*
▶ **programmable read-only memory**

/prɒm/

☆**prompt** *noun* (system operation)
a message on screen to show that the computer requires input
from the user: *enter 'Y' for 'yes' in response to the prompt* ○ *type
in 'WHATPC' at the floppy drive prompt* ○ *Invalid input will result
in the prompt being displayed again.*

/prɒmpt/
pl prompts
◄ type *at*, wait *for* the **prompt**; a
prompt character, symbol
syn system prompt

---

propagate *verb*
to spread something to different places: *propagate a virus*

/ˈprɒpəɡeɪt/
**propagate, propagating,
propagated**
note transitive verb
◄ **propagate** an effect, error

---

propagated error *noun*
an error in a mathematical calculation that is caused by using
data that contains errors: *The propagated error got bigger as the
calculation continued.*

/ˌprɒpəɡeɪtɪd ˈerə(r)/
pl propagated errors
◄ compensate *for*, reduce a
propagated error

---

propagation delay *noun*
▶ **gate delay**

/ˌprɒpəˈɡeɪʃn dɪˌleɪ/

---

propagation time *noun*
▶ **gate delay**

/ˌprɒpəˈɡeɪʃn taɪm/

---

proportional font *noun*
a font which has characters that can occupy a different
amount of horizontal space: *The letter 'i' occupies less space than
the letter 'w' in a proportional font.*

/prəˌpɔːʃnl ˈfɒnt/
pl proportional fonts
▶ **font, kerning, monospace
font**

---

abbr abbreviation   **pl** plural   **syn** synonym   ▶ see   ◄ collocate (*word often used with the headword*)

proprietary software *noun*
a program that an individual or company, etc owns the
COPYRIGHT of; buying a copy of the program is the only legal
way to use it: *proprietary software that runs on a range of
hardware*

/prə,praɪətri ˈsɒftweə(r)/

note not used with *a* or *an*. No
plural and used with a singular
verb only.

◪ buy, purchase, use
proprietary software

▶ **freeware, public domain
software, shareware**

protect *verb*
▶ **write protect²**

/prəˈtekt/

protected field *noun* (software)
an area in a data record which can only have data written to it
by users with special access rights

/prə,tektɪd ˈfiːld/

pl protected fields

◪ access, define data, etc *in*, read
data, etc *from* a **protected field**

protocol *noun* (communications)
the agreed signals and rules that control data format, control
signals and the timing of data transmissions, etc between
computers, either directly or over a network

/ˈprəʊtəkɒl/

pl protocols

◪ conform *to*, design, follow,
obey, use a **protocol**

prototyping *noun*
the preparation of a model of a new program or system so that
it can be tested and improved: *accuracy of processing was
established during prototyping*

/ˈprəʊtətaɪpɪŋ/

note not used with *a* or *an*. No
plural and used with a singular
verb only.

◪ a **prototyping** method,
schedule

pseudocode *noun* (software/programming)
code that contains a combination of a programming language
such as C, and natural language such as English. Some
programmers write new programs in pseudocode first and
then translate them into a programming language: *The
program logic was defined using pseudocode, before being coded in
FORTRAN.* ○ *write a draft version of the program in pseudocode*

/ˈsjuːdəʊ ˌkəʊd/

note not used with *a* or *an*. No
plural and used with a singular
verb only.

◪ program *in*, read, write
pseudocode

pseudo-random number generator *noun*
software that creates PSEUDO-RANDOM NUMBERS

/ˈsjuːdəʊ ˌrændəm ˈnʌmbə
ˌdʒenəreɪtə(r)/

pl pseudo-random number
generators

◪ call *on*, use a **random number
generator**

pseudo-random numbers *noun*
a string of numbers in a certain order that is selected by a
computer. Each string will appear more than once, but this
will only happen after a very long time: *Games and simulations
use pseudo-random numbers.*

/ˈsjuːdəʊ ˌrændəm ˈnʌmbəz/

note only plural

◪ generate, seed a **pseudo-
random numbers**

PSN *abbr*
packet switched network

/ˌpiː es ˈen/

note pronounced as individual
letters

public access terminal *noun* (hardware)
a terminal linked to a network or central database that is
placed where members of the public can use it: *use a public
access terminal in a library to search the catalogue*

/ˌpʌblɪk ˈækses ˌtɜːmɪnl/

pl public access terminals

◪ access information *via* a **public
access terminal**

public carrier *noun*
▶ **common carrier**

/ˌpʌblɪk ˈkæriə(r)/

---

public domain software *noun* (software)
a program that has been made available for anyone to use and is usually free of charge: *a graphical user interface built with public domain software* ○ *access public domain software from a bulletin board*

/ˈpʌblɪk dəˈmeɪn ˈsɒftweə(r)/
note no plural
▶ **freeware, proprietary software, shareware**

---

public key cipher *noun*
a system for sending secret messages that uses two KEYS (2). One key is known to everyone, and is used to turn a message into a CIPHER (2), the other key is secret and is used to change the cipher back into its original form so the message can be read.

/ˈpʌblɪk ˈkiː ˈsaɪfə(r)/
pl public key ciphers
ᴹ decipher messages, etc *using*, encipher messages, etc *using* a **public key cipher**
▶ **cipher**

---

puck *noun* (hardware)
a small device that is moved over a GRAPHICS TABLET to input data into a computer. When the puck is placed over a certain point in a drawing, the user presses the button on the puck and the position is read and stored by the computer: *transfer the architectural plans into the computer using a puck*

/pʌk/
pl pucks

---

pull-down menu *noun* (applications)
a menu that the user selects from the MENU BAR in a graphical user interface: *The 'save' command is on the pull-down menu called FILE.*

/ˌpʊl daʊn ˈmenjuː/
pl pull-down menus
▶ **pop-up menu**

---

pulse code modulation *noun*
a way of transmitting analog data as a digital signal. This is done by turning the values of the analog signal into codes which are then stored or transmitted as digits.

/ˌpʌls kəʊd mɒdjuˈleɪʃn/
note no plural
▶ **amplitude modulation, frequency modulation, modulation, phase modulation**

---

punched card *noun* (hardware)
a piece of card with small holes that represent data

/ˌpʌntʃt ˈkɑːd/
pl punched cards

---

punched card reader *noun* (hardware)
a device that reads the information on a PUNCHED CARD and changes it into a form that can be processed by a computer

/ˌpʌntʃt ˈkɑːd ˌriːdə(r)/
pl punched card readers

---

pure code *noun* (software)
a computer program that does not change any of its instructions when it is executed

/ˌpjʊə ˈkəʊd/
note not used with *a* or *an*. No plural and used with a singular verb only.
ᴹ execute, program, run, write **pure code**
▶ **code**

---

purge *verb*
to delete data from a file: *purge the master file of old records*

/pɜːdʒ/
purge, purging, purged
note transitive verb

---

push *verb*
to add a new data item to a STACK. The item becomes the TOP OF STACK and no other items on the stack can be accessed until it is removed: *push the value onto the stack*

/pʊʃ/
push, pushing, pushed
note transitive verb

---

abbr abbreviation   **pl** plural   **syn** synonym   ▶ see   ᴹ collocate (*word often used with the headword*)

| | ⋈ **push** a data item, value |
| | ▶ **pop** |

push-down list *noun*
▶ **stack**

/ˈpʊʃ daʊn lɪst/

push-down stack *noun*
▶ **stack**

/ˈpʊʃ daʊn stæk/

push-up list *noun*
▶ **queue**

/ˈpʊʃ ʌp lɪst/

Qq

QBE *abbr*
▶ **Query by Example**

/ˌkjuː biː ˈiː/
note pronounced as individual letters

QL *abbr*
▶ **query language**

/ˌkjuː ˈel/
note pronounced as individual letters
pl QLs

quantize *verb*
to process an analog signal and turn it into a sequence of numbers: *During recording of a digital CD, the music is quantized to produce numbers which are recorded onto the disk.*

/ˈkwɒntaɪz/
quantize, quantizing, quantized
note transitive verb
⋈ **quantize** a signal
▶ **analog, digital**

query¹ *noun*
a request that is made by a user to a database asking it to provide a list of the records that match certain conditions: *The search query can be presented as sentences, phrases or lists of items.* ○ *run the query and the results will appear as data in two columns*

/ˈkwɪəri/
pl queries
⋈ formulate a **query**

query² *verb*
to make a database search for all records that match certain conditions: *query the database for records of all unpaid bills in the last financial year*

/ˈkwɪəri/
query, querying, queried
note transitive verb

Query by Example *noun*
(*trade mark*) (*software*) a high-level computer programming language designed for accessing large databases

note Query by Example is a non-procedural query language. It was designed by IBM in 1975.

/ˌkwɪəri baɪ ɪɡˈzɑːmpl/
note not used with *a* or *an*. No plural and used with a singular verb only.
abbr QBE
⋈ **Query by Example** syntax, variables

query language *noun* (*software*)
a high-level computer programming language that is designed for accessing databases

/ˈkwɪəri ˌlæŋgwɪdʒ/
pl query languages
abbr QL
⋈ access a database *using*, interrogate a database *using*,

use, write *in* a **query language**: **query language** grammar, syntax

▶ **database language, data manipulation language**

☆**queue**[1] *noun*
1 a collection of things waiting for attention and which will be processed in order: *a queue of print jobs waiting for the network printer* **2** a DATA STRUCTURE arranged as a list of data items in order. Items may only be added at one end of the list and accessed at the other end: *a queue of data items to be processed*

/kjuː/
pl queues
1 ᴍ have a place *in*, join, wait *in* a **queue**
2 ᴍ access, define, empty, implement, update, use a **queue**
syn first in, first out queue, push-up list
▶ **dequeue, dynamic data structure**

☆**queue**[2] *verb* (system operation)
1 to add tasks to other tasks so they are ready to be processed or printed in order: *The system is programmed to queue the jobs before they are processed.* **2** (of tasks) to come together to be processed in a certain order: *The print jobs are queueing.*

/kjuː/
queue, queuing, queued
note transitive or intransitive verb

---

quicksort *noun* (software)
an ALGORITHM for sorting data

/ˈkwɪksɔːt/
note no plural

☆**quit** *verb* (user operation)
to leave a program or system: *quit the application and return to the directory* ○ *quit from the current program*

/kwɪt/
quit, quitting, quit
note transitive or intransitive verb
ᴍ **quit** *from* a program, etc
▶ **escape, exit**

---

qwerty keyboard *noun* (hardware)
a keyboard where the top row of letter keys starts from the left with QWERTY

/ˌkwɜːti ˈkiːbɔːd/
pl qwerty keyboards
▶ **azerty keyboard, keyboard**[1]

Rr

---

rack *noun* (hardware)
a metal frame that supports and holds circuit boards and other devices, such as disk drives

/ræk/
pl racks

---

ragged left *adjective*
(of text) that is arranged on the page so that the left side is not JUSTIFIED **(1)**

/ˌrægɪd ˈleft/

---

ragged right *adjective*
(of text) that is arranged on the page so that the right side is not JUSTIFIED **(1)**

/ˌrægɪd ˈraɪt/

---

abbr abbreviation   **pl** plural   **syn** synonym   ▶ see   ᴍ collocate (*word often used with the headword*)

ragged text *noun*
text which had not been JUSTIFIED **(1)** on the right or left side

/ˌrægɪd ˈtekst/

note not used with *a* or *an*. No plural and used with a singular verb only

---

☆**RAM** *noun* (hardware)
random access memory. Memory in which locations may be accessed in any order. All RAM locations take the same amount of time to access: *The computer needs 16Mb of RAM to run the program.* ○ *The program is resident in RAM.*

note RAM is semiconductor-based memory and can be written to and read from. Main memory is often just called 'RAM'.

/ræm/

note not used with *a* or *an*. No plural and used with a singular verb only.

◄ **RAM** chips, circuits

▶ **random access**

RAM chip *noun*
▶ **memory chip**

/ˈræm tʃɪp/

RAM disk *noun* (hardware)
a part of RAM that functions like a physical disk drive

/ˈræm dɪsk/

pl RAM disks

◄ read data *from*, write data *to* a **RAM disk**

syn silicon disk, virtual disk

▶ **disk cache**

RAM refresh *noun*
▶ **refresh 1**

/ˈræm rɪˌfreʃ/

☆**random access** *noun* (system operation)
an access method where the computer can go directly to individual data items without having to search through all data items in memory: *Random access allows data items to be written to disk in any order.*

/ˌrændəm ˈækses/

note not used with *a* or *an*. No plural and used with a singular verb only.

◄ a **random access** data structure, device

syn direct access, parallel access

---

random access file *noun*
a file where each data item can be accessed without reading other data items first: *Random access files are usually stored on disk.*

/ˈrændəm ˈækses ˈfaɪl/

pl random access files

◄ **random access file** storage, structure

---

random access memory *noun*
▶ **RAM**

/ˈrændəm ˈækses ˈmeməri/

---

random access storage device *noun* (hardware)
a form of backing store or auxiliary memory that allows access to any memory location in any order: *Magnetic disks are random access storage devices.*

/ˈrændəm ˈækses ˈstɔːrɪdʒ dɪˌvaɪs/

pl random access storage devices

◄ install, use a **random access storage device**

syn direct access storage device

---

range *noun*
a group of selected CELLS **(2)** in a spreadsheet that are next to each other and are processed as a single unit: *a range of cells with the same format* ○ *one command affects the range*

/reɪndʒ/

pl ranges

---

range check *noun*
a method of data VALIDATION; the computer looks at data and if it is not within certain limits the data is rejected

/ˈreɪndʒ tʃek/

pl range checks

rank *verb*
to put something in a particular order, especially according to importance or size: *rank the data in order of date*

/ræŋk/
rank, ranking, ranked
note transitive verb
Ⱶ **rank** data, information

---

raster *noun* (hardware)
a method of displaying an image by drawing horizontal lines, made of PIXELS, on a screen

/ˈræstə(r)/
note not used with *a* or *an*. No plural and used with a singular verb only.
Ⱶ **raster** graphics; a **raster** format, grid, image, representation, scan

---

raster display *noun* (hardware)
a screen that shows images as horizontal lines made of PIXELS: *TV screens and computer monitors are usually raster displays.*

/ˈræstə dɪˌspleɪ/
note not used with *a* or *an*. No plural and used with a singular verb only.
► **vector display**

---

raster image processor *noun* (hardware)
a raster device that converts instructions into an image or a page of text that can be printed

/ˈræstə(r) ˌɪmɪdʒ ˌprəʊsesə(r)/
pl raster image processors

---

raw data *noun*
data that has not been processed: *convert raw data from documents into a form that the computer can process*

/ˌrɔː ˈdeɪtə/
note not used with *a* or *an*. No plural and used with a singular verb only.
Ⱶ analyse, assemble, evaluate, input, process, sort, validate the **raw data**

---

ray tracing *noun*
a way of producing very high-quality computer graphics where the the objects on screen look very similar to real objects. One of the most important parts of this process is making light and colour look natural: *Ray tracing and lighting effects were used in the computer animation to make the water look real.*

/ˈreɪ ˌtreɪsɪŋ/
note not used with *a* or *an*. No plural and used with a singular verb only.

R & D *abbr*
► **research and development**

/ˌɑːr ənd ˈdiː/

☆**read** *verb* (system operation)
to access data in main memory of a storage device such as a disk: *The disk drive reads data from a disk into the computer's RAM.* ○ *read the data block by block* ○ *a program that can read files in different formats*

/riːd/
read, reading, read
note transitive verb
Ⱶ **read** data *from* disk, a file, tape
► copy², ROM, write

☆**readable** *adjective*
able to be read and processed by a computer or a device: *The instructions must be converted into a computer-readable format for processing.*

/ˈriːdəbl/
Ⱶ a **readable** instruction, program
syn machine-readable

---

read channel *noun* (hardware)
a hardware path that carries data that has been accessed from memory

/ˈriːd ˌtʃænl/
pl read channels

---

abbr abbreviation   **pl** plural   **syn** synonym   ► see   Ⱶ collocate (*word often used with the headword*)

read cycle *noun*
the amount of time taken for data to be read from memory, processed and returned to memory

/ˈriːd ˌsaɪkl/
pl read cycles

---

reader *noun* (hardware)
a device that reads data stored in one form and changes it into another form so that it can be processed by a computer: *A punched card reader converts holes in cards into data for computer processing.*

/ˈriːdə(r)/
pl readers

---

read error *noun* (software)
an error that occurs when the computer accesses data from memory

/ˈriːd ˌerə(r)/
pl read errors
Ⓜ cause, detect a **read error**
▶ **write error**

---

read head *noun* (hardware)
the part of a disk or tape drive that reads data from a disk or tape and transfers it to the computer: *There is a pause of half a second while the read head moves from one track on the disk to another track.*

/ˈriːd hed/
pl read heads

☆**read only memory** *noun*
▶ **ROM**

/ˈriːd ˌəʊnli ˈmeməri/

---

readout *noun*
a display of information on a screen: *a readout of the results of the experiment*

/ˈriːdaʊt/
pl readouts
▶ **printout**

---

read/write head *noun* (hardware)
the part of a disk or tape drive that reads data from the disk or tape to the computer, or writes data from the computer to the disk or tape

/ˌriːd ˈraɪt hed/
pl read/write heads

☆**read/write memory** *noun* (hardware)
memory such as RAM that a computer can write data to and read data from

/ˈriːd ˈraɪt ˈmeməri/
note no plural

---

real number *noun* (mathematics)
a number that is a whole number or a FRACTION

note In some programming languages, real numbers are those stored in floating point form.

/ˌriːəl ˈnʌmbə(r)/
pl real numbers
▶ **floating point**

☆**real-time** *adjective* (software/operations/system)
able to respond immediately so that the user is not aware of a delay: *A real-time program in the flight simulator makes it respond immediately to the user's actions.*

/ˈriːəl taɪm/
Ⓜ a **real-time** operating system, program

---

real-time clock *noun* (hardware)
a BATTERY BACKED device in a PC that keeps a record of the date and time, rather than taking this information from a network

/ˌriːəl taɪm ˈklɒk/
pl real-time clocks
Ⓜ read, reset, set the **real-time clock**
syn internal clock   •
▶ **system clock**

☆**real-time processing** *noun*
(software/operations/system)
a method of running programs or computing data to obtain an immediate response: *Air-traffic control systems operate through real-time processing.*

/ˌriːəl taɪm ˈprəʊsesɪŋ/
note no plural
▶ **batch processing**

real-time system *noun*
a computer system that can receive and process data about an
event very quickly so that the output can affect the event
before it finishes: *Real-time systems are used in air-traffic control.*

/ˌriːəl taɪm ˈsɪstəm/
pl real-time systems

☆**reboot** *verb* (software)
to boot a computer again: *reboot the computer if it crashes* ○ *The
system would not reboot after the power failure.*

/ˌriːˈbuːt/
reboot, rebooting, rebooted

note transitive or intransitive
verb
◖ **reboot** the machine, system
▶ **boot, cold boot, warm boot**

---

receiver *noun* (hardware)
a device that accepts data from a transmission channel: *The
receiver the message was sent to was a fax machine.*

/rɪˈsiːvə(r)/
pl receivers
◖ a digital, radar, radio, satellite
receiver; receiver equipment,
hardware, software
▶ **transmission channel,
transmitter**

---

rechargeable battery *noun* (hardware)
a BATTERY that is able to be filled with electricity each time the
electricity it contains is used: *The portable computer runs on a
rechargeable battery.* ○ *The PC can run off a rechargeable battery.*

/riːˌtʃɑːdʒəbl ˈbætri/
pl rechargeable batteries
◖ fit, replace the **rechargeable
battery**; an additional, a high-
capacity, an optional, a spare
rechargeable battery

---

recompile *verb* (software)
to COMPILE **1** a program again, usually after changes have been
made to it

/ˌriːkəmˈpaɪl/
**recompile, recompiling,
recompiled**
note transitive verb

---

reconfigure *verb*
to CONFIGURE software and hardware again

/ˌriːkənˈfɪɡə(r)/
**reconfigure, reconfiguring,
reconfigured**
note transitive verb
◖ **reconfigure** a circuit board,
computer system, package,
printer, program

☆**record¹** *noun* (software)
a part of a data file that holds related data about one item

/ˈrekɔːd/
pl records
◖ access, print, update a **record**;
a **record** count, format, layout
syn data record
▶ **field, file**

☆**record²** *verb* (system operation)
to store data or information in permanent form on disk or
magnetic tape: *backup the computer records onto floppy disk*

/rɪˈkɔːd/
record, recording, recorded
note transitive verb
◖ **record** data *in* electronic form
▶ **save**

---

abbr abbreviation   **pl** plural   **syn** synonym   ▶ see   ◖ collocate (*word often used with the headword*)

record format *noun*
the particular way in which a record is structured

/'rekɔːd ˌfɔːmæt/
pl record formats
▶ **record**

---

record head *noun*
▶ **write head**

/rɪ'kɔːd hed/

---

recording density *noun* (hardware)
the number of bits of data that can be held in a certain area of a magnetic tape or disk

/rɪ'kɔːdɪŋ ˌdensəti/
pl recording densities

☆**recover** *verb*
1 (*systems operation*) to return to normal operation after a crash or fault: *The system recovered after the software problem had been solved.* **2** to find lost or damaged data: *Some of the files were recovered after the system crash.*

/rɪ'kʌvə(r)/
recover, recovering, recovered
1 note intransitive verb
2 note transitive verb

---

recoverable error *noun*
an error that occurs while a program is running but does not stop the program running: *Entering the wrong filename is a recoverable error because the system prompts the user to re-enter the correct filename.*

/rɪˌkʌvərəbl 'erə(r)/
pl recoverable errors

---

recovery *noun*
1 (*systems operation*) the process of returning to normal operation after an error or fault has occurred: *The recovery of the system was delayed because the virus had not been completely destroyed.* **2** the process of finding lost or damaged data: *Recovery of the files was difficult without the correct software.*

/rɪ'kʌvəri/
note not used with *a* or *an*. No plural and used with a singular verb only.

---

recursion *noun* (software)
the ability of a SUBROUTINE, function or procedure to CALL² (2) itself

/rɪ'kɜːʃn/
note not used with *a* or *an*. No plural and used with a singular verb only.
◄ allow, implement, permit **recursion**

---

recursive *adjective*
(of a subroutine, function or procedure) that is able to CALL² (2) itself

/rɪ'kɜːsɪv/
◄ a **recursive** call, program, routine

---

red-green-blue *noun*
a way of displaying colour images on screen. The image is in the form of three separate signals that are transferred to the screen and each signal controls the red, green and blue colours: *display an image in red-green-blue* ○ *save the image in red-green-blue format*

/ˌred griːn 'bluː/
note no plural
abbr RGB
◄ a **red-green-blue** beam, connection, monitor, signal

---

redirection *noun*
the process of sending a signal or message to its destination by using a route which is different from the one that would normally be used

/ˌriːdə'rekʃn/
note not used with *a* or *an*. No plural and used with a singular verb only.

☆**reduced instruction set computer** *noun*
▶ **RISC**

/rɪ'djuːst ɪnˌstrʌkʃn set kəm'pjuːtə(r)/

redundant code *noun* (software)

statements in a computer program that are never executed and which can be removed without changing the way the program operates: *Comment statements are redundant code but are worth retaining for documentation purposes.*

/rɪˌdʌndənt ˈkəʊd/

note not used with *a* or *an*. No plural and used with a singular verb only.

◄ delete, identify, remove **redundant code**

---

re-entrant *adjective*
► **relocatable**

/ri ˈentrənt/

---

re-entrant code *noun*
► **relocatable code**

/ri ˌentrənt ˈkəʊd/

---

re-entrant program *noun*
► **relocatable code**

/ri ˌentrənt ˈprəʊgræm/

---

re-entrant routine *noun*
► **relocatable routine**

/riː ˌentrənt ruːˈtiːn/

---

reference *noun*

1 a data item that contains information such as an address or an index which shows where another data item may be found: *a reference parameter* ○ *a reference address* 2 a fixed value that is compared with other values

/ˈrefərəns/

pl references

1 ◄ access, call *by*, give, follow a **reference**

2 ◄ a **reference** date, mark, value

---

reference file *noun*

a file that holds fixed data: *Names and addresses of employees are held in the reference file.*

/ˈrefərəns faɪl/

pl reference files

◄ access a **reference file**

► **master file**

---

reference manual *noun*
► **manual**

/ˈrefərəns ˌmænjuəl/

---

reformat *verb* (hardware)

to format a disk that has already been formatted: *reformat the floppy disk so it can be used again* ○ *If the disk is reformatted all the data it contains will be deleted.*

/ˌriː ˈfɔːmæt/

reformat, reformatting, reformatted

note transitive verb

► **format²**

☆**refresh** *verb* (hardware)

1 to constantly renew the data held in RAM so that it does not get lost 2 to constantly renew data displayed on screen so that it does not fade

/rɪˈfreʃ/

refresh, refreshing, refreshed

note transitive verb

1 ◄ **refresh** memory, RAM

syn RAM refresh, rewrite

2 ◄ **refresh** the display, screen

syn screen refresh

---

refresh rate *noun* (hardware)

the number of times each second that the computer renews information in memory or on screen: *The refresh rate of the screen is 60HZ, so the image is refreshed 60 times per second.*

/rɪˈfreʃ reɪt/

pl refresh rates

◄ decrease, increase the **refresh rate**

---

region fill *verb*
► **fill 2**

/ˈriːdʒən fɪl/

---

abbr abbreviation   **pl** plural   **syn** synonym   ► see   ◄ collocate (*word often used with the headword*)

☆**register** noun (hardware)
a small high-speed memory circuit in a microprocessor that holds binary data: *The register holds the address of a location in memory.*

/ˈredʒɪstə(r)/
pl registers
ᴍ hold bytes *in*, hold results *in* a **register**
▶ address register, general-purpose register

---

relational adjective
that has a connection or link with something

/rɪˈleɪʃənl/

---

relational database noun (applications)
a database in which information is stored in files that have a connection or link with one another: *construct a relational database to link inventories*

/rɪˌleɪʃənl ˈdeɪtəbeɪs/
pl relational databases
ᴍ access, create, search, set up, transfer data *into* a **relational database**

---

relational expression noun (software)
an expression in a computer programming language that uses comparisons such as 'less than' and 'greater than or equal to', etc with variables and constants. The value of a relational expression is either TRUE or FALSE: *the relational expression AGE <65*

/rɪˌleɪʃənl ɪkˈspreʃn/
pl relational expressions
ᴍ evaluate, program, write a **relational expression**

---

relational operator noun
a symbol in a statement, etc that is processed by a computer and allows two or more values to be compared: *The relational operator '=' shows the relation 'equal to'.*

/rɪˌleɪʃənl ˈɒpəreɪtə(r)/
pl relational operators
▶ operator

---

relative address noun
an ADDRESS[1] that is defined in relation to a reference address

/ˌrelətɪv əˈdres/
pl relative addresses
▶ absolute address

---

relative addressing noun
a way of addressing memory in which the address contained in the instruction code is added to the BASE ADDRESS to obtain the ABSOLUTE ADDRESS: *The task of the compiler is simplified by using relative addressing.*

/ˌrelətɪv əˈdresɪŋ/
note not used with *a* or *an*. No plural and used with a singular verb only.
ᴍ allow, employ, make use *of* **relative addressing**
syn base addressing
▶ relocatable code

---

relative coordinates noun
information about position that is given in relation to a particular reference point: *The pixels on the display screen have relative coordinates based on the upper left corner of the screen.*

/ˌrelətɪv kəʊˈɔːdɪnəts/
note plural noun used with a plural verb

---

relay[1] noun (hardware)
a switch controlled by an electrical signal: *Relays can be used to control mains voltages.*

/ˈriːleɪ/
pl relays
ᴍ operate, switch a **relay**

---

relay[2] verb
to pass data or signals from one place to another: *Data is relayed from node to node around the network.* ○ *The satellite can relay 300 million bits of information.*

/ˈriːleɪ/
relay, relaying, relayed
note transitive verb
ᴍ relay data, electronic mail

---

release[1] noun
a new version of a product, especially software: *The latest release of the spreadsheet package is version 2.2.*

/rɪˈliːs/
pl releases
ᴍ the latest, new, recent **release**

release² *verb*

1 to make a new version of a product available to buy: *The new application will be released in the autumn.* 2 to stop using a resource so that it can be used by other users or processes: *Closing an application releases enough memory to allow a different application to run.*

/rɪˈliːs/

release, releasing, released

note transitive verb

1 ⋈ **release** a CD, game, program, word processing package
▶ **ship**

2 ⋈ **release** memory, peripherals, resources

reliability *noun*

the ability of a piece of equipment to work well without breaking down: *The new computer has a good reputation for reliability.*

/rɪˌlaɪəˈbɪləti/

note no plural

⋈ good, poor **reliability**; a **reliability** record, test

reload *verb* (hardware/software)

to load again: *The operating system reloaded after the warm boot.* ○ *Reload the program if it doesn't work the first time it is loaded.*

/ˌriːˈləʊd/

reload, reloading, reloaded

note transitive or intransitive verb

⋈ **reload** a disk, program; **reload** information, software
▶ **load**

relocatable *adjective*

(of a computer program) that can be moved to another area of memory and still execute correctly

/ˌriːləʊˈkeɪtəbl/

⋈ a **relocatable** function, procedure, subroutine

syn re-entrant

relocatable code *noun* (software)

code that can be loaded into any part of the memory and then executed by the computer

/ˈriːləʊˌkeɪtəbl ˈkəʊd/

note not used with *a* or *an*. No plural and used with a singular verb only.

⋈ program, write **relocatable code**

syn relocatable program, re-entrant code, re-entrant program
▶ **relative addressing**

relocatable program *noun*
▶ **relocatable code**

/ˈriːləʊˌkeɪtəbl ˈprəʊɡræm/

relocatable routine *noun*

a ROUTINE that will execute in any part of memory that it is loaded into

/ˈriːləʊˌkeɪtəbl ruːˈtiːn/

pl relocatable routines

⋈ program, write a **relocatable routine**

syn re-entrant routine

relocation *noun*

the act of changing address references in a computer program so the program will execute when loaded into a different area of memory

/ˌriːləʊˈkeɪʃn/

note usually singular

⋈ permanent, temporary **relocation**

remote *adjective*

(of a computer or system, etc) that is in another place in the building, country or world and can be accessed through a communications link: *access remote databases and e-mail facilities* ○ *remote login services*

/rɪˈməʊt/

⋈ a **remote** database, machine, node, server, terminal
▶ **local**

---

abbr abbreviation   **pl** plural   **syn** synonym   ▶ see   ⋈ collocate (*word often used with the headword*)

remote access *noun*

the use of a computer system that is in another place in the building, country or world, usually by using a terminal and communications links, such as telephone lines: *use a modem for remote access to the office computer network* ○ *All the data is stored on computer in New York with remote access from Hong Kong and London.*

/rɪ,məʊt 'ækses/

note not used with *a* or *an*. No plural and used with a singular verb only.

ᛝ **remote access** capability

remote device *noun* (hardware)

a device such as a printer that is not close to the computer system it is connected to

/rɪ,məʊt dɪ'vaɪs/

pl remote devices

remote job entry *noun*

a method of BATCH PROCESSING in which instructions are sent to a central computer from a terminal that is not close to the central computer

/rɪ,məʊt 'dʒɒb ,entri/

pl remote job entries

abbr RJE

remote terminal *noun* (hardware)

a computer terminal that is able to access a computer system or server that it is not close to: *The remote terminal uses a modem to communicate with the system it is connected to.*

/rɪ,məʊt 'tɜːmɪnl/

pl remote terminals

ᛝ access, connect *to* a **remote terminal**

removable *adjective*

(of a device, etc) that can be taken out or removed: *a removable floppy disk* ○ *The outer casing of the printer is removable so it can be easily repaired.*

/rɪ'muːvəbl/

ᛝ a **removable** component, hard disk

removable disk *noun* (hardware)

a disk that can be taken out of a computer

/rɪ,muːvəbl 'dɪsk/

pl removable disks

rendering *noun* (software/graphics)

a way of making an image that is created by a graphics program look real: *Rendering shows how an object reflects light.*

/'rendərɪŋ/

note not used with *a* or *an*. No plural and used with a singular verb only.

repaginate *verb*

to insert page breaks into a document again, usually because the document has been changed: *A number of amendments have been made to the contract so it will have to be repaginated.* ○ *This word-processing package allows documents to be automatically repaginated.*

/,riː'pædʒɪneɪt/

repaginate, repaginating, repaginated

note transitive verb

ᛝ **repaginate** a document, file

repeat *verb*

to do something more than once: *repeat the data transmission* ○ *Holding down the key makes the character repeat.*

/rɪ'piːt/

repeat, repeating, repeated

note transitive or intransitive verb

ᛝ **repeat** an action, a loop, a procedure

repeat counter *noun*

a variable that stores the number of times a DO LOOP has been executed: *When the repeat counter reaches 100, the loop terminates.*

/rɪ'piːt ,kaʊntə(r)/

pl repeat counters

ᛝ initialize, update the **repeat counter**

▶ **loop variable**

repeater *noun* (hardware)
a device that is used in a network to increase the strength of the messages passed between the computers: *use repeaters if a network has to be extended to incorporate more terminals*

/rɪ'piːtə(r)/
pl repeaters
◄ amplify a signal *with*, transmit a signal *through* a **repeater**
► **network**

repeat key *noun* (hardware)
a key on a computer keyboard that must be held down at the same time as another key to continue to enter the same character

/rɪ'piːt kiː/
pl repeat keys
◄ hold *down*, press, strike a **repeat key**

repeat loop *noun*
► **repeat until loop**

/rɪ'piːt luːp/

repeat until loop *noun* (software)
a block of statements in a computer programming language that is executed again and again until a TEST[1] **(2)** at the end of the block shows that the rest of the program can be executed: *A repeat until loop is always executed at least once.*

/rɪ,piːt ən'tɪl luːp/
pl repeat until loops
◄ execute, perform, repeat a **repeat until loop**
syn repeat loop
► **loop[1] 2**

replace string *noun* (applications)
a group of characters in a certain order that replaces another group of characters in a SEARCH AND REPLACE operation

/rɪ'pleɪs strɪŋ/
pl replace strings
◄ alter, define a **replace string**
► **search string, string**

report generator *noun* (applications)
a program that produces the results of a database search in a way that is easy to read. Report generators are often designed so that they can be used by people without programming skills.

/rɪ'pɔːt ,dʒenəreɪtə(r)/
pl report generators
◄ an automatic, a database, an interactive **report generator**

reprogram *verb* (software/programming)
to program again, usually by changing the instructions controlling a computer, etc so that it operates in a different way: *reprogram the computer's operating system*

/,riː'prəʊɡræm/
reprogram, reprogramming, reprogrammed
note transitive verb
◄ **reprogram** a computer, printer
► **program[2]**

request to send signal *noun*
a signal which is sent by a transmitting device to a receiving device to ask if the receiving device is ready to accept a data transmission: *Before the computer sends data to be printed, it first sends a request to send signal to check if the printer is ready to receive the data.*

/rɪ,kwest tə 'send ,sɪɡnəl/
pl request to send signals
abbr RTS
◄ receive, send, transmit a **request to send signal**

requirements specification *noun*
a part of the process of systems analysis and design in which the tasks that a new system will perform are listed, together with the time, memory and other RESOURCES that will be needed: *The problems of the system were assessed and a requirements specification was produced for a more effective system.* ○ *The requirements specification gives guidelines for tailoring a system to a client's requirements.* ○ *functions described in a requirements specification*

/rɪ'kwaɪəmənts ,spesɪfɪ,keɪʃn/
note usually singular
◄ consult *over*, develop, prepare, produce a **requirements specification**
► **acceptance testing**

rerun¹ *noun*

any execution of a computer program after the first execution: *There was a rerun of the program with new data.* ○ *The rerun gave different results from the first execution of the program.*

/'ri:rʌn/
pl reruns

---

rerun² *verb*

to execute a program again: *rerun the payroll program with new data*

/ˌri:'rʌn/
rerun, rerunning, reran, rerun

note transitive verb

---

res *abbr*
▶ **resolution**

/rez/

---

research and development *noun*

the process of developing and testing new products: *invest in research and development*

/rɪˌsɜːtʃ ənd dɪ'veləpmənt/

note not used with *a* or *an*. No plural and used with a singular verb only.

abbr R and D, R & D

◄ **research and development** expenditure, personnel

---

reserved *adjective*

kept for a specific use: *This block of memory is reserved for the operating system.*

/rɪ'zɜːvd/

---

reserved word *noun* (software/programming)

a natural language word that has a special meaning in a computer programming language and so cannot be chosen by a programmer as the name for a variable: *A reserved word in BASIC is 'input'.*

/rɪˌzɜːvd 'wɜːd/
pl reserved words

◄ avoid, use a **reserved word**

☆**reset** *verb*

to make a computer ready to use again, usually after an error: *The computer had to be reset after the screen froze.*

/'ri:set/
resets, resetting, reset

note transitive verb
▶ **reboot**

---

reset button *noun* (hardware)

a button on a computer that makes a program stop running so that it can start again from the beginning: *If the computer crashes, try pressing the reset button.* ○ *Press the reset button if the program gets into an infinite loop.*

/'ri:set ˌbʌtn/
pl reset buttons

◄ hit, press, strike the **reset button**

---

resident font *noun*

a font that is programmed permanently into a printer: *The resident font is stored in ROM.*

/ˌrezɪdənt 'fɒnt/
pl resident fonts

---

resident program *noun* (software)

a computer program that remains in memory when other programs are being executed so that it can quickly be executed without the delay of loading it from disk or BACKING STORE: *A PC operating system is a resident program whenever the computer is switched on.*

/ˌrezɪdənt 'prəʊgræm/
pl resident programs

◄ delete, execute, load, remove a **resident program**

▶ **terminate and stay resident program**

☆**resolution** *noun*
a measure of the quality of an image on screen or an image printed on paper: *a screen with a resolution of 640 by 480 pixels* ○ *a printer with a resolution of 406 dots per inch*

/ˌrezə'luːʃn/
pl resolutions
abbr res
▶ **high resolution, low resolution**

---

resource *noun* (hardware/software)
any part of a computer system that is used by a program while the program is running: *System resources include disk drives, printers, workstations and memory.*

/rɪ'sɔːs/
pl resources
◪ allocate, divide, share a **resource**

---

resource allocation *noun*
the process of dividing a computer system's resources between different programs: *The operating system is responsible for resource allocation between competing programs.*

/rɪ'sɔːs æləˌkeɪʃn/
note not used with *a* or *an*. No plural and used with a singular verb only.
◪ efficient, inefficient **resource allocation**

---

response time *noun*
the amount of time a computer takes to react to an action or request: *The response time between striking a key and seeing the information on screen is less than one second.*

/rɪ'spɒns taɪm/
pl response times
◪ an excellent, a fast, a slow **response time**

---

restart *verb*
to start again, especially to start a computer after it has crashed: *The program had to be restarted because of an error.*

/ˌriː'stɑːt/
restart, restarting, restarted
note transitive verb
◪ **restart** a computer, printer, program

---

restore *verb*
to return something to its original state: *restore the deleted documents so they can be accessed*

/rɪ'stɔː(r)/
restore, restoring, restored
note transitive verb
◪ **restore** a directory, document, file

---

retrieval *noun*
the process of searching for and obtaining data from a computer system

/rɪ'triːvl/
note not used with a *a* or *an*. No plural and used with a singular verb only.
◪ document, file, information **retrieval**

☆**retrieve** *verb* (system operation)
to obtain data or information from a computer system or database, etc

/rɪ'triːv/
retrieve, retrieving, retrieved
note transitive verb
◪ **retrieve** data, information
▶ **recover**

☆**return¹** *noun*
1 (*hardware*) a name for the return key which is used to put the cursor in a different place, such as the beginning of a new line: *press return to start a new paragraph* ○ *use return to move to the next command* **2** (*software/programming*) a statement in a program that marks the end of a SUBROUTINE (= an ordered group of programming language statements): *This program has more than one return statement.*

/rɪ'tɜːn/
1 note usually singular
▶ **enter¹, space bar**
2 pl returns

---

abbr abbreviation   **pl** plural   **syn** synonym   ▶ see   ◪ collocate (*word often used with the headword*)

☆**return²** *verb* (user operation)
to move the cursor to a different place, usually the beginning of a new line: *Type the name and then return to type the address on the next line.*

/rɪˈtɜːn/
return, returning, returned
note intransitive verb
► **newline character**

---

return address *noun* (software/programming)
the address of the machine code instruction that will be the next to be executed after a SUBROUTINE or function is called: *The return address is stored on a stack.*

/rɪˈtɜːn əˌdres/
pl return addresses
ᴎ access, retrieve, store the **return address**
► **call, parameter passing**

☆**return key** *noun*
► **return¹ 1**

/rɪˈtɜːn ˌkiː/

---

return to zero *noun*
a way of sending binary data (bits) as positive or negative VOLTAGES with the signal returning to zero VOLTS after each bit has been sent

/rɪˌtɜːn tə ˈzɪərəʊ/
note singular noun, used with a singular verb
abbr RTZ
ᴎ a **return to zero** protocol, system
► **non return to zero**

---

reverse Polish notation *noun*
a POSTFIX NOTATION for mathematical and logical operations in which the operator is written after the OPERANDS: *In reverse Polish notation, the operation of adding 2 to 3 is written '2 3 +'.*

/rɪˈvɜːs ˈpəʊlɪʃ nəʊˈteɪʃn/
note not used with *a* or *an*. No plural and used with a singular verb only.
abbr RPN
ᴎ use, write *in* **reverse Polish notation**
► **Polish notation**

---

reverse video *noun*
► **inverse video**

/rɪˌvɜːs ˈvɪdiəʊ /

---

rewind *verb* (operations)
to make a tape or film, etc go backwards towards the beginning: *The video rewinds automatically when it reaches the end of the tape.* ○ *rewind the film before taking it out of the camera*

/ˌriːˈwaɪnd/
rewind, rewinding, rewound
note transitive or intransitive verb
ᴎ **rewind** a film, magnetic tape

---

rewrite *verb*
► **refresh 1**

/ˌriːˈraɪt/

RGB *abbr*
► **red-green-blue**

/ˌɑː dʒiː ˈbiː/
note pronounced as individual letters

RGB monitor *noun* (hardware)
a monitor that can receive information relating to colour as three separate signals of red, green and blue

/ˈɑː dʒiː ˌbiː ˌmɒnɪtə(r)/
pl RGB monitors

ribbon cable *noun* (hardware) a flat cable found inside computers or computer equipment that is made of small wires that are next to each other. A ribbon cable is usually used to connect the computer's disk drives to the computer system.	/ˈrɪbən ˌkeɪbl/ **pl** ribbon cables
Rich Text Format *noun* (*trade mark*) a standard for sending documents between computers **note** RTF works by coding the font and layout, etc of a document as ordinary text. Text can be transmitted successfully across networks without special software. This means that the document will look the same when it has reached the place it was sent to, even if it is sent from one type of computer to another.	/ˌrɪtʃ ˈtekst ˌfɔːmæt/ **note** no plural **abbr** RTF
right arrow *noun* (hardware) the CURSOR CONTROL KEY with an arrow pointing to the right: *hit the right arrow to move the cursor to the right*	/ˌraɪt ˈærəʊ/ **pl** right arrows ◄ hold *down*, press the **right arrow** ► **down arrow, left arrow, up arrow**
right justify *verb* to arrange text, etc on screen or on paper so that the right side of the text is parallel with the edge of the paper or screen	/ˌraɪt ˈdʒʌstɪfaɪ/ **right justify, right justifying, right justified** **note** transitive verb ◄ **right justify** a document; **right justify** text ► **justify, left justify**
ring network *noun* (hardware/networks) a network where the NODES (**2**) (= computers) are linked in a circle, with each node communicating with two neighbours. Messages may pass through several nodes before they reach their destination: *The topology is a ring network.*	/ˈrɪŋ ˌnetwɜːk/ **pl** ring networks ◄ configure a network *as*, use a **ring network** ► **bus network, network, network topology, star network, tree network**
ripple through carry *noun* ► **cascade carry**	/ˌrɪpl θruː ˈkæri/
☆**RISC** *abbr* (hardware) a reduced instruction set computer. A computer designed to use a microprocessor with a small INSTRUCTION SET to make processing time fast: *a single-chip RISC microprocessor*	/rɪsk/ **abbr** Risc, risc ◄ a **RISC** application, chip, platform, processor, system; **RISC** architecture ► **CISC**
RJE *abbr* ► **remote job entry**	/ˌɑː dʒeɪ ˈiː/ **note** pronounced as individual letters
robot *noun* (hardware) an electronic or mechanical device that is designed to do work, usually in industry: *The car factory uses robots at certain stages of the manufacturing process.*	/ˈrəʊbɒt/ **pl** robots ◄ build, construct, engineer, invent, program a **robot**; a computerized, an intelligent **robot**

abbr abbreviation   **pl** plural   **syn** synonym   ► see   ◄ collocate (*word often used with the headword*)

robotics *noun* (science)
the theory and practice of how robots can be developed to do
different types of work

/rəʊˈbɒtɪks/

note not used with *a* or *an*. No
plural and used with singular
verb only.

◄ study, work *in* the field of
robotics

robust *adjective*
(of hardware or software) that works well and is not easily
damaged

/rəʊˈbʌst/

◄ a **robust** construction, hard
disk, program, system

rogue value *noun*
▶ **terminator 1**

/ˌrəʊg ˈvæljuː/

rollback *noun*
a return to the condition that existed before an error occurred
in a computer system: *The system includes a rollback recovery
feature.*

/ˈrəʊlbæk/

note no plural

roll in *verb*
to transfer data from the BACKING STORE (= a separate memory
with a record of the data in main memory) to the main
memory

/ˈrəʊl ɪn/

roll in, rolling in, rolled in

note transitive verb

roll out *verb*
1 to transfer information from the main memory to the
BACKING STORE (= a separate memory which holds a record of
the data in main memory) **2** to make a new application, etc
available to computer users in a company or organization: *The
information technology department will roll out upgraded e-mail
software to all PC users by the end of the month.*

/ˈrəʊl aʊt/

**roll out, rolling out, rolled
out**

note transitive verb

☆**ROM** *abbr* (hardware)
read only memory. A part of memory that contains permanent
instructions or data which the computer can access but
cannot change: *This type of computer has a 32-bit ROM already
installed.*

/rɒm/

◄ a **ROM** chip

▶ **memory, programmable
read-only memory, RAM**

Roman number *noun*
▶ **Roman numeral**

/ˌrəʊmən ˈnʌmbə(r)/

Roman numeral *noun*
one of the figures 'I, V, X, L, C, D, M' used in writing numbers,
usually in official documents and copyright statements

/ˌrəʊmən ˈnjuːmərəl/

pl Roman numerals

◄ express something *in*, write
something *in* **Roman
numerals**

syn Roman number

▶ **Arabic numeral**

ROM cartridge *noun* (hardware)
software in ROM chips on a printed circuit board which is put
into a container called a cartridge that can be plugged into a
computer or system: *plug the ROM cartridge into the video game
system*

/ˈrɒm ˌkɑːtrɪdʒ/

pl ROM cartridges

root *noun*
the one data item in a tree that has only DESCENDANTS, and is
not the descendant of any other item

/ruːt/
pl roots
⋈ access, update the **root**
▶ data structure, tree

---

root directory *noun*
the main directory from which other directories, subdirectories
and files can be accessed: *The root directory 'A:Ø' contains the
directory 'business data'.* ○ *select the root directory of drive D*

/ˈruːt dəˌrektəri/
pl root directories

ROT *abbr*
▶ rotate operation

/rɒt/
note pronounced as a word

---

rotate operation *noun*
an operation in which the individual bits of a data item are
moved (shifted) left or right. The bits which are moved out of
one end of the storage location are moved in at the other end:
*Performing a rotate operation on the pattern 1000101 gives
0001011.*

/ˌrəʊˌteɪt ɒpəˈreɪʃn/
pl rotate operations
abbr ROT
⋈ carry out, perform, program a
rotate operation; a **rotate
operation** *by* two places
syn circular shift, cyclic shift,
rotation
▶ arithmetic shift, logical shift

---

rotation *noun*
▶ rotate operation

/rəʊˈteɪʃn/

---

rotational delay *noun*
the time between a request for data from a disk and the
moment when the data is underneath the READ HEAD (= the
part of the drive that reads data from a disk and transfers it to
the computer) and can be accessed: *a fast disk with a small
average rotational delay*

/rəʊˌteɪʃənl dɪˈleɪ/
pl rotational delays

---

round *verb* (mathematics)
to represent a number by one of less PRECISION: *3.14159
rounded to two decimal places is 3.14* ○ *3.14159 rounded to three
decimal places is 3.142*

/raʊnd/
round, rounding, rounded
note transitive verb
⋈ round a number *down/up*
syn round off
▶ truncate

---

round brackets *noun*
a pair of symbols represented as '()'

/ˌraʊnd ˈbrækɪts/
note plural noun
⋈ delete, enclose something *in*,
insert **round brackets**
▶ brackets

---

rounding error *noun* (mathematics)
an error that occurs when numbers which have been ROUNDED
are used in calculations

/ˈraʊndɪŋ ˌerə(r)/
pl rounding errors
syn round off error

---

round off *verb*
▶ round

/ˌraʊnd ˈɒf/

---

round off error *noun*
▶ rounding error

/ˈraʊnd ɒf ˌerə(r)/

---

abbr abbreviation   **pl** plural   **syn** synonym   **▶** see   **⋈** collocate (*word often used with the headword*)

round robin *noun*

/ˌraʊnd ˈrɒbɪn/

pl round robins

an ALGORITHM that controls the amount of time that is given to each process in a MULTI-USER SYSTEM

note A round robin algorithm treats each user in the same way. It gives them a fixed amount of time to work on the system in a certain order.

---

routine *noun* (software/programming)

/ruːˈtiːn/

pl routines

a set of programming language statements that is not a complete program but which performs a particular job when it is part of a complete program: *A well-designed program is broken up into separate routines.* ○ *modify code in the routine*

⋈ call, input *to* a **routine**

syn procedure, subprogram

note 'Routine' is often used as a general term for 'function', 'procedure' or 'subroutine'.

---

routine call *noun*

/ruːˈtiːn kɔːl/

▶ **procedure call**

---

row *noun*

/rəʊ/

pl rows

a horizontal line consisting of a series of items that are placed next to each other: *a row of figures*

▶ **column, line**

RPN *abbr*

/ˌɑː piː ˈen/

▶ **reverse Polish notation**

note pronounced as individual letters

RS-232C *noun*

/ˈɑːr es ˈtuː ˈθriː ˈtuː ˈsiː/

note no plural

a common standard interface used by most modems for SERIAL COMMUNICATION (= the transmission of one bit of data following another in order): *Many personal computers have an RS-232C connection.* ○ *connect a device via an RS-232C interface*

⋈ an **RS-232C** connection, interface, port

▶ **RS-422, RS-423**

RS-422 *noun*

/ˈɑːr es ˈfɔː tuː ˈtuː/

note no plural

an improved form of the RS-232C standard interface which allows higher transmission rates

⋈ an **RS-422** connection, interface, port

RS-423 *noun*

/ˈɑːr es ˈfɔː tuː ˈθriː/

note no plural

an improved form of the RS-232C standard interface which allows higher transmission rates

⋈ an **RS-423** connection, interface, port

RTF *abbr*

/ˌɑː tiː ˈef/

▶ **Rich Text Format**

note pronounced as individual letters

☆**RTN** *abbr*

▶ **return¹ 1**

note used in written English only

RTS *abbr*

/ˌɑː tiː ˈes/

▶ **request to send signal**

note pronounced as individual letters

RTZ *abbr*

/ˌɑː tiː ˈzed/

▶ **return to zero**

note pronounced as individual letters

rubber banding *noun* ▶ **elastic banding**	/ˌrʌbə ˈbændɪŋ/
rule-based system *noun* a type of EXPERT SYSTEM which uses rules that are stored as part of a KNOWLEDGE BASE	/ˌruːl beɪst ˈsɪstəm/ **pl** rule-based systems ⵂ build, feed data *into*, use, write a **rule-based system**; a diagnostic **rule-based system**
☆**run¹** *noun* (software/system operation) one complete execution of a program	/rʌn/ **pl** runs **syn** program run ▶ **job, task**
☆**run²** *verb* (system operation) to execute a program: *The program was set to run overnight.* ○ *run the error analysis program*	/rʌn/ **run, running, ran, run** **note** transitive or intransitive verb ⵂ **run** a job, program
run around *verb* to fit text around an image when designing a page with word processing and graphics software: *The text of the story has been run around the photograph.*	/ˌrʌn əˈraʊnd/ **run around, running around, ran around, run around** **note** transitive verb
running head *noun* ▶ **header 2**	/ˌrʌnɪŋ ˈhed/
run time *noun* **1** the period of time during which a program is executing: *The run time was scheduled for late evening.* **2** the time a program takes to execute: *The run time was only a few milliseconds.*	/ˈrʌn taɪm/ **pl** run times **1** ⵂ schedule the **run time** **2** ⵂ note, record the **run time**
run-time error *noun* an error that is made when a program is running	/ˈrʌn taɪm ˌerə(r)/ **pl** run-time errors ⵂ detect a **run-time error**
run-time library *noun* (software) software that is present in memory when a particular program is executing, so that the program can CALL² (2), ROUTINES in this software: *The run-time library includes sorting routines.*	/ˌrʌn taɪm ˈlaɪbrəri/ **pl** run-time libraries ⵂ load the **run-time library** ▶ **library, library program, library routine**
run-time system *noun* software and operating system ROUTINES that must be present in memory before a particular program can execute: *The run-time system does not occupy much memory.*	/ˈrʌn taɪm ˌsɪstəm/ **pl** run-time systems ⵂ load the **run-time system**
R/W *abbr* read/write	**note** used in written English only

abbr abbreviation　　**pl** plural　　**syn** synonym　　▶ see　　ⵂ collocate (*word often used with the headword*)

sampling rate *noun*
the speed at which data can be read from an external device or SENSOR: *a sampling rate of up to 22KHz*

/ˈsɑːmplɪŋ reɪt/
pl sampling rates
⋈ a high, low **sampling rate**

---

satellite computer *noun* (hardware)
a small computer that is linked to a larger one: *The satellite computer works under the control of the mainframe.*

/ˈsætəlaɪt kəmˌpjuːtə(r)/
pl satellite computers

---

saturation *noun*
a part of a television signal that carries information about the amount of colour in a picture

/ˌsætʃəˈreɪʃn/
note not used with *a* or *an*. No plural and used with a singular verb only.
⋈ high, low **saturation**
▶ **hue**

☆**save** *verb* (user operation/system operation)
to store data or information on disk or magnetic tape: *The word processing software can be set to prompt the user to save data every 5 minutes.* ○ *save the data to disk*

/seɪv/
save, saving, saved
note transitive verb
▶ **storage, record²**

SBC *abbr*
▶ **single board computer**

/ˌes biː ˈsiː/
note pronounced as individual letters

---

scalar *noun*
a variable that holds one value: *a scalar multiplier*

/ˈskeɪlə(r)/
pl scalars
syn scalar variable

---

scalar processor *noun*
a processor that calculates scalar values at high speeds: *The supercomputer contains a scalar processor.* ○ *The system can be configured with up to eight scalar processors.*

/ˌskeɪlə ˈprəʊsesə(r)/
pl scalar processors

---

scalar variable *noun*
▶ **scalar**

/ˌskeɪlə ˈveəriəbl/

---

scale¹ *noun*
a graded system that is used for measuring something: *The graphics package allows images to be drawn to scale to give a realistic view of their actual size.* ○ *The scale on the axes of the graph is 1cm to 500m.*

/skeɪl/
pl scales

---

scale² *verb*
to change the size of something: *Bitmaps scale badly as enlargement breaks up a pattern and compression makes the details impossible to see.* ○ *scale up the picture so it covers the whole screen* ○ *scale down the text so it occupies less space on the page*

/skeɪl/
scale, scaling, scaled
note transitive or intransitive verb
⋈ **scale** something *down/up*, a drawing, picture, plan

---

scan *verb*
1 to transfer images and text, etc to a computer by moving a device called a scanner over the images and text: *scan the text into the computer* **2** to move light or electricity across the PHOSPHORUS inside a screen to produce an image: *The electron beam scans the inside of the screen a line at a time.*

/skæn/
scan, scanning, scanned
note transitive verb
1 ⋈ **scan** a document, picture

scan line *noun*
one of the horizontal lines that is part of an image on screen:
There are 625 scan lines on a UK TV screen and 525 in the USA.

/ˈskæn laɪn/
pl scan lines
◄ draw a **scan line**

☆**scanner** *noun* (hardware)
an electronic device that is moved over a document so the
contents of the document can be transferred to a computer:
The scanner captures the image as a bitmap. ○ *The add-on scanner
enables users to read printed information into their systems very
quickly.*

/ˈskænə(r)/
pl scanners
◄ a laser **scanner**
syn image scanner
► **bar code reader, optical
scanner**

scan rate *noun*
the number of times per second the image on screen is
renewed: *a scan rate of 50 frames per second*

/ˈskæn reɪt/
pl scan rates
◄ adjust, synchronize the **scan
rate**
► **refresh**

scheduler *noun*
► **scheduling algorithm**

/ˈʃedjuːlə(r)/

scheduling algorithm *noun* (software)
the part of the systems software in a TIME-SHARING SYSTEM that
decides which program will execute next: *The scheduling
algorithm allocated an amount of time for each program to execute.*

/ˈʃedjuːlɪŋ ˌælɡərɪðəm/
pl scheduling algorithms
syn scheduler

schema *noun*
a diagram or chart that shows the layout of types of data in a
database and the links between them: *Drawing up a schema is
an early step in database design.*

/ˈskiːmə/
pl schemas
pl schemata
◄ compile, draw *up* a **schema**
► **logical schema, physical
schema, subschema**

scope *noun* (software/programming)
the parts of a computer program in which a particular variable
may be accessed; this can be the whole program or only
smaller parts of it: *The scope of the variable is local to the print
subroutine.*

/skəʊp/
note not used with *a* or *an*. No
plural and used with a singular
verb only.
◄ contradict, define **scope**;
global, local **scope**
► **local scope, local variable,
global scope, global variable**

SCR *abbr*
► **sequence control register**

/ˌes siː ˈɑː/
note pronounced as individual
letters

scramble *verb*
to change the order of data while it is being transmitted so that
it cannot be understood. When the data reaches the correct
place, it is put into the correct order so that it can be
understood: *a set of chips that scramble and decode a satellite
signal* ○ *The program scrambles secret transmissions for extra
security.*

/ˈskræmbl/
**scramble, scrambling,
scrambled**
note transitive verb

scrapbook *noun* (software)
software available on some systems that allows a user to keep
permanent copies of useful items such as pieces of text or
graphics from different applications: *A template for a memo is in
the scrapbook.*

/ˈskræpbʊk/
pl scrapbooks
◄ copy something *from/to*, paste
something *from/to* a
scrapbook

---

abbr abbreviation   **pl** plural   **syn** synonym   ► see   ◄ collocate (*word often used with the headword*)

scratch[1] *adjective*
(of memory) that is used for holding temporary results while a program is being executed

/skrætʃ/

---

scratch[2] *verb*
to delete, remove or erase: *scratch the data file*

/skrætʃ/
scratch, scratching, scratched

note transitive verb

---

scratch file *noun*
▶ **temporary file**

/'skrætʃ faɪl/

---

scratchpad *noun*
▶ **temporary file**

/'skrætʃpæd/

---

scratch tape *noun* (hardware)
a magnetic tape that is used to hold TEMPORARY FILES

/'skrætʃ teɪp/
pl scratch tapes

◪ overwrite, recycle the **scratch tape**

☆**screen** *noun* (hardware)
a device with a surface made of clear glass or plastic that is attached to a computer and displays text and graphics, etc: *several windows were open on the screen*

/skriːn/
pl screens

◪ a colour, high-resolution, low-resolution, monochrome **screen**

▶ **liquid crystal display, monitor, VDU**

---

screen buffer *noun*
an area of memory that holds the contents of the screen display

/'skriːn ˌbʌfə(r)/
pl screen buffers

◪ access, read data *from*, update, write data *to* the **screen buffer**

---

screen dump *noun*
text or images on a computer screen that have been saved to a file: *The screen dump can be printed and included in publicity material for the software.*

/'skriːn dʌmp/
pl screen dumps

◪ edit, print, view the **screen dump**

---

screen editor *noun* (software)
software that allows a user to change data displayed on the screen; changes made to the data on screen will also be made to the permanent stored copy of the data: *use a screen editor to make changes to the file*

/'skriːn ˌedɪtə(r)/
pl screen editors

---

screen grabber *noun* (software)
software that will take a copy of the screen as a graphic so that it can be printed out or inserted into a document

/'skriːn ˌgræbə(r)/
pl screen grabbers

▶ **video digitizer**

---

screen layout *noun*
▶ **layout**

/'skriːn ˌleɪaʊt/

---

screen refresh *noun*
▶ **refresh**

/'skriːn rɪˌfreʃ/

☆**scroll** *verb*

to move up and down through text, etc displayed on a screen: *scroll up or down the text line by line or page by page*

/skrəʊl/

scroll, scrolling, scrolled

note transitive verb

▶ **horizontal scrolling, page down, page up, vertical scrolling**

---

scroll bar *noun*

a dark border, usually around two sides of a window in a graphical user interface, that allows the user to move around a document: *click in the scroll bar to move a page at a time* ○ *click on the arrow at the end of the scroll bar to move a line at a time* ○ *drag the box along the scroll bar to move to another part of the window*

/ˈskrəʊl bɑ:(r)/

pl scroll bars

ℍ a horizontal, vertical **scroll bar**

SCSI *abbr*

small computer system interface

/ˈskʌzi/

note pronounced as a word

SD *abbr*

▶ **single density disk**

/ˌes ˈdi:/

note pronounced as individual letters

SDLC *abbr*

▶ **synchronous data link control**

note used in written English only

☆**search**[1] *noun*

the act of looking for data in a computer system: *the search yielded no results*

/sɜ:tʃ/

pl searches

ℍ a case sensitive, a case insensitive, a string, a successful, an unsuccessful **search**

☆**search**[2] *verb* (system operation)

to look for data in a computer system: *The spellcheck facility loads dictionaries and searches for spelling mistakes in text.* ○ *search for a specified string in a document*

/sɜ:tʃ/

search, searching, searched

note transitive verb

ℍ **search** the database, spreadsheet

▶ **retrieve**

---

search and replace *noun* (software/system operation)

an operation in most applications, especially word processing packages, that searches text for a string of characters which is deleted and replaced by another string: *use the search and replace function to replace the word 'secretary' with 'administrator'*

/ˌsɜ:tʃ ənd rɪˈpleɪs/

note not used with *a* or *an*. No plural and used with a singular verb only.

ℍ a **search and replace** function, operation, option, tool

▶ **replace string, search string**

---

search key *noun*

a value of a field in a record that is used when searching a database or spreadsheet, etc to access the complete record: *The search key 'January' can be used by the database to access full records of transactions processed in January.*

/ˈsɜ:tʃ ki:/

pl search keys

ℍ look up, match, use a **search key**

▶ **index**

---

search path *noun*

the group of directories and subdirectories that are examined in a certain order so that a file can be found

/ˈsɜ:tʃ pɑ:θ/

pl search paths

ℍ examine, follow the **search path**

---

abbr abbreviation   **pl** plural   **syn** synonym   ▶ see   ℍ collocate (*word often used with the headword*)

search string *noun* (applications)
a group of characters in a certain order that software looks for, usually in a SEARCH AND REPLACE operation: *The search string included wild cards.*

/'sɜːtʃ strɪŋ/
pl search strings
▶ **replace string**

secondary channel *noun* (communications)
a DATA CHANNEL that carries CONTROL CHARACTERS with a data transmission: *The secondary channel carries timing and handshaking signals separately from data.*

/ˌsekəndri 'tʃænl/
pl secondary channels
◄ send control characters *over*, transmit control characters *via* a **secondary channel**

secondary index *noun* (software/data structure)
a table used to access data items held in a SEQUENTIAL FILE ; the data items in the file are not in the same order as the entries in the index: *The primary index is a table of employees' insurance numbers and secondary indexes contain names and job titles.*

/ˌsekəndri 'ɪndeks/
pl secondary indexes
pl secondary indices
◄ access, build, construct, make, update a **secondary index**
▶ **inverted file, primary index, primary key**

secondary key *noun*
a field in a data record that can be used with an INDEX (= a list that contains information about the location of a data item) to access records; the value of the field may be the same in different records, so the secondary key may not identify just one record in a field: *use a secondary key to refine a search*

/ˌsekəndri 'kiː/
pl secondary keys
◄ access, use a **secondary key**
▶ **primary key**

secondary storage *noun*
▶ **secondary store**

/ˌsekəndri 'stɔːrɪdʒ/

☆**secondary store** *noun* (hardware)
memory which holds information permanently but is of lower cost, lower speed and higher capacity than main memory: *The system uses floppy disks as a secondary store.*

/ˌsekəndri 'stɔː(r)/
pl secondary stores
syn backing store, secondary storage
▶ **memory, primary memory**

☆**second generation** *noun* (hardware)
a stage in computer design when the TRANSISTOR replaced the valve

note Second generation computers were built in the early1960s.

/'sekənd ˌdʒenə'reɪʃn/
note no plural
▶ **fifth generation, first generation, fourth generation, third generation**

☆**sector** *noun*
▶ **disk sector**

/'sektə(r)/

secure system *noun*
a computer system that is protected by passwords or other security devices so that it can only be accessed by users with the right to use the system: *Sensitive data should be held on a secure system.* ○ *The secure system could not be accessed by unauthorized users.*

/sɪˌkjʊə 'sɪstəm/
pl secure systems
◄ access, store data *in a* **secure system**

security *noun*
▶ **data security**

/sɪ'kjʊərəti/

security backup *noun*
a copy of a data file that is kept away from the main computer system in case the original is damaged or lost: *Security backups of the day's work are made on tape and stored in a fire-proof safe.*

/sɪˌkjʊərəti 'bækʌp/
pl security backups
◄ make, update a **security backup**

seed *noun*
a number used by a PSEUDO-RANDOM NUMBER GENERATOR to stop it calculating the same string of numbers each time it is used

/siːd/
pl seeds
ℍ generate, specify, use a **seed**

---

seek *verb*
to move the READ/WRITE HEAD to the correct place on a disk: *seek the correct disk track*

/siːk/
seek, seeking, sought
note transitive verb

---

seek area *noun* (hardware)
an area of memory that is examined during a search operation: *The seek area includes extended memory.*

/ˈsiːk eəriə/
pl seek areas
ℍ examine, search, traverse the **seek area**

---

seek time *noun*
the time taken for the READ/WRITE HEAD on a disk to physically move to the correct track: *Seek time is only part of the unavoidable delay in accessing data on a rotating storage device.*

/ˈsiːk taɪm/
pl seek times
ℍ improve, measure the **seek time**
▶ latency

---

segment¹ *noun* (software)
a part of a large computer program that can be loaded into main memory by itself, and which will execute without all of the program being present

/ˈsegmənt/
pl segments
ℍ load a **segment**
syn overlay

---

segment² *verb*
to divide something into separate parts, especially to divide a computer program into SEGMENTS¹: *segment a program which is too large to fit into memory* ○ *segment the program into independent modules*

/segˈment/
segment, segmenting, segmented
note transitive verb

---

segment address *noun* (hardware)
the memory location where a SEGMENT¹ must be loaded so that it will execute successfully

/segˌment əˈdres/
pl segment addresses
ℍ load *at* the **segment address**

---

segmentation *noun*
the process of dividing something into separate parts, especially dividing a computer program into SEGMENTS¹

/ˌsegmenˈteɪʃn/
note not used with *a* or *an*. No plural and used with a singular verb only.
ℍ efficient **segmentation**

---

select *verb* (user operation)
to choose something that is usually on screen: *select the text to be deleted by highlighting it* ○ *select the menu option by clicking on it*

/sɪˈlekt/
select, selecting, selected
note transitive verb

---

selectable *adjective*
able to be chosen at a certain time: *The 'paste' menu option is not selectable because no text has been cut.*

/sɪˈlektəbl/
ℍ a **selectable** feature, function, menu, option

---

selection *noun*
a piece of text, etc that is chosen in a document, usually by highlighting it: *The selection was highlighted so that it could be copied to the clipboard.*

/sɪˈlekʃn/
pl selections
ℍ alter, copy, delete, replace the **selection**

---

self-adapting system *noun*
hardware and/or software that is able to change its actions to respond to different conditions outside the system: *The computer system that controls traffic signals is a self-adapting system because it behaves in different ways as traffic flow changes.*

/ˈself əˌdæptɪŋ ˈsɪstəm/
pl self-adapting systems
ℍ program a **self-adapting system**
▶ heuristic

---

abbr abbreviation   **pl** plural   **syn** synonym   ▶ see   ℍ collocate (*word often used with the headword*)

self-checking *adjective*
▶ **self-diagnostic**

/ˌself ˈtʃekɪŋ/

---

self-diagnostic *adjective*
(of a system or process) that is able to check its own functions
and to find and report errors: *The self-diagnostic routines built in
to the laser printer are executed each time the printer is switched
on.*

/ˈself ˌdaɪəgˈnɒstɪk/

Ħ a **self-diagnostic** device,
system; **self-diagnostic**
software

syn self-checking

---

self-documenting code *noun* (software/programming)
a computer program that is written in a high-level language
by a computer programmer so that it can be understood by
other computer programmers: *In this self-documenting code
functions and variables have names that described their purpose.*

/ˈself ˈdɒkjumentɪŋ ˈkəʊd/

note not used with *a* or *an*. No
plural and used with a singular
verb only.

Ħ produce, write **self-
documenting code**

---

self test *noun* (hardware)
an examination of a device that happens automatically when
it is switched on to check that it is working correctly: *The
printer's self test didn't identify any errors.*

/ˌself ˈtest/

pl self tests

Ħ carry out, perform a **self test**

▶ **test¹**

---

semantic error *noun* (software/programming)
a mistake in a programming language statement that causes it
to have no sensible meaning. Semantic errors can exist in
programs that have no SYNTAX ERRORS: *A typical semantic error is
a reference to an undefined variable.*

/sɪˌmæntɪk ˈerə(r)/

pl semantic errors

Ħ correct, detect, make a
semantic error

▶ **semantics, syntax error**

---

semantics *noun* (software/programming)
the meaning of a programming language statement, not its
structure

/sɪˈmæntɪks/

note not used with *a* or *an*. No
plural and used with a singular
verb only.

Ħ define the **semantics**

▶ **grammar**

---

semaphore *noun*
▶ **flag**

/ˈseməfɔː(r)/

---

semiconductor *noun* (hardware)
a material such as SILICON that allows a certain amount of
electrical current to pass through it

note 'Semiconductor' is also used to refer to components such
as transistors and integrated circuits that are made from
semiconductor material.

/ˌsemikənˈdʌktə(r)/

pl semiconductors

Ħ **semiconductor** memory

---

sensor *noun* (hardware)
an electronic device that can recognize signals or light, etc: *The
sensor detects electrical pulses.*

/ˈsensə(r)/

pl sensors

Ħ a heat, a light, an optical, a
temperature **sensor**

---

sentinel *noun*
▶ **terminator 1**

/ˈsentɪnl/

---

separator *noun*
a symbol that is used to separate two things such as items of
data or parts of a program instruction written on a single line:
*The separator in the instructions FOR I=1 TO 10:PRINT I:NEXT I
is the ':' symbol.*

/ˈsepəreɪtə(r)/

pl separators

Ħ a **separator** character, symbol

sequence *noun*
a group of items that are in a certain order: *a sequence of figures arranged in numerical order* ○ *The command sequence is 'ESC/ [?1;4;5]'.*

/'si:kwəns/
pl sequences
◄ an alphabetical, a command, a complex, a consecutive, an escape, a linear, a logical **sequence**

---

sequence check *noun*
a process that ensures data has been correctly arranged or sorted

/'si:kwəns tʃek/
pl sequence checks
◄ carry out, implement a **sequence check**

---

sequence control register *noun*
▶ **current address register**

/ˌsi:kwəns kən'trəʊl ˌredʒɪstə(r)/

---

sequential access *noun*
an access method where individual items are accessed in a certain order. All the previous items must first be read before locating the particular item required: *The master file is updated from the transaction file by sequential access.*

/sɪˌkwenʃl 'ækses/
note not used with *a* or *an*. No plural and used with a singular verb only.
◄ a **sequential access** file
▶ **random access storage device, random access, serial access**

---

sequential file *noun* (software)
a file stored in memory containing data that is accessed in a certain order. All the previous items must first be read before locating the particular item required.

/sɪˌkwenʃl 'faɪl/
pl sequential files
◄ access, add records *to*, search, update a **sequential file**
syn serial file

---

sequential flow *noun*
the movement of bits in a DATA STREAM where one bit follows another bit in a certain order: *a sequential flow of instructions* ○ *a sequential flow of data*

/sɪˌkwenʃl 'fləʊ/
pl sequential flows

---

sequential logic *noun*
LOGIC CIRCUITS that are arranged so that the inputs to one circuit depend on the outputs of other circuits

note Sequential logic is the basis of devices such as adders and shift registers.

/sɪˌkwenʃl 'lɒdʒɪk/
note not used with *a* or *an*. No plural and used with a singular verb only.
◄ **sequential logic** circuits, devices
▶ **adder, shift register, gate**

---

sequential processing *noun*
a method of processing where each piece of data is processed in the order in which it is accessed

/sɪˌkwenʃl 'prəʊsesɪŋ/
note not used with *a* or *an*. No plural and used with a singular verb only
◄ **sequential processing** methods, techniques

---

sequential search *noun*
a way of finding an item by starting at the top of a list and looking through the list in order until the item is found: *a sequential search that moves from A to B to C* ○ *start the sequential search from the beginning of the list*

/sɪˌkwenʃl 'sɜːtʃ/
pl sequential searches
◄ a **sequential search** algorithm
syn linear search

---

abbr abbreviation   **pl** plural   **syn** synonym   ▶ see   ◄ collocate (*word often used with the headword*)

serial access *noun*
an access method where data items can only be accessed by reading all earlier items first: *Serial access is used to locate items stored on tape.*

/ˌsɪəriəl ˈækses/
note not used with *a* or *an*. No plural and used with a singular verb only.
⋈ a **serial access** data structure, device, file
▶ **random access**

---

serial adder *noun* (hardware)
an adder that adds the digits of two binary numbers one after the other and not all at the same time

/ˌsɪəriəl ˈædə(r)/
pl serial adders
▶ **adder, parallel adder**

---

serial communication *noun*
the transmission of one bit or one data item after another in a fixed order

/ˌsɪəriəl kəˌmjuːnɪˈkeɪʃn/
note not used with *a* or *an*. No plural and used with a singular verb only.
⋈ **serial communication** methods, protocols

---

serial data transmission *noun*
▶ **serial transmission**

/ˌsɪəriəl ˈdeɪtə trænsˌmɪʃn/

---

serial file *noun*
▶ **sequential file**

/ˌsɪəriəl ˈfaɪl/

---

serial input *noun*
▶ **serial transmission**

/ˌsɪəriəl ˈɪnpʊt/

---

serial interface *noun*
a device that transfers data and CONTROL CHARACTERS one after the other over a transmission channel: *The printer is available with an optional serial interface.*

/ˌsɪəriəl ˈɪntəfeɪs/
pl serial interfaces
⋈ attach a connector *to*, fit, insert, set the parameters *of* the **serial interface**
syn serial port
▶ **parallel interface**

---

serial output *noun*
▶ **serial transmission**

/ˌsɪəriəl ˈaʊtpʊt/

---

serial port *noun*
▶ **serial interface**

/ˈsɪəriəl pɔːt/

---

serial printer *noun* (hardware)
a printer that is connected to a computer by a SERIAL INTERFACE

/ˌsɪəriəl ˈprɪntə(r)/
pl serial printers
▶ **parallel printer, printer**

☆**serial processing** *noun* (system operation)
1 (*data processing*) the processing of data items in the order they are stored or input into a computer **2** (*programming*) the execution of one program instruction after another in a fixed order

/ˌsɪəriəl ˈprəʊsesɪŋ/
note no plural
1,2 ⋈ first-in, first-out **serial processing**
▶ **parallel processing**

serial transmission *noun*

the process of sending data over a communications channel where the binary digits that form the message are sent one bit at a time (serial output) or are received one bit at a time (serial input): *The computers send data to each other as serial transmissions over telephone lines.*

note Serial transmission takes longer than parallel transmission but requires less expensive communication lines.

/ˌsɪəriəl trænsˈmɪʃn/

pl serial transmissions

⋈ a **serial transmission** channel, connection, line, method, protocol

syn serial data transmission, serial input, serial output

▶ **parallel transmission**

☆**server** *noun* (hardware)

a computer in a network that is used for storing and managing access to shared files: *The e-mail server is down for maintenance.*

/ˈsɜːvə(r)/

pl servers

⋈ a printer **server**

syn file server

▶ **client-server**

---

session *noun*

an amount of time that is spent working on a computer: *book the computer in the resources room for a 3-hour session*

/ˈseʃn/

pl sessions

⋈ the current, work **session**

---

session layer *noun*

one of the levels of structure of the International Standards Organization PROTOCOL for data communications. The session layer describes standards that make communication between different systems possible: *The session layer deals with synchronization and requesting permission to send data.*

/ˈseʃn ˌleɪə(r)/

note not used with *a* or *an*. No plural and used with a singular verb only.

⋈ define, specify the **session layer**

▶ **application layer, data link layer, ISO OSI, network layer, physical layer, presentation layer, transport layer**

---

set¹ *noun*

a collection data items, etc which usually share some features

/set/

pl sets

⋈ a data **set**; a **set** of data items/ numbers

▶ **union**

---

set² *verb*

to give something a position or a value: *set the variable to its initial value* ○ *set the bit to 0*

/set/

set, setting, set

note transitive verb

⋈ **set** something *in* position, something *back* to zero; **set** a flip-flop, an input *to* 1, etc

---

set up *verb*

to INSTALL (1,2) a program or device so that it is ready to be used: *The instructions on how to set up the computer are in the manual.*

/ˌset ˈʌp/

set up, setting up, set up

note transitive verb

⋈ **set up** a computer, a printer, a system

---

set-up option *noun*

a choice that is available when preparing a system for use: *One of the set-up options is to have the window covering the whole screen.* ○ *One set-up option is to reserve some memory for a RAM disk.*

/ˈset ʌp ˌɒpʃn/

pl set-up options

⋈ choose, select a **set-up option**

---

abbr abbreviation   **pl** plural   **syn** synonym   ▶ see   ⋈ collocate (*word often used with the headword*)

seven segment display noun (hardware)
a digital display that can display the decimal digits 0 to 9: *The liquid crystal display is a seven segment display.*

note The seven segments are the three vertical and four horizontal lines that form the number 8.

/ˈsevn ˈsegmənt dɪˈspleɪ/
pl seven segment displays

---

shared file noun
a file stored in memory that can be accessed by more than one user or system

/ˌʃeəd ˈfaɪl/
pl shared files
ℍ access, edit, store, retrieve a **shared file**

---

shared line noun (hardware)
a transmission channel that is used by two or more different users: *Using a shared line cuts the cost of connecting to a network.* ○ *It is impossible for two users to use a shared line at the same time.*

/ˌʃeəd ˈlaɪn/
pl shared lines
ℍ install, transmit data *over*, use a **shared line**

---

shared memory noun (hardware)
memory that is shared between processors: *The three processors have shared memory.*

/ˌʃeəd ˈmeməri/
note no plural

---

shared resource noun
any part of a computer system that can be used by more than one device, program or user: *Printers that are made available to all users on the network are a shared resource.*

/ˌʃeəd rɪˈsɔːs/
pl shared resources
▶ **resource**

---

shareware noun (software)
software that is available free for a user to test; if the user likes the software and wants to keep using it, they must buy it from the author

/ˈʃeəweə(r)/
note not used with *a* or *an*. No plural and used with a singular verb only.
ℍ a **shareware** author, game, program, title, utility
▶ **freeware, proprietary software, public domain software**

---

sheet feeder noun (hardware)
a part of a printer where the sheets of paper are placed so that they can move into the printer: *The automatic sheet feeder holds 400 pieces of paper.*

/ˈʃiːt ˌfiːdə(r)/
pl sheet feeders

---

shell noun (software)
a piece of software such as a utility program that helps a user to use a very difficult program or operating system: *enter the Unix command in a C shell*

/ʃel/
pl shells

---

shield¹ noun
material that is placed around COMPONENTS or circuits to protect them

/ʃiːld/
pl shields
ℍ an electrostatic, a metal, a non-conducting, a plastic **shield**

---

shield² verb
to protect a COMPONENT from electricity, dirt or anything that can cause damage: *These sensitive devices must be shielded from electrical interference.*

/ʃiːld/
shield, shielding, shielded
note transitive verb
ℍ **shield** a circuit, component, device
▶ **clean room**

☆**shift** noun (hardware)

the key on a computer keyboard that is used to produce capital letters or the character that is the highest of two characters printed on a key. It is also used with other keys to produce other characters or to access other functions: *press 'shift' and '4' to get the '$' symbol*

/ʃɪft/

note not used with *a* or *an*. No plural and used with a singular verb only.

◄ hold *down*, press, use **shift**

syn shift key

► **backspace¹, cursor control key, delete¹, insert¹**

---

shift instruction noun (software)

an instruction, usually in machine code, that moves the bits held in a register to the left or right

/ˈʃɪft ɪnˌstrʌkʃn/

pl shift instructions

◄ a left, right **shift instruction**

► **logical left shift, logical right shift, logical shift**

☆**shift key** noun
► **shift**

/ˈʃɪft kiː/

---

shift register noun

an electronic circuit which hold bits that are moved one position to the left or right

/ˈʃɪft ˌredʒɪstə(r)/

pl shift registers

◄ a cycling, linear, looped, serial **shift register**

► **logical left shift, logical right shift, logical shift**

---

ship verb

to make software or hardware available to buy in shops: *The company plans to ship the latest version of the application in the autumn.* ○ *The new hardware is scheduled to ship next year.* ○ *read the instructions shipped with the software*

/ʃɪp/

ship, shipping, shipped

note transitive or intransitive verb

---

short card noun (hardware)

an EXPANSION BOARD that is small in size

/ˌʃɔːt ˈkɑːd/

pl short cards

---

short haul modem noun (hardware)

a modem that is used for communication over short distances and can operate without using a CARRIER SIGNAL. Short haul modems are used instead of local area networks: *A short haul modem is used between computers in the same building.*

/ˌʃɔːt hɔːl ˈməʊdem/

pl short haul modems

◄ receive data *through*, send data *via*, transmit data *by* a **short haul modem**

SI abbr

Système International. The international system of units of measurement: *The SI unit of temperature is the kelvin.*

/ˌes ˈaɪ/

note pronounced as individual letters

---

side effect noun

an unexpected effect that occurs in addition to the one that was originally expected: *The tabulation subroutine had the side effect of resetting the printer.*

/ˈsaɪd ɪˌfekt/

pl side effects

◄ correct, experience, suffer a **side effect**; a possible, serious **side effect**

---

sideways ROM noun (software)

software that allows a particular area of memory be accessed in order to carry out a certain function

/ˌsaɪdweɪz ˈrɒm/

note not used with *a* or *an*. No plural and used with a singular verb only.

---

abbr abbreviation   **pl** plural   **syn** synonym   ► see   ◄ collocate (*word often used with the headword*)

sign *noun* (mathematics) /saɪn/

1 a symbol that is used to show a mathematical operation: *To make the equation correct, replace the multiplication sign with a division sign.* **2** the positive or negative state of a number: *Test the sign of the number.*

pl signs

1 ᴍ an addition, a division, a multiplication, a plus, a subtraction **sign**

2 ᴍ a negative, positive **sign**

☆**signal¹** *noun* /ˈsɪgnəl/

an electrical wave that is usually used to carry data: *a signal with a frequency of 10MHz* ○ *The strong signal modulates the weak one.*

pl signals

ᴍ input, receive, send, transmit a **signal**; an analog, a digital **signal**

---

signal² *verb* /ˈsɪgnəl/

to send a message, especially to or from a computer: *The modem signalled that it had detected a carrier wave.* ○ *The bleep signalled an error.*

signal, signalling, signalled

note transitive or intransitive verb

(*US* **signal, signaling, signaled**)

---

signal conversion *noun* /ˈsɪgnəl kənˌvɜːʃn/

the process of changing a signal so that it can carry data or so that it will be accepted by a device or communications channel: *The signal conversion of a steady carrier by modulation allows data to be sent.*

note usually singular

ᴍ effect, perform **signal conversion**

▶ **carrier signal, modulation**

---

sign and magnitude *noun* /ˌsaɪn ənd ˈmægnɪtjuːd/

a method of representing numbers in which the sign of the MOST SIGNIFICANT BIT represents the sign of the number: *The mantissa is stored as a binary fraction in sign and magnitude format.*

note not used with *a* or *an*. No plural and used with a singular verb only.

---

sign bit *noun* /ˈsaɪn bɪt/

a single bit that is used to show the SIGN (2) of a number: *a pattern whose sign bit is 1*

pl sign bits

---

signed *adjective* /saɪnd/

(of a number) that has a positive (+) or negative (-) sign

ᴍ a **signed** digit, figure, number

▶ **sign**

---

signed integer *noun* /ˌsaɪnd ˈɪntɪdʒə(r)/

a whole number that has a positive (+) or negative (-) sign

pl signed integers

---

significant digit *noun* /sɪgˌnɪfɪkənt ˈdɪdʒɪt/

▶ **significant figure**

---

significant figure *noun* (mathematics) /sɪgˌnɪfɪkənt ˈfɪgə(r)/

a digit in a number which gives information about the PRECISION of the number

pl significant figures

syn significant digit

---

sign off *verb* /ˌsaɪn ˈɒf/

▶ **log off**

---

sign on *verb* /ˌsaɪn ˈɒn/

▶ **log on**

---

silicon *noun* (hardware) /ˈsɪlɪkən/

a light metal that is used to make chips: *use silicon as a semiconductor*

note not used with *a* or *an*. No plural and used with a singular verb only.

▶ **wafer**

☆**silicon chip** *noun* ▶ **chip**	/ˌsɪlɪkən ˈtʃɪp/
silicon disk *noun* ▶ **RAM disk**	/ˌsɪlɪkən ˈdɪsk/
simplex *adjective* (data transmission) able to be sent over a data channel in one direction only: *The simplex transmission travelled from sender to receiver.*	/ˈsɪmpleks/ **note** no plural ◄ **simplex** mode, operation, transmissions ▶ **duplex**
simplex channel *noun* (hardware) a data channel that allows transmission of data in one direction only	/ˈsɪmpleks ˈtʃænl/ **pl** simplex channels ◄ send data *over*, transmit data *via*, use a **simplex channel** ▶ **duplex channel, half duplex channel**
simulate *verb* to create a particular condition or situation by using a computer model or program to represent it: *The likely path of the hurricane can be simulated using a specially-developed computer program.*	/ˈsɪmjuleɪt/ **simulate, simulating, simulated** **note** transitive verb ◄ **simulate** an action, a condition, an effect, a process
simulation *noun* the act or process of reproducing a particular condition or situation by using a computer model or program to represent it: *Pilots are expected to continue their training with flight simulation.*	/ˌsɪmjuˈleɪʃn/ **pl** simulations ◄ a computer, flight, traffic, weather **simulation** ▶ **virtual reality**
☆**simulator** *noun* (hardware) a machine that runs a computer program to create the conditions of a certain situation: *The flight simulator had a screen that showed the runway.*	/ˈsɪmjuleɪtə(r)/ **pl** simulators ▶ **emulator, virtual reality**
simultaneous processing *noun* the processing of two or more tasks at the same time: *The tasks are distributed across different CPUs for simultaneous processing.*	/ˈsɪml̩ˌtemiəs ˈprəʊsesɪŋ/ **note** not used with *a* or *an*. No plural and used with a singular verb only. ▶ **multitasking**
single board computer *noun* (hardware) a small computer which has all its circuits on one printed circuit board: *The single board computer provides additional processing power for the system.*	/ˌsɪŋgl bɔːd kəmˈpjuːtə(r)/ **pl** single board computers **abbr** SBC ◄ assemble, make, manufacture a **single board computer** ▶ **chip**
single chip computer *noun* (hardware) a computer where the central processing unit and memory are provided on a single integrated circuit (chip)	/ˌsɪŋgl tʃɪp kəmˈpjuːtə(r)/ **pl** single chip computers ◄ assemble, make, manufacture a **single chip computer**

abbr abbreviation   **pl** plural   **syn** synonym   ▶ see   ◄ collocate (*word often used with the headword*)

single density disk *noun*
a magnetic disk that can store information

/'sɪŋgl ˌdensəti 'dɪsk/
pl single density disks
abbr SD
▶ **double density disk, high density disk**

---

single length word *noun*
a WORD **(1)** that stores a single unit of data

/ˌsɪŋgl leŋθ 'wɜːd/
pl single length words
▶ **double length word**

---

single precision *noun*
the way of storing numerical data using a single WORD **(1)** for each number

/ˌsɪŋgl prɪ'sɪʒn/
note not used with a *a* or *an*. No plural and used with a singular verb only.
◄ **single-precision** arithmetic, data, storage
▶ **double precision, extended precision, precision**

---

single-sided disk *noun* (hardware)
a magnetic disk that can store information on one side only

/'sɪŋgl ˌsaɪdɪd 'dɪsk/
pl single-sided disks
abbr SSD
▶ **double-sided disk**

---

single step *verb*
to execute a computer program one instruction at a time, stopping after each instruction so that the programmer can check that the program is working correctly

/ˌsɪŋgl 'step/
single step, single stepping, single stepped
note transitive verb
◄ **single step** a procedure, program, subroutine
syn walk through

---

single threading *noun* (software/programming)
the process of executing one part (thread) of a program at a time

/ˌsɪŋgl 'θredɪŋ/
note not used with *a* or *an*. No plural and used with a singular verb only.
▶ **multithreading**

---

single-user *adjective* (hardware/software)
(of a computer or system) that can only be used by one user at a time

/ˌsɪŋgl 'juːzə(r)/
◄ a **single-user** licence, terminal
▶ **multi-user**

---

single-user computer *noun* (hardware)
a computer that can only be used by one user at a time

/'sɪŋgl ˌjuːzə kəm'pjuːtə(r)/
pl single-user computers

---

single-user system *noun*
a system that can only be used by one user at a time

/'sɪŋgl ˌjuːzə 'sɪstəm/
pl single-user systems
▶ **multi-user system**

---

sink *noun* (hardware)
the part of a system that receives data or signals, etc from another device: *Data travels from the source to the sink.*

/sɪŋk/
pl sinks
▶ **source**

site *noun* /saɪt/
1 a place such as a company or school where computers and software are used: *All computers on the site were down because of a power failure.* **2** a place on the INTERNET where an individual or company puts information: *The company's net site has downloadable software demos.*

pl sites
1 ▶ node 2, site licence
2 ▶ browser, World Wide Web

site licence *noun* /ˈsaɪt ˌlaɪsns/
an agreement that allows a certain number of people to use a single piece of software in one place: *The electronic dictionary is available with a site licence for 10 users.*

pl site licences
H apply *for*, authorize, grant, obtain, pay *for* a **site licence**

site network *noun* /ˈsaɪt ˌnetwɜːk/
a type of local area network that connects users on one SITE (1) to each other and to the central computer

pl site networks
H access, install, maintain a **site network**
▶ backbone network, wide area network

slave processor *noun* (hardware) /ˈsleɪv ˌprəʊsesə(r)/
a computer or device that is controlled by another computer or device: *The slave processor is controlled by the master computer.*

pl slave processors
▶ master/slave system

sleep *noun* /sliːp/
the state of a computer or system before a user has LOGGED ON

note not used with *a* or *an*. No plural and used with a singular verb only.

sleeve *noun* (hardware) /sliːv/
a cover for a magnetic disk: *The details of what the disk holds are written on the sleeve.* ○ *The sleeve protects the disk from dust and damage.*

pl sleeves

SLSI *abbr* /ˌes el es ˈaɪ/
▶ super large scale integration

note pronounced as individual letters

small scale integration *noun* (hardware) /ˌsmɔːl skeɪl ɪntɪˈgreɪʃn/
the process of putting one to ten components on an integrated circuit

note not used with *a* or *an*. No plural and used with a singular verb only.
abbr SSI
▶ circuit board, large scale integration, medium scale integration, printed circuit board, super large scale integration, ultra large scale integration, very large scale integration, wafer scale integration

smart *adjective* /smɑːt/
(of software and hardware) that can work in an intelligent way, sometimes without instructions from the user: *The smart CPU can turn down processor speed from 20MHz to 2.5MHz to save energy when no one is using the computer.*

smart card *noun* (hardware) /ˈsmɑːt kɑːd/
a plastic card containing a microprocessor that can hold and process information: *The patients' medical records are kept on small plastic smart cards.*

pl smart cards

abbr abbreviation   **pl** plural   **syn** synonym   ▶ see   H collocate (*word often used with the headword*)

smart terminal *noun*
▶ **intelligent terminal**

/ˌsmɑːt ˈtɜːmɪnl/

SNA *abbr*

(*trade mark*) ▶ **Systems Network Architecture**

/ˌes en ˈeɪ/

note pronounced as individual letters

---

snapshot *noun*
a copy of all the registers and important memory locations of a computer at a particular moment in time

/ˈsnæpʃɒt/

pl snapshots

✂ make, store, take a **snapshot**

---

snapshot dump *noun*
a printout of everything displayed on a computer screen at one time

/ˈsnæpʃɒt dʌmp/

pl snapshot dumps

✂ make, take a **snapshot dump**

---

soak-test *verb*
to test a device or a program to make sure it works properly by running it continuously for some time: *All the products are soak-tested before being delivered to the customer.*

/ˈsəʊk test/

soak-test, soak-testing, soak-tested

note transitive verb

✂ **soak-test** a computer, device, mouse, printer, program

---

socket *noun* (hardware)
a single device or one part of another device with a set of holes which a plug fits into: *put the plug in the socket and turn the switch on* ○ *Connect the mouse to the socket in the keyboard.*

/ˈsɒkɪt/

pl sockets

✂ an electrical, a keyboard, a mouse, a printer, a tape **socket**

---

soft copy *noun*
text or information held in the computer's memory and displayed on screen, not printed on paper

/ˌsɒft ˈkɒpi/

note not used with *a* or *an*. No plural and used with a singular verb only.

▶ **hard copy, printout**

---

soft error *noun*
an error that can be corrected by a program or operating system so the program does not stop running

/ˌsɒft ˈerə(r)/

pl soft errors

▶ **hard error**

---

soft hyphen *noun*
a HYPHEN (= the character '-') that some programs will automatically put into a word if it cannot fit onto a single line: *The program inserted a soft hyphen into the middle of the word 'computer' when it ran over the end of the line.*

/ˌsɒft ˈhaɪfn/

pl soft hyphens

✂ delete, insert a **soft hyphen**

---

soft return *noun* (applications/word processing)
a line break that is put into text by a program so that text does not appear in the margins. If the text is changed, then the position of this line break will also change.

/ˌsɒft rɪˈtɜːn/

pl soft returns

✂ insert a **soft return**

▶ **hard return, newline character**

---

soft-sectored disk *noun* (hardware)
a disk that has its SECTORS (= areas of storage space) marked by data that is recorded onto the disk, and not by a hole that is made in the disk

/ˈsɒft ˌsektəd ˈdɪsk/

pl soft-sectored disks

✂ format a **soft-sectored disk**

▶ **format² 1, track**

soft space *noun* (applications/word processing)
a space that is put into text by a program when creating JUSTIFIED (1) text. If the text is changed, the location of this space will also change.

/ˌsɒft ˈspeɪs/
pl soft spaces
◄ delete, insert a **soft space**
► **nonbreaking space, kerning**

☆**software** *noun* (software)
programs that run on a computer. Different types of software include SYSTEM SOFTWARE that controls how the computer operates; APPLICATIONS SOFTWARE that does certain jobs such as word processing; software such as games or electronic dictionaries, etc and FREEWARE that can be any type of software and is available for little or no money.

/ˈsɒftweə(r)/
note no plural
◄ configure, edit, run, write **software**; computer, licensed, management **software**; a **software** application, package, product, system, vendor; **software** compatibility, development, technology
► **firmware, hardware, portable software, program, proprietary software, public domain software, shareware**

---

software base *noun* (software/applications)
all of the application programs used on a computer: *The company has expanded its software base to include networking capabilities.*

/ˈsɒftweə beɪs/
note usually singular
◄ expand, replace, revise the **software base**; an accounting, a computer-aided design, a scientific, a protocol-independent **software base**

---

software compatible *adjective*
(of a computer) that can work with software written for a different model of computer

/ˌsɒftweə kəmˈpætəbl/

---

software conversion *noun* (software)
the process of changing software written for one computer so that it will run on another computer

/ˈsɒftweə kənˌvɜːʃn/
note no plural
◄ a **software conversion** utility

---

software development *noun* (software)
the processes involved in inventing, writing and testing new programs

/ˈsɒftweə dɪˌveləpmənt/
note not used with *a* or *an*. No plural and used with a singular verb only.
◄ a **software development** environment, kit, package, tool

---

software engineer *noun* (personnel)
a person who writes and tests computer programs: *The software engineer debugged the program during the final stages of beta testing.*

/ˈsɒftweə(r) endʒɪˌnɪə(r)/
pl software engineers
◄ consult, employ a **software engineer**

---

software engineering *noun*
the processes involved in writing computer software such as designing, coding and testing programs

/ˈsɒftweə(r) endʒɪˈnɪərɪŋ/
note not used with *a* or *an*. No plural and used with a singular verb only.

---

software house *noun*
a company that invents, writes and sells computer programs: *order the new e-mail software from the software house*

/ˈsɒftweə haʊs/
pl software houses

---

abbr abbreviation   **pl** plural   **syn** synonym   ► see   ◄ collocate (*word often used with the headword*)

software interrupt *noun*
a signal that is sent by a program asking the CPU for attention

/ˌsɒftweə(r) ˈɪntərʌpt/
pl software interrupts

⋈ handle, issue, respond *to* a **software interrupt**; a **software interrupt** request, service routine, signal

▶ **hardware interrupt, interrupt[1]**

---

software licence *noun* (software)
an official document that shows a person or organization can use a piece of software: *The software licence refers to installation and use of the software package on one computer only.*

/ˈsɒftweə laɪsəns/
pl software licences

⋈ apply *for*, buy, obtain, pay *for* a **software licence**; **software licence** fees

▶ **site licence**

---

software maintenance *noun* (software)
the process of keeping software working as efficiently as possible by correcting errors that have been found or by UPGRADING[2] **(2)** the software to newer versions

/ˈsɒftweə ˌmeɪntənəns/
note not used with *a* or *an*. No plural and used with singular verb only.

⋈ carry out **software maintenance**

☆**software package** *noun* (applications)
a single application that contains a set of related programs or MODULES **(2)** such as a word processing application that contains a spellcheck module: *The software package came with a licence, manual and telephone helpline number.* ○ *The system was bundled with a database software package.*

/ˈsɒftweə ˌpækɪdʒ/
pl software packages

⋈ bundle, buy, purchase, sell a **software package**

syn package

▶ **suite**

---

software piracy *noun* (software)
copying and/or selling software without the permission of the person or company who owns the COPYRIGHT

/ˈsɒftweə ˌpaɪrəsi/
note not used with *a* or *an*. No plural and used with a singular verb only.

⋈ combat, detect, deter, fight, prosecute *for*, stop **software piracy**

---

software release *noun* (software)
software that is made available for people to buy. A software release is usually a new piece of software, or an UPGRADE[1] (= an improved version of a piece of software): *New software releases are coming on to the market every day.* ○ *The company has doubled its profits with its latest software release.*

/ˈsɒftweə rɪˌliːs/
pl software releases

⋈ buy, issue, publish, sell a **software release**; the latest, new, recent **software release**

---

software reliability *noun* (software)
the ability of a piece of software to work correctly: *Constant copying can reduce software reliability.*

/ˈsɒftweə rɪˌlaɪəˈbɪləti/
note not used with *a* or *an*. No plural and used with a singular verb only.

⋈ excellent, poor **software reliability**

---

software tool *noun* (software)
a program that is used to develop and write new software: *a software tool that helps non-programmers to program* ○ *commercial software tools aimed at developing new client/server applications*

/ˈsɒftweə ˌtuːl/
pl software tools

SOH *abbr*
▶ **start of header character**

note used in written English only

---

solid-state *adjective*
(of electronic circuits) that are made from solid material with connections and devices burnt into the material

note Most solid-state devices are made from silicon or similar elements.

/ˈsɒlɪd steɪt/
◢ a **solid-state** computer, detector, device, laser, transistor; **solid-state** electronics, circuitry, memory, physics
▶ **chip**

---

son file *noun*
the most up-to-date working version of a file

/ˈsʌn faɪl/
pl son files

---

sort¹ *noun* (software/system operation)
a program that puts data in a certain order: *run a sort to arrange data in alphabetical order*

/sɔːt/
pl sorts
◢ a **sort** algorithm, key
▶ **index**

☆**sort²** *verb* (system operation)
to put data into a certain order using a computer program

/sɔːt/
sorts, sorting, sorted
note transitive verb
◢ **sort** alphabetically, *by* date, *by* letter, *by* name, *by* number, chronologically, numerically, thematically
▶ **bubble sort, index, insertion sort, merge sort**

SOT *abbr*
▶ **start of text character**

note used in written English only

---

source *noun*
the part of a system that transmits data or signals, etc to another device: *Data travels from the source to the sink. ○ The source of the signal was a satellite.*

/sɔːs/
pl sources
▶ **sink**

☆**source code** *noun* (software/programming)
a computer program written in a high-level language that must be translated into OBJECT CODE before it can be executed

/ˈsɔːs kəʊd/
note not used with *a* or *an*. No plural and used with a singular verb only.
◢ list **source code**
syn source program
▶ **compiler, interpreter, machine code, translator**

---

source data *noun*
the original data from which information is taken

/ˈsɔːs ˌdeɪtə/
note used with a plural or a singular verb

---

source document *noun*
the original document from which information is taken: *various source documents were used to produce the statistics*

/ˈsɔːs ˌdɒkjumənt/
pl source documents
◢ consult, read, use a **source document**

---

source file *noun*
a program written in SOURCE LANGUAGE which must then be translated into a language the computer can understand

/ˈsɔːs faɪl/
pl source files

---

abbr abbreviation   **pl** plural   **syn** synonym   ▶ see   ◢ collocate (*word often used with the headword*)

source language *noun*
the language which is used to write the SOURCE CODE of a program

note Source language is usually a high-level language.

/ˈsɔːs ˌlæŋgwɪdz/
pl source languages
◄ compile something *from*, translate the **source language**
► **object language**

---

source program *noun*
► **source code**

/ˈsɔːs ˌprəʊgræm/

---

space¹ *noun*
a gap between words or lines of text, etc: *reduce the space between the words so that more text fits on a page*

/speɪs/
◄ delete, insert, leave a **space**; a large, narrow, small, thin **space**

---

space² *verb*
to put gaps between words or lines of text, etc: *space the text so that the lines are not too close together* ○ *space the letters evenly*

/speɪs/
space, spacing, spaced
note transitive verb
◄ **space** a document, letter, line; **space** text, work

☆**space bar** *noun* (hardware)
the longest key on a keyboard that is used for making a space between characters: *Press the space bar after a full stop.*

/ˈspeɪs bɑː(r)/
pl space bars
◄ hit, press, use the **space bar**
► **return¹ 1, tab¹**

---

space character *noun*
the character that is sent to the computer when the space bar is pressed

/ˈspeɪs ˌkærəktə(r)/
pl space characters

---

spacing *noun*
the amount of space between words or lines of text, etc: *adjust the spacing between the heading and the first line* ○ *use single-line spacing in a letter*

/ˈspeɪsɪŋ/
note not used with *a* or *an*. No plural and used with a singular verb only.
◄ adjust, increase, reduce the **spacing**

---

sparse array *noun*
an array which contains many items that have the same value, which is often zero

/ˌspɑːs əˈreɪ/
pl sparse arrays
◄ access, store data *in* a **sparse array**
► **array, band matrix, data structure**

---

special purpose *adjective*
(of a computer or system, etc) that is designed to do a particular job: *The special purpose computers only process the high-security data on the network.*

/ˌspeʃl ˈpɜːpəs/

---

specification *noun*
the technical details relating to hardware and software: *The computer's technical specifications include a 540 MB hard disk.* ○ *The software specifications explain which platform it will run on.*

/ˌspesɪfɪˈkeɪʃn/
pl specifications
abbr spec
◄ draw up, list, meet the **specifications**; a detailed, technical **specification**

speech generation *noun*
▶ **speech synthesis**

/ˈspiːtʃ dʒenəˌreɪʃn/

---

speech output *noun*
the sound produced by a computer that is similar to human speech

/ˌspiːtʃ ˈaʊtpʊt/

note not used with *a* or *an*. No plural and used with a singular verb only.

syn voice output

---

speech recognition *noun*
the ability of a computer to understand human speech: *The system's speech recognition capabilities are limited.*

/ˈspiːtʃ ˌrekəgˈnɪʃn/

note not used with *a* or *an*. No plural and used with a singular verb only.

◄ a **speech recognition** device, facility, research program, system; **speech recognition** software

syn voice recognition

▶ **continuous speech recognition, continuous speech understanding**

---

speech synthesis *noun*
the ability of a computer to produce spoken words: *The hand-held translator has speech synthesis capabilities.*

/ˌspiːtʃ ˈsɪnθəsɪs/

note not used with *a* or *an*. No plural and used with a singular verb only.

syn speech generation

---

speech synthesizer *noun* (hardware)
a device connected to a computer that can produce spoken words

/ˈspiːtʃ ˌsɪnθəsaɪzə(r)/

pl speech synthesizers

syn voice synthesizer

---

spellcheck¹ *noun* (applications/word processing)
a tool in a word processing application that searches a document to find words which do not match the computer's dictionary: *configure the spellcheck to ignore all proper names* ○ *run the document through the spellcheck*

/ˈspeltʃek/

pl spellchecks

(also **spelling checker**)

◄ access, load the **spellcheck**

---

spellcheck² *verb*
to use a tool in a word processing application that searches a document to find words which do not match the computer's dictionary

/ˈspeltʃek/

spellcheck, spellchecking, spellchecked

note transitive verb

◄ **spellcheck** a document, letter

---

spike *noun*
▶ **surge**

/spaɪk/

---

spindle *noun* (hardware)
the central part of a disk drive which holds the surface of the disk in order to make it move round

/ˈspɪndl/

pl spindles

◄ drive the disk *by*, load the disk *onto* a **spindle**

---

split baud rate *noun*
the two speeds of data transmission, measured in BAUD, for a transmission channel which uses different transmission rates for sending data in one direction and receiving data from another direction: *Viewdata transmissions use a split baud rate of 1 200/75.*

/ˌsplɪt ˈbɔːd reɪt/

pl split baud rates

◄ transmit *at*, use a **split baud rate**

▶ **baud rate**

---

abbr abbreviation **pl** plural **syn** synonym ▶ see ◄ collocate (*word often used with the headword*)

split screen *noun*

a display screen or window that is divided into two or more areas, each showing different information: *The two documents can be compared by displaying them as a split screen.*

/ˌsplɪt ˈskriːn/

pl split screens

⋈ arrange *as*, display *as* a **split screen**

---

spool¹ *noun* (hardware)

a round container which holds tape, etc: *a spool of printer ribbon* ○ *wind the magnetic tape onto the spool*

/spuːl/

pl spools

---

spool² *verb*

1 to move tape on a SPOOL¹: *spool the tape backwards and forwards* **2** to move data to temporary storage such as a disk or buffer, usually before it is printed or before the next stage of processing: *The print server spools the documents.*

/spuːl/

spool, spooling, spooled

note transitive verb

2 ⋈ **spool** the file

▶ **print spooling**

---

spooler *noun* (software)

software that moves data to a temporary storage place on disk, usually before it is printed

/ˈspuːlə(r)/

pl spoolers

⋈ invoke, load, use a **spooler**; a **spooler** module

☆**spreadsheet** *noun* (applications)

a program that displays data in rows and columns and is used to perform calculations on the data: *change one item of data to see the effect on all the other data in the spreadsheet* ○ *enter a formula in the cell of the spreadsheet*

/ˈspredʃiːt/

pl spreadsheets

⋈ enter data *in*, extract data *from*, fill, manipulate a **spreadsheet**; a **spreadsheet** calculation, formula, program

▶ **cell 2**

---

sprite *noun* (software)

an object in computer graphics which can be programmed to move across the screen in a certain direction at a certain speed: *program the character in a computer game as a sprite*

/spraɪt/

pl sprites

⋈ manipulate, program a **sprite**; a **sprite** attribute, command

▶ **turtle**

---

sprocket *noun* (hardware)

a wheel with teeth that fit into the holes in computer paper. It is used to make sure that paper moves correctly through a printer, etc: *use a sprocket to position continuous stationery accurately*

/ˈsprɒkɪt/

pl sprockets

⋈ a **sprocket** drive, hole, wheel

---

sprocket feed *noun* (hardware)

a part of the printer that holds the paper in place while it is being printed

/ˈsprɒkɪt fiːd/

pl sprocket feeds

syn pin feed, tractor feed

SQL *abbr*

Structured Query Language. A high-level computer programming language designed for accessing large databases.

note SQL is a non-procedural query language that was designed in the 1970s.

/ˌes kjuː ˈel/

note pronounced as individual letters

note not used with *a* or *an*. No plural and used with a singular verb only.

⋈ access data using, write queries *in* **SQL**; **SQL** syntax

---

square brackets *noun*

the characters '[ ]' found on a computer keyboard: *Square brackets are often used in formal syntax definitions to enclose optional elements.*

/ˌskweə ˈbrækɪts/

pl square brackets

⋈ enclose something *in*, surround something *by/with* **square brackets**

SSD *abbr*
► **single sided disk**

note used in written English only

SSI *abbr*
► **small scale integration**

/ˌes es ˈaɪ/

note pronounced as individual letters

---

stack *noun* (software/programming)
a DATA STRUCTURE (= a collection of data items considered as one single item) where only one data item, called the TOP OF STACK, can be accessed. A new data item added to the stack becomes the top of stack, but the original item is still held, although it cannot be accessed until the present top of stack is removed.

/stæk/

pl stacks

M access, define, empty, implement, pop, push, update a **stack**

syn last in, first out stack, LIFO stack, push-down list, push-down stack

► **bottom of stack, dynamic data structure, parse, pop, push, top of stack**

---

stack base *noun* (software/programming)
the address in memory used by the first item placed on a STACK. The stack will get larger and smaller, but the stack base will be the one fixed location that is always used by the stack.

/ˈstæk beɪs/

pl stack bases

---

stack overflow *noun*
an error that happens when a program tries to add a new item to a STACK but there is no space on the stack to store the extra item: *Stack overflow caused the program to crash.*

/ˈstæk ˌəʊvəfləʊ/

note no plural

M cause, encounter, recover *from* **stack overflow**

---

stack pointer *noun*
a memory location that holds the address of the next free location in a STACK: *The stack pointer is updated whenever a new data item is added to the stack.*

/ˈstæk ˌpɔɪntə(r)/

pl stack pointers

M access, decrement, increment, update the **stack pointer**

---

stack underflow *noun*
the error that occurs when a program tries to remove an item from the top of a STACK that is empty

/ˌstæk ˈʌndəfləʊ/

note not used with *a* or *an*. No plural and used with a singular verb only.

M cause, detect **stack underflow**

☆**stand-alone** *adjective* (hardware)
(of a computer or system) that can work without being connected to other computers: *a stand-alone microcomputer*

/ˈstænd əˌləʊn/

► **multi-user system**

---

standard function *noun* (software/programming)
a FUNCTION or SUBROUTINE that is part of a high-level programming language: *Trigonometric routines are provided as standard functions in most scientific programming languages.*

/ˌstændəd ˈfʌŋkʃn/

pl standard functions

M call, provide, use a **standard function**

---

standard interface *noun*
hardware and software that operates to an agreed standard: *The written specification defines a standard interface between applications using different protocols.* ○ *The use of a standard interface means that software packages will all work in the same way.*

/ˌstændəd ˈɪntəfeɪs/

pl standard interfaces

---

abbr abbreviation   **pl** plural   **syn** synonym   ► see   **M** collocate (*word often used with the headword*)

standards *noun*
an agreed set of features that hardware and software must have to reach a certain level of quality and work in an acceptable way

/'stændədz/
note usually plural
⋈ conform *to*, develop, fail to meet, formulate, meet, monitor, specify **standards**; acceptable, clearly-defined, international, realistic, strict **standards**
▶ compatible, protocol

---

star network *noun* (hardware)
a network where the NODES (2) are each linked directly to a central computer. All communication must pass through this computer: *The star network has a server as the central node.* ○ *The star network closed down because the central computer failed.*

/'stɑː ,netwɜːk/
pl star networks
⋈ configure as, use a **star network**
▶ bus network, network, network topology, ring network, tree network

---

start bit *noun*
a binary digit used in ASYNCHRONOUS COMMUNICATION to show the beginning of a piece of data: *Each data word is preceded by a start bit.*

/'stɑːt bɪt/
pl start bits
⋈ receive, send, transmit a **start bit**
▶ stop bit

---

start of header character *noun*
the CONTROL CHARACTER with ASCII code number 1 which is used to mark the beginning of the HEADER (1) information in a message

/,stɑːt əv 'hedə ,kærəktə(r)/
pl start of header characters
abbr SOH
⋈ receive, send, transmit, type a **start of header character**

---

start of text character *noun*
the CONTROL CHARACTER with ASCII code number 2, which is used to mark the beginning of a message after any HEADER (1) information

/,stɑːt əv 'tekst ,kærəktə(r)/
pl start of text characters
abbr SOT, STX
⋈ receive, send, transmit, type a **start of text character**
▶ end of text character

---

start up[1] *noun*
▶ boot[1]

/'stɑːt ʌp/

---

start up[2] *verb*
▶ boot[2]

/'stɑːt ʌp/

---

state *noun*
the condition of a device, computer or system at a certain time, especially the condition of all registers, switches and memory locations: *The modem is in a state ready to receive data.*

/steɪt/
pl states
⋈ initial **state**
syn status

☆**statement** *noun* (software/programming)
the smallest executable part of a program: *The program was written with each statement starting on a new line.*

/'steɪtmənt/
pl statements
⋈ a comment, control **statement**
syn program statement

▶ **argument, assertion, assignment statement, command**

☆**state-of-the-art** *adjective*
connected with the most modern technology or equipment: *State-of-the-art computer simulators are used to train personnel.* ○ *install a state-of-the-art electronic system to control the railway network*

/ˌsteɪt əv ði ˈɑːt/
ᴍ **state-of-the-art** equipment, hardware, software, technology
▶ **high-tech**

---

state transition diagram *noun*
a chart showing the possible states of a system and the way the system moves between states in response to different inputs: *a state transition diagram of a Turing machine*

/ˌsteɪt tranˈzɪʃn ˌdaɪəgræm/
pl state transition diagrams
ᴍ display *as*, draw a **state transition diagram**

---

static *noun*
a loud noise in a transmitted signal, especially a radio signal: *It was almost impossible to hear the radio broadcast because of the static.*

/ˈstætɪk/
note not used with *a* or *an*. No plural and used with a singular verb only.
ᴍ filter out **static**

---

static allocation *noun*
a situation where a fixed amount of memory for a program is reserved. The amount of memory does not change during the execution of the program.

/ˈstætɪk ˌæləˈkeɪʃn/
note not used with *a* or *an*. No plural and used with a singular verb only.
ᴍ implement, use **static allocation**
▶ **dynamic allocation**

---

static data structure *noun*
a DATA STRUCTURE (= a collection of data items that behaves as a single item) that is fixed in size and cannot grow larger or smaller during the execution of a program

/ˌstætɪk ˈdeɪtə ˌstrʌktʃə(r)/
pl static data structures
ᴍ access, choose, define, implement, traverse, update a **static data structure**
▶ **dynamic data structure**

---

static memory *noun* (hardware)
memory that keeps data as long as an electric current flows. Static memory does not need to be REFRESHED (1).

/ˌstætɪk ˈmeməri/
note no plural
syn static RAM
▶ **DRAM**

---

static RAM *noun*
▶ **static memory**

/ˌstætɪk ˈræm/

---

stationery *noun* (hardware)
equipment for writing or printing, such as pens, paper, envelopes and labels: *computer stationery* ○ *stationery supplies*

/ˈsteɪʃənri/
note not used with *a* or *an*. No plural and used with a singular verb only.
ᴍ continuous, pre-printed **stationery**
▶ **multipart stationery**

---

status *noun*
▶ **state**

/ˈsteɪtəs/

---

status bit *noun*
a single bit which shows if a computer operation has been completed successfully: *The status bit is checked after each data transfer to see if it has been reported as successful.*

/ˈsteɪtəs bɪt/
pl status bits
ᴍ clear, set, unset the **status bit**

---

abbr abbreviation   **pl** plural   **syn** synonym   ▶ see   ᴍ collocate (*word often used with the headword*)

status line *noun*
1 the part of a screen display, usually at the top or bottom of the screen, that gives a report on what the computer is doing at any time during the execution of a program **2** one of the CONTROL LINES (= a wire in a data bus that carries control signals) in a parallel data link that carries information about how a system is operating

/ˈsteɪtəs laɪn/
pl status lines
1 ᴍ read, update the **status line**
2 ᴍ read, test the **status line**

---

status register *noun*
a register that contains STATUS BITS: *an 8-bit status register*

/ˈsteɪtəs ˌredʒɪstə(r)/
pl status registers
ᴍ examine the **status register**
syn status word

---

status word *noun*
▶ **status register**

/ˈsteɪtəs wɜːd/

---

step¹ *noun*
a single fixed operation, usually a basic operation: *The complex program could be broken down into individual steps.*

/step/
pl steps
ᴍ carry out, execute a **step**
▶ **single step**

---

step² *verb*
to move by a fixed amount usually to execute one single operation: *step through the program to examine the contents of the registers*

/step/
step, stepping, stepped
note intransitive verb
ᴍ **step** *through* a program, *through* a subroutine
▶ **single step**

---

stepwise refinement *noun* (software/programming)
a method of TOP DOWN DESIGN where each part of the program is first described generally and is then developed in a more and more detailed way: *Executable code is written at the final stage of stepwise refinement.*

/ˌstepwaɪz rɪˈfaɪnmənt/
pl stepwise refinements
▶ **structured programming**

---

stop bit *noun*
a binary digit used in ASYNCHRONOUS COMMUNICATION to indicate the end of a piece of data: *Each data word ends with a stop bit.*

/ˈstɒp bɪt/
pl stop bits
ᴍ receive, send, transmit a **stop bit**
▶ **start bit**

---

stop list *noun*
a set of items that are ignored when a database is searched: *The stop list included very common words such as 'and', 'the' and 'a' to shorten search time.*

/ˈstɒp lɪst/
pl stop lists
ᴍ add something *to*, delete something *from* a **stop list**

---

storage *noun* (hardware)
places where data and programs are held so that they are available to a computer: *The computer's storage includes RAM, ROM, disks and buffers.*

/ˈstɔːrɪdʒ/
note no plural
syn data storage, store
▶ **external memory**

---

storage allocation *noun* (software)
the process of choosing which memory locations will be used to hold different programs that execute on the same computer

/ˌstɔːrɪdʒ æləˌkeɪʃn/
note not used with *a* or *an*. No plural and used with a singular verb only.

⋈ dynamic, static **storage
allocation; storage
allocation** algorithms,
methods, procedures, routines

▶ **dynamic allocation**

---

storage capacity noun
the maximum amount of data, measured in bits and bytes, etc
that can be held in storage devices such as memory, disk and
tape: *The disk has a storage capacity of 1 gigabyte.*

/ˌstɔːrɪdʒ kəˌpæsəti/
note usually singular

---

storage device noun (hardware)
a piece of equipment such as tape or disk, etc which can hold
computer data

/ˌstɔːrɪdʒ dɪˈvaɪs/
pl storage devices
⋈ auxiliary, backing, data, mass,
optical **storage device**

---

storage location noun
▶ **address¹ 1**

/ˌstɔːrɪdʒ ləʊˈkeɪʃn/

---

storage media noun (hardware)
the different types of STORAGE DEVICES that can be used by a
computer, especially as a backing store

/ˈstɔːrɪdʒ ˌmiːdiə/
note plural noun, used with a
plural verb

☆**store** noun
▶ **storage**

/stɔː(r)/

---

store address noun
▶ **address¹**

/ˈstɔː(r) əˌdres/

---

store and forward switching noun
▶ **message switching**

/ˈstɔː(r) ənd ˈfɔːwəd ˈswɪtʃɪŋ/

---

stored program noun
▶ **program**

/ˌstɔːd ˈprəʊgræm/

---

straight line code noun (software/programming)
a computer program whose statements are always executed
one after the other in the order they are written

/ˈstreɪt ˈlaɪn ˈkəʊd/
note not used with *a* or *an*. No
plural and used with a singular
verb only.
⋈ insert *as*, program, write
straight line code

---

stream noun
▶ **data stream**

/striːm/

---

streamer noun (hardware)
a continuous piece of magnetic tape that is used for making
backup copies of data: *backup data onto a streamer*

/ˈstriːmə(r)/
pl streamers
syn tape streamer

☆**string** noun
a group of letters, numbers or characters, etc in a certain
order: *search for a particular character string* ○ *change the order of
bytes in a string* ○ *a string of consecutive characters*

/strɪŋ/
pl strings
⋈ an alphabetic, an input, a
numeric, a search, a sequential,
a text **string**
syn character string
▶ **array**

---

abbr abbreviation   **pl** plural   **syn** synonym   ▶ see   ⋈ collocate (*word often used with the headword*)

string array *noun*
an array in which each individual data item is a string:
initialize a string array with null strings

/ˈstrɪŋ ə,reɪ/
pl string arrays

ᴴ access, declare, define a **string array**

---

string concatenation *noun*
the process of adding one string to the end of another string to make a single string

/ˈstrɪŋ kən,kætə,neɪʃn/
note usually singular

ᴴ carry out, perform a **string concatenation**

▶ **concatenation**

---

string handling *noun*
the operations that can be performed on data items stored as strings

note Common operations in string handling are concatenation and truncation.

/ˈstrɪŋ ,hændlɪŋ/
note not used with *a* or *an*. No plural and used with a singular verb only.

ᴴ carry out, perform **string handling; string handling** algorithms, methods

syn string manipulation

---

string length *noun*
the number of characters or bytes, etc in a string

/ˈstrɪŋ leŋθ/
pl string lengths

ᴴ assign a, read the **string length**

---

string manipulation *noun*
▶ **string handling**

/ˈstrɪŋ mə,nɪpju,leɪʃn/

---

string variable *noun*
the name used in a computer programming language for a set of locations in the computer's memory which can hold a string. Data is stored in a string variable by using an ASSIGNMENT STATEMENT (= a statement that gives a value to a variable): *a programming language that supports string variables*

/ˈstrɪŋ ,veəriəbl/
pl string variables

ᴴ assign a name *to*, read the value *of*, reference a **string variable**; concatenate two **string variables**

▶ **logical variable, numeric variable, variable**

---

strip¹ *noun* (hardware)
a narrow piece of something such as paper: *The bank card has a strip of magnetic material on the back.*

/strɪp/
pl strips

syn stripe

▶ **magnetic strip**

---

strip² *verb*
to remove something that has been added, leaving a central part behind: *strip away the header information from an e-mail message* ○ *strip off the leading zeros*

/strɪp/
strip, stripping, stripped
note transitive verb

---

stripe *noun*
▶ **strip**

/straɪp/

---

strobe¹ *noun*
1 a single pulse sent to an electronic component **2** a light source that pulses at a regular rate

/strəʊb/
pl strobes

1 ᴴ assert, send a **strobe**

2 ᴴ adjust, use a **strobe**

strobe² *verb*   /strəʊb/

1 to pulse at regular intervals: *The display strobed badly and was uncomfortable to look at.* **2** to send a single pulse to one of the inputs of an electronic component: *The system clock strobes the READ input.*

strobe, strobing, strobed

1 note intransitive verb

◣ **strobe** at high frequency

2 note transitive verb

◣ **strobe** an input, output

---

strongly typed *adjective* (programming)   /ˌstrɒŋli ˈtaɪpt/

(of a programming language) that cannot change the DATA TYPE of a variable: *Pascal is a strongly-typed language.*

◣ a **strongly typed** language, variable

▶ **weakly typed**

---

structure¹ *noun*   /ˈstrʌktʃə(r)/

the way the parts of something are put together or organized: *The structure of the program was not clear.*

pl structures

◣ design, implement the **structure**; a complex, a data, an elaborate, a simple, a tree-like **structure**

---

structure² *verb*   /ˈstrʌktʃə(r)/

to put something together in an organized way: *The program was structured so that it was easy to understand.*

structure, structuring, structured

note transitive verb

◣ **structure** a presentation, program

---

structured design *noun*

▶ **structured programming**

/ˌstrʌktʃəd dɪˈzaɪn/

---

structure diagram *noun*   /ˈstrʌktʃə ˌdaɪəɡræm/

a drawing showing how the parts of a program or the COMPONENTS of a computer system are organized

pl structure diagrams

◣ draft, draw up a **structure diagram**

---

structured programming *noun* (software/programming)   /ˌstrʌktʃəd ˈprəʊɡræmɪŋ/

a method of designing a computer program so that it is easy to understand, change and maintain. This is usually done by making each part of the program an individual PROCEDURE **(2)** which is programmed separately: *Separate modules of code are often used in structured programming.* ○ *Structured programming should avoid the GOTO instruction.*

note not used with *a* or *an*. No plural and used with a singular verb only.

◣ **structured programming** methods, techniques, methodology

syn structured design

▶ **top-down**

Structured Query Language *noun*

▶ **SQL**

/ˌstrʌktʃəd ˈkwɪəri ˌlæŋɡwɪdʒ/

STX *abbr*

▶ **start of text character**

note used in written English only

---

style sheet *noun* (applications/word processing)   /ˈstaɪl ʃiːt/

a file that contains instructions for FORMATS¹ **(2)** that can be used in word-processed documents. A style sheet usually includes instructions for line-spacing, margin size and the type of FONT to be used: *save the style sheet so it can be reused for future documents*

pl style sheets

◣ create, design, save, use a **style sheet**

---

abbr abbreviation   **pl** plural   **syn** synonym   ▶ see   ◣ collocate (*word often used with the headword*)

stylus *noun* (hardware)
a device shaped like a pen that is used for pointing to a TOUCH SCREEN or GRAPHICS TABLET: *select a command from the menu using the stylus*

/ˈstaɪləs/
pl styli
pl styluses
ℍ draw *with*, point *with* a **stylus**

☆**subdirectory** *noun* (software)
a directory that is inside another directory: *The letters are stored in a subdirectory called 'correspondence' on the C drive.*

/ˈsʌbdəˌrektəri/
pl subdirectories
▶ file, directory

sublist *noun*
a list that is a data item in another list: *The sublist (C, D) is in the list (A, B, (C, D))*

/ˈsʌblɪst/
pl sublists
ℍ access, insert a **sublist**

subprogram *noun*
▶ routine

/ˈsʌbprəʊɡræm/

subroutine *noun* (software/programming)
a ROUTINE that is CALLED² (2) several times to execute a small task: *The subroutine checks the password.*

/ˈsʌbruːtiːn/
pl subroutines
ℍ call, define, invoke a **subroutine**; an add-on, a built-in, a user-defined **subroutine**
▶ closed subroutine, function¹ 2, nested subroutine, open subroutine, parameter

subroutine call *noun* (software)
the statement in a computer programming language that causes a SUBROUTINE to be executed

/ˈsʌbruːtiːn kɔːl/
pl subroutine calls
ℍ make a **subroutine call**
▶ calling sequence, function call, parameter, return¹ 2

subroutine library *noun* (software)
a collection of SUBROUTINES or FUNCTIONS that is stored centrally and can be used by any programmer: *Utility and housekeeping routines are stored in a subroutine library so they don't have to be rewritten each time they are needed.*

/ˈsʌbruːtiːn ˌlaɪbrəri/
pl subroutine libraries
ℍ access, store *in* a **subroutine library**
▶ library routine

subschema *noun*
a diagram or chart showing the layout of types of data in a part of a database and the links between the data items as a user sees them

note The subschema may not be the same as the overall layout of the data (the schema). It may be specially designed for a particular type of user.

/ˈsʌbskiːmə/
pl subschemas
pl subschemata
ℍ compile, draw up a **subschema**
▶ schema, logical schema, physical schema

subscript *noun*
a printed character such as the '₂' in 'H₂O': *use a subscript to denote a value* ○ *an array subscript*

/ˈsʌbskrɪpt/
pl subscripts
ℍ add, format something *as*, insert a **subscript**
▶ superscript

subscripted variable *noun*
▶ array

/ˌsʌbskrɪptɪd ˈveəriəbl/

substrate *noun* (hardware)
the bottom layer of a CHIP: *The electronic connections and gates of an integrated circuit are fabricated onto the substrate.*

/ˈsʌbstreɪt/
pl substrates
◄ assemble something *onto* the **substrate**

---

substring *noun*
a string that forms part of a longer string: *'X1Y2' is a substring of 'X1Y2Z3'*

/ˈsʌbstrɪŋ/
pl substrings
◄ access, extract, separate *out* a **substring**

---

subsystem *noun* (hardware/software)
a part of a hardware or software SYSTEM: *The input subsystem is responsible for passing data to the processing modules.*

/ˈsʌbsɪstəm/
pl subsystems
◄ design, implement a **subsystem**

---

suffix *noun*
a code at the end of a message or record: *The suffix '.EXE' at the end of the file TEXT.EXE shows that it is an executable file.*

/ˈsʌfɪks/
pl suffixes
► **postfix notation, prefix**

---

suite *noun* (applications)
a collection of related applications that are sold as a unit: *an office suite of spreadsheet, word processing and database applications* ○ *a suite of software development tools*

/swiːt/
pl suites
◄ design, implement a **suite**
► **software package**

Sun *noun* (organizations)
(*trade mark*) a US manufacturer of workstations that are usually used in networks

/sʌn/
◄ a **Sun** terminal, workstation

☆**supercomputer** *noun* (hardware)
a powerful computer with a large amount of memory and a very fast CPU: *Some mathematical calculations require the power that only supercomputers can provide.* ○ *use a supercomputer for scientific modelling*

/ˈsuːpəkəmpjuːtə(r)/
pl supercomputers
◄ a parallel-processing **supercomputer**

---

super large scale integration *noun* (hardware)
the process of putting 100 000 or more components on an integrated circuit

/ˈsuːpə ˈlɑːdʒ skeɪl ˌɪntɪˈɡreɪʃn/
note not used with *a* or *an*. No plural and used with a singular verb only.
abbr SLSI
◄ **super large scale integration** methods, techniques
► **circuit board, large scale integration, medium scale integration, printed circuit board, small scale integration, ultra large scale integration, very large scale integration, wafer scale integration**

---

supermini *noun* (hardware)
a powerful minicomputer

/ˈsuːpəmɪni/
pl superminis

---

superscript *noun*
a printed character such as the '³' in 'x³': *The item number is indicated by a superscript figure.* ○ *The superscript 'e' denotes an expected variable.*

/ˈsuːpəskrɪpt/
pl superscripts
◄ add, format something *as*, insert a **superscript**
► **subscript**

---

abbr abbreviation   **pl** plural   **syn** synonym   ► see   ◄ collocate (*word often used with the headword*)

supervisor *noun*
▶ operating system

/ˈsuːpəvaɪzə(r)/

---

supervisor state *noun*
the period of time when the operating system, not the user's program, has control of the computer: *The system entered the supervisor state to process an interrupt.*

/ˈsuːpəvaɪzə steɪt/

note not used with *a* or *an*. No plural and used with singular verb only.

✣ enter, leave the **supervisor state**

---

support¹ *noun*
the help offered to the user by a company who makes or sells a computer: *telephone support is available 24 hours a day*

/səˈpɔːt/

note not used with *a* or *an*. No plural and used with a singular verb only.

✣ offer, receive **support**; telephone, user **support**

---

support² *verb*
1 the ability of a system to work with other systems, devices or programs: *The computer supports 32 dial-in user terminals.* 2 the ability of a computer or system to use certain methods to do calculations on data: *The CPU supports floating-point arithmetic.*

/səˈpɔːt/

support, supporting, supported

note transitive verb

---

support group *noun* (personnel)
a team of people who help users solve problems with computers, systems or software

/səˈpɔːt gruːp/

pl support groups

✣ ask, call, telephone the **support group**; an end-user, a technical **support group**

---

suppression *noun*
the removal or hiding of unwanted data: *The suppression of HTML tags in a hypertext document makes them invisible to the user.*

/səˈpreʃn/

note not used with *a* or *an*. No plural and used with a singular verb only.

✣ carry out, perform a **suppression**

---

surge *noun*
a sudden increase in power which may damage a computer or make it lose data: *A power surge blew a lot of fuses.*

/sɜːdʒ/

pl surges

✣ protect *against* a **surge**

syn power surge, spike

▶ **fuse¹, transient**

---

surge protector *noun* (hardware)
a device that can sense a sudden increase in electrical power and stop it reaching computers so that equipment is not damaged and data is not lost

/ˈsɜːdʒ prə,tektə(r)/

pl surge protectors

▶ **fuse¹**

---

suspend *verb*
to stop something for a short time so that it can be continued later: *The printer interrupt suspended the program while it was executing.*

/səˈspend/

suspend, suspending, suspended

note transitive verb

✣ **suspend** an operation, a process, a program

---

swap *verb*
to change the program which is being executed. This is done by copying it to disk and loading another program from disk into memory: *The operating system swaps the program when a peripheral interrupt occurs.*

/swɒp/

swap, swapping, swapped

note transitive verb

▶ **multiprogramming, time slice**

switch *noun*
1 (*hardware*) a mechanical or electronic device that can complete an electrical circuit in order to allow a current to pass, or break an electrical circuit which stops a current from passing **2** (*software*) an instruction in a program that can pass control to different statements

/swɪtʃ/
pl switches
1 ⋈ an off, an on, a two-way **switch**
▶ **circuit breaker**
2 ⋈ execute a **switch**
syn switch statement
▶ **conditional branch**

switched network *noun*
a network where messages can be sent to any one of a number of different locations described in the HEADER **(1)** information

/ˌswɪtʃt ˈnetwɜːk/
pl switched networks
⋈ install, maintain, use a **switched network**
▶ **unswitched network**

switching *noun*
the process of making a connection over a network or telephone system. Data can be sent over this connection along one fixed path for the whole time of the transmission (circuit switching), or the data can travel over over several different paths and can be put together by the receiving device (packet switching).

/ˈswɪtʃɪŋ/
note no plural
⋈ a **switching** delay, mechanism; **switching** apparatus

switching centre *noun*
a place in a network that receives messages and passes them to another place

/ˈswɪtʃɪŋ ˌsentə(r)/
pl switching centres
⋈ receive data *from*, send data *via*, transmit data *via* a **switching centre**
▶ **gateway**

switching speed *noun*
a measure of how fast a memory location or LOGIC CIRCUIT can change from one state to another

note Modern computers measure switching speeds in millions of operations per second.

/ˈswɪtʃɪŋ spiːd/
pl switching speeds
⋈ improve, measure the **switching speed**; fast, slow **switching speed**

switch statement *noun*
▶ **switch 2**

/ˈswɪtʃ ˌsteɪtmənt/

symbol *noun*
1 any character that is not an ALPHANUMERIC character: *Common symbols are ? * & $.* **2** a label or identifier in a computer program: *Among the symbols in this program are the labels START and END.*

/ˈsɪmbl/
pl symbols
1 ⋈ print a **symbol**
2 note In this sense, symbols are often made up from alphanumeric characters.
⋈ identify, parse a **symbol**

symbolic *adjective*
connected with or using symbols

/sɪmˈbɒlɪk/
⋈ a **symbolic** expression, statement

symbolic address *noun*
an address in a MACHINE CODE program that is written using a name of the programmer's choice; the true address will be inserted automatically when the program is translated

/sɪmˌbɒlɪk əˈdres/
pl symbolic addresses
⋈ give, insert, write a **symbolic address**
▶ **absolute address**

---

abbr abbreviation   **pl** plural   **syn** synonym   ▶ see   ⋈ collocate (*word often used with the headword*)

symbolic addressing *noun*
the use of names of the programmer's choice to stand for
addresses in a MACHINE CODE program

/sɪmˌbɒlɪk əˈdresɪŋ/
note not used with *a* or *an*. No
plural and used with a singular
verb only.
◄ employ, use **symbolic
addressing**

---

symbolic language *noun* (software/programming)
a computer programming language that allows the
programmer to choose names for variables or addresses

note Most languages, especially high-level languages, are
symbolic languages; only machine code is truly non-symbolic.

/sɪmˌbɒlɪk ˈlæŋgwɪdʒ/
pl symbolic languages
◄ program *in*, use, write *in* a
symbolic language

---

symbol table *noun*
▶ **name table**

/ˈsɪmbl ˌteɪbl/

---

symmetric traversal *noun* (software/programming)
a path through a BINARY TREE that accesses each data item in
turn. Any particular item is accessed only after all items
reached through its left DESCENDANT are accessed and before
those reached through its right descendant are accessed:
*Symmetric traversal of a properly constructed binary tree produces
the data in ascending order.*

/sɪˌmetrɪk trəˈvɜːsl/
pl symmetric traversals
◄ perform a **symmetric
traversal**
▶ **post-order traversal, pre-
order traversal**
syn enorder traversal, inorder
traversal

SYN *abbr*
▶ **synchronous idle character**

note used in written English only

---

sync *abbr*
▶ **synchronization**

/sɪŋk/

---

sync bit *abbr*
▶ **synchronization bit**

/ˈsɪŋk bɪt/

---

sync character *abbr*
▶ **synchronization character**

/ˈsɪŋk ˌkærəktə(r)/

---

synchronization *noun*
a situation where two or more devices or processes operate at
the same time or speed as each other or something else:
*Because a printer is much slower than a computer, software is used
to keep them in synchronization.*

/ˌsɪŋkrənaɪˈzeɪʃn/
note no plural
◄ be *in* **synchronization** *with*
something

---

synchronization bit *noun*
a binary digit that is sent as part of a data transmission to
provide a common reference mark for two devices that need to
be in synchronization: *Several synchronization bits are sent at
predetermined intervals to adjust the clock speeds of the two devices.*

/ˌsɪŋkrənaɪˈzeɪʃn bɪt/
pl synchronization bits
abbr sync bit
◄ receive, send, transmit a
synchronization bit

---

synchronization character *noun*
a character that is sent as part of a data transmission to
provide a common reference mark for two devices that need to
be in synchronization

/ˌsɪŋkrənaɪˈzeɪʃn ˌkærəktə(r)/
pl synchronization characters
abbr sync character
◄ receive, send, transmit a
synchronization character

synchronization pulse noun

a single pulse that is sent as part of a data transmission to provide a common reference mark for two devices that need to be in synchronization: *A series of synchronization pulses are recorded as part of a video recording.*

/ˌsɪŋkrənaɪˈzeɪʃn pʌls/

pl synchronization pulses

abbr sync pulse

◄ receive, record, send, transmit a **synchronization pulse**

synchronize verb

to make something operate at the same time or speed as something else: *The oscillator produces a regular signal that can be used to synchronize other devices.* ○ *The wheels must synchronize as they revolve.* ○ *A common clock synchronizes the transmission of data between the devices.*

/ˈsɪŋkrənaɪz/

synchronize, synchronizing, synchronized

note transitive and intransitive verb

◄ **synchronize** a device *with* a signal

synchronous adjective

(of a device or process) that operates at the same time or speed as something else: *The entire operation of a computer is synchronous as every component is driven by a master clock.*

/ˈsɪŋkrənəs/

◄ a **synchronous** operation, port; **synchronous** access, communication, mode

► asynchronous

synchronous communication noun

the sending and receiving of data at fixed times under the control of a timing clock

/ˈsɪŋkrənəs kəˌmjuːnɪˈkeɪʃn/

note not used with *a* or *an*. No plural and used with a singular verb only.

◄ employ, use **synchronous communication**

► **asynchronous communication**

synchronous data link control noun

a set of rules that must be obeyed by both devices involved in SYNCHRONOUS COMMUNICATION

/ˌsɪŋkrənəs ˈdeɪtə lɪŋk kənˌtrəʊl/

pl synchronous data link controls

abbr SDLC

◄ define, design, implement **synchronous data link control**

► **synchronous protocol**

synchronous idle character noun

the CONTROL CHARACTER that is used in synchronous communication when no message is being sent to keep the sending device and receiving device in SYNCHRONIZATION: *The synchronous idle character is sent by typing CONTROL-V.*

/ˌsɪŋkrənəs ˈaɪdl ˌkærəktə(r)/

pl synchronous idle characters

abbr SYN

◄ receive, send, transmit, type a **synchronous idle character**

synchronous mode noun

the state that two devices are in when they exchange data at fixed times

note Synchronous mode needs special timing hardware but does not need any special stop and start signals.

/ˈsɪŋkrənəs məʊd/

note not used with *a* or *an*. No plural and used with a singular verb only.

◄ communicate *in*, operate *in*, use **synchronous mode**

► **asynchronous mode**

synchronous orbit satellite noun

a satellite whose orbit matches the speed of rotation of the earth, and which appears to remain stationary above one place on the earth's surface: *A network of synchronous orbit satellites covers the globe.*

/ˈsɪŋkrənəs ˈɔːbɪt ˈsætəlaɪt/

pl synchronous orbit satellites

◄ launch, transmit data *via* **synchronous orbit satellite**

syn geostationary orbit satellite

---

abbr abbreviation   **pl** plural   **syn** synonym   ► see   ◄ collocate (*word often used with the headword*)

synchronous protocol *noun*
a set of rules that must be obeyed by both devices involved in
SYNCHRONOUS COMMUNICATION

/ˌsɪŋkrənəs ˈprəʊtəkɒl/
pl synchronous protocols

ⵉ conform *to*, define, implement, use a **synchronous protocol**

---

synchronous TDM *noun*
▶ **synchronous time division multiplexing**

/ˌsɪŋkrənəs ˌtiː diː ˈem/

---

synchronous transmission *noun*
1 the exchange of data between COMPONENTS or devices in
SYNCHRONOUS MODE so data is exchanged at fixed times: *The
synchronous transmission of data inside a computer.* **2** one
particular message that is transmitted at a fixed time: *Transfers
between CPU registers are synchronous transmissions.*

/ˌsɪŋkrənəs trænsˈmɪʃn/
note not used with *a* or *an*. No plural and used with a singular verb only.

1 ⵉ **synchronous transmission** protocols, methods

▶ **asynchronous transmission 1**

2 pl synchronous transmissions

ⵉ make, send a **synchronous transmission**

▶ **asynchronous transmission 2**

---

sync pulse *abbr*
▶ **synchronization pulse**

/ˈsɪŋk pʌls/

---

syntactic error *noun*
▶ **syntax error**

/sɪnˌtæktɪk ˈerə(r)/

---

syntax *noun*
▶ **grammar**

/ˈsɪntæks/

---

syntax analysis *noun*
the process of checking a computer program to see if it obeys
the GRAMMAR rules of the programming language: *Syntax
analysis is an early stage of compilation.*

/ˈsɪntæks əˌnæləsɪs/
note not used with *a* or *an*. No plural and used with a singular verb only.

ⵉ carry out, perform **syntax analysis**

▶ **parsing**

---

syntax check *noun*
▶ **grammar check**

/ˈsɪntæks tʃek/

---

syntax error *noun*
a mistake in a programming language statement caused by
breaking the grammar rules of the language: *A typical syntax
error is to spell a command incorrectly.*

/ˈsɪntæks ˌerə(r)/
pl syntax errors

ⵉ commit, correct, detect, make a **syntax error**

syn syntactic error

▶ **grammar, semantic error**

---

synthesize *verb*
to make something from a number of smaller things, such as
words from individual sounds

/ˈsɪnθəsaɪz/
synthesize, synthesizing, synthesized

	note transitive verb
	◄ **synthesize** music, speech
	► **speech synthesis**

synthesizer *noun*
a device which makes something from a number of smaller things, such as words from individual sounds

/ˈsɪnθəsaɪzə(r)/
pl synthesizers
◄ a music, speech **synthesizer**
► **speech synthesizer**

sysgen *abbr*
► **system generation**

/ˈsɪsdʒen/

☆**system** *noun* (hardware)
a computer installation including a central processing unit, peripherals and software that are designed to work together: *The complete system incorporates six networked personal computers and two laser printers.*

/ˈsɪstəm/
pl systems
◄ an AI, a CAD, a computer, an interactive **system**

system administrator *noun* (personnel)
the person in charge of running a computer system: *The system administrator is responsible for all aspects of the operation of the system including data entry, security and maintenance.*

/ˌsɪstəm ədˈmɪnɪstreɪtə(r)/
pl system administrators

system board *noun* (hardware)
the printed circuit board that holds the CPU: *The system board is the main component of the computer.*

/ˈsɪstəm bɔːd/
pl system boards
◄ install, manufacture a **system board**
► **daughter board**

system clock *noun* (hardware)
an electronic device inside a computer which sends out signals at fixed intervals of time. These signals are used to keep all the parts of a computer system operating at the correct speed: *The rate at which the system clock runs is a significant feature in assessing the power of a computer.* ○ *a clock speed of 60 MHz*

note The speed of a system clock is measured in Hertz.

/ˌsɪstəm ˈklɒk/
pl system clocks
► **real-time clock**

system console *noun* (hardware)
the main control panel of a computer system: *Operator commands are issued from the system console.*

/ˌsɪstəm ˈkɒnsəʊl/
pl system consoles

system crash *noun* (hardware)
a sudden failure of a computer system: *The system crash happened when the network became overloaded.*

/ˈsɪstəm kræʃ/
pl system crashes
► **crash**

system design *noun*
the process of choosing computer hardware and software to work together to do certain type of work: *The system design meets the requirements of the scientists who will use it to do detailed calculations.*

/ˈsɪstəm dɪˌzaɪn/
note not used with *a* or *an*. No plural and used with a singular verb only.
(also **systems design**)
◄ carry out, perform **system design**
► **systems analysis**

system development *noun*
the process of designing, installing and perhaps testing a computer system

/ˈsɪstəm dɪˌveləpmənt/
note not used with *a* or *an*. No plural and used with a singular verb only.

abbr abbreviation   **pl** plural   **syn** synonym   ► see   ◄ collocate (*word often used with the headword*)

> ⋈ **system development** tools, methods, methodology

system disk *noun*
the storage device that holds the OPERATING SYSTEM and other system software

/'sɪstəm dɪsk/
pl system disks
⋈ access, use the **system disk**

system error *noun*
an error that is detected by the operating system

/'sɪstəm ˌerə(r)/
pl system errors

system generation *noun*
the process of creating an OPERATING SYSTEM from separate modules, including only those needed for the particular computer system in use: *System generation is designed to optimize the most heavily-used part of the system software.*

/'sɪstəm dʒenəˌreɪʃn/
note not used with *a* or *an*. No plural and used with a singular verb only.
⋈ carry out, perform **system generation**
syn sysgen

system life cycle *noun*
the amount of time that passes from designing a new system to when the system is no longer used

/ˌsɪstəm 'laɪf ˌsaɪkl/
pl system life cycles
▶ **sytems analysis**

system program *noun*
▶ **systems program**

/'sɪstəm ˌprəʊgræm/

system prompt *noun*
▶ **prompt**

/'sɪstəm prɒmpt/

system routine *noun*
▶ **systems routine**

/ˌsɪstəm ruː'tiːn/

systems analysis *noun*
the process of examining an existing system to see if it could be improved, or designing new systems

/ˌsɪstəmz ə'næləsɪs/
note not used with *a* or *an*. No plural and used with singular verb only.
⋈ **systems analysis** methods, professionals
▶ **systems design**

☆**systems analyst** *noun* (personnel)
a person who assesses a computer system in order to find ways in which it can be developed and improved: *The systems analyst wrote a report about improvements that were needed in the computer system.* ○ *The systems analyst determined the hardware and software requirements of the system.*

/ˌsɪstəmz 'ænəlɪst/
pl systems analysts
▶ **database administrator**

systems chart *noun*
▶ **data flowchart**

/'sɪstəmz tʃɑːt/

systems integration *noun*
the process of building a computer system from computer parts made by different ORIGINAL EQUIPMENT MANUFACTURERS: *a systems integration solution to meet the requirements of particular customers*

/'sɪstəmz ɪntɪˌgreɪʃn/
note singular noun, used with a singular verb

Systems Network Architecture *noun*
(*trade mark*) a way of linking computers and PERIPHERALS in networks which was developed by IBM: *conform to Systems Network Architecture protocols*

/ˌsɪstəmz ˈnetwɜːk ˌɑːkɪtektʃə(r)/

note no plural

abbr SNA

◄ implement **Systems Network Architecture**; **Systems Network Architecture** methods, protocols

► **Open Systems Interconnection**

☆**system software** *noun* (software)
the programs that control the operation of the computer or computer system: *The system software that handles the peripheral devices, input from the user and screen updates.*

/ˌsɪstəm ˈsɒftweə(r)/

note not used with *a* or *an*. No plural and used with a singular verb only.

◄ install the **system software**

► **applications software, systems program**

systems program *noun*
one of the computer programs making up the SYSTEM SOFTWARE: *There are various utilities among the systems programs.*

/ˈsɪstəmz ˌprəʊɡræm/

pl systems programs

◄ install, update, use a **systems program**

syn system program

► **applications program**

☆**systems programmer** *noun* (personnel)
a person who writes systems software: *A systems programmer can often write a new program using portions of existing programs.*

/ˈsɪstəmz ˌprəʊɡræmə(r)/

pl systems programmers

► **applications programmer**

systems routine *noun* (software)
one of the ROUTINES that form the SYSTEMS SOFTWARE: *There are various utilities among the systems routines.*

/ˈsɪstəmz ruːˌtiːn/

pl systems routines

◄ install, update, use a **systems routine**

syn system routine

☆**systems software** *noun* (software)
the set of programs including the operating system and utility programs that control the operations of a computer system

/ˈsɪstəmz ˌsɒftweə(r)/

note plural noun used with a singular verb

► **applications software**

system support *noun*
the department of a company which maintains and services the computer system: *System support functions include an advice service for users.*

/ˌsɪstəm səˈpɔːt/

note not used with *a* or *an*. No plural and used with singular verb only.

◄ call *on*, offer **system support**

system testing *noun*
the stage at which a new computer system is checked to make sure that it works correctly

/ˌsɪstəm ˈtestɪŋ/

note not used with *a* or *an*. No plural and used with a singular verb only.

◄ carry out, perform **system testing**

► **acceptance testing, system specification**

---

abbr abbreviation   **pl** plural   **syn** synonym   ► see   ◄ collocate (*word often used with the headword*)

T *abbr*
▶ **tera**

/tiː/

☆**tab¹** *noun*
▶ **tab stop**

/tæb/

☆**tab²** *verb* (user operation)
to move the cursor to a certain part of a text such as a new paragraph or to the next column in a table: *tab across to the next column*

/tæb/
tab, tabbing, tabbed
note intransitive verb
M **tab** *across/down* a document, etc

☆**tab character** *noun* (hardware)
a character which moves the cursor to a certain part of a text such as a new paragraph or the next column in a table

/tæb ˈkæræktə(r)/
pl tab characters
(also **tabulator**)
M a horizontal, vertical **tab**; a **tab** stop
▶ **space bar**

☆**tab key** *noun* (hardware)
a key that moves the cursor to a certain part of a text such as a new paragraph or the next column in a table

/ˈtæb kiː/
pl tab keys
M hit, press the **tab key**

---

table *noun*
▶ **two-dimensional array**

/ˈteɪbl/

---

tablet *noun*
▶ **graphics tablet**

/ˈtæblət/

---

tab stop *noun*
a position in a line of a document that is fixed. It shows where a piece of text or a column of figures, etc will begin: *The default tab stop is at 3cm.* ○ *set tab stops at 2cm intervals*

/ˈtæb stɒp/
pl tab stops
M alter, set the **tab stops**
syn tab

---

tabulate *verb*
to arrange data as a list or table: *analyse and tabulate data for modelling and forecasting*

/ˈtæbjuleɪt/
tabulate, tabulating, tabulated
note transitive verb
M **tabulate** data, numbers

---

tag¹ *noun*
1 a code describing the type of item in a SOURCE CODE statement: *There are separate tags for variables, operators and keywords and other items.* **2** a code that is added to a data item to describe that data item: *each word in the corpus has a part of speech tag*

/tæg/
pl tags
1,2 M attach a **tag**: a data **tag**
▶ **parsing, syntax analysis**

---

tag² *verb*
to attach something that carries extra information to a larger object: *tag each syntactic item with an identifying code*

/tæg/
tag, tagging, tagged
note transitive verb
M **tag** an item, object

---

tail *noun*
a list made from the items in an existing list after the HEAD **(1)** (= the first item in a list) has been removed: *The new list (B, (C, D)) is the tail of the list (A, B, (C, D))*

/teɪl/
pl tails
M access, delete, print the **tail**

tandem processors *noun* (hardware)
two computer systems that operate together to provide more processing power: *Tandem processors provide the speed and power necessary for real-time weather forecasting.*

/ˌtændəm ˈprəʊsesəz/
note plural noun used with a plural verb
ꟼ configure *as*, employ, use **tandem processors**
▶ **in tandem**

tape *noun* (hardware)
a long narrow strip of material that is used for storing data that can be read by a machine or a computer: *rewind the audio tape and play the song again* ○ *The backups of the day's work are made on tape.*

/teɪp/
pl tapes
ꟼ load, rewind, spool, wind a **tape**; a **tape** cassette, code, drive, guide
▶ **CD, magnetic tape, paper tape**

tape backup *noun*
1 the process of copying data onto magnetic tape so that it can be used if original data is lost or damaged: *do a tape backup over night* **2** a copy of data on magnetic tape that can be used if the original data is lost or damaged: *The tape backup was needed when the system accidentally erased all the data.*

/ˌteɪp ˈbæk ʌp/
pl tape backups

tape cartridge *noun* (hardware)
a container that holds magnetic tape: *back up the hard disk to a tape cartridge*

/ˈteɪp ˌkɑːtrɪdʒ/
pl tape cartridges

tape cassette *noun*
▶ **cassette**

/ˈteɪp kəˌset/

tape deck *noun* (hardware)
a device that records or plays back information held on magnetic tape: *a 1 600 bpi tape deck* ○ *a tape deck with AMS (automatic music search)* ○ *eject the cassette from the tape deck*

note A tape deck is a type of magnetic tape unit but 'tape deck' is often used to talk about a machine for playing audio (music) cassettes.

/ˈteɪp dek/
pl tape decks

tape device *noun*
▶ **magnetic tape unit**

/ˈteɪp dɪˌvaɪs/

tape drive *noun* (hardware)
a device that moves a tape across a READ/WRITE HEAD so that data can be written to the tape or read from the tape: *The tape drive is supplied with pre-formatted tapes.* ○ *a 525Mb tape drive*

/ˈteɪp draɪv/
pl tape drives
ꟼ an audio, a cartridge, a portable **tape drive**

tape format *noun*
the way data or information is stored on tape

/ˈteɪp ˌfɔːmæt/
pl tape formats
▶ **format¹ 1**

tape label *noun*
data written at the start of a piece of magnetic tape which describes the information held on the tape

note A tape label is not the piece of paper on the container of a tape.

/ˈteɪp ˌleɪbl/
pl tape labels
ꟼ read, write the **tape label**

---

abbr abbreviation　　**pl** plural　　**syn** synonym　　▶ see　　ꟼ collocate (*word often used with the headword*)

tape library *noun*
a place where computer tapes are kept: *The backup tapes are stored in the tape library.*

/'teɪp ˌlaɪbrəri/
pl tape libraries

tape punch *noun* (hardware)
a machine that makes small holes in paper tape

/'teɪp pʌntʃ/
pl tape punches
▶ **paper tape**

tape reader *noun* (hardware)
a device that reads data on paper tape or magnetic tape so that the data can be passed to a computer for processing

/'teɪp ˌriːdə(r)/
pl tape readers

tape recorder *noun* (hardware)
a machine that records or plays data held on magnetic tape: *The home computer uses a tape recorder which relays the program from the tape into the computer's memory.*

/'teɪp rɪˌkɔːdə(r)/
pl tape recorders
ℍ plug *in*, switch *off/on* the **tape recorder**; an audio, a digital, a multi-track, a voice-activated **tape recorder**

tape streamer *noun*
▶ **streamer**

/'teɪp ˌstriːmə(r)/

tape transport *noun*
▶ **transport**[1]

/'teɪp ˌtrænspɔːt/

tape unit *noun*
▶ **magnetic tape unit**

/'teɪp ˌjuːnɪt/

target computer *noun*
▶ **object computer**

/'tɑːgɪt kəmˌpjuːtə(r)/

target language *noun*
▶ **object language**

/'tɑːgɪt ˌlæŋgwɪdʒ/

target program *noun*
▶ **object program**

/'tɑːgɪt ˌprəʊgræm/

☆**task** *noun*
a group of instructions or a subprogram that the computer executes as a single unit

/tɑːsk/
pl tasks
ℍ a complex, simple **task**; a **task** queue
▶ **job, multitasking**

tasking *noun*
▶ **multitasking**

/'tɑːskɪŋ/

TAT *abbr*
▶ **turnaround time**

/ˌtiː eɪ 'tiː/
note pronounced as individual letters

Tb *abbr*
▶ **terabyte**

note used in written English only

TCP/IP *abbr*
transmission control protocol/Internet protocol

/'tiː siː ˌpiː aɪ 'piː/
note pronounced as individual letters

(also **transmission control protocol/interface program,**

transport control protocol/
interface program,
transport control protocol/
Internet protocol)

TDM *abbr*
▶ **time division multiplexing**

/ˌtiː diː ˈem/

note pronounced as individual letters

---

technology *noun*
1 the study and use of science for practical purposes in industry, etc **2** the use of science in a particular area, such as computing: *Advances in computer technology mean minicomputers can now do what mainframes used to do.* ○ *Videotex and videodisk are technologies that can be used in education.* ○ *introduce new printing technologies*

/tekˈnɒlədʒi/

1 note not used with *a*, or *an*. No plural and used with a singular verb only.

◪ develop, exploit, invest *in*, study **technology**; advanced, modern, new **technology**

2 pl technologies

◪ aviation, computer, nuclear, microchip, military, multimedia, software **technology**

1,2 ▶ **hi-tech, IT, state-of-the-art**

---

telecommunications *noun*
the transmission of data over long distances using radio, television, telephone, satellite or computer links: *Local terminals are linked to a central database via a telecommunications network.* ○ *invest in the telecommunications infrastructure*

/ˌtelikəˌmjuːnɪˈkeɪʃnz/

note not used with *a* or *an*. No plural and used with a singular verb only.

◪ a **telecommunications** link, network, service, system; **telecommunications** equipment, technology

---

teleconferencing *noun*
the use of computer equipment and communications links to allow a group of people who are in different places to talk to each other at the same time: *use desktop video teleconferencing for face-to-face meetings* ○ *link telephones to home computers to allow teleconferencing*

/ˌteliˈkɒnfərənsɪŋ/

note not used with *a* or *an*. No plural and used with a singular verb only.

(also **videoconferencing**)

---

teleprocessing *noun*
the use of a terminal to access a remote computer: *Sales data from stores is collected centrally by teleprocessing.*

/ˌteliˈprəʊsesɪŋ/

note not used with *a* or *an*. No plural and used with a singular verb only.

◪ **teleprocessing** hardware, software, systems

▶ **transaction processing**

---

telesoftware *noun* (software)
software which can be copied from a VIDEOTEX system or from a network to a user's computer: *Telesoftware can be found on many bulletin boards.*

/ˌteliˈsɒftweə(r)/

note not used with *a* or *an*. No plural and used with a singular verb only.

◪ download **telesoftware**

---

teletext *noun*
a system that displays information on specially adapted television screens: *dial up the teletext pages on news and weather*

/ˈtelitekst/

note not used with *a* or *an*. No plural and used with a singular verb only.

---

abbr abbreviation   **pl** plural   **syn** synonym   ▶ see   ◪ collocate (*word often used with the headword*)

⋈ access, broadcast *on*, view **teletext**; **teletext** hardware, software
▶ **videotex**

---

teletypewriter *noun* (hardware)
a computer terminal without a screen that shows information
only in printed form

note Teletypewriters have mostly been replaced by modern
computers.

/ˌteliˈtaɪpraɪtə(r)/
pl teletypewriters
abbr TTY

---

teleworking *noun*
working from home and communicating with the office and
other places by phone, fax and e-mail, etc: *Advances in
telecommunications will make teleworking more common.*

/ˈteliwɜːkɪŋ/
note not used with *a* or *an*. No
plural and used with a singular
verb only.
▶ **home computer**

---

template *noun*
1 an incomplete document or spreadsheet which contains
standard text or data. The user adds their own data to the
template in order to produce a document in a standard style.
2 a piece of plastic or card with shapes that have been cut out
of it. This is used as an easy way of producing the shapes to
make FLOW CHART symbols: *draw round the shapes in the template*
○ *The template contains diamonds, rectangles and other standard
shapes.*

/ˈtempleɪt/
pl templates
1 ⋈ base a document *on*, edit,
load a **template**; a letter,
memo, text **template**
▶ **boilerplate**

---

temporary file *noun*
a data file containing data that is needed only while a program
is executing and which may be deleted when execution has
finished: *In the DOS operating system, temporary files usually
have the extension .TMP.*

/ˌtemprəri ˈfaɪl/
pl temporary files
⋈ create, delete, store data in a
temporary file
syn scratch file, scratchpad,
volatile file, work file

---

temporary storage *noun* (hardware)
any form of memory that is used to hold data for a short time:
*A utility manages a section of memory that is used as temporary
storage.*

/ˌtemprəri ˈstɔːrɪdʒ/
note no plural

---

ten's complement *noun*
a system for recording positive and negative numbers using
the base ten numerals

note In ten's complement notation, small negative numbers
are represented as large positive ones. For example, using eight
decimal digits, -1 will be represented as 99999999. Addition
of ten's complement numbers will give the correct positive or
negative answer as long as the calculation does not cause
overflow.

/ˌtenz ˈkɒmplɪmənt/
note no plural
(also **10's complement**)
⋈ employ, use **ten's
complement**; **ten's
complement** arithmetic,
notation, representation
▶ **two's complement, one's
complement, nine's
complement, overflow**

---

tera *prefix*
one million million, 10^{12}

note In computing, where binary arithmetic is often used,
'tera' can also mean the near equivalent 2^{40}.

/ˈterə/
abbr T
▶ **giga, kilo, mega**

terabit *noun* (hardware)
one million million bits

note In computing, because of the use of the binary system, a terabit is 2^{40}, or 1 099 511 627 776 bits. There are 8 terabits in a terabyte.

/'terəbɪt/
pl terabits

---

terabyte *noun* (hardware)
one million million bytes

note In computing, because of the use of the binary system, a terabyte is 2^{40}, or 1 099 511 627 776 bytes.

/'terəbaɪt/
pl terabytes
abbr Tb
▶ **kilobyte, megabyte, gigabyte**

☆**terminal** *noun* (hardware)
a VDU and a keyboard that are connected to a central computer system. A terminal does not process data but is used to access data held on a central computer.

/'tɜːmɪnl/
pl terminals
syn dumb terminal
▶ **intelligent terminal, local intelligence, public access terminal**

---

terminal emulation *noun*
the ability of a computer to function as a terminal, usually so it can communicate with another computer: *use the PC in terminal emulation mode when accessing the mainframe*

/'tɜːmɪnl ˌemjuˈleɪʃn/
note not used with *a* or *an*. No plural and used with a singular verb only.

---

terminal session *noun*
a period of time spent working at a computer terminal: *The system records resources used during each terminal session.*

/'tɜːmɪnl ˌseʃn/
pl terminal sessions

---

terminate *verb*
1 to end something, especially the execution of a computer program: *The operator terminated the program after it entered an infinite loop.* ○ *The program terminated normally.* **2** to add an electronic device to the end of a cable linking several computers in order to avoid the problem of unwanted signals travelling through the cable: *The picture on the monitor screens around the room was poor because the connection was not terminated correctly.*

/'tɜːmɪneɪt/
terminate, terminating, terminated
note transitive or intransitive verb
1 ⋈ **terminate** an execution, a process, a run
2 ⋈ **terminate** the bus, daisy chain

---

terminate and stay resident program *noun* (software)
a RESIDENT PROGRAM that is always available to the user to perform simple tasks even when another piece of software is running: *A continually updated clock display is provided by a terminate and stay resident program.*

/ˌtɜːmɪneɪt ənd steɪ ˈrezɪdənt ˌprəʊɡræm/
pl terminate and stay resident programs
abbr TSR

---

terminator *noun*
1 a value inserted at the end of a list of data items that shows where the list ends: *use any negative number as a terminator for the input data* **2** (hardware) an electronic device added to the end of a cable that connects several computers. Terminators stop extra signals (noise) that travel through a cable from damaging the important signals travelling through the cable: *Without the terminator, the picture on the chain of the monitors spread around the room is very poor.*

/'tɜːmɪneɪtə(r)/
pl terminators
1 ⋈ insert, read the **terminator**
syn rogue value, sentinel
2 ⋈ fix, install a **terminator**

---

ternary *adjective*
connected with a system of numbers based on the number 3

note In ternary notation, the only digits used are 0, 1 and 2.

/'tɜːnəri/
⋈ **ternary** arithmetic, logic, notation

---

abbr abbreviation **pl** plural **syn** synonym ▶ see ⋈ collocate (*word often used with the headword*)

test¹ *noun*
/test/

1 an examination of a device or software to see that it is
working correctly: *The printer test was satisfactory.* **2** a logical
expression that is used to decide which statement in a program
will be executed next: *In a repeat until loop, the test comes at the
end.*

pl tests

1,2 ⋈ carry out, perform a **test**

1 ▶ **beta testing, self test**

test² *verb*
/test/

to examine hardware or software to see if it is working
correctly: *Modern operating systems usually test the memory
when the computer is switched on.* ○ *test the payroll program*

test, testing, tested

note transitive verb

⋈ **test** a computer, printer,
program; **test** software

test data *noun*
/'test ˌdeɪtə/

a set of data that should produce known results when input to
a computer program, and which can be used to test if the
program is working correctly: *The installation package includes
test data to verify the program's operation.* ○ *Test data should
include values not expected to occur in normal running, to ensure
that the program recovers correctly.*

note not used with *a* or *an*. No
plural and used with a singular
verb only.

⋈ a suite of, set of **test data**

▶ **test run**

test equipment *noun* (hardware)
/'test ɪˌkwɪpmənt/

equipment used to check that the hardware of a computer
system is operating correctly: *Test equipment is used in the final
stages of computer manufacture.*

note not used with *a* or *an*. No
plural and used with a singular
verb only.

⋈ automatic, electronic **test
equipment**

▶ **automatic test equipment**

test run *noun*
/'test rʌn/

the execution of a computer program using data designed to
produce known results so that the program can be checked to
make sure it operates correctly

pl test runs

⋈ do, perform a **test run**

▶ **test data**

☆**text** *noun*
/tekst/

1 data that consists of letters, numbers and symbols, etc that
represent words and other information: *How much text can the
disk store?* **2** a document such as a letter or report: *How many
texts are stored on the disk?*

1 note not used with *a* or *an*. No
plural and used with a singular
verb only.

abbr TXT

⋈ edit, print **text**; electronic,
machine-readable **text**; **text**
encoding, handling,
manipulation, recognition

2 pl texts

⋈ edit, print the **text**; an
electronic, a machine-readable
text

▶ **hypertext**

text editing *noun*
▶ **text processing**
/'tekst ˌedɪtɪŋ/

text editor *noun*
/'tekst ˌedɪtə(r)/

software that can be used for processing text: *a text editor
designed for editing program source code*

note The term 'text editor' is sometimes used to talk about a
simple word processor without advanced functions.

pl text editors

⋈ use, load text *into*, print *from* a
text editor

▶ **editor, line editor, word
processor**

text file *noun*
a data file that contains text but no formatting codes: *format the text file before sending it to the printer*

/'tekst faɪl/
pl text files

⋈ print, read, save data *as* a **text file**

▶ format¹ 1

---

text processing *noun*
the use of a computer to store and edit text: *Most office computers are used solely for text processing.*

/'tekst ˌprəʊsesɪŋ/
note not used with *a* or *an*. No plural and used with a singular verb only.

⋈ a **text processing** program; **text processing** software

syn text editing

▶ word processing

---

text retrieval system *noun*
a computer that is used for storing and indexing documents which can be searched for and examined: *The archives are held in a text retrieval system.*

/ˌtekst rɪˈtriːvl ˌsɪstəm/
pl text retrieval systems

⋈ access, use a **test retrieval system**

▶ information retrieval

---

text-to-sound converter *noun* (hardware)
an electronic device that changes a piece of text into sound: *The text-to-sound converter can reproduce music.*

/ˌtekst tə ˈsaʊnd kənˌvɜːtə(r)/
pl text-to-sound converters

---

thermal paper *noun* (hardware)
special paper used in a THERMAL PRINTER

/ˌθɜːml ˈpeɪpə(r)/
note not used with *a* or *an*. No plural and used with a singular verb only.

---

thermal printer *noun* (hardware)
a printer that uses heat to create characters on THERMAL PAPER

/ˌθɜːml ˈprɪntə(r)/
pl thermal printers

---

thesaurus *noun* (applications)
a function in a word processing program that allows the user to look for words with similar meanings: *The thesaurus provided the synonyms 'details', 'information' and 'facts' for the word 'data'.*

/θɪˈsɔːrəs/
pl thesauri, but thesauruses is often used

⋈ access, look up a word *in*, use a **thesaurus**; an on-line **thesaurus**

▶ dictionary

---

thick Ethernet *noun*
(*trade mark*) (*network*) an Ethernet network using CO-AXIAL CABLES to carry signals over a distance of approximately 1 000 metres

/ˌθɪk ˈiːθənet/
note no plural

(also **thick ethernet**)

▶ Ethernet

---

thin Ethernet *noun*
(*trade mark*) (*network*) an Ethernet network using CO-AXIAL CABLES to carry signals over a distance of approximately 300 metres

/ˌθɪn ˈiːθənet/
note no plural

(also **thin ethernet**)

▶ Ethernet

☆**third generation** *noun* (hardware)
a stage in computer design when the chip replaced the TRANSISTOR

/'θɜːd ˌdʒenəˈreɪʃn/
note no plural

note Third generation computers were built in the 1960s.

---

abbr abbreviation   **pl** plural   **syn** synonym   **▶** see   **⋈** collocate (*word often used with the headword*)

▶ **fifth generation, first generation, fourth generation, second generation**

---

third party *noun*

a company that makes and sells small devices or PERIPHERALS that can be used with larger devices and peripherals produced by a bigger company. The third party is not usually part of the larger company: *The computers were from IBM but the mice and keyboards were bought from a third party at a reduced price.*

/ˌθɜːd ˈpɑːti/

pl third parties

M **third party** equipment, risks, services

▶ **original equipment manufacturer**

---

thrashing *noun*

a situation where VIRTUAL MEMORY is constantly moving data in and out of main memory and so cannot execute any programs. This is usually because of a design fault.

/ˈθræʃɪŋ/

note Not used with *a* or *an*. No plural and used with a singular verb only.

---

thread *noun* (software/programming)

one of the parts of a program that may be executed at the same time as another part of a program in MULTITHREADING

/θred/

pl threads

▶ **multithreading**

---

threaded tree *noun*

a tree DATA STRUCTURE in which each node contains POINTERS to other nodes which help to TRAVERSE the tree more efficiently

/ˌθredɪd ˈtriː/

pl threaded trees

M construct, traverse a **threaded tree**

---

threading *noun*

▶ **multithreading**

/ˈθredɪŋ/

3D *abbr*

▶ **three-dimensional**

/ˌθriː ˈdiː/

---

three-dimensional *adjective*

(of an image, etc) that looks solid and whose points can be identified by three values: *The points of the three-dimensional shape can be described by giving x, y and z coordinates.* ○ *3D computer games* ○ *images in 3D*

/ˌθriː daɪˈmenʃənl/

abbr 3D

M a **three-dimensional** data structure, figure

▶ **multi-dimensional, one-dimensional, two dimensional**

---

three-dimensional array *noun* (software/programming)

a DATA STRUCTURE made up of data items of the same type. All items share the same name and individual items are accessed by giving three numbers to locate their position in the array: *The element LOC(5, 7, 7) is part of the three-dimensional array called LOC.* ○ *RSC(5, 12, 4) is the twelfth element in the fifth row of the fourth table in the three-dimensional array called RSC.*

note A programmer may think of a three-dimensional array as a number of tables.

/ˌθriː daɪˈmenʃənl əˈreɪ/

pl three-dimensional arrays

M access, define, use a **three-dimensional array**

▶ **array, array dimension, array bounds, matrix, one-dimensional array, two-dimensional array**

---

three-dimensional model *noun*

information about a solid shape that is stored in a computer so that the shape can be viewed from different positions: *In the virtual reality software, the user can walk around a three-dimensional model of the city.*

/ˈθriː daɪˌmenʃənl ˈmɒdl/

pl three-dimensional models

M construct, store a **three-dimensional model**

▶ **two-dimensional model**

throughput *noun*
the rate of the processing which is done by a computer or peripheral device which can be measured as instructions-per-minute, jobs-per-day or bits per second, etc: *The throughput of this printer is 10 pages per minute.*

/'θru:pʊt/
note no plural and used with a singular verb only
⋈ **throughput** rate
▶ **burst rate, MIPS**

tile *verb*
to arrange several windows on a display screen so that they fill the screen but do not overlap: *When windows are tiled, only one is active, even though all are visible.*

/taɪl/
tile, tiling, tiled
note transitive verb
⋈ **tile** applications, windows
▶ **cascade**

time division multiplexing *noun*
a way of transmitting different signals over the same channel by giving each signal a part of the available transmission time

/'taɪm dɪ,vɪʒn 'mʌltɪpleksɪŋ/
note not used with *a* or *an*. No plural and used with a singular verb only.
abbr TDM
⋈ asynchronous, synchronous **time division multiplexing**
▶ **asynchronous transmission, frequency division multiplexing, multiplexing, synchronous transmission**

timeout *noun*
the automatic disconnection of a device that receives data if no data has been sent for a fixed time: *There is a timeout after five minutes of inactivity.*

/'taɪmaʊt/
pl timeouts
⋈ cause, initiate a **timeout**

timer *noun*
any device that counts units of time such as seconds and minutes: *The timer in the multitasking system causes an interrupt so that processing time is not spent on just one task.*

/'taɪmə(r)/
pl timers
⋈ initiate, reset, set a **timer**

time-sharing *noun*
the use of a computer system by more than one user at the same time. The system appears to process the each user's request at the same time. This is done by giving each user a TIME SLICE so the system executes small parts of each user's request one after the other, so in reality the computer does not process all requests at the same time.

/'taɪm ,ʃeərɪŋ/
note not used with *a* or *an*. No plural and used with a singular verb only.
⋈ implement, use **time-sharing**
▶ **multiprogramming, multitasking**

time-sharing system *noun*
a computer system that is used by more than one user at the same time: *The time-sharing system can accommodate up to 32 simultaneous users.*

/'taɪm ʃeərɪŋ ,sɪstəm/
pl time-sharing systems
⋈ access, work *on* a **time sharing system**

time slice *noun* (software/system software)
the short period of time during which part of a program is executed in a MULTIPROGRAMMING or TIME-SHARING system before it is stopped so that part of another program can be executed: *The time slice is very small compared with disk access times, keyboard speeds and printer speeds.*

/'taɪm slaɪs/
pl time slices
⋈ execute a program *for*, suspend a program *after*, use *up* a **time slice**

---

abbr abbreviation   **pl** plural   **syn** synonym   ▶ see   ⋈ collocate (*word often used with the headword*)

timing loop *noun* (programming)
a short section of a computer program that is executed over and over again to provide a fixed delay: *The delay caused by executing the timing loop can be very accurately determined.*

/ˈtaɪmɪŋ luːp/
pl timing loops
◣ execute, initiate a **timing loop**

---

timing signal *noun*
a regular pulse that is sent from the central computer system CLOCK in order to keep all other components working at the correct rate: *The timing signal keeps the computer operating in synchronization.*

/ˈtaɪmɪŋ ˌsɪɡnəl/
pl timing signals
◣ broadcast, send a **timing signal**

☆**toggle** *verb*
to switch between two states by pressing a certain key on the keyboard: *It is possible to toggle between magnified and normal views in this graphics program.* ○ *toggle the paragraph markers on or off in the word processing application*

/ˈtɒɡl/
toggles, toggling, toggled
note transitive or intransitive verb
▶ **hot key**

---

token *noun*
1 (*programming*) a code used in a high-level language for RESERVED WORDS or other program statements: *The lexical analyser converts the source code into tokens.* **2** (*networks*) a bit pattern that passes from NODE (2) to node in a ring or bus network. A node can only send a message if it controls the token.

/ˈtəʊkən/
pl tokens
1 ◣ insert, substitute a **token**
▶ **lexical analysis**
2 ◣ pass, release, take control *of* the **token**
▶ **token passing**

---

token bus network *noun*
a bus network that prevents messages from interfering with each other by use of a special bit pattern called a TOKEN (2). The token travels over the network and messages can only be sent by the node that controls the token: *This local area network is organized as a token bus network.*

/ˈtəʊkən bʌs ˌnetwɜːk/
pl token bus networks
◣ install, send data *over*, transmit data *via* a **token bus network**
▶ **bus network**

---

token passing *noun* (networks)
a method of preventing interference between messages on a network. A special bit pattern called a TOKEN (2) passes from NODE (2) to node and messages may be sent by the node just after the token has been received and before it is passed on to the next node: *message collision is prevented by token passing*

/ˈtəʊkən ˌpɑːsɪŋ/
note no plural
◣ a **token passing** protocol

---

token ring network *noun*
a ring network that prevents messages from interfering with each other by use of a special bit pattern called a TOKEN 2. The token travels over the network and messages can only be sent by the NODE (2) that controls the token: *This local area network is organized as a token ring network.*

/ˈtəʊkən rɪŋ ˌnetwɜːk/
pl token ring networks
◣ install, send over, transmit *via* a **token ring network**
▶ **ring network**

---

tool *noun*
1 a program that is used by a programmer to write other programs **2** a part of an applications package that allows a user to do a certain job: *The graphics package has a paintbrush tool and a line drawing tool.* ○ *The word processing application has a hyphenation and word count tool.*

/tuːl/
pl tools
1,2 ◣ select, use a **tool**
2 ◣ a **tool** bar

top-down design *noun*

a method of creating software or computer systems by starting with the largest units and breaking them down into smaller and smaller units

/ˌtɒp daʊn dɪˈzaɪn/

note not used with *a* or *an*. No plural and used with a singular verb only.

Ⓜ **top-down design** methods, principles, techniques

syn top-down development

▶ **bottom-up design, top-down programming**

top-down development *noun*
▶ **top-down design**

/ˌtɒp daʊn dɪˈveləpmənt/

top-down programming *noun*

a method of developing computer programs by starting with details of the whole program and breaking this into smaller and smaller units: *Structured programming requires top-down programming methods.*

/ˌtɒp daʊn ˈprəʊɡræmɪŋ/

note not used with *a* or *an*. No plural and used with a singular verb only.

Ⓜ **top-down programming** methods, principles, techniques

▶ **top-down design, bottom-up programming**

top of stack *noun*

the newest item that has been added to a STACK. The top of stack is the only item that may be accessed, and until it is removed no other items already on the stack can be accessed: *push a data item onto the top of stack*

/ˌtɒp əv ˈstæk/

note not used with *a* or *an*. No plural and used with a singular verb only.

Ⓜ access, pop the **top of stack**

▶ **last in, first out, bottom of stack, pop, push**

topology *noun*
▶ **network topology**

/təˈpɒlədʒi/

total[1] *noun*

the value formed by adding up a number of things: *The total of 6+5+3 is 14.* ○ *The total is computed in two ways to make certain that no errors have occurred.*

/ˈtəʊtl/

pl totals

Ⓜ a check, control, hash **total**

▶ **checksum, control total, hash total**

total[2] *verb*

to add together a number of things to get a single amount: *A checksum is created by totalling various parts of the individual data items.* ○ *total the column of figures*

/ˈtəʊtl/

total, totalling, totalled

note transitive verb

(*US* **total, totaling, totaled**)

touch pad *noun* (hardware)

a flat pad which a user touches to control the position of the cursor on screen

/ˈtʌtʃ pæd/

pl touch pads

touch screen *noun* (hardware)

a computer screen responds to someone touching it with their finger or a STYLUS (= a device shaped like a pen): *The touch screen in the tourist information centre gives details of local hotels.* ○ *a point-of-information system with a touch screen*

/ˈtʌtʃ skriːn/

pl touch screens

syn touch-sensitive screen

touch-sensitive *adjective*

(of a device) that responds to someone touching it with their finger or a STYLUS (= a device shaped like a pen): *use the touch-sensitive screen to select information*

/ˌtʌtʃ ˈsensətɪv/

Ⓜ a **touch-sensitive** graphics tablet, screen

abbr abbreviation   **pl** plural   **syn** synonym   ▶ see   Ⓜ collocate (*word often used with the headword*)

touch-sensitive screen *noun*
▶ **touch screen**

/'tʌtʃ ˌsensətɪv 'skriːn/

TP *abbr*
▶ **transaction processing**

/ˌtiː 'piː/
note pronounced as individual letters

---

trace¹ *noun*
1 the process of recording the order in which program instructions are executed when a program is run: *Carrying out a trace can help identify flaws in program logic.* **2** the record that is made of the order in which program instructions are executed when a program is run: *Use the trace to isolate problems in the execution of the program.*

/treɪs/
pl traces
1 ◄ perform a **trace**
2 ◄ print out, read, study a **trace**
▶ TROFF, TRON

---

trace² *verb*
to record the order in which program instructions are executed when a program is run: *trace the logic flow in a subroutine*

/treɪs/
trace, tracing, traced
note transitive verb
◄ **trace** a program, subroutine
▶ **dry run**

---

trace program *noun*
a program that automatically produces a TRACE (2) of another program that is running: *use a trace program to check the logic flow* ○ *identify errors using a trace program*

/'treɪs ˌprəʊgræm/
pl trace programs
◄ employ, use a **trace program**
syn tracing software
▶ TROFF, TRON

---

trace statement *noun*
a DECLARATION in a program that causes a TRACE (2) to be produced for all parts of the program

/'treɪs ˌsteɪtmənt/
pl trace statements
◄ insert, use a **trace statement**
▶ TROFF, TRON

---

trace table *noun*
a printed display of the values that are assigned to variables as a program is executed: *The trace table showed that the variables were not being correctly initialized.*

/'treɪs ˌteɪbl/
pl trace tables
◄ print out, read, study a **trace table**

---

tracing software *noun*
▶ **trace program**

/'treɪsɪŋ ˌsɒftweə(r)/

---

track *noun*
▶ **disk track**

/træk/

---

trackball *noun* (hardware)
a small ball in a box that is used to control the position of a cursor on a screen: *The laptop computer has a built-in trackball.*

/'trækbɔːl/
pl trackballs
◄ move, roll the **trackball**
▶ **mouse**

---

tractor feed *noun*
▶ **sprocket feed**

/'træktə fiːd/

---

traffic *noun*
all messages and other signals that are processed by a network or communications channel: *All the network traffic is handled in digital form.*

/'træfɪk/
note not used with *a* or *an*. No plural and used with a singular verb only.

	⋈ cut down *on*, manage, monitor, reduce the flow *of* **traffic**; heavy, light **traffic**; **traffic** control
	▶ **incoming traffic, traffic density, outgoing traffic**

---

traffic density *noun*
the number of messages and other signals that are processed by a network or communication channel: *The traffic density is low at weekends.*

/'træfɪk ˌdensəti/
pl traffic densities
⋈ high, low **traffic density**
▶ **outgoing traffic**

---

trailer *noun*
the final data item in a file which often contains CHECK SUMS or CONTROL TOTALS: *A trailer is written and maintained by the applications software.*

/'treɪlə(r)/
pl trailers
⋈ access, write a **trailer**
syn trailer label

---

trailer label *noun*
▶ **trailer**

/'treɪlə(r) ˌleɪbl/

---

transaction *noun*
1 a single item of data that can be processed on its own: *The system is capable of dealing with 7 000 transactions per hour.* **2** any single activity inside a computer or system: *the transaction of deleting a file*

/træn'zækʃn/
pl transactions
1 ⋈ input, process a **transaction**

---

transaction file *noun*
a data file holding all new items of data waiting to be processed

/træn'zækʃn ˌfaɪl/
pl transaction files
⋈ access, read the **transaction file**
syn update file
▶ **master file**

---

transaction processing *noun*
a way of organizing a large computer system so that requests for processing are sent as single transactions, each of which is completely processed before the next one

/træn'zækʃn ˌprəʊsesɪŋ/
note not used with *a* or *an*. No plural and used with a singular verb only.
abbr TP
⋈ on-line **transaction processing**; a **transaction processing** system; **transaction processing** software

---

transceiver *noun* (hardware)
a communications device which acts as both a transmitter and a receiver: *The field engineer carries a voice transceiver – a mobile telephone – out on the road.*

/træn'siːvə(r)/
pl transceivers
⋈ receive messages, etc *via*, transmit messages, etc *via* a **transceiver**

---

transducer *noun* (hardware)
a device which converts one form of energy into another form of energy: *The transducer was coupled to the amplifier to convert (transduce) electric energy into sound.*

note Transducers may convert one type of electric energy into another type of electric energy, or they may convert nonelectric energy into electric energy.

/træns'djuːsə(r)/
pl transducers
⋈ calibrate, connect a **transducer**

---

abbr abbreviation   **pl** plural   **syn** synonym   **▶** see   **⋈** collocate (*word often used with the headword*)

transfer¹ *noun*

a move from one place to another: *The transfer of data from one computer to the other took place overnight.*

/ˈtrænsfɜː(r)/
pl transfers
M data, file **transfer**

---

transfer² *verb*

1 to move something from one place to another: *Data is transferred over a wide area network.* **2** to pass the control of program execution from one part of the program to another part of the program: *transfer control to a routine or module*

/trænsˈfɜː(r)/
transfer, transferring, transferred
note transitive verb

---

transfer rate *noun*

the speed at which data is moved between main memory and a PERIPHERAL, or over a communications channel: *a data transfer rate of 995KB per second* ○ *A sustained data transfer rate of 100Mbs can be achieved over a communications channel with high bandwidth.*

/ˈtrænsfɜː reɪt/
pl transfer rates
M improve, optimize the **transfer rate**
▶ **RAM disk**

---

transfer time *noun*

the time taken to transfer data from one device to another: *The execution speed will always be limited by the transfer time over the network.*

/ˈtrænsfɜː taɪm/
pl transfer times
M improve, shorten the **transfer time**

---

transient¹ *noun*

an increase in electrical power for a short time which may damage a computer: *Special circuitry has been installed to protect against transients.*

/ˈtrænziənt/
pl transients
M remove, suppress a **transient**
syn power transient
▶ **surge**

---

transient² *adjective*

only present for a short period of time: *A transient area is reserved for temporary use by user programs.*

/ˈtrænziənt/
M a **transient** effect, error, program

---

transient error *noun* (hardware)

a hardware error which only occurs for a short time

/ˌtrænziənt ˈerə(r)/
pl transient errors
M detect a **transient error**
syn intermittent error

☆**transistor** *noun* (hardware)

an electronic device which is able to operate in many ways and is often used as a switch to turn an electric current on or off, or as a device that MODULATES an electric current: *The transistor switches on and off at very high frequencies.*

/trænˈzɪstə(r)/
pl transistors
▶ **field effect transistor**

---

transistor-transistor logic *noun* (hardware)

a family of logic circuits made as chips

note Transistor-transistor logic is cheap and operates at high speed; it is probably the commonest logic design in modern integrated circuits.

/trænˈzɪstə trænˈzɪstə ˈlɒdʒɪk/
note not used with *a* or *an*. No plural and used with a singular verb only.
abbr TTL
M design, fabricate, implement **transistor-transistor logic**

---

translate *verb*

to change something from one form to another, especially to change a computer program written in a high-level language into machine code by compiling or assembling it: *translate the program into machine code .*

/trænsˈleɪt/
translate, translating, translated
note transitive verb

	⋈ **translate** a program; **translate** data, source code

translation table *noun*
▶ **conversion table**

/trænsˈleɪʃn ˌteɪbl/

---

translator *noun*
a program which changes a high-level language into machine code

/trænsˈleɪtə(r)/
pl translators
⋈ use, pass code, etc *through* a **translator**
▶ **compiler, interpreter**

☆**transmission** *noun*
1 the process of sending signals that carry data and messages, etc between two or more devices. Transmission can either be over fixed links such as cables or over non-fixed links such as radio waves, etc: *High-speed links such as satellite are used for the transmission of pictures.* **2** a single message or block of data that is sent between two devices: *five data transmissions took place overnight* ○ *an e-mail transmission*

/trænsˈmɪʃn/
abbr TX
1 note not used with *a* or *an*. No plural and used with a singular verb only.
⋈ a **transmission** line, protocol
2 pl transmissions
⋈ receive, send a **transmission**

---

transmission channel *noun* (hardware)
a link between two or more devices that allows data and messages, etc to be sent between them. There may be more than one transmission channel in a physical link such as a cable: *Fibre optic cables can carry hundreds or thousands of transmission channels.*

/trænsˈmɪʃn ˌtʃænl/
pl transmission channels
⋈ receive data *over*, use a **transmission channel**
▶ **frequency division multiplexing, time division multiplexing, transmission line**

---

transmission control protocol *noun*
a set of standards that control the transfer of data across a network: *Software that recognizes the TCP/IP transmission control protocol must be running on the computer to allow connection to the Internet.*

/trænsˌmɪʃn kənˈtrəʊl ˌprəʊtəkɒl/
note not used with *a* or *an*. No plural and used with a singular verb only.
abbr TCP
⋈ conform *to*, follow, obey the **transmission control protocol**; **transmission control protocol** software
▶ **Internet**

---

transmission error *noun*
a mistake in data that is caused by the TRANSMISSION CHANNEL it is sent over: *The noisy telephone line caused the transmission error.*

/trænsˈmɪʃn ˌerə(r)/
pl transmission errors
⋈ correct, identify a **transmission error**

---

transmission line *noun*
a link between two or more devices that allows data to be sent between them. Several data transmissions may use a link at the same time if it is divided into separate TRANSMISSION CHANNELS: *Transmission lines that could be used to send the data include telephone lines, satellite links and fixed cabling.*

/trænsˈmɪʃn laɪn/
pl transmission lines
⋈ receive data *over*, send data *over*, use a **transmission line**

---

abbr abbreviation   **pl** plural   **syn** synonym   ▶ see   **⋈** collocate (*word often used with the headword*)

transmission rate *noun*

the amount of data sent over a transmission channel in a
certain amount of time: *a transmission rate of 9 600 baud*

note Transmission rates may be measured in bits per second,
baud or kilobaud.

/træns'mɪʃn reɪt/
pl transmission rates
◄ achieve, measure a
transmission rate
► **baud, kilobaud**

---

transmit *verb*

to send data from one device to another device, especially from
one computer to another over a TRANSMISSION CHANNEL: *The
computer transmits data over the network.* ○ *use satellite
communications to transmit computer data from one device to
another* ○ *transmit data and video signals across television
networks*

/træns'mɪt/
**transmit, transmitting,
transmitted**
note transitive verb
► **broadcast²**

---

transmitter *noun*

a device that sends data over a TRANSMISSION CHANNEL to
another device

/træns'mɪtə(r)/
pl transmitters
◄ identify the **transmitter**;
transmitter equipment,
hardware, software
► **receiver**

---

transparent *adjective*

1 (of a process or part of a computer or system) that happens
or works without the user noticing: *the transparent use of files
by one application that were created by a different application* ○ **2**
(*communications*) (of data transmission) that happens without
problems between the sending and receiving devices: *The size of
data bus is transparent to applications programs as they function
identically whether running on a machine with a 16-bit bus or on
one with 32-bit bus.*

/træns'pærənt/

---

transport *noun* (hardware)

the machinery that moves something, especially tape or disk
past the READ/WRITE HEAD of a device: *The tape transport needs
regular maintenance if read errors are to be avoided.*

/'trænspɔːt/
pl transports
◄ disk, tape, continuous
stationery **transport**
syn tape transport
► **disk drive**

---

transportable computer *noun*

► **portable computer**

/træn,spɔːtəbl kəm'pjuːtə(r)/

---

transport layer *noun*

one of the sections of the International Standards Organization
PROTOCOL for data communications. The transport layer
describes standards to move data in the most efficient way over
different types of networks: *The transport layer will try to find the
cheapest route possible for sending data, possibly by multiplexing
signals.*

/'trænspɔːt ˌleɪə(r)/
note usually singular
◄ define, specify the **transport
layer**
► **application layer, data link
layer, ISO OSI, network
layer, physical layer,
presentation layer, session
layer**

---

transpose *verb*

to change the order in which things occur or appear: *The day
and month fields in the English date 8.1.96 (the 8th of January
1996) are transposed in an American date to 1.8.96.*

/træn'spəʊz/
**transpose, transposing,
transposed**
note transitive verb
◄ **transpose** data items, fields,
elements

transputer *noun* (hardware)

a computer that is contained in a single chip. It is used for PARALLEL PROCESSING (= the execution of several programs at the same time): *build a supercomputer from transputers* ○ *Add a transputer to the computer to improve its performance.*

/træn'spjuːtə(r)/
pl transputers

---

trap *verb*

to detect an error and correct it before it does any damage: *The accounting software traps division by zero errors.*

/træp/
trap, trapping, trapped
note transitive verb
◄ **trap** an error

---

trapping *noun*

the process of finding and correcting an error before it causes problems: *Error trapping is much improved in the latest version of the software.*

/'træpɪŋ/
note not used with *a* or *an*. No plural and used with a singular verb only.

---

traversal *noun*

the process of accessing all the data items in a DATA STRUCTURE in order: *The tree traversal produced the data in ascending order.*

/trə'vɜːsl/
pl traversals
◄ carry out, effect, perform a **traversal**
► pre-order traversal, post-order traversal, symmetric traversal

---

traverse *verb*

to access all the data items in a DATA STRUCTURE in order: *traverse the tree to remove the data in ascending order* ○ *count the data items by traversing the tree*

/trə'vɜːs/
traverse, traversing, traversed
note transitive verb
◄ **traverse** a list, tree
► post-order traversal, pre-order traversal, symmetric traversal

---

☆**tree** *noun*

a DATA STRUCTURE where each data item is linked by POINTERS to one or more data items, called DESCENDANTS, which are also linked to other data items: *The highest level of a tree is the root.*

/triː/
pl trees
◄ access, define, implement, traverse, update a **tree**
syn tree structure
► binary tree, branch 1, node 1, pointer, root, traverse

---

tree and branch network *noun*
► **tree network**

/,triː ənd 'brɑːntʃ ,netwɜːk/

---

tree network *noun*

a network where NODES (1) are linked in a TREE structure where each node is linked to a more important node: *Messages pass up the tree network and then down again to reach their destination.*

/'triː ,netwɜːk/
pl tree networks
◄ configure something *as*, use a **tree network**
► bus network, network, network topology, ring network, star network
syn tree and branch network

---

tree structure *noun*
► **tree**

/'triː ,strʌktʃə(r)/

---

abbr abbreviation   **pl** plural   **syn** synonym   ► see   ◄ collocate (*word often used with the headword*)

TROFF *abbr*

trace off. A TRACE STATEMENT in many programming languages that stops the production of a TRACE (2) (= the record that is made of the order in which program instructions are executed when a program is run): *insert a TROFF statement*

/trɒf/
note pronounced as a word

Trojan horse *noun* (software)

a virus which is designed to copy or corrupt data in a secure computer system. A Trojan horse appears to be a simple utility or other useful program, but when it is executed it also performs some illegal act, such as copying security information for future use.

/ˌtrəʊdʒən ˈhɔːs/
pl Trojan horses
⋈ execute, load a **Trojan horse**
▶ virus

TRON *abbr*

trace on. A TRACE STATEMENT in many languages that starts the production of a TRACE[1] (2) (= the record that is made of the order in which program instructions are executed when a program is run).

/trɒn/
note pronounced as a word

TRUE *noun* (logic)

one of the two values that a logical expression can have in formal logic

note The logical TRUE is written in capital letters to show that it is different from the word 'true' used in ordinary language.

/truː/
note not used with *a* or *an*. No plural and used with a singular verb only.
⋈ assign the value, evaluate *to*, take the value **TRUE**
▶ FALSE

truncate *verb*

to shorten something, especially a number, by removing part of it: *The denary number 3.14159 truncated to three decimal places becomes 3.142.*

/trʌŋˈkeɪt/
truncate, truncating, truncated
note transitive verb
⋈ **truncate** a field, number, string
syn chop round to zero
▶ round, truncation error

truncation *noun*

the process of making something shorter by removing part of it: *Truncation of a number to a fixed number of decimal places makes it less precise.*

/trʌŋˈkeɪʃn/
note not used with *a* or *an*. No plural and used with a singular verb only.
⋈ **truncation** algorithm, rules
▶ rounding

truncation error *noun*

an error caused by using a truncated number instead of the full number: *The use of 3.142 instead of 3.14159 introduces a truncation error of 0.00041.*

/trʌŋˈkeɪʃn ˌerə(r)/
pl truncation errors
⋈ minimize, propagate **truncation errors**
▶ round off error

trunk *noun*
▶ bus

/trʌŋk/

trunk network *noun*
▶ backbone network

/ˈtrʌŋk ˌnetwɜːk/

☆**truth table** *noun* (mathematics and logic)

a table with a list of logic operations and their possible truth values: *the truth table for the AND operation*

/ˈtruːθ ˌteɪbl/
pl truth tables
⋈ draw up, refer *to* a **truth table**
▶ Boolean algebra

truth value *noun* (mathematics and logic)
one of the values TRUE or FALSE used as a LOGIC OPERAND: *The truth value of '1=2' is FALSE.*

/'tru:θ ˌvælju:/
pl truth values
Ⱶ access, calculate a **truth value**
▶ **logical variable**

TSR *abbr*
▶ **terminate and stay resident program**

/ˌti: es 'ɑ:(r)/
note pronounced as individual letters

TTL *abbr*
▶ **transistor-transistor logic**

/ˌti: ti: 'el/
note pronounced as individual letters

TTY *abbr*
▶ **teletypewriter**

/ˌti: ti: 'waɪ/
note pronounced as individual letters

tuple *noun*
a set of numbers in order: *A point in space can be represented as a 3-tuple of coordinates.*

/'tju:pl/
pl tuples
Ⱶ represent something *as* a **tuple**

Turing machine *noun*
a computing device which used a tape containing squares which had a 1, 0 or nothing in each square. The device would read a symbol and then change its state according to which symbol it had read. This kind of action was shown to be enough to carry out any computational task.

note The Turing machine was created by the British mathematician Alan Turing in 1936.

/'tjʊərɪŋ məˌʃi:n/
pl Turing machines
Ⱶ compute a result using, design a **Turing machine**
▶ **automaton**

Turing test *noun*
a test that is used to decide if a computer is intelligent. A computer and a person both communicate with another person (the tester), and if the tester cannot find differences between the responses of the computer and the person, the computer has some intelligence.

note The Turing test is a philosophical way of exploring ideas about machine intelligence.

/'tjʊərɪŋ test/
pl Turing tests
Ⱶ apply, discuss, perform the **Turing test**
▶ **artificial intelligence**

turnaround time *noun*
the amount of time between inputting data into a computer for processing and receiving the result: *Turnaround time must be improved as the payroll takes far too long to process.*

note Turnaround time is sometimes used when talking about the amount of time it takes a commercial computing business to receive and process data.

/'tɜ:nəraʊnd taɪm/
pl turnaround times
abbr TAT
Ⱶ measure, shorten **turnaround time**

turnkey system *noun*
a complete system of hardware and software which can be bought as a unit and which can do a certain type of work: *The finance department had a turnkey accounting system installed last year.* ○ *a turnkey system for a doctor's surgery*

/ˌtɜ:nki: 'sɪstəm/
pl turnkey systems

turtle *noun*
a small shape on screen which can be used to draw graphics in the LOGO language

/'tɜ:tl/
pl turtles

abbr abbreviation   **pl** plural   **syn** synonym   ▶ see   Ⱶ collocate (*word often used with the headword*)

> ⋈ draw *with*, hide, show, use the **turtle**; a floor, screen **turtle**

turtle graphics *noun*
pictures and shapes created by the LOGO language using a TURTLE: *These graphs were drawn as turtle graphics.*

/ˌtɜːtl ˈɡræfɪks/
note plural noun used with a plural verb
⋈ draw, sketch **turtle graphics**; **turtle graphics** commands, procedures

☆**tutorial** *noun* (hardware)
a way of teaching a person how to use a computer or program, etc: *an on-screen tutorial is included in the price of the software* ○ *The program has an on-line tutorial but the manual contains more details of each task.*

/tjuːˈtɔːriəl/
pl tutorials
▶ **documentation, manual**

twisted pair *noun*
the simplest transmission line between two devices. Two wires are contained in an insulated cover and are twisted around each other to improve the electrical quality of the signal: *Telephone extensions use twisted pair cables.*

/ˌtwɪstɪd ˈpeə(r)/
pl twisted pairs
⋈ connect devices, etc *with*, install a **twisted pair**

2D *abbr*
▶ **two-dimensional**

/ˌtuː ˈdiː/

two-dimensional *adjective*
(of an image, etc) that looks flat and whose points are able to be identified by two values: *The points in a two-dimensional drawing have x and y coordinates.*

/ˌtuː daɪˈmenʃənəl/
abbr 2D
⋈ a **two-dimensional** data structure, figure
▶ **three-dimensional**

two-dimensional array *noun* (software/programming)
a DATA STRUCTURE that is made up of data items of the same type. All items share the same name and individual items are accessed by giving two numbers to locate their position in the array: *The element MATRIX(5, 7) is part of the two-dimensional array called MATRIX.* ○ *SCR(5, 12) is the twelfth element in the fifth row of the two-dimensional array called SCR.*

note A programmer may think of a two-dimensional array as a table with rows and columns.

/ˈtuː daɪˌmenʃənəl əˈreɪ/
pl two-dimensional arrays
⋈ access, define, use a **two-dimensional array**
syn table
▶ **array, array dimension, array bounds, matrix, one-dimensional array, three-dimensional array**

two-dimensional model *noun*
a shape that is stored in a computer in such a way that information about any third dimension (such as depth) is lost

/ˈtuː daɪˌmenʃənəl ˈmɒdl/
pl two-dimensional models
⋈ construct, store a **two-dimensional model**
▶ **three-dimensional model**

two's complement *noun*
a system for recording positive and negative binary numbers

note In two's complement notation, small negative numbers are represented as large positive ones. For example, using eight bits, -1 will be represented as 11111111. The addition of two's complement numbers will give the correct positive or negative answer as long as the calculation does not cause overflow.

/ˌtuːz ˈkɒmplɪmənt/
note no plural
(also **2's complement**)
⋈ employ, use **two's complement**; **two's complement** arithmetic, notation, representation
▶ **ten's complement, one's complement, nine's complement, overflow**

TX *abbr*
▶ **transmission**

/ˌtiː ˈeks/
note pronounced as individual letters

TXT *abbr*
▶ **text**

/ˌtiː eks ˈtiː/
note pronounced as individual letters

---

type-ahead *noun*
the ability of software to record key strokes made by the user while the software is still working on a previous task. When the software is free to deal with the characters typed, they will not have been lost.

/ˌtaɪp əˈhed/
note not used with *a* or *an*. No plural and used with a singular verb only.

---

type checking *noun*
the action of a high-level language translator or RUN-TIME SYSTEM in checking that a memory location or program contains the correct DATA TYPE: *Type checking prevents the user from inadvertently assigning a string to a numeric variable.*

/ˈtaɪp ˌtʃekɪŋ/
note not used with *a* or *an*. No plural and used with a singular verb only.
◄ implement, use **type checking**

---

type declaration *noun*
a statement in a programming language that defines a new DATA TYPE

/ˈtaɪp ˌdekləˌreɪʃn/
pl type declarations
◄ make, include, insert a **type declaration**
▶ **declaration**

☆**typeface** *noun*
the design of letters and characters: *The standard typeface for reports is Geneva.*

/ˈtaɪpfeɪs/
pl typefaces
◄ change the **typeface**
syn face
▶ **font**

Uu

UART *abbr*
▶ **universal asynchronous receiver/transmitter**

/ˈjuːɑːt/
note pronounced as a word

ULA *abbr*
▶ **uncommitted logic array**

/ˌjuː el ˈaɪ/
note pronounced as individual letters

ULSI *abbr*
▶ **ultra large scale integration**

/ˌjuː el es ˈaɪ/
note pronounced as individual letters

---

ultra large scale integration *noun* (hardware)
the process of putting more than 100 000 COMPONENTS on an integrated circuit

/ˈʌltrə ˈlɑːdʒ skeɪl ˌɪntɪˈgreɪʃn/
note no plural
▶ **circuit board, large scale integration, medium scale integration, printed circuit board, small scale integration, super large scale integration, very large scale integration, wafer scale integration**

---

abbr abbreviation   **pl** plural   **syn** synonym   ▶ see   ◄ collocate (*word often used with the headword*)

unary minus *noun*
the process of turning a positive number into a negative number, for example 3 into -3

/ˌjuːnəri ˈmaməs/
pl unary minuses
⋈ perform the operation *of* **unary minus**

---

unary operation *noun*
an operation that is performed on one OPERAND

/ˈjuːnəri ɒpəˌreɪʃn/
pl unary operations
▶ **logic operation, unary minus**

---

unary operator *noun*
an operator that uses one OPERAND in a calculation

/ˌjuːnəri ˈɒpəreɪtə(r)/
pl unary operators
⋈ define, use a **unary operator**
syn monadic operator
▶ **binary operator**

---

unbundled software *noun* (software)
software that is not supplied with a computer system and has to be bought separately: *Unbundled software that can be used by the system includes network data management software.*

/ˌʌnbʌndld ˈsɒftweə(r)/
note not used with *a* or *an*. No plural and used with a singular verb only.
▶ **bundled software**

---

uncommitted logic array *noun* (hardware)
a chip made of a large number of separate GATES that are not connected together. This is to allow the user to make the connections between the gates to make a CUSTOM-BUILT chip: *The user can turn an uncommitted logic array into a purpose-built chip.*

/ˈʌnkəˌmɪtɪd ˈlɒdʒɪk əˌreɪ/
pl uncommitted logic arrays
abbr ULA
⋈ burn code *into*, configure, install an **uncommitted logic array**
syn programmable logic array

---

unconditional *adjective*
not depending on the state of other parts of a system

/ˌʌnkənˈdɪʃənl/
▶ **conditional**

---

unconditional branch *noun* (software/programming)
an instruction that always makes the computer change the order of executing instructions. Instead of executing instructions in the order they appear, the computer jumps to another part of the program and continues executing instructions from there: *The BASIC instruction GOTO is an unconditional branch.* ○ *The simplest transfer of control instruction is the unconditional branch.*

/ˈʌnkənˌdɪʃənl ˈbrɑːntʃ/
pl unconditional branches
⋈ follow, insert, obey, remove an **unconditional branch**
syn unconditional jump
▶ **conditional branch**

---

unconditional jump *noun*
▶ **unconditional branch**

/ˈʌnkənˌdɪʃənl ˈdʒʌmp/

---

underflow *noun*
an error which occurs because the result of a mathematical calculation is too close to zero for the computer to represent it with PRECISION

/ˈʌndəfləʊ/
note not used with *a* or *an*. No plural and used with a singular verb only.
⋈ cause, detect **underflow**
▶ **floating point underflow, overflow, stack underflow**

underscore *noun*

the character '_' found on a computer keyboard and often used as part of names where a space would not be allowed: *The underscore inserted into the e-mail address 'Benjamin_Wegener@studio.com' takes the place of a space to separate first name from family name.*

/ˈʌndəskɔː(r)/

pl underscores

ᴍ insert, print an **underscore**

---

unformatted *adjective*

1 (of a disk) that has not had the storage space it contains organized in a way that makes it ready to use: *The computer cannot read an unformatted disk.* **2** (of text) that has not been given a certain layout: *The text on the screen was unformatted.*

/ˌʌnˈfɔːmætɪd/

▶ **format**

---

uninterruptible power supply *noun* (hardware)

a device that controls the supply of electricity to a computer so that if the main power supply fails, the device provides battery power so no data is lost: *The uninterruptible power supply monitors the electricity flow to the PC.*

/ˌʌnɪntəˌrʌptəbl ˈpaʊə səˌplaɪ/

pl uninterruptible power supplies

abbr UPS

---

union *noun*

an operation on two sets of things which makes a new set containing one of every item found in each set without repeating an item: *The union of the sets {1, 2, 3} and {3, 4, 5} is the set {1, 2, 3, 4, 5}.*

/ˈjuːniən/

pl unions

ᴍ set, set theoretic **union**

▶ **set**[1]

---

unipolar *adjective*

having only one state: *The unipolar device has the same voltage polarity to represent ON and OFF.*

/ˌjuːniˈpəʊlə(r)/

ᴍ a **unipolar** signal, transistor

▶ **bipolar**

---

unipolar signal *noun*

a signal that is passed between logic devices which uses only positive and zero VOLTAGES, not positive and negative voltages

/ˈjuːniˌpəʊlə ˈsɪgnəl/

pl unipolar signals

ᴍ receive, send a **unipolar signal**

▶ **bipolar signal**

---

unique identifier *noun*

▶ **primary key**

/juːˌniːk aɪˈdentɪfaɪə(r)/

---

unit *noun* (hardware)

1 a single machine or device **2** a part of something: *The basic unit of a string is a character.*

/ˈjuːnɪt/

pl units

2 ᴍ a basic, fundamental **unit**

---

unit cost *noun*

the cost of producing one item. This is found by dividing the total production costs by the number of items produced: *The unit cost of integrated circuits has fallen as technology has improved.*

/ˌjuːnɪt ˈkɒst/

pl unit costs

ᴍ estimate, quote a **unit cost**

---

universal asynchronous receiver/transmitter *noun* (hardware)

a LOGIC CIRCUIT that allows two devices to communicate in a way that is not controlled by time. The data that is transmitted contains information about when to start and stop transmission: *The modem in the PC contains a universal asynchronous receiver/transmitter.*

/juːnɪˈvɜːsl eɪˈsɪŋkrənəs rɪˈsiːvə trænsˈmɪtə(r)/

pl universal asynchronous receiver/transmitters

abbr UART

ᴍ build, design a **universal asynchronous receiver/transmitter**

---

abbr abbreviation   **pl** plural   **syn** synonym   ▶ see   ᴍ collocate (*word often used with the headword*)

universal product code *noun*

a number that is given to many items for sale in shops and is usually printed on the packaging as a BAR CODE: *The universal product code is used for stock control and inventory management.*

/ˈjuːnɪˌvɜːsl ˈprɒdʌkt kəʊd/
pl universal product codes
abbr UPC
⋈ scan the **universal product code**

---

universal synchronous receiver/transmitter *noun*

a single integrated circuit that contains receiving and transmitting circuits. The data that is transmitted is SYNCHRONIZED by a clock.

/juːnɪˈvɜːsl ˈsɪŋkrənəs rɪˌsiːvə(r)/trænsˈmɪtə(r)/
pl universal synchronous receiver/transmitters
abbr USRT
⋈ build, design a **universal synchronous receiver/transmitter**

Unix *noun*

(*trade mark*) (*software*) an operating system for different computers from mainframes to personal computers. Unix is often used in multi-user networks and is written in C (1).

/ˈjuːnɪks/
note no plural
⋈ a **Unix** command, environment, server
▶ **operating system**

---

unpack *verb*

to separate something into parts: *unpack the byte into individual bits*

/ˌʌnˈpæk/
unpack, unpacking, unpacked
note transitive verb
⋈ **unpack** a data item, word
▶ **pack²**

---

unprotected *adjective*

able to be changed: *Cells on the spreadsheet that the user can change are unprotected.*

/ˌʌnprəˈtektɪd/
⋈ an **unprotected** field, record
▶ **write protect**

---

unprotected field *noun*

part of a data record, etc that can be changed by the user: *The cursor only moves between the unprotected fields - the ones that the user cannot change are ignored.*

/ˈʌnprəˌtektɪd ˈfiːld/
pl unprotected fields
⋈ change, enter, update an **unprotected field**
▶ **protected field**

---

unrecoverable error *noun*

an error in the execution of a program that makes it impossible for execution to continue: *Attempting to access a non-existent file is an unrecoverable error.*

/ˈʌnrɪˌkʌvərəbl ˈerə(r)/
pl unrecoverable errors
⋈ cause, detect an **unrecoverable error**

---

unset *verb*

to make a single bit equal to zero: *unset the carry bit*

/ˌʌnˈset/
unset, unsetting, unset
note transitive verb
▶ **clear¹ 1**

---

unsigned *adjective*

(of a number) that has no information about its positive or negative value: *An unsigned number is usually assumed to be positive.*

/ˌʌnˈsaɪnd/
⋈ an **unsigned** fraction, integer

---

unswitched network *noun* (*hardware*)

a network where messages can be sent from a terminal only to a fixed destination: *Cash dispensers form an unswitched network.*

/ˌʌnswɪtʃt ˈnetwɜːk/
pl unswitched networks

| | ⋈ install, maintain, use an **unswitched network** |
| | ▶ **switched network** |

---

up arrow *noun* (hardware)
the CURSOR CONTROL KEY on a keyboard marked with an arrow pointing up: *The up arrow can be used to move between lines.*

/ˈʌp ˌærəʊ/
pl up arrows
⋈ hold, press the **up arrow**
▶ **down arrow, left arrow, page up, page down, right arrow**

UPC *abbr*
▶ **universal product code**

/ˌjuː piː ˈsiː/
note pronounced as individual letters

☆**update¹** *noun* (software)
a piece of new data that replaces old data: *The latest update added the names and addresses of all new clients to the database.*

/ˈʌpdeɪt/
pl updates
▶ **upgrade¹**

☆**update²** *verb*
to replace old data with data that is current

/ˌʌpˈdeɪt/
update, updating, updated
note transitive verb
⋈ **update** the database, records, spreadsheet
▶ **upgrade²**

---

update file *noun*
▶ **transaction file**

/ˈʌpdeɪt faɪl/

☆**upgrade¹** *noun* (hardware)
an improved computer, computer system or piece of software: *The upgrade of the software has fewer bugs.*

/ˈʌpɡreɪd/
pl upgrades
⋈ a hardware, software, system **upgrade**

☆**upgrade²** *verb*
1 to make a computer system more powerful, usually by adding or replacing parts: *upgrade the capability of the networks*
2 to improve a piece of software: *upgrade the video game so it has more variations*

/ˌʌpˈɡreɪd/
upgrade, upgrading, upgraded
note transitive verb
▶ **update**

☆**upload** *verb* (system operation)
to transfer programs, data or information from a computer to a larger computer or mainframe: *This piece of software enables a PC to upload a graphics file.* ○ *Assignments are completed offline, then uploaded to a central computer.*

/ˌʌpˈləʊd/
upload, uploading, uploaded
note transitive verb
⋈ **upload** a message
▶ **download**

---

upper case *noun*
▶ **capital**

/ˌʌpə ˈkeɪs/

UPS *abbr*
▶ **uninterruptible power supply**

/ˌjuː piː ˈes/
note pronounced as individual letters

---

abbr abbreviation   **pl** plural   **syn** synonym   ▶ see   ⋈ collocate (*word often used with the headword*)

up time *noun*

the period of time during which a computer system is available for use: *There has been a marked improvement in the percentage of up time since the new operating system was installed.*

/ˈʌp taɪm/

note not used with *a* or *an*. No plural and used with a singular verb only.

(also **uptime**)

ꓭ improve, maximize **up time**

▶ **down time**

---

upwards compatible *adjective*

(of software or hardware) that will be able to operate with newer versions of software or hardware: *The programs are upwards compatible to the new computer.* ○ *The fibre optic cable links will be upwards compatible in the future.*

/ˌʌpwədz kəmˈpætəbl/

(*US* **upward compatible**)

ꓭ **upwards compatible** *to/with* something; **upwards compatible** hardware, software

▶ **downwards compatible**

---

usability *noun*

how easy or difficult it is to use something: *The keyboard was redesigned to improve its usability.* ○ *identify usability problems in the new systems*

/ˌjuːzəˈbɪləti/

note not used with *a* or *an*. No plural and used with a singular verb only.

ꓭ assess, determine, enhance, improve **usability**

---

usable *adjective*

able to be used: *The network is usable again now the server is working properly.*

/ˈjuːzəbl/

☆**user** *noun* (personnel)

a person who uses a device, computer or computer system: *a workstation that suit the user's needs* ○ *a database user group* ○ *The information technology department provides user support.*

/ˈjuːzə(r)/

pl users

ꓭ a **user** group, guide, manual, name; **user** needs, requirements

syn end user

---

user-definable *adjective*

able to be changed by a user: *The background screen colour and the default directory are user-definable.*

/ˌjuːzə dɪˈfaɪnəbl/

ꓭ a **user-definable** parameter

▶ **customize**

---

user-defined *adjective*

(of something) that has been changed by the user: *The printer operates with several user-defined defaults.*

/ˌjuːzə dɪˈfaɪnd/

ꓭ a **user-defined** option, parameter

---

user-defined data type *noun* (software)

a DATA TYPE which is not built in to the programming language and which must be defined by DECLARATIONS made by the user

/ˈjuːzə dɪˌfaɪnd ˈdeɪtə taɪp/

pl user-defined data types

ꓭ define, use a **user-defined data type**

---

user documentation *noun*

▶ **manual**

/ˈjuːzə ˌdɒkjumenˈteɪʃn/

☆**user-friendly** *adjective*

connected with a program, computer or system, etc that is easy to use, especially for someone with little technical knowledge: *a user-friendly accounting package*

/ˌjuːzə ˈfrendli/

ꓭ a **user-friendly** application, feature, language; **user-friendly** software

user group *noun* (personnel)

a group of people who use the same computer system or software and meet to talk about ways of using the system or software more efficiently: *a user group newsletter and helpline*

/'ju:zə gru:p/

pl user groups

ꓶ belong *to*, form, join a **user group**

▶ **closed user group**

---

user interface *noun* (applications)

the boundary between a user and a computer or program: *Updates of the software will include an improved user interface.*

/ˌju:zə(r) 'ɪntəfeɪs/

pl user interfaces

ꓶ a command line, an intuitive, a menu-driven **user interface**

▶ **graphical user interface**

---

user manual *noun*

▶ **manual**

/'ju:zə ˌmænjuəl/

---

user name *noun*

the identification that a user gives to log on to a computer system: *a user name consisting of a string of alphanumeric characters* ○ *Users have to change their user names regularly for security reasons.* ○ *Some users have different user names, each associated with different passwords and different sets of privileges.*

/'ju:zə neɪm/

pl user names

ꓶ choose, enter, use a **user name**

▶ **password**

---

user program *noun*

a program written by the user of a computer, rather than by a manufacturer

/'ju:zə ˌprəʊgræm/

pl user programs

ꓶ execute, load, run, write a **user program**

USRT *abbr*

▶ **universal synchronous receiver/transmitter**

/ˌju: es ɑ: 'ti:/

note pronounced as individual letters

---

utility *noun*

▶ **utility program**

/ju:'tɪləti/

---

utility program *noun* (software)

a program that performs a common task needed by most computer users, such as formatting a disk or printing a list of files: *a utility program that converts files*

/ju:'tɪləti ˌprəʊgræm/

pl utility programs

ꓶ call, execute, use a **utility program**

syn utility

▶ **systems software**

Vv

V *abbr*

▶ **volt**

/vi:/

---

vaccine *noun*

▶ **virus checking program**

/'væksi:n/

---

validate *verb* (system operations)

to check that data entered into a computer is complete and reasonable: *validate the contents of the directory* ○ *validate the data files before they are handed over for further text processing* ○ *The computer system uses various methods to validate data.*

/'vælɪdeɪt/

validate, validating, validated

note transitive verb

ꓶ **validate input**

---

abbr abbreviation   **pl** plural   **syn** synonym   ▶ see   **ꓶ** collocate (*word often used with the headword*)

	▶ **data integrity, error checking, verify, vet**
validation *noun* the process of checking that data which has been input into a computer system is complete and reasonable: *Validation happens when all files have been corrected.*	/,vælɪ'deɪʃn/ **note** no plural ◪ data **validation**; a **validation** algorithm, routine ▶ **verification, range check**
validation suite *noun* (software) software that is used to test whether programming languages meet certain STANDARDS	/,vælɪ'deɪʃn swiːt/ **pl** validation suites ◪ execute, use the **validation suite**
validity check *noun* a test that shows whether something will work correctly: *run a validity check to make sure that data has been encoded in a way that is compatible with the database*	/və'lɪdəti tʃek/ **pl** validity checks ◪ carry out, perform a **validity check**
value *noun* the quantity that a VARIABLE represents: *The variable X has the value 3.*	/'væljuː/ **pl** values ◪ assign, give a **value** to something; a default, an initial, a numeric, a string **value**
value-added network *noun* (hardware/networks) a network which provides more services than just the transfer of data; this may be access to an information service, or managing the user's network communications: *The value-added network provides conversion facilities for computers that use different protocols.*	/,væljuː 'ædɪd ,netwɜːk/ **pl** value added networks **abbr** VAN ◪ link computers *over*, send data *over*, share data *on*, use a **value-added network**
VAN *abbr* ▶ **value-added network**	/væn/ **note** pronounced as a word
vanilla *adjective* (of hardware and software) that is very basic and does not have any extra features or ADD-ONS: *The vanilla word processor does not have a spellcheck.*	/və'nɪlə/
VAR *abbr* ▶ **variable**	/,viː eɪ 'ɑː(r)/ **note** pronounced as individual letters
☆**variable** *noun* the name used in a programming language for a set of locations in the computer's memory which can hold one data item. Data is stored in a variable by using an ASSIGNMENT STATEMENT: *a logical variable*	/'veəriəbl/ **pl** variables **abbr** VAR ◪ assign a value *to*, increment, read the value *of* a **variable**; a **variable** type, value ▶ **constant[1], numeric variable, string variable, strongly typed**
variable-length *adjective* not having a fixed length; able to change length when needed: *variable-length records use space effectively*	/,veəriəbl 'leŋθ/ ◪ a **variable-length** field, record, word ▶ **word length**

variable name *noun* (software)
the IDENTIFIER that is given to a variable: *variable names are restricted to six characters*

/ˈveəriəbl neɪm/
pl variable names
⧓ declare, define a **variable name**

☆**VDU** *abbr* (hardware)
a visual display unit. A screen for displaying information from a computer: *Stored information can be called up at any time on the computer's visual display unit.*

/ˌviː diː ˈjuː/
note pronounced as individual letters
pl VDUs
⧓ a **VDU** operator
syn visual display terminal
▶ **monitor**

vector *noun*
▶ **one-dimensional array**

/ˈvektə(r)/

vector display *noun* (hardware)
a screen that shows images that are lines which are not made of PIXELS: *The oscilloscope uses a vector display.*

/ˈvektə dɪˌspleɪ/
note not used with *a* or *an*. No plural and used with a singular verb only.
▶ **raster display**

vector graphics *noun* (applications/graphics)
text or an image that is produced on a screen by drawing each line of the text or image individually. This gives very good DEFINITION **(1)**.

/ˈvektə ˌɡræfɪks/
note plural noun used with a plural verb
⧓ 3D **vector graphics**; a **vector graphics** application, package

Venn diagram *noun* (mathematics)
a picture showing the result of an operation on two or more sets of things: *The Venn diagram shows the intersection of three sets of numbers.*

/ˈven ˌdaɪəɡræm/
pl Venn diagrams
⧓ draw a **Venn diagram**

verification *noun*
the process of checking that data transferred from one place to another has not been changed, especially data that has been keyed into a computer from paper

/ˌverɪfɪˈkeɪʃn/
note not used with *a* or *an*. No plural and used with a singular verb only.
⧓ carry out, perform **verification**; data **verification**; a **verification** check
▶ **checksum, control total, validation**

☆**verify** *verb* (system operation)
to check that data entered into a computer or recorded on a disk is correct: *The hard disk backup utility formats and verifies all new disks.*

/ˈverɪfaɪ/
verify, verifying, verified
note transitive verb
⧓ **verify** a cassette, disk, tape
▶ **authenticate, error checking, validate, vet**

vertical redundancy check *noun*
a method of checking errors in transmitted data. If the PARITY BIT generated by the vertical redundancy check does not correspond with the PARITY used, an error has occurred.

/ˌvɜːtɪkl rɪˈdʌndənsi tʃek/
pl vertical redundancy checks
abbr VRC

	◄ apply a **vertical redundancy check**
	► **horizontal redundancy check**

---

vertical refresh rate *noun*
the number of times each second that a RASTER DISPLAY begins a new picture

/ˌvɜːtɪkl rɪ'freʃ reɪt/
pl vertical refresh rates
◄ specify the **vertical refresh rate**
► **refresh rate**

---

vertical scrolling *noun*
the process of moving information on screen or in a window up or down

/ˌvɜːtɪkl 'skrəʊlɪŋ/
note not used with *a* or *an*. No plural and used with a singular verb only.
► **horizontal scrolling**

---

very large scale integration *noun*
the process of putting 10 000 to 100 000 components on an integrated circuit

/'veri 'lɑːdʒ 'skeɪl ˌɪntɪ'greɪʃn/
note not used with *a* or *an*. No plural and used with a singular verb only.
abbr VLSI
◄ **very large scale integration** methods, techniques
► **circuit board, large scale integration, medium scale integration, printed circuit board, small scale integration, super large scale integration, ultra large scale integration, wafer scale integration**

---

vet *verb* (system operation)
to check that data entered into a computer is reliable and not CORRUPT[2]

/vet/
vet, vetting, vetted
note transitive verb
◄ **vet input**
► **error checking, validate, verify**

VGA *abbr*
► **video graphics array**

/ˌviː dʒiː 'eɪ/
note pronounced as individual letters

---

video *noun*
images displayed on a television set or other RASTER DISPLAY: *full motion video*

/'vɪdiəʊ/
note not used with *a* or *an*. No plural and used with a singular verb only.
◄ display, process, transmit **video**
► **audio**

---

video adaptor *noun* (hardware)
a device that connects a computer to a video display unit: *The video adaptor must be compatible with the display unit.*

/'vɪdiəʊ əˌdæptə(r)/
pl video adaptors
(also **video adapter**)
◄ install a **video adaptor**; a **video adaptor** board, card

video digitizer noun (hardware)
a device used for transferring moving pictures to a computer: *a full authoring package that combines a video digitizer with compression software*

/ˌvɪdiəʊ ˈdɪdʒɪtaɪzə(r)/
pl video digitizers
syn frame grabber

videodisk noun (hardware)
a read-only optical storage device that is able to store video pictures

/ˈvɪdiəʊdɪsk/
pl videodisks
◄ access, play a **videodisk**
► **CD-ROM**

video display noun (hardware)
any device that displays text or images on screen: *a colour video display*

/ˈvɪdiəʊ dɪˌspleɪ/
pl video displays

video graphics array noun
(*trade mark*) a video adaptor that gives a colour display on a computer screen: *standard VGA resolution of 640X480 pixels* ○ *a video graphics array that supports 256 colours*

/ˌvɪdiəʊ ˈɡræfɪks əˌreɪ/
note usually singular
abbr VGA

video memory noun (hardware)
a set of locations in memory that is permanently allocated to the video display. To display a character in a particular position on the screen, the program writes the code for that character to the corresponding memory location.

/ˌvɪdiəʊ ˈmeməri/
note no plural
syn video RAM, video storage

video RAM noun
► **video memory**

/ˌvɪdiəʊ ˈræm/

video signal noun
a signal which carries video information to be displayed on screen

/ˈvɪdiəʊ ˌsɪɡnəl/
pl video signals
◄ process, transmit a **video signal**

video storage noun
► **video memory**

/ˈvɪdiəʊ ˌstɔːrɪdʒ/

video terminal noun (hardware)
a computer that is able to display video: *Video terminals are now standard on all computer systems.*

/ˈvɪdiəʊ ˌtɜːmɪnl/
pl video terminals
◄ install, use a **video terminal**

videotex noun
a system that accesses information from a central database and displays this information on specially adapted television screens. The information travels through phone lines and is decoded before it appears on screen.

note Originally known as Viewdata.

/ˈvɪdiəʊteks/
note not used with *a* or *an*. No plural and used with a singular verb only.
(also **videotext**)
◄ **videotex** hardware, software
► **teletext**

view¹ noun
a display of information or graphics on screen: *The view of the three-dimensional plan of the building is on the computer screen.*

/vjuː/
pl views
◄ a close, detailed **view**

view² verb
to display information or graphics on a screen: *view the document in print preview mode* ○ *view the file before it is edited*

/vjuː/
view, viewing, viewed
note transitive verb

	⋈ **view** a display, picture, printout
viewport *noun* the way a graphic image looks on screen from different angles. The software controls the way the user sees the object on the screen.	/'vju:pɔ:t/ **pl** viewports ⋈ change, define the **viewport**
virtual *adjective* (of a device or process) that works in a different way to the way the user experiences it working: *The computer can make a piece of memory into a virtual disk which it uses in the same way as a hard disk.*	/'vɜ:tʃuəl/ ⋈ a **virtual** library, machine, network, processor, storage system
virtual address *noun* an address in VIRTUAL MEMORY	/ˌvɜ:tʃuəl ə'dres/ **pl** virtual addresses ⋈ compute, decode a **virtual address**
virtual circuit *noun* the path between transmitter and receiver in a packet switched network. This path is not fixed and may be different for each packet of data that is sent, so the circuit is a virtual circuit, rather than a real fixed circuit: *connect over a virtual circuit*	/ˌvɜ:tʃuəl 'sɜ:kɪt/ **pl** virtual circuits ⋈ break, establish a **virtual circuit** ▶ **packet switching**
virtual disk *noun* ▶ **RAM disk**	/ˌvɜ:tʃuəl 'dɪsk/
virtual machine *noun* (software) software that copies the way a computer system works: *In a time-sharing system each user is working on a virtual machine.*	/ˌvɜ:tʃuəl mə'ʃi:n/ **pl** virtual machines ⋈ use, work *on* a **virtual machine**
virtual memory *noun* a form of memory that seems bigger than it is. This is done by storing some data on backing store so that it can be moved into main memory very quickly without slowing down processing speed very much.	/ˌvɜ:tʃuəl 'meməri/ **note** not used with *a* or *an*. No plural and used with a singular verb only. **syn** virtual storage ▶ **paging**
☆**virtual reality** *noun* an environment created by a computer that a person can experience by wearing special equipment	/ˌvɜ:tʃuəl ri'æləti/ **note** no plural **abbr** VR ⋈ experience **virtual reality**; a **virtual reality** game, helmet, interface, simulation application
virtual storage *noun* ▶ **virtual memory**	/ˌvɜ:tʃuəl 'stɔ:rɪdʒ/
☆**virus** *noun* (software) instructions that are hidden in a program and are designed to cause errors or destroy data in a computer system: *The virus that infected the computer was programmed to corrupt the hard disk.*	/'vaɪrəs/ **pl** viruses ⋈ **virus** detection, protection ▶ **Trojan horse, worm**[2]

virus checking
the process of checking a computer to see if it has any VIRUSES:
*Virus checking is undertaken on a regular basis to protect the
system.*

/'vaɪrəs ˌtʃekɪŋ/
note not used with *a* or *an*. No
plural and used with a singular
verb only.
ᴎ carry out, perform **virus
checking**
▶ **disinfect**

---

virus checking program *noun* (software)
software that tries to find any VIRUSES in a computer

/'vaɪrəs ˌtʃekɪŋ ˌprəʊgræm/
pl virus checking programs
ᴎ install, run, use a **virus
checking program**
syn virus scanner, vaccine, virus
shield

---

virus scanner *noun*
▶ **virus checking program**

/'vaɪrəs ˌskænə(r)/

---

virus shield *noun*
▶ **virus checking program**

/'vaɪrəs ʃiːld/

---

visual display terminal *noun*
▶ **VDU**

/ˌvɪʒuəl dɪˈspleɪ ˌtɜːmɪnl/

☆**visual display unit** *noun*
▶ **VDU**

/ˌvɪʒuəl dɪˈspleɪ ˌjuːnɪt/

VLSI *abbr*
▶ **very large scale integration**

/ˌviː el es ˈaɪ/
note pronounced as individual
letters

---

voice answer back *noun* (software/communications)
the use of recorded messages on a computer to answer
enquiries over the telephone. The user presses keys on the
telephone keypad to choose the information they want to hear:
*In the embassy's voice answer back service, pressing the star button
on the phone accesses information about visas.* ○ *The telephone
network provides users with voice answer back.*

/ˌvɔɪs ˈɑːnsə bæk/
note not used with *a* or *an*. No
plural and used with a singular
verb only.
ᴎ implement, use **voice answer
back**
▶ **voice mail**

---

voice data entry *noun*
▶ **voice input**

/ˌvɔɪs ˈdeɪtə ˌentri/

---

voice input *noun*
the process of transferring information to a computer by
talking to it. The computer uses a SPEECH RECOGNITION system to
convert the sound into data.

/ˌvɔɪs ˈɪnpʊt/
note not used with *a* or *an*. No
plural and used with a singular
verb only.
syn voice data entry

---

voice mail *noun*
a system for recording telephone messages as computer data;
REMOTE ACCESS can allow the user to listen to the messages

/'vɔɪs meɪl/
note not used with *a* or *an*. No
plural and used with a singular
verb only.
ᴎ receive, send, transmit, use
voice mail
▶ **e-mail**

---

abbr abbreviation   **pl** plural   **syn** synonym   ▶ see   ᴎ collocate (*word often used with the headword*)

voice output *noun* ▶ **speech ouput**	/ˌvɔɪs ˈaʊtpʊt/
voice recognition *noun* ▶ **speech recognition**	/ˈvɔɪs ˌrekəgˈnɪʃn/
voice synthesizer *noun* ▶ **speech synthesizer**	/ˈvɔɪs ˌsmθəsaɪzə(r)/
volatile file *noun* ▶ **temporary file**	/ˌvɒlətaɪl ˈfaɪl/
volatile memory *noun* (hardware) memory that loses the data it contains when the power is switched off	/ˌvɒlətaɪl ˈmeməri/ **note** no plural ▶ **primary memory**
volt *noun* (hardware/electricity) the unit used to measure VOLTAGE: *The mains current supply in the UK is 240 volts.*	/vəʊlt/ **pl** volts **abbr** V
voltage *noun* the electrical force in a circuit that is measured in VOLTS	/ˈvəʊltɪdʒ/ **pl** voltages **⋈** fluctuating, high, low, steady **voltage**
voltmeter *noun* an instrument for measuring the electrical force in a circuit: *The engineer used the voltmeter to check the potential across the input terminals.*	/ˈvəʊltmiːtə(r)/ **pl** voltmeters **⋈** use a **voltmeter**
volume *noun* (hardware) a disk or tape that stores computer data: *The volume needed is disk number 8.*	/ˈvɒljuːm/ **pl** volumes **⋈** dismount, mount a **volume**
volume label *noun* a data item that is placed at the start of the data on a VOLUME so that it can be identified: *The volume label includes the volume name.*	/ˈvɒljuːm ˌleɪbl/ **pl** volume labels **⋈** access, read, write the **volume label** **syn** volume name ▶ **tape label**
volume name *noun* ▶ **volume label**	/ˈvɒljuːm neɪm/
VR *abbr* ▶ **virtual reality**	/ˌviː ˈɑː(r)/ **note** pronounced as individual letters
VRAM *abbr* ▶ **video RAM**	/ˈviː ræm/
VRC *abbr* ▶ **vertical redundancy check**	/ˌviː ɑː ˈsiː/ **note** pronounced as individual letters

wafer *noun* (hardware) a very thin slice of SILICON onto which integrated circuits are placed **note** A wafer usually contains more than one integrated circuit.	/ˈweɪfə(r)/ **pl** wafers ◄ etch a circuit *onto*, fabricate a circuit *onto* a **wafer**
wafer scale integration *noun* (hardware) the process of making a single integrated circuit from one WAFER	/ˈweɪfə skeɪl ˌɪntɪˈɡreɪʃn/ **note** not used with *a* or *an*. No plural and used with a singular verb only.
wait condition *noun* (hardware) the pause while a computer waits for input: *The wait condition lasted for several clock cycles.*	/ˈweɪt kənˌdɪʃn/ **pl** wait conditions **syn** wait state
wait state ► **wait condition**	/ˈweɪt steɪt/
walk through *verb* ► **single-step**	/ˌwɔːk ˈθruː/
☆**WAN** *abbr* ► **wide area network**	/wæn/ **note** pronounced as a word
wand *noun* ► **bar code reader**	/wɒnd/
warm boot *verb* to return of a computer system to the state it was in immediately after it was switched on: *Warm boot the computer with the command ALT+CTRL+DEL.*	/ˌwɔːm ˈbuːt/ **warm boot, warm booting, warm booted** **note** transitive verb **syn** warm start ► **boot**
☆**warm start** *verb* ► **warm boot**	/ˌwɔːm ˈstɑːt/
weakly typed *adjective* (programming) (of a programming language) that can change the DATA TYPE of a variable: *a weakly typed language*	/ˌwiːkli ˈtaɪpt/ ► **strongly typed**
well-behaved *adjective* (of software) that works correctly with an operating system	/ˌwel bɪˈheɪvd/ ◄ a **well-behaved** program, routine, module
while loop *noun* (software/programming) a block of statements in a computer programming language that is executed again and again if a TEST[1] **(2)** at the start of the block shows that the execution should happen: *execute a while loop*	/ˈwaɪl luːp/ **pl** while loops ◄ perform, repeat a **while loop** ► **loop[1] 2**
☆**wide area network** *noun* a network that covers a large area with NODES **(2)** that are linked together: *The wide area network is linked by telephone, satellite and radio.* ○ *connect to JANET, the Internet and other international wide area networks* ○ *run data through a WAN*	/ˈwaɪd eəriə ˈnetwɜːk/ **pl** wide area networks **abbr** WAN ◄ download data *from*, link computers *over*, send data *over*, send electronic mail *over*, share data *on*, use a **wide area network**

abbr abbreviation   **pl** plural   **syn** synonym   ► see   ◄ collocate (*word often used with the headword*)

	syn long haul network
	▶ **Arpanet, Bitnet, bulletin board, gateway, Internet, local area network, network**

widow *noun* the last line of a piece of text which is printed on its own at the top of a new page: *The layout of the text is designed to avoid widows.*	/'wɪdəʊ/ **pl** widows ◄ allow, suppress **widows** ▶ **orphan**
☆**wildcard** *noun* (software) a symbol that represents any character or group of characters: *An asterisk is commonly used as a wildcard.*	/'waɪldkɑːd/ **pl** wildcards ◄ a **wildcard** character, search ▶ **search and replace**
☆**WIMP** *abbr* (applications) windows, icons, mice and pull-down menus. The software and hardware that forms a USER INTERFACE that is designed to be easy to use.	/wɪmp/ **pl** WIMPs ◄ a **WIMP** environment ▶ **graphical user interface, icon, menu, mouse, window**
Winchester disk *noun* (hardware) a small hard disk used in microcomputers	/'wɪntʃɪstə dɪsk/ **pl** Winchester disks
☆**window**[1] *noun* (applications) an area on a screen showing data or information from a program or file, etc: *Several windows containing different applications were open at the same time.* ○ *click on the window to make it active*	/'wɪndəʊ/ **pl** windows ◄ enlarge, move, open, shrink a **window**; **window** control, management
☆**window**[2] *verb* (user operation) to divide the screen into windows: *The screen was windowed to allow the user to look at the output from three applications at the same time.*	/'wɪndəʊ/ **window, windowing, windowed** **note** transitive verb ▶ **cascade**[2]
windowing *noun* the process of displaying the output from a program in a window on the screen	/'wɪndəʊɪŋ/ **note** no plural ◄ a **windowing** interface, routine
windowing software *noun* (software) software that allows programs to display output in windows on screen	/'wɪndəʊɪŋ ˌsɒftweə(r)/ **note** not used with *a* or *an*. No plural and used with a singular verb only. ◄ install, use **windowing software**
wire *noun* (hardware) a thin piece of metal that is used to carry an electrical current	/'waɪə(r)/ **pl** wires ◄ join components *with* a **wire**
wire frame model *noun* a way of representing a complicated three-dimensional object on screen by only drawing the outline	/'waɪə 'freɪm 'mɒdl/ **pl** wire frame models ◄ draw, represent something *as* a **wire frame model**

---

wire wrap *noun* (hardware)

a way of making part of a circuit by winding wires around a connector: *Wire wrap was one of the methods used to produce a prototype circuit.*

/ˈwaɪə ræp/

note not used with *a* or *an*. No plural and used with a singular verb only.

☆**word** *noun*

1 (hardware) a unit of memory that is processed as a single unit by the CPU **2** (data representation) the written or printed letters that form a unit of a language: *There are about 200 words in the document.*

/wɜːd/

pl words

1 ⋈ an 8-bit, a 16-bit, a 32-bit **word**

▶ **byte, character, gulp, nibble, storage, word processing**

---

word length *noun*

the number of bits in a WORD

/ˈwɜːd lenθ/

pl word lengths

⋈ fixed, variable **word length**

---

word machine *noun*

a computer which has a WORD **1** as a basic unit of storage and processing

/ˈwɜːd məˌʃiːn/

pl word machines

⋈ design, program a **word machine**

▶ **byte machine**

☆**word processing** *noun* (applications)

the use of a computer to edit, format, store a piece of text entered into the computer from a keyboard. This text may also be printed.

/ˈwɜːd ˌprəʊsesɪŋ/

note no plural

abbr WP

⋈ a **word processing** application, operation, package, system; be familiar *with* **word processing**

▶ **text processing, desktop publishing**

---

word processor *noun* (hardware)

a computer that runs a WORD PROCESSING application and is usually used to produce documents such as letters and reports: *type and edit the letter on the word processor* ○ *key the text into the word processor*

/ˈwɜːd ˌprəʊsesə(r)/

pl word processors

abbr WP

---

word wrap *noun*

the feature of a word processing program that allows the user to ignore the end of each line; when a word being typed does not fit onto one line, the whole word is automatically moved to the next line

/ˈwɜːd ræp/

note not used with *a* or *an*. No plural and used with a singular verb only.

⋈ a **word wrap** algorithm, facility

syn wraparound

---

work area *noun*

▶ **workspace**

/ˈwɜːk ˌeəriə/

---

work file *noun*

▶ **temporary file**

/ˈwɜːk faɪl/

---

working store *noun* (hardware)

a group of memory locations used by a program to hold results of a calculation before the calculation is completely finished

/ˈwɜːkɪŋ stɔː(r)/

note no plural

---

abbr abbreviation   **pl** plural   **syn** synonym   ▶ see   ⋈ collocate (*word often used with the headword*)

workspace *noun*
the computer memory that is reserved for a user or for an application program

/'wɜːkspeɪs/
pl workspaces
⋈ claim, define, use a **workspace**
syn work area

☆**workstation** *noun* (hardware)
1 the place where a person works. This is usually a desk in an office with a computer. **2** a computer that is used for COMPUTER AIDED DESIGN or to create computer graphics. This is usually a very expensive and powerful computer. **3** any type of computer that is connected to a network

/'wɜːksteɪʃn/
pl workstations
2 ⋈ a high-end **workstation**

World Wide Web *noun*
a HYPERMEDIA system for finding and accessing information on the INTERNET: *download a software demo from the World Wide Web* ○ *browse a site on the World Wide Web*

note The World Wide Web is often referred to as just 'the Web'.

/ˌwɜːld waɪd 'web/
note no plural
⋈ a **World Wide Web** address, browser, presence, search engine, site
▶ **browser, home page, Internet**

WORM¹ *abbr*
write once, read many (times)

/wɜːm/
note pronounced as a word

---

worm² *noun*
a type of virus which makes many copies of itself in different computers: *The worm made the machine crash.*

/wɜːm/
pl worms
▶ **Trojan horse, virus**

WP *abbr*
1 ▶ **word processing**
2 ▶ **word processor**

/ˌdʌblju: 'pi:/
note pronounced as individual letters

☆**wrap** *verb* (system operation)
to continue automatically, especially to start a new line when the end of the line is reached in a WORD PROCESSING operation: *The word processing package wraps the text onto the next line.*

/ræp/
wrap, wrapping, wrapped
note transitive verb
▶ **word processing, newline character**

---

wraparound *noun*
▶ **word wrap**

/'ræpəraʊnd/

☆**write** *verb* (system operation)
to transfer data to a storage device such as a disk, or to an output device such as a screen or printer: *The computer is writing the file to tape.*

/raɪt/
write, writing, wrote, written
note transitive verb
⋈ **write** data *to* disk, data *to* file, data *to* screen, data *to* tape
▶ **enter², read**

---

write error *noun* (software)
an error caused by the failure of a write instruction to execute correctly: *The write error was caused because the disk was write protected.*

/'raɪt ˌerə(r)/
pl write errors
⋈ cause, detect a **write error**
▶ **read error**

write head *noun* (hardware) the part of a disk or tape drive that transfers information to a tape or disk	/ˈraɪt hed/ **pl** write heads **syn** record head ▶ **read/write head**
write instruction *noun* (software/programming) an instruction in MACHINE CODE that causes the contents of a register to be copied to a storage location	/ˈraɪt ɪnˌstrʌkʃn/ **pl** write instructions ᴎ execute, program a **write instruction**
write permit ring *noun* (hardware) a device on a magnetic tape container. When the device is in position the user is allowed to erase or OVERWRITE data on the tape. To protect the data, the device is removed.	/ˌraɪt pəˈmɪt rɪŋ/ **pl** write permit rings
write protect[1] *adjective* able to stop data being written to or erased from a disk or magnetic tape: *use the write protect tab on the disk so the data is not lost*	/ˌraɪt prəˈtekt/ ᴎ a **write protect** mechanism, notch, system, tab
write protect[2] *verb* to protect information stored on disk or tape by making it impossible to write data to or erase data from the disk or tape: *The error was caused by trying to write to a file that had been write protected.*	/ˌraɪt prəˈtekt/ **write protect, write protecting, write protected** **note** transitive verb ᴎ **write protect** a disk, file, tape **syn** protect
WWW *abbr* ▶ **World Wide Web**	**note** used in written English only
☆**WYSIWYG** *abbr* (applications) what you see is what you get. A feature of some word processing applications where the way the text looks on screen is the same as it will look when it is printed on paper.	/ˈwɪziwɪg/ **note** pronounced as a word ᴎ a **WYSIWYG** display, feature, package, screen, system ▶ **desktop publishing, word processing**

Xx

X-axis *noun* the horizontal scale in a two- or three-dimensional graph or drawing: *plot 'time' on the x-axis*	/ˈeks ˌæksɪs/ **pl** X-axes ᴎ align something *with*, distance something *along*, distance something *from* the **X-axis** **syn** horizontal axis ▶ **Y-axis, Y-coordinate, Z-axis, Z-coordinate**
X-coordinate *noun* the position of a point in a graph measured on the X-AXIS: *The X-coordinate is quoted first when giving the coordinates of a point.*	/ˈeks kəʊˌɔːdɪnət/ **pl** X-coordinates ᴎ give, measure, state the **X-coordinate**

abbr abbreviation   **pl** plural   **syn** synonym   ▶ see   ᴎ collocate (*word often used with the headword*)

▶ **Y-axis, Y-coordinate, Z-axis, Z-coordinate**

---

xerographic paper *noun* (hardware)
special paper used with a XEROGRAPHIC PRINTER

/ˈzɪərəʊˌɡræfɪk ˈpeɪpə(r)/

note not used with *a* or *an*. No plural and used with a singular verb only.

---

xerographic printer *noun* (hardware)
a printer that uses electricity to make ink stick to paper in order to produce high-quality printed text and graphics

/ˈzɪərəʊˌɡræfɪk ˈprɪntə(r)/

pl xerographic printers

XNOR *abbr*
▶ **XNOR gate**

/ˌeksˈnɔː(r)/

XNOR circuit *abbr*
▶ **XNOR gate**

/ˌeks ˈnɔː ˌsɜːkɪt/

XNOR gate *noun*
an exclusive NOR gate. A logic circuit with two inputs and a single output. There is a signal on the output only when the inputs are both the same.

note An XNOR gate is the same as an EQ gate.

/ˌeks ˈnɔː ɡeɪt/

pl XNOR gates

◄ assert the input *to*, read ouput *from* an **XNOR gate**

syn XNOR, XNOR circuit

XON/XOFF *noun*
a PROTOCOL for ASYNCHRONOUS TRANSMISSION. The receiving device sends the XON code to the transmitting device to start data transmission, and the XOFF code to stop data transmission: *XON/XOFF is often used between two personal computers.*

/eksˌɒn eksˈɒf/

note not used with *a* or *an*. No plural and used with a singular verb only.

▶ **handshake**

XOR *abbr*
▶ **EXOR operation**

/ˌeksˈɔː(r)/

XOR gate *noun*
▶ **EXOR gate**

/ˌeksˈɔː ɡeɪt/

XT *abbr* (hardware)
extended technology

/ˌeks ˈtiː/

note pronounced as individual letters

▶ **AT**

Yy

Y-axis *noun*
the vertical scale in a two- or three-dimensional graph or drawing

/ˈwaɪ æksɪs/

pl Y-axes

◄ align something *with*, distance something *along*, distance something *from* the **Y-axis**

▶ **X-coordinate, Y-coordinate, Z-axis, Z-coordinate**

Y-coordinate *noun*
the position of a point in a graph measured on the Y-AXIS

/ˈwaɪ kəʊˌɔːdɪnet/

pl Y-coordinates

◄ give, measure, state the **Y-coordinate**

▶ **X-axis, X-coordinate, Z-axis, Z-coordinate**

Z-axis *noun*
the scale in a three-dimensional graph or drawing that represents depth

/ˈzed ˌæksɪs/
pl Z-axes
⋈ align something *with*, distance something *along*, distance something *from* the **Z-axis**
▶ X-axis, X-coordinate, Y-axis, Y-coordinate

Z-coordinate *noun*
the position of a point in a graph measured on the Z-AXIS: *The Z-coordinate is quoted third when giving the coordinates of a point.*

/ˈzed kəʊˌɔːdɪnət/
pl Z-coordinates
⋈ give, measure, state the **Z-coordinate**
▶ X-axis, X-coordinate, Y-axis, Y-coordinate

zero *noun*
the digit 0: *'One million' is written as 1 followed by six zeroes.*

/ˈzɪərəʊ/
pl zeroes

zero fill *verb*
to write or print a number to a fixed number of decimal places by adding zeroes at the front of the number. Zero filling a number does not change its value: *123 zero filled to six places is 000123*

/ˈzɪərəʊ fɪl/
zero fill, zero filling, zero filled
note transitive verb
⋈ **zero fill** a field, store location

zero flag *noun*
a single bit in the CPU that is set to 1 when the contents of the ACCUMULATOR are zero

/ˈzɪərəʊ flæg/
pl zero flags
⋈ test, clear the **zero flag**

zero suppression *noun*
a method of saving space in a data file by not storing zeroes that are not needed: *Zero supression reduces the number 000003856.34 to 3856.34*

/ˈzɪərəʊ səˌpreʃn/
note not used with *a* or *an*. No plural and used with a singular verb only.
⋈ implement **zero suppression** : a **zero suppression** algorithm

zoom *verb*
to change the size of an image on a display screen so more can be seen or so that details become clearer: *zoom the image to enlarge it*

/zuːm/
zoom, zooming, zoomed
note transitive verb
⋈ **zoom** an image. etc *by* a fixed amount

---

abbr abbreviation　　**pl** plural　　**syn** synonym　　▶ see　　⋈ collocate (*word often used with the headword*)

Core vocabulary

The words that form the core vocabulary appear in the dictionary with the ☆ symbol in front of each item. The core vocabulary consists of the most important words that are used in the English of computing.

abbreviation
abort
accept
access
accumulator
accuracy
acoustic coupler
acronym
active
adaptor
ADC
adder
address
address bus
addressing
AI
ALGOL
alphanumeric
ALU
analog
analog computer
analog-to-digital converter
application
applications program
applications programmer
applications software
archive
archived file
argument
arithmetic and logic unit
arithmetic unit
array
array processor
artificial intelligence
ASCII
ASCII file
assembler
assembly
assembly language

assembly program
assign
assignment
backing store
backspace
backspace key
backup
base
BASIC
batch
batch processing
binary
binary digit
binary notation
binary number
binary system
bit
BkSp
block
Boolean algebra
boot
bootstrap loader
breakpoint
bridge
bubble memory
buffer
bug
bus
byte
C
cache
CAD
CADCAM
CAI
CAL
CALL
CAM
cancel
capacity

capture
cartridge
CD
CD-I
CD-ROM
central processing unit
character
chip
circuit
CISC
clear
click
COBOL
code
cold boot
command
comment
communications
compact disc
compatible
complex instruction set
  computer
computer
computer aided design
computer aided instruction
computer assisted
  manufacturing
computer aided manufacturing
computer assisted design
computerization
computerize
computer program
computer programmer
configuration
connect
connection
continuous
control unit
convert
copy
copy
CPU
crash
cursor
cursor control key

cut
cut and paste
data
databank
database
data channel
debug
decimal
decision support system
decoder
dedicated
default
delete
delete key
delimiter
demodulator
design
desktop publishing
device
dialog box
digital computer
digital-to-analog-converter
digitize
direct access
directory
disassembler
disc
disk
disk access
disk drive
disk operating system
disk sector
display
document
documentation
DOS
dot matrix printer
dots per inch
double density disk
down arrow
download
down time
DP
dpi
DRAM

DSS
DTP
dumb terminal
dump
duplex
dynamic RAM
edit
electronic mail
e-mail
embed
emulator
encode
end
end key
enter
environment
erase
error
escape
escape key
execute
exit
expanded memory
expert system
export
extended memory
extension
facsimile transmission
failure
fault
fax
field
fifth generation
file
filename
file server
filter
firmware
first generation
fixed-point arithmetic
Fkey
floating-point arithmetic
floppy disk
flowchart
font

format
FORTRAN
fourth generation
front-end processor
function
function key
G
gate
gateway
generate
generation
generator
giga
glitch
global
graphical user interface
graphics
graph plotter
GUI
gulp
hack
hacker
hard copy
hard disk
hardware
header
help
HEX
hexadecimal
hierarchy
hierarchical database
high-level language
highlight
high-tech
home
home computer
home key
host computer
housekeeping
hypermedia
hypertext
icon
identification
identifier
illegal operation

image
import
incompatible
index
information retrieval
information technology
input
input device
input/output
insert
insert key
install
instruction
instruction set
integrated circuit
intelligent terminal
interactive
interface
interrupt
I/O
IT
jack
job
joystick
justify
K
key
keyboard
keyboard
keyboarder
keypad
KHz
kilo
kilobyte
kilohertz
knowledge base
LAN
laptop
laser disk
laser printer
layout
LCD
LED
light emitting diode
line printer

liquid crystal display
load
local area network
log
logarithm
logic
log on
LOGO
log off
low-level language
M
machine
machine code
machine language
machine-readable
macro
magnetic bubble memory
magnetic disk
magnetic tape
mail merge
mainframe
management information
  system
manual
MAR
MB
MBR
Mbyte
mega
megabyte
megahertz
memory
memory address register
memory buffer register
memory map
menu
merge
message
micro
microchip
microcomputer
microinstruction
microprocessor
microsecond
minicomputer

MIS
mode
modem
modulator
module
monitor
mouse
multimedia
multiplexer
multitasking
multi-user
multi-user system
network
network database
nibble
node
notation
number
number crunching
Num Lock key
OCR
off-line
on-line
operating system
operation
operational
operator
optical character recognition
optical disc
option
output
output device
overwrite
page down
page up
parallel processing
Pascal
password
paste
path
pathname
PC
PCB
peripheral
personal computer

personal identification number
Pg Dn
Pg Up
PIN
plotter
portable computer
power supply
primary memory
printed circuit board
printer
printout
process
processing
processor
program
programmer
programming
programming language
PROLOG
prompt
queue
quit
RAM
random access
read
readable
read only memory
read/write memory
real-time
real-time processing
reboot
record
recover
reduced instruction set
    computer
refresh
register
reset
resolution
retrieve
return
return key
RISC
ROM
RTN

run
save
scanner
screen
scroll
search
secondary store
second generation
sector
serial processing
server
shift
shift key
signal
silicon chip
simulator
software
software package
sort
source code
space bar
spreadsheet
stand-alone
statement
state-of-the-art
store
string
subdirectory
supercomputer
system
systems analyst
systems programmer
systems software
tab
tab character
tab key
task

terminal
text
third generation
toggle
transistor
transmission
tree
truth table
tutorial
typeface
update
upgrade
upload
user
user-friendly
user interface
utility program
validate
variable
VDU
verify
virtual reality
virus
visual display unit
WAN
warm start
wide area network
wildcard
WIMP
window
word
word processing
workstation
wrap
write
WYSIWYG

ASCII in decimal, hexadecimal

DEC. NO.	HEXADECIMAL CHARACTER		DEC. NO.	HEXADECIMAL CHARACTER		DEC. NO.	HEXADECIMAL CHARACTER		DEC. NO.	HEXADECIMAL CHARACTER	
0	00	NUL	32	20	SP	64	40	@	96	60	'
1	01	SOH	33	21	!	65	41	A	97	61	a
2	02	STX	34	22	"	66	42	B	98	62	b
3	03	ETX	35	23	#	67	43	C	99	63	c
4	04	EOT	36	24	$	68	44	D	100	64	d
5	05	ENQ	37	25	%	69	45	E	101	65	e
6	06	ACK	38	26	&	70	46	F	102	66	f
7	07	BEL	39	27	'	71	47	G	103	67	g
8	08	BS	40	28	(	72	48	H	104	68	h
9	09	HT	41	29	)	73	49	I	105	69	i
10	0A	LF	42	2A	*	74	4A	J	106	6A	j
11	0B	VT	43	2B	+	75	4B	K	107	6B	k
12	0C	FF	44	2C	,	76	4C	L	108	6C	l
13	0D	CR	45	2D	-	77	4D	M	109	6D	m
14	0E	SO	46	2E	.	78	4E	N	110	6E	n
15	0F	SI	47	2F	/	79	4F	O	111	6F	o
16	10	DLE	48	30	0	80	50	P	112	70	p
17	11	DC1	49	31	1	81	51	Q	113	71	q
18	12	DC2	50	32	2	82	52	R	114	72	r
19	13	DC3	51	33	3	83	53	S	115	73	s
20	14	DC4	52	34	4	84	54	T	116	74	t
21	15	NAK	53	35	5	85	55	U	117	75	u
22	16	SYN	54	36	6	86	56	V	118	76	v
23	17	ETB	55	37	7	87	57	W	119	77	w
24	18	CAN	56	38	8	88	58	X	120	78	x
25	19	EM	57	39	9	89	59	Y	121	79	y
26	1A	SUB	58	3A	:	90	5A	Z	122	7A	z
27	1B	ESC	59	3B	;	91	5B	[	123	7B	{
28	1C	FS	60	3C	>	92	5C	\	124	7C	l
29	1D	GS	61	3D	=	93	5D	]	125	7D	}
30	1E	RS	62	3E	>	94	5E	↑	126	7E	~
31	1F	US	63	3F	?	95	5F	_	127	7F	DEL

The ASCII symbols

ACK	Acknowledge	GS	Group Separator
BEL	Bell	HT	Horizontal Tabulation
BS	Backspace	LF	Line Feed
CAN	Cancel	NAK	Negative Acknowledgement
CR	Carriage Return	NUL	Null
DC	Device Control	RS	Record Separator
DEL	Delete	SI	Shift In
DLE	Data Link Escape	SO	Shift Out
EM	End of Medium	SOH	Start of Heading
ENQ	Enquiry	SP	Space (Blank)
EOT	End of Transmission	STX	Start of Text
ESC	Escape	SUB	Substitute
ETB	End of Transmission Block	SYN	Synchronous Idle
ETX	End of Text	US	Unit Separator
FF	Form Feed	VT	Vertical Tabulation
FS	File Separator		

Numeric Equivalents

Decimal (Base 10)	Hexa-decimal (Base 16)	Octal (Base 8)	Binary (Base 2)	Decimal (Base 10)	Hexa-decimal (Base 16)	Octal (Base 8)	Binary (Base 2)
1	01	1	00000001	42	2A	52	00101010
2	02	2	00000010	43	2B	53	00101011
3	03	3	00000011	44	2C	54	00101100
4	04	4	00000100	45	2D	55	00101101
5	05	5	00000101	46	2E	56	00101110
6	06	6	00000110	47	2F	57	00101111
7	07	7	00000111	48	30	60	00110000
8	08	10	00001000	49	31	61	00110001
9	09	11	00001001	50	32	62	00110010
10	0A	12	00001010	51	33	63	00110011
11	0B	13	00001011	52	34	64	00110100
12	0C	14	00001100	53	35	65	00110101
13	0D	15	00001101	54	36	66	00110110
14	0E	16	00001110	55	37	67	00110111
15	0F	17	00001111	56	38	70	00111000
16	10	20	00010000	57	39	71	00111001
17	11	21	00010001	58	3A	72	00111010
18	12	22	00010010	59	3B	73	00111011
19	13	23	00010011	60	3C	74	00111100
20	14	24	00010100	61	3D	75	00111101
21	15	25	00010101	62	3E	76	00111110
22	16	26	00010110	63	3F	77	00111111
23	17	27	00010111	64	40	100	01000000
24	18	30	00011000	65	41	101	01000001
25	19	31	00011001	66	42	102	01000010
26	1A	32	00011010	67	43	103	01000011
27	1B	33	00011011	68	44	104	01000100
28	1C	34	00011100	69	45	105	01000101
29	1D	35	00011101	70	46	106	01000110
30	1E	36	00011110	71	47	107	01000111
31	1F	37	00011111	72	48	110	01001000
32	20	40	00100000	73	49	111	01001001
33	21	41	00100001	74	4A	112	01001010
34	22	42	00100010	75	4B	113	01001011
35	23	43	00100011	76	4C	114	01001100
36	24	44	00100100	77	4D	115	01001101
37	25	45	00100101	78	4E	116	00100111
38	26	46	00100110	79	4F	117	01001111
39	27	47	00100111	80	50	120	01010000
40	28	50	00101000	81	51	121	01010001
41	29	51	00101001	82	52	122	01010010

Decimal (Base 10)	Hexa-decimal (Base 16)	Octal (Base 8)	Binary (Base 2)	Decimal (Base 10)	Hexa-decimal (Base 16)	Octal (Base 8)	Binary (Base 2)
83	53	123	01010011	126	7E	176	01111110
84	54	124	01010100	127	7F	177	01111111
85	55	125	01010101	128	80	200	10000000
86	56	126	01010110	129	81	201	10000001
87	57	127	01010111	130	82	202	10000010
88	58	130	01011000	131	83	203	10000011
89	59	131	01011001	132	84	204	10000100
90	5A	132	01011010	133	85	205	10000101
91	5B	133	01011011	134	86	206	10000110
92	5C	134	01011100	135	87	207	10000111
93	5D	135	01011101	136	88	210	10001000
94	5E	136	01011110	137	89	211	10001001
95	5F	137	01011111	138	8A	212	10001010
96	60	140	01100000	139	8B	213	10001011
97	61	141	01100001	140	8C	214	10001100
98	62	142	01100010	141	8D	215	10001101
99	63	143	01100011	142	8E	216	10001110
100	64	144	01100100	143	8F	217	10001111
101	65	145	01100101	144	90	220	10010000
102	66	146	01100110	145	91	221	10010001
103	67	147	01100111	146	92	222	10010010
104	68	150	01101000	147	93	223	10010011
105	69	151	01101001	148	94	224	10010100
106	6A	152	01101010	149	95	225	10010101
107	6B	153	01101011	150	96	226	10010110
108	6C	154	01101100	151	97	227	10010111
109	6D	155	01101101	152	98	230	10011000
110	6E	156	01101110	153	99	231	10011001
111	6F	157	01101111	154	9A	232	10011010
112	70	160	01110000	155	9B	233	10011011
113	71	161	01110001	156	9C	234	10011100
114	72	162	01110010	157	9D	235	10011101
115	73	163	01110011	158	9E	236	10011110
116	74	164	01110100	159	9F	237	10011111
117	75	165	01110101	160	A0	240	10100000
118	76	166	01110110	161	A1	241	10100001
119	77	167	11101111	162	A2	242	10100010
120	78	170	01111000	163	A3	243	10100011
121	79	171	01111001	164	A4	244	10100100
122	7A	172	01111010	165	A5	245	10100101
123	7B	173	01111011	166	A6	246	10100110
124	7C	174	01111100	167	A7	247	10100111
125	7D	175	01111101	168	A8	250	10101000

Decimal	Hexa-decimal	Octal	Binary	Decimal	Hexa-decimal	Octal	Binary
(Base 10)	(Base 16)	(Base 8)	(Base 2)	(Base 10)	(Base 16)	(Base 8)	(Base 2)
169	A9	251	10101001	213	D5	325	11010101
170	AA	252	10101010	214	D6	326	11010110
171	AB	253	10101011	215	D7	327	11010111
172	AC	254	10101100	216	D8	330	11011000
173	AD	255	10101101	217	D9	331	11011001
174	AE	256	10101110	218	DA	332	11011010
175	AF	257	10101111	219	DB	333	11011011
176	B0	260	10110000	220	DC	334	11011100
177	B1	261	10110001	221	DD	335	11011101
178	B2	262	10110010	222	DE	336	11011110
179	B3	263	10110011	223	DF	337	11011111
180	B4	264	10110100	224	E0	340	11100000
181	B5	265	10110101	225	E1	341	11100001
182	B6	266	10110110	226	E2	342	11100010
183	B7	267	10110111	227	E3	343	11000011
184	B8	270	10111000	228	E4	344	11100100
185	B9	271	10111001	229	E5	345	11100101
186	BA	272	10111010	230	E6	346	11100110
187	BB	273	10111011	231	E7	347	11100111
188	BC	274	10111100	232	E8	350	11101000
189	BD	275	10111101	233	E9	351	11101001
190	BE	276	10111110	234	EA	352	11101010
191	BF	277	10111111	235	EB	353	11101011
192	C0	300	11000000	236	EC	354	11101100
193	C1	301	11000001	237	ED	355	11101101
194	C2	302	11000010	238	EE	356	11101110
195	C3	303	11000011	239	EF	357	11101111
196	C4	304	11000100	240	F0	360	11110000
197	C5	305	11000101	241	F1	361	11110001
198	C6	306	11000110	242	F2	362	11110010
199	C7	307	11000111	243	F3	363	11110011
200	C8	310	11001000	244	F4	364	11110100
201	C9	311	11001001	245	F5	365	11110101
202	CA	312	11001010	246	F6	366	11110110
203	CB	313	11001011	247	F7	367	11110111
204	CC	314	11001100	248	F8	370	11111000
205	CD	315	11001101	249	F9	371	11111001
206	CE	316	11001110	250	FA	372	11111010
207	CF	317	11001111	251	FB	373	11111011
208	D0	320	11010000	252	FC	374	11111100
209	D1	321	11010001	253	FD	375	11111101
210	D2	322	11010010	254	FE	376	11111110
211	D3	323	11010011	255	FF	377	11111111
212	D4	324	11010100				

KEY TO THE DICTIONARY

headword (ordered letter-by-letter ignoring all spaces and hyphens)

difficult words in capitals

numbers to show the different meanings of a word

realistic examples showing grammar patterns

helpful notes with extra information

a cross reference to the definition of the full form of the word

part of speech

definitions written in words that are easy to understand

a gloss which explains some difficult words

different forms of the verb: present, -ing form, past tense/past participle

grammar notes

phonetic symbols and a note about pronunciation

/ˈrəʊl aʊt/
roll out, rolling out, rolled out
note transitive verb

roll out *verb*
1 to transfer information from the main memory to the BACKING STORE (= a separate memory which holds a record of the data in main memory) **2** to make a new application, etc available to computer users in a company or organization: *The information technology department will roll out upgraded e-mail software to all PC users by the end of the month.*

/ˌbləʊ ˈʌp/
blow up, blowing up, blew up, blown up
1 note transitive or intransitive verb
2 note transitive verb
⊭ **blow up** graphics, pictures

blow up *verb*
1 to make something explode: *The power surge blew up the computer and caused a small fire.* ○ *The printer blew up.* **2** to make an image, etc larger: *blow up the picture so it fills the whole screen*

/ˈɪntənet/
note no plural
⊭ access, surf the **Internet**; an Internet protocol, service, site
▶ **World Wide Web**

Internet *noun*
many small networks which are connected together to make a larger network that covers the world: *send international electronic mail via the Internet* ○ *buy a PC that is Internet-enabled for full access to Internet services*
note Always referred to as 'the Internet'.

/ˌaɪ ˈəʊ/
note pronounced as individual letters

☆**I/O** *abbr*
▶ **input/output**